Microsoft Excel 2013: Data Analysis and Business Modeling

Wayne L. Winston

Published with the authorization of Microsoft Corporation by:
O'Reilly Media, Inc.
1005 Gravenstein Highway North
Sebastopol, California 95472

ISBN: 978-0-7356-6913-0

1 2 3 4 5 6 7 8 9 LSI 8 7 6 5 4 3

Printed and bound in the United States of America.

Microsoft Press books are available through booksellers and distributors worldwide. If you need support related to this book, email Microsoft Press Book Support at *mspinput@microsoft.com*. Please tell us what you think of this book at *http://www.microsoft.com/learning/booksurvey*.

Microsoft and the trademarks listed at *http://www.microsoft.com/about/legal/en/us/IntellectualProperty/Trademarks/EN-US.aspx* are trademarks of the Microsoft group of companies. All other marks are property of their respective owners.

The example companies, organizations, products, domain names, email addresses, logos, people, places, and events depicted herein are fictitious. No association with any real company, organization, product, domain name, email address, logo, person, place, or event is intended or should be inferred.

This book expresses the author's views and opinions. The information contained in this book is provided without any express, statutory, or implied warranties. Neither the author, O'Reilly Media, Inc., Microsoft Corporation, nor its resellers, or distributors will be held liable for any damages caused or alleged to be caused either directly or indirectly by this book.

Acquisitions and Developmental Editor: Kenyon Brown

Production Editor: Kara Ebrahim

Editorial Production: nSight, Inc.

Technical Reviewer: Peter Myers

Copyeditor: nSight, Inc.

Indexer: nSight, Inc.

Cover Design: Twist Creative • Seattle

Cover Composition: Ellie Volckhausen

Illustrator: Rebecca Demarest

Contents at a glance

	Introduction	xxi
CHAPTER 1	Range names	1
CHAPTER 2	Lookup functions	15
CHAPTER 3	INDEX function	23
CHAPTER 4	MATCH function	27
CHAPTER 5	Text functions	35
CHAPTER 6	Dates and date functions	51
CHAPTER 7	Evaluating investments by using net present value criteria	59
CHAPTER 8	Internal rate of return	67
CHAPTER 9	More Excel financial functions	75
CHAPTER 10	Circular references	87
CHAPTER 11	IF statements	93
CHAPTER 12	Time and time functions	111
CHAPTER 13	The Paste Special command	117
CHAPTER 14	Three-dimensional formulas	123
CHAPTER 15	The Auditing tool and Inquire add-in	127
CHAPTER 16	Sensitivity analysis with data tables	139
CHAPTER 17	The Goal Seek command	149
CHAPTER 18	Using the Scenario Manager for sensitivity analysis	155
CHAPTER 19	The COUNTIF, COUNTIFS, COUNT, COUNTA, and COUNTBLANK functions	161
CHAPTER 20	The SUMIF, AVERAGEIF, SUMIFS, and AVERAGEIFS functions	169
CHAPTER 21	The OFFSET function	175
CHAPTER 22	The INDIRECT function	187
CHAPTER 23	Conditional formatting	195
CHAPTER 24	Sorting in Excel	223
CHAPTER 25	Tables	231
CHAPTER 26	Spinner buttons, scroll bars, option buttons, check boxes, combo boxes, and group list boxes	245
CHAPTER 27	The analytics revolution	261
CHAPTER 28	Introducing optimization with Excel Solver	267
CHAPTER 29	Using Solver to determine the optimal product mix	273
CHAPTER 30	Using Solver to schedule your workforce	285

CHAPTER 31	Using Solver to solve transportation or distribution problems	291
CHAPTER 32	Using Solver for capital budgeting	297
CHAPTER 33	Using Solver for financial planning	305
CHAPTER 34	Using Solver to rate sports teams	313
CHAPTER 35	Warehouse location and the GRG Multistart and Evolutionary Solver engines	319
CHAPTER 36	Penalties and the Evolutionary Solver	329
CHAPTER 37	The traveling salesperson problem	335
CHAPTER 38	Importing data from a text file or document	339
CHAPTER 39	Importing data from the Internet	345
CHAPTER 40	Validating data	349
CHAPTER 41	Summarizing data by using histograms	359
CHAPTER 42	Summarizing data by using descriptive statistics	369
CHAPTER 43	Using PivotTables and slicers to describe data	385
CHAPTER 44	The Data Model	441
CHAPTER 45	PowerPivot	455
CHAPTER 46	Power View	469
CHAPTER 47	Sparklines	485
CHAPTER 48	Summarizing data with database statistical functions	491
CHAPTER 49	Filtering data and removing duplicates	501
CHAPTER 50	Consolidating data	521
CHAPTER 51	Creating subtotals	527
CHAPTER 52	Charting tricks	533
CHAPTER 53	Estimating straight-line relationships	569
CHAPTER 54	Modeling exponential growth	577
CHAPTER 55	The power curve	581
CHAPTER 56	Using correlations to summarize relationships	589
CHAPTER 57	Introduction to multiple regression	597
CHAPTER 58	Incorporating qualitative factors into multiple regression	605
CHAPTER 59	Modeling nonlinearities and interactions	615
CHAPTER 60	Analysis of variance: one-way ANOVA	623
CHAPTER 61	Randomized blocks and two-way ANOVA	629
CHAPTER 62	Using moving averages to understand time series	641
CHAPTER 63	Winters's method	645
CHAPTER 64	Ratio-to-moving-average forecast method	651
CHAPTER 65	Forecasting in the presence of special events	655
CHAPTER 66	An introduction to random variables	663

CHAPTER 67   The binomial, hypergeometric, and negative binomial
random variables   669

CHAPTER 68   The Poisson and exponential random variable   679

CHAPTER 69   The normal random variable   683

CHAPTER 70   Weibull and beta distributions: modeling machine
life and duration of a project   691

CHAPTER 71   Making probability statements from forecasts   697

CHAPTER 72   Using the lognormal random variable to model
stock prices   701

CHAPTER 73   Introduction to Monte Carlo simulation   705

CHAPTER 74   Calculating an optimal bid   715

CHAPTER 75   Simulating stock prices and asset allocation modeling   721

CHAPTER 76   Fun and games: simulating gambling and sporting
event probabilities   731

CHAPTER 77   Using resampling to analyze data   739

CHAPTER 78   Pricing stock options   743

CHAPTER 79   Determining customer value   757

CHAPTER 80   The economic order quantity inventory model   763

CHAPTER 81   Inventory modeling with uncertain demand   769

CHAPTER 82   Queuing theory: the mathematics of waiting in line 777

CHAPTER 83   Estimating a demand curve   785

CHAPTER 84   Pricing products by using tie-ins   791

CHAPTER 85   Pricing products by using subjectively determined
demand   797

CHAPTER 86   Nonlinear pricing   803

CHAPTER 87   Array formulas and functions   813

Index   831

Contents

Introduction . . . . *xxi*

    Errata xxvi

    We want to hear from you xxvi

    Stay in touch xxvi

Chapter 1   Range names   1

    How can I create named ranges? 1

        Using the Name box to create a range name 2

        Creating named ranges by using Create From Selection 4

        Creating range names by using Define Name 5

        Name Manager 6

    Answers to this chapter's questions 7

    Remarks 13

    Problems 13

Chapter 2   Lookup functions   15

    Syntax of the lookup functions 15

        VLOOKUP syntax 15

        HLOOKUP syntax 16

    Answers to this chapter's questions 16

    Problems 20

Chapter 3   INDEX function   23

    Syntax of the *INDEX* function 23

    Answers to this chapter's questions 23

    Problems 25

What do you think of this book? We want to hear from you!

Microsoft is interested in hearing your feedback so we can continually improve our
books and learning resources for you. To participate in a brief online survey, please visit:

microsoft.com/learning/booksurvey

Chapter 4   MATCH function   **27**

    Answers to this chapter's questions...............................29

    Problems...32

Chapter 5   Text functions   **35**

    Text function syntax..36

        The *LEFT* function..37

        The *RIGHT* function...37

        The *MID* function...37

        The *TRIM* function..37

        The *LEN* function...37

        The *FIND* and *SEARCH* functions 37

        The *REPT* function 37

        The *CONCATENATE* and & functions...........................38

        The *REPLACE* function...38

        The *VALUE* function 38

        The *UPPER*, *LOWER*, and *PROPER* functions 38

        The *CHAR* function 38

        The *CLEAN* Function 39

        The *SUBSTITUTE* FUNCTION 39

    Answers to this chapter's questions...............................40

        Extracting data by using the Convert Text To Columns Wizard ...43

    Problems...47

Chapter 6   Dates and date functions   **51**

    Answers to this chapter's questions...............................52

    Problems...57

**Chapter 7   Evaluating investments by using net present
value criteria**   **59**

    Answers to this chapter's questions...............................60

    Problems...64

Chapter 8 Internal rate of return   **67**

    Answers to this chapter's questions. 68

    Problems. 73

Chapter 9 More Excel financial functions   **75**

    Answers to this chapter's questions. 75

    CUMPRINC and *CUMIPMT* functions 81

    Problems. 83

Chapter 10 Circular references   **87**

    Answers to this chapter's questions. 87

    Problems. 90

Chapter 11 IF statements   **93**

    Answers to this chapter's questions. 94

    Problems. 106

Chapter 12 Time and time functions   **111**

    Answers to this chapter's questions. 111

    Problems. 115

Chapter 13 The Paste Special command   **117**

    Answers to this chapter's questions. 117

    Problems. 121

Chapter 14 Three-dimensional formulas   **123**

    Answer to this chapter's question 123

    Problem 125

Chapter 15 The Auditing tool and Inquire add-in   **127**

   Answers to this chapter's questions. 130

   Problems. 138

Chapter 16 Sensitivity analysis with data tables   **139**

   Answers to this chapter's questions. 140

   Problems. 146

Chapter 17 The Goal Seek command   **149**

   Answers to this chapter's questions. 149

   Problems. 152

Chapter 18 Using the Scenario Manager for sensitivity analysis   **155**

   Answer to this chapter's question 155

   Remarks 158

   Problems. 158

Chapter 19 The COUNTIF, COUNTIFS, COUNT, COUNTA, and COUNTBLANK functions   **161**

   Answers to this chapter's questions. 163

   Remarks 166

   Problems. 166

Chapter 20 The SUMIF, AVERAGEIF, SUMIFS, and AVERAGEIFS functions   **169**

   Answers to this chapter's questions. 170

   Problems. 172

Chapter 21 The OFFSET function   **175**

   Answers to this chapter's questions. 176

   Remarks 184

   Problems. 185

Chapter 22 The INDIRECT function   **187**

Answers to this chapter's questions...............................188

Problems...193

Chapter 23 Conditional formatting   **195**

Answers to this chapter's questions...............................197

Problems...219

Chapter 24 Sorting in Excel   **223**

Answers to this chapter's questions...............................223

Problems...230

Chapter 25 Tables   **231**

Answers to this chapter's questions...............................231

Problems...244

Chapter 26 Spinner buttons, scroll bars, option buttons, check boxes, combo boxes, and group list boxes   **245**

Answers to this chapter's questions...............................247

Problems...258

Chapter 27 The analytics revolution   **261**

Answers to this chapter's questions...............................261

Chapter 28 Introducing optimization with Excel Solver   **267**

Problems...270

Chapter 29 Using Solver to determine the optimal product mix   **273**

Answers to this chapter's questions...............................273

Problems...283

Chapter 30 Using Solver to schedule your workforce   **285**

Answer to this chapter's question 285

Problems...288

Chapter 31 Using Solver to solve transportation or distribution problems   **291**

Answer to this chapter's question 291

Problems...294

Chapter 32 Using Solver for capital budgeting   **297**

Answer to this chapter's question 297

    Handling other constraints...................................300

    Solving binary and integer programming problems...........301

Problems...303

Chapter 33 Using Solver for financial planning   **305**

Answers to this chapter's questions...............................305

Problems...310

Chapter 34 Using Solver to rate sports teams   **313**

Answer to this chapter's question 314

Problems...318

Chapter 35 Warehouse location and the GRG Multistart and Evolutionary Solver engines   **319**

Understanding the GRG Multistart and Evolutionary Solver engines...319

    How does Solver solve linear Solver problems?................319

    How does the GRG Nonlinear engine solve nonlinear optimization models? 320

    How does the Evolutionary Solver engine tackle nonsmooth optimization problems? 323

Answers to this chapter's questions...............................323

Problems...328

Chapter 36 Penalties and the Evolutionary Solver   **329**

Answers to this chapter's questions. 329

Using conditional formatting to highlight each employee's ratings 332

Problems. 333

Chapter 37 The traveling salesperson problem   **335**

Answers to this chapter's questions. 335

Problems. 338

Chapter 38 Importing data from a text file or document   **339**

Answer to this chapter's question 339

Problems. 344

Chapter 39 Importing data from the Internet   **345**

Answer to this chapter's question 345

Problems. 348

Chapter 40 Validating data   **349**

Answers to this chapter's questions. 349

Remarks 355

Problems. 356

Chapter 41 Summarizing data by using histograms   **359**

Answers to this chapter's questions. 359

Problems. 367

Chapter 42 Summarizing data by using descriptive statistics   **369**

Answers to this chapter's questions. 370

Using conditional formatting to highlight outliers 375

Problems. 382

Chapter 43 Using PivotTables and slicers to describe data   **385**

    Answers to this chapter's questions. 386

        Remarks about grouping 424

    Problems. 437

Chapter 44 The Data Model   **441**

    Answers to this chapter's questions. 441

    Problems. 453

Chapter 45 PowerPivot   **455**

    Answers to this chapter's questions. 456

    Problems. 468

Chapter 46 Power View   **469**

    Answers to this chapter's questions. 470

    Problems. 483

Chapter 47 Sparklines   **485**

    Answers to this chapter's questions. 485

    Problems. 490

**Chapter 48 Summarizing data with database statistical
          functions**   **491**

    Answers to this chapter's questions. 493

    Problems. 498

Chapter 49 Filtering data and removing duplicates   **501**

    Answers to this chapter's questions. 503

    Problems. 518

Chapter 50 Consolidating data   **521**

    Answer to this chapter's question 521

    Problems. 525

Chapter 51 Creating subtotals   **527**

    Answers to this chapter's questions. 527

    Problems. 532

Chapter 52 Charting tricks   **533**

    Answers to this chapter's questions. 534

    Problems. 566

Chapter 53 Estimating straight-line relationships   **569**

    Answers to this chapter's questions. 571

    Problems. 575

Chapter 54 Modeling exponential growth   **577**

    Answer to this chapter's question 577

    Problems. 580

Chapter 55 The power curve   **581**

    Answer to this chapter's question 584

    Problems. 586

Chapter 56 Using correlations to summarize relationships   **589**

    Answer to this chapter's question 591

        Filling in the correlation matrix 593

        Using the *CORREL* function 594

        Relationship between correlation and R^2 .594

        Correlation and regression toward the mean. 595

    Problems. 595

Chapter 57 Introduction to multiple regression   **597**

    Answers to this chapter's questions. 597

Chapter 58 Incorporating qualitative factors into multiple regression **605**

Answers to this chapter's questions. 605

Chapter 59 Modeling nonlinearities and interactions **615**

Answers to this chapter's questions. 615

Problems for Chapters 57 and 58. 619

Chapter 60 Analysis of variance: one-way ANOVA **623**

Answers to this chapter's questions. 624

Problems. 628

Chapter 61 Randomized blocks and two-way ANOVA **629**

Answers to this chapter's questions. 630

Problems. 638

Chapter 62 Using moving averages to understand time series **641**

Answer to this chapter's question 641

Problem 643

Chapter 63 Winters's method **645**

Time series characteristics. 645

Parameter definitions. 645

Initializing Winters's method 646

Estimating the smoothing constants. 647

Remarks 649

Problems. 649

Chapter 64 Ratio-to-moving-average forecast method **651**

Answers to this chapter's questions. 651

Problem 654

Chapter 65 Forecasting in the presence of special events   **655**

Answers to this chapter's questions. 655

Problems. 662

Chapter 66 An introduction to random variables   **663**

Answers to this chapter's questions. 663

Problems. 667

**Chapter 67 The binomial, hypergeometric, and negative
binomial random variables**   **669**

Answers to this chapter's questions. 670

Problems. 676

Chapter 68 The Poisson and exponential random variable   **679**

Answers to this chapter's questions. 679

Problems. 682

Chapter 69 The normal random variable   **683**

Answers to this chapter's questions. 683

Problems. 689

**Chapter 70 Weibull and beta distributions: modeling machine
life and duration of a project**   **691**

Answers to this chapter's questions. 691

Problems. 696

Chapter 71 Making probability statements from forecasts   **697**

Answers to this chapter's questions. 698

Problems. 699

Chapter 72 Using the lognormal random variable to model stock prices   **701**

    Answers to this chapter's questions. 701

    Remarks 704

    Problems. 704

Chapter 73 Introduction to Monte Carlo simulation   **705**

    Answers to this chapter's questions. 706

        The impact of risk on your decision 712

        Confidence interval for mean profit. 713

    Problems. 713

Chapter 74 Calculating an optimal bid   **715**

    Answers to this chapter's questions. 715

    Problems. 718

Chapter 75 Simulating stock prices and asset allocation modeling   **721**

    Answers to this chapter's questions. 722

    Problems. 729

Chapter 76 Fun and games: simulating gambling and sporting event probabilities   **731**

    Answers to this chapter's questions. 731

    Problems. 737

Chapter 77 Using resampling to analyze data   **739**

    Answer to this chapter's question 739

    Problems. 742

Chapter 78 Pricing stock options   **743**

    Answers to this chapter's questions. 744

    Problems. 754

Chapter 79 Determining customer value   **757**

     Answers to this chapter's questions. 757

     Problems. 761

Chapter 80 The economic order quantity inventory model   **763**

     Answers to this chapter's questions. 763

     Problems. 767

Chapter 81 Inventory modeling with uncertain demand   **769**

     Answers to this chapter's questions. 770

     Problems. 775

Chapter 82 Queuing theory: the mathematics of waiting in line   **777**

     Answers to this chapter's questions. 777

     Problems. 782

Chapter 83 Estimating a demand curve   **785**

     Answers to this chapter's questions. 785

     Problems. 789

Chapter 84 Pricing products by using tie-ins   **791**

     Answer to this chapter's question 791

     Problems. 794

Chapter 85 Pricing products by using subjectively determined demand   **797**

     Answers to this chapter's questions. 797

     Problems. 800

Chapter 86 Nonlinear pricing   **803**

     Answers to this chapter's questions. 803

     Problems. 810

Chapter 87 Array formulas and functions   **813**

  Answers to this chapter's questions. 814

  Problems. 827

  Index   *831*

What do you think of this book? We want to hear from you!

Microsoft is interested in hearing your feedback so we can continually improve our
books and learning resources for you. To participate in a brief online survey, please visit:

microsoft.com/learning/booksurvey

Introduction

Whether you work for a Fortune 500 corporation, a small company, a government agency, or a not-for-profit organization, if you're reading this introduction the chances are you use Microsoft Excel in your daily work. Your job probably involves summarizing, reporting, and analyzing data. It might also involve building analytic models to help your employer increase profits, reduce costs, or manage operations more efficiently.

Since 1999, I've taught thousands of analysts at organizations such as 3M, Booz Allen Hamilton consulting, Bristol-Myers Squibb, Broadcom Cisco Systems, Deloitte Consulting, Drugstore.com, eBay, Eli Lilly, Ford, General Electric, General Motors, Intel, Microsoft, Morgan Stanley, NCR, Owens Corning, Pfizer, Proctor & Gamble, PWC, Schlumberger, Tellabs, the U.S. Army, the U.S. Department of Defense, and Verizon how to use Excel more efficiently and productively in their jobs. Students have often told me that the tools and methods I teach in my classes have saved them hours of time each week and provided them with new and improved approaches for analyzing important business problems.

I've used the techniques described in this book in my own consulting practice to solve many business problems. For example, I have used Excel to help the Dallas Mavericks and New York Knickers NBA basketball teams evaluate referees, players, and lineups. During the last 15 years I have also taught Excel business modeling and data analysis classes to MBA students at Indiana University's Kelley School of Business. (As proof of my teaching excellence, I have won over 45 teaching awards, and have won the school's overall MBA teaching award six times.) I would like to also note that 95 percent of MBA students at Indiana University take my spreadsheet modeling class even though it is an elective.

The book you have in your hands is an attempt to make these successful classes available to everyone. Here is why I think the book will help you learn how to use Excel more effectively:

- The materials have been tested while teaching thousands of analysts working for Fortune 500 corporations and government agencies, including the U.S. Army.

- I've written the book as though I am talking to the reader. I hope this approach transfers the spirit of a successful classroom environment to the written page.

- I teach by example, which makes concepts easier to master. These examples are constructed to have a real-world feel. Many of the examples are based on questions sent to me by employees of Fortune 500 corporations.

- For the most part, I lead you through the approaches I take in Excel to set up and answer a wide range of data analysis and business questions. You can follow along with my explanations by referring to the sample worksheets that accompany each example. However, I have also included template files for the book's examples on the companion website. If you want to, you can use these templates to work directly with Excel and complete each example on your own.

- For the most part, the chapters are short and organized around a single concept. You should be able to master the content of most chapters with at most two hours of study. By looking at the questions that begin each chapter, you'll gain an idea about the types of problems you'll be able to solve after mastering a chapter's topics. .

- In addition to learning about Excel formulas, you will learn some important math in a fairly painless fashion. For example, you'll learn about statistics, forecasting, optimization models, Monte Carlo simulation, inventory modeling, and the mathematics of waiting in line. You will also learn about some recent developments in business thinking, such as real options, customer value, and mathematical pricing models.

- At the end of each chapter, I've provided a group of practice problems (over 600 in total) that you can work through on your own. These problems will help you master the information in each chapter. Answers to all problems are included in files on the book's companion website. Many of these problems are based on actual problems faced by business analysts at Fortune 500 companies.

- Most of all, learning should be fun. If you read this book, you will learn how to predict U.S. presidential elections, how to set football point spreads, how to determine the probability of winning at craps, and how to determine the probability of a specific team winning an NCAA tournament. These examples are interesting and fun, and they also teach you a lot about solving business problems with Excel.

 Note To follow along with this book, you must have Excel 2013. Previous versions of this book can be used with Excel 2003, Excel 2007, or Excel 2010.

What's new in this edition

This edition of the book contains the following changes:

- An explanation of Excel's 2013 exciting Flash Fill feature

- An explanation of how to delete invisible characters which often mess up calculations.

- An explanation of the following new Excel 2013 functions: SHEET, SHEETS, FORMULATEXT, and ISFORMULA.

- A simple method for listing all of a workbook's worksheet names.

- A chapter describing the exciting new field of analytics.

- How to create PivotTables from data in disparate locations or based on another PivotTable.

- How to use Excel 2013's new Timeline feature to filter PivotTables based on dates.

- A description of Excel 2013's Data Model.

- A description of Excel 2013's PowerPivot add-in.

- How to use Power View to create mind blowing charts and graphics.

- A new chapter on charting tricks and a general description of charting in Excel 2013.

- Over 30 new problems have been added.

What you should know before reading this book

To follow the examples in this book you do not need to be an Excel guru. Basically, the two key actions you should know how to do are the following:

- **Enter a formula**   You should know that formulas must begin with an equals sign (=). You should also know the basic mathematical operators. For example, you should know that an asterisk (*) is used for multiplication, a forward slash (/) is used for division, and the caret key (^) is used to raise a quantity to a power.

- **Work with cell references**   You should know that when you copy a formula that contains a cell reference such as $A$4 (an absolute cell reference, which is created by including the dollar signs), the formula still refers to cell A4 in the cells you copy it to. When you copy a formula that contains a cell reference such as $A4 (a mixed cell address), the column remains fixed, but the row changes. Finally, when you copy a formula that contains a cell reference such as A4 (a relative cell reference), both the row and the column of the cells referenced in the formula change.

How to use this book

As you read along with the examples in this book, you can take one of two approaches:

- You can open the template file that corresponds to the example you are studying and complete each step of the example as you read the book. You will be surprised how easy this process is and amazed with how much you learn and retain. This is the approach I use in my corporate classes.

- Instead of working in the template, you can follow my explanations as you look at the final version of each sample file.

Using the companion content

This book features a companion website that makes available to you all the sample files you use in the book's examples (both the final Excel workbooks and starting templates you can work with on your own). The workbooks and templates are organized in folders named for each chapter. The answers to all chapter-ending problems in the book are also included with the sample files. Each answer file is named so that you can identify it easily. For example, the file containing the answer to Problem 2 in Chapter 10 is named s10_2.xlsx.

To work through the examples in this book, you need to copy the book's sample files to your computer. These practice files, and other information, can be downloaded from the book's detail page, located at:

http://aka.ms/Excel2013Data/files

Display the detail page in your Web browser, and follow the instructions for downloading the files.

Your companion eBook

The eBook edition of this book allows you to:

- Search the full text
- Print
- Copy and paste

To download your eBook, please see the instruction page at the back of this book.

Acknowledgments

I am eternally grateful to Jennifer Skoog and Norm Tonina, who had faith in me and first hired me to teach Excel classes for Microsoft finance. Jennifer in particular was instrumental in helping design the content and style of the classes on which the book is based. Keith Lange of Eli Lilly, Pat Keating and Doug Hoppe of Cisco Systems, and Dennis Fuller of the U.S. Army also helped me refine my thoughts on teaching data analysis and modeling with Excel.

Editors Kenyon Brown and Rachel Roumeliotis did a great job of keeping me (and the book) on schedule. Peter Myers did a great job with the technical editing. Thanks also to Production Editors Kara Ebrahim and Chris Norton for managing the book's production. I am grateful to my many students at the organizations where I've taught and at the Indiana University Kelley School of Business. Many of them have taught me things I did not know about Excel.

Alex Blanton, formerly of Microsoft Press, championed this project at the start and shared my vision of developing a user-friendly text designed for use by business analysts.

Finally, my lovely and talented wife, Vivian, and my wonderful children, Jennifer and Gregory, put up with my long weekend hours at the keyboard.

Support & feedback

The following sections provide information on errata, book support, feedback, and contact information.

Errata

We've made every effort to ensure the accuracy of this book and its companion content. If you do find an error, please report it on our Microsoft Press site at oreilly.com:

1. Go to *http://microsoftpress.oreilly.com*.

2. In the **Search** box, enter the book's ISBN or title.

3. Select your book from the search results.

4. On your book's catalog page, under the cover image, you'll see a list of links.

5. Click **View/Submit Errata.**

You'll find additional information and services for your book on its catalog page. If you need additional support, please e-mail Microsoft Press Book Support at *mspinput@microsoft.com*.

Please note that product support for Microsoft software is not offered through the addresses above.

We want to hear from you

At Microsoft Press, your satisfaction is our top priority, and your feedback our most valuable asset. Please tell us what you think of this book at:

http://www.microsoft.com/learning/booksurvey

The survey is short, and we read *every one* of your comments and ideas. Thanks in advance for your input!

Stay in touch

Let's keep the conversation going! We're on Twitter: *http://twitter.com/MicrosoftPress*.

CHAPTER 1

Range names

Questions answered in this chapter:

- I want the total sales in Arizona, California, Montana, New York, and New Jersey. Can I use a formula to compute the total sales in a form such as AZ+CA+MT+NY+NJ instead of SUM(A21:A25) and still get the right answer?

- What does a formula such as Average(A:A) do?

- What is the difference between a name with workbook scope and one with worksheet scope?

- I really am getting to like range names. I have started defining range names for many of the workbooks I have developed at the office. However, the range names do not show up in my formulas. How can I make recently created range names show up in previously created formulas?

- How can I paste a list of all range names (and the cells they represent) into my worksheet?

- I am computing projected annual revenues as a multiple of last year's revenue. Is there a way to have the formula look like (1+growth)*last year?

- For each day of the week, we are given the hourly wage and hours worked. Can we compute total salary for each day with the wages*hours formula?

You have probably worked with worksheets that use formulas such as SUM(A5000:A5049). Then you have to find out what's contained in cells A5000:A5049. If cells A5000:A5049 contain sales in each US state, wouldn't the formula SUM(USSales) be easier to understand? In this chapter, you learn how to name individual cells or ranges of cells and how to use range names in formulas.

How can I create named ranges?

There are three ways to create named ranges:

- By entering a range name in the **Name** box

- By clicking **Create From Selection** in the **Defined Names** group on the **Formulas** tab

- By clicking **Name Manager** or **Define Name** in the **Defined Names** group on the **Formulas** tab

Using the Name box to create a range name

The Name box (shown in Figure 1-1) is located directly above the label for column A. (To see the Name box, click the **Formula** bar.) To create a range name in the Name box, simply select the cell or range of cells that you want to name, click in the **Name** box, and then type the range name you want to use. Press Enter, and you've created the range name. Clicking the drop-down arrow in the Name box displays the range names defined in the current workbook. You can display all the range names in a workbook by pressing the F3 key to open the **Paste Name** dialog box. When you select a range name from the Name box, Microsoft Excel 2013 selects the cells corresponding to that range name. This enables you to verify that you've chosen the cell or range that you intended to name. Range names are not case sensitive.

A1	▾

FIGURE 1-1 You can create a range name by selecting the cell range you want to name and then typing the range name in the Name box.

For example, suppose you want to name cell F3 *east* and cell F4 *west*. See Figure 1-2 and the Eastwestempt.xlsx file. Select cell F3, type **east** in the **Name** box, and then press Enter. Select cell F4, type **west** in the **Name** box, and press Enter. If you now reference cell F3 in another cell, you see =east instead of =F3. This means that whenever you see the reference *east* in a formula, Excel will insert whatever is in cell F3.

	E	F	G
1			
2			
3	east	5	
4	west	10	

FIGURE 1-2 Name cell F3 east and cell F4 west.

Suppose you want to assign a rectangular range of cells (such as A1:B4) the name *Data*. Select the cell range A1:B4, type **Data** in the **Name** box, and press Enter. Now a formula such as =AVERAGE(Data) would average the contents of cells A1:B4. See the Data.xlsx file and Figure 1-3.

data	fx	1

	A	B	C
1	1	2	
2	3	2	
3	1	1	
4	2	-1	
5			1.375
6		cell C5	=AVERAGE(data)
7		contains	

FIGURE 1-3 Name the A1:B4 range Data.

Sometimes, you want to name a range of cells made up of several noncontiguous rectangular ranges. For example, in Figure 1-4 and the Noncontig.xlsx file, you might want to assign the name *Noncontig* to the range consisting of cells B3:C4, E6:G7, and B10:C10. To assign this name, select any one of the three rectangles making up the range (B3:C4 for now). Hold down the Ctrl key and then select the other two ranges (E6:G7 and B10:C10). Now release the Ctrl key, type the name **Noncontig** in the Name box, and press Enter. Using *Noncontig* in any formula will now refer to the contents of cells B3:C4, E6:G7, and B10:C10. For example, entering the formula =AVERAGE(Noncontig) in cell E11 yields 4.75 (because the 12 numbers in your range add up to 57, and 57/12 = 4.75).

	B	C	D	E	F	G
1						
2						
3	1	2				
4	3	4				
5						
6				6	7	10
7				8	9	1
8						
9						
10	2	4				
11				4.75		
12				Cell E11 contains formula		
13				=AVERAGE(noncontig)		

FIGURE 1-4 This is how to name a noncontiguous range of cells.

Creating named ranges by using Create From Selection

The Statestemp.xlsx worksheet contains sales during March for each of the 50 US states. Figure 1-5 shows a subset of this data. You would like to name each cell in the B6:B55 range with the correct state abbreviation. To do this, select the A6:B55 range and click **Create From Selection** in the **Defined Names** group on the **Formulas** tab (see Figure 1-6) and then select the Left Column check box, as indicated in Figure 1-7.

	A	B
5	State	March Sales
6	AL	$ 915.00
7	AK	$ 741.00
8	AZ	$ 566.00
9	AR	$ 754.00
10	CA	$ 687.00
11	CO	$ 757.00
12	CT	$ 786.00
13	DE	$ 795.00
14	FL	$ 944.00
15	GA	$ 624.00
16	HI	$ 663.00
17	ID	$ 895.00
18	IL	$ 963.00

FIGURE 1-5 By naming the cells that contain state sales with state abbreviations, you can use the abbreviation rather than the cell's column letter and row number when you refer to the cell.

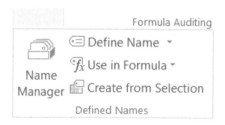

FIGURE 1-6 Select Create From Selection.

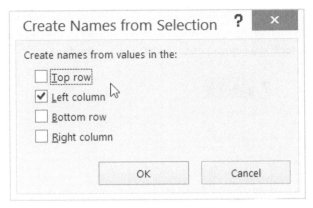

FIGURE 1-7 Select the Left Column check box.

Excel now knows to associate the names in the first column of the selected range with the cells in the second column of the selected range. Thus, B6 is assigned the range name *AL*, B7 is named *AK*, and so on. Creating these range names in the Name box would have been incredibly tedious! Click the drop-down arrow in the **Name** box to verify that these range names have been created.

Creating range names by using Define Name

If you choose **Name Manager** on the **Formulas** tab and select **Define Name** from the menu shown in Figure 1-6, the New Name dialog box shown in Figure 1-8 opens.

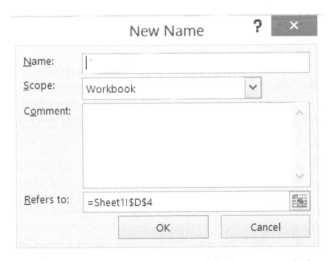

FIGURE 1-8 This is how the New Name dialog box appears before creating any range names.

Suppose you want to assign the name *range1* (range names are not case sensitive) to the cell range A2:B7. Type **range1** in the **Name** box and then point to the range or type **=A2:B7** in the **Refers To** area. The New Name dialog box will now look like Figure 1-9. Click **OK**, and you're done.

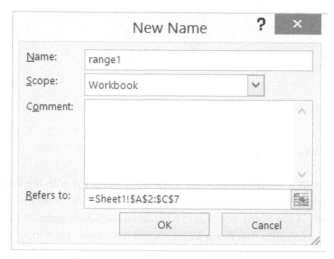

FIGURE 1-9 The New Name dialog box looks like this after creating a range name.

If you click the Scope arrow, you can select **Workbook** or any worksheet in your workbook. This decision is discussed later in this chapter, so for now, just choose the default scope of **Workbook**. You can also add comments for any of your range names.

Name Manager

If you now click the **Name** arrow, the name *range1* (and any other ranges you have created) appears in the Name box. In Excel 2013, there is an easy way to edit or delete your range names. Open **Name Manager** by selecting the **Formulas** tab and then click **Name Manager** from the menu shown in Figure 1-6. You now see a list of all range names. For example, for the States.xlsx file, the Name Manager dialog box will look like Figure 1-10.

To edit any range name, double-click the range name or select the range name and click Edit; you can then change the name of the range, the cells the range refers to, or the scope of the range.

To delete any subset of range names, first select the range names you want to delete. If the range names are listed consecutively, select the first range name in the group you want to delete, hold down the Shift key, and select the last range name in the group. If the range names are not listed consecutively, you can select any range name you want to delete and then hold down the Ctrl key while you select the other range names for deletion. Then press the Delete key to delete the selected range names.

Now look at some specific examples of how to use range names.

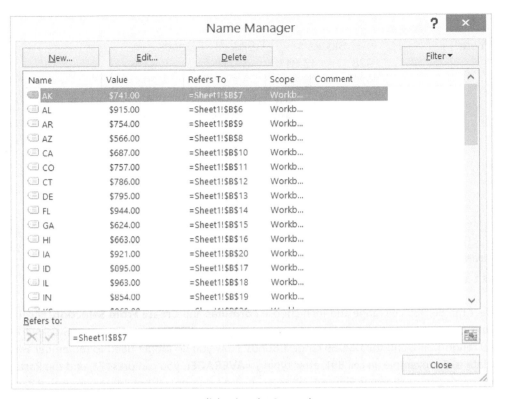

FIGURE 1-10 This is the Name Manager dialog box for States.xlsx.

Answers to this chapter's questions

This section provides the answers to the questions that are listed at the beginning of the chapter.

I want the total sales in Arizona, California, Montana, New York, and New Jersey. Can I use a formula to compute the total sales in a form such as AZ+CA+MT+NY+NJ instead of SUM(A21:A25) and still get the right answer?

Return to the States.xlsx file, in which you assigned each state's abbreviation as the range name for the state's sales. If you want to compute total sales in Alabama, Alaska, Arizona, and Arkansas, clearly you could use the formula SUM(B6:B9). You could also point to cells B6, B7, B8, and B9, and the formula would be entered as =AL+AK+AZ+AR. The latter formula is self-describing.

As another illustration of how to use range names, look at the Historicalinvesttemp.xlsx file, shown in Figure 1-11, which contains annual percentage returns on stocks, T-bills, and bonds. (Some rows are hidden in this figure; the data ends in row 89.)

	A	B	C	D
7	Year	Stocks	T.Bills	T.Bonds
8	1928	43.81%	3.08%	0.84%
9	1929	-8.30%	3.16%	4.20%
10	1930	-25.12%	4.55%	4.54%
11	1931	-43.84%	2.31%	-2.56%
12	1932	-8.64%	1.07%	8.79%
13	1933	49.98%	0.96%	1.86%
14	1934	-1.19%	0.30%	7.96%
15	1935	46.74%	0.23%	4.47%
88	2008	-37.00%	25.87%	1.60%
89	2009	26.46%	-14.90%	0.10%
90		stocks	tbills	bonds
91	averages	11.28%	4.28%	4.91%

FIGURE 1-11 This figure shows historical investment data.

Select the B8:D89 cell range and then choose **Formulas** and **Create From Selection**. For this example, names are created in the top row of the range. The B8:B89 range is named Stocks, the C8:C89 range T.Bills, and the D8:D89 range T.Bonds. Now you no longer need to remember where your data is. For example, in cell B91, after typing **=AVERAGE(**, you can press F3, and the Paste Name dialog box opens, as shown in Figure 1-12. You can also bring up a list of range names that can be pasted in formulas if you start typing and click **Use In Formula** on the **Formulas** tab.

FIGURE 1-12 You can add a range name to a formula by using the Paste Name dialog box.

You can select **Stocks** in the **Paste Name** list and click **OK**. After entering the closing parenthesis, the formula, =AVERAGE(Stocks), computes the average return on stocks (11.28 percent). The beauty of this approach is that even if you don't remember where the data is, you can work with the stock return data anywhere in the workbook!

This chapter would be remiss if it did not mention the exciting AutoComplete capabilities of Excel 2013. If you begin typing =Average(T, Excel shows you a list of range names and functions that begin with T, and you can just double-click **T.Bills** to complete the entry of the range name.

What does a formula such as Average(A:A) do?

If you use a column name (in the form of A:A, C:C, and so on) in a formula, Excel treats an entire column as a named range. For example, entering the =AVERAGE(A:A) formula averages all numbers in column A. Using a range name for an entire column is very helpful if you frequently enter new data in a column. For example, if column A contains monthly sales of a product, as new sales data are entered each month, your formula computes an up-to-date monthly sales average. Use caution, however, because if you enter the =AVERAGE(A:A) formula in column A, you will get a circular reference message because the value of the cell containing the average formula depends on the cell containing the average. You learn how to resolve circular references in Chapter 10, "Circular references." Similarly, entering the =AVERAGE(1:1) formula averages all numbers in row 1.

What is the difference between a name with workbook scope and one with worksheet scope?

The Sheetnames.xlsx file will help you understand the difference between range names that have workbook scope and range names that have worksheet scope. When you create names with the Name box, the names default to workbook scope. For example, suppose you use the Name box to assign the name *sales* to the cell range E4:E6 in Sheet3, and these cells contain the numbers 1, 2, and 4, respectively. If you enter a formula such as =SUM(sales) in any worksheet, you obtain an answer of 7 because the Name box creates names with workbook scope, so anywhere in the workbook you refer to the name *sales* (which has workbook scope), the name refers to cells E4:E6 of Sheet3. In any worksheet, if you now enter the =SUM(sales) formula, you will obtain 7 because anywhere in the workbook, Excel links *sales* to cells E4:F6 of Sheet3.

Now suppose that you type 4, 5, and 6 in cells E4:E6 of Sheet1 and 3, 4, and 5 in cells E4:E6 of Sheet2, and then you open Name Manager, give the name *jam* to cells E4:E6 of Sheet1, and define the scope of this name as Sheet1. Then you move to Sheet2, open Name Manager, give the name *jam* to cells E4:E6, and define the scope of this name as Sheet2. The Name Manager dialog box now looks like Figure 1-13.

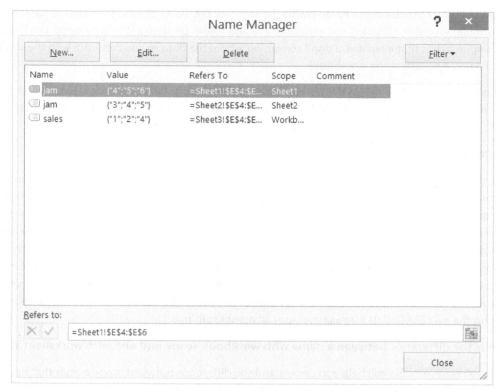

FIGURE 1-13 The Name Manager dialog box displays worksheet and workbook names.

Now, what if you enter the =SUM(jam) formula in each sheet? In Sheet 1, =SUM(jam) will total cells E4:E6 of Sheet1. Because those cells contain 4, 5, and 6, you obtain 15. In Sheet2, =SUM(jam) will total cells E4:E6 of Sheet2, yielding *3 + 4 + 5 = 12*. In Sheet3, however, the =SUM(jam) formula will yield a #NAME? error because no range is named *jam* in Sheet3. If you enter the =SUM(Sheet2!jam) formula anywhere in Sheet3, Excel will recognize the worksheet-level name that represents cell range E4:E6 of Sheet2 and yield a result of *3 + 4 + 5 = 12*. Thus, by prefacing a worksheet-level name by its sheet name followed by an exclamation point (!), you can refer to a worksheet-level range in a worksheet other than the sheet in which the range is defined.

I really am getting to like range names. I have started defining range names for many of the workbooks I have developed at the office. However, the range names do not show up in my formulas. How can I make recently created range names show up in previously created formulas?

Look at the Applynames.xlsx file and Figure 1-14.

	E	F
1		
2		
3	price	$5.00
4	demand	8500
5	unit cost	$4.00
6	fixed cost	$3,000.00
7	profit	$5,500.00

FIGURE 1-14 This figure shows how to apply range names to formulas.

The price of a product was entered in cell F3 and product demand of *=10000–300*F3* in cell F4. The unit cost and fixed cost are entered in cells F5 and F6, respectively, and profit is computed in cell F7 with the =F4*(F3–F5)–F6 formula. In this example, **Formulas**, **Create From Selection**, and then **Left Column** are used to name cell F3 *price*, cell F4 *demand*, cell F5 *unit cost*, cell F6 *fixed cost*, and cell F7 *profit*. You would like these range names to show up in the cell F4 and cell F7 formulas. To apply the range names, first select the range where you want the range names applied (in this case, F4:F7). Now open the **Defined Names** group on the **Formulas** tab, click the **Define Name** arrow, and then choose **Apply Names**. Highlight the names you want to apply and then click **OK**. Note that cell F4 now contains the =10000–300*price formula, and cell F7 contains the =demand*(price–unit_cost)–fixed_cost formula, as you wanted.

By the way, if you want the range names to apply to the entire worksheet, select the entire worksheet by clicking the **Select All** button at the intersection of the column and row headings.

How can I paste a list of all range names (and the cells they represent) into my worksheet?

Press F3 to open the **Paste Name** box and then click the **Paste List** button. (See Figure 1-12.) A list of range names and the cells each corresponds to will be pasted into your worksheet, beginning at the current cell location.

I am computing projected annual revenues as a multiple of last year's revenue. Is there a way to have the formula look like (1+growth)*last year?

The Last year.xlsx file contains the solution to this problem. As shown in Figure 1-15, you want to compute revenues for 2012–2018 that grow at 10 percent per year off a base level of $300 million in 2011.

	A	B	C	D
1				
2				
3	growth	0.1		
4				
5		revenue		
6	2011	300		
7	2012	330		
8	2013	363		
9	2014	399.3		
10	2015	439.23		
11	2016	483.153		
12	2017	531.4683		
13	2018	584.6151		

FIGURE 1-15 Create a range name for the previous year.

To begin, use the **Name** box to name cell B3 *growth*. Now comes the good part! Move the cursor to B7 and open the **New Name** dialog box by clicking **Define Name** in the **Defined Names** group on the **Formulas** tab. Fill in the **New Name** dialog box as shown in Figure 1-16.

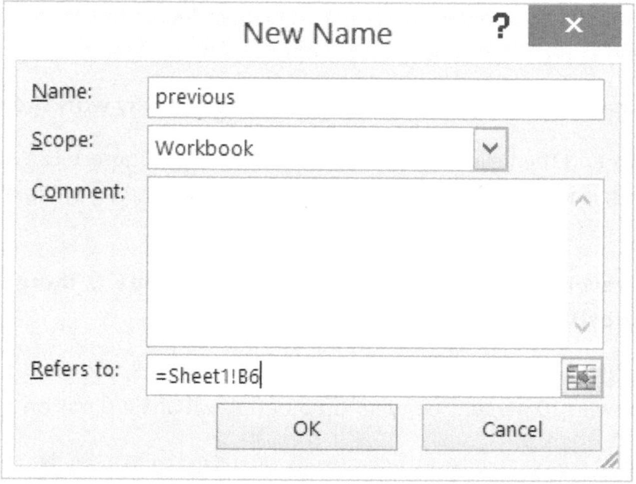

New Name ? ✕
Name: previous
Scope: Workbook ⌄
Comment:
Refers to: =Sheet1!B6
OK   Cancel

FIGURE 1-16 In any cell, this name refers to the cell above the active cell.

Because you are in cell B7, Excel interprets this range name always to refer to the cell above the current cell. This would not work if, in the B6 cell reference, the 6 were dollar signed because dollar signing the 6 would prevent the row reference from changing to pick up the row directly above the active cell. If you enter the =previous*(1+growth) formula in cell B7 and copy it down to the B8:B13 range, each cell will contain the formula you want and will multiply 1.1 by the contents of the cell directly above the active cell.

For each day of the week, we are given the hourly wage and hours worked. Can we compute total salary for each day with the wages*hours formula?

As shown in Figure 1-17 (see the Namedrows.xlsx file), row 12 contains daily wage rates, and row 13 contains hours worked each day.

	E	F	G	H	I	J	K	L
11		Monday	Tuesday	Wednesda	Thursday	Friday	Saturday	Sunday
12	wage	$ 5.00	$ 6.00	$ 7.00	$ 8.00	$ 9.00	$ 15.00	$ 15.00
13	hours	55	65	75	65	77	88	36
14	payroll	$ 275.00	$ 390.00	$ 525.00	$ 520.00	$ 693.00	$ 1,320.00	$ 540.00

FIGURE 1-17 In any cell, this name refers to the cell above the active cell.

You can select row 12 (by clicking the 12) and use the **Name** box to enter the name **wage**. Select row 13 and type the name **hours** in the **Name** box. If you now enter the wage*hours formula in cell F14 and copy this formula to the G14:L14 range, you can see that Excel finds the wage and hour values and multiplies them in each column.

Remarks

- Excel does not allow you to use the letters r and c as range names.

- The only symbols allowed in range names are periods (.) and underscores (_).

- If you use Create From Selection to create a range name, and your name contains spaces, Excel inserts an underscore (_) to fill in the spaces. For example, Product 1 is created as Product_1.

- Range names cannot begin with numbers or look like a cell reference. For example, 3Q and A4 are not allowed as range names. Because Excel 2013 has more than 16,000 columns, a range name such as cat1 is not permitted because there is a CAT1 cell. If you try to name a cell CAT1, Excel tells you the name is invalid. Probably your best alternative is to name the cell cat1_.

Problems

1. The Stock.xlsx file contains monthly stock returns for General Motors and Microsoft. Name the ranges containing the monthly returns for each stock and compute the average monthly return on each stock.

2. Open a new blank workbook and name the range containing the A1:B3 and A6:B8 cells as Red.

3. In cells Q5 and Q6 in the Citydistances.xlsx file, you can enter the latitude and longitude of any city and, in Q7 and Q8, the latitude and longitude of a second city. Cell Q10 computes the distance between the two cities. Define range names for the latitude and longitude of each city and ensure that these names show up in the formula for total distance.

4. The Sharedata.xlsx file contains the numbers of shares you own of each stock and the price of each stock. Compute the value of the shares of each stock with the shares*price formula.

5. Create a range name that averages the past five years of sales data. Assume annual sales are listed in a single column. Use data in the Last5.xlsx file.

CHAPTER 2

Lookup functions

Questions answered in this chapter:

- How can I write a formula to compute tax rates based on income?

- Given a product ID, how can I look up the product's price?

- Suppose that a product's price changes over time. I know the date the product was sold. How can I write a formula to compute the product's price?

Syntax of the lookup functions

Lookup functions enable you to look up values from worksheet ranges. In Microsoft Excel 2013, you can perform both vertical lookups (by using the *VLOOKUP* function) and horizontal lookups (by using the *HLOOKUP* function). In a vertical lookup, the lookup operation starts in the first column of a worksheet range. In a horizontal lookup, the operation starts in the first row of a worksheet range. Because the majority of formulas using lookup functions involve vertical lookups, this chapter concentrates on *VLOOKUP* functions.

VLOOKUP syntax

The syntax of the *VLOOKUP* function is as follows. The brackets ([ ]) indicate optional arguments.

```
VLOOKUP(lookup value,table range,column index,[range lookup])
```

- *Lookup value* is the value you want to look up in the first column of the table range.

- *Table range* is the range that contains the entire lookup table. The table range includes the first column, in which you try to match the lookup value, and any other columns in which you want to look up formula results.

- *Column index* is the column number in the table range from which the value of the lookup function is obtained.

- *Range lookup* is an optional argument. The point of *range lookup* is to specify an exact or approximate match. If the *range lookup* argument is *True* or omitted, the first column of the table range must be in ascending numerical order. If the *range lookup* argument is *True* or omitted and an exact match to the lookup value is found in the first column of the table range, Excel bases the lookup on the row of the table in which the exact match is found. If the *range lookup* argument is *True* or omitted and an exact match does not exist, Excel bases the lookup on the largest value in the first column that is less than the lookup value. If the *range lookup* argument is *False* and an exact match to the lookup value is found in the first column of the table range, Excel bases the lookup on the row of the table in which the exact match is found. If no exact match is obtained, Excel returns an #N/A (Not Available) response. Note that a *range lookup* argument of *1* is equivalent to *True*, whereas a *range lookup* argument of *0* is equivalent to *False*.

HLOOKUP syntax

In an *HLOOKUP* function, Excel tries to locate the lookup value in the first row (not the first column) of the table range. For an *HLOOKUP* function, use the *VLOOKUP* syntax and change *column* to *row*.

Now, explore some interesting examples of lookup functions.

Answers to this chapter's questions

This section provides the answers to the questions that are listed at the beginning of the chapter.

How can I write a formula to compute tax rates based on income?

The following example shows how a *VLOOKUP* function works when the first column of the table range consists of numbers in ascending order. Suppose that the tax rate depends on income, as shown in Table 2-1.

TABLE 2-1 Tax rate on income

Income level	Tax rate
$0–$9,999	15%
$10,000–$29,999	30%
$30,000–$99,999	34%
$100,000 and over	40%

To see an example of how to write a formula that computes the tax rate for any income level, open the Lookup.xlsx file, shown in Figure 2-1.

	C	D	E	F	G
3	**Lookup Tables**				
4					
5		Income	Tax rate		Lookup=D6:E9
6		0	0.15		
7		10000	0.3		
8		30000	0.34		
9		100000	0.4		
10					
11			TRUE	FALSE	
12		Income	Rate		
13		-1000	#N/A	#N/A	
14		30000	0.34	0.34	
15		29000	0.3	#N/A	
16		98000	0.34	#N/A	
17		104000	0.4	#N/A	

FIGURE 2-1 Use a lookup function to compute a tax rate. The numbers in the first column of the table range are sorted in ascending order.

First, the relevant information (tax rates and break points) was entered in cell range D6:E9. The table range is named D6:E9 *lookup*. It's recommended always to name the cells you're using as the table range. If you do so, you need not remember the exact location of the table range, and when you copy any formula involving a lookup function, the lookup range will always be correct. To illustrate how the lookup function works, some incomes were entered in the D13:D17 range. By copying the *VLOOKUP(D13,Lookup,2,True)* formula from E13 to E14:E17, the tax rate was computed for the income levels listed in D13:D17. Examine how the lookup function worked in cells E13:E17. Note that because the column index in the formula is *2*, the answer always comes from the second column of the table range.

- In D13, the income of –$1,000 yields #N/A because –$1,000 is less than the lowest income level in the first column of the table range. If you want a tax rate of 15 percent associated with an income of –$1,000, replace the 0 in D6 with a number that is –1,000 or smaller.

- In D14, the income of $30,000 exactly matches a value in the first column of the table range, so the function returns a tax rate of 34 percent.

- In D15, the income level of $29,000 does not exactly match a value in the first column of the table range, which means the lookup function stops at the largest number less than $29,000 in the first column of the range $10,000 in this case. This function returns the tax rate in column 2 of the table range opposite $10,000, or 30 percent.

- In D16, the income level of $98,000 does not yield an exact match in the first column of the table range. The lookup function stops at the largest number less than $98,000 in the first column of the table range. This returns the tax rate in column 2 of the table range opposite $30,000—34 percent.

- In D17, the income level of $104,000 does not yield an exact match in the first column of the table range. The lookup function stops at the largest number less than $104,000 in the first column of the table range, which returns the tax rate in column 2 of the table range opposite $100,000—40 percent.

In F13:F17, the value of the *range lookup* argument was changed from *True* to *False*, and the VLOOKUP(D13,Lookup,2,False) formula was copied from F13 to F14:F17. Cell F14 still yields a 34 percent tax rate because the first column of the table range contains an exact match to $30,000. All the other entries in F13:F17 display #N/A because none of the other incomes in D13:D17 has an exact match in the first column of the table range.

Given a product ID, how can I look up the product's price?

Often, the first column of a table range does not consist of numbers in ascending order. For example, the first column of the table range might list product ID codes or employee names. In my experience teaching thousands of financial analysts, I've found that many people don't know how to deal with lookup functions when the first column of the table range does not consist of numbers in ascending order. In these situations, remember only one simple rule: Use *False* as the value of the *range lookup* argument.

Here's an example. In the Lookup.xlsx file (see Figure 2-2), you can see the prices for five products, listed by their product ID code. How do you write a formula that takes a product ID code and returns the product price?

	H	I	J
9			Lookup2=H11:I15
10	Product ID	Price	
11	A134	$ 3.50	
12	B242	$ 4.20	
13	X212	$ 4.80	
14	C413	$ 5.00	
15	B2211	$ 5.20	
16			
17	ID	Price	
18	B2211	3.5	
19	B2211	5.2	

FIGURE 2-2 Look up prices from product ID codes. When the table range isn't sorted in ascending order, enter *False* as the last argument in the lookup function formula.

Many people would enter the formula as in cell I18: VLOOKUP(H18,Lookup2,2). However, note that when you omit the fourth argument (the *range lookup* argument), the value is assumed to be *True*.

Because the product IDs in the *Lookup2* (H11:I15) table range are not listed in alphabetical order, an incorrect price ($3.50) is returned. If you enter the VLOOKUP(H18,Lookup2,2,False) formula in cell I18, the correct price ($5.20) is returned.

You would also use *False* in a formula designed to find an employee's salary by using the employee's last name or ID number.

By the way, you can see in Figure 2-2 that columns A to G are hidden. To hide columns, you begin by selecting the columns you want to hide. Click the **Home** tab on the ribbon. In the **Cells** group, choose Format, point to **Hide & Unhide** (under Visibility), and then choose **Hide Columns**.

Suppose that a product's price changes over time. I know the date the product was sold. How can I write a formula to compute the product's price?

Suppose the price of a product depends on the date the product was sold. How can you use a lookup function in a formula that will pick up the correct product price? More specifically, suppose the price of a product is as shown in the following table:

Date sold	Price
January–April 2005	$98
May–July 2005	$105
August–December 2005	$112

Write a formula to determine the correct product price for any date on which the product is sold in the year 2005. For variety, use an *HLOOKUP* function. The dates when the price changes are in the first row of the table range. See the Datelookup.xlsx file, shown in Figure 2-3.

	A	B	C	D	E
1					
2	Date	1/1/2005	5/1/2005	8/1/2005	
3	Price	98	105	112	
4					
5			Lookup:B2:D3		
6					
7		Date	Price		
8		1/4/2005	98		
9		5/10/2005	105		
10		9/12/2005	112		
11		5/1/2005	105		

FIGURE 2-3 Use an *HLOOKUP* function to determine a price that changes depending on the date it's sold.

The HLOOKUP(B8,lookup,2,TRUE) formula is copied from C8 to C9:C11. This formula tries to match the dates in column B with the first row of the B2:D3 range. At any date between 1/1/05 and 4/30/05, the lookup function stops at 1/1/05 and returns the price in B3; for any date between 5/1/05 and

7/31/05, the lookup stops at 5/1/05 and returns the price in C3; and for any date later than 8/1/05, the lookup stops at 8/1/05 and returns the price in D3.

Problems

1. The Hr.xlsx file gives employee ID codes, salaries, and years of experience. Write a formula that yields the employee's salary from a given ID code. Write another formula that yields the employee's years of experience from a given ID code.

2. The Assign.xlsx file gives the assignment of workers to four groups. The suitability of each worker for each group (on a scale from 0 to 10) is also given. Write a formula that gives the suitability of each worker for the group to which the worker is assigned.

3. You are thinking of advertising Microsoft products on a sports telecast. As you buy more ads, the price of each ad decreases as shown in the following table:

Number of ads	Price per ad
1–5	$12,000
6–10	$11,000
11–20	$10,000
21 and higher	$9,000

For example, if you buy 8 ads, you pay $11,000 per ad, but if you buy 14 ads, you pay $10,000 per ad. Write a formula that yields the total cost of purchasing any number of ads.

4. You are thinking of advertising Microsoft products on a popular TV music program. You pay one price for the first group of ads, but as you buy more ads, the price per ad decreases as shown in the following table:

Ad number	Price per ad
1–5	$12,000
6–10	$11,000
11–20	$10,000
21 or higher	$9,000

For example, if you buy 8 ads, you pay $12,000 per ad for the first 5 ads and $11,000 for each of the next 3 ads. If you buy 14 ads, you pay $12,000 for each of the first 5 ads, $11,000 for each of the next 5 ads, and $10,000 for each of the last 4 ads. Write a formula that yields the total cost of purchasing any number of ads. Hint: You probably need at least three columns in your table range, and your formula might involve two lookup functions.

5. The annual rate your bank charges you to borrow money for 1, 5, 10, or 30 years is shown in the following table:

Duration of loan	Annual loan rate
1 year	6%
5 years	7%
10 years	9%
30 years	10%

If you borrow money from the bank for any duration from 1 through 30 years that's not listed in the table, your rate is found by interpolating between the rates given in the table. For example, you borrow money for 15 years. Because 15 years is one quarter of the way between 10 years and 30 years, the annual loan rate would be calculated as follows:

$$\frac{1}{4}(9) + \frac{3}{4}(10) = 9.75\%$$

Write a formula that returns the annual interest rate on a loan for any period between 1 and 30 years.

6. The distance between any two US cities (excluding cities in Alaska and Hawaii) can be approximated by this formula:

$$69 * \sqrt{(lat1 - lat2)^2 + (long1 - long2)^2}$$

The Citydata.xlsx file contains the latitude and longitude of selected US cities. Create a table that gives the distance between any two of the listed cities.

7. In the Pinevalley.xlsx file, the first worksheet contains the salaries of several employees at Pine Valley University, the second worksheet contains the age of the employees, and the third worksheet contains the years of experience. Create a fourth worksheet that contains the salary, age, and experience for each employee.

8. The Lookupmultiplecolumns.xlsx file contains information about several sales made at an electronics store. A salesperson's name will be entered in B17. Write an Excel formula that can be copied from C17 to D17:F17 that extracts each salesperson's radio sales to C17, TV sales to D17, printer sales to E17, and CD sales to F17.

9. The Grades.xlsx file contains students' grades on an exam. Suppose the curve is as follows:

Score	Grade
Below 60	F
60–69	D
70–79	C
80–89	B
90 and above	A

Use Excel to return each student's letter grade on this exam.

10. The Employees.xlsx file contains the ranking each of 35 workers has given (on a 0–10 scale) to three jobs. The file also gives the job to which each worker is assigned. Use a formula to compute each worker's ranking for the job to which the worker is assigned.

11. Suppose one dollar can be converted to 1,000 yen, 5 pesos, or 0.7 euros. Set up a spreadsheet in which the user can enter an amount in US dollars and a currency, and the spreadsheet converts dollars to the entered currency.

CHAPTER 3

INDEX function

Questions answered in this chapter:

- I have a list of distances between US cities. How can I write a function that returns the distance between, for example, Seattle and Miami?

- Can I write a formula that references the entire column containing the distances between each city and Seattle?

Syntax of the *INDEX* function

The *INDEX* function enables you to return the entry in any row and column within an array of numbers. The most commonly used syntax for the *INDEX* function is the following:

```
INDEX(Array,Row Number,Column Number)
```

To illustrate, the INDEX(A1:D12,2,3) formula returns the entry in the second row and third column of the A1:D12 array. This entry is the one in cell C2.

Answers to this chapter's questions

This section provides the answers to the questions that are listed at the beginning of the chapter.

I have a list of distances between US cities. How can I write a function that returns the distance between, for example, Seattle and Miami?

The Index.xlsx file (see Figure 3-1) contains the distances between eight US cities. The C10:J17 range, which contains the distances, is named *Distances*.

A	B	C	D	E	F	G	H	I	J
4	Boston-Denver	1991			T Dist to Seattle	15221			
5	Seattle- Miami	3389							
6									
7									
8									
9		Boston	Chicago	Dallas	Denver	LA	Miami	Phoenix	Seattle
10 1	Boston	0	983	1815	1991	3036	1539	2664	2612
11 2	Chicago	983	0	1205	1050	2112	1390	1729	2052
12 3	Dallas	1815	1205	0	801	1425	1332	1027	2404
13 4	Denver	1991	1050	801	0	1174	2100	836	1373
14 5	LA	3036	2112	1425	1174	0	2757	398	1909
15 6	Miami	1539	1390	1332	2100	2757	0	2359	3389
16 7	Phoenix	2664	1729	1027	836	398	2359	0	1482
17 8	Seattle	2612	2052	2404	1373	1909	3389	1482	0

FIGURE 3-1 You can use the *INDEX* function to calculate the distance between cities.

Suppose that you want to enter the distance between Boston and Denver in a cell. Because distances from Boston are listed in the first row of the array named *Distances*, and distances to Denver are listed in the fourth column of the array, the appropriate formula is INDEX(distances,1,4). The results show that Boston and Denver are 1,991 miles apart. Similarly, to find the (much longer) distance between Seattle and Miami, you would use the INDEX(distances,6,8) formula. Seattle and Miami are 3,389 miles apart.

Imagine that a resident of Seattle, Kurt Sovain is embarking on a road trip to visit relatives in Phoenix, Los Angeles (USC!), Denver, Dallas, and Chicago. At the conclusion of the road trip, Kurt returns to Seattle. Can you easily compute how many miles Kurt travels on the trip? As you can see in Figure 3-2, you simply list the cities Kurt visited (*8-7-5-4-3-2-8*) in the order he visited them, starting and ending in Seattle, and copy the INDEX(distances,C21,C22) formula from D21 to D26. The formula in D21 computes the distance between Seattle and Phoenix (city number 7), the formula in D22 computes the distance between Phoenix and Los Angeles, and so on. Kurt will travel a total of 7,112 miles on his road trip. Just for fun, use the *INDEX* function to show that the Miami Heat travel more miles during the NBA season than any other team.

	C	D	E
19	Road Trip!!		
20	City	Distance	
21	8	1482	
22	7	398	
23	5	1174	
24	4	801	
25	3	1205	
26	2	2052	
27	8		
28	Total	7112	

FIGURE 3-2 These are the distances for Kurt's road trip.

Can I write a formula that references the entire column containing the distances between each city and Seattle?

The *INDEX* function makes it easy to reference an entire row or column of an array. If you set the row number to 0, the *INDEX* function references the listed column. If you set the column number to 0, the *INDEX* function references the listed row. To illustrate, suppose you want to total the distances from each listed city to Seattle. You could enter either of the following formulas:

```
SUM(INDEX(distances,8,0))
```

```
SUM(INDEX(distances,0,8))
```

The first formula totals the numbers in the eighth row (row 17) of the Distances array; the second formula totals the numbers in the eighth column (column J) of the Distances array. In either case, you find that the total distance from Seattle, to the other cities, and back to Seattle is 15,221 miles, as you can see in Figure 3-1.

Problems

1. Use the *INDEX* function to compute the distance between Los Angeles and Phoenix and the distance between Denver and Miami.

2. Use the *INDEX* function to compute the total distance from Dallas to the other cities.

3. A resident of Dallas, Texas, is embarking on a road trip that takes her to Chicago, Denver, Los Angeles, Phoenix, and Seattle. How many miles will she travel on this trip?

4. The Product.xlsx file contains monthly sales for six products. Use the *INDEX* function to compute the sales of Product 2 in March. Use the *INDEX* function to compute total sales during April.

5. The Nbadistances.xlsx file shows the distance between any pair of NBA arenas. Suppose you begin in Atlanta, visit the arenas in the order listed, and then return to Atlanta. How far would you travel?

6. Use the *INDEX* function to solve problem 10 of Chapter 2, "Lookup functions."

CHAPTER 4

MATCH function

Questions answered in this chapter:

- Given monthly sales for several products, how can I write a formula that returns the sales of a product during a specific month? For example, how much of Product 2 did I sell during June?

- Given a list of baseball players' salaries, how can I write a formula that yields the player with the highest salary? How about the player with the fifth-highest salary?

- Given the annual cash flows from an investment project, how do I write a formula that returns the number of years required to pay back the project's initial investment cost?

Suppose you have a worksheet with 5,000 rows containing 5,000 names. You need to find the name *John Doe*, which you know appears somewhere (and only once) in the list. Wouldn't you like to know of a formula that would return the row number that contains that name? The *MATCH* function enables you to find the first occurrence of a match to a given text string or number within a given array. You should use the *MATCH* function instead of a lookup function when you want the position of a number in a range rather than the value in a particular cell. The syntax of the match function is:

```
Match(lookup value,lookup range,[match type])
```

In the explanation that follows, assume that all cells in the lookup range are in the same column. In this syntax:

- Lookup value is the value you're trying to match in the lookup range.

- Lookup range is the range you're examining for a match to the lookup value. The lookup range must be a row or column.

- Match type=1 requires the lookup range to consist of numbers listed in ascending order. The *MATCH* function then returns the row location in the lookup range (relative to the top of the lookup range) that contains the largest value in the range that is less than or equal to the lookup value.

- Match type=−1 requires the lookup range to consist of numbers listed in descending order. The *MATCH* function returns the row location in the lookup range (relative to the top of the lookup range) that contains the last value in the range that is greater than or equal to the lookup value.

- Match type=0 returns the row location in the lookup range that contains the first exact match to the lookup value. (Chapter 19, "COUNTIF, COUNTIFS, COUNT, COUNTA, and COUNTBLANK functions," discusses how to find the second or third match.) When no exact match exists and match type=0, Excel returns the error message #N/A. Most MATCH function applications use match type=0, but if match type is not included, match type=1 is assumed. Thus, use match type=0 when the cell contents of the lookup range are unsorted. This is the situation you usually face.

The Matchex.xlsx file, shown in Figure 4-1, contains three examples of the MATCH function's syntax.

	A	B	C	D	E	F	G
4		Boston			-5		6
5		Chicago			-4		5
6		Dallas			-3		4
7		Denver			-1		3
8		LA			3		-1
9		Miami			4		-3
10		Phoenix			5		-4
11		Seattle			6		-5
12				last number<=0	4	last number>=-4	7
13	Boston	1					
14	Phoenix	7					
15	Pho*	7					

FIGURE 4-1 Use the MATCH function to locate the position of a value in a range.

In cell B13, the MATCH("Boston",B4:B11,0) formula returns 1 because the first row in the B4:B11 range contains the value Boston. Text values must be enclosed in quotation marks (""). In cell B14, the MATCH("Phoenix",B4:B11,0) formula returns 7 because cell B10 (the seventh cell in B4:B11) is the first cell in the range that matches Phoenix. In cell E12, the MATCH(0,E4:E11,1) formula returns 4 because the last number that is less than or equal to 0 in the E4:E11 range is in cell E7 (the fourth cell in the lookup range). In cell G12, the MATCH(-4,G4:G11,-1) formula returns 7 because the last number that is greater than or equal to -4 in the G4:G11 range is contained in cell G10 (the seventh cell in the lookup range).

The MATCH function can also work with an inexact match. For example, the MATCH("Pho*",B4:B11,0) formula returns 7. The asterisk is treated as a wildcard, which means that Microsoft Excel searches for the first text string in the B4:B11 range that begins with Pho. Incidentally, this same technique can be used with a lookup function. For example, in the price lookup exercise in Chapter 2, "Lookup functions," the VLOOKUP("x*",lookup2,2) formula would return the price of product X212 ($4.80).

If the lookup range is contained in a single row, Excel returns the relative position of the first match in the lookup range, moving from left to right. As shown in the following examples, the MATCH function is often very useful when it is combined with other Excel functions such as VLOOKUP, INDEX, or MAX.

Answers to this chapter's questions

This section provides the answers to the questions that are listed at the beginning of the chapter.

Given monthly sales for several products, how can I write a formula that returns the sales of a product during a specific month? For example, how much of Product 2 did I sell during June?

The Productlookup.xlsx file (shown in Figure 4-2) lists sales of four NBA bobble-head dolls from January through June. How can you write a formula that computes the sales of a given product during a specific month? The trick is to use one *MATCH* function to find the row that contains the given product and another *MATCH* function to find the column that contains the given month. You can then use the *INDEX* function to return the product sales for the month.

	A	B	C	D	E	F	G
3		January	February	March	April	May	June
4	Shaq	831	685	550	965	842	804
5	Kobe	719	504	965	816	639	814
6	MJ	916	906	851	912	964	710
7	T-Mac	844	509	991	851	742	817
8							
9	Product	Month	Row # of product	Column # of month	Product Sales		
10	Kobe	June	2	6	814		

FIGURE 4-2 The *MATCH* function can be used in combination with functions such as *INDEX* and *VLOOKUP*. The range B4:G7 contains sales data for the dolls and is named *Sales*.

This figure shows how *MATCH* and *INDEX* functions can be combined to look up sales for any month and player combination. The range B4:G7 contains sales data for the dolls and is named *Sales*. The product you want to know about is in cell A10 and the month is in cell B10. In C10, you use the MATCH(A10,A4:A7,0) formula to determine which row number in the *Sales* range contains sales figures for the Kobe doll. Then, in cell D10, use the MATCH(B10,B3:G3,0) formula to determine which column number in the *Sales* range contains June sales. Now that you have the row and column numbers that contain the sales figures you want, you can use the INDEX(Sales,C10,D10) formula in cell E10 to yield the piece of sales data that's needed. For more information on the *INDEX* function, see Chapter 3, "The INDEX function."

Given a list of baseball players' salaries, how can I write a formula that yields the player with the highest salary? How about the player with the fifth-highest salary?

The Baseball.xlsx file (see Figure 4-3) lists the salaries paid to 401 Major League Baseball players during the 2001 season. The data is not sorted by salary, and you want to write a formula that returns the name of the player with the largest salary as well as the name of the player with the fifth-highest salary.

To find the name of the player with the highest salary, proceed as follows:

1. Use the *MAX* function to determine the value of the highest salary.

2. Use the *MATCH* function to determine the row that contains the player with the highest salary.

3. Use a *VLOOKUP* function (keying off the data row containing the player's salary) to look up the player's name.

The range C12:C412 includes players' salaries and is named *Salaries*. The range used in the *VLOOKUP* function (range A12:C412) is named Lookup.

	A	B	C	D
6		name	Alex Rodriguez	dl-Derek Jeter
7			highest	5th highest
8		player position	345	232
9		amount	22000000	12600000
10				
11		name	salary	
12	1	dl-Mo Vaughn	13166667	
13	2	Tim Salmon	5683013	
14	3	Garret Anderson	4500000	
15	4	Darin Erstad	3450000	
16	5	Troy Percival	3400000	
17	6	Ismael Valdes	2500000	
18	7	Pat Rapp	2000000	
19	8	Glenallen Hill	1500000	
20	9	Troy Glaus	1250000	
21	10	Shigetoshi Hasegawa	1150000	
22	11	Scott Spiezio	1125000	
23	12	Orlando Palmeiro	900000	
24	13	Alan Levine	715000	
25	14	Mike Holtz	705000	
26	15	Jorge Fabregas	500000	

FIGURE 4-3 This example uses the *MAX, MATCH,* and *VLOOKUP* functions to find and display the highest value in a list.

In cell C9, you find the highest player salary ($22 million) with the MAX(Salaries) formula. Next, in cell C8, you use the MATCH(C9,Salaries,0) formula to determine the player number of the player with the highest salary. Variable *match type=0* was used because the salaries are not listed in either ascending or descending order. Player number 345 has the highest salary. Finally, in cell C6, you use the VLOOKUP(C8,Lookup,2) function to find the player's name in the second column of the lookup range. Not surprisingly, Alex Rodriguez was the highest-paid player in 2001.

To find the name of the player with the fifth-highest salary, you need a function that yields the fifth-largest number in an array. The *LARGE* function does that job. The syntax of the *LARGE* function is *LARGE(cell range,k)*. When it is entered this way, it returns the *k*th-largest number in a cell range. Thus, the LARGE(salaries,5) formula in cell D9 yields the fifth-largest salary ($12.6 million). Proceeding as before, you find that Derek Jeter is the player with the fifth-highest salary. (The *dl* before Jeter's name indicates that at the beginning of the season, Jeter was on the disabled list.) The *SMALL(salaries,5)* function would return the fifth-lowest salary.

Given the annual cash flows from an investment project, how can I write a formula that returns the number of years required to pay back the project's initial investment cost?

The Payback.xlsx file, shown in Figure 4-4, shows the projected cash flows for an investment project over the next 15 years. Assume that in Year 1, the project required a cash outflow of $100 million. During Year 1, the project generated a cash inflow of $14 million. You expect cash flows to grow at 10 percent per year. How many years will pass before the project pays back its investment?

The number of years required for a project to pay back an investment is called the *payback period*. In high-tech industries, the payback period is often used to rank investments. (You learn in Chapter 7, "Evaluating investments by using net present value criteria," that payback is flawed as a measure of investment quality because it ignores the value of money over time.) For now, concentrate on how to determine the payback period for this simple investment model.

	A	B	C	D	E
1	Year 1 cash flow	14			Payback Period
2	Growth	0.1			6
3	Initial Investment	-100			
4	Year	Annual Cash flow	Cumulative cash flow		
5	0	-100	-100		
6	1	14	-86		
7	2	15.4	-70.6		
8	3	16.94	-53.66		
9	4	18.634	35.026		
10	5	20.4974	-14.5286		
11	6	22.54714	8.01854		
12	7	24.801854	32.820394		
13	8	27.2820394	60.1024334		
14	9	30.01024334	90.11267674		
15	10	33.01126767	123.1239444		
16	11	36.31239444	159.4363389		
17	12	39.94363389	199.3799727		
18	13	43.93799727	243.31797		
19	14	48.331797	291.649767		
20	15	53.1649767	344.8147437		

FIGURE 4-4 Use the *MATCH* function to calculate an investment's payback period.

To determine the payback period for the project, proceed as follows:

1. In column B, compute the cash flows for each year.

2. In column C, compute the cumulative cash flows for each year.

Now you can use the *MATCH* function (with *match type=1*) to determine the row number of the first year in which cumulative cash flow is positive. This calculation gives you the payback period.

The cells in B1:B3 have the range names listed in A1:A3. Year 0 cash flow (–Initial_investment) is entered in cell B5. Year 1 cash flow (Year_1_cf) is entered in cell B6. Copying the B6*(1+Growth) formula from B7 to B8:B20 computes the cash flow for Year 2 through Year 15.

To compute the Year 0 cumulative cash flow, use the B5 formula in cell C5. For later years, you can calculate cumulative cash flow by using a formula such as Year t cumulative cash flow=Year t–1 cumulative cash flow+Year t cash flow. To implement this relationship, copy the =C5+B6 formula from C6 to C7:C20.

To compute the payback period, use the *MATCH* function (with *match type=1*) to compute the last row of the C5:C20 range containing a value less than 0. This calculation always gives you the payback period. For example, if the last row in C5:C20 that contains a value less than 0 is the sixth row in the range, the seventh value marks the cumulative cash flow for the first year the project is paid back. Because your first year is Year 0, the payback occurs during Year 6. Therefore, the formula in cell E2, MATCH(0,C5:C20,1), yields the payback period (6 years). If any cash flows after Year 0 are negative, this method fails because the range of cumulative cash flows would not be listed in ascending order.

Problems

1. Using the distances between US cities given in the Index.xlsx file, write a formula using the *MATCH* function to determine (based on the names of the cities) the distance between any two of the cities.

2. The Matchtype1.xlsx file lists the dollar amounts of 30 transactions in chronological order. Write a formula that yields the first transaction for which total volume to date exceeds $10,000.

3. The Matchthemax.xlsx file gives the product ID codes and unit sales for 265 products. Use the *MATCH* function in a formula that yields the product ID code of the product with the largest unit sales.

4. The Buslist.xlsx file gives the amount of time between bus arrivals (in minutes) at 45th Street and Park Avenue in New York City. Write a formula that, for any arrival time after the first bus, gives the amount of time you have to wait for a bus. For example, if you arrive 12.4 minutes from now, and buses arrive 5 minutes and 21 minutes from now, you wait 21 – 12.4 = 8.6 minutes for a bus.

5. The Salesdata.xlsx file contains the number of computers each salesperson sold. Create a formula that returns the units a given salesperson sold.

6. Suppose the *VLOOKUP* function was removed from Excel. Explain how you could still get along by using the *MATCH* and *INDEX* functions.

CHAPTER 5

Text functions

Questions answered in this chapter:

- I have a worksheet in which each cell contains a product description, a product ID, and a product price. How can I put all the product descriptions in column A, all the product IDs in column B, and all the prices in column C?

- Every day, I receive data about total US sales, which is computed in a cell as the sum of East, North, and South regional sales. How can I extract East, North, and South sales to separate cells?

- At the end of each school semester, my students evaluate my teaching performance on a scale from 1 to 7. I know how many students gave me each possible rating score. How can I easily create a bar graph of my teaching evaluation scores?

- I have downloaded numerical data from the Internet or a database. When I try to do calculations with the data, I always get a #VALUE error. How can I solve this problem?

- I like text functions, but is there an easy way (not involving text functions) to extract first or last names from data, create an email list from a list of names, or perform other routine operations on text data?

When someone sends you data or you download data from the web, it often isn't formatted the way you want. For example, in sales data you download, dates and sales amounts might be in the same cell, but you need them to be in separate cells. How can you manipulate data so that it appears in the format you need? The answer is to become good at using the Microsoft Excel text functions. In this chapter, you learn how to use the following Excel text functions and the new Flash Fill feature to manipulate your data so that it looks the way you want:

- *LEFT*

- *RIGHT*

- *MID*

- *TRIM*

- *LEN*

- *FIND*

- *SEARCH*

- *REPT*

- *CONCATENATE*

- *REPLACE*

- *VALUE*

- *UPPER*

- *LOWER*

- *PROPER*

- *CHAR*

- *CLEAN*

- *SUBSTITUTE*

Text function syntax

The Textfunctions.xlsx file, shown in Figure 5-1, includes examples of text functions. You see how to apply these functions to a specific problem later in the chapter but begin by seeing what each of the text functions does. Then you can combine the functions to perform some complex manipulations of data.

	A	B	C	D	E
1	Radim	Patralur			
2					
3	Radim Patralur	Left 4	Radi		
4		Right 4	alur		
5		Trim spaces	Radim Patralur		
6		Number of characters	16		
7		Number of characters in trimmed result	14		
8		5 characters starting at space 2	adim		
9		Find first space	6		
10		Find first r (case sensitive)	12		
11		Find first r (not case sensitive)	1		
12		Combining first and Last Name	Radim Patralur	Radim Patralur	
13		Replace an with gg	Raggm Patralur		
14	Text 31	Number 31			
15	31		31		
16		Change to lower case	radim patralur		
17		Change to Upper case	RADIM PATRALUR	I LOVE EXCEL 2013!	
18		Change to Proper case	Radim Patralur		
19		Replace all spaces by *	I*LOVE*EXCEL*2013!		
20		Replace only third space by *	I LOVE EXCEL*2013!		

FIGURE 5-1 This figure shows examples of text functions.

The *LEFT* function

The LEFT(text,k) function returns the first *k* characters in a text string. For example, cell C3 contains the LEFT(A3,4) formula. Excel returns *Regg*.

The *RIGHT* function

The RIGHT(text,k) function returns the last *k* characters in a text string. For example, in cell C4, the RIGHT(A3,4) formula returns *ller*.

The *MID* function

The MID(text,k,m) function begins at character *k* of a text string and returns the next *m* characters. For example, the MID(A3,2,5) formula in cell C8 returns characters 2–6 from cell A3; the result is *eggie*.

The *TRIM* function

The TRIM(text) function removes all spaces from a text string except for single spaces between words. For example, in cell C5, the TRIM(A3) formula eliminates two of the three spaces between Reggie and Miller and yields *Reggie Miller*. The *TRIM* function also removes spaces at the beginning and end of a cell's contents.

The *LEN* function

The LEN(text) function returns the number of characters in a text string (including spaces). For example, in cell C6, the LEN(A3) formula returns 15 because cell A3 contains 15 characters. In cell C7, the LEN(C5) formula returns 13. Because two spaces have been removed in the trimmed result in cell C5, cell C5 contains two fewer characters than the original text in A3.

The *FIND* and *SEARCH* functions

The FIND(text_to_find,actual_text,k) function returns the location at or after character *k* of the first character of *text to find* in *actual text*. *FIND* is case sensitive. *SEARCH* has the same syntax as *FIND*, but it is not case sensitive. For example, the FIND("r",A3,1) formula in cell C10 returns 15, the location of the first lowercase *r* in the Reggie Miller text string. (The uppercase *R* is ignored because *FIND* is case sensitive.) Entering SEARCH("r",A3,1) in cell C11 returns 1 because *SEARCH* matches *r* to either a lowercase character or an uppercase character. Entering FIND(" ",A3,1) in cell C9 returns 7 because the first space in the Reggie Miller string is the seventh character.

The *REPT* function

You can use the *REPT* function to repeat a text string a specified number of times. The syntax is REPT(text,number_of_times). For example REPT("|",3) produces output |||.

The *CONCATENATE* and *&* functions

The *CONCATENATE(text1,text2, . . .,text30)* function can be used to join up to 30 text strings into a single string. The *&* operator can be used instead of *CONCATENATE*. For example, entering the A1&" "&B1 formula in cell C12 returns Reggie Miller. Entering the CONCATENATE(A1," ",B1) formula in cell D12 yields the same result.

The *REPLACE* function

The *REPLACE(old_text,k,m,new_text)* function begins at character *k* of old text and replaces the next *m* characters with new text. For example, in cell C13, the REPLACE(A3,3,2,"nn") formula replaces the third and fourth characters (gg) in cell A3 with nn. This formula yields *Rennie Miller*.

The *VALUE* function

The *VALUE(text)* function converts a text string that represents a number to a number. For example, entering the VALUE(A15) formula in cell B15 converts text string 31 in cell A15 to numerical value *31*. You can identify value *31* in cell A15 as English text because it is left justified. Similarly, you can identify value *31* in cell B15 as a number because it is right justified.

The *UPPER*, *LOWER*, and *PROPER* functions

The *UPPER(text)* function changes *text* to all uppercase. For example, in cell C16, the LOWER(C12) formula changes the capital letters to small and yields *reggie miller*. In cell C17, the UPPER(C16) formula changes all letters to uppercase and yields *REGGIE MILLER*. Finally, in cell C18, the PROPER(C17) formula restores the proper case and yields *Reggie Miller*.

The *CHAR* function

The *CHAR(number)* function yields (for a number between 1 and 255) the ASCII character with that number. For example, CHAR(65) yields *A*, CHAR(66) yields *B*, and this sequence continues. The ASCIIcharacters.xlsx file contains a list of ASCII characters. A partial listing is shown in Figure 5-2.

	C	D
3	Character #	Character
4	1	
5	2	ꓶ
6	3	ꓡ
7	4	ꓳ
8	5		
9	6	—
10	7	•
11	8	◘
12	9	
13	10	
14	11	♂
15	12	♀
16	13	
17	14	♫
18	15	☼
19	16	†
20	17	◄
21	18	↕
22	19	‼
23	20	¶

FIGURE 5-2 Here is a partial list of ASCII characters.

The *CLEAN* Function

As you can see in Figure 5-2, certain characters, such as character number 10 (which represents a line feed), are invisible. Applying the *CLEAN* function to a cell removes some but not all the invisible (or nonprinting) ASCII characters. The *CLEAN* function will not remove, for example, CHAR(160), which is a nonbreaking space. Later in this chapter, you examine how to remove troublesome characters such as CHAR(160) from a cell.

The *SUBSTITUTE* FUNCTION

The *SUBSTITUTE* function replaces specific text in a cell when you do not know the position of the text. The syntax of the *SUBSTITUTE* function is SUBSTITUTE(cell,old_text,new_text,[instance_number]). The last argument is optional. If omitted, every occurrence of old text in the cell is replaced by new text. If the last argument is included (say with a value of *n*), only the *n*th instance of old text is replaced by new text. To illustrate the use of the *SUBSTITUTE* function, suppose you want to replace the spaces in cell C17 with asterisks. First, you enter the SUBSTITUTE(D17," ","*") formula in cell C19.

This replaces each space with an * and yields *I* LOVE* EXCEL* 2013!* Entering the SUBSTITUTE(D17, "","*",3) formula in cell C20 replaces only the third space with an * and yields *I LOVE EXCEL*2013!*

Answers to this chapter's questions

You can see the power of text functions by using them to solve some actual problems that former students have experienced working for Fortune 500 corporations. Often, the key to solving problems is to combine multiple text functions into a single formula.

I have a worksheet in which each cell contains a product description, a product ID, and a product price. How can I put all the product descriptions in column A, all the product IDs in column B, and all the prices in column C?

In this example, the product ID is always defined by the first 12 characters, and the price is always indicated in the last 8 characters (with two spaces following the end of each price). The solution, contained in the Lenora.xlsx file and shown in Figure 5-3, uses the *LEFT, RIGHT, MID, VALUE, TRIM,* and *LEN* functions.

It's always a good idea to begin by trimming excess spaces, which you can do by copying the TRIM(A4) formula from B4 to B5:B12. The only excess spaces in column A turn out to be the two spaces inserted after each price. To see this, put the cursor in cell A4 and press F2 to edit the cell. If you move to the end of the cell, you see two blank spaces. The results of using the *TRIM* function are shown in Figure 5-3. To prove that the *TRIM* function removed the two extra spaces at the end of cell A4, you can use formulas =LEN(A4) and =LEN(B4) to show that cell A4 contains 52 characters, and cell B4 contains 50 characters.

	A	B	
1	length of A4	length of B4	
2	52		50
3	Untrimmed	Trimmed	
4	32592100AFES CONTROLLERPENTIUM/100,(2)1GB H 304.00	32592100AFES CONTROLLERPENTIUM/100,(2)1GB H 304.00	
5	32592100JCP9 DESKTOP UNIT 225.00	32592100JCP9 DESKTOP UNIT 225.00	
6	325927008990 DESKTOP WINDOWS NT 4.0 SERVER 232.00	325927008990 DESKTOP WINDOWS NT 4.0 SERVER 232.00	
7	325926008990 DESKTOP WINDOWS NT 4.0 WKST 232.00	325926008990 DESKTOP WINDOWS NT 4.0 WKST 232.00	
8	325921008990 DESKTOP, DOS OS 232.00	325921008990 DESKTOP, DOS OS 232.00	
9	325922008990 DESKTOP, WINDOWS DESKTOP OS 232.00	325922008990 DESKTOP, WINDOWS DESKTOP OS 232.00	
10	325925008990 DESKTOP, WINDOWS NT OS 232.00	325925008990 DESKTOP, WINDOWS NT OS 232.00	
11	325930008990 MINITOWER, NO OS 232.00	325930008990 MINITOWER, NO OS 232.00	
12	32593000KEYY MINI TOWER 232.00	32593000KEYY MINI TOWER 232.00	

FIGURE 5-3 Use the *TRIM* function to trim away excess spaces.

To capture the product ID, you need to extract the 12 leftmost characters from column B. To do this, copy the LEFT(B4,12) formula from C4 to C5:C12. This formula extracts the 12 leftmost characters from the text in cell B4 and the following cells, yielding the product ID, as you can see in Figure 5-4.

	B	C	D	E	F
1	length of B4				
2		50			
3	Trimmed	Product ID	Price	Product Description	Concatenation
4	32592100AFES CONTROLLERPENTIUM/100,(2)1G	32592100AFI	304	CONTROLLERPENTIUM/100,(2	32592100AFES CONTROLLERPENTIUM/100,(2)1GB H 304
5	32592100JCP9 DESKTOP UNIT 225.00	32592100JCI	225	DESKTOP UNIT	32592100JCP9 DESKTOP UNIT 225
6	32592700899O DESKTOP WINDOWS NT 4.0 SER	3259270089S	232	DESKTOP WINDOWS NT 4.0 S	32592700899O DESKTOP WINDOWS NT 4.0 SERVER 232
7	325926008990 DESKTOP WINDOWS NT 4.0 WKS	3259260089S	232	DESKTOP WINDOWS NT 4.0 V	325926008990 DESKTOP WINDOWS NT 4.0 WKST 232
8	325921008990 DESKTOP, DOS OS 232.00	3259210089S	232	DESKTOP, DOS OS	325921008990 DESKTOP, DOS OS 232
9	325922008990 DESKTOP, WINDOWS DESKTOP	3259220089S	232	DESKTOP, WINDOWS DESKT	325922008990 DESKTOP, WINDOWS DESKTOP OS 232
10	325925008990 DESKTOP, WINDOWS NT OS 232.	3259250089S	232	DESKTOP, WINDOWS NT OS	325925008990 DESKTOP, WINDOWS NT OS 232
11	325930008990 MINITOWER, NO OS 232.00	3259300089S	232	MINITOWER, NO OS	325930008990 MINITOWER, NO OS 232
12	32593000KEYY MINI TOWER 232.00	32593000KE	232	MINI TOWER	32593000KEYY MINI TOWER 232

FIGURE 5-4 Use text functions to extract the product ID, price, and product description from a text string.

To extract the product price, you know that the price occupies the last six digits of each cell, so you need to extract the rightmost six characters from each cell. To do so, the VALUE(RIGHT(B4,6) formula was copied from cell D4 to D5:D12. The *VALUE* function was used to turn the extracted text into a numerical value. If you don't convert the text to a numerical value, you can't perform mathematical operations on the prices.

Extracting the product description is much trickier. By examining the data, you can see that if you begin your extraction with the thirteenth character and continue until you are six characters from the end of the cell, you can get the data you want. Copying the MID(B4,13,LEN(B4)−6−12) formula from E4 to E5:E12 does the job. LEN(B4) returns the total number of characters in the trimmed text. This formula (MID for middle) begins with the thirteenth character and then extracts the number of characters equal to the total number less the 12 characters at the beginning (the product ID) and the 6 characters at the end (price). This subtraction leaves only the product description.

Now suppose you are given the data with the product ID in column C, the price in column D, and the product description in column E. Can you put these values together to recover your original text?

Text can easily be combined by using the *CONCATENATE* function. Copying the CONCATENATE(C4,E4,D4) formula from F4 to F5:F12 recovers your original (trimmed) text, which you can see in Figure 5-4.

The concatenation formula starts with the product ID in cell C4. Next, you add the product description from cell E4. Finally, you add the price from cell D4. You have now recovered the entire text describing each computer! Concatenation can also be performed by using the & sign. You could recover the original product ID, product description, and price in a single cell with the C4&E4&D4 formula. Note that cell E4 contains a space before the product description and a space after the product description. If cell E4 did not contain these spaces, you could use the C4&" "&E4&" "&D4 formula to insert the necessary spaces. The space between each pair of quotation marks results in the insertion of a space.

If the product IDs did not always contain 12 characters, this method of extracting the information would fail. You could, however, extract the product IDs by using the *FIND* function to discover the location of the first space. Then you could obtain the product ID by using the *LEFT* function to extract all characters to the left of the first space. The example in the next section shows how this approach works.

If the price did not always contain precisely six characters, extracting the price would be a little tricky. See Problem 15 for an example of how to extract the last word in a text string.

Every day, I receive data about total US sales, which is computed in a cell as the sum of East, North, and South regional sales. How can I extract East, North, and South sales to separate cells?

This problem was expressed by an employee in the Microsoft finance department. She received a worksheet each day containing formulas such as =50+200+400, =5+124+1025, and other such formulas. She needed to extract each number into a cell in its own column. For example, she wanted to extract the first number (East sales) in each cell to column C, the second number (North sales) to column D, and the third number (South sales) to column E. What makes this problem challenging is that you don't know the exact location of the character at which the second and third numbers start in each cell. In cell A3, North sales begin with the fourth character. In cell A4, North sales begin with the third character.

The data for this example is in the Salesstripping.xlsx file, shown in Figure 5-5. You can identify the locations of the different regions' sales as follows:

- East sales are represented by every character to the left of the first plus sign (+).

- North sales are represented by every character between the first and second plus signs.

- South sales are represented by every character to the right of the second plus sign.

By combining the *FIND*, *LEFT*, *LEN*, and *MID* functions, you can easily solve this problem as follows:

- Use the **Edit, Replace** command to replace each equal sign (=) with a space. To remove the equal signs, select the A3:A6 range. Then, on the **Home** tab in the **Editing** group, choose **Find & Select** and then choose **Replace**. In the **Find What** field, enter an equal sign and insert a space in the **Replace With** field. Then choose **Replace All**. This converts each formula into text by replacing the equal sign with a space.

- Use the *FIND* function to locate the two plus signs in each cell.

	A	B	C	D	E	F	G
1	**Extracting Sales in Three Regions**						
2	East+North+South	First +	Second +	East	North	Total Length	South
3	10+300+400	3	7	10	300	10	400
4	4+36.2+800	2	7	4	36.2	10	800
5	3+23+4005	2	5	3	23	9	4005
6	18+1+57.31	3	5	18	1	10	57.31

FIGURE 5-5 Extract East, North, and South sales with a combination of the *FIND*, *LEFT*, *LEN*, and *MID* functions.

Begin by finding the location of the first plus sign for each piece of data. By copying the FIND("+",A3,1) formula from B3 to B4:B6, you can locate the first plus sign for each data point. To find the second plus sign, begin one character after the first plus sign, copying the FIND("+",A3,B3+1) formula from C3 to C4:C6.

To find East sales, you can use the *LEFT* function to extract all the characters to the left of the first plus sign, copying the LEFT(A3,B3-1) formula from D3 to D4:D6. To extract North sales, use the *MID* function to extract all the characters between the two plus signs. Begin one character after the first plus sign and extract the number of characters equal to (*Position of 2nd plus sign*) – (*Position of 1st plus sign*) – 1. If you leave out the –1, you'll get the second plus sign. (Go ahead and check this.) So, to get North sales, you copy the MID(A3,B3+1,C3–B3–1) formula from E3 to E4:E6.

To extract South sales, you use the *RIGHT* function to extract all the characters to the right of the second plus sign. South sales will have the number of characters equal to (*Total characters in cell*) – (*Position of 2nd plus sign*). You compute the total number of characters in each cell by copying the LEN(A3) formula from F3 to F4:F6. Finally, you can obtain South sales by copying the RIGHT(A3,F3–C3) formula from G3 to G4:G6.

Extracting data by using the Convert Text To Columns Wizard

There is an easy way to extract East, North, and South sales (and data similar to this example) without using text functions. Select cells A3:A6 and then, on the **Data** tab on the ribbon, in the **Data Tools** group, click **Text To Columns**. Select **Delimited**, click **Next**, and then fill in the dialog box as shown in Figure 5-6.

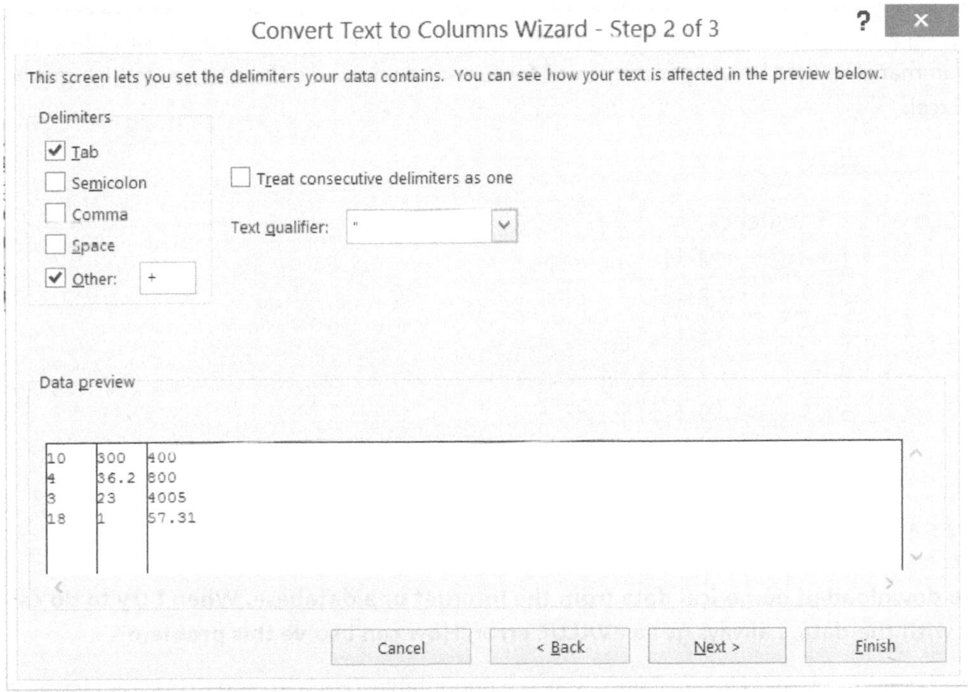

FIGURE 5-6 This figure shows the Convert Text To Columns Wizard.

Entering the plus sign in the **Delimiters** area directs Excel to separate each cell into columns, breaking at each occurrence of the plus sign. Note that options are provided for breaking data at tabs, semicolons, commas, or spaces. Now click **Next**, select the upper-left corner of your destination range (in the example, cell A8 is chosen), and click **Finish**. The result is shown in Figure 5-7.

	A	B	C
8	10	300	400
9	4	36.2	800
10	3	23	4005
11	18	1	57.31
12			
13	**Results of Data Text to Columns**		

FIGURE 5-7 Here are the results of the Convert Text To Columns Wizard.

At the end of each school semester, my students evaluate my teaching performance on a scale from 1 to 7. I know how many students gave me each possible rating score. How can I easily create a bar graph of my teaching evaluation scores?

The Repeatedhisto.xlsx file contains teaching evaluation scores (on a scale from 1 to 7). Two people gave scores of 1, three people gave scores of 2, and so on. Using the *REPT* function, you can easily create a graph to summarize this data. Copy the =REPT("|",C4) formula from D4 to D5:D10. This formula places as many "|" characters in column D as the entry in column C. Figure 5-8 makes clear the preponderance of good scores (6s and 7s) and the relative rarity of poor scores (1s and 2s). Repeating a character such as | enables you to mimic a bar graph or histogram easily. See Chapter 41, "Summarizing data by using histograms," for further discussion of how to create histograms with Excel.

	B	C	D
3	Score	Frequency	
4	1	2	||
5	2	3	|||
6	3	6	||||||
7	4	7	|||||||
8	5	9	|||||||||
9	6	33	|||||||||||||||||||||||||||||||||
10	7	28	||||||||||||||||||||||||||||

FIGURE 5-8 Use the *REPT* function to create a frequency graph.

I have downloaded numerical data from the Internet or a database. When I try to do calculations with the data, I always get a #VALUE error. How can I solve this problem?

In the Cleanexample.xlsx file (see Figure 5-9), the unprintable CHAR(10) and CHAR(160) have been concatenated in front of the number 33 in cells E5 and H6, respectively. In cells E8 and H8, you apply the *VALUE* function in an attempt to transform the contents of E5 and H6 into numbers, but the result is the #VALUE error, which indicates that Excel cannot figure out that you want these cells treated as numbers. In cell E11, the contents of cell E5 were cleaned with the CLEAN(E5) formula. In cell E12, you see the numerical value *33*, so the VALUE(E11) formula succeeds after CHAR(10) was cleaned. However, in cell H10, an attempt was made to clean the contents of cell H6 with the CLEAN(H6) formula. In cell H11, the VALUE(H10) formula fails because the CLEAN function does not remove CHAR(160). You can, however, use the SUBSTITUTE function to replace CHAR(160) with an empty space, and all is well. In cell H14, use the FIND(CHAR(160),H10) formula to verify that CHAR(160) is present in cell H10. You find that the first character in cell H10 was CHAR(160); if the FIND function returned an error, you would know that CHAR(160) was not present in cell H10. In cell H15, the SUBSTITUTE(H6,CHAR(160),"") formula replaces all occurrences of CHAR(160) with an empty space. In cell H16, the VALUE(H15) formula yields the number 33, so we can now perform mathematical operations on the contents of cell H15!

	E	F	G	H	I	J
4	char 10					
5	33			char 160		
6				33		
7						
8	#VALUE!			#VALUE!		
9				CLEAN?		
10	cleaned			33		
11	33			#VALUE!		
12		33		CLEAN and VALUE DO NOT WORK		
13				SUBSTITUTE		
14			FIND CHAR 160	1		
15			SUBSTITUTE	33		
16			VALUE	33		
17				160		

FIGURE 5-9 Use the *CLEAN* and *SUBSTITUTE* functions to remove unprintable characters.

I like text functions, but is there an easy way (not involving text functions) to extract first or last names from data, create an email list from a list of names, or perform other routine operations on text data?

Flash Fill uses sophisticated pattern recognition technology to mimic many tasks that were previously performed with text functions. The Flashfill.xlsx file contains the following examples of Flash Fill in action:

- Extracting first and last names

- Creating email addresses for UXYZ University by appending @UXYZ.edu to a person's last name

- Extracting the dollar and cents amounts from a list of prices

To use the Flash Fill feature, look at a column near your data and in the row containing the first row of data type in an example of what you want to accomplish. Usually, if you press Enter and then

Ctrl+E, Flash Fill correctly anticipates your wishes and fills in the remaining cells. Sometimes, however, it takes more than one example for Flash Fill to get things right.

As shown in Figure 5-10, you want to extract each person's first and last name in columns E and F. Type **Tricia** in cell E6 of the first and last worksheet and press Enter. Press Ctrl+E, and Excel fills in each person's first name in E7:E13. Similarly, if you type **Lopez** in F6, press Enter, and then press Ctrl+E, Flash Fill enters each person's last name in F7:F13.

	D	E	F
5	Full	First	Last
6	Tricia Lopez	Tricia	Lopez
7	Will Wong	Will	Wong
8	Jack Spratt	Jack	Spratt
9	Vivian Hibbits	Vivian	Hibbits
10	Jose Gomez	Jose	Gomez
11	April Chou	April	Chou
12	Tanya Walters	Tanya	Walters
13	James Jones	James	Jones

FIGURE 5-10 Flash Fill automatically fills in first and last names.

As shown in Figure 5-11, you want to create an email address for each person by appending @UXYZ.edu to each person's last name. Begin by typing **Lopez@UXYZ.edu** in cell E6 of the worksheet email. After pressing Enter, press Ctrl+E, and Flash Fill magically creates email addresses in the E7:E13 range.

	D	E
5	Name	Email
6	Tricia Lopez	Lopez@UXYZ.edu
7	Will Wong	Wong@UXYZ.edu
8	Jack Spratt	Spratt@UXYZ.edu
9	Vivian Hibbits	Hibbits@UXYZ.edu
10	Jose Gomez	Gomez@UXYZ.edu
11	April Chou	Chou@UXYZ.edu
12	Tanya Walters	Walters@UXYZ.edu
13	James Jones	Jones@UXYZ.edu

FIGURE 5-11 Create email addresses with Flash Fill.

As shown in Figure 5-12, you want to extract the dollar and cents amounts of the prices shown in the D6:D11 cell range of the Dollars and Cents worksheet. To begin, type **6** in cell E6 and press Enter. After pressing Ctrl+E, the correct dollar amounts are inserted in E7:E11. Similarly, if you type **56** in F6 and press Enter followed by Ctrl+E, Flash Fill fills in the correct cents amounts in F7:F11.

	D	E	F
4			
5	Price	Dollars	Cents
6	$6.56	6	56
7	$7.43	7	43
8	$9.86	9	86
9	$15.43	15	43
10	$173.32	173	32
11	$4.21	4	21

FIGURE 5-12 Use Flash Fill to extract dollars and cents.

Flash Fill can make mistakes, especially when the data is not very consistent. Also (unlike formulas involving text functions), the results from Flash Fill are not dynamic and will not update if the original data is changed.

If you wish, you may disable Flash Fill by selecting **Options** from **FILE** on the ribbon. Under **Advanced,** open the Editing Options section of the dialog box and clear **Automatically Flash Fill**.

Problems

1. Cells B2:B5 of the Showbiz.xlsx workbook contain the fictitious addresses of some of our favorite people. Use text functions to extract each person's name to one column and each person's street address to another.

2. The IDprice.xlsx workbook contains the product ID and prices for various products. Use text functions to put the product IDs and prices in separate columns and then use the **Text To Columns** command on the **Data** tab on the ribbon to accomplish the same goal.

3. The Quarterlygnpdata.xlsx workbook contains quarterly GNP data for the United States (in billions of 1996 dollars). Extract this data to three columns so that the first column contains the year, the second column contains the quarter number, and the third column contains the GNP. The Textstylesdata.xlsx file contains information about the style, color, and size of a variety of shirts. For example, the first shirt is style 100 (indicated by digits between the colon and the hyphen). Its color is 65, and its size is L. Use text functions to extract the style, color, and size of each shirt.

4. The file Textstylesdata.xlsx contains information about the style, color, and size for a variety of shirts. For example, the first shirt is style 100 (indicated by digits between the colon and the hyphen). Its color is 65, and its size is 1. Use text functions to extract the size, color, and style of each shirt.

5. The Emailproblem.xlsx file gives first and last names of several new Microsoft employees. To create an email address for each employee, follow the first letter of the employee's first name by the employee's last name and add @microsoft.com to the end. Use text functions to create the email addresses efficiently.

6. The Lineupdata.xlsx file gives the number of minutes played by five-player combinations (lineups). (Lineup 1 played 10.4 minutes, for instance.) Use text functions to put this data into a form suitable for numerical calculations; for example, transform 10.4m into the number 10.4.

7. The Reversenames.xlsx file gives the first names, middle names or initials, and last names of several people. Transform these names so that the last name appears first, followed by a comma, and then followed by the first and middle names. For example, transform Gregory William Winston into Winston, Gregory William.

8. The Incomefrequency.xlsx file contains the distribution of starting salaries for MBA graduates of Faber College. Summarize this data by creating a frequency graph.

9. Recall that CHAR(65) yields the letter A, CHAR(66) yields the letter B, and so on. Use these facts to populate cells B1:B26 efficiently with the sequence of A, B, C, and so on through Z.

10. The Capitalizefirstletter.xlsx file contains various song titles or phrases, such as, "The rain in Spain falls mainly in the plain." Ensure that the first letter of each song title is capitalized.

11. The Ageofmachine.xlsx file contains data in the following form:

    - S/N: 160768, vib roller,84" smooth drum,canopy Auction: 6/2–4/2005 in Montgomery, Alabama

    - Each row refers to a machine purchase. Determine the year of each purchase.

12. When downloading corporate data from the Security and Exchange Commission's EDGAR site, you often obtain data for a company that looks something like this:

    - Cash and Cash Equivalents: $31,848, $31,881

    - How would you extract Cash and Cash Equivalents efficiently for each company?

13. The Lookuptwocolumns.xlsx file gives the model, year, and price for each of a series of cars. Set up formulas that enable you to enter the model and year of a car and return its price.

14. The Moviedata.xlsx file contains the names of several movies followed by the number of copies of the movie DVD purchased by a local video store. Extract the title of each movie from this data.

15. The Moviedata.xlsx file contains the names of several movies followed by the number of copies of the movie DVD purchased by a local video store. For each movie, extract the number of copies purchased from this data. Hint: You probably want to use the *SUBSTITUTE* function. The syntax of the *SUBSTITUTE* function is SUBSTITUTE(text,old_text,new_text,[instance_num]). If instance num is omitted, every occurrence of old text in text is replaced by new text. If instance num is given, then only that occurrence of old text is replaced by new text. For example, SUBSTITUTE(A4,1,2) would replace each 1 in cell A4 with a 2, but SUBSTITUTE(A4,1,2,3) would replace only the third occurrence of a 1 in cell A4 with a 2.

16. The Problem16data.xlsx file contains the number of people who responded 1–5 on a marketing questionnaire (1 = Very unlikely to buy product, . . . , 5 = Very likely to buy product). Summarize this data graphically by using the asterisk symbol. To make your summary look more appealing, on the **Home** tab on the ribbon, choose **Orientation** in the **Alignment** group and make the text vertical. Right-click the row number and increase the row height. Finally, in the **Alignment** group, choose **Wrap Text** so that you make the text of your graph vertical.

17. The Problem17data.xlsx file contains people's names (such as Mr. John Doe). Use text functions to extract each person's title and first name to separate columns.

18. The Weirddata.xls file contains three numbers imported from an Internet site. Add up the numbers and see that the total is incorrect. Modify the data so that the *SUM* function can obtain the correct sum of the three numbers. Hint: Use the *FIND* function to find out which invisible character is present!

19. Use Flash Fill to change the names in the Flashfilltemplate.xls worksheet to lowercase.

20. Use Flash Fill to extract the number from each row in the Movienumbers.xlsx file.

21. For the data in Movienumbers.xlsx, use Flash Fill to create a column that inserts the number in the movie title at the end of the phrase, "The number in the title of this movie is . . . ".

CHAPTER 6

Dates and date functions

Questions answered in this chapter:

- When I enter dates in Excel, I often see a number such as 37625 rather than a date such as 1/4/2003. What does this number mean, and how can I change it to a normal date?

- Can I use a formula to display today's date automatically?

- How can I determine a date that is 50 workdays after another date? How can I exclude holidays if I want to?

- How can I determine the number of workdays between two dates?

- I have 500 dates entered in an Excel worksheet. How can I write formulas to extract from each date the month, year, day of the month, and day of the week?

- I am given the year, month, and day of the month for a date. Is there an easy way to recover the actual date?

- My business has purchased and sold machines. For some, I have the date the machine was purchased and the date the machine was sold. Can I easily determine how many months we kept these machines?

To illustrate the most commonly used month-day-year formats in Microsoft Excel 2013, suppose today is January 4, 2004. You can enter this date as any of the following:

- 1/4/2004

- 4-Jan-2004

- January 4, 2004

- 1/4/04

If you enter only two digits to represent a year, and the digits are 30 or higher, Excel assumes the digits represent years in the twentieth century; if the digits are lower than 30, Excel assumes they represent years in the twenty-first century. For example, 1/1/29 is treated as January 1, 2029, but 1/1/30 is treated as January 1, 1930. Each year, the year treated as dates in the twenty-first century increases by one.

Answers to this chapter's questions

This section provides the answers to the questions that are listed at the beginning of the chapter.

When I enter dates in Excel, I often see a number such as 37625 rather than a date such as 1/4/2003. What does this number mean, and how can I change it to a normal date?

The way Excel treats calendar dates is sometimes confusing to the novice. The key is understanding that Excel can display a date in a variety of month-day-year formats, or it can display a date in *serial format*. A date in serial format, such as 37625, is simply a positive integer that represents the number of days between the given date and January 1, 1900. Both the current date and January 1, 1900 are included in the count. For example, Excel displays January 3, 1900, in serial format as the number 3, which means there are three days between January 1, 1900, and January 3, 1900 (including both days).

> **Note** Excel assumes that 1900 was a leap year containing 366 days. In reality, 1900 contained only 365 days. For some fascinating information on the origin of this bug, see *www. joelonsoftware.com/items/2006/06/16.html*.

Figure 6-1 shows the worksheet named Serial Format in the Dates.xlsx file. Suppose you are given the dates shown in cells D5:D14 in serial format. For example, value *37622* in cell D5 indicates a date that is 37,622 days after January 1, 1900 (including both January 1, 1900, and day 37,622). To display these serial dates in month-day-year format, copy them to E5:E14. Select the E5:E14 cell range, right-click the selection, and choose **Format Cells**. At any time, by the way, you can open the Format Cells dialog box by pressing Ctrl+1. Now select the date format you want from the list shown in Figure 6-2. The dates in E5:E14 are displayed in date format, as you can see in Figure 6-1. If you want to format dates in the serial number format, select E5:E14, right-click the selection, and choose **Format Cells**, **General**.

	D	E
4	Dates	Reformatted
5	37622	1/1/2003
6	37623	1/2/2003
7	37624	1/3/2003
8	37625	1/4/2003
9	37626	1/5/2003
10	37627	1/6/2003
11	37628	1/7/2003
12	37629	1/8/2003
13	37630	1/9/2003
14	37631	1/10/2003

FIGURE 6-1 Use the Format Cells command to change dates from serial number format to month-day-year format.

Simply changing the date format of a cell to General will yield the date in serial format. Another way to obtain the date in serial format is to use the *DATEVALUE* function and enclose the date in quotation marks. For example, in the Date Format worksheet of the Dates.xlsx file, cell I5 contains the DATEVALUE("1/4/2003") formula. Excel yields 37625, which is the serial format for January 4, 2003.

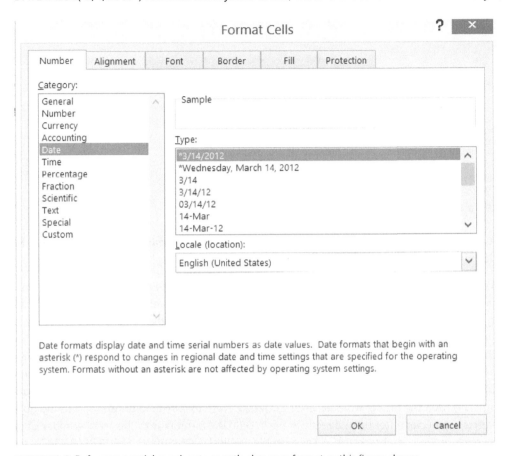

FIGURE 6-2 Reformat a serial number to month-day-year format as this figure shows.

Can I use a formula to display today's date automatically?

Displaying today's date with a formula is easy, as you can see by looking at cell C13 of the Date Format worksheet shown in Figure 6-3. Entering the *TODAY()* function in a cell displays today's date. This screenshot was created on July 7, 2013.

	B	C	D	E	F	G	H	I
			Year	Month	Day	Day of Week	Putting date together	Serial Number
5	1/4/2003	1/4/2003	2003	1	4	7	1/4/2003	37625
6	2/1/1901	2/1/1901	1901	2	1	6	2/1/1901	398
7	4-Jan-2003	4-Jan-03	2003	1	4	7	1/4/2003	
8	January 4, 2003	4-Jan-03	2003	1	4	7	1/4/2003	
9	1/4/03	4-Jan-03	2003	1	4	7	1/4/2003	
10		3-Jan-01	1900	1	0	7	1/0/1900	3
11								
12								
13	Today's date	7/7/2013	50 workdays from start date	excluding holidays				
14	Start date	1/3/2003	3/14/2003	3/17/2003				
15	Later date	8/4/2003						
16					Holidays			
17	Workdays between (excluding	150			7/4/2003			
18	Workdays between (no holidays)	152			1/20/2003			

FIGURE 6-3 Here are examples of date functions.

How can I determine a date that is 50 workdays after another date? How can I exclude holidays if I want to?

The *WORKDAY(start_date,#days,[holidays])* function displays the date that is the number of workdays (a workday is a nonweekend day) indicated by #days after a given start date. Holidays is an optional argument for the function by which you can exclude from the calculation any dates that are listed in a cell range. Thus, entering the WORKDAY(C14,50) formula in cell D14 of the Date Format worksheet tells you that 3/14/2003 is 50 workdays after 1/3/2003. If you believe that the only two holidays that matter are Martin Luther King Day and Independence Day, you can change the formula to WORKDAY(C14,50,F17:F18). With this addition, Excel does not count 1/20/2003 in its calculations, making 3/17/2003 the fiftieth workday after 1/3/2003. Note that instead of referring to the holidays in other cells, you can enter them directly in the WORKDAY formula with the serial number of each holiday enclosed in curly brackets ({ }). For example, WORKDAY(38500,10,{38600,38680,38711}) would find the tenth workday after the date with serial number 38500, ignoring Labor Day, Thanksgiving, and Christmas 2005.

The *WORKDAY.INTL* function was introduced in Excel 2010. Use this function to choose your own definition of a workday. The syntax is WORKDAY.INTL(start_date,days,weekend,[holidays]). Use the third argument to specify the definition of a day off. You can use the following codes to specify the definition of a day off:

1 or omitted	Saturday, Sunday
2	Sunday, Monday
3	Monday, Tuesday
4	Tuesday, Wednesday
5	Wednesday, Thursday
6	Thursday, Friday

7	Friday, Saturday
11	Sunday only
12	Monday only
13	Tuesday only
14	Wednesday only
15	Thursday only
16	Friday only
17	Saturday only

For example, in worksheet Date Format of the Dates.xlsx file, the date 100 workdays after 3/14/2011 was computed in cell C27 (see Figure 6-4), with Sunday and Monday as days off, with the WORKDAY.INTL(C23,100,2) formula. In cell C28, the date 100 workdays after 3/14/2011 when only Sunday is a day off was computed by using the WORKDAY.INTL(C23,100,11) formula. You can also enter the definition of days off with a string of seven ones and zeroes; a one indicates a day off, and the first entry in the string is Monday, the second is Tuesday, and so on. Thus, in cells D26 and D27, the previous results were duplicated with the WORKDAY.INTL(C23,100,"1000001") and WORKDAY. INTL(C23,100,"0000001") formulas, respectively.

How can I determine the number of workdays between two dates?

The key to solving this problem is to use the *NETWORKDAYS* function. The syntax for this function is NETWORKDAYS(start_date,end_date,[holidays]), where *holidays* is an optional argument identifying a cell range that lists the dates you want to count as holidays. The *NETWORKDAYS* function returns the number of working days between *start date* and *end date*, excluding weekends and any listed holidays. As an illustration of the *NETWORKDAYS* function, look at cell C18 in the Date Format worksheet, which contains the NETWORKDAYS(C14,C15) formula. This formula yields the number of working days between 1/3/2003 and 8/4/2003, which is 152. The NETWORKDAYS(C14,C15,F17:F18) formula in cell C17 yields the number of workdays between 1/3/2003 and 8/4/2003, excluding Martin Luther King Day and Independence Day. The answer is 152–2=150.

The *NETWORKDAYS.INTL* function was introduced with Excel 2010. Like the *WORKDAYS.INTL* function, *NETWORKDAYS.INTL* enables you to customize the definition of a weekend. For example, in cell C31 of the Date Format worksheet in the Dates.xlsx file, the number of workdays (373) between 3/14/2011 and 8/16/2012 was computed, when Sunday and Monday are days off, with the NETWORKDAYS.INTL(C23,C24,2) formula. (See Figure 6-4.) In cell D31, the same result was computed with the NETWORKDAYS.INTL(C23,C24,"1000001") formula.

	B	C	D
21	**International Functions**		
22			
23	Start Date	3/14/2011	
24	End Date	8/16/2012	
25			
26	**100 workdays later**		
27	Sunday Monday as weekend	7/30/2011	7/30/2011
28	Sunday as weekend	7/8/2011	7/8/2011
29			
30	**Days Between Start and End Date**		
31	Sunday Monday as weekend	373	373
32	Sunday as weekend	448	448

FIGURE 6-4 This figure shows examples of international date functions.

I have 500 dates entered in an Excel worksheet. How can I write formulas that will extract from each date the month, year, day of the month, and day of the week?

The Date Format worksheet of the Dates.xlsx file (see Figure 6-3) lists several dates in the B5:B10 cell range. In B5 and B7:B9, four formats were used to display January 4, 2003. In columns D:G, the year, month, day of the month, and day of the week for each date were extracted. By copying the YEAR(B5) formula from D5 to D6:D10, the year for each date was extracted. By copying the MONTH(B5) formula from E5 to E6:E10, the month (1=January, 2=February, and so on) portion of each date was extracted. By copying the DAY(B5) formula from F5 to F6:F10, the day of the month for each date was extracted. Finally, by copying the WEEKDAY(B5,1) formula from G5 to G6:G10, the day of the week for each date was extracted. Note that this process might not work for non-US regional settings.

When the last argument of the *WEEKDAY* function is 1, 1=Sunday, 2=Monday, and so on. When the last argument is 2, 1=Monday, 2=Tuesday, and so on. When the last argument is 3, 0=Monday, 1=Tuesday, and so on.

I am given the year, month, and day of the month for a date. Is there an easy way to recover the actual date?

The *DATE* function, whose arguments are DATE(year,month,day), returns the date with the given year, month, and day of the month. In the Date Format worksheet, copying the DATE(D5,E5,F5) formula from cell H5 to cells H6:H10 recovers the dates you started with.

My business has purchased and sold machines. For some, I have the date the machine was purchased and the date the machine was sold. Can I easily determine how many months we kept these machines?

The *DATEDIF* function can easily determine the number of complete years, months, or days between two dates. In file Datedif.xlsx (see Figure 6-5), you can see that a machine was bought on 10/15/2006 and was sold on 4/10/2008. How many complete years, months, or days was the machine kept? The syntax of the *DATEDIF* function is DATEDIF(startdate,enddate,time_unit). If the unit is written as "y," you get the number of complete years between the start and end dates; if the unit is written as "m," you get the number of complete months between the start and end dates; and if the unit is written as "d," you get the number of complete days between the start and end dates. Thus, entering DATEDIF(D4,D5,"y") in cell D6 shows that the machine was kept for one full year. Entering the DATEDIF(D4,D5,"m") formula in cell D7 shows the machine was kept for 17 complete months. Entering the DATEDIF(D4,D5,"d") formula in cell D7 shows the machine was kept for 543 complete days.

	C	D
4	bought	10/15/2006
5	sold	4/10/2008
6	years	1
7	months	17
8	days	543

FIGURE 6-5 This figure shows use of the *DATEDIF* function.

Problems

1. What is the serial format for January 25, 2006?

2. What is the serial format for February 14, 1950?

3. To what actual date does a serial format of 4526 correspond?

4. To what actual date does a serial format of 45000 correspond?

5. Determine the day that occurs 74 workdays after today's date (including holidays).

6. Determine the day that occurs 74 workdays after today's date (including holidays but excluding the current year's Christmas, New Year's Day, and Independence Day).

7. How many workdays (including holidays) are there between July 10, 2005, and August 15, 2006?

8. How many workdays (including holidays but excluding Christmas, New Year's Day, and Independence Day) are there between July 10, 2005, and August 15, 2006?

 Note The Datep.xlsx file contains several hundred dates. Use this file for the next set of problems.

9. Determine the month, year, day of the month, and day of the week for each date.

10. Express each date in serial format.

11. A project begins on December 4, 2005. The project consists of Activities 1, 2, and 3. Activity 2 can start the day after Activity 1 finishes. Activity 3 can start the day after Activity 2 finishes. Set up a worksheet that accepts as inputs the duration (in days) of the three activities and outputs both the month and year during which each activity is completed.

12. You bought a stock on July 29, 2005, and sold it on December 30, 2005. The stock exchange is closed on Labor Day, Christmas, and Thanksgiving. Create a list of dates of when the stock market was open during the time you owned the stock.

13. The Machinedates.xlsx file contains dates on which several machines were bought and sold. Determine how many months and years each machine was kept.

14. Given any date, find a way to have Excel compute the day of the week of the first day of the date's month.

15. Given any date, find a way to have Excel compute the last day of the date's month. Hint: DATE(2005,13,1), surprisingly, returns 1/1/2006.

16. Given any date, how can you compute which day of the year it is? For example, what day of the year will 4/15/2020 be? Hint: The DATE(2020,1,0) formula will return the serial number for day 0 of January 2020, and Excel will treat this as December 31, 2019.

17. In the country of Fredonia, employees have Tuesday and Wednesday off. What date is 200 workdays after 5/3/2013?

18. In the country of Lower Ampere, employees have Friday and Saturday off. In addition, Valentine's Day is a holiday. How many workdays are there between 1/10/2014 and 5/31/2015?

19. Suppose the first quarter of each year is January–March, the second quarter is April–June, and so on. Write a formula that returns the first day of the quarter for a given date.

20. Use the definitions of quarters given in problem 19 and write a formula that computes the last day of the previous quarter for any given date.

21. Set up a spreadsheet in which a person can enter his date of birth, and the spreadsheet returns the person's actual age.

22. Memorial Day is always the last Monday in May. Set up a spreadsheet in which you can enter the year, and the spreadsheet determines the date of Memorial Day.

23. Create a spreadsheet that always lists the next 50 workdays (assuming no holidays and that Monday through Friday are the workdays.)

CHAPTER 7

Evaluating investments by using net present value criteria

Questions answered in this chapter:

- What is net present value (NPV)?

- How can I use the Excel *NPV* function?

- How can I compute NPV when cash flows are received at the beginning of a year or in the middle of a year?

- How can I compute NPV when cash flows are received at irregular intervals?

Consider the following two investments, whose cash flows are listed in the NPV.xlsx file and shown in Figure 7-1:

- Investment 1 requires a cash outflow of $10,000 today and $14,000 two years from now. One year from now, this investment will yield $24,000.

- Investment 2 requires a cash outflow of $6,000 today and $1,000 two years from now. One year from now, this investment will yield $8,000.

Which is the better investment? Investment 1 yields total cash flow of $0, whereas Investment 2 yields a total cash flow of $1,000. At first glance, Investment 2 appears to be better, but wait a minute. Most of the cash outflow for Investment 1 occurs two years from now, whereas most of the cash outflow for Investment 2 occurs today. Spending $1 two years from now doesn't seem as costly as spending $1 today, so maybe Investment 1 is better than first appears. To determine which investment is better, you need to compare the values of cash flows received at different points in time. That's where the concept of net present value proves useful.

	A	B	C	D	E	F
1						
2						
3		r	0.2			
4	NPV	Time	0	1	2	Total cash flow
5	277.7778	Investment 1 Cash flow	-10000	24000	-14000	0
6	-27.7778	Investment 2 Cash Flow	-6000	8000	-1000	1000
7		Present V alue Inv 1	-10000	20000	-9722.22	
8		Present Value Inv 2	-6000	6666.667	-694.444	
9						
10		Present Value beginning of Year				
11		Investment 1	$277.78	$277.78		
12		Investment 2	($27.78)	($27.78)		
13		Present Value End of Year				
14		Investment 1	$231.48			
15		Investment 2	($23.15)			
16		Present Value Middle of year				
17		Investment 1	$253.58			
18		Investment 2	($25.36)			

FIGURE 7-1 To determine which investment is better, you need to calculate net present value.

Answers to this chapter's questions

This section provides the answers to the questions that are listed at the beginning of the chapter.

What is net present value?

The net present value (NPV) of a stream of cash flow received at different points in time is simply the value *measured in today's dollars*. Suppose you have $1 today, and you invest this dollar at an annual interest rate of r percent. This dollar will grow to $1+r$ dollars in the first year, $(1+r)^2$ dollars in two years, and so on. You can say, in some sense, that $1 today equals $(1+r)$ a year from now and $(1+r)^2$ two years from now. In general, you can say that $1 today is equal to $(1+r)^n$ n years from now. As an equation, this calculation can be expressed as follows:

$1 now = $(1+r)^n$ received n years from now

If you divide both sides of this equation by $(1 + r)^n$, you get the following important result:

$1/(1 + r)^n$ now = $1 received n years from now

This result tells you how to compute (in today's dollars) the NPV of any sequence of cash flows. You can convert any cash flow to today's dollars by multiplying the cash flow received n years from now (n can be a fraction) by $1/(1 + r)^n$.

You then add up the value of the cash flows (in today's dollars) to find the investment's NPV. Assume r is equal to 0.2. You could calculate the NPV for the two investments you're considering as follows:

$$= \text{Investment1NPV} = -10,000 + \frac{24,000}{(1 + 0.20)^1} + \frac{-14,000}{(1 + 0.20)^2} = \$277.78$$

$$= \text{Investment2NPV} = -6,000 + \frac{8,000}{(1 + 0.20)^1} + \frac{-1,000}{(1 + 0.20)^2} = \$-27.78$$

Based on NPV, Investment 1 is superior to Investment 2. Although total cash flow for Investment 2 exceeds total cash flow for Investment 1, Investment 1 has a better NPV because a greater proportion of Investment 1's negative cash flow comes later, and the NPV criterion gives less weight to cash flows that come later. If you use a value of .02 for r, Investment 2 has a larger NPV because when r is very small, later cash flows are not discounted as much, and NPV returns results similar to those derived by ranking investments according to total cash flow.

Note The interest rate of r = 0.2 was randomly chosen, skirting the issue of how to determine an appropriate value of r. You need to study finance for at least a year to understand the issues involved in determining an appropriate value for r. The appropriate value of r used to compute NPV is often called the company's *cost of capital*. Suffice it to say that most US companies use an annual cost of capital between 0.1 (10 percent) and 0.2 (20 percent). If the annual interest rate is chosen according to accepted finance practices, projects with NPV > 0 increase the value of a company, projects with NPV < 0 decrease the value of a company, and projects with NPV = 0 keep the value of a company unchanged. A company should (if it had unlimited investment capital) invest in every available investment having positive NPV.

To determine the NPV of Investment 1 in Microsoft Excel, assign the range name r_ to the interest rate (located in cell C3). Copy the Time 0 cash flow from C5 to C7. You can determine the NPV for Investment 1's Year 1 and Year 2 cash flows by copying the D5/(1+r_)^D$4 formula from D7 to L7. The caret symbol (^), located over the number 6 on the US keyboard, raises a number to a power. In cell A5, compute the NPV of Investment 1 by adding the NPV of each year's cash flow with the SUM(C7:E7) formula. To determine the NPV for Investment 2, copy the formulas from C7:E7 to C8:E8 and from A5 to A6.

How can I use the Excel *NPV* function?

The Excel *NPV* function uses the NPV(rate,range of cells) syntax. This function determines the NPV for the given rate of the cash flows in the range of cells. The function's calculation assumes that the first cash flow is one period from now. In other words, entering the NPV(r_,C5:E5) formula will not determine the NPV for Investment 1. Instead, this formula (entered in cell C14) computes the NPV of the following sequence of cash flows: –$10,000 a year from now, $24,000 two years from now, and –$14,000 three years from now. Call this Investment 1 (End of Year). The NPV of Investment 1 (End of Year) is $231.48. Assuming beginning of year cash flows, to compute the actual cash NPV of

Investment 1, enter the C7+NPV(r_,D5:E5) formula in cell C11. This formula does not discount the Time 0 cash flow at all (which is correct because Time 0 cash flow is already in today's dollars) but first multiplies the cash flow in D5 by 1/1.2 and then multiplies the cash flow in E5 by $1/1.2^2$.

The formula in cell C11 yields the correct NPV of Investment 1, $277.78.

How can I compute NPV when cash flows are received at the beginning of a year or in the middle of a year?

To use the *NPV* function to compute the net present value of a project whose cash flows always occur at the beginning of a year, you can use the approach described to determine the NPV of Investment 1: Separate out the Year 1 cash flow and apply the *NPV* function to the remaining cash flows. Alternatively, observe that for any year n, $1 received at the beginning of year n is equivalent to $(1 + r)$ received at the end of year n. Remember that in one year, a dollar will grow by a factor of $(1 + r)$. Thus, if you multiply the result obtained with the *NPV* function by $(1 + r)$, you can convert the NPV of a sequence of year-end cash flows to the NPV of a sequence of cash flows received at the beginning of the year. You can also compute the NPV of Investment 1 in cell D11 with the (1+r_)*C14 formula. Of course, you again obtain an NPV of $277.78.

Now suppose the cash flows for an investment occur in the middle of each year. For an organization that receives monthly subscription revenues, you can approximate the 12 monthly revenues received during a given year as a lump sum received in the middle of the year. How can you use the *NPV* function to determine the NPV of a sequence of mid-year cash flows? For any Year n,

$$\$\sqrt{1+r}$$

received at the end of Year n is equivalent to $1 received at the middle of Year n because in half a year, $1 will grow by a factor of

$$\sqrt{1+r}$$

If you assume the cash flows for Investment 1 occur mid-year, you can compute the NPV of the mid-year version of Investment 1 in cell C17 with the SQRT(1+r_)*C14 formula. You obtain a value of $253.58.

How can I compute NPV when cash flows are received at irregular intervals?

Cash flows often occur at irregular intervals, which makes computing the NPV or internal rate of return (IRR) of these cash flows more difficult. Fortunately, the Excel *XNPV* function makes computing the NPV of irregularly timed cash flows a snap.

The *XNPV* function uses the XNPV(rate,values,dates) syntax. The first date listed must be the earliest, but other dates need not be listed in chronological order. The *XNPV* function computes the NPV of the given cash flows, assuming the current date is the first date in the sequence. For example, if the first listed date is 4/8/13, the NPV is computed in April 8, 2013, dollars.

To illustrate the use of the *XNPV* function, look at the example on the NPV as of First Date worksheet in the XNPV.xlsx file, which is shown in Figure 7-2. Suppose that on April 8, 2015, you paid out $900. Later, you receive the following amounts:

- $300 on August 15, 2015

- $400 on January 15, 2016

- $200 on June 25, 2016

- $100 on July 3, 2016

If the annual interest rate is 10 percent, what is the NPV of these cash flows? Enter the dates (in Excel date format) in D3:D7 and the cash flows in E3:E7. Entering the XNPV(A9,E3:E7,D3:D7) formula in cell D11 computes the project's NPV in April 8, 2015, dollars because that is the first date listed. This project would have an NPV, in April 8, 2015, dollars, of $28.64.

	A	B	C	D	E	F	G
1							
2	XNPV Function		Code	Date	Cash Flow	Time	discount factor
3			42102.00	4/8/2015	-900		1
4			42231.00	8/15/2015	300	0.353425	0.966876054
5			42384.00	1/15/2016	400	0.772603	0.92900895
6			42546.00	6/25/2016	200	1.216438	0.890529581
7			42554.00	7/3/2016	100	1.238356	0.888671215
8	Rate						
9		0.1					
10				XNPV	Direct		
11				28.63943	28.639434		

FIGURE 7-2 This figure shows the use of the *XNPV* function.

The computations the *XNPV* function performs are as follows:

1. Compute the number of years after April 8, 2015, that each date occurred. (This was done in column F.) For example, August 15 is 0.3534 years after April 8.

2. Discount cash flows at the rate of $1/(1+rate)$years after.

    For example, the August 15, 2015 cash flow is discounted by

    $$\frac{1}{(1 + 0.1)^{3534}} = 0.967$$

3. Sum up overall cash flows in cell E11: (cash flow value)*(discount factor).

Suppose that today's date is actually July 8, 2013. How would you compute the NPV of an investment in today's dollars? Simply add a row with today's date and 0 cash flow and include this row in the range for the *XNPV* function. (See Figure 7-3 and the Today worksheet.) The NPV of the project in today's dollars is $106.99.

	A	B	C	D	E
1					
2	**XNPV Function**		**Code**	**Date**	**Cash Flow**
3			41463.00	7/8/2013	0
4			42102.00	4/8/2015	-900
5			42231.00	8/15/2015	300
6			42384.00	1/15/2016	400
7			42546.00	6/25/2016	200
8			42554.00	7/3/2016	100
9			42188.00	7/3/2015	100
10	**Rate**				
11		0.1			
12				**XNPV**	
13				106.9907	

FIGURE 7-3 NPV is converted to today's dollars.

Note that if a cash flow is left blank, the *NPV* function ignores both the cash flow and the period, and the *XNPV* function returns a #NUM error.

Problems

1. An NBA player is to receive a $1,000,000 signing bonus today and $2,000,000 one year, two years, and three years from now. Assuming $r = 0.10$ and ignoring tax considerations, would he be better off receiving $6,000,000 today?

2. A project has the following cash flows:

Now	One year from now	Two years from now	Three years from now
-$4 million	$4 million	$4 million	-$3 million

If the company's cost of capital is 15 percent, should it proceed with the project?

3. Beginning one month from now, a customer will pay his Internet provider $25 per month for the next five years. Assuming all revenue for a year is received at the middle of a year, estimate the NPV of these revenues. Use $r = 0.15$.

4. Beginning one month from now, a customer will pay $25 per month to her Internet provider for the next five years. Assuming all revenue for a year is received at the middle of a year, use the *XNPV* function to obtain the exact NPV of these revenues. Use $r = 0.15$.

5. Consider the following set of cash flows over a four-year period. Determine the NPV of these cash flows if $r = 0.15$ and cash flows occur at the end of the year:

Year	1	2	3	4
	-$600	$550	-$680	$1,000

Solve Problem 5, assuming cash flows occur at the beginning of each year.

6. Consider the following cash flows:

Date	Cash flow
12/15/01	-$1,000
1/11/02	$300
4/7/03	$600
7/15/04	$925

If today is November 1, 2001, and r = 0.15, what is the NPV of these cash flows?

7. After earning an MBA, a student will begin working at an $80,000-per-year job on September 1, 2005. He expects to receive a 5 percent raise each year until he retires on September 1, 2035. If the cost of capital is 8 percent a year, determine the total present value of his before-tax earnings.

8. Consider a 30-year bond that pays $50 at the end of Years 1–29 and $1,050 at the end of Year 30. If the appropriate discount rate is 5 percent per year, what is a fair price for this bond?

CHAPTER 8

Internal rate of return

Questions answered in this chapter:

- How can I find the IRR of cash flows?

- Does a project always have a unique IRR?

- Are there conditions that guarantee a project will have a unique IRR?

- If each of two projects has a single IRR, how can I use the projects' IRRs?

- How can I find the IRR of irregularly spaced cash flows?

- What is the MIRR, and how can I compute it?

The net present value (NPV) of a sequence of cash flows depends on the interest rate (r) used. For example, if you consider cash flows for Projects 1 and 2 (see the IRR worksheet in the IRR.xlsx file, shown in Figure 8-1), you find that for $r = 0.2$, Project 2 has a larger NPV, and for $r = 0.01$, Project 1 has a larger NPV. When you use NPV to rank investments, the outcome can depend on the interest rate. It is the nature of human beings to want to boil everything in life down to a single number. The internal rate of return (IRR) of a project is simply the interest rate that makes the NPV of the project equal to 0. If a project has a unique IRR, the IRR has a nice interpretation. For example, if a project has an IRR of 15 percent, you receive an annual rate of return of 15 percent on the cash flow you invested. In this chapter's examples, you'll find that Project 1 has an IRR of 47.5 percent, which means that the $400 invested at Time 1 is yielding an annual rate of return of 47.5 percent. Sometimes, however, a project might have more than one IRR or even no IRR. In these cases, speaking about the project's IRR is useless.

	A	B	C	D	E	F	G	H	I	J	K
1		Time	1	2	3	4	5	6	7	NPV r=.2	NPV r= .01
2	Project 1		-400	200	600	-900	1000	250	230	$268.54	$918.99
3	Project 2		-200	150	150	200	300	100	80	$297.14	$741.07
4	Project 1	IRR Proj 1 No Guess	IRR Proj 2 No Guess								
5	no guess	47.5%	80.1%								
6											
7	guess	Guess Proj 1	Guess proj 2								
8	-0.9	47.5%	80.1%								
9	-0.7	47.5%	80.1%								
10	-0.5	47.5%	80.1%								
11	-0.3	47.5%	80.1%								
12	-0.1	47.5%	80.1%								
13	0.1	47.5%	80.1%								
14	0.3	47.5%	80.1%								
15	0.5	47.5%	80.1%								
16	0.7	47.5%	80.1%								

FIGURE 8-1 This figure shows an example of the IRR function.

Answers to this chapter's questions

This section provides the answers to the questions that are listed at the beginning of the chapter.

How can I find the IRR of cash flows?

The *IRR* function calculates internal rate of return. The function has the IRR(range_of_cash_
flows,[guess]) syntax, in which guess is an optional argument. If you do not enter a guess for a project's IRR, Excel begins its calculations with a guess that the project's IRR is 10 percent and then varies
the estimate of the IRR until it finds an interest rate that makes the project's NPV equal 0 (the project's
IRR). If Excel can't find an interest rate that makes the project's NPV equal 0, Excel returns #NUM. In
cell B5, enter the *IRR(C2:I2)* formula to compute Project 1's IRR. Excel returns 47.5 percent. Thus, if you
use an annual interest rate of 47.5 percent, Project 1 will have an NPV of 0. Similarly, you can see that
Project 2 has an IRR of 80.1 percent.

Even if the *IRR* function finds an IRR, a project might have more than one IRR. To check whether
a project has more than one IRR, you can vary the initial guess of the project's IRR (for example, from −90 percent to 90 percent). You can vary the guess for Project 1's IRR by copying the
IRR($C$2:$I$2,A8) formula from B8 to B9:B17. Because all the guesses for Project 1's IRR yield 47.5
percent, you can be fairly confident that Project 1 has a unique IRR of 47.5 percent. Similarly, you can
be fairly confident that Project 2 has a unique IRR of 80.1 percent.

Does a project always have a unique IRR?

In the Multiple IRR worksheet in the IRR.xlsx file (see Figure 8-2), you can see that Project 3 (cash flows
of −20, 82, −60, 2) has two IRRs. The guess was varied about Project 3's IRR from −90 percent to 90
percent by copying the IRR($B$4:$E$4,B8) formula from C8 to C9:C17.

	A	B	C	D	E	F
1	**Multiple IRR's**					
2						
3		1	2	3	4	
4	Project 3	-20	82	-60	2	
5			plain irr	-9.6%		
6						
7		guess				
8		-0.9	-9.6%		npv at -9.6%	($0.01)
9		-0.7	-9.6%		npv at 216.1%	$0.00
10		-0.5	-9.6%			
11		-0.3	-9.6%			
12		-0.1	-9.6%			
13		0.1	-9.6%			
14		0.3	-9.6%			
15		0.5	216.1%			
16		0.7	216.1%			
17		0.9	216.1%			

FIGURE 8-2 This project has more than one IRR.

Note that when a guess is 30 percent or less, the IRR is –9.6 percent. For other guesses, the IRR is 216.1 percent. For both these interest rates, Project 3 has an NPV of 0

In the No IRR worksheet in the IRR.xlsx file (shown in Figure 8-3), you can see that no matter what guess you use for Project 4's IRR, you receive the #NUM message. This message indicates that Project 4 has no IRR.

When a project has multiple IRRs or no IRR, the concept of IRR loses virtually all meaning. Despite this problem, however, many companies still use IRR as their major tool for ranking investments.

	A	B	C	D
1				
2		No IRR		
3				
4		0	1	2
5	Project 4	10	-30	35
6				
7		guess		
8		-0.9	#NUM!	
9		-0.8	#NUM!	
10		-0.7	#NUM!	
11		-0.6	#NUM!	
12		-0.5	#NUM!	
13		-0.4	#NUM!	
14		-0.3	#NUM!	
15		-0.2	#NUM!	
16		-0.1	#NUM!	
17		0	#NUM!	
18		0.1	#NUM!	
19		0.2	#NUM!	
20		0.3	#NUM!	
21		0.4	#NUM!	
22		0.5	#NUM!	
23		0.6	#NUM!	
24		0.7	#NUM!	
25		0.8	#NUM!	
26		0.9	#NUM!	

FIGURE 8-3 This is a project with no IRR.

Are there conditions that guarantee a project will have a unique IRR?

If a project's sequence of cash flows contains exactly one change in sign, the project is guaranteed to have a unique IRR. For example, for Project 2 in the IRR worksheet, the sign of the cash flow sequence is − + + + + +. There is only one change in sign (between Time 1 and Time 2), so Project 2 must have a unique IRR. For Project 3 in the Multiple IRR worksheet, the signs of the cash flows are − + − +. Because the sign of the cash flows changes three times, a unique IRR is not guaranteed. For Project 4 in the No IRR worksheet, the signs of the cash flows are + − +. Because the signs of the cash flows change twice, a unique IRR is not guaranteed in this case either. Most capital investment projects (such as building a plant) begin with a negative cash flow followed by a sequence of positive cash flows. Therefore, most capital investment projects do have a unique IRR.

If each of two projects has a single IRR, how can I use the projects' IRRs?

If a project has a unique IRR, you can state that the project increases the value of the company *if and only if* the project's IRR exceeds the annual cost of capital. For example, if the cost of capital for a company is 15 percent, both Project 1 and Project 2 would increase the value of the company.

Suppose two projects are under consideration (both having unique IRRs), but you can undertake at most one project. It's tempting to believe that you should choose the project with the larger IRR. To illustrate that this belief can lead to incorrect decisions, look at Figure 8-4 and the Which Project worksheet in IRR.xlsx. Project 5 has an IRR of 40 percent, and Project 6 has an IRR of 50 percent. If you rank projects based on IRR and can choose only one project, you would choose Project 6. Remember, however, that a project's NPV measures the amount of value the project adds to the company. Clearly, Project 5 will (for virtually any cost of capital) have a larger NPV than Project 6. Therefore, if only one project can be chosen, Project 5 is it. IRR is problematic because it ignores the scale of the project. Whereas Project 6 is better than Project 5 on a per-dollar-invested basis, the larger scale of Project 5 makes it more valuable to the company than Project 6.

	B	C	D	E
1				
2	Project	Time 0	Time 1	IRR
3	5	-100	140	40%
4	6	-1	1.5	50%

FIGURE 8-4 IRR can lead to an incorrect choice of which project to pursue.

How can I find the IRR of irregularly spaced cash flows?

Cash flows occur on actual dates, not just at the start or end of the year. The *XIRR* function has the XIRR(cash_flow,dates,[guess]) syntax. The *XIRR* function determines the IRR of a sequence of cash flows that occur on any set of irregularly spaced dates. As with the *IRR* function, guess is an optional argument. For an example of how to use the *XIRR* function, look at Figure 8-5 and worksheet XIRR of the IRR.xlsx file.

	A	B	C	D	E	F
1					Project 7	
2	XIRR Function			Date	Cash Flow	
3				Code	Date	Cash Flow
4				4/8/2011	4/8/2011	-1500
5				8/15/2011	8/15/2011	300
6				1/15/2012	1/15/2012	400
7				6/25/2012	6/25/2012	200
8				XIRR		
9				-48.69%		

FIGURE 8-5 This is an example of the *XIRR* function.

The XIRR(F4:F7,E4:E7) formula in cell D9 shows that the IRR of Project 7 is −48.69 percent.

What is the MIRR, and how can I compute it?

In many situations, the rate at which a company borrows funds is different from the rate at which the company reinvests funds. IRR computations implicitly assume that the rate at which a company borrows and reinvests funds is equal to the IRR. If you know the actual rate at which you borrow money and the rate at which you can reinvest money, the modified internal rate of return (*MIRR*) function computes a discount rate that makes the NPV of all your cash flows (including paying back your loan and reinvesting your proceeds at the given rates) equal to 0. The syntax of MIRR is MIRR(cash flow values,borrowing rate,reinvestment rate). A nice thing about MIRR is that it is always unique. Figure 8-6 in worksheet MIRR of the IRR.xlsx file contains an example of MIRR. Suppose you borrow $120,000 today and receive the following cash flows: Year 1: $39,000; Year 2: $30,000; Year 3: $21,000; Year 4: $37,000; Year 5: $46,000. Assume you can borrow at 10 percent per year and reinvest your profits at 12 percent per year.

After entering these values in cells E7:E12 of worksheet MIRR, you can find the MIRR in cell D15 with the MIRR(E7:E12,E3,E4) formula. Thus, this project has an MIRR of 12.61 percent. The actual IRR of 13.07 percent was computed in cell D16.

	C	D	E	F
1				
2				
3		borrow	0.1	
4		invest	0.12	
5				
6		Year	Amt	
7		0	-120000	
8		1	39000	
9		2	30000	
10		3	21000	
11		4	37000	
12		5	46000	
13			total	
14				
15	MIRR	12.6094%		
16	IRR	13.0736%		

FIGURE 8-6 This is an example of the *MIRR* function.

Note that if a cash flow is left blank, the *IRR* function ignores both the cash flow and the period and returns a #NUM error.

Problems

1. Compute all IRRs for the following sequence of cash flows:

Year 1	Year 2	Year 3	Year 4	Year 5	Year 6	Year 7
−$10,000	$8,000	$1,500	$1,500	$1,500	$1,500	−$1,500

Consider a project with the following cash flows. Determine the project's IRR. If the annual cost of capital is 20 percent, would you undertake this project?

Year 1	Year 2	Year 3
−$4,000	$2,000	$4,000

Find all IRRs for the following project:

Year 1	Year 2	Year 3
$100	−$300	$250

Find all IRRs for a project having the given cash flows on the listed dates:

1/10/2003	7/10/2003	5/25/2004	7/18/2004	3/20/2005	4/1/2005	1/10/2006
−$1,000	$900	$800	$700	$500	$500	$350

Consider the following two projects and assume a company's cost of capital is 15 percent. Find the IRR and NPV of each project. Which projects add value to the company? If the company can choose only a single project, which project should it choose?

	Year 1	Year 2	Year 3	Year 4
Project 1	−$40	$130	$19	$26
Project 2	−$80	$36	$36	$36

Twenty-five year old Meg Prior intends to invest $10,000 in her retirement fund at the beginning of each of the next 40 years. Assume that during each of the next 30 years, Meg will earn 15 percent on her investments and during the last 10 years before she retires, her investments will earn 5 percent. Determine the IRR associated with her investments and her final retirement position. How do you know there will be a unique IRR? How would you interpret the unique IRR?

2. Give an intuitive explanation of why Project 6 (on the Which Project worksheet in the IRR.xlsx file) has an IRR of 50 percent.

3. Consider a project having the following cash flows:

Year 1	Year 2	Year 3
–$70,000	$12,000	$15,000

Try to find the IRR of this project without simply guessing. What problem arises? What is the IRR of this project? Does the project have a unique IRR?

4. For the cash flows in Problem 1, assume you can borrow at 12 percent per year and invest profits at 15 percent per year. Compute the project's MIRR.

5. Suppose today that you paid $1,000 for the bond described in Problem 9 of Chapter 7, "Evaluating investments by using net present value criteria." What would be the bond's IRR? A bond's IRR is often called the *yield* of the bond.

CHAPTER 9

More Excel financial functions

Questions answered in this chapter:

- You are buying a copier. Would you rather pay $11,000 today or $3,000 a year for five years?

- If at the end of each of the next 40 years I invest $2,000 a year toward my retirement and earn 8 percent a year on my investments, how much will I have when I retire?

- I am borrowing $10,000 for 10 months with an annual interest rate of 8 percent. What are my monthly payments? How much principal and interest am I paying each month?

- I want to borrow $80,000 and make monthly payments for 10 years. The maximum monthly payment I can afford is $1,000. What is the maximum interest rate I can afford?

- If I borrow $100,000 at 8 percent interest and make payments of $10,000 per year, how many years will it take me to pay back the loan?

When you borrow money to buy a car or house, you always wonder whether you are getting a good deal. When you save for retirement, you are curious about how large a nest egg you'll have when you retire. In our daily work and personal lives, financial questions similar to these often arise. Knowledge of the Microsoft Excel *PV, FV, PMT, PPMT, IPMT, CUMPRINC, CUMIPMT, RATE,* and *NPER* functions makes it easy to answer these types of questions.

Answers to this chapter's questions

This section provides the answers to the questions that are listed at the beginning of the chapter.

You are buying a copier. Would you rather pay $11,000 today or $3,000 a year for five years?

The key to answering this question is being able to value the annual payments of $3,000 per year. Assume the cost of capital is 12 percent per year. You could use the *NPV* function to answer this question, but the Excel *PV* function provides a much quicker way to solve it. A stream of cash flows that involves the same amount of cash outflow (or inflow) each period is called an *annuity*. Assuming that each period's interest rate is the same, you can easily value an annuity by using the Excel *PV* function. It returns the value in today's dollars of a series of future payments, under the assumption of periodic, constant payments and a constant interest rate. The syntax of the *PV* function is PV(rate,#per,[pmt],[fv],[type]), where pmt, fv, and type are optional arguments.

Note When working with Excel financial functions, you can use the following conventions for the signs of pmt (payment) and fv (future value): money received has a positive sign, and money paid out has a negative sign.

- *Rate* is the interest rate per period. For example, if you borrow money at 6 percent per year and the period is a year, then rate = 0.06. If the period is a month, then rate = 0.06/12 = 0.005.

- *#per* is the number of periods in the annuity. For this copier example, #per = 5. If payments on the copier are made each month for five years, #per = 60. Your rate must, of course, be consistent with #per. That is, if #per implies a period is a month, you must use a monthly interest rate; if #per implies a period is a year, you must use an annual interest rate.

- *Pmt* is the payment made each period. For this copier example, pmt = –$3,000. A payment has a negative sign, whereas money received has a positive sign. At least one of pmt or fv must be included.

- *Fv* is the cash balance (or future value) you want to have after the last payment is made. For this copier example, fv = 0. For example, if you want to have a $500 cash balance after the last payment, fv = $500. If you want to make an additional $500 payment at the end of the last period, fv = –$500. If fv is omitted, it is assumed to equal 0.

- *Type* is either 0 or 1 and indicates when payments are made. When type is omitted or equal to 0, payments are made at the end of each period. When type = 1, payments are made at the beginning of each period. Note that you may also write True instead of 1 and False instead of 0 in all functions discussed in this chapter.

Figure 9-1 indicates how to solve the copier problem. (See the PV worksheet of the Excelfinfunctions.xlsx file.)

The present value of paying $3,000 at the end of each year for five years with a 12 percent cost of capital was computed in cell B3 by using the =PV(0.12,5,–3000,0,0) formula. Excel returns an NPV of $10,814.33. By omitting the last two arguments, you can obtain the same answer with the =PV(0.12,5,–3000) formula. Thus, it is a better deal to make payments at the end of the year than to pay out $11,000 today.

If you make payments on the copier of $3,000 at the beginning of each year for five years, the NPV of the payments is computed in cell B4 with the =PV(0.12,5,–3000,0,1) formula. Note that changing the last argument from a 0 to a 1 changed the calculations from end of year to beginning of year. You can see that the present value of your payments is $12,112.05. Therefore, it's better to pay $11,000 today than make payments at the beginning of the year.

Suppose you pay $3,000 at the end of each year and must include an extra $500 payment at the end of Year 5. You can now find the present value of all your payments in cell B5 by including a future value of $500 with the =PV(0.12,5,–3000,–500,0) formula. Note that the $3,000 and $500 cash flows have negative signs because you are paying out the money. The present value of all these payments is equal to $11,098.04.

	A	B
1		
2	PMT	
3	Pay $3000 for 5 years end of year	$10,814.33
4	Pay $3000 for 5 years beginning of year	$12,112.05
5	Extra $500 payment end of year 5;end of year payments	$11,098.04

FIGURE 9-1 This is an example of the *PV* function.

If at the end of each of the next 40 years I invest $2,000 a year toward my retirement and earn 8 percent a year on my investments, how much will I have when I retire?

In this situation, you want to know the value of an annuity in terms of future dollars (40 years from now) and not today's dollars. This is a job for the Excel *FV* (future value) function The FV function gives the future value of an investment assuming periodic, constant payments with a constant interest rate. The syntax of the *FV* function is FV(rate,#per,[pmt],[pv],[type]), where pmt, pv, and type are optional arguments.

- Rate is the interest rate per period. In this case, rate equals 0.08.

- #Per is the number of periods in the future at which you want the future value computed. #Per is also the number of periods during which the annuity payment is received. In this case, #per = 40.

- Pmt is the payment made each period. In this case, pmt equals –$2,000. The negative sign indicates that you are paying money into an account. At least one of pmt or pv must be included.

- Pv is the amount of money (in today's dollars) owed right now. In this case, pv equals $0. If today you owe someone $10,000, then pv equals $10,000 because the lender gave you $10,000, and you received it. If today you had $10,000 in the bank, then pv equals –$10,000 because you must have paid $10,000 into your bank account. If pv is omitted, it is assumed to equal 0.

- Type is a 0 or 1 and indicates when payments are due or money is deposited. If type equals 0 or is omitted, money is deposited at the end of the period. In this case, type is 0 or omitted. If type equals 1, payments are made or money is deposited at the beginning of the period.

In worksheet FV of file Excelfinfunctions.xlsx (see Figure 9-2), you can enter the =FV(0.08,40,–2000) formula in cell B3 to find that, in 40 years, your nest egg will be worth $518,113.04. Note that you should enter a negative value for the annual payment because the $2,000 is paid into your account. You could obtain the same answer by entering the last two unnecessary arguments with the FV(0.08,40,–2000,0,0) formula.

If deposits were made at the beginning of each year for 40 years, the =FV(0.08,40,–2000,0,1) formula (entered in cell B4) would yield the value in 40 years of your nest egg: $559,562.08.

	A	B
1		
2	FV	
3	Invest $2000 end of year for 40 years	$518,113.04
4	Invest $2000 beginning of year for 40 years	$559,562.08
5	We start with $30000 and invest $2000 per year at end of year for 40 years	$1,169,848.68

FIGURE 9-2 This is an example of the *FV* function.

Finally, suppose that, in addition to investing $2,000 at the end of each of the next 40 years, you initially have $30,000 to invest. If you earn 8 percent per year on your investments, how much money will you have when you retire in 40 years? You can answer this question by setting pv equal to –$30,000 in the *FV* function. The negative sign is used because you have deposited, or paid, $30,000 into your account. In cell B5, the =FV(0.08,40,–2000,–30000,0) formula yields a future value of $1,169,848.68.

I am borrowing $10,000 for 10 months with an annual interest rate of 8 percent. What are my monthly payments? How much principal and interest am I paying each month?

The Excel *PMT* function computes the periodic payments for a loan, assuming constant payments and a constant interest rate. The syntax of the *PMT* function is PMT(rate,#per,pv,[fv],[type]), where fv and type are optional arguments.

- Rate is the per-period interest rate of the loan. In this example, use one month as a period; rate equals 0.08/12 = 0.006666667.

- #Per is the number of payments made. In this case, #per equals 10.

- Pv is the present value of all the payments. That is, pv is the amount of the loan. In this case, pv equals $10,000. Pv is positive because you are receiving the $10,000.

- Fv indicates the final loan balance you want to have after making the last payment. In this case, fv equals 0. If fv is omitted, Excel assumes that it equals 0. Suppose you have taken out a balloon loan for which you make payments at the end of each month, but at the conclusion of the loan, you pay off the final balance by making a $1,000 balloon payment. Then fv equals –$1,000. The $1,000 is negative because you are paying it out.

- Type is a 0 or 1 and indicates when payments are due. If type equals 0 or is omitted, payments are made at the end of the period. If you first assumed end-of-month payments, type is 0 or omitted. If type equals 1, payments are made or money is deposited at the beginning of the period.

In cell G1 of the PMT worksheet of the Excelfinfunctions.xlsx file (see Figure 9-3), compute the monthly payment on a 10-month loan for $10,000, assuming an 8 percent annual interest rate and end-of-month payments with the =–PMT(0.08/12,10,10000,0,0) formula. The monthly payment is $1,037.03. The *PMT* function by itself returns a negative value because you are making payments to the company giving you the loan.

If you want to, you can use the Excel *IPMT* and *PPMT* functions to compute the amount of interest paid each month toward the loan and the amount of the balance paid down each month. (This is called payment on the principal.)

To determine the interest paid each month, use the *IPMT* function. The syntax of the *IPMT* function is IPMT(rate,per,#per,pv,[fv],[type]), where fv and type are optional arguments. The per argument indicates the period number for which you compute the interest. The other arguments mean the same as they do for the *PMT* function. Similarly, to determine the amount paid toward the principal each month, you can use the *PPMT* function. The syntax of the *PPMT* function is PPMT(rate,per,#per,pv,[fv],[type]). The meaning of each argument is the same as it is for the *IPMT* function. By copying the =–PPMT(0.08/12,C6,10,10000,0,0) formula from F6 to F7:F16, you can compute the amount of each month's payment that is applied to the principal. For example, during Month 1, you pay only $970.37 toward the principal. As expected, the amount paid toward the principal increases each month. The minus sign is needed because the principal is paid to the company giving you the loan, and *PPMT* will return a negative number. By copying the =–IPMT(0.08/12,C6,10,10000,0,0) formula from G6 to

G7:G16, you can compute the amount of interest paid each month. For example, in Month 1, you pay $66.67 in interest. Of course, the amount of interest paid each month decreases.

	B	C	D	E	F	G	H
1			rate	0.00666667	payment	$1,037.03	
2	PMT,PPMT,IPMT Functions		months	10	end of month		
3	CUMPRINC CUMIPMT		loan amount	$ 10,000.00			
4							
5		Time	Beginning balance	Monthly Payment	Principal	Interest	Ending Balance
6		1	$ 10,000.00	$1,037.03	$970.37	$66.67	$9,029.63
7		2	$9,029.63	$1,037.03	$976.83	$60.20	$8,052.80
8		3	$8,052.80	$1,037.03	$983.35	$53.69	$7,069.45
9		4	$7,069.45	$1,037.03	$989.90	$47.13	$6,079.55
10		5	$6,079.55	$1,037.03	$996.50	$40.53	$5,083.05
11		6	$5,083.05	$1,037.03	$1,003.15	$33.89	$4,079.90
12		7	$4,079.90	$1,037.03	$1,009.83	$27.20	$3,070.07
13		8	$3,070.07	$1,037.03	$1,016.56	$20.47	$2,053.51
14		9	$2,053.51	$1,037.03	$1,023.34	$13.69	$1,030.16
15		10	$1,030.16	$1,037.03	$1,030.16	$6.87	($0.00)
16							
17		NPV of payments	$10,000.00				
18					cum int months 2-4	cumprinc months 2-4	
19		payment beginning of each month	$1,030.16		-161.0125862	-2950.083682	
20		monthly payment if we make $1000 ending payment	$940.00				

FIGURE 9-3 These are examples of *PMT, PPMT, CUMPRINC, CUMIPMT*, and *IPMT* functions.

Note that each month (Interest Paid) + (Payment Toward Principal) = (Total Payment). Sometimes the total is off by a cent due to rounding.

You can also create the ending balances for each month in column H by using the relationship (Ending Month t Balance) = (Beginning Month t Balance) – (Month t Payment toward Principal). Note that in Month 1, Beginning Balance equals $10,000. In column D, you can create each month's beginning balance by using the relationship of (for t = 2, 3, . . . 10)(Beginning Month t Balance) = (Ending Month t – 1 Balance). Of course, Ending Month 10 Balance equals $0, as it should.

Interest each month can be computed as (Month t Interest) = (Interest rate) * (Beginning Month t Balance). For example, the Month 3 interest payment can be computed as = (0.0066667) * ($8,052.80), which equals $53.69.

Of course, the NPV of all payments is exactly $10,000. You can check this in cell D17 with the NPV(0.08/12,E6:E15) formula. (See Figure 9-3.)

If the payments are made at the beginning of each month, the amount of each payment is computed in cell D19 with the =–PMT(0.08/12,10,10000,0,1) formula. Changing the last argument to 1 changes each payment to the beginning of the month. Because the lender is getting her money earlier, monthly payments are less than the end-of-month case. If she pays at the beginning of the month, the monthly payment is $1,030.16.

Finally, suppose that you want to make a balloon payment of $1,000 at the end of 10 months. If you make your monthly payments at the end of each month, the =−PMT(0.08/12,10,10000,−1000,0) formula in cell D20 computes your monthly payment. The monthly payment turns out to be $940. Because $1,000 of the loan is not being paid with monthly payments, it makes sense that your new monthly payment is less than the original end-of-month payment of $1,037.03.

CUMPRINC and CUMIPMT functions

You'll often want to accumulate the interest or principal paid during several periods. The CUMPRINC and CUMIPMT functions make this easy.

The CUMPRINC function computes the principal paid between two periods (inclusive). The syntax of the CUMPRINC function is CUMPRINC(rate,#per,pv,start_period,end_period,type). Rate, #per, pv, and type have the same meanings as described previously.

The CUMIPMT function computes the interest paid between two periods (inclusive). The syntax of the CUMIPMT function is CUMIPMT(rate,#nper,pv,start_period,end_period,type). Rate, #per, pv, and type have the same meanings as described previously. For example, in cell F19 on the PMT worksheet, you can compute the interest paid during months 2 through 4 ($161.01) by using the =CUMIPMT(0.08/12,10,10000,2,4,0) formula. In cell G19, compute the principal paid off in months 2 through 4 ($2,950.08) by using the =CUMPRINC(0.08/12,10,10000,2,4,0) formula.

I want to borrow $80,000 and make monthly payments for 10 years. The maximum monthly payment I can afford is $1,000. What is the maximum interest rate I can afford?

Given a borrowed amount, the length of a loan, and the payment each period, the RATE function tells you the rate of the loan. The syntax of the RATE function is RATE(#per,pmt,pv,[fv],[type],[guess]), where fv, type, and guess are optional arguments. #Per, pmt, pv, fv, and type have the same meanings as previously described. Guess is simply a guess at what the loan rate is. Usually, guess can be omitted. Entering the =RATE(120,−1000,80000,0,0) formula in cell D9 of the Rate worksheet (in the Excelfinfunctions.xlsx file) yields .7241 percent as the monthly rate. Assume payments are made at the end of the month. (See Figure 9-4.)

You can verify the RATE function calculation in cell D15. The =PV(.007241,120,−1000,0,0) formula yields $80,000.08. This shows that payments of $1,000 at the end of each month for 120 months have a present value of $80,000.08.

If you could pay back $10,000 during month 120, the maximum rate you could handle would be given by the =RATE(120,−1000,80000,−10000,0,0) formula. In cell D12, this formula yields a monthly rate of 0.818 percent.

	D	E	F	G	H
4					
5					
6	**BORROWING $80,000**				
7	**120 MONTHLY PAYMENTS OF $1000 PER MONTH**				
8	**WHAT IS MAX RATE YOU CAN HANDLE?**				
9	0.72410%	=RATE(120,-1000,80000,0,0)			
10	**IF YOU CAN PAY $10,000 AT END**				
11	**WHAT IS MAX RATE YOU CAN HANDLE?**				
12	0.818%				
13					
14					
15	$80,000.08				
16		CHECK!			
17		=PV(0.007241,120,-1000,0,0)			

FIGURE 9-4 This is an example of the *RATE* function.

If I borrow $100,000 at 8 percent interest and make payments of $10,000 per year, how many years will it take me to pay back the loan?

Given the size of a loan, the payments each period, and the loan rate, the *NPER* function tells you how many periods it takes to pay back a loan. The syntax of the *NPER* function is NPER(rate,pmt,pv,[fv],[type]), where fv and type are optional arguments.

Assuming end-of-year payments, the =NPER(0.08,–10000,100000,0,0) formula in cell D7 of worksheet Nper (in the Excelfinfunctions.xlsx file) yields 20.91 years. (See Figure 9-5.) Thus, 20 years of payments will not quite pay back the loan, but 21 years will overpay the loan. To verify the calculation, use the *PV* function in cells D10 and D11 to show that paying $10,000 per year for 20 years pays back $98,181.47, and paying $10,000 for 21 years pays back $100,168.03.

Suppose that you are planning to pay back $40,000 in the final payment period. How many years will it take to pay back the loan? Entering the =NPER(0.08,–10000,100000,–40000,0) formula in cell D14 shows that it will take 15.90 years to pay back the loan. Thus, 15 years of payments will not quite pay off the loan, and 16 years of payments will slightly overpay the loan.

	C	D
1		
2		
3		Borrow $100000 8%
4		ANNUAL PAYMENTS OF $10,000 PER YEAR
5		END OF YEAR PAYMENT
6		HOW MANY YEARS?
7		20.91237188
8		20 YEARS WILL NOT PAY IT OFF; 21 WILL
9		CHECK
10	20 YEARS	$98,181.47
11	21 YEARS	$100,168.03
12		
13		IF WE PAY $40,000 AT END OF PROBLEM
14		15.9012328
15		15 YEARS WILL NOT PAY IT OFF; 16 YEARS WILL

FIGURE 9-5 This is an example of the *NPER* function.

Problems

Unless otherwise mentioned, all payments are made at the end of the period.

1. You have just won the lottery. At the end of each of the next 20 years, you will receive a payment of $50,000. If the cost of capital is 10 percent per year, what is the present value of your lottery winnings?

2. A *perpetuity* is an annuity that is received forever. If I rent out my house and, at the beginning of each year, I receive $14,000, what is the value of this perpetuity? Assume an annual 10 percent cost of capital. (Hint: Use the *PV* function and let the number of periods be many!)

3. I now have $250,000 in the bank. At the end of each of the next 20 years, I withdraw $15,000. If I earn 8 percent per year on my investments, how much money will I have in 20 years?

4. I deposit $2,000 per month (at the end of each month) over the next 10 years. My investments earn 0.8 percent per month. I would like to have $1 million in 10 years. How much money should I deposit now?

5. A Premier League soccer player is receiving $15 million at the end of each of the next seven years. He can earn 6 percent per year on his investments. What is the present value of his future revenues?

6. At the end of each of the next 20 years, I will receive the following amounts:

Years	Amounts
1–5	$200
6–10	$300
11–20	$400

Use the *PV* function to find the present value of these cash flows if the cost of capital is 10 percent. Hint: Begin by computing the value of receiving $400 a year for 20 years and then subtract the value of receiving $100 a year for 10 years and continue in that way.

7. You are borrowing $200,000 on a 30-year mortgage with an annual interest rate of 10 percent. Assuming end-of-month payments, determine the monthly payment, interest payment each month, and amount paid toward principal each month.

8. Answer each question in Problem 7, assuming beginning-of-month payments.

9. Use the *FV* function to determine the value to which $100 accumulates in three years if you are earning 7 percent per year.

10. You have a liability of $1,000,000 due in 10 years. The cost of capital is 10 percent per year. What amount of money do you need to set aside at the end of each of the next 10 years to meet this liability?

11. You are planning to buy a new car. The cost of the car is $50,000. You have been offered two payment plans:

- A 10 percent discount on the sales price of the car, followed by 60 monthly payments financed at 9 percent per year.

- No discount on the sales price of the car, followed by 60 monthly payments financed at 2 percent per year.

If you believe your annual cost of capital is 9 percent, which payment plan is a better deal? Assume all payments occur at the end of the month.

12. I presently have $10,000 in the bank. At the beginning of each of the next 20 years, I will invest $4,000, and I expect to earn 6 percent per year on my investments. How much money will I have in 20 years?

13. A *balloon mortgage* requires you to pay off part of a loan during a specified period and then make a lump sum payment to pay off the remaining portion of the loan. Suppose you borrow $400,000 on a 20-year balloon mortgage, and the interest rate is .5 percent per month. Your end-of-month payments during the first 20 years are required to pay off $300,000 of your loan, at which point, you have to pay off the remaining $100,000. Determine your monthly payments for this loan.

14. An adjustable rate mortgage (ARM) ties monthly payments to a rate index (for instance, the US T-bill rate). Suppose you borrow $60,000 on an ARM for 30 years (360 monthly payments).

The first 12 payments are governed by the current T-bill rate of 8 percent. In years 2–5, monthly payments are set at the year's beginning monthly T-bill rate + 2 percent. Suppose the T-bill rates at the beginning of years 2–5 are as follows:

Beginning of year	T-bill rate
2	10 percent
3	13 percent
4	15 percent
5	10 percent

Determine monthly payments during years 1–5 and each year's ending balance.

15. Suppose you have borrowed money at a 14.4 percent annual rate, and you make monthly payments. If you have missed four consecutive monthly payments, how much should next month's payment be to catch up?

16. You want to replace a machine in 10 years and estimate the cost will be $80,000. If you can earn 8 percent annually on your investments, how much money should you put aside at the end of each year to cover the cost of the machine?

17. You are buying a motorcycle. You pay $1,500 today and $182.50 a month for three years. If the annual rate of interest is 18 percent, what was the original cost of the motorcycle?

18. Suppose the annual rate of interest is 10 percent. You pay $200 a month for two years, $300 a month for a year, and $400 for two years. What is the present value of all your payments?

19. You can invest $500 at the end of each six-month period for five years. If you want to have $6,000 after five years, what is the annual rate of return you need on your investments?

20. I borrow $2,000 and make quarterly payments for two years. The annual rate of interest is 24 percent. What is the size of each payment?

21. I have borrowed $15,000. I am making 48 monthly payments, and the annual rate of interest is 9 percent. What is the total interest paid over the course of the loan?

22. I am borrowing $5,000 and plan to pay back the loan with 36 monthly payments. The annual rate of interest is 16.5 percent. After one year, I pay back $500 extra and shorten the period of the loan to two years total. What will my monthly payment be during the second year of the loan?

23. With an adjustable rate mortgage, you make monthly payments depending on the interest rates at the beginning of each year. You have borrowed $60,000 on a 30-year ARM. For the first year, monthly payments are based on the current annual T-bill rate of 9 percent. In years 2–5, monthly payments will be based on the following annual T-bill rates +2 percent.

- Year 2: 10 percent

- Year 3: 13 percent

- Year 4: 15 percent

- Year 5: 10 percent

The catch is that the ARM contains a clause that ensures that monthly payments can increase a maximum of 7.5 percent from one year to the next. To compensate the lender for this provision, the borrower adjusts the ending balance of the loan at the end of each year based on the difference between what the borrower actually paid and what he should have paid. Determine monthly payments during Years 1–5 of the loan.

24. You have a choice of receiving $8,000 each year beginning at age 62, and ending when you die, or receiving $10,000 each year beginning at age 65 and ending when you die. If you think you can earn an 8 percent annual return on your investments, which will net the larger amount?

25. You have just won the lottery and will receive $50,000 a year for 20 years. What rate of interest would make these payments the equivalent of receiving $500,000 today?

26. A bond pays a $50 coupon at the end of each of the next 30 years and pays $1,000 face value in 30 years. If you discount cash flows at an annual rate of 6 percent, what would be a fair price for the bond?

27. You have borrowed $100,000 on a 40-year mortgage with monthly payments. The annual interest rate is 16 percent. How much will you pay over the course of the loan? With four years left on the loan, how much will you still owe?

28. I need to borrow $12,000. I can afford payments of $500 per month, and the annual rate of interest is 4.5 percent. How many months will it take to pay off the loan?

29. You are considering borrowing $50,000 on a 180-month loan. The annual interest rate on the loan depends on your credit score in the following fashion:

Write a formula that gives your monthly payments as a function of your credit score.

30. You intend to borrow $40,000 for a new car. You want to determine the monthly payments and total interest paid in the following situations:

- 48-month loan, 6.85% annual rate

- 60-month loan, 6.59% annual rate

CHAPTER 10

Circular references

Questions answered in this chapter:

- I often get a circular reference message from Excel. Does this mean I've made an error?

- How can I resolve circular references?

When Microsoft Excel 2013 displays a message stating that your workbook contains a circular reference, it means there is a loop, or dependency, between two or more cells in a workbook. For example, a circular reference occurs if the value in cell A1 influences the value in D3, the value in cell D3 influences the value in cell E6, and the value in cell E6 influences the value in cell A1. Figure 10-1 illustrates the pattern of a circular reference.

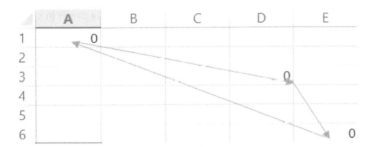

FIGURE 10-1 This is a loop causing a circular reference.

As you'll soon see, you can resolve circular references by clicking the **File** tab on the ribbon and then choosing **Options**. Choose **Formulas** and then select the **Enable Iterative Calculation** check box.

Answers to this chapter's questions

This section provides the answers to the questions that are listed at the beginning of the chapter.

I often get a circular reference message from Excel. Does this mean I've made an error?

A circular reference usually arises from a logically consistent worksheet in which several cells exhibit a looping relationship similar to that illustrated in Figure 10-1. Look at a simple example of a problem that cannot easily be solved in Excel without creating a circular reference.

A small company earns $1,500 in revenues and incurs $1,000 in costs. It wants to give 10 percent of its after-tax profits to charity. Its tax rate is 40 percent. How much money should it give to charity? The solution to this problem is in worksheet Sheet1 in the Circular.xlsx file, shown in Figure 10-2.

	C	D	E	F
1		Charity=10%*After tax profits		
2				
3	Revenues	$1,500.00		
4	tax rate	0.4		
5	costs	$1,000.00		
6	charity	28.301887		
7	before tax profit	471.69811		
8	after tax profit	283.01887		

FIGURE 10-2 A circular reference can occur when you're calculating taxes.

Begin by naming the cells in D3:D8 with the corresponding names in cells C3:C8. Enter the firm's revenue, tax rate, and costs in D3:D5. To compute a contribution to charity as 10 percent of after-tax profit, enter the 0.1*after_tax_profit formula in cell D6. Determine before-tax profit in cell D7 by subtracting costs and the charitable contribution from revenues. The formula in cell D7 is Revenues–Costs–Charity. Finally, compute after-tax profit in cell D8 as (1–tax_rate)*before_tax_profit.

Excel indicates a circular reference in cell D8. (See the bottom-left corner of the Circular. xlsx file). What's going on?

1. Charity (cell D6) influences before-tax profit (cell D7).

2. Before-tax profit (cell D7) influences after-tax profit (cell D8).

3. After-tax profit (cell D8) influences charity.

Thus, you have a loop of form D6-D7-D8-D6 (indicated by the blue arrows in Figure 10-2), which causes the circular reference message. The worksheet is logically correct; you have done nothing wrong. Still, you can see from Figure 10-2 that Excel is calculating an incorrect answer for charitable contributions.

How can I resolve circular references?

Resolving a circular reference is easy. Simply click the **File** tab at the left end of the ribbon and then choose **Options** to open the **Excel Options** dialog box. Choose **Formulas** in the left pane and then select the **Enable Iterative Calculation** check box in the **Calculation Options** section, as shown in Figure 10-3.

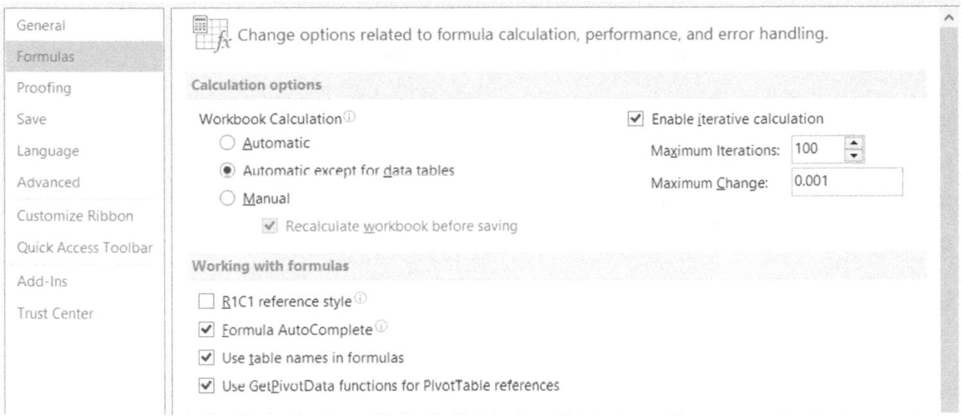

FIGURE 10-3 Use Enable Iterative Calculation to resolve a circular reference.

When you activate Enable Iterative Calculation, Excel recognizes that your circular reference has generated the following system of three equations with three unknowns:

```
Charity=0.1*(AfterTax Profit)
BeforeTax Profit=Revenue-Charity-Costs
AfterTax Profit=(1-Tax rate)*(BeforeTax Profit)
```

The three unknowns are Charity, BeforeTax Profit, and AfterTax Profit. When you activate Enable Iterative Calculation, Excel iterates (based on my experience with circular references, 100 iterations should be used) to seek a solution to all equations generated by the circular reference. From one iteration to the next, the values of the unknowns are changed by a complex mathematical procedure (Gauss-Seidel Iteration). Excel stops if the maximum change in any worksheet cell from one iteration to the next is smaller than the Maximum Change value (0.001 by default). You can reduce the Maximum Change setting to a smaller number, such as 0.000001. If you do not reduce the Maximum Change setting to a smaller number, you might find Excel assigning a value of, for example, 5.001 to a cell that should equal 5, and this is annoying. In addition, some complex worksheets might require more than 100 iterations before converging to a resolution of the circularity. For this example, however, the circularity is almost instantly resolved, and you can see the solution given in Figure 10-4.

Note The charitable contribution of $28.30 is now exactly 10 percent of the after-tax profit of $283.01. All other cells in the worksheet are now correctly computed.

Note that the Excel iteration procedure is only guaranteed to work when solving systems of *linear* equations. In other situations, convergence to a solution is not always guaranteed. In the tax example, resolving the circular references requires solving a system of linear equations, so you know Excel will find the correct answer.

	C	D	E	F
1		Charity=10%*After tax profits		
2				
3	Revenues	$1,500.00		
4	tax rate	0.4		
5	costs	$1,000.00		
6	charity	28.301887		
7	before tax profit	471.69811		
8	after tax profit	283.01887		

FIGURE 10-4 Excel runs the calculations to resolve the circular reference.

Here's one more example of a circular reference. In any Excel formula, you can refer to an entire column or row by name. For example, the AVERAGE(B:B) formula averages all cells in column B. The =AVERAGE(1:1) formula averages all cells in row 1. This shortcut is useful if you're continually dumping new data (such as monthly sales) into a column or row. The formula always computes average sales, and you do not ever need to change it. The problem is that if you enter this formula in the column or row that it refers to, you create a circular reference. By activating Enable Iterative Calculation, circular references such as these are resolved quickly.

Problems

1. Before paying employee bonuses and state and federal taxes, a company earns profits of $60,000. The company pays employees a bonus equal to 5 percent of after-tax profits. State tax is 5 percent of profits (after bonuses are paid). Federal tax is 40 percent of profits (after bonuses and state tax are paid). Determine the amount paid in bonuses, state tax, and federal tax.

2. On January 1, 2002, I have $500. At the end of each month, I earn 2 percent interest. Each month's interest is based on the average of the month's beginning and ending balances. How much money will I have after 12 months?

3. My airplane is flying the following route: Houston–Los Angeles–Seattle–Minneapolis–Houston. On each leg of the journey, the plane's fuel usage (expressed as miles per gallon) is 40–.02*(average fuel en route). Here, average fuel en route is equal to .5*(initial fuel en route+final fuel en route). My plane begins in Houston with 1,000 gallons of fuel. The distance flown on each leg of the journey is as follows:

Leg	Miles
Houston to Los Angeles	1,200
Los Angeles to Seattle	1,100
Seattle to Minneapolis	1,500
Minneapolis to Houston	1,400

How many gallons of fuel remain when I return to Houston?

4. A common method used to allocate costs to support departments is the *reciprocal cost allocation method*. This method can easily be implemented by use of circular references. To illustrate, suppose Wingtip Toys has two support departments: Accounting and Consulting. The company also has two product divisions: Division 1 and Division 2. It has decided to allocate $600,000 of the cost of operating the Accounting department and $116,000 of the cost of operating the Consulting department to the two divisions. The fraction of accounting and consulting time each part of the company uses is as follows:

	Accounting	Consulting	Division 1	Division 2
Percentage of accounting work done for other parts of the company	0%	20%	30%	50%
Percentage of consulting work done for other parts of the company	10%	0%	80%	10%

How much of the accounting and consulting costs should be allocated to other parts of the company? You need to determine two quantities: total cost allocated to accounting and total cost allocated to consulting. Total cost allocated to accounting equals $600,000+.1*(total cost allocated to consulting) because 10 percent of all consulting work was done for the Accounting department. A similar equation can be written for the total cost allocated to consulting. You should now be able to calculate the correct allocation of both accounting and consulting costs to each other part of the company.

5. We start a year with $200 and receive $100 during the year. We also receive 10 percent interest at the end of the year with the interest based on our starting balance. In this case, we end the year with $320. Determine the ending balance for the year if interest accrues on the average of our starting and ending balances.

CHAPTER 11

IF statements

Questions answered in this chapter:

- If I order up to 500 units of a product, I pay $3.00 per unit. If I order from 501 through 1,200 units, I pay $2.70 per unit. If I order from 1,201 through 2,000 units, I pay $2.30 per unit. If I order more than 2,000 units, I pay $2.00 per unit. How can I write a formula that expresses the purchase cost as a function of the number of units purchased?

- I just purchased 100 shares of stock at a cost of $55 per share. To hedge the risk that the stock might decline in value, I purchased 60 six-month European put options. Each option has an exercise price of $45 and costs $5. How can I develop a worksheet that indicates the six-month percentage return on my portfolio for a variety of possible future prices?

- Many stock market analysts believe that moving-average trading rules can outperform the market. A commonly suggested moving-average trading rule is to buy a stock when the stock's price moves above the average of the past 15 months and to sell a stock when the stock's price moves below the average of the past 15 months. How would this trading rule have performed against the Standard & Poor's 500 Stock Index (S&P)?

- In the game of craps, two dice are tossed. If the total of the dice on the first roll is 2, 3, or 12, you lose. If the total of the dice on the first roll is 7 or 11, you win. Otherwise, the game keeps going. How can I write a formula to determine the status of the game after the first roll?

- In most pro forma financial statements, cash is used as the plug to make assets and liabilities balance. I know that using debt as the plug would be more realistic. How can I set up a pro forma statement having debt as the plug?

- When I copy a VLOOKUP formula to determine salaries of individual employees, I get a lot of #NA errors. Then when I average the employee salaries, I cannot get a numerical answer because of the #NA errors. Can I easily replace the #NA errors with a blank space so I can compute average salary?

- My worksheet contains quarterly revenues for Wal-Mart. Can I easily compute the revenue for each year and place it in the row containing the first quarter's sales for that year?

- IF statements can get rather large. How many IF statements can I nest in a cell? What is the maximum number of characters allowed in an Excel formula?

The situations listed here seem to have little, if anything, in common. However, setting up Microsoft Excel 2013 models for each of these situations requires the use of an IF statement. The IF formula is probably the single most useful formula in Excel. With IF formulas, you can conduct conditional tests on values and formulas, mimicking (to a limited degree) the conditional logic provided by computing languages such as C, C++, and Java.

An IF formula begins with a condition such as A1>10. If the condition is true, the formula returns the first value listed in the formula; otherwise, you move on within the formula and repeat the process. The easiest way to show you the power and utility of IF formulas is to use them to help answer each of this chapter's questions.

Answers to this chapter's questions

This section provides the answers to the questions that are listed at the beginning of the chapter.

If I order up to 500 units of a product, I pay $3.00 per unit. If I order from 501 through 1,200 units, I pay $2.70 per unit. If I order from 1,201 through 2,000 units, I pay $2.30 per unit. If I order more than 2,000 units, I pay $2.00 per unit. How can I write a formula that expresses the purchase cost as a function of the number of units purchased?

You can find the solution to this question on the Quantity Discount worksheet in the Ifstatement.xlsx file. The worksheet is shown in Figure 11-1.

	A	B	C	D
1		cutoff	price	
2	cut1	500	$ 3.00	price1
3	cut2	1200	$ 2.70	price2
4	cut3	2000	$ 2.30	price3
5			$ 2.00	price4
6				
7				
8	order quantity	cost	per unit cost	
9	450	$1,350.00	$ 3.00	
10	900	$2,430.00	$ 2.70	
11	1450	$3,335.00	$ 2.30	
12	2100	$4,200.00	$ 2.00	

FIGURE 11-1 You can use an IF formula to model quantity discounts.

Suppose cell A9 contains your order quantity. You can compute an order's cost as a function of the order quantity by implementing the following logic:

- If A9 is less than or equal to 500, the cost is 3*A9.

- If A9 is from 501 through 1,200, the cost is 2.70*A9.

- If A9 is from 1,201 through 2,000, the cost is 2.30*A9.

- If A9 is more than 2,000, the cost is 2*A9.

Begin by linking the range names in A2:A4 to cells B2:B4 and linking the range names in cells D2:D5 to cells C2:C5. Then you can implement this logic in cell B9 with the following formula:

```
IF(A9<=_cut1,price1*A9,IF(A9<=_cut2,price2*A9,IF(A9<=_cut3,price3*A9,price4*A9)))
```

To understand how Excel computes a value from this formula, recall that IF statements are evaluated from left to right. If the order quantity is less than or equal to 500 (cut1), the cost is given by price 1*A9. If the order quantity is not less than or equal to 500, the formula checks to see whether the order quantity is less than or equal to 1,200. If this is the case, the order quantity is from 501 through 1,200, and the formula computes a cost of price 2*A9. Next, the formula checks whether the order quantity is less than or equal to 2,000. If this is true, the order quantity is from 1,201 through 2,000, and the formula computes a cost of price 3*A9. Finally, if the order cost has not yet been computed, the formula defaults to the value price 4*A9. In each case, the IF formula returns the correct order cost. Note that three other order quantities are entered in cells A10:A12, and the cost formula is copied to B10:B12. For each order quantity, the formula returns the correct total cost.

An IF formula containing more than one IF statement is called a *nested IF formula*.

I just purchased 100 shares of stock at a cost of $55 per share. To hedge the risk that the stock might decline in value, I purchased 60 six-month European put options. Each option has an exercise price of $45 and costs $5. How can I develop a worksheet that indicates the six-month percentage return on my portfolio for a variety of possible future prices?

Before tackling this problem, I want to review some basic concepts from the world of finance. A European put option allows you to sell a share of a stock at a given time in the future (in this case, six months) for the exercise price (in this case, $45). If the stock's price in six months is $45 or higher, the option has no value. Suppose, however, that the price of the stock in 6 months is below $45. Then you can make money by buying a share and immediately reselling the stock for $45. For example, if in 6 months the stock is selling for $37, you can make a profit of $45 – $37, or $8 per share, by buying a share for $37 and then using the put to resell the share for $45. You can see that put options protect you against downward moves in a stock price. In this case, whenever the stock's price in six months is below $45, the puts start accruing some value. This cushions a portfolio against a decrease in value of the shares it owns. Note also that the percentage return on a portfolio (assume that the stocks in the portfolio do not pay dividends) is computed by dividing the number of the change in the portfolio's value (final portfolio value–initial portfolio value) by the portfolio's initial value.

With this background, look at how the six-month percentage return on this portfolio, consisting of 60 puts and 100 shares of stock, varies as the share price varies between $20 and $65. You can find this solution on the Hedging worksheet in the Ifstatement.xlsx file. The worksheet is shown in Figure 11-2.

The labels in A2:A7 are linked to cells B2:B7. The initial portfolio value is equal to 100($55)+60($5)=*$5,800*, shown in cell B7. By copying the IF(A9<exprice,exprice–A9,0)*Nputs formula from B9 to B10:B18, you can compute the final value of the puts. If the six-month price is less than

the exercise price, you can value each put as *exercise price–six-month price*. Otherwise, each put will have a value of $0 in six months. Copy the Nshares*A9 formula from C9 to C10:C18 and compute the final value of the shares. Copying the ((C9+B9)–startvalue)/startvalue) formula from D9 to D10:D18 computes the percentage return on the hedged portfolio. Copying the (C9–Nshares*pricenow)/ (Nshares*pricenow) formula from E9 to E10:E18 computes the percentage return on the portfolio if you are unhedged (that is, you have no puts).

	A	B	C	D	E
1					
2	Nputs	60			
3	Nshares	100			
4	exprice	$ 45.00			
5	pricenow	$ 55.00			
6	putcost	$ 5.00			
7	startvalue	$5,800.00			
8	final stock price	final put value	final share value	percentage return hedged	percentage return unhedged
9	$ 20.00	$1,500.00	$2,000.00	-39.7%	-63.6%
10	$ 25.00	$1,200.00	$2,500.00	-36.2%	-54.5%
11	$ 30.00	$ 900.00	$3,000.00	-32.8%	-45.5%
12	$ 35.00	$ 600.00	$3,500.00	-29.3%	-36.4%
13	$ 40.00	$ 300.00	$4,000.00	-25.9%	-27.3%
14	$ 45.00	$ -	$4,500.00	-22.4%	-18.2%
15	$ 50.00	$ -	$5,000.00	-13.8%	-9.1%
16	$ 55.00	$ -	$5,500.00	-5.2%	0.0%
17	$ 60.00	$ -	$6,000.00	3.4%	9.1%
18	$ 65.00	$ -	$6,500.00	12.1%	18.2%

FIGURE 11-2 This is a hedging example that uses IF statements.

In Figure 11-2, you can see that if the stock price drops below $45, the hedged portfolio has a larger expected return than the unhedged portfolio. Note also that if the stock price does not decrease, the unhedged portfolio has a larger expected return. This is why the purchase of puts is often referred to as *portfolio insurance*.

Many stock market analysts believe that moving-average trading rules can outperform the market. A commonly suggested moving-average trading rule is to buy a stock when the stock's price moves above the average of the previous 15 months and to sell a stock when the stock's price moves below the average of the previous 15 months' price. How would this trading rule have performed against the Standard & Poor's 500 Stock Index (S&P)?

In this example, compare the performance of the moving-average trading rule (in the absence of transaction costs for buying and selling stock) to a buy-and-hold strategy. The strength of a moving-average trading rule is that it helps you follow market trends. A moving-average trading rule lets you ride up with a bull market and sell before a bear market destroys you.

The data set contains the monthly value of the S&P 500 Index for the period of January, 1871, through October, 2002. To track the performance of the moving-average trading strategy, you need to track the following information each month:

- What is the average of the S&P 500 Index over the past 15 months?

- Do I own stock at the beginning of each month?

- Do I buy stock during the month?

- Do I sell stock during the month?

- What is the cash flow for the month (positive if I sell stock, negative if I buy stock, and 0 otherwise)?

The worksheet for this situation requires you to scroll down many rows. It helps to keep columns A and B, as well as the headings in row 8, visible as you scroll down. To do this, in the Matradingrule .xlsx file, move the cursor to cell C9, choose **View** on the ribbon, and then select **Freeze Panes** in the **Windows** group. This presents the choices shown in Figure 11-3.

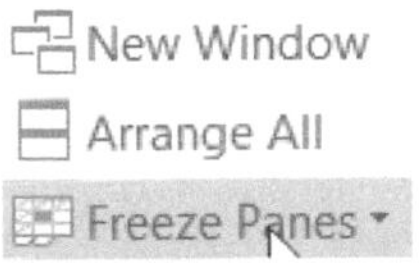

New Window
Arrange All
Freeze Panes ▾

FIGURE 11-3 Choose from the Freeze Panes options.

Here you choose **Freeze Panes**, which keeps columns A and B and rows 6–8 visible as you scroll through the worksheet. **Freeze Top Row** keeps just the top row visible while scrolling through the rest of the worksheet. For example, if the visible top row is row 6, you see row 6 no matter how far down you scroll. If you choose **Freeze First Column**, you always see the leftmost column as you scroll through the worksheet. Selecting **Unfreeze Panes** from the menu returns you to normal worksheet view.

The Matradingrule.xlsx file, shown in Figure 11-4, includes the formulas needed to track the effectiveness of a moving-average strategy. Tackling this problem requires several IF formulas, and some of the IF formulas require an *AND* operator. For example, you buy the stock during a month if and only if you don't own the stock at the beginning of the month, and the current month's price is higher than the 15-month moving average for the stock's price. The first month for which you can compute a 15-month moving average is April 1872, so begin your calculations in row 24.

Date	S&P Comp. P	Own?	MA	Buy?	Sell?	Cash flow
				MA profit	$1,319.75	
				Buy and hold profit	$849.45	
1872.02	4.88					
1872.03	5.04					
1872.04	5.18	Yes	4.739	no	no	0
1872.05	5.18	Yes	4.788	no	no	0
1872.06	5.13	Yes	4.833	no	no	0
1872.07	5.1	Yes	4.868	no	no	0
1872.08	5.04	Yes	4.892	no	no	0
1872.09	4.95	Yes	4.904	no	no	0
1872.1	4.97	Yes	4.913	no	no	0
1872.11	4.95	Yes	4.929	no	no	0
1872.12	5.07	Yes	4.939	no	no	0
1873.01	5.11	Yes	4.955	no	no	0
1873.02	5.15	Yes	4.989	no	no	0
1873.03	5.11	Yes	5.023	no	no	0
1873.04	5.04	Yes	5.048	no	yes	5.04
1873.05	5.05	no	5.06	no	no	0
1873.06	4.98	no	5.071	no	no	0
1873.07	4.97	no	5.067	no	no	0
1873.08	4.97	no	5.053	no	no	0
1873.09	4.59	no	5.039	no	no	0

FIGURE 11-4 The moving-average trading rule beats buy-and-hold.

Assume that you first owned the stock in April 1872, so enter **Yes** in cell C24.

- By copying the AVERAGE(B9:B23) formula from D24 to D25:D1590, you compute the 15-month moving average for each month.

Note An easy way to copy the formula from D24 to D25:D1590 is to point at the lower-right corner of cell D24 (the pointer appears as a crosshair) and then double-click the left mouse button. Double-clicking copies the formula to all the cells in the column with a value in the column to the left. You can use this trick to copy formulas in multiple columns also.

- By copying the IF(AND(C24="No",B24>D24),"yes","no") formula from E24 to E25:E1590, you determine for each month whether the S&P share is purchased during the month. Remember that you purchase the share only if you did not own the stock at the beginning of the month, and the current value of the S&P exceeds its 15-month moving average. Notice the AND portion of the formula. It contains two conditions (more than two are allowed) separated by a comma. If both conditions are satisfied, the formula returns Yes; otherwise, it returns No. For an IF formula to recognize text, place quotation marks (" ") around the text.

- By copying the IF(AND(C24="Yes",B24<D24),"yes","no") formula from F24 to F25:F1590, you determine for each month whether the S&P share is sold. The stock is sold if and only if you owned the S&P share at the beginning of the month and the current value of the S&P share is below the 15-month moving average. April 1873 is the first month in which you sell your S&P stock.

- During any month before October 2002, if you buy a share of the S&P during the month, the cash flow is negative the value of the S&P share you bought. If you sell a share of the S&P during the month, the cash flow equals the value of the S&P. Otherwise, the cash flow is 0. During October 2002, you sell any S&P share you own to get credit for its value. Therefore, by copying the IF(E24="yes",−B24,IF(F24="yes",B24,0)) formula from G24 to G25:G1589, you record the cash flow for all months before October 2002. Entering the IF(C1590="yes",B1590,0) formula in cell G1590 gives you credit for selling any stock you own at the beginning of the past month.

- In cell G6, compute total profit from the moving-average trading strategy with the SUM(G24:G1590) formula. You can see that the 15-month moving-average strategy earns a profit of $1,319.75.

- The profit from buying and holding shares is simply the October 2002 S&P value minus the April 1872 S&P value. Compute the profit from the buy-and-hold strategy in cell G7 with the B1590–B24 formula.

As you can see, the buy-and-hold profit of $849.45 is far worse than the profit from the moving-average trading rule. Of course, this solution ignores the transaction costs incurred in buying and selling stocks. If transaction costs are large, this might wipe out the excess profits the moving-average trading strategy earns.

In the game of craps, two dice are tossed. If the total of the dice on the first roll is 2, 3, or 12, you lose. If the total of the dice on the first roll is 7 or 11, you win. Otherwise, the game keeps going. How can I write a formula to determine the status of the game after the first roll?

The fact that you lose in craps if you throw a 2, 3, or 12 can be conveniently modeled by placing an OR formula within an IF formula. In cell B5 of the Craps worksheet of the Ifstatement.xlsx file, shown in Figure 11-5, enter the IF(OR(A5=2,A5=3,A5=12),"lose",IF(OR(A5=7,A5=11),"win","keep_going")) formula. This formula is then copied from B5 to B6:B7. The formula displays lose if a 2, 3, or 12 is entered in cell A5. It displays win if a 7 or 11 is entered, and it displays keep going for any other value.

FIGURE 11-5 Use IF statements to model the first roll in craps.

In most pro forma financial statements, cash is used as the plug to make assets and liabilities balance. I know that using debt as the plug would be more realistic. How can I set up a pro forma statement having debt as the plug?

A pro forma statement is basically a prediction of a company's financial future. A pro forma requires construction of a company's future balance sheets and income statements. The balance sheet provides a snapshot of the company's assets and liabilities at any point in time; an income statement tells you how the company's financial status is changing at any point in time. Pro forma statements can help a company determine its future needs for debt; they are also key parts of models that stock analysts use to determine whether a stock is properly valued. In the Proforma.xlsx file, the free cash flows (FCFs) were generated for a company for the next four years. Figure 11-6 shows the balance sheet, and Figure 11-7 shows the income statement.

B	C	D	E	F	G	H
3 Sales growth	SG	0.02		CA/Sales		0.15
4 Initial sales	IS	1,000.00		CL/Sales		0.07
5 Interest rate on debt	IRD	0.10		NFA/Sales		0.60
6 Dividend payout	DIV	0.05		GFA/Sales		0.90
7 Tax rate	TR	0.53				
8 COGS/Sales	COGS	0.75				
9 Depreciation rate	DEP	0.10				
10 Liquid asset interest rate	LAIR	0.09				
11 Balance sheet						
12		0.00	1.00	2.00	3.00	4.00
13 Cash and marketable securities			0.00	0.00	0.00	52.56
14 Current assets		150.00	153.00	156.06	159.18	162.36
15 Gross fixed assets		900.00	1,001.33	1,115.29	1,243.29	1,386.93
16 Acc. dep.		300.00	400.13	511.66	635.99	774.68
17 Net fixed assets		600.00	601.20	603.62	607.30	612.24
18 Total assets		750.00	754.20	759.68	766.48	827.17
19						
20 Current liabilities		70.00	71.40	72.83	74.28	75.77
21 Debt		180.00	118.96	59.33	1.80	0.00
22 Stock		400.00	400.00	400.00	400.00	400.00
23 Retained earnings		100.00	163.84	227.52	290.39	351.40
24 Equity		500.00	563.84	627.52	690.39	751.40
25 Total liabilities		750.00	754.20	759.68	766.48	827.17

FIGURE 11-6 This is a pro forma assumptions statement and balance sheet.

B	C	D	E	F	G	H
27 Income statement		0.00	1.00	2.00	3.00	4.00
28 Sales		1,000.00	1,020.00	1,040.40	1,061.21	1,082.43
29 Cost of goods sold		700.00	765.00	780.30	795.91	811.82
30 Depreciation			100.13	111.53	124.33	138.69
31 Operating income			154.87	148.57	140.97	131.92
32 Interest income			0.00	0.00	0.00	4.73
33 Interest expense			11.90	5.93	0.18	0.00
34 Income before taxes			142.97	142.64	140.79	136.65
35 Taxes			75.77	75.60	74.62	72.42
36 Net income			67.20	67.04	66.17	64.22
37						
38 Beg. retained earnings			100.00	163.84	227.52	290.39
39 Dividends			3.36	3.35	3.31	3.21
40 Ending retained earnings			163.84	227.52	290.39	351.40

FIGURE 11-7 This is a pro forma income statement.

Column D contains information about the company's status (during year 0). The basic assumptions are as follows:

- Sales growth (SG) is 2 percent per year.

- Initial sales are $1,000.

- Interest rate on debt is 10 percent.

- Dividend payout is 5 percent of net income.

- The tax rate is 53 percent.

- Cost of goods sold (COGS) is 75 percent of sales.

- Depreciation is 10 percent of gross fixed assets.

- Liquid assets earn 9 percent.

- Current assets are 15 percent of sales.

- Current liabilities are 7 percent of sales.

Assign the names in the cell range C3:C10 to the cells in the range D3:D10. Then, during each Year *t*, basic finance and accounting imply the following relationships, which are then implemented in a series of formulas:

- **Formula 11.1** Year *t*+1 sales=(Year *t* sales)*(1+SG). You can compute sales during each year by copying the D28*(1+SG) formula from E28 to F28:H28.

- **Formula 11.2** Year *t* COGS=COGS*(Year *t* sales). Each year's COGS is computed by copying the formula COGS*E28 from E29 to F29:H29.

- **Formula 11.3** If Year *t* assets>Year *t* liabilities, Year *t* debt must be set equal to Year *t* total assets – Year *t* current liabilities – Year *t* equity. Otherwise, Year *t* debt equals 0. You can compute each year's debt in E21:H21 with the IF(E18>E20+E24,E18–E20–E24,0) formula. If Year *t* total assets are greater than Year *t* total liabilities, this formula sets Year *t* debt to Year *t* total assets – Year *t* current liabilities – Year *t* equity. This equalizes, or balances, assets and liabilities. Otherwise, you set Year *t* debt equal to 0. In this case, Year *t* cash and marketable securities are used to balance assets and liabilities.

- **Formula 11.4** Year *t* current liabilities = (CL/Sales ratio)*(Year *t* sales). In E20:H20, use the $H$4*E28 formula to compute current liabilities for each year (copying this formula from E20 to F20:H20).

- **Formula 11.5** Year *t* equity = Year *t* stock +Year *t* retained earnings. In E24:H24, you can compute equity by copying the SUM(E22:E23) formula from E24 to F24:H24.

- **Formula 11.6** If Year *t* debt is greater than 0, Year *t* cash and marketable securities equals 0. Otherwise, Year *t* cash and marketable securities equals MAX(0,Year *t* total liabilities – Year *t* current assets – Year *t* net fixed assets). In E13:H13, compute cash and marketable securities for each year by copying the IF(E21>0,0,MAX(0,E25–E14–E17)) formula from E13 to F13:H13. If Year *t* debt is greater than 0, you need not use Year *t* cash and marketable securities to balance assets and liabilities. In this case, set Year *t* cash and marketable securities equal to 0. Otherwise, set Year *t* cash and marketable securities equal to Year *t* total assets – Year *t* current liabilities – Year *t* equity. This balances assets and liabilities if Year *t* assets (without cash and marketable securities) are less than Year *t* liabilities. If debt does not balance assets and liabilities, this creates liquid assets as the plug that does balance assets and liabilities.

- **Formula 11.7** Year *t* interest expense = (Year *t* debt)*IRD. In E33, compute interest expense by using the IRD*E21 formula, copying this formula again to F33:H33.

- **Formula 11.8** Year *t* interest income = (Year *t* cash and marketable securities)*LAIR. In E32:H32, compute interest income by copying the LAIR*E13 formula from E32 to F32:H32.

- **Formula 11.9** Year *t* operating income = Year *t* sales – Year *t* COGS – Year *t* depreciation. In E31:H31, operating income is computed by copying the E28–E29–E30 formula from E31 to F31:H31.

- **Formula 11.10** Year *t* dividends = (Year *t* net income)*DIV. In E39:H39, copy the E36*DIV formula from E39 to F39:H39 to compute dividends for each year.

- **Formula 11.11** Year $t + 1$ beginning retained earnings = Year t ending retained earnings. Compute beginning retained earnings each year in F38:H38, copying the E40 formula from F38 to G38:H38.

- **Formula 11.12** Year t end of year retained earnings = Year t beginning retained earnings + Year t net income – Year t dividends. In E40:H40, compute each year's ending retained earnings by copying the E38+E36–E39 formula from E40 to F40:H40.

- **Formula 11.13** Year t income before taxes = Year t operating income – Year t interest expense + Year t cash income. Compute income before taxes by copying the E31–E33+E32 formula from E34 to F34:H34.

- **Formula 11.14** Year t taxes = (Year t income before taxes)*TR. Compute each year's taxes in E35:H35 by copying the TR*E34 formula from E35 to F35:H35.

- **Formula 11.15** Year t net income after taxes = (Year t income before taxes) – (Year t taxes). In E36:H36, compute each year's net income by copying the E34–E35 formula from E36 to F36:H36.

- **Formula 11.16** Year t gross fixed assets = Year t net fixed assets + Year t accumulated depreciation. In cells E15:H15, compute gross fixed assets for each year by copying the E17+E16 formula.

- **Formula 11.17** Year t depreciation = (Year t net fixed assets)*DEP. For each year, you can use the DEP*E15 formula to compute depreciation, copying the formula from E30 to F30:H30.

- **Formula 11.18** Year t accumulated depreciation = Year $t – 1$ accumulated depreciation + Year t depreciation. For each year, use the D16+E30 formula to compute accumulated depreciation by copying the formula from E16 to F16:H16.

- **Formula 11.19** Year t net fixed assets = Year t gross fixed assets – Year t accumulated depreciation. In row 17, to compute net fixed assets, copy the E15–E16 formula from E17 to F17:H17.

- **Formula 11.20** Year t total assets = Year t liquid assets + Year t net fixed assets + Year t cash and marketable securities. By adding liquid assets, current assets, and net fixed assets, you can compute total assets by copying the SUM(E13,E14,E17) formula from E18 to F18:H18.

- **Formula 11.21** Year t total liabilities = Year t current liabilities + Year t debt + Year t equity. By copying the SUM(E20,E21,E24) formula from E25 to F25:H25, you can compute total liabilities for each period. Each year will balance because of your debt and liquid asset statements.

Formulas 11.3 and 11.6 require the use of IF statements. This worksheet will also contain circular references. (For more information about solving circular references, see Chapter 10, "Circular references.") For example, the following relationships create a circular reference:

- Year t cash affects Year t total assets.

- Year t total assets affect Year t debt.

- Year t debt affects Year t cash.

Because the worksheet contains circular references, you need to click the **File** tab, choose **Options** and then **Formulas**, and select the **Enable Iterative Calculations** check box. As explained in Chapter 10, this enables Excel to resolve circular references. Note that for each Year t, total assets in row 18 equal total liabilities in row 25. This shows the power of IF formulas combined with circular references.

When I copy a VLOOKUP formula to determine salaries of individual employees, I get a lot of #N/A errors. Then when I average the employee salaries, I cannot get a numerical answer because of the #N/A errors. Can I easily replace the #N/A errors with a blank space so I can compute average salary?

The Errortrap.xlsx file (see Figure 11-8) contains salaries and names of five employees in the D3:E7 cell range. In D11:D15 is a list of five people; compute their salary by copying the =VLOOKUP(D11,$D3:$E$7,2,False) formula from E11 to E12:E15. Unfortunately, in cells E13 and E14, Excel displays an #N/A error. NA is the acronym for "not available." Excel returns an #N/A error value when a formula cannot return an appropriate result. Because JR and Josh have no listed salary, VLOOKUP cannot return a salary value for them. Thus, when you compute average salary in E16 with the =AVERAGE(E11:E15) formula, you get an #N/A error. Many people manually replace the #N/A errors with spaces so that their average formula will calculate properly (by ignoring the spaces). The IFERROR function makes replacing errors with a character (such as a space or a 0) easy. The syntax of IFERROR is IFERROR(value,value_if_error).

The first argument is the formula you want calculated, and the second argument is the value to insert in the cell if your formula returns an error value. (Other common error values are #DIV/0, #NAME, #NUM, #REF, #VALUE; more on these later in the section.) Therefore, copying the IFERROR(VLOOKUP(D11,$D$3:$E3:$E7,2,False)," ") formula from F11 to F12:F15 computes salary correctly for each actual employee and enters a blank space for people who are not actual employees. The =AVERAGE(F11:F15) formula now correctly computes the average salary for all listed employees.

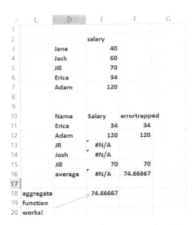

FIGURE 11-8 Here is an example of how error-trapping formulas trap formulas.

Excel 2010 and Excel 2013 provide a new function, the *AGGREGATE* function, that enables you to perform calculations and ignore rows that contain errors. The syntax of the AGGREGATE function is AGGREGATE(function_number,option,array). *Function number* is a code between 1 and 19 that gives the function involved in your calculations. For example, 1 = AVERAGE, and 9 = SUM. See the Help topic on this function (by clicking **Help On This Function** in the Function Wizard) for a complete list of available functions. *Option* gives the type of cells that should be ignored in your calculations. (See Table 11-1.) Option 6 ignores error values. *Array* is simply the range of cells used in your calculations. As shown in cell E18, the AGGREGATE(1,6,E11:E15) formula correctly computes the average (74.6667) of the listed salaries.

TABLE 11-1 Types of cells that should be ignored

Option	Behavior
0 or omitted	Ignore nested *SUBTOTAL* and *AGGREGATE* functions..
1	Ignore hidden rows and nested *SUBTOTAL* and *AGGREGATE* functions.
2	Ignore error values and nested *SUBTOTAL* and *AGGREGATE* functions.
3	Ignore hidden rows, error values, and nested *SUBTOTAL* and *AGGREGATE* functions.
4	Ignore nothing.
5	Ignore hidden rows.
6	Ignore error values.
7	Ignore hidden rows and error values.

The Errortypes.xlsx file, shown in Figure 11-9, contains examples of other common error values.

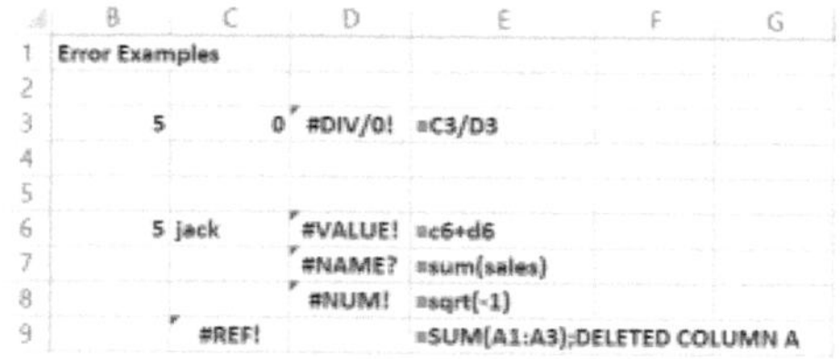

FIGURE 11-9 These are examples of Excel error values.

- In cell D3, the =C3/B3 formula yields a #DIV/0! value because you can't divide by 0.

- In cell D6, the =C6+D6 formula yields a #VALUE! error because *Jack* is not the appropriate type of data for the entered formula. (*Jack* is text.)

- In cell D7, the =SUM(Sales) formula returns a #NAME? error, indicating that the Sales range name referred to in the formula is not defined.

- In cell D8, the =SQRT(–1) formula results in a #NUM! error, which results when you enter an unacceptable argument in a function. Because negative numbers do not have square roots, Excel displays the #NUM! error.

- In cell C9, entering the SUM(A1:A3) formula and then deleting column A results in a #REF! error because the cells that are referred to in the formula (cells A1:A3) are no longer in the worksheet.

You can use the *IFERROR* function to replace any of these error values by a number or text string.

My worksheet contains quarterly revenues for Wal-Mart. Can I easily compute the revenue for each year and place it in the row containing the first quarter's sales for that year?

The Walmartrev.xlsx file contains quarterly revenues (in millions of dollars) for Wal-Mart. (See Figure 11-10.) Rows 6, 10, 14, and so on contain the revenues for the first quarter of each year. In each of these rows, you will compute total revenues for the year in column E. In other rows, column E should be blank. You could enter the SUM(D6:D9) formula in cell E6 and copy this formula to E10, E14, E18, and so on, but there must be a better way. Using an IF statement with two neat Excel functions, (*ROW* and *MOD*), gives you an easy way to enter the formula once and then copy it. The *ROW(cell reference)* function yields the row of reference. The *=ROW(A6)* function yields a 6; if you are in row 6, the *=ROW()* function would also yield a 6. The *MOD(number,divisor)* function yields the remainder when *number* is divided by *divisor*. For example, MOD(9,4) yields 1, whereas MOD(6,3) yields 0. You want your formula to work only in rows that leave a remainder of 2 when divided by 4. Therefore, copying the =IF(MOD(ROW(),4)= 2,SUM(D6:D9)," ") formula from E6 to E7:E57 ensures that you add up revenues for the current year only in rows that leave a remainder of 2 when divided by 4. This means that you compute annual revenues only in the first quarter of each year, which is the goal.

	B	C	D	E
3	Wal-Mart revenues			
4				
5	Year	Quarter	revenue	Annual revenues
6	1991	1	9,281	43886.76096
7	1991	2	10,340	
8	1991	3	10,628	
9	1991	4	13,639	
10	1992	1	11,649	55483.59296
11	1992	2	13,028	
12	1992	3	13,684	
13	1992	4	17,122	
14	1993	1	13,920	67344.29593
15	1993	2	16,237	
16	1993	3	16,827	
17	1993	4	20,361	
18	1994	1	17,686	82493.89093
19	1994	2	19,942	
20	1994	3	20,418	
21	1994	4	24,448	
22	1995	1	20,440	93627

FIGURE 11-10 This is a summary of Wal-Mart, annual revenues.

IF statements can get rather large. How many IF statements can I nest in a cell? What is the maximum number of characters allowed in an Excel formula?

In Excel 2013, you can nest up to 64 IF statements in a cell. In previous versions of Excel, you could nest a maximum of seven IF statements. In Excel 2010 (and Excel 2007), a cell can contain up to 32,000 characters.

Problems

1. Suppose the price of a product will change at dates in the future as follows:

Date	Price
On or before February 15, 2004	$8
From February 16, 2004, through April 10, 2005	$9
From April 11, 2005, through January 15, 2006	$10
After January 15, 2006	$11

   Write a formula that computes the price of the product based on the date the product is sold.

2. The Blue Yonder Airlines flight from Seattle to New York has a capacity of 250 people. The airline sold 270 tickets for the flight at a price of $300 per ticket. Tickets are nonrefundable. The variable cost of flying a passenger (mostly food costs and fuel costs) is $30 per passenger. If more than 250 people show up for the flight, the flight is overbooked, and Blue Yonder must pay overbooking compensation of $350 per person to each overbooked passenger. Develop a worksheet that computes Blue Yonder's profit based on the number of customers who show up for the flight.

3. A major drug company is trying to determine the correct plant capacity for a new drug. A unit of annual capacity can be built for a cost of $10. Each unit of the drug sells for $12 and incurs variable costs of $2. The drug will be sold for 10 years. Develop a worksheet that computes the company's 10-year profit, given the chosen annual capacity level and the annual demand for the drug. Assume demand for the drug is the same each year. You can ignore the time value of money in this problem.

4. The drug company is producing a new drug. The company has made the following assumptions:

   - During Year 1, 100,000 units will be sold.

   - Sales will grow for three years and then decline for seven years.

   - During the growth period, sales will grow at a rate of 15 percent per year. During the decline, sales will drop at a rate of 10 percent per year.

   Develop a worksheet that uses the values for Year 1 sales, the length of the growth cycle, the length of the decline cycle, the growth rate during the growth cycle, and the rate of decrease during the decline cycle to compute unit sales for Years 1–11.

5. You are bidding on a construction project. The low bid gets the project. You estimate the project cost at $10,000. Four companies are bidding against you. It costs $400 to prepare the bid. Write a formula that (given the bids of your four competitors and your bid) computes your profit.

6. We are bidding on a valuable painting. The high bid gets the painting. We estimate the painting's value at $10,000. Four companies are bidding against us. It costs $400 to prepare the bid. Write a formula that (given the bids of our four competitors and our bid) determines whether we get the painting.

7. A drug company believes its new drug will sell 10,000 units during 2004. It expects two competitors to enter the market. The year in which the first competitor enters, the company expects to lose 30 percent of its market share. The year in which the second competitor enters, the company expects to lose 15 percent of its market share. The size of the market is growing at 10 percent per year. Given values for the years in which the two competitors enter, develop a worksheet that computes the annual sales for years 2004–2013.

8. A clothing store has ordered 100,000 swimsuits. It costs $22 to produce a swimsuit. It plans to sell them until August 31 at a price of $40 and then mark the price down to $30. Given values for demand through August 31 and after August 31, develop a worksheet to compute the profit from this order.

9. On each roll of the dice after the first roll in a game of craps, the rules are as follows: If the game has not ended and the current roll matches the first roll, you win the game. If the game has not ended and the current roll is a 7, you lose. Otherwise, the game continues. Develop a worksheet that tells you (given knowledge of the first four rolls) the status of the game after four dice rolls.

10. On the S&P moving-average example, suppose you still buy shares if the current price exceeds the 15-month moving average, but you sell if the current price is less than the 5-month moving average. Is this strategy more profitable than selling when the current price is less than the 15-month moving average?

11. A European call option gives you the right to buy a share of stock at a specified future date for a given exercise price. A *butterfly spread* involves buying one call option with a low exercise price, buying one call option with a high exercise price, and selling two call options with an exercise price midway between the low and high exercise prices. Here is an example of a butterfly spread: The current stock price is $60. You buy a $54 six-month European call option for $9, buy a $66 six-month European call option for $4, and sell two $60 European call options for the price of $6. Compute the profit (in dollars, not percentage) for this transaction as a function of six-month stock prices ranging from $40 to $80. When a trader purchases a butterfly spread, which type of movement in the stock price during the next six months is the trader betting on?

12. Suppose a stock is currently selling for $32. You buy a six-month European call option with an exercise price of $30 for $2.50 and sell a six-month European call option with an exercise price of $35 for $1. Compute the profit of this strategy (in dollars) as a function of a six-month stock price ranging from $25 to $45. Why is this strategy called a *bull spread*? How would you modify this strategy to create a *bear spread*?

13. Reconsider your pro forma example. Suppose the interest rate on your debt depends on your financial well-being. More specifically, suppose that if your earnings before interest and

taxes (EBIT) are negative, your interest rate on debt is 16 percent. If your interest expense is more than 10 percent of EBIT and EBIT is positive, your interest rate on debt is 13 percent. Otherwise, your interest rate is 10 percent. Modify the pro forma to account for this variable interest rate.

14. Do this problem independently of problem 13. Suppose your firm wants a debt-to-equity ratio of 50 percent during each year. How would you modify the pro forma? Hint: You must keep each year's stock nonnegative and use stock and cash or marketable securities to balance assets and liabilities.

15. Martin Luther King Day occurs on the third Monday in January. Write a formula that computes (given the year) the date of Martin Luther King Day. Hint: First determine the day of the week for January 1 of the given year.

16. Thanksgiving occurs on the fourth Thursday in November. Write a formula that computes (given the year) the date of Thanksgiving. Hint: First determine the day of the week for November 1 of the given year.

17. The first quarter of the year is January–March; the second quarter, April–June; the third quarter, July–September; and the fourth quarter, October–December. Write a formula that returns (for any given date) the quarter of the year.

18. Write a formula that returns a person's age, given her date of birth.

19. Labor Day is the first Monday in September. Write a formula that determines the date of Labor Day for a given year.

20. The Nancybonds.xlsx file gives the bond rating for several bonds in a previous and future month. You want to count efficiently how many bonds were downgraded. Unfortunately, each company is listed in more than one row. Assuming you have sorted the data on the company name, how would you determine the number of downgraded bonds?

21. The Addresses.xlsx file gives people's names on one line, their street address on the next line, and their city, state, and ZIP code on the following line. How could you put each person's information on one line?

22. The FormattingDDAnum.xlsx file gives a bunch of text strings, such as DDA, D, DDA1250045, and so on. A cell is properly formatted if the first three characters are DDA and the last seven characters are a number one million or larger. Determine which cells are properly formatted.

23. Suppose the number of Group 1 members is listed in cell B1, the number of Group 2 members is listed in cell B2, and the number of Group 3 members is listed in cell B3. The total number of group members is always 100. Suppose that Group 1 has 50 members, Group 2 has 30 members, and Group 3 has 20 members. Efficiently place a 1 for each Group 1 member in column D, a 2 for each Group 2 member in column D, and a 3 for each Group 3 member in column D. Thus, column D should (in this example) have a 1 in D1:D50, a 2 in D51:D80, and a 3 in D81:D100.

24. The Dividebyprice.xlsx file contains units sold of each product and total revenue. You want to determine the average price for each product. Of course, if units sold is 0, then there is no average price. Error-trap the Dividebyprice.xlsx file to ensure that all products with zero sales yield the No Sales message instead of a #DIV!0 error.

25. The School of Fine Art has 100 lockers numbered 1 to 100. At present, all lockers are open. Begin by closing every locker whose number evenly divides by 3. Then toggle (toggling means opening a closed locker and closing an open locker) each locker whose number is divisible by 4; then toggle each locker whose number is divisible by 5, . . . , and, finally, toggle each locker whose number is divisible by 100. How many lockers are now open?

26. The Matchlist.xlsx file contains a list of people who bought your product in February and a list of people who bought it in March. Determine how many of your February customers purchased your product in March.

27. Set up a calendar worksheet that takes a given month and year as inputs and tells you the day of the week on which each day of the month occurs.

28. Some rows of column C of the Problem28data.xlsx file contain the word *and*. Create formulas in column D that place an X in a row of column D if and only if column C in that row contains the word *and*.

29. Suppose you toss two 20-sided dice. The 400 possible outcomes are (1, 1), (1, 2), . . . , (20, 20). Use IF statements to generate all 400 possible outcomes systematically.

30. Using the data in the Catsanddogs.xlsx file, determine how many times the text string cat or dog occurs.

CHAPTER 12

Time and time functions

Questions answered in this chapter:

- How can I enter times in Excel?

- How can I enter a time and date in the same cell?

- How does Excel do computations with times?

- How can I have my worksheet always display the current time?

- How can I use the *TIME* function to create times?

- How can I use the *TIMEVALUE* function to convert a text string to a time?

- How can I extract the hour, minute, or second from a given time?

- Given work starting and ending times, how can I determine the number of hours an employee worked?

- I added up the total time an employee worked, and I never get more than 24 hours. What did I do wrong?

- How can I easily create a sequence of regularly spaced time intervals?

Recall from Chapter 6, "Dates and date functions," that Microsoft Excel 2013 gives the date January 1, 1900, the serial number 1; January 2, 1900, the serial number 2; and so on. Excel also assigns serial numbers to times (as a fraction of a 24-hour day). The starting point is midnight, so 3:00 A.M. has a serial number of .125, noon has a serial number of .5, 6:00 P.M. has a serial number of .75, and so on. If you combine a date and time in a cell, the serial number is the number of days after January 1, 1900, plus the time fraction associated with the given time. Thus, entering January 1, 2007 in a cell yields (when formatted as General) a serial number of 39083, whereas January 1, 2007, 6:00 A.M. yields a serial number of 39083.25.

Answers to this chapter's questions

This section provides the answers to the questions that are listed at the beginning of the chapter.

How can I enter times in Excel?

To indicate times, you enter a colon (:) after the hour and another colon before the seconds. For example, in file Time.xlsx (see Figure 12-1), the time of 8:30 A.M. in cell C2 is entered simply as 8:30 or 8:30 AM. In cell C3, 8:30 P.M. is entered as 8:30 PM. As shown in cell D3, you could also enter 8:30 P.M. with 24-hour military time as 20:30. In cell A4, the time is entered as 3:10:30 PM. This represents 30 seconds after 3:10 P.M.

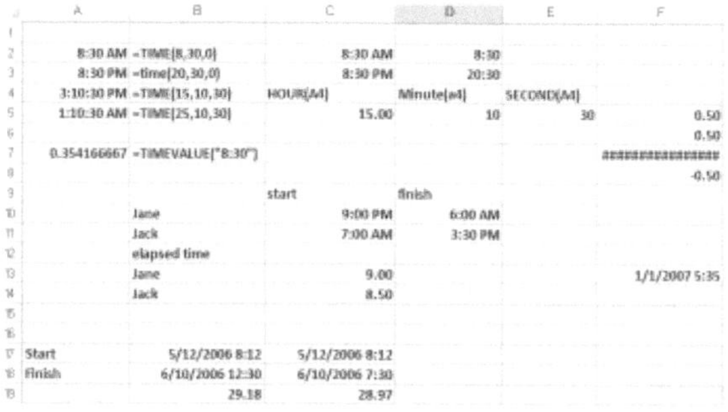

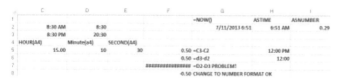

FIGURE 12-1 This figure shows examples of time formats.

How can I enter a time and date in the same cell?

Simply put a space after the date and enter the time. In cell F13 of file Time.xlsx, January 1, 2007 5:35 is entered. Of course, this represents 5:35 A.M. on January 1, 2007. Excel immediately reformatted this to 1/1/2007 5:35.

How does Excel do computations with times?

When Excel computes differences in times, the result displayed depends on the format used in the cell. Figure 12-2 displays the various Excel time formats.

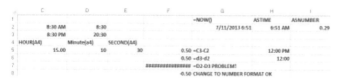

FIGURE 12-2 This figure shows the different Excel time formats.

In the Time.xlsx file (see Figure 12-2), the difference between 8:30 P.M. and 8:30 A.M. in cells F5 and H5 are displayed with the =C3−C2 formula. If you do not change the format, Excel thinks these times are 12 hours apart and enters 12:00 PM, as shown in cell H5. In most cases, you'll want Excel to portray these times as .5 days apart. (Multiplying by 24, you could convert this time difference to hours.) To make Excel show .5 in cell F5, format cell F5 as a number.

In cell F7, the user tried to subtract an earlier time from a later time with the =D2−D3 formula. Because he did not reformat the cell, Excel displays the dreaded #############. If he changes the cell containing the formula to the Number format (as in cell F8), he obtains the correct time difference, –.5 days.

Cells B17 and C17 give the start times for two jobs, whereas cells B18 and C18 give the finish times for the jobs. (See Figure 12-3.) If you want to calculate how many hours it takes to complete each job, copy the =B18–B17 formula from B19 to C19 and reformat the cell as Number. Thus, the first job took 29.18 days, and the second job took 28.97 days.

	A	B	C
17	Start	5/12/2006 8:12	5/12/2006 8:12
18	Finish	6/10/2006 12:30	6/10/2006 7:30
19		29.18	28.97
20			

FIGURE 12-3 Determine the time needed to complete jobs.

How can I have my worksheet always display the current time?

The Excel =NOW() formula gives today's date and the current time. For example, in cell G2 (see Figure 12-4) of file Time.xlsx, entering =NOW() yielded 7/11/2013 6:51 because the screen capture was created at 6:50 A.M. on July 11, 2013. To compute the current time, enter the =NOW()–TODAY() formula in cell H2 or I2. Cell H2 is formatted to show a time (9:50 P.M.), whereas cell I2 is formatted to show a number (.91 days). This represents the fact that 9:50 P.M. is 91 percent of the way between midnight of one day and midnight of the next day.

	G	H	I
1	=NOW()	ASTIME	ASNUMBER
2	7/11/2013 6:51	6:51 AM	0.29
3			

FIGURE 12-4 Use the Now() and Today() functions.

How can I use the *TIME* function to create times?

The *TIME* function has the TIME(hour,minute,second) syntax. Given an hour, minutes, and seconds, the *TIME* function returns a time of day. The *TIME* function never returns a value exceeding 24 hours.

In cell A2 (see Figure 12-1), the =TIME(8,30,0) formula yields 8:30 A.M. In cell A3, the =TIME(20,30,0) formula yields 8:30 P.M. In cell A4, the =TIME(15,10,30) formula yields 3:10:30 P.M. Finally, note that in cell A5, the =TIME(25,10,30) formula treats the 25 as though it is 25 – 24 = 1 and yields 1:10:30 A.M.

If the number of seconds does not show up in a cell, just select a Time format that displays seconds.

How can I use the *TIMEVALUE* function to convert a text string to a time?

The *TIMEVALUE* function has the =TIMEVALUE(timetext) syntax, where timetext is a text string that gives a time in a valid format. Then TIMEVALUE returns the time as a fraction between 0 and 1. (This means that the *TIMEVALUE* function ignores any date in timetext.) For example, in cell A7 (see Figure 12-1), the =TIMEVALUE("8:30") formula yields 0.354166667 because 8:30 A.M. is 35.4 percent of the way between midnight of one day and midnight of the next day.

How can I extract the hour, minute, or second from a given time?

The Excel *HOUR*, *MINUTE*, and *SECOND* functions extract the appropriate time unit from a cell containing time. For example (as shown in Figure 12-1), entering the =HOUR(A4) formula in cell C5 yields 15 (3:00 P.M. is 15:00 military time). Entering the =Minute(A4) formula in cell D5 yields 10, whereas entering =SECOND(A4) in cell E5 yields 30.

Given work starting and ending times, how can I determine the number of hours an employee worked?

In cells C10:D11 (see Figure 12-5), you can enter the times that Jane and Jack started and ended work. You want to figure out how long each of them worked. The problem is that Jane finished work the day after she started, so simple subtraction does not give the actual number of hours she worked. Copying the =IF(D10>C10,24*(D10–C10),24+24*(D10–C10)) formula from C13 to C14 yields the correct result. These cells are formatted as Number. If the finish time is after the start time, subtracting the start time from the finish time and multiplying by 24 yields hours worked. If the finish time is before the start time, then 24*(finish time – start time) yields a negative number of hours, but adding 24 hours fixes things, assuming the end of the shift was one day later. Thus, Jane worked 9 hours, and Jack worked 8.5 hours.

	A	B	C	D
9			start	finish
10		Jane	9:00 PM	6:00 AM
11		Jack	7:00 AM	3:30 PM
12		elapsed time		
13		Jane	9.00	
14		Jack	8.50	

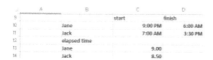

FIGURE 12-5 Compute the length of time employees worked.

I added up the total time an employee worked, and I never get more than 24 hours. What did I do wrong?

Cells C31:D35 in Figure 12-6 give the number of hours (formatted as h:mm) an employee worked on each day of her workweek. In cell D36, the =SUM(D31:D35) formula computes the total number of hours worked during the week. Excel displays 14:48. This is clearly wrong, but the fault is not with the SUM function but with the cell formatting. With the h:mm format, Excel never displays a value exceeding 24 hours. You can choose a format (38:48:00) that displays more than 24 hours, as cell D38 shows. Then, summing up the hours worked each day displays the correct number of hours worked (38 hours and 48 minutes).

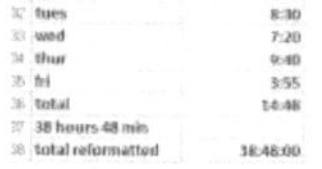

	C	D
30		
31	mon	9:23
32	tues	8:30
33	wed	7:20
34	thur	9:40
35	fri	3:55
36	total	14:48
37	38 hours 48 min	
38	total reformatted	38:48:00

FIGURE 12-6 Determine the total hours worked during the week.

How can I easily create a sequence of regularly spaced time intervals?

Suppose a doctor takes appointments from 8:00 A.M. in 20-minute segments up to 5:00 P.M. How can you enter the list of possible appointment times in different rows? Use the great AutoFill feature in Excel. (See Figure 12-7.) Enter the first two times (8:00 A.M. and 8:20 A.M.) in cells L15:L16. Now select cells L15:L16 and move the cursor to the lower-right corner of cell L16 until you see the black cross. Drag the pointer down until you see 5:00 P.M. (the last appointment time). From cells L15:L16, Excel has guessed (correctly!) that you want to enter times that are 20 minutes apart. Entering Monday in a cell and Tuesday below it and using AutoFill will yield a sequence of Monday, Tuesday, Wednesday, . . . , eventually restarting at Monday. Entering 1/1/2007 in one cell, 2/1/2007 in another cell, selecting these two cells, and using AutoFill yields a sequence of dates such as 1/1/2007, 2/1/2007, 3/1/2007, and so on.

L
14	sequence of times
15	8:00 AM
16	8:20 AM
17	8:40 AM
18	9:00 AM
19	9:20 AM
20	9:40 AM
21	10:00 AM
22	10:20 AM
23	10:40 AM
24	11:00 AM
25	11:20 AM
26	11:40 AM
27	12:00 PM
28	12:20 PM
29	12:40 PM
30	1:00 PM

FIGURE 12-7 Enter a sequence of times.

Problems

1. Write a formula that will return a time 18 hours after the current time.

2. The Marathon.xlsx file gives marathon race times for four runners. Problems (a) through (c) refer to this data. Compute the average time of the runners.

   a. How much faster was John than Jill?

   b. How many total minutes did each runner take?

   c. How many total seconds did each runner take?

3. The Jobshop.xlsx file gives the start time and date for several jobs and the time required to complete each job. Determine the completion time for each job.

CHAPTER 13

The Paste Special command

Questions answered in this chapter:

- How can I move the results of calculations (not the formulas) to a different part of a worksheet?

- I have a list of names in a column. How can I make the list appear in a row instead of a column?

- I've downloaded US T-bill interest rates from a website into Excel. The data displays a 5 when the interest rate is 5 percent, 8 when the interest rate is 8 percent, and so on. How can I easily divide my results by 100 so that a 5 percent interest rate, for example, is displayed as .05?

With the Paste Special command in Microsoft Excel 2013, you can easily manipulate worksheet data. In this chapter, you see how to use the Paste Special command to perform the following types of operations:

- Paste only the values in cells (not the formulas) in a different part of a worksheet.

- Transpose data in columns to rows and vice versa.

- Transform a range of numbers by adding, subtracting, dividing, or multiplying each number in the range by a given constant.

Answers to this chapter's questions

This section provides the answers to the questions that are listed at the beginning of the chapter.

How can I move the results of calculations (not the formulas) to a different part of a worksheet?

In the Paste Special Value worksheet in the Pastespecial.xlsx file, the E4:H9 cell range contains the names, games, total points, and points per game for five 10- to 11-year-old basketball players from Bloomington, Indiana. In the H5:H9 cell range, use the data in cells F5:G9 to compute each child's points per game, as shown in Figure 13-1. Suppose you want to copy this data and the calculated points per game—but not the formulas that perform the calculations—to a different cell range (E13:H18, for example). Just select the E4:H9 range, press Ctrl+C, and then move to the upper-left corner of the range where you want to copy the data (cell E13 in this example). Next, right-click the upper-left corner cell in the target range, choose **Paste Special**, and then fill in the **Paste Special** dialog box as indicated in Figure 13-2. After clicking **OK**, the E13:H18 range contains the data but not the formulas from the E4:H9 cell range. You can check this by clicking cell H16. You see a value (7) but not the formula that was used to compute Gregory's average points per game. Note that if you use the Paste Special command, select **Values**, and then paste the data into the same range from which you copied the data, your formulas disappear from the worksheet.

	E	F	G	H	I
3					
4		Games	Points	Points/game	
5	Dan	4	28	7.00	
6	Gabe	4	28	7.00	
7	Gregory	5	35	7.00	
8	Christian	6	22	3.67	
9	Max	6	15	2.50	
10					
11					
12					
13		Games	Points	Points/game	
14	Dan	4	28	7	
15	Gabe	4	28	7	
16	Gregory	5	35	7	
17	Christian	6	22	3.666666667	
18	Max	6	15	2.5	

FIGURE 13-1 Use the Paste Special command to paste only values.

FIGURE 13-2 The Paste Special dialog box with Values selected. Selecting Values pastes only values and not formulas.

I have a list of names in a column. How can I make the list appear in a row instead of a column?

To realign data from a row to a column (or vice versa), copy the data and then use the Paste Special command with **Transpose** selected. Essentially, Transpose in the Paste Special dialog box flips selected cells around so that the first row of the copied range becomes the first column of the range you paste data into and vice versa. For an example, look at the Paste Special Transpose worksheet in the Pastespecial.xlsx file, shown in Figure 13-3.

Suppose that you want to list the players' names in one row (starting in cell E13). Select the E5:E9 range and then press Ctrl+C to copy the data. Right-click cell E13, click **Paste Special**, and select **Transpose** in the **Paste Special** dialog box. After you click **OK**, Excel transposes the players' names into one row.

	Games	Points	Points/game
Dan	4	28	7.00
Gabe	4	28	7.00
Gregory	5	35	7.00
Christian	6	22	3.67
Max	6	15	2.50

Dan	Gabe	Gregory	Christian	Max

	Dan	Gabe	Gregory	Christian	Max
Games	4	4	5	6	6
Points	28	28	35	22	15
Points/game	7.00	7.00	7.00	3.67	2.50

FIGURE 13-3 Use the Transpose option in the Paste Special dialog box to transpose a row of data into a column or a column of data into a row.

Suppose you want to transpose the spreadsheet content in E4:H9 to a range beginning in cell E17. Begin by selecting the E4:H9 range. Next, press Ctrl+C. Now move to the upper-left corner of the range where you want to put the transposed information (E17). Right-click and choose **Paste Special**, select **Transpose**, and then click **OK**. You see that the content of E4:H9 is transposed (turned on its side), as shown in Figure 13-3. Note that in F20:J20, Excel was smart enough to adjust the points-per-game formula so that the average for each player is now computed from data in the same column instead of in the same row.

> **Note** When you select **Paste Special** and click **Paste Link** instead of OK, the transposed cells are linked to the original cells, and changes you make to the original data are reflected in the copy. By changing the value in cell F5 to 7, the value in cell F18 becomes 7 as well, and cell F20 will display Dan's average as 4 points per game.

I've downloaded US T-bill interest rates from a website into Excel. The data displays a 5 when the interest rate is 5 percent, 8 when the interest rate is 8 percent, and so on. How can I easily divide my results by 100 so that a 5 percent interest rate, for example, is displayed as .05?

The Paste Special Divide Before worksheet in the Pastespecial.xlsx file (see Figure 13-4) contains the annual rate of interest paid by three-month US T-bills for each month between January 1970 and February 1987. In January 1970, the annual rate on a three-month T-bill was 8.01 percent. Suppose you want to earn annual interest on $1 invested at the current T-bill rate. The formula to calculate the rate is (1 + (annual rate)/100). It would be easier to compute earned interest if the column of annual interest rates were divided by 100.

The Operations area of the Paste Special dialog box enables you to add, subtract, multiply, or divide each number in a range by a given number, providing an easy way to divide each interest rate by 100. Here you want to divide each number in column D. To begin, enter your divisor (100). You can enter it anywhere in the worksheet—F5 in this instance. (See Figure 13-4.) With F5 selected, press **Ctrl+C**. You see the moving ants surrounding cell F5. Select the range of numbers you want to modify. To select all the data in column D, click in cell D10, press **Ctrl+Shift,** and then press the **down arrow** key. This shortcut is a useful trick for selecting a tall cell range. (To select a wide set of data listed in one row, move to the first data point, press **Ctrl+Shift,** and then press the **right arrow** key.) Right-click and choose **Paste Special** and then select **Divide** in the Paste Special dialog box, as shown in Figure 13-5.

	C	D	E	F
5				100
6				
7				
8				
9	date	3mo		
10	1.1970	8.01		
11	2.1970	7.01		
12	3.1970	6.48		
13	4.1970	7.03		
14	5.1970	7.04		
15	6.1970	6.52		
16	7.1970	6.43		
17	8.1970	6.38		
18	9.1970	6.03		
19	10.1970	5.96		
20	11.1970	5.07		
21	12.1970	4.9		
22	1.1971	4.17		
23	2.1971	3.43		
24	3.1971	3.64		
25	4.1971	4.04		
26	5.1971	4.38		

FIGURE 13-4 This figure shows the data for using Divide in the Paste Special dialog box to divide a data range by a constant.

FIGURE 13-5 You can apply an option in the Operation area of the Paste Special dialog box to a range of cells.

After you click **OK**, Excel divides each selected number in column D by 100. The results are shown in Figure 13-6. If you had selected Add, D10 would display 108.01; if you had selected Subtract, D10 would display –91.99; and if you had selected Multiply, D10 would display 801.

	C	D
9	date	3mo
10	1.1970	0.0801
11	2.1970	0.0701
12	3.1970	0.0648
13	4.1970	0.0703
14	5.1970	0.0704
15	6.1970	0.0652
16	7.1970	0.0643
17	8.1970	0.0638
18	9.1970	0.0603
19	10.1970	0.0596
20	11.1970	0.0507
21	12.1970	0.049
22	1.1971	0.0417
23	2.1971	0.0343
24	3.1971	0.0364
25	4.1971	0.0404
26	5.1971	0.0438

FIGURE 13-6 These are the results of using Divide in the Paste Special dialog box.

Problems

1. The Mavs.xlsx file contains statistics for the great 2002–2003 Dallas Mavericks basketball team. Player names are listed in column A, statistical categories are listed in row 3, and statistical results are listed in rows 4–20. Change the worksheet so that all player names are listed in the same row and all statistical categories are listed in the same column.

2. Field goal percentage, free throw percentage, and three point percentage are listed as decimals. For example, Steve Nash made 91.9 percent of his free throws, which is listed as .919. Change the worksheet so that all shooting percentages are listed as a number from 1 through 100.

3. The Productpaste.xlsx file contains data on quarterly sales for four products. Copy this data to another range so that quarterly sales are read across instead of down. Link your copied data to the original data so that your computation of annual sales in the copied data range reflect changes entered in rows 5–8.

4. The Productsalespaste.xlsx file contains sales of Products X, Y, and Z (in thousands of units). Convert this sales data to sales in actual units. Hint: Remember you can use the Ctrl key (as explained in Chapter 1, "Range names") to select a noncontiguous range of cells.

CHAPTER 14

Three-dimensional formulas

Question answered in this chapter:

- Is there an easy way to set up a multiple-worksheet workbook in which each worksheet has a similar structure? Can I easily create formulas that involve cells in multiple worksheets?

In many business situations, you have to set up workbooks in which each worksheet has a similar format or structure. Here are some examples:

- You want to track your company's sales in each region of the country in a separate worksheet and then summarize total sales in a summary worksheet.

- You want to track your company's sales for each month in a separate worksheet and then summarize year-to-date sales in a summary worksheet.

In this chapter, you learn how to set up workbooks in which the individual worksheets have a similar structure. This chapter also discusses three-dimensional formulas, which enable you to write formulas easily to perform calculations on cells in multiple worksheets.

Answer to this chapter's question

This section provides the answer to the question that is listed at the beginning of the chapter.

Is there an easy way to set up a multiple-worksheet workbook in which each worksheet has a similar structure? Can I easily create formulas that involve cells in multiple worksheets?

Suppose you want to set up a workbook that contains a separate worksheet to track sales in each region (East, South, Midwest, and West) of the United States. You also want to summarize total sales in a summary worksheet. In each worksheet, you want to track your product's price, unit cost, and units sold as well as your fixed cost and profits. In the summary worksheet, you want to track just total profit and units sold. You want your individual region worksheets to look like Figure 14-1.

	A	B	C
1	East		
2			
3		Price	10
4		Unit cost	5
5		Units sold	35
6		Fixed cost	100
7		Profit	75

FIGURE 14-1 This figure shows sales in the East.

To set up this structure, you enter the product price in cell C3 of each worksheet, the unit cost in cell C4, the units sold in cell C5, and the fixed cost in cell C6. Then, in cell C7, you compute the East region profit with the (C3-C4)*C5-C6 formula. You want the same structure in the worksheets for the other regions. It turns out you need to enter the headings and formula in only one worksheet, and then Excel automatically copies them to the other region's worksheets.

To begin, open a blank workbook, which by default contains one worksheet. By clicking the **Insert Worksheet** icon to the right of the last-named worksheet (or by pressing Shift+F11), insert four new worksheets so that your workbook contains five worksheets. Name the first four worksheets **East**, **South**, **Midwest**, and **West**. Name the last worksheet **Summary**. All sales will be totaled in the Summary worksheet. (By the way, if you select **Options** on the **File** tab and then choose **General**, you can change the number of worksheets included in a workbook by default.)

To set up the regional worksheets, select the first worksheet (**East**); hold down the Shift key and select the last individual worksheet (**West**). Now, whatever you enter in the East worksheet is duplicated in the other regional worksheets. Simply type Price in cell B3, Unit Cost in cell B4, Units Sold in cell B5, Fixed Cost in cell B6, and Profit in cell B7. Finally, enter the (C3-C4)*C5-C6 formula in cell C7. Now click the last sheet to leave this data entry procedure. You see that each regional worksheet has the same headings in column B and the correct Profit formula in cell C7.

You are now ready to use three-dimensional formulas to compute total units sold and profit. In cell C5, you compute total units sold. Remember that you entered units sold for each region in cell C5. Move your cursor to cell C5 of the Summary worksheet where you want to compute total units sold. Type =SUM(and then move your cursor to the first cell you want to total (cell C5 of sheet **East**). Next, hold down the **Shift** key and click the name of the last worksheet you want to total (in this case, **West**). Last, enter a right (closing) parenthesis in the formula bar, and you see the SUM(east:west!C5) formula entered in cell C5 of the Summary sheet. This formula is an example of a three-dimensional formula. Most Excel formulas operate in two dimensions (rows and columns). A three-dimensional formula operates in a third dimension: across worksheets. This formula tells Excel to sum cell C5 in all worksheets, starting with the East worksheet and ending with the West worksheet. If you wanted to, you could have typed this formula in cell C5 of the Summary worksheet. Copying this formula and pasting it to cell C7 of the Summary worksheet computes your company's total profit. (See Figure 14-2.)

FIGURE 14-2 This figure summarizes unit sales and profit.

In Chapter 22, "The *INDIRECT* function," you learn how the *INDIRECT* function can summarize data in different worksheets. Later, you learn about four other methods you can use to summarize data in multiple worksheets and or workbooks.

- PivotTables (Chapter 43)

- Data Consolidate (Chapter 52)

- Data Model (Chapter 44)

- PowerPivot (Chapter 45)

Problem

1. You own six local coffee shops. The revenues and customer count for each coffee shop are given in the following table:

Shop	Revenues	Customer Count
1	$8,000	1,950
2	$7,000	1,800
3	$9,000	2,200
4	$8,400	2,000
5	$5,900	1,400
6	$10,100	2,500

Set up a workbook that makes it easy to enter revenue and customer count for each store and create a summary worksheet (using three-dimensional formulas) that computes total weekly revenue and customer count.

CHAPTER 15

The Auditing tool and Inquire add-in

Questions answered in this chapter:

- I've just been handed a five thousand–row worksheet that computes the net present value (NPV) of a new car. In the worksheet, my financial analyst made an assumption about the annual percentage of the growth in the product's price. Which cells in the worksheet are affected by this assumption?

- I think my financial analyst made an error computing Year 1 before-tax profit. Which cells in the worksheet model were used for this calculation?

- How does the auditing tool work when I'm working with data in more than one worksheet or workbook?

- What is the new Inquire add-in and how can I install it?

- What information does the Inquire add-in show about a workbook?

- How does the Inquire add-in compare workbooks?

- How does the Inquire add-in show the relationships between cell formulas?

- How does the Inquire add-in show the relationships between worksheets?

When you hear the word structure, you might often think about the structure of a building. The structure of a worksheet model refers to the way input assumptions (data such as unit sales, price, and unit cost) are used to compute outputs of interest such as NPV, profit, or cost. The Microsoft Excel 2013 auditing tool provides an easy method for documenting the structure of a worksheet or workbook, which makes understanding the logic underlying complex worksheet models easier. To view the auditing options in Excel, click the **Formulas** tab on the ribbon and then view the **Formula Auditing** group. (See Figure 15-1.)

This chapter discusses the Trace Precedents, Trace Dependents, and Remove Arrows commands. Here, this chapter holds a brief discussion of the other elements of the Formula Auditing group. The Evaluate Formula command is discussed in Chapter 21, "The OFFSET function."

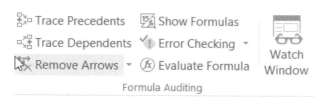

FIGURE 15-1 This figure shows the Formula Auditing toolbar.

Clicking the Show Formulas icon, shown in Figure 15-1, serves as a switch that toggles the display of formulas in cells and the display of the values that result from the formulas. You can also press Ctrl+~ to toggle between showing formulas in cells and showing the formulas' results. Formulas can also be shown in a spreadsheet by using the new *FORMULATEXT* function in Excel 2013. The ISFORMULATEXT.xlsx file (see Figure 15-2) illustrates the use of this function.

	A	B	C	D	E
1					
2					
3	x	y	Column A ISFORMULA?	Column B ISFORMULA?	FORMULATEXT
4	1	5	FALSE	TRUE	=5*A4
5	2	10	FALSE	TRUE	=5*A5
6	3	15	FALSE	TRUE	=5*A6

FIGURE 15-2 This figure shows the usage of the *ISFORMULA* and *FORMULATEXT* functions.

The numbers 1, 2, and 3 are entered in column A and, in column B, they are multiplied by 5. Copying the =FORMULATEXT(B4) formula from E4 to E5:E6 causes the formulas from column B to appear in column E.

Columns C and D illustrate the use of another new Excel 2013 function, *ISFORMULA*. This formula returns TRUE if a cell contains a formula and FALSE otherwise. If you copy the =ISFORMULA(A4) formula from C4 to C4:D6, you see that column B contains formulas, and column A does not.

Error Checking, shown in Figure 15-1, checks your worksheet for errors and gives you help on the errors. To illustrate how the Excel Error Trap capability works, look again at the Errortrap.xlsx file from Chapter 10, "Circular references." (See Figure 15-3.)

Clicking the drop-down arrow yields three options: Error Checking, Trace Errors, and Circular References. Your workbook contains no circular references, so Circular Reference is dimmed. If the workbook contained any circular references, Excel would highlight them. If you select Error Checking, Excel begins to check for errors. The first error it finds is in cell E13; the dialog box shown in Figure 15-4 opens. Clicking Help On This Error leads you to further information about the error. Show Calculation Steps enables you to step through the calculation of the formula. Ignore Error closes the dialog box. Edit In Formula Bar enables you to edit the formula. Selecting Previous returns you to the previously found error, and Next sends you to the dialog box for the next error.

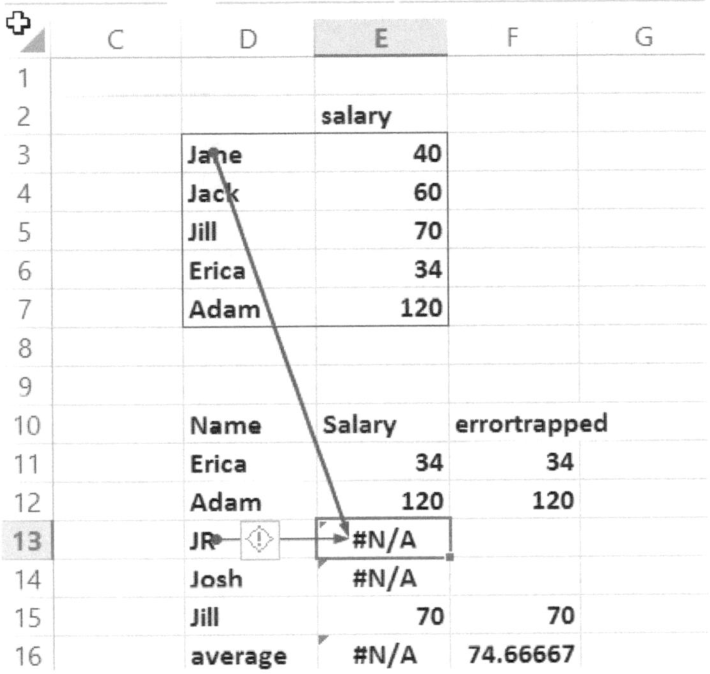

	C	D	E	F	G
1					
2			salary		
3		Jane	40		
4		Jack	60		
5		Jill	70		
6		Erica	34		
7		Adam	120		
8					
9					
10		Name	Salary	errortrapped	
11		Erica	34	34	
12		Adam	120	120	
13		JR	#N/A		
14		Josh	#N/A		
15		Jill	70	70	
16		average	#N/A	74.66667	

FIGURE 15-3 This figure illustrates Error Checking and Trace Errors.

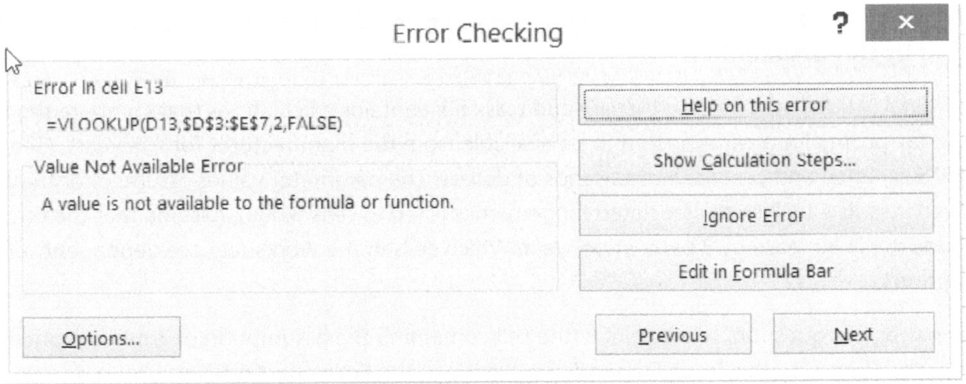

Error Checking

Error In cell E13
=VLOOKUP(D13,$D$3:$E$7,2,FALSE)

Value Not Available Error

A value is not available to the formula or function.

Help on this error

Show Calculation Steps...

Ignore Error

Edit in Formula Bar

Options...

Previous   Next

FIGURE 15-4 This figure shows the Error Checking dialog box.

If you select Trace Errors from the drop-down menu and the active cell contains an error, the cells needed to compute the active cell are indicated by blue arrows or a blue rectangle. For example, in Figure 15-3, cell D13 and the D3:E7 cell range are needed to compute cell E13. (This cell generated an #N/A error.)

By using the Watch Window, you can select a cell or cells and then, no matter where you are in the workbook, you see how the value of the selected cells changes. For example, after selecting the Watch Window, you can select Add Watch and add a formula (say to cell C3 in Sheet 1). Now, even if you are working in a different workbook, the Watch Window shows you how cell C3 of Sheet 1 changes.

Trace Precedents and Trace Dependents locate and display precedents and dependents for worksheet cells or formulas. A *precedent* is any cell whose value is needed to compute a selected formula's value. For example, if you were analyzing a direct-mail campaign, you would make assumptions about the number of letters mailed and the response rate for the mailing. Then you could compute the number of responses as *response rate*letters mailed*. In this case, the response rate and total letters mailed are precedents of the cell containing the formula used to compute total responses. A *dependent* is any cell containing a formula whose values can't be computed without knowledge of a selected cell. In the previous example, the cell containing the total number of responses is a dependent of the cell containing the response rate. Excel marks precedents and dependents with blue arrows when you use the auditing tool. The Remove Arrows button clears the display of the arrows.

Let's apply the auditing tool to some practical problems.

Answers to this chapter's questions

This section provides the answers to the questions that are listed at the beginning of the chapter.

I've just been handed a five thousand–row worksheet that computes the net present value (NPV) of a new car. In the worksheet, my financial analyst made an assumption about the annual percentage of the growth in the product's price. Which cells in the worksheet are affected by this assumption?

The Original Model worksheet in the NPVaudit.xlsx file contains calculations that compute the NPV of after-tax profits for a car expected to be available from the manufacturer for five years. (See Figure 15-5.) Price and cost are in thousands of dollars. The parameter values assumed for the analysis are given in cells C1:C8 (with associated range names listed in cells B1:B8). Assume that the price of the product will increase by 3 percent per year. Which cells in the worksheet are dependents of this assumption?

To answer this question, select cell C8 (the cell containing the assumption of 3 percent price growth) and then click the **Trace Dependents** button in the **Formula Auditing** group on the **Formulas** tab. Excel displays the set of arrows, shown in Figure 15-6, pointing to direct dependents of cell C8. Note that for Trace Dependents or Trace Precedents (see the following) to work correctly, the entire ribbon must show before clicking **Trace Dependents**. Pressing Control+F1 serves as a toggle between just the ribbon tabs and all options showing on the ribbon.

	A	B	C	D	E	F
1		taxrate	0.4			
2		Year1sales	10000			
3		Sales growth	0.1			
4		Year1price	$ 9.00			
5		Year1cost	$ 6.00			
6		intrate	0.15			
7		costgrowth	0.05			
8		pricegrowth	0.03			
9	Year	1	2	3	4	5
10	Unit Sales	10000	11000	12100	13310	14641
11	unit price	$ 9.00	$ 9.27	$ 9.55	$ 9.83	$ 10.13
12	unit cost	$ 6.00	$ 6.30	$ 6.62	$ 6.95	$ 7.29
13	Revenues	$ 90,000.00	$ 101,970.00	$ 115,532.01	$ 130,897.77	$ 148,307.17
14	Costs	$ 60,000.00	$ 69,300.00	$ 80,041.50	$ 92,447.93	$ 106,777.36
15	Before Tax Profits	$ 30,000.00	$ 32,670.00	$ 35,490.51	$ 38,449.83	$ 41,529.81
16	Tax paid	$ 12,000.00	$ 13,068.00	$ 14,196.20	$ 15,379.93	$ 16,611.92
17	Aftertax Profits	$ 18,000.00	$ 19,602.00	$ 21,294.31	$ 23,069.90	$ 24,917.89
18						
19	NPV	$70,054.34				

FIGURE 15-5 You can use the auditing tool to trace formulas in complex spreadsheets.

By clicking the Trace Dependents button once, Excel points to the cells that *directly* depend on the price growth assumption. In Figure 15-6, you can see that only the unit prices for Years 2–5 depend directly on this assumption. Clicking Trace Dependents repeatedly shows all formulas whose calculation requires the value for annual price growth, as shown in Figure 15-7.

	A	B	C	D	E	F
1		taxrate	0.4			
2		Year1sales	10000			
3		Sales growth	0.1			
4		Year1price	$ 9.00			
5		Year1cost	$ 6.00			
6		intrate	0.15			
7		costgrowth	0.05			
8		pricegrowth	0.03			
9	Year	1	2	3	4	5
10	Unit Sales	10000	11000	12100	13310	14641
11	unit price	$ 9.00	$ 9.27	$ 9.55	$ 9.83	$ 10.13
12	unit cost	$ 6.00	$ 6.30	$ 6.62	$ 6.95	$ 7.29
13	Revenues	$ 90,000.00	$ 101,970.00	$115,532.01	$ 130,897.77	$ 148,307.17
14	Costs	$ 60,000.00	$ 69,300.00	$ 80,041.50	$ 92,447.93	$ 106,777.36
15	Before Tax Profits	$ 30,000.00	$ 32,670.00	$ 35,490.51	$ 38,449.83	$ 41,529.81
16	Tax paid	$ 12,000.00	$ 13,068.00	$ 14,196.20	$ 15,379.93	$ 16,611.92
17	Aftertax Profits	$ 18,000.00	$ 19,602.00	$ 21,294.31	$ 23,069.90	$ 24,917.89

FIGURE 15-6 Trace directly dependent cells.

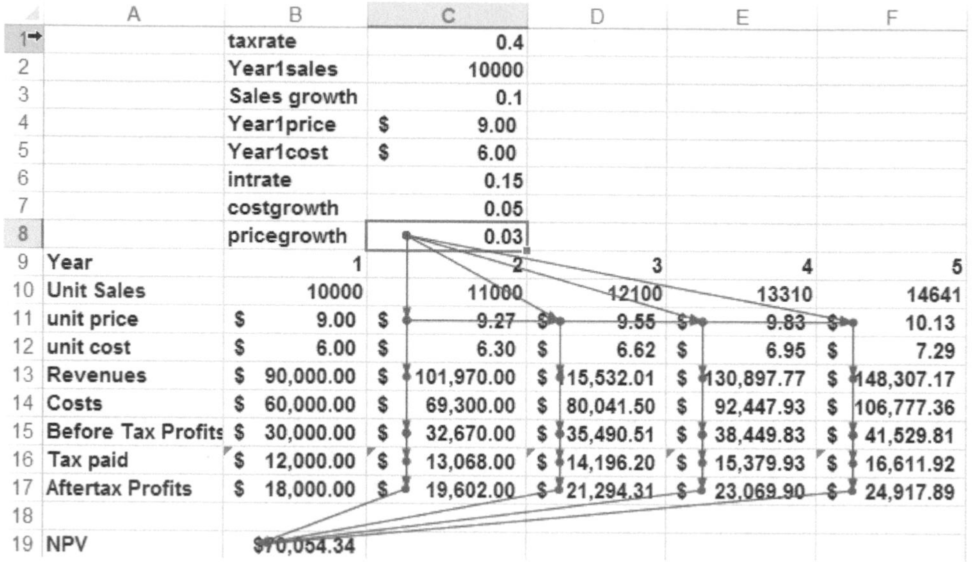

FIGURE 15-7 Clicking Trace Dependents repeatedly shows all the dependents of the price growth assumption.

You can see that in addition to unit price in Years 2–5, the price growth assumption affects Years 2–5 revenue, before-tax profits, tax paid, after-tax profits, and NPV. You can remove the arrows by clicking the Remove Arrows button.

The keystroke combination of CONTROL+] highlights all direct dependents of the active cell in blue; the keystroke combination of CONTROL+SHIFT+] highlights in blue all dependents of the active cell.

I think my financial analyst made an error in computing Year 1 before-tax profit. Which cells in the worksheet model were used for this calculation?

Now you want to find the precedents for cell B15, the cells needed to compute Year 1 before-tax profit. Select cell B15 and then click the **Trace Precedents** button once. You see the arrows shown in Figure 15-8.

As you can see, the cells needed to compute before-tax Year 1 profit directly are Year 1 revenues and Year 1 cost. (Before-tax Year 1 profit equals Year 1 revenue minus Year 1 cost.) Repeatedly clicking the **Trace Precedents** button yields all precedents of Year 1 before-tax profit, as shown in Figure 15-9.

	A	B	C	D	E	F
1		taxrate	0.4			
2		Year1sales	10000			
3		Sales growth	0.1			
4		Year1price	$ 9.00			
5		Year1cost	$ 6.00			
6		intrate	0.15			
7		costgrowth	0.05			
8		pricegrowth	0.03			
9	Year	1	2	3	4	5
10	Unit Sales	10000	11000	12100	13310	14641
11	unit price	$ 9.00	$ 9.27	$ 9.55	$ 9.83	$ 10.13
12	unit cost	$ 6.00	$ 6.30	$ 6.62	$ 6.95	$ 7.29
13	Revenues	$ 90,000.00	$ 101,970.00	$115,532.01	$ 130,897.77	$ 148,307.17
14	Costs	$ 60,000.00	$ 69,300.00	$ 80,041.50	$ 92,447.93	$ 106,777.36
15	Before Tax Profits	$ 30,000.00	32,670.00	$ 35,490.51	$ 38,449.83	$ 41,529.81
16	Tax paid	$ 12,000.00	13,068.00	$ 14,196.20	$ 15,379.93	$ 16,611.92
17	Aftertax Profits	$ 18,000.00	$ 19,602.00	$ 21,294.31	$ 23,069.90	$ 24,917.89

FIGURE 15-8 These are the direct precedents for Year 1 before-tax profit.

	A	B	C	D	E	F
1		taxrate	0.4			
2		Year1sales	10000			
3		Sales growth	0.1			
4		Year1price	$ 9.00			
5		Year1cost	$ 6.00			
6		intrate	0.15			
7		costgrowth	0.05			
8		pricegrowth	0.03			
9	Year	1	2	3	4	5
10	Unit Sales	10000	11000	12100	13310	14641
11	unit price	$ 9.00	$ 9.27	$ 9.55	$ 9.83	$ 10.13
12	unit cost	$ 6.00	$ 6.30	$ 6.62	$ 6.95	$ 7.29
13	Revenues	$ 90,000.00	$ 101,970.00	$ 115,532.01	$ 130,897.77	$ 148,307.17
14	Costs	$ 60,000.00	$ 69,300.00	$ 80,041.50	$ 92,447.93	$ 106,777.36
15	Before Tax Profits	$ 30,000.00	32,670.00	$ 35,490.51	$ 38,449.83	$ 41,529.81
16	Tax paid	$ 12,000.00	13,068.00	$ 14,196.20	$ 15,379.93	$ 16,611.92
17	Aftertax Profits	$ 18,000.00	$ 19,602.00	$ 21,294.31	$ 23,069.90	$ 24,917.89
18						
19	NPV	$70,054.34				

FIGURE 15-9 Click Trace Precedents repeatedly to show all precedents of Year 1 before-tax profit.

Here the only input assumptions that influence Year 1 before-tax profit are Year 1 sales, Year 1 price, and Year 1 cost.

How does the auditing tool work when I'm working with data in more than one worksheet or workbook?

Consider the simple worksheet model in the Audittwosheets.xlsx workbook, shown in Figure 15-10. The formula in the Profit worksheet computes a company's profit (unit sales*(price – variable cost) – fixed cost) from information contained in the Data worksheet.

FIGURE 15-10 This figure shows data for using the auditing tool on multiple worksheets.

Suppose you want to know the precedents of the profit formula. Select cell D7 in the Profit worksheet and then click **Trace Precedents** in the **Formula Auditing** group on the **Formulas** tab. You see a dotted line, an arrow, and the worksheet icon shown in Figure 15-11.

FIGURE 15-11 This is the result of tracing precedents with data on multiple worksheets.

The worksheet icon indicates that the precedents of the profit formula lie in another worksheet. Double-clicking the dotted line opens the Go To dialog box, shown in Figure 15-12.

Now you can click any of the listed precedents (cells D4:D7 in the Data worksheet), and Excel will send you to the precedent you selected.

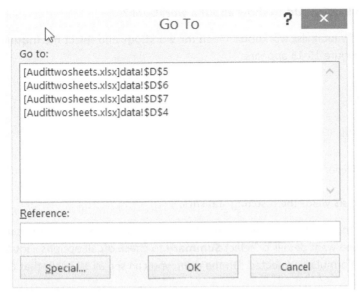

FIGURE 15-12 With the Go To dialog box, you can audit data in multiple worksheets.

What is the new Inquire add-in and how can I install it?

If you own Excel 2013 Professional Plus, you have access to the Inquire add-in, a more sophisticated version of the auditing tool that enables you to:

- Derive many interesting statistics about the current workbook.

- Compare two workbooks to determine how they differ.

- Create a sophisticated diagram of the cells that are precedents or dependents of the current cell.

- Create a sophisticated diagram of the interrelationships between worksheets in the current workbook.

- Clean excess formatting from a workbook.

- List the passwords associated with the workbook.

- To install the Inquire add-in, proceed as follows:

    1. Select **File** on the ribbon and choose **Options**.

    2. Choose **Add-Ins**. Select **COM Add-ins** and click **GO**.

    3. Select **Inquire Add-in** and click **OK**. You should now see the INQUIRE tab on the ribbon.

What information does the Inquire add-in show about a workbook?

Use Inquire to analyze your NPVaudit.xlsx workbook. Open the workbook and select the **Inquire** ribbon tab. The menu shown in Figure 15-13 appears.

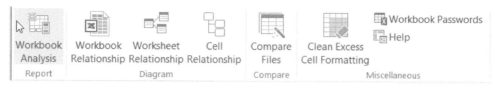

FIGURE 15-13 This is the Inquire menu.

Selecting **Workbook Analysis** yields the resulting statistics.

After selecting Workbook Analysis, the Workbook Analysis Report dialog box opens. You can check any features for which you want details or select **Summary** to check off all options. Figure 15-14 shows the results when Formulas is selected. On the right, you can see all 123 cells that contain formulas in the workbook.

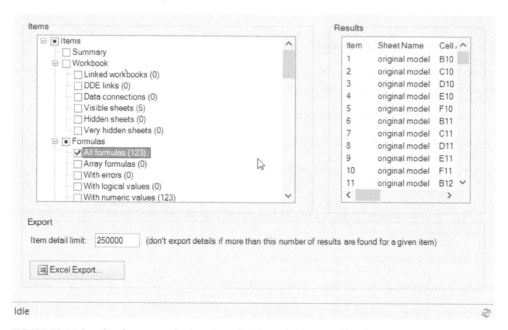

FIGURE 15-14 Inquire shows you the location of all formulas in a workbook.

How does Inquire compare workbooks?

Often, the analyst hands his workbook off to a colleague who makes changes in the workbook. The Inquire add-in makes it easy to compare two workbooks and identify differences between them. To illustrate how Inquire compares workbooks, open the Prodmixtemp.xlsx file. This workbook (which is discussed further in Chapter 29, "Using Solver to determine the optimal product mix") contains data but no formulas, which are needed to determine a profit-maximizing product mix. The Prodmix.xlsx file contains formulas needed to evaluate the product mix. After opening this workbook, the Inquire add-in can be used to compare these workbooks. Select **Compare Files**; you are prompted to list the files you want compared. After selecting the files, you obtain the results shown in Figure 15-15. On the right, the cells in Prodmix.xlsx that were changed are highlighted.

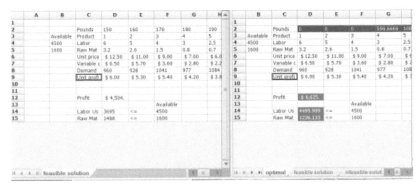

FIGURE 15-15 Inquire compares two workbooks.

How does Inquire show the relationships between cell formulas?

To illustrate how Inquire displays cell relationships, return to the NPVaudit.xlsx file. If you want to look at the cell relationships involving cell B15, place your cursor in cell B15 and select **Cell Relationship**; choose **Trace Both** to display both the dependents and precedents of cell B15. The resulting diagram is shown in Figure 15-16.

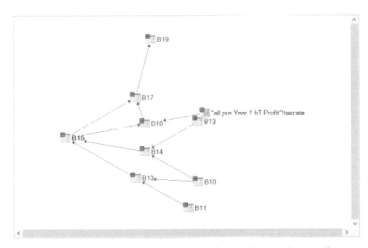

FIGURE 15-16 This figure shows the cell relationships involving cell B15.

How does Inquire show the relationships between worksheets?

When a workbook involves multiple worksheets, it is often difficult to understand how the worksheets are related. The Inquire add-in makes it easy to determine how worksheets are related. To illustrate how Inquire sheds light on the relationship between two worksheets, reopen the Audittwosheetstemp.xlsx file and select **Worksheet Relationships** from the Inquire ribbon tab.

Figure 15-17 shows the results. From Figure 15-17, it is apparent that information from the Data worksheet is needed to compute the results in the Profit worksheet.

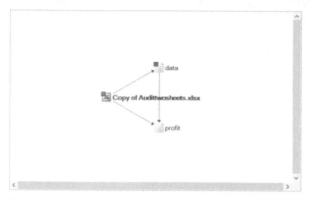

FIGURE 15-17 Inquire shows relationships between worksheets.

Problems

1. In the car NPV example, determine the following:

   - The direct dependents and all dependents of the interest rate

   - The direct dependents and all dependents of the tax rate

   - The direct precedents and all precedents for Year 4 unit sales

   - The direct precedents and all precedents for Year 3 costs

2. For the Prodmix.xlsx file, determine:

   - The precedents of profit.

   - The dependents of amount of Product 1 produced.

3. In the Prodmix.xlsx file, use the Inquire add-in to diagram the dependents of Product 1 produced.

4. In the Prodmix.xlsx file, use the Inquire add-in to diagram the precedents of profit.

CHAPTER 16

Sensitivity analysis with data tables

Questions answered in this chapter:

- I'm thinking of starting a store in the local mall to sell gourmet lemonade. Before opening the store, I'm curious about how my profit, revenue, and variable costs will depend on the price I charge and the unit cost.

- I intend to build a new house. The amount of money I need to borrow (with a 15-year repayment period) depends on the price for which I sell my current house. I'm also unsure about the annual interest rate I'll receive when I close. Can I determine how my monthly payments will depend on the amount borrowed and the annual interest rate?

- A major Internet company is thinking of purchasing another online retailer. The retailer's current annual revenues are $100 million, with expenses of $150 million. Current projections indicate that the retailer's revenues are growing at 25 percent per year, and its expenses are growing at 5 percent per year. You know projections might be in error, however, and would like to know, for a variety of assumptions about annual revenue and expense growth, the number of years before the retailer will show a profit.

Most worksheet models contain assumptions about certain parameters or inputs to the model. In the lemonade example, the inputs include:

- The price for which a glass of lemonade is sold.

- The unit cost of producing a glass of lemonade.

- The sensitivity of demand for lemonade to price charged.

- The annual fixed cost of running a lemonade stand.

Based on input assumptions, you can compute outputs of interest. For the lemonade example, the outputs of interest might include:

- Annual profit.

- Annual revenue.

- Annual variable cost.

Despite best intentions, assumptions about input values can be in error. For example, your best guess about the variable cost of producing a glass of lemonade might be $0.45, but it's possible that your assumption is in error. *Sensitivity analysis* determines how a spreadsheet's outputs vary in response to changes to its inputs. For example, you might want to see how a change in product price affects yearly profit, revenue, and variable cost. With a data table in Microsoft Excel 2013, you can easily vary one or two inputs and perform a sensitivity analysis. With a *one-way* data table, you can determine how changing one input changes any number of outputs. With a *two-way* data table, you can determine how changing two inputs changes a single output. This chapter's three examples show how easy it is to use a data table and obtain meaningful sensitivity results.

Answers to this chapter's questions

This section provides the answers to the questions that are listed at the beginning of the chapter.

I'm thinking of starting a store in the local mall to sell gourmet lemonade. Before opening the store, I'm curious about how my profit, revenue, and variable costs will depend on the price I charge and the unit cost.

The work required for this analysis is in the Lemonade.xlsx file. (See Figure 16-1, Figure 16-2, and Figure 16-4.) The input assumptions are given in the D1:D4 range. Assume that annual demand for lemonade (see the formula in cell D2) equals 65000–9000*price. (Chapter 83, "Estimating a demand curve," contains a discussion of how to estimate a demand curve.) The names created in C1:C7 correspond to cells D1:D7.

Annual revenue was computed in cell D5 with the demand*price formula. In cell D6, the annual variable cost was computed with the unit_cost*demand formula. Finally, in cell D7, profit was computed by using the revenue – fixed_cost – variable_cost formula.

	C	D
1	price	$ 4.00
2	demand	29000
3	unit cost	$ 0.45
4	fixed cost	$ 45,000.00
5	revenue	$ 116,000.00
6	variable cost	$ 13,050.00
7	profit	$ 57,950.00

FIGURE 16-1 These are the inputs that change the profitability of a lemonade store.

Suppose that you want to know how changes in price (for example, from $1.00 through $4.00 in $0.25 increments) affect annual profit, revenue, and variable cost. Because you're changing only one input, a one-way data table will solve the problem. The data table is shown in Figure 16-2.

To set up a one-way data table, begin by listing input values in a column. The prices of interest (ranging from $1.00 through $4.00 in $0.25 increments) are listed in the C11:C23 range. Next, move over one column and up one row from the list of input values, and there the formulas are listed that you want the data table to calculate. The formula for profit is entered in cell D10, the formula for revenue in cell E10, and the formula for variable cost in cell F10.

	C		D	E	F
		profit		revenue	variable cost
0			57950	116000	13050
1	$ 1.00	$	(14,200.00)	$ 56,000.00	$ 25,200.00
2	$ 1.25	$	(2,000.00)	$ 67,187.50	$ 24,187.50
3	$ 1.50	$	9,075.00	$ 77,250.00	$ 23,175.00
4	$ 1.75	$	19,025.00	$ 86,187.50	$ 22,162.50
5	$ 2.00	$	27,850.00	$ 94,000.00	$ 21,150.00
6	$ 2.25	$	35,550.00	$100,687.50	$ 20,137.50
7	$ 2.50	$	42,125.00	$106,250.00	$ 19,125.00
8	$ 2.75	$	47,575.00	$110,687.50	$ 18,112.50
9	$ 3.00	$	51,900.00	$114,000.00	$ 17,100.00
0	$ 3.25	$	55,100.00	$116,187.50	$ 16,087.50
1	$ 3.50	$	57,175.00	$117,250.00	$ 15,075.00
2	$ 3.75	$	58,125.00	$117,187.50	$ 14,062.50
3	$ 4.00	$	57,950.00	$116,000.00	$ 13,050.00

FIGURE 16-2 This is a one-way data table with varying prices.

Now select the table range (C10:F23). The table range begins one row above the first input; its last row is the row containing the last input value. The first column in the table range is the column containing the inputs; its last column is the last column containing an output. After selecting the table range, click the **Data** tab on the ribbon. In the **Data Tools** group, choose **What-If Analysis** and then choose **Data Table**. Now fill in the **Data Table** dialog box as shown in Figure 16-3.

FIGURE 16-3 Create a data table.

For the column input cell, you use the cell in which you want the listed inputs—that is, the values listed in the first column of the data table range—to be assigned. Because the listed inputs are prices, you can choose D1 as the column input cell. After you click **OK**, Excel creates the one-way data table shown in Figure 16-4.

	B	C		D	E	F
1		price	$	4.00		
2		demand		29000		
3		unit cost	$	0.45		
4		fixed cost	$	40,000.00		
5		revenue	$	116,000.00		
6		variable cost	$	13,050.00		
7		profit	$	57,950.00		
8						
9			profit		revenue	variable cost
10	price			57950	116000	13050
11		$	1.00	$ (14,200.00)	$ 56,000.00	$ 25,200.00
12		$	1.25	$ (2,000.00)	$ 67,187.50	$ 24,187.50
13		$	1.50	$ 9,075.00	$ 77,250.00	$ 23,175.00
14		$	1.75	$ 19,025.00	$ 86,187.50	$ 22,162.50
15		$	2.00	$ 27,850.00	$ 94,000.00	$ 21,150.00
16		$	2.25	$ 35,550.00	$ 100,687.50	$ 20,137.50
17		$	2.50	$ 42,125.00	$ 106,250.00	$ 19,125.00
18		$	2.75	$ 47,575.00	$ 110,687.50	$ 18,112.50
19		$	3.00	$ 51,900.00	$ 114,000.00	$ 17,100.00
20		$	3.25	$ 55,100.00	$ 116,187.50	$ 16,087.50
21		$	3.50	$ 57,175.00	$ 117,250.00	$ 15,075.00
22		$	3.75	$ 58,125.00	$ 117,187.50	$ 14,062.50
23		$	4.00	$ 57,950.00	$ 116,000.00	$ 13,050.00

FIGURE 16-4 This is a one-way data table with varying prices.

In the D11:F11 range, profit, revenue, and variable cost are computed for a price of $1.00. In cells D12:F12, profit, revenue, and variable cost are computed for a price of $1.25 and on through the range of prices. The profit-maximizing price among all listed prices is $3.75. A price of $3.75 would produce an annual profit of $58,125.00, annual revenue of $117,187.50, and an annual variable cost of $14,062.50.

Suppose you want to determine how annual profit varies as price varies from $1.50 through $5.00 (in $0.25 increments) and unit cost varies from $0.30 through $0.60 (in $0.05 increments). Because you're changing two inputs here, you need a *two-way* data table. (See Figure 16-5.) List the values for one input down the first column of the table range (use the H11:H25 range for the price values) and the values for the other input in the first row of the table range. (In this example, the I10:O10 range holds the list of unit cost values.) A two-way data table can have only one output cell, and the formula for the output must be placed in the upper-left corner of the table range. Therefore, place the profit formula in cell H10.

	H	I	J	K	L	M	N	O
9		unit cost						
10	57950	$ 0.30	$ 0.35	$ 0.40	$ 0.45	$ 0.50	$ 0.55	$ 0.60
11	$ 1.50	$16,800.00	$14,225.00	$11,650.00	$ 9,075.00	$ 6,500.00	$ 3,925.00	$ 1,350.00
12	$ 1.75	$26,412.50	$23,950.00	$21,487.50	$19,025.00	$16,562.50	$14,100.00	$11,637.50
13	$ 2.00	$34,900.00	$32,550.00	$30,200.00	$27,850.00	$25,500.00	$23,150.00	$20,800.00
14	$ 2.25	$42,262.50	$40,025.00	$37,787.50	$35,550.00	$33,312.50	$31,075.00	$28,837.50
15	$ 2.50	$48,500.00	$46,375.00	$44,250.00	$42,125.00	$40,000.00	$37,875.00	$35,750.00
16	$ 2.75	$53,612.50	$51,600.00	$49,587.50	$47,575.00	$45,562.50	$43,550.00	$41,537.50
17	$ 3.00	$57,600.00	$55,700.00	$53,800.00	$51,900.00	$50,000.00	$48,100.00	$46,200.00
18	$ 3.25	$60,462.50	$58,675.00	$56,887.50	$55,100.00	$53,312.50	$51,525.00	$49,737.50
19	$ 3.50	$62,200.00	$60,525.00	$58,850.00	$57,175.00	$55,500.00	$53,825.00	$52,150.00
20	$ 3.75	$62,812.50	$61,260.00	$59,687.50	$58,125.00	$56,562.50	$55,000.00	$53,437.50
21	$ 4.00	$62,300.00	$60,850.00	$59,400.00	$57,950.00	$56,500.00	$55,050.00	$53,600.00
22	$ 4.25	$60,662.50	$59,325.00	$57,987.50	$56,650.00	$55,312.50	$53,975.00	$52,637.50
23	$ 4.50	$57,900.00	$56,675.00	$55,450.00	$54,225.00	$53,000.00	$51,775.00	$50,550.00
24	$ 4.75	$54,012.50	$52,900.00	$51,787.50	$50,675.00	$49,562.50	$48,450.00	$47,337.50
25	$ 5.00	$49,000.00	$48,000.00	$47,000.00	$46,000.00	$45,000.00	$44,000.00	$43,000.00

FIGURE 16-5 A two-way data table shows profit as a function of price and unit variable cost.

Select the table range (cells H10:O25) and click the **Data** tab. In the **Data Tools** group, choose **What-If Analysis** and then select **Data Table**. Cell D1 (price) is the column input cell, and cell D3 (unit variable cost) is the row input cell. These settings ensure that the values in the first column of the table range are used as prices, and the values in the first row of the table range are used as unit variable costs. After clicking **OK**, you see the two-way data table shown in Figure 16-5. As an example, in cell K19, when you charge $3.50 and the unit variable cost is $0.40, the annual profit equals $58,850.00. For each unit cost, the profit-maximizing price has been highlighted. Note that as the unit cost increases, the profit-maximizing price increases because some of the cost increase is passed on to customers. Of course, you can only guarantee that the profit-maximizing price in the data table is within $0.25 of the actual profit-maximizing price. When you learn about Excel Solver in Chapter 83, you learn how to determine (to the penny) the exact profit-maximizing price.

Here are some other notes on this problem:

- As you change input values in a worksheet, the values calculated by a data table change, too. For example, if you increased fixed cost by $10,000, all profit numbers in the data table would be reduced by $10,000.

- You can't delete or edit a portion of a data table. If you want to save the values in a data table, select the table range, copy the values, and then right-click and select **Paste Special**. Choose **Values** from the **Paste Special** menu. If you take this step, however, changes to your worksheet inputs no longer cause the data table calculations to update.

- When setting up a two-way data table, be careful not to mix up your row and column input cells. A mix-up will cause nonsensical results.

- Most people set their worksheet calculation mode to Automatic. With this setting, any change in your worksheet will cause all your data tables to be recalculated. Usually, you want this, but if your data tables are large, automatic recalculation can be incredibly slow. If the constant recalculation of data tables is slowing your work down, click the **File** tab on the ribbon, choose **Options**, and then click the **Formulas** tab. Select **Automatic Except For Data Tables**. When Automatic Except For Data Tables is selected, all your data tables recalculate only when you press the F9 (recalculation) key. Alternatively, you can click the **Calculation Options** button (in the **Calculation** group on the **Formulas** tab) and then choose **Automatic Except For Data Tables**.

I intend to build a new house. The amount of money I need to borrow (with a 15-year repayment period) depends on the price for which I sell my current house. I'm also unsure about the annual interest rate I'll receive when I close. Can I determine how my monthly payments will depend on the amount borrowed and the annual interest rate?

The real power of data tables becomes evident when you combine a data table with one of the Excel functions. In this example, you use a two-way data table to vary two inputs (the amount borrowed and the annual interest rate) to the Excel *PMT* function and determine how the monthly payment varies as these inputs change. (The *PMT* function is discussed in detail in Chapter 9, "More Excel financial functions.") The work for this example is in the Mortgagedt.xlsx file, shown in Figure 16-6.

Suppose you're borrowing money on a 15-year mortgage, for which monthly payments are made at the end of each month. Input the amount borrowed in cell D2, the number of months in the mortgage (180) in D3, and annual interest rate in D4. Associate the range names in cells C2:C4 with cells D2:D4. Based on these inputs, compute the monthly payment in D5 with the -PMT(Annual_int_rate/12,Number_of_Months,Amt_Borrowed) formula,

	C	D	E	F	G	H	I	J
2	Amt Borrowed	$400,000.00						
3	Number of Months	180						
4	Annual int rate	6%						
5	Monthly Payment	$3,375.43						
6			Annual	Interest	Rate			
7	$3,375.43	5.0%	5.5%	6.0%	6.5%	7.0%	7.5%	8.0%
8	$ 300,000.00	$2,372.38	$2,451.25	$2,531.57	$2,613.32	$2,696.48	$2,781.04	$2,866.96
9	$ 350,000.00	$2,767.78	$2,859.79	$2,953.50	$3,048.88	$3,145.90	$3,244.54	$3,344.78
10	$ 400,000.00	$3,163.17	$3,268.33	$3,375.43	$3,484.43	$3,595.31	$3,708.05	$3,822.61
11	$ 450,000.00	$3,558.57	$3,676.88	$3,797.36	$3,919.98	$4,044.73	$4,171.56	$4,300.43
12	$ 500,000.00	$3,953.97	$4,085.42	$4,219.28	$4,355.54	$4,494.14	$4,635.06	$4,778.26
13	$ 550,000.00	$4,349.36	$4,493.96	$4,641.21	$4,791.09	$4,943.56	$5,098.57	$5,256.09
14	$ 600,000.00	$4,744.76	$4,902.50	$5,063.14	$5,226.64	$5,392.97	$5,562.07	$5,733.91
15	$ 650,000.00	$5,140.16	$5,311.04	$5,485.07	$5,662.20	$5,842.38	$6,025.58	$6,211.74

FIGURE 16-6 You can use a data table to determine how mortgage payments vary as the amount borrowed and the interest rate change.

You think that the amount borrowed will range (depending on the price for which you sell your current house) between $300,000 and $650,000 and that your annual interest rate will range between 5 percent and 8 percent. In preparation for creating a data table, enter the amounts borrowed in the C8:C15 range and possible interest rate values in the D7:J7 range. Cell C7 contains the output you want to recalculate for various input combinations. Therefore, set cell C7 equal to cell D5. Select the table range (C7:J15), choose **What-If Analysis** on the **Data** tab, and then select **Data Table**. Because numbers in the first column of the table range are amounts borrowed, the column input cell is D2. Numbers in the first row of the table are annual interest rates, so your row input cell is D4. After you click **OK**, you see the data table shown in Figure 16-6. This table shows, for example, that if you borrow $400,000 at an annual rate of 6 percent, your monthly payments would be just over $3,375. The data table also shows that at a low interest rate (for example, 5 percent), an increase of $50,000 in the amount borrowed raises the monthly payment by around $395, whereas at a high interest rate (such as 8 percent), an increase of $50,000 in the amount borrowed raises the monthly payment by about $478.

A major Internet company is thinking of purchasing another online retailer. The retailer's current annual revenues are $100 million, with expenses of $150 million. Current projections indicate that the retailer's revenues are growing at 25 percent per year, and its expenses are growing at 5 percent per year. You know projections might be in error, however, and would like to know, for a variety of assumptions about annual revenue and expense growth, the number of years before the retailer will show a profit.

You want to determine the number of years needed to break even, using annual growth rates in revenue from 10 percent through 50 percent and annual expense growth rates from 2 percent through 20 percent. Assume also that if the firm cannot break even in 13 years, you'll say it cannot break even. Your work is in the Bezos.xlsx file, shown in Figure 16-7 and Figure 16-8.

Hide columns A and B and rows 16–18. To hide columns A and B, first select any cells in columns A and B (or select the column headings) and then click the **Home** tab. In the **Cells** group, click **Format**, point to **Hide & Unhide**, and select **Hide Columns**. To hide rows 16–18, select any cells in those rows (or select the row headings) and repeat the previous procedure, selecting **Hide Rows**. The Format Visibility options also include Unhide Rows and Unhide Columns. If you receive a worksheet with many hidden rows and columns and want to display all of them quickly, you can select the entire worksheet by clicking the **Select All** button at the intersection of the column and row headings. Now selecting Unhide Rows or Unhide Columns will display all hidden rows or columns in the worksheet.

In row 11, project the firm's revenue out 13 years (based on the annual revenue growth rate assumed in E7) by copying the E11*(1+$E$7) formula from F11 to G11:R11. In row 12, project the firm's expenses out 13 years (based on the annual expense growth rate assumed in E8) by copying the E12*(1+$E$8) formula from F12 to G12:R12. (See Figure 16-7.)

	C	D	E	F	G	H	P	Q	R
7	Revenue	1E+08	0.25						
8	Expenses	1.50E+08	0.05						
9									
10			0	1	2	3	11	12	13
11	Revenue:	1E+08	1.25E+08	1.56E+08	1.95E+08	1.16E+09	1.46E+09	1.82E+09
12	Expenses	2E+08	1.58E+08	1.65E+08	1.74E+08	2.57E+08	2.69E+08	2.83E+08
13	Breakeven		0	0	3	0	0	0
14									
15	Total	3							

FIGURE 16-7 You can use a data table to calculate how many years it will take to break even.

You would like to use a two-way data table to determine how varying the growth rates for revenues and expenses affects the years needed to break even. You need one cell whose value always tells you the number of years needed to break even. Because you can break even during any of the next 13 years, this might seem like a tall order.

Begin by using an IF statement for each year in row 13 to determine whether you break even during the year. The IF statement returns the number of the year if you break even during the year or 0 otherwise. Determine the year you break even in cell E15 by adding all the numbers in row 13. Finally, you can use cell E15 as the output cell for a two-way data table.

Copy the IF(AND(E11<E12,F11>F12),F10,0) formula from cell F13 to G13:R13. This formula shows that you break even for the first time during a year if, and only if, during the previous year, revenues are less than expenses and, during the current year, revenues are greater than expenses. If this is the case, the year number is entered in row 13; otherwise, 0 is entered.

Now, in cell E15, you can determine the break even year (if any) with the IF(SUM(F13:R13)>0,SUM (F13:R13),"No BE") formula. If you do not break even during the next 13 years, the formula returns the "No BE" text string.

Now, enter the annual revenue growth rates (10 percent through 50 percent) in the E21:E61 range. Enter annual expense growth rates (2 percent to 20 percent) in the F20:X20 range. Ensure that the year-of-break even formula is copied to cell E20 with the =E15 formula. Select the E20:X61 table range, click **What-If Analysis** on the **Data** tab, and then choose **Data Table**. Select cell E7 (revenue growth rate) as the column input cell and cell E8 (expense growth rate) as the row input cell. With these settings, you obtain the two-way data table shown in Figure 16-8.

	D	E	F	G	H	P	Q	R	S	T	U	V	W	X
19				Expense	Growth									
20			3	0.02	0.03	0.04	0.12	0.13	0.14	0.15	0.16	0.17	0.18	0.19	0.2
21			0.1	6	7	8 No BE	No BE	No BE	No BE No BE	No BE	No BE	No BE No BE		
22	Revenue	0.11	5	6	7 No BE	No BE	No BE	No BE No BE	No BE	No BE	No BE No BE		
23	growth	0.12	5	5	6 No BE	No BE	No BE	No BE No BE	No BE	No RF	No BE		
24			0.13	4	5	5 No BE	No BE	No BE	No BE No BE	No BE	No BE	No BE No BE		
25			0.14	4	4	5 No BE	No BE	No BE	No BE No BE	No BE	No BE	No BE No BE		
55			0.44	2	2	2	2	2	2	2	2	3	3	3
56			0.45	2	2	2	2	2	2	2	2	3	3	3
57			0.46	2	2	2	2	2	2	2	2	2	2	3
58			0.47	2	2	2	?	2	2	2	2	2	2	2
59			0.48	2	2	2	2	2	2	2	2	2	2	2
60			0.49	2	2	2	2	2	2	2	2	2	2	2
61			0.5	2	2	2	2	2	2	2	2	2	2	2

FIGURE 16-8 This figure shows a two-way data table.

Note, for example, that if expenses grow at 4 percent a year, a 10-percent annual growth in revenue will result in breaking even in eight years, whereas a 50-percent annual growth in revenue will result in breaking even in only two years! Also note that if expenses grow at 12 percent per year and revenues grow at 14 percent per year, you will not break even by the end of 13 years.

Problems

1. You've been assigned to analyze the profitability of Bill Clinton's autobiography. The following assumptions have been made:

   - Bill is receiving a one-time royalty payment of $12 million.

   - The fixed cost of producing the hardcover version of the book is $1 million.

   - The variable cost of producing each hardcover book is $4.

   - The publisher's net from book sales per hardcover unit sold is $15.

   - The publisher expects to sell 1 million hardcover copies.

   - The fixed cost of producing the paperback is $100,000.

   - The variable cost of producing each paperback book is $1.

   - The publisher's net from book sales per paperback unit sold is $4.

   - Paperback sales will be double hardcover sales.

   Use this information to answer the following questions:

   - How will the publisher's before-tax profit vary as hardcover sales vary from 100,000 through 1 million copies?

   - How does the publisher's before-tax profit vary as hardcover sales vary from 100,000 through 1 million copies and the ratio of paperback sales to hardcover sales varies from 1 through 2.4?

2. The annual demand for a product equals $500 - 3p + 10a.5$ where p is the price of the product in dollars and a is hundreds of dollars spent on advertising the product. The annual fixed cost of selling the product is $10,000, and the unit variable cost of producing the product is $12. Determine a price (within $10) and amount of advertising (within $100) that maximizes profit.

3. Reconsider your hedging example from Chapter 11, "IF statements." For stock prices in six months that range from $20 through $65 and the number of puts purchased varies from 0 through 100 (in increments of 10), determine the percentage return on your portfolio.

4. For your mortgage example, suppose you know the annual interest rate will be 5.5 percent. Create a table that shows the difference in payments among a 15-year, 20-year, and 30-year mortgage for amounts borrowed from $300,000 through $600,000 (in $50,000 increments).

5. Currently, you sell 40,000 units of a product for $45 each. The unit variable cost of producing the product is $5. You are thinking of cutting the product price by 30 percent. You are sure this will increase sales by an amount from 10 percent through 50 percent. Perform a sensitivity analysis to show how profit will change as a function of the percentage increase in sales. Ignore fixed costs.

6. Assume that at the end of each of the next 40 years, you put the same amount in your retirement fund and earn the same interest rate each year. Show how the amount of money you will have at retirement changes as you vary your annual contribution from $5,000 through $25,000 and the rate of interest varies from 3 percent through 15 percent.

7. The *payback period* for a project is the number of years needed for a project's future profits to pay back the project's initial investment. A project requires a $300 million investment at Time 0. The project yields profit for 10 years, and Time 1 cash flow will be between $30 million and $100 million. Annual cash flow growth will be from 5 percent through 25 percent a year. How does the project payback depend on the Year 1 cash flow and cash flow growth rates?

8. A software development company is thinking of translating a software product into Swahili. Currently, 200,000 units of the product are sold per year at a price of $100 each. Unit variable cost is $20. The fixed cost of translation is $5 million. Translating the product into Swahili will increase sales during each of the next three years by some unknown percentage over the current level of 200,000 units. Show how the change in profit resulting from the translation depends on the percentage increase in product sales. You can ignore the time value of money and taxes in your calculations.

9. The Citydistances.xlsx file gives latitude and longitude for several US cities. It also has a formula that determines the distance between two cities by using a given latitude and longitude. Create a table that computes the distance between any pair of cities listed.

10. You have begun saving for your child's college education. You plan to save $5,000 per year and want to know the amount of money you will have in the college fund for annual rates of return on your investment from 4 percent through 12 percent after saving for 10–15 years.

11. If you earn interest at percentage rate r per year and compound your interest n times per year, then in y years, $1 will grow to $(1 + (r/n))^{ny}$ dollars. Assuming a 10 percent annual interest rate, create a table showing the factor by which $1 will grow in 5–15 years for daily, monthly, quarterly, and semiannual compounding.

12. Assume you have $100 in the bank. Each year, you withdraw x percent (ranging from 4 percent through 10 percent) of your original balance. For annual growth rates of 3 percent through 10 percent per year, determine how many years it will take before you run out of money. Hint: You should use the *IFERROR* function (discussed in Chapter 11) because if your annual growth rate exceeds the withdrawal rate, you will never run out of money.

13. If you earn interest at an annual rate of x percent per year, in n years, $1 will become $(1 + x)^n$ dollars. For annual rates of interest from 1 percent through 20 percent, determine exactly when (in years) $1 will double.

14. You are borrowing $200,000 and making payments at the end of each month. For an annual interest rate ranging from 5 percent through 10 percent and loan durations of 10, 15, 20, 25, and 30 years, determine the total interest paid on the loan.

15. You are saving for your child's college fund. You will contribute the same amount of money to the fund at the end of each year. Your goal is to end up with $100,000. For annual investment returns ranging from 4 percent through 15 percent and number of years investing varying from 5–15 years, determine your required annual contribution.

16. The Antitrustdata.xlsx file gives the starting and ending years for many court cases. Determine the number of court cases active during each year.

17. You can retire at age 62 and receive $8,000 per year or retire at age 65 and receive $10,000 per year. What is the difference (in today's dollars) between these two choices as you vary the annual rate at which you discount cash flows between 2 percent and 10 percent and vary age of death between 70 and 84?

CHAPTER 17

The Goal Seek command

Questions answered in this chapter:

- For a given price, how many glasses of lemonade does a lemonade store need to sell per year to break even?

- We want to pay off our mortgage in 15 years. The annual interest rate is 6 percent. The bank told us we can afford monthly payments of $2,000. How much can we borrow?

- I always had trouble with story problems in high school algebra. Can Excel make solving story problems easier?

The Goal Seek feature in Microsoft Excel 2013 enables you to compute a value for a worksheet input that makes the value of a given formula match the goal you specify. For example, in the lemonade store example in Chapter 16, "Sensitivity analysis with data tables," suppose you have fixed overhead costs, fixed per-unit costs, and a fixed sales price. Given this information, you can use Goal Seek to calculate the number of glasses of lemonade you need to sell to break even. Essentially, Goal Seek embeds a powerful equation solver in your worksheet. To use Goal Seek, you need to provide Excel with three pieces of information:

- **Set Cell**   Specifies that the cell contains the formula that calculates the information you're seeking. In the lemonade example, Set Cell would contain the formula for profit.

- **To Value**   Specifies the numerical value for the goal that's calculated in Set Cell. In the lemonade example, because you want to determine the sales volume that represents the break-even point, To Value would be 0.

- **By Changing Cell**   Specifies the input cell that Excel changes until Set Cell calculates the goal defined in the To Value cell. In the lemonade example, By Changing Cell would contain annual lemonade sales.

Answers to this chapter's questions

This section provides the answers to the questions that are listed at the beginning of the chapter.

For a given price, how many glasses of lemonade does a lemonade store need to sell per year to break even?

The work for this section is in the Lemonadegs.xlsx file, which is shown in Figure 17-1. As in Chapter 16, assume an annual fixed cost of $45,000.00 and a variable unit cost of $0.45. Assume a price of $3.00. The question is how many glasses of lemonade do you need to sell each year to break even.

	C	D
1	price	$ 3.00
2	demand	17647.05882
3	unit cost	$ 0.45
4	fixed cost	$ 45,000.00
5	revenue	$ 52,941.18
6	variable cost	$ 7,941.18
7	profit	$ -

FIGURE 17-1 Use this data to set up the Goal Seek feature to perform a break-even analysis.

To start, insert any number for demand in cell D2. In the **What-If Analysis** group on the **Data** tab, click **Goal Seek**. Now fill in the Goal Seek dialog box as shown in Figure 17-2.

FIGURE 17-2 The Goal Seek dialog box is filled in with entries for a break-even analysis.

The dialog box indicates that you want to change cell D2 (annual demand, or sales) until cell D7 (profit) hits a value of 0. After you click **OK**, you get the result that's shown in Figure 17-1. If you sell approximately 17,647 glasses of lemonade per year (or 48 glasses per day), you'll break even. To find the value you're seeking, Excel varies the demand in cell D2 (alternating between high and low values) until it finds a value that makes profit equal $0. If a problem has more than one solution, Goal Seek will still display only one answer.

We want to pay off our mortgage in 15 years. The annual interest rate is 6 percent. The bank told us we can afford monthly payments of $2,000. How much can we borrow?

You can begin to answer this question by setting up a worksheet to compute the monthly payments on a 15-year loan (assume payments at the end of the month) as a function of the annual interest rate and a trial loan amount. Look at the work done in the Paymentgs.xlsx file and in Figure 17-3.

In cell E6, the $-PMT$(annual_int_rate/12,years,amt._borrowed) formula computes the monthly payment associated with the amount borrowed, which is listed in cell E5. Filling in the Goal Seek dialog box as shown in Figure 17-4 calculates the amount borrowed that results in monthly payments equal to $2,000. With a limit of $2,000 for monthly payments, you can borrow up to $237,007.03.

	D	E
1		
2		
3	Years	180
4	Annual int rate	0.06
5	Amount borrowed	$ 237,007.03
6	Monthly payment	$2,000.00

FIGURE 17-3 You can use data such as this with the Goal Seek feature to determine the amount you can borrow based on a set monthly payment.

FIGURE 17-4 The Goal Seek dialog box is set up to calculate the mortgage example.

I always had trouble with story problems in high school algebra. Can Excel make solving story problems easier?

If you think back to high school algebra, most story problems required you to choose a variable (it was usually called x) that solved a particular equation. Goal Seek is an equation solver, so it's perfectly suited to solving story problems. Here's a typical high school algebra problem:

> *Maria and Edmund have a lover's quarrel while honeymooning in Seattle. Maria storms into her Mazda Miata and drives 64 miles per hour toward her mother's home in Los Angeles. Two hours after Maria leaves, Edmund jumps into his BMW in hot pursuit, driving 80 miles per hour. How many miles will each person have traveled when Edmund catches Maria?*

You can find the solution in the Maria.xlsx file, shown in Figure 17-5.

	C	D
1		
2	Time Maria drives	10
3	Maria speed	64
4	Time Edmund drives	8
5	Edmund speed	80
6	Maria distance	640
7	Edmund distance	640
8	Difference	0

FIGURE 17-5 Goal Seek can help you solve story problems.

Set Cell will be the difference between the distances Maria and Edmund have traveled. You can set this to a value of *0* by changing the number of hours Maria drives. Of course, Edmund drives two hours less than Maria.

Enter a trial number of hours that Maria drives in cell D2. Associate the range names in the C2:C8 cell range with cells D2:D8. Because Edmund drives two fewer hours than Maria, enter the Time_Maria_drives–2 formula in cell D4. In cells D6 and D7, use the fact that *distance = speed*time* to compute the total distance Maria and Edmund travel. The difference between the distances is computed in cell D8 with the Maria_distance–Edmund_distance formula. Now you can fill in the Goal Seek dialog box as shown in Figure 17-6.

FIGURE 17-6 The Goal Seek dialog box is filled in to solve an algebra story problem.

Change Maria's hours of driving (cell D2) until the difference between the miles each travels (cell D8) equals 0. As you can see, after Maria drives 10 hours and Edmund 8 hours, they will each have driven a distance of 640 miles.

Problems

1. From Problem 1 in Chapter 16, determine how many hardcover books must be sold to break even.

2. From the car net present value (NPV) example in Chapter 15, "The auditing tool and Inquire add-in," by what rate do annual sales need to grow for total NPV to equal $1 million?

3. What value of Year 1 unit cost would increase your NPV in the car example in Chapter 15 to $1 million?

4. In your mortgage example, suppose you need to borrow $200,000 for 15 years. If your maximum payments are limited to $2,000 per month, how high an annual interest rate can you tolerate?

5. How could you use Goal Seek to determine a project's internal rate of return (IRR)?

6. At the end of each of the next 40 years, you will put $20,000 in your retirement fund. What rate of return on your investments do you need to have $2 million available for retirement in 40 years?

7. You expect to earn 10 percent per year on your retirement investments. At the end of each of the next 40 years, you want to put the same amount of money in your retirement portfolio. How much money do you need to put in each year to have $2 million in your account when you retire?

8. Consider two projects with the following cash flows:

	Year 1	Year 2	Year 3	Year 4
Project 1	−$1,000	$400	$350	$400
Project 2	−$900	$100	$100	$1,000

For what rate of interest will Project 1 have a larger NPV? (Hint: Find the interest rate that makes both projects have the same NPV.)

9. You are managing a conference at your college. Your fixed costs are $15,000. You must pay the 10 speakers $700 each and the college union $300 per conference participant for food and lodging costs. You are charging each conference participant who is not also a speaker $900, which includes the conference fee and food and lodging costs. How many paid registrants need to attend for you to break even?

10. You are buying 40 pounds of candy. Some of the candy sells for $10 per pound, and some sells for $6 per pound. How much candy at each price should you buy to result in an average cost of $7 per pound?

11. Three electricians are wiring your new home. Electrician 1 by himself will need 11 days to do the job. Electrician 2 by himself will need 5 days to do the job. Electrician 3 by herself will need 9 days to do the job. If all three electricians work on the job, how long will the job take to complete?

12. To celebrate the Lewis and Clark expedition, you are traveling 40 miles upstream and then 40 miles downstream in a canoe. The speed of the river current is 5 miles per hour. If the trip takes you 5 hours total, how fast do you travel if the river has no current?

13. In the NPV.xlsx file in Chapter 7, "Evaluating investments by using net present value criteria," you found that for high interest rates, Project 1 has a larger NPV and, for small interest rates, Project 2 has a larger NPV. For what interest rate would the two projects have the same NPV?

CHAPTER 18

Using the Scenario Manager for sensitivity analysis

Question answered in this chapter:

- I'd like to create best, worst, and most likely scenarios for a firm's sales of an automobile model by varying the values of Year 1 sales, annual sales growth, and Year 1 sales price. Data tables for sensitivity analysis enable me to vary only one or two inputs, so I can't use a data table. Does Excel have a tool I can use to vary more than two inputs in a sensitivity analysis?

You can use the Scenario Manager to perform sensitivity analysis by varying as many as 32 input cells. With the Scenario Manager, you first define the set of input cells you want to vary. Name your scenario and enter the value of each input cell for each scenario. Finally, select the output cells (also called *result cells*) that you want to track. The Scenario Manager then creates a beautiful report containing the inputs and the values of the output cells for each scenario.

Answer to this chapter's question

This section provides the answer to the question that is listed at the beginning of the chapter.

I'd like to create best, worst, and most likely scenarios for a firm's sales of an automobile model by varying the values of Year 1 sales, annual sales growth, and Year 1 sales price. Data tables for sensitivity analysis enable me to vary only one or two inputs, so I can't use a data table. Does Excel have a tool I can use to vary more than two inputs in a sensitivity analysis?

Suppose you want to create the following three scenarios related to the net present value (NPV) of a car, using the example in Chapter 15, "The Auditing tool and Inquire add-in."

	Year 1 sales	Annual sales growth	Year 1 sales price
Best case	$20,000	20%	$10.00
Most likely case	$10,000	10%	$7.50
Worst case	$5,000	2%	$5.00

For each scenario, you want to look at the firm's NPV and each year's after-tax profit. The work is in the NPVauditscenario.xlsx file. Figure 18-1 shows the worksheet model (contained in the Original

Model worksheet), and Figure 18-2 shows the scenario report (contained in the Scenario Summary worksheet).

	A	B	C	D	E	F
1		taxrate	0.4			
2		Year1sales	12000			
3		Sales growth	0.05			
4		Year1price	$ 7.50			
5		Year1cost	$ 6.00			
6		intrate	0.15			
7		costgrowth	0.05			
8		pricegrowth	0.03			
9	Year	1	2	3	4	5
10	Unit Sales	12000	12600	13230	13891.5	14586.075
11	unit price	$ 7.50	$ 7.73	$ 7.96	$ 8.20	$ 8.44
12	unit cost	$ 6.00	$ 6.30	$ 6.62	$ 6.95	$ 7.29
13	Revenues	$ 90,000.00	$ 97,335.00	$ 105,267.80	$ 113,847.13	$ 123,125.67
14	Costs	$ 72,000.00	$ 79,380.00	$ 87,516.45	$ 96,486.89	$ 106,376.79
15	Before Tax Profit	$ 18,000.00	$ 17,955.00	$ 17,751.35	$ 17,360.24	$ 16,748.88
16	Tax	$ 7,200.00	$ 7,182.00	$ 7,100.54	$ 6,944.10	$ 6,699.55
17	Aftertax Profits	$ 10,800.00	$ 10,773.00	$ 10,650.81	$ 10,416.15	$ 10,049.33
18						
19	NPV	$35,492.08				

FIGURE 18-1 This is the data on which the scenarios are based.

	A	B	C	D	E	F	G
2		Scenario Summary					
3				Current Values	Best	Most Likely	Worst
5		Changing Cells:					
6			Year1sales	12000	20000	10000	5000
7			Sales_growth	0.05	0.2	0.1	0.02
8			Year1price	$ 7.50	$ 10.00	$ 7.50	$ 5.00
9		Result Cells:					
10			$B$17	$ 10,800.00	$ 48,000.00	$ 9,000.00	$ (3,000.00)
11			$C$17	$ 10,773.00	$ 57,600.00	$ 9,405.00	$ (3,519.00)
12			$D$17	$ 10,650.81	$ 69,016.32	$ 9,741.10	$ (4,090.33)
13			$E$17	$ 10,416.15	$ 82,560.80	$ 9,980.12	$ (4,718.50)
14			$F$17	$ 10,049.33	$ 98,588.50	$ 10,087.17	$ (5,408.35)
15			$B$19	$35,492.08	$226,892.87	$32,063.83	($13,345.75)
16		Notes: Current Values column represents values of changing cells at					
17		time Scenario Summary Report was created. Changing cells for each					
18		scenario are highlighted in gray.					

FIGURE 18-2 This is the scenario summary report.

To begin defining the best-case scenario, click the **Data** tab and then choose **Scenario Manager** in the **What-If Analysis** menu in the **Data Tools** group. Click the **Add** button and fill in the **Add Scenario** dialog box as shown in Figure 18-3.

FIGURE 18-3 These are the data inputs for the best-case scenario.

Enter a name for the scenario (**Best**) and select C2:C4 as the input cells containing the values that define the scenario. After you click **OK** in the **Add Scenario** dialog box, fill in the **Scenario Values** dialog box with the input values that define the best case, as shown in Figure 18-4.

FIGURE 18-4 Define the input values for the best-case scenario.

When you click **Add** in the **Scenario Values** dialog box, you can enter the data for the most-likely and worst-case scenarios. After entering data for all three scenarios, click **OK** in the **Scenario Values** dialog box. The **Scenario Manager** dialog box, shown in Figure 18-5, lists the scenarios you created. When you click **Summary** in the **Scenario Manager** dialog box, you can choose the result cells that will be displayed in scenario reports. Figure 18-6 shows how you indicated that you want the scenario summary report in the Scenario Summary dialog box to track each year's after-tax profit (cells B17:F17) as well as total NPV (cell B19).

FIGURE 18-5 The Scenario Manager dialog box displays each scenario you define.

FIGURE 18-6 Use the Scenario Summary dialog box to select the result cells for the summary report.

Because the result cells come from more than one range, you can separate the B17:F17 and B19 ranges with a comma. (You could also have pressed the Ctrl key to select and enter multiple ranges.) After selecting **Scenario Summary** (instead of PivotTable), click **OK**, and Excel creates the beautiful

Scenario Summary report pictured earlier, in Figure 18-2. Notice that Excel includes a column, labeled Current Values, for the values that were originally placed in the worksheet. The worst case loses money (a loss of $13,345.75), whereas the best case is quite profitable (a profit of $226,892.67). Because the worst-case price is less than your variable cost, the worst case loses money in each year.

Remarks

- Scenario PivotTable Report in the Scenario Summary dialog box presents the scenario results in a PivotTable format.

- Suppose you select a scenario in the Scenario Manager dialog box and then click the **Show** button. The input cells' values for the selected scenario then appear in the worksheet, and Excel recalculates all formulas. This tool is great for presenting a slide show of your scenarios.

- It's hard to create a lot of scenarios with the Scenario Manager because you need to input each individual scenario's values. Monte Carlo simulation (see Chapter 73, "Introduction to Monte Carlo simulation") makes it easy to create many scenarios. When you use the Monte Carlo simulation method, you can find information such as the probability that the NPV of a project's cash flows is nonnegative—an important measure because it is the probability that the project adds value to the company.

- Clicking the minus (–) sign in row 5 of the Scenario Summary report hides the Assumption cells and shows only results. Clicking the plus (+) sign restores the full report.

- Suppose you send a file to several people, and each adds his own scenarios. After each person returns the file containing the scenarios to you, you can merge all the scenarios into one workbook by opening each person's version of the workbook, clicking the **Merge** button in the **Scenario Manager** dialog box in the original workbook, and then selecting the workbooks containing the scenarios you want to merge. Excel merges the selected scenarios in the original workbook.

Problems

1. Delete the best-case scenario and run another scenario report.

2. Add a scenario named High Price, in which Year 1 price equals $15, and the other two inputs remain at their most-likely values.

3. For the lemonade stand example in Chapter 16, "Sensitivity analysis with data tables," use the Scenario Manager to display a report summarizing profit for the following scenarios:

Scenario	Price	Unit cost	Fixed cost
High cost/high price	$5.00	$1.00	$65,000.00
Medium cost/medium price	$4.00	$0.75	$45,000.00
Low cost/low price	$2.50	$0.40	$25,000.00

For the mortgage payment example in Chapter 16, use the Scenario Manager to create a report tabulating monthly payments for the following scenarios:

Scenario	Amount borrowed	Annual rate	Number of monthly payments
Lowest payment	$300,000	4%	360
Most-likely payment	$400,000	6%	240
Highest payment	$550,000	8%	180

CHAPTER 19

The COUNTIF, COUNTIFS, COUNT, COUNTA, and COUNTBLANK functions

Questions answered in this chapter:

■ Suppose I have a list of songs that were played on the radio. For each song, I know the singer, the date the song was played, and the length of the song. How can I answer questions such as these about the songs in the list:

- How many were sung by each singer?

- How many were not sung by my favorite singer?

- How many were at least four minutes long?

- How many were longer than the average length of all songs on the list?

- How many were sung by singers whose last names begin with S?

- How many were sung by singers whose last names contain exactly six letters?

- How many were played after June 15, 2005?

- How many were played before 2009?

- How many were exactly four minutes long?

- How many were sung by my favorite singer and were exactly four minutes long?

- How many were sung by my favorite singer and were three to four minutes long?

■ In a more general context, how can I perform operations such as the following:

- Count the number of cells in a range containing numbers.

- Count the number of blank cells in a range.

- Count the number of nonblank cells in a range.

You often need to count the number of cells in a range that meet a given criterion. For example, if a worksheet contains information about makeup sales, you might want to count the number of sales transactions made by the salesperson named Jennifer or the number of sales transactions that occurred after June 10. The *COUNTIF* function enables you to count the number of cells, in a range that meet criteria that are defined based on one row or column of the worksheet.

The syntax of the *COUNTIF* function is COUNTIF(range,criterion):

- Range is the range of cells in which you want to count cells meeting a given criterion.

- Criterion is a number, date, or expression that determines whether to count a given cell in the range.

The syntax of *COUNTIFS* is COUNTIFS(range1,criterion1,range2,criterion2,...,range_n,criterion_n).

COUNTIFS counts the number of rows for which the range1 entry meets criterion1, the range2 entry meets criterion2, the range_n entry meets criterion_n, and so on. Thus, *COUNTIFS* allows the criteria to involve more than one column or multiple conditions in one column. Other functions that allow for multiple criteria are discussed in Chapter 20, "The *SUMIF, AVERAGEIF, SUMIFS*, and *AVERAGEIFS* functions," and Chapter 48, "Summarizing data with database statistical functions."

The key to using the *COUNTIF* function (and similar functions) successfully is understanding the wide variety of criteria that Microsoft Excel accepts. The types of criteria you can use are best explained through the use of examples. In addition to examples of the *COUNTIF* function, this chapter provides examples of the *COUNT, COUNTA,* and *COUNTBLANK* functions:

- The *COUNT* function counts the number of cells in a range containing numbers.

- The *COUNTA* function counts the number of nonblank cells in a range.

- The *COUNTBLANK* function counts the number of blank cells in a range.

As an illustration of how to use these functions, consider a database (Rock.xlsx file) that gives the following information for each song played on radio station WKRP:

- The singer

- The date the song was played

- The length of the song

Figure 19-1 shows a subset of the data.

	D	E	F	G
6	Song Number	Singer	Date	Minutes
7	1	Eminem	5/21/2004	4
8	2	Eminem	4/15/2004	2
9	3	Cher	1/28/2005	2
10	4	Eminem	1/28/2005	4
11	5	Moore	11/5/2004	2
12	6	Cher	9/18/2004	4
13	7	Spears	4/15/2004	3
14	8	Spears	3/17/2005	3
15	9	Manilow	1/16/2005	4
16	10	Eminem	4/10/2005	4
17	11	Madonna	2/15/2004	3
18	12	Eminem	1/10/2004	4
19	13	Springsteen	4/10/2005	2
20	14	Spears	4/15/2004	4
21	15	Moore	7/8/2004	3
22	16	Madonna	6/26/2004	4
23	17	Spears	5/28/2005	3
24	18	Mellencamp	7/27/2005	5
25	19	Spears	9/18/2004	5
26	20	Madonna	7/8/2004	4

FIGURE 19-1 This is the song database used for the *COUNTIF* examples.

Answers to this chapter's questions

This section provides the answers to the questions that are listed at the beginning of the chapter.

How many songs were sung by each singer?

To begin, select the first row of the database, the D6:G6 range. Select the whole database by pressing Ctrl+Shift+down arrow. In the **Defined Names** group on the **Formulas** tab, click **Create From Selection** and then choose **Top Row**. This names the D7:D957 range Song Numb, the E7:E957 range Singer, the F7:F957 range Date, and the G7:G957 range Minutes. To determine how many songs were sung by each singer, copy the COUNTIF(Singer,B5) formula from C5 to C6:C12. In cell C5, this formula now displays the number of cells in the Singer range that match the value in B5 (Eminem). The database contains 114 songs sung by Eminem. Similarly, Cher sang 112 songs, and so on, as you can see in Figure 19-2. You could also have found the number of songs sung by Eminem with the COUNTIF(Singer,"Eminem") formula. Note that you must enclose text such as Eminem in quotation marks ("") and that criteria are not case sensitive.

	B	C
2	count	9
3	counta	18
4	countblank	2
5	Eminem	114
6	Cher	112
7	Moore	131
8	Spears	129
9	Mellencamp	115
10	Madonna	133
11	Springsteen	103
12	Manilow	114
13	Total	951

FIGURE 19-2 Use *COUNTIF* to determine how many songs were sung by each singer.

How many songs were not sung by Eminem?

To solve this problem, you need to know that Excel interprets the character combination <> as "not equal to." The COUNTIF(Singer,"<>Eminem") formula, entered in cell C15, tells you that 837 songs in the database were not sung by Eminem, as you can see in Figure 19-3. You must enclose <>Eminem in quotation marks because Excel treats the not-equal-to (<>) character combination as text, and Eminem is, of course, text. You could obtain the same result by using the COUNTIF(Singer,"<>"&B5) formula, which uses the ampersand (&) symbol to concatenate the reference to cell B5 and the <> operator.

	B	C
15	Not by Eminem	837
16	Songs >= 4 minutes	477
17	Songs longer than average	477
18	Singer begins with S	232
19	Singer has six letters in name	243
20	Songs after 6/15/2005	98
21	Songs Before 2009	951
22	Songs exactly 4 minutes	247
23	Songs exactly 5 minutes	230
24	Springsteen songs 4 minutes	24
25	Madonna songs 3 or 4 minutes	70

FIGURE 19-3 You can combine the *COUNTIF* function with the not-equal-to operator (<>).

How many songs were at least four minutes long?

In cell C16, you can compute the number of songs played that lasted at least four minutes by using the COUNTIF(Minutes,">=4") formula. You need to enclose >=4 in quotation marks because the greater-than or equal-to (>=) character combination, like <>, is treated as text. You can see that 477 songs lasted at least four minutes.

How many songs were longer than the average length of all songs on the list?

To answer this question, first compute the average length of a song with the AVERAGE(Minutes) formula in cell G5. Then, in cell C17, compute the number of songs that last longer than the average with the COUNTIF(Minutes,">"&G5) formula. You can refer to another cell (in this case, G5) in the criteria by using the & character. You can see that 477 songs lasted longer than average, which matches the number of songs lasting at least 4 minutes. These numbers match because it is assumed the length of each song was an integer. For a song to last at least 3.48 minutes, it has to last at least 4 minutes.

How many songs were sung by singers whose last names begin with S?

To answer this question, use a wildcard character, the asterisk (*), in the criteria. An asterisk represents any sequence of characters. Thus, the COUNTIF(Singer,"S*") formula in cell C18 picks up any song sung by a singer whose last name begins with S. (The criteria are not case sensitive.) Two hundred thirty-two songs were sung by singers with last names that begin with S. This number is simply the total of the songs sung by Bruce Springsteen and Britney Spears (103 + 129 = 232).

How many songs were sung by singers whose last names contain exactly six letters?

This example uses the question mark (?) wildcard character. The question mark matches any character. Therefore, entering the COUNTIF(Singer,"??????") formula in cell C19 counts the number of songs sung by singers having six letters in their last name. The result is 243. (Two singers have last names of six characters, Britney Spears and Eminem, who together sang a total of 243 songs—129 + 114 = 243.)

How many songs were played after June 15, 2005?

The criteria you use with *COUNTIF* functions handle dates based on a date's serial number. (A later date is considered larger than an earlier date.) The COUNTIF(Date,">6/15/2005") formula in cell C20 tells you that 98 songs were played after June 15, 2005.

How many songs were played before 2009?

Here, you want your criteria to pick up all dates on or before December 31, 2008. Enter the COUNTIF(Date,"<=12/31/2008") formula in cell C21. You can see that 951 songs (which turns out to be all the songs) were played before the start of 2009.

How many songs were exactly four minutes long?

In cell C22, compute the number of songs lasting exactly four minutes with the COUNTIF(Minutes,4) formula. This formula counts the number of cells in the G7:G957 range containing a 4. As you can see, 247 songs lasted exactly four minutes. In a similar fashion, cell C23 shows that 230 songs lasted exactly five minutes.

How many songs played were sung by Bruce Springsteen and were exactly four minutes long?

You want to count each row in which an entry in the Singer column is Springsteen and an entry in the Minutes column is 4. Because this question involves more than one criterion, this is a job for the wonderful *COUNTIFS* function. Enter the =COUNTIFS(Singer,"Springsteen",Minutes,4) formula in cell C24.

This formula counts any row in which Singer is Springsteen and Minutes equals 4. Bruce Springsteen sang 24 songs that were exactly four minutes long. Your favorite Springsteen song might be "Thunder Road," but that song is more than four minutes long. Use the function wizard to input formulas involving the *COUNTIFS* function. Don't forget that you can paste range names into your formula with the F3 key.

How many songs played were sung by Madonna and were three to four minutes long?

Because you are dealing with multiple criteria, this is again a job for *COUNTIFS*. Entering the =COUNTIFS(Singer,"Madonna",Minutes,"<=4",Minutes,">=3") formula in cell C25 counts all rows in which Madonna sang a song that was from three to four minutes long. These are exactly the rows you want to count. It turns out that Madonna sang 70 songs that were from three to four minutes long. (Maybe your favorite one is "Crazy for You!")

How can I count the number of cells in a range containing numbers?

The *COUNT* function counts the number of cells in a range containing a numeric value. For example, the COUNT(B5:C14) formula in cell C2 displays *9* because nine cells (the cells in C5:C13) in the B5:C14 range contain numbers. (See Figure 19-2.)

How can I count the number of blank cells in a range?

The *COUNTBLANK* function counts the number of blank cells in a range. For example, the COUNTBLANK(B5:C14) formula entered in cell C4 returns a value of *2* because two cells (B14 and C14) in the B5:C14 range contain blanks.

How do I count the number of nonblank cells in a range?

The *COUNTA* function returns the number of nonblank cells in a range. For example, the COUNTA(B5:C14) formula in cell C3 returns *18* because 18 cells in the B5:C14 range are not blank.

Remarks

In the remainder of the book, alternative methods are discussed to answer questions involving two or more criteria (such as how many Britney Spears songs were played before June 10, 2005):

- Database statistical functions are discussed in Chapter 48.

- Array formulas are discussed in Chapter 87, "Array formulas and functions."

Problems

The following questions refer to the Rock.xlsx file:

1. How many songs were not sung by Britney Spears?

2. How many songs were played before June 15, 2004?

3. How many songs were played between June 1, 2004, and July 4, 2006? Hint: Take the difference between two *COUNTIF* functions.

4. How many songs were sung by singers whose last names begin with M?

5. How many songs were sung by singers whose names contain an e?

6. Create a formula that always yields the number of songs played today. Hint: Use the *TODAY()* function.

7. For the D4:G15 cell range, count the cells containing a numeric value. Count the number of blank cells. Count the number of nonblank cells.

8. How many songs sung by Barry Manilow were played in 2004?

9. How many songs at least 4 minutes long and sung by Mandy Moore were played in 2007 or earlier?

10. How many songs exactly three minutes long and sung by Britney Spears were played later than 2004?

11. The NBA.xlsx file contains the following information:

    - Columns A and B contain the name of each NBA team and a code number for each team. For example, Team 1 is Atlanta.

    - Column C contains the home team for each game.

- Column D contains the visiting team for each game.

- Column E contains points scored by the home team.

- Column F contains points scored by the visiting team.

From this data, compute the number of games played by each team.

12. The Matchthesecond.xlsx file gives a list of names. Some names occur more than once. Determine the row in which, for example, the second occurrence of the name "Dave" occurs. Set up a worksheet in which you can enter a person's name and a positive integer (such as *n*) and it returns the row in which the name occurs for the *n*th time.

13. The Numbers.xlsx file contains a set of numbers. Count how many of these numbers are between 1 and 12, inclusive.

CHAPTER 20

The SUMIF, AVERAGEIF, SUMIFS, and AVERAGEIFS functions

Questions answered in this chapter:

- I'm a sales manager for a makeup company and have summarized the following information for each sales transaction: salesperson, date of sale, units sold (or returned), and total price received (or paid out for returns). How can I answer the following questions?

  - What is the total dollar amount of merchandise sold by each salesperson?

  - How many units were returned?

  - What is the total dollar amount of sales in or after 2005?

  - How many units of lip gloss were sold? How much revenue did lip gloss sales bring in?

  - What is the total dollar amount of sales by someone other than a specific salesperson?

  - What is the average number of units sold in each transaction by a specific salesperson?

  - What is the total dollar amount of lipstick sold by a specific salesperson?

  - What is the average quantity (in units) of lipstick in each sale by a specific salesperson?

  - Among transactions involving at least 50 units, what is the average quantity of lipstick in each sale by a specific salesperson?

  - Among transactions of more than $100, what is the total dollar amount of lipstick sold by a specific salesperson? What is the total dollar amount from transactions of less than $100?

If you want to sum all the entries in one column (or row) that match criteria that depend on another column (or row), the *SUMIF* function gets the job done. The syntax of the *SUMIF* function is SUMIF(range,criterion,[sum_range]):

- Range is the range of cells that you want to evaluate with a criterion.

- Criterion is a number, date, or expression that determines whether a given cell in the sum range is added.

- Sum range is the range of cells that are added. If sum range is omitted, it is assumed to be the same as range.

The rules for criteria you can use with the *SUMIF* function are identical to the rules used for the *COUNTIF* function. For information about the *COUNTIF* function, see Chapter 19, "The *COUNTIF*, *COUNTIFS*, *COUNT*, *COUNTA*, and *COUNTBLANK* functions."

The *AVERAGEIF* function has the AVERAGEIF(range,criterion,[average_range]) syntax. *AVERAGEIF* averages the range of cells meeting a criterion.

Microsoft Excel 2013 includes three functions (introduced in Excel 2007) that you can use to flag rows that involve multiple criteria: *COUNTIFS* (discussed in Chapter 19), *SUMIFS*, and *AVERAGEIFS*. Other functions you can use to do calculations involving multiple criteria are discussed in Chapter 48, "Summarizing data with database statistical functions." Array functions (see Chapter 87, "Array functions and formulas") can also be used to handle calculations involving multiple criteria.

The syntax of *SUMIFS* is SUMIFS(sum_range,range1,criterion1,range2,criterion2, . . . , rangeN, criterionN). *SUMIFS* sums up every entry in the *sum_range* for which criterion1 (based on range1) and criterion2 (based on range2), . . . , criterion*N* (based on range*N*) are all satisfied. In a similar fashion, the *AVERAGEIFS* function has the AVERAGEIFS(sum_range,range1,criterion1,range2,-criterion2, . . . ,rangeN,criterionN) syntax. *AVERAGEIFS* averages every entry in the sumrange for which criterion1 (based on range1) and criterion2 (based on range2), . . . , criterion*N* (based on range*N*) are all satisfied.

Answers to this chapter's questions

This section provides the answers to the questions that are listed at the beginning of the chapter.

What is the total dollar amount of merchandise sold by each salesperson?

The work for the problems in this chapter is in the Makeup2007.xlsx file. Figure 20-1 shows a subset of the data.

	G	H	I	J	K	L
4	Trans Number	Name	Date	Product	Units	Dollars
5	1	Betsy	4/1/2004	lip gloss	45	$ 137.20
6	2	Hallagan	3/10/2004	foundation	50	$ 152.01
7	3	Ashley	2/25/2005	lipstick	9	$ 28.72
8	4	Hallagan	5/22/2006	lip gloss	55	$ 167.08
9	5	Zaret	6/17/2004	lip gloss	43	$ 130.60
10	6	Colleen	11/27/2005	eye liner	58	$ 175.99
11	7	Cristina	3/21/2004	eye liner	8	$ 25.80
12	8	Colleen	12/17/2006	lip gloss	72	$ 217.84
13	9	Ashley	7/5/2006	eye liner	75	$ 226.64
14	10	Betsy	8/7/2006	lip gloss	24	$ 73.50
15	11	Ashley	11/29/2004	mascara	43	$ 130.84
16	12	Ashley	11/18/2004	lip gloss	23	$ 71.03
17	13	Emilee	8/31/2005	lip gloss	49	$ 149.59
18	14	Hallagan	1/1/2005	eye liner	18	$ 56.47
19	15	Zaret	9/20/2006	foundation	-8	$ (21.99)
20	16	Emilee	4/12/2004	mascara	45	$ 137.39
21	17	Colleen	4/30/2006	mascara	66	$ 199.65
22	18	Jen	8/31/2005	lip gloss	88	$ 265.19

FIGURE 20-1 This is the data you'll use for SUMIF examples.

As usual, begin by labeling the data in columns G through L with the corresponding names in cells G4:L4. For example, the Product range name corresponds to the J5:J1904 range. To compute the total amount sold by each salesperson (see Figure 20-2), copy the SUMIF(Name,A5,Dollars) formula from cell B5 to B6:B13. This formula adds up every entry in the Dollars column that contains the name Emilee in the Name column and shows that Emilee sold $25,258.87 worth of makeup. Of course, the =SUMIF(Name,"Emilee",Dollars) formula would yield the same result.

	A	B	C
4	Name	Dollar Volume	
5	Emilee	$ 25,258.87	
6	Hallagan	$ 28,705.16	
7	Ashley	$ 25,947.24	
8	Zaret	$ 26,741.31	
9	Colleen	$ 24,890.66	
10	Cristina	$ 23,849.56	
11	Betsy	$ 28,803.15	
12	Jen	$ 29,050.53	
13	Cici	$ 27,590.57	
14			
15			
16	Units returned	922	
17	Total dollars sold 2005 or later	$ 157,854.32	
18	Units of lip gloss sold	16333	
19	$s of lip gloss sold	$ 49,834.64	
20	$s sold not by Jen	$ 211,786.51	
21	Lipstick $s by Jen	3953	
22	avg units lipstick by Zaret	33	
23	avg units lipstick Zaret units >=50	68	
24	Lipstick $s >=$100 Jen	3583	
25	Lipstick $s <$100 Jen	370 check	
26	average units by Jen	43.548	43.548

FIGURE 20-2 These are the results of *SUMIF* computations.

How many units were returned?

In cell B16, the SUMIF(Units,"<0",Units) formula totals every number less than 0 in the Units column (column K). The result is −922. Inserting a minus sign in front of the SUMIF formula shows that 922 units were returned. (Recall that when the sum range argument is omitted from a *SUMIF* function, Excel assumes that sum range equals range. Therefore, the −SUMIF(Units,"<0") formula would also yield 922.)

What is the total dollar amount of sales in or after 2005?

In cell B17, the SUMIF(Date,">=1/1/2005",Dollars) formula totals every entry in the Dollar column (column L) that contains a date on or after 1/1/2005 in the Date column. The formula shows that $157,854.32 worth of makeup was sold in 2005 or later.

How many units of lip gloss were sold? How much revenue did lip gloss sales bring in?

In cell B18, the SUMIF(Product,"lip gloss",Units) formula totals every cell in the Units column that contains the text "lip gloss" in the Product column (column J). You can see that 16,333 units of lip gloss were sold. This is the net sales amount; transactions in which units of lip gloss were returned are counted as negative sales.

In a similar fashion, in cell B19, the SUMIF(Product,"lip gloss",Dollars) formula tells you that a net amount of $49,834.64 worth of lip gloss was sold. This calculation counts refunds associated with returns as negative revenue.

What is the total dollar amount of sales by someone other than Jen?

In cell B20, the SUMIF(Name,"<>Jen",Dollars) formula sums the dollar amount of all transactions that do not have Jen in the Name column. You find that salespeople other than Jen sold $211,786.51 worth of makeup.

What is the average number of units sold in each transaction by a specific salesperson?

This is a job for the *AVERAGEIF* function. Entering the =AVERAGEIF(Name,"Jen",Units) formula in cell B26 averages every entry in the Units column that contains Jen in the Name column. Jen's average transaction size was 43.548 units. You can verify this in cell C26 with the =SUMIF(Name,"Jen",Units) /COUNTIF(Name,"Jen") formula.

What is the total dollar amount of lipstick sold by Jen?

This calculation involves two criteria (Name="Jen" and Product="lipstick"). Therefore, you need to compute the quantity you're looking for in cell B21 with the =SUMIFS(Dollars,Name,"Jen",Product, "lipstick") formula. The total dollar amount of all transactions in which Jen sold lipstick is $3,953.

What is the average quantity (in units) of lipstick in each sale by Zaret?

This calculation requires the *AVERAGEIFS* function. Compute the quantity in cell B22 with the =AVERAGEIFS(Units,Name,"Zaret",Product,"lipstick") formula. For the sales transactions in which Zaret sold lipstick, the average number of units sold is 33.

Among transactions involving at least 50 units, what is the average quantity of lipstick in each sale by Zaret?

Here again, use *AVERAGEIFS* but add a criterion to ensure that the number of units sold in each transaction was at least 50. In cell B23, enter the =AVERAGEIF(Units,Name,"Zaret",Product,"lipstick", Units,">=50") formula. In all transactions in which Zaret sold at least 50 units of lipstick, the average transaction size is 68 units.

Among transactions of more than $100, what is the total dollar amount of lipstick sold by Jen? What is the total dollar amount from transactions of less than $100?

Because the criteria are Name=Jen, Product=lipstick, and some statement about the dollar size of each order, you need to use the *SUMIFS* function. In cell B24, compute the total amount in transactions in which Jen sold lipstick and the dollar amount was at least $100 with the =SUMIFS(Dollars,- Name,"Jen",Product,"lipstick",Dollars">=100") formula. Jen sold $3,583 worth of lipstick in such transactions. In lipstick transactions involving less than $100, you can see in cell B25 that the answer is $370. (The formula is =SUMIFS(Dollars,Name,"Jen",Product,"lipstick",Dollars,"<100".) Note that $370 + $3,583 equals the total revenue Jen generated from lipstick sales (computed in cell B21).

Problems

1. For each product, determine the total number of units and dollar volume sold.

2. Determine the total revenue earned before December 10, 2005.

3. Determine the total units sold by salespeople whose last names begin with C.

4. Determine the total revenue earned by people who have five letters in their names.

5. How many units were sold by people other than Colleen?

6. How many units of makeup were sold from January 15, 2004, through February 15, 2005?

7. The NBA.xlsx file contains the following information:

   - Columns A and B list the name of each NBA team and a code number for each team. For example, team 1 is Atlanta and so on.

   - Column C lists the home team for each game.

   - Column D lists the visiting team for each game.

   - Column E lists points scored by the home team.

   - Column F lists points scored by the visiting team.

   From this data, compute for each team the average number of points the team scored per game and the average number of points the team gave up.

8. The Toysrus.xlsx file contains sales revenue (in millions of dollars) during each quarter for the years 1997–2001 and the first two quarters of 2002. Use this data to compute a seasonal index for each quarter of the year. For example, if average sales during the first quarter were 80 percent of the overall average sales per quarter, the first quarter would have a seasonal index of 0.8.

9. The Sumifrows.xlsx file contains sales data during several winter, spring, summer, and fall quarters. Determine average sales during the winter, spring, summer, and fall quarters.

10. Again, by using the Makeup2007.xlsx file, determine how much revenue was made on sales transactions involving at least 50 units of makeup.

11. How many units of lip gloss did Cici sell in 2004?

12. What is the average number of units of foundation sold by Emilee?

13. What is the average dollar size of a foundation sale by Betsy after the end of 2004?

14. In transactions in which Ashley sold at least 40 units of lipstick, what is the total dollar amount?

15. Create a table that contains sales of each product by each person.

16. Create a table that, when you enter a year in your worksheet, contains sales of each product by a person during that year.

17. From the Numbers.xlsx file, find the total of all numbers between 5 and 15, inclusive.

18. From the Numbers.xlsx file, find the average of all numbers between 10 and 25, inclusive.

CHAPTER 21

The OFFSET function

Questions answered in this chapter:

- How can I create a reference to a range of cells that is a specified number of rows and columns from a cell or another range of cells?

- How can I perform a lookup operation based on the right most column in a table range instead of the left most column?

- I often download software product sales information listed by country. I need to track revenues from Iran as well as costs and units sold, but the data about Iran isn't always in the same location in the worksheet. Can I create a formula that will always pick out Iran's revenues, costs, and units sold?

- Each drug my company develops goes through three stages of development. I have a list of the cost by month for each drug, and I know the length in months of each development stage. Can I create formulas that compute the total cost incurred for each drug during each stage of development?

- I run a small video store. In a worksheet, my accountant has listed the name of each movie and the number of copies in stock. Unfortunately, he combined this information in one cell for each movie. How can I extract the number of copies of each movie in stock to a separate cell?

- How does the Excel Evaluate Formula feature work?

- How can I write a formula that always returns the last number in a column?

- How can I set up a range name that automatically includes new data?

- I am charting my company's monthly unit sales. Each month, I download the most recent month's unit sales. I would like my chart to update automatically. Is there an easy way to accomplish this?

Use the *OFFSET* function to create a reference to a range that is a specified number of rows and columns away from a cell or range of cells. Basically, to create a reference to a range of cells, you first specify a reference cell. You then indicate the number of rows and columns away from the reference cell that you want to create your range. For example, by using the *OFFSET* function, I can create a reference to a cell range that contains two rows and three columns and begins two columns to the right and one row above the current cell. You can calculate the specified number of rows and columns to move from a reference cell by using other Microsoft Excel functions.

The syntax of the *OFFSET* function is OFFSET(reference,rows_moved,columns_moved,height,width).

- Reference is a cell or range of cells from which the offset begins. If you specify a range of cells, the cells must be adjacent to each other.

- Rows moved is the number of rows away from the reference cell or range that you want the range reference to start (the upper-left cell in the offset range). A negative number of rows moves you up from the reference; a positive number of rows moves you down. For example, if reference equals C5 and rows moved equals –1, you move to row 4. If rows moved equals +1, you move to row 6. If rows moved equals 0, you stay at row 5.

- Columns moved is the number of columns away from the reference cell or range that you want the range reference to start. A negative number of columns moves you left from the reference; a positive number of columns moves you right. For example, if reference equals C5 and columns moved equals –1, you move to column B. If columns moved equals +1, you move to column D. If columns moved equals 0, you stay at column C.

- Height and width are optional arguments that give the number of rows and columns in the offset range. If height or width is omitted, the OFFSET function creates a range for which the value of height or width equals the height or width of the reference cell or range.

Answers to this chapter's questions

This section provides the answers to the questions that are listed at the beginning of the chapter.

How can I create a reference to a range of cells that is a specified number of rows and columns from a cell or another range of cells?

The Offsetexample.xlsx file, shown in Figure 21-1, provides some examples of the *OFFSET* function in action.

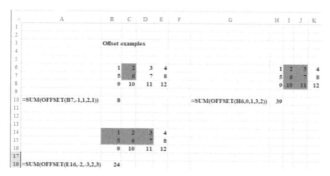

FIGURE 21-1 This figure shows the use of the *OFFSET* function in combination with the *SUM* function.

For example, in cell B10, enter the formula shown in cell A10: SUM(OFFSET(B7,–1,1,2,1)). This formula begins in cell B7. It moves one row up and one column to the right, which takes you to cell C6. The formula now selects a range consisting of two rows and one column, which yields range C6:C7.

The *SUM* function adds the numbers in this range, which yields 2 + 6 = 8. The other two examples shown in Figure 21-1 work the same way. The following sections show you how to apply the *OFFSET* function to solve some problems from major US companies.

How can I perform a lookup operation based on the right most column in a table range instead of the left most column?

In Figure 21-2 (see the Lefthandlookup.xlsx workbook) are listed the members of the 2002–2003 Dallas Mavericks NBA basketball team and their field goal percentages. If you're asked to find the player with a specific field goal percentage, you could easily solve that problem by using a *VLOOKUP* function. But what you really want to do is a *left-side lookup*, which involves finding the field goal percentage for a player by using his name. A *VLOOKUP* function can't perform a left-side lookup, but a left-side lookup is simple if you combine the *MATCH* and *OFFSET* functions.

	B	C	D	E
4				
5		Left-hand lookup		
6			Name	FG %age
7	FG%	Player	Walt Williams	0.397
8	45.8%	Dirk Nowitzki		
9	41.8%	Michael Finley		
10	46.3%	Steve Nash		
11	39.5%	Nick Van Exel		
12	53.5%	Raef LaFrentz		
13	60.2%	Eduardo Najera		
14	51.2%	Shawn Bradley		
15	39.7%	Walt Williams		
16	44.4%	Adrian Griffin		
17	48.4%	Avery Johnson		
18	47.6%	Raja Bell		
19	66.7%	Evan Eschmeyer		
20	41.0%	Popeye Jones		
21	40.0%	Mark Strickland		
22	23.5%	Adam Harrington		

FIGURE 21-2 You can do a left-side lookup by using the *MATCH* and *OFFSET* functions

First, enter the player's name in cell D7 and then use a reference cell of B7 (the field goal percentage column header) with the *OFFSET* function. To find the player's field goal percentage, move down to the row below row 7, where the player's name appears. This is a job for the *MATCH* function. The *MATCH* function portion of the OFFSET(B7,MATCH(D7,$C$8:$C$22,0),0) formula moves down to the row containing the specified player's name and then moves over 0 columns. Because the reference consists of one cell, omitting the height and width arguments of the *OFFSET* function ensures that the range this formula returns is also one cell. Thus, you pick up the player's field goal percentage.

I often download software product sales information listed by country. I need to track revenues from Iran as well as costs and units sold, but the data about Iran isn't always in the same location in the worksheet. Can I create a formula that will always pick out Iran's revenues, costs, and units sold?

The Asiansales.xlsx file (see Figure 21-3) contains data for units sold, sales revenue, and variable cost for software sold to several countries in Asia and the Middle East. Each month, when you download the monthly financial reports, the location of each country in the worksheet changes, so you need formulas that always return (for a given country) the correct units sold, revenue, and variable cost.

	C	D	E	F
6	Country/Region	Units sold	Revenue	Variable Cost
7	India	541	$ 4,328	$ 1,082
8	China	1000	$ 5,000	$ 2,000
9	Iran	577	$ 2,308	$ 1,731
10	Israel	454	$ 3,632	$ 1,362
11	Japan	141	$ 705	$ 423
12	Taiwan	221	$ 1,105	$ 663
13	Thailand	223	$ 1,115	$ 446
14	Indonesia	524	$ 2,620	$ 1,048
15	Malaysia	328	$ 1,968	$ 984
16	Vietnam	469	$ 2,814	$ 1,407
17	Cambodia	398	$ 1,990	$ 796
18				
19		Units sold	Revenue	Variable Cost
20	Country/Region	1	2	3
21	Iran	577	2308	1731

FIGURE 21-3 You can use the *OFFSET* function in calculations when you're working with data that aren't always in the same location in a worksheet.

By copying the OFFSET($C$6,MATCH($C21,$C$7:$C$17,0),D20) formula from D21 to E21:F21, you can compute the result you want. This formula sets reference equal to cell C6 (which contains the words Country/Region) and then moves over one column (to cell D20) to find units sold and down to the row containing the country listed in C21. In cell E21, the reference to D20 now refers to E20 and becomes a 2, so you move over two columns to the right of column C to find revenue. In cell E21, the reference to D20 now refers to F20 and becomes a 3, so you move three columns to the right of column C to find variable cost.

Each drug my company develops goes through three stages of development. I have a list of the cost by month for each drug, and I know how many months each development stage took for each drug. Can I create formulas that compute the total cost incurred for each drug during each stage of development?

The Offsetcost.xlsx file contains the monthly costs incurred to develop five drugs and, for each drug, the number of months required to complete each phase. A subset of the data is shown in Figure 21-4.

The goal is to determine for each drug the total cost incurred during each development phase. In cells D4:D6, you compute the total development costs for Phases 1–3 for Drug 1. Compute Phase 1 costs for Drug 1 by using a cell reference of D10, with rows moved and columns moved equal to 0. Setting height equal to the number of months in Phase 1 and width equal to 1 captures all Phase 1 costs. Compute Phase 1 costs for Drug 1 in cell D4 with the SUM(OFFSET(D10,0,0,D1,1)) formula. Next, in cell D5, compute Phase 2 total costs for Drug 1 by using the SUM(OFFSET(D10,D1,0,D2,1)) formula. Start with a cell reference of D10 (the first month of costs) and move down the number of rows equal to the length of Phase 1. This takes you to the beginning of Phase 2. Setting height equal to the value in cell D2 ensures that you include all Phase 2 costs. Finally, in cell D6, find the Phase 3 development costs for Drug 1 by using the SUM(OFFSET(D10,D1+D2,0,D3,1)) formula. In this formula, you start from the first month of sales and move down the number of rows equal to the total time needed for Phases 1 and 2. This takes you to the beginning of Phase 3 where, in cell D3, you total the number of rows to capture Phase 3 costs. Then, by copying the formulas in D4:D6 to E4:H6, you can compute total costs for Phase 1 through Phase 3 for Drug 2 through Drug 5. For example, for Drug 2, total Phase 1 costs equal $313, total Phase 2 costs equal $789, and total Phase 3 costs equal $876.

	B	C	D	E	F	G	H
1		Dur Phase 1	2	3	9	12	6
2		Dur Phase 2	2	8	5	4	12
3		Dur Phase 3	2	11	4	11	15
4		Phase 1 Cost	110	313	795	1167	615
5		Phase 2 Cost	142	789	465	397	1096
6		Phase 3 Cost	234	876	401	1135	1588
7							
8							
9	Code	Month	Drug 1	Drug 2	Drug 3	Drug 4	Drug 5
10	1	Jan-98	52	135	131	121	69
11	2	Feb-98	58	120	77	60	68
12	3	Mar-98	80	58	66	52	113
13	4	Apr-98	62	56	78	61	146
14	5	May-98	130	126	98	118	94
15	6	Jun-98	104	102	64	117	125
16	7	Jul-98	121	59	115	112	137
17	8	Aug-98	107	123	56	102	77
18	9	Sep-98	80	88	110	85	93
19	10	Oct-98	51	111	72	118	89
20	11	Nov-98	74	124	82	143	66
21	12	Dec-98	76	107	99	78	66
22	13	Jan-99	97	97	129	77	142
23	14	Feb-99	118	63	83	148	94
24	15	Mar-99	83	59	90	108	62

FIGURE 21-4 Use the *OFFSET* function to compute development costs for Phase 1 through Phase 3.

I run a small video store. In a worksheet, my accountant has listed the name of each movie and the number of copies in stock. Unfortunately, he combined this information into one cell for each movie. How can I extract the number of copies of each movie in stock to a separate cell?

The Moviestemp.xlsx file contains the name of each movie and the number of copies in stock in the C2:C12 range.

	A	B	C	D	E	F	G	H	I
1	count words	Number	Movie and Number of Copies						
2	2	40	Seabiscuit 40	Seabiscuit	40				
3	4	12	Lara Croft Tombraider 12	Lara	Croft	Tombraider	12		
4	6	36	Raiders of the Lost Ark 36	Raiders	of	the	Lost	Ark	36
5	3	5	Annie Hall 5	Annie	Hall	5			
6	2	4	Manhattan 4	Manhattan	4				
7	3	112	Star Wars 112	Star	Wars	112			
8	4	128	How to Deal 128	How	to	Deal	128		
9	4	1	The Matrix Reloaded 1	The	Matrix	Reloaded	1		
10	3	1040	Johnny English 1040	Johnny	English	1040			
11	3	12	Rosemary's Baby 12	Rosemary's	Baby	12			
12	3	1002	High Noon 1002	High	Noon	1002			

FIGURE 21-5 Use the *OFFSET* function to show this movie example.

As shown in Column B of Figure 21-5 (see the Movies worksheet of the Movies.xlsx workbook), you want to extract the number of copies owned of each movie to a separate cell. If the number of copies were listed to the left of a movie's title, this problem would be easy; you could use the *FIND* function to locate the first space and then use the *LEFT* function to return all the data to the left of the first space. (See Chapter 5, "Text functions," for a discussion of how to use the *LEFT* and *FIND* functions as well as other functions you can use to work with text.) Unfortunately, this technique doesn't work when the number of copies is listed to the right of the movie title. For a one-word movie title, for example, the number of copies is to the right of the first space, but for a four-word movie title, the number of copies is to the right of the fourth space.

One way to solve this problem is to click the Data tab on the ribbon and, in the Data Tools group, click Text To Columns to place each word in a title and the number of copies in separate columns. You can use the *COUNTA* function to count the total number of words in a title, including the number of items as a word, for each movie. You can then use the OFFSET function to locate the number of items.

To begin, insert enough columns to the right of the data to allow each word in the movies' titles and the number of items to be extracted to a separate column. You could use six columns (Raiders of the Lost Ark requires six columns), as you can see in Figure 21-5. Then you can select the C2:C12 cell range and choose **Text To Columns** on the **Data** tab. Select **Delimited** in the **Convert Text To Columns Wizard** and use the space character as the delimiting character. After selecting cell D2 as the destination cell, the results show in columns D through I of Figure 21-5.

Now, count the number of words in each movie's cell (counting the number of items as a word) by copying the COUNTA(D2:I2) formula from A2 to A3:A12. The results are shown in Figure 21-5.

Finally, by copying the OFFSET(C2,0,A2) formula from B2 to B3:B12, you can locate the number of copies of each movie in stock. This formula begins at the reference cell containing the movie title and moves over the number of columns equal to the number of words in the title cell. Because the reference cell contains only one cell, you can omit the height and width arguments of the *OFFSET* function so that the function uses only the cell containing the last word (the number of copies) of the title cell.

Of course, as shown in Figure 21-6 and the worksheet, you could use Flash Fill to extract the number of copies of each movie. Enter 40 in cell D2 and 12 in cell D3; press Enter and then press Ctrl+E.

	C	D
1	Movie and Number of Copies	
2	Seabiscuit 40	Seabiscuit
3	Lara Croft Tombraider 12	Lara
4	Raiders of the Lost Ark 36	Raiders
5	Annie Hall 5	Annie
6	Manhattan 4	Manhattan
7	Star Wars 112	Star
8	How to Deal 128	How
9	The Matrix Reloaded 1	The
10	Johnny English 1040	Johnny
11	Rosemary's Baby 12	Rosemary's
12	High Noon 1002	High

FIGURE 21-6 Use Flash Fill to extract the number of items in stock.

How does the Excel Evaluate Formula feature work?

If you select any portion of a cell formula and then press F9, Excel displays the value created by that portion of the formula. When you have finished reviewing the evaluated value, you must press Esc, or the value will replace the formula. This trick makes debugging and understanding complex formulas easier. Thus, it might be easier to understand what the *OFFSET* portion of the formula does if you apply this trick to any of the formulas in this chapter. For example, in the Offsetcost.xlsx file, cell E4 generates total Phase 1 cost with the =SUM(OFFSET(E10,0,0,E1,1)) formula. If you move the cursor over OFFSET(E10,0,0,E1,1), highlight this part of the formula, and then select F9, you see =SUM({135,120,58}), which indicates that the *OFFSET* portion of the formula in cell D4 uses the correct cells (D10:D12). Be sure you press Esc to exit this procedure, or you will modify the formula!

Another way to see how a complex formula works is to use the Evaluate Formula command. Move the cursor to E4 and click the **Formulas** tab on the ribbon. In the **Formula Auditing** group, choose **Evaluate Formula**. (See Figure 21-7.) Click the **Evaluate** button (it looks like a magnifying glass), and Excel simplifies the formula step by step until you see the formula's result. After clicking **Evaluate** twice, the formula appears as =SUM($E$10:E$12), so you know that in cell E4, you have selected the Phase 1 cells for Drug 2, which is what you wanted.

FIGURE 21-7 This is the Evaluate Formula dialog box.

How can I write a formula that always returns the last number in a column?

You often download new data into a worksheet. Can you write a formula that always returns sales during the most recent month? (See the Mostrecent.xlsx file and Figure 21-8.)

FIGURE 21-8 Find the last number in a column.

Enter the OFFSET(B6,COUNT(B:B),0,1,1) formula in cell D4.

This formula begins in cell B6 and moves down the number of rows equal to the number of numerical entries in column B. This takes you to the most recent month of sales, which is selected because 1,1 returns only one cell.

How can I set up a range name that automatically includes new data?

People who use Excel often add rows or columns of data to a range of data they use to create a PivotTable or to perform another type of analysis. Usually, they simply update the range of cells referred to in their formula and then rerun the analysis. However, you can use dynamic range names and never have to update the range of data referred to in a formula or PivotTable. The range automatically updates. Here is an example.

The Dynamicrange.xlsx file shows entries from a human resources (HR) database. (See Figure 21-9.)

	A	B	C	D	E	F	G
1	Name	Salary	Exp	Gender			
2	John	35500	3	M			
3	Jack	42300	4	M			
4	Jill	53426	5	F			
5	Erica	56000	6	F			
6	JR	62000	8	M			
7	Bianca	49000	10	F			
8	Francis	52000	5	M			
9	Roger	56000	7	M			
10	Maggie	42000	4				
11							448278

FIGURE 21-9 This figure shows an example of a dynamic range.

Currently, nine rows and four columns contain data. Wouldn't it be nice if you could create a range name that would automatically include more rows and columns when you add people or fields of information to the database?

To create a dynamic range, click the **Formulas** tab and, in the **Defined Names** group, choose **Name Manager**. Click **New** and define a range, as shown in Figure 21-10.

FIGURE 21-10 Create a dynamic range.

The range starts in the upper-left corner: cell A1. Because you want cell A1 to be the upper-left corner of the named range, you choose rows moved and columns moved to equal 0. The selected range has number of rows=number of nonblank entries in column A, and number of columns=number of nonblank entries in row 1. Thus, if you add people or data fields, the formula automatically expands to include them. The dollar signs ($) are needed so that the defined range will not shift if you move around the worksheet.

To try this out, enter the =SUM(data) formula in cell G11. At present, this formula totals all numbers in the A1:D10 range and yields $448,278.

Now add the name Meredith to row 11, enter a salary of $10,000 in B11, enter a variable for Mistakes (add the word Mistakes) in E1, and enter 1,000 in E11. The =SUM(data) formula now includes the 10,000 and 1,000 and automatically updates to $459,278.

I am charting my company's monthly unit sales. Each month, I download the most recent month's unit sales. I would like my chart to update automatically. Is there an easy way to accomplish this?

The Chartdynamicrange.xlsx workbook (see Figure 21-11) contains the units sold of your company's product. As you can see, the units sold have been charted using an XY (scatter) chart.

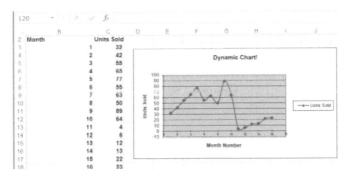

FIGURE 21-11 You can use the *OFFSET* function to update this chart dynamically.

Beginning in row 19, you download new sales data. Is there an easy way to ensure that the chart automatically includes the new data?

The key to updating the chart is to use the *OFFSET* function to create dynamic range names for both the Months column and the Units Sold column. As new data is entered, the dynamic range for unit sales automatically includes all sales data, and the dynamic range for months includes each month number. After creating these ranges, you can modify the chart, replacing the data ranges used in the chart with the dynamic ranges. The chart now updates as new data is entered.

To begin, click **Define Names** on the **Formulas** tab on the ribbon to open the **New Name** dialog box. Create a range named Units by filling in the dialog box as shown in Figure 21-12.

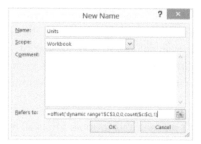

FIGURE 21-12 Create a dynamic range name for the units sold.

Entering =OFFSET('dynamic range'!$C$3,0,0,COUNT(!$C:$C),1) in the **Refers To** area of the dialog box creates a range one column wide beginning in cell C3, which contains the first unit sales data point. The range will contain as many numbers as there are in column C, which is derived by the portion of the formula that reads COUNT('dynamic range'!$C:$C). As new data is entered in column C, the data is automatically included in the range named Units.

Next, create a dynamic range named Month for the months entered in column B. The formula is shown in Figure 21-13.

FIGURE 21-13 This is the formula that defines a dynamic range named Month.

Now click any point in the chart. In the formula box, you see the SERIES('dynamic range'!$C$2,'dynamic range'!$B$3:$B$18,'dynamic range'!$C$3:$C$18,1) formula. This formula is the way Excel retrieves the data required to plot the chart. Replace the $B$3:$B$18 and $C$3:$C18 ranges with the dynamic range names as follows:

```
SERIES('dynamic range'!$C$2,Chartdynamicrange.xlsx!Month,Chartdynamicrange
.xlsx!Units,1)
```

If a blank space is listed above any new data, this method won't work. Enter some new data, and you'll see that it is included in the chart.

Remarks

The Excel Table feature makes it easy to set things up so that charts and formulas automatically incorporate new data. See Chapter 25, "Tables," for a discussion of this feature.

Problems

1. The C21p1.xlsx file contains data about unit sales for 11 products from 1999 to 2003. Write a formula using the *MATCH* and *OFFSET* functions that determines the sales of a given product during a given year. Can you think of a way to solve this problem without using the *MATCH* and *OFFSET* functions?

2. A commonly suggested moving average trading rule is to buy a stock when its price moves above the average of the past D months and to sell it when its price moves below the average of the past D months. Chapter 11, "IF statements," showed that for D = 15, this trading rule outperformed the Standard & Poor's 500 by a substantial amount. By combining a one-way data table with the *OFFSET* function, determine the value of D that maximizes trading profit (excluding transactions costs). You can find pertinent data in the Matradingrule.xlsx file.

3. A commonly suggested moving average trading rule is to buy a stock when its price moves above the average of the past B months and to sell it when its price moves below the average of the past S months. Chapter 11 shows that for B = S = 15, this trading rule outperformed the Standard & Poor's 500 by a substantial amount. By combining a two-way data table with the *OFFSET* function, determine the values of B and S that maximize trading profit (excluding transactions costs). You'll find data for this problem in the Matradingrule.xlsx file.

4. The Lagged.xlsx file contains data about the number of magazine ads placed by US Army recruiting during each of 60 consecutive months. For each month, the *k*-month lagged number of ads is defined to equal the number of ads placed *k* months ago. For months 7–60, you want to compute the 1-month lagged and 2-month through 6-month lagged values of the number of ads. Use the *OFFSET* function to compute these lagged values efficiently.

5. The Verizondata.xlsx file gives sales of four Verizon phones in five regions. Determine an efficient method to enter the region, type of phone, and sales of each phone for each of the 20 region–product combinations into one row.

6. The Agingdata.xlsx file gives the number of insurance claims projected to be received daily and the number of insurance company workers available. Each day, a worker can process up to 30 claims. Workers process the oldest claims in the system first. Cells H6:AL6 contain the number of claims already in the system on January 1, before new claims arrive. Set up a worksheet to track the aging of the claims. That is, for each day, how many 1-day-old , 2-day-old, . . . 30-day-old, and over-30-day-old claims will be in the system?

7. Each row of the DVDsales.xlsx file contains monthly sales of a DVD. Write a formula to determine sales for each DVD during its first six months on the market.

8. To obtain a golfer's handicap, you average the 10 lowest of the golfer's last 20 rounds. Then you subtract 80 and round to the nearest integer. Thus, if the 10 lowest of the last 20 rounds add up to 864, the handicap would be 6. The Golfdata.xlsx file contains a golfer's scores. Beginning in row 24, compute the golfer's handicap after each round. Assume that if the tenth best score in the last 20 rounds occurs more than once, all rounds including that score will be

included in the handicap calculation. Note that the =ROUND(x,0) Excel function will round *x* to the nearest integer.

9. Each row of the Carsumdata.xlsx file contains sales data for a product (car, train, or plane) from January through July, and you enter a month and a product in the worksheet. Write a formula that gives the total sales of that product during the given month.

10. The Verizon.xlsx file contains monthly returns on Verizon stock. Use the *OFFSET* function to extract all the January returns to one column, all the February returns to one column, and so on.

11. The Casesensitive.xlsx file contains product codes and product prices. Note that the product codes are case sensitive. For example, DAG32 is not the same product as dag32. Write a formula that gives the product price for any product code. Hint: You might need to use the *EXACT* function. The EXACT(cell1,cell2) formula yields True if cell1 and cell2 have exactly the same contents. *EXACT* differentiates between uppercase and lowercase letters.

12. The Reversed.xlsx file contains a column of numbers. Use the *OFFSET* function to reverse the numbers so that the number on the bottom occurs on the top and so on.

13. The Diagonal.xlsx file contains a matrix of numbers. Determine how to put the diagonal elements of the matrix in a single column.

14. The Yeartodate.xlsx file contains a company's monthly sales from 2008 through 2014. Write a formula that returns the year's cumulative sales to date for a given year and month of a year. For example, if you enter a 6 for the month and 2010 for the year, your formula should compute total sales for the January–June 2010 period.

15. Show how you might create a graph of monthly sales that always displays just the last six months of sales.

16. The Transactiondata.xlsx file contains sales transactions in divisions A, B, C, D, and E of a drug company. Use the *OFFSET* function to modify this data so that the sales for each division appear in a single row.

CHAPTER 22

The INDIRECT function

Questions answered in this chapter:

- My worksheet formulas often contain references to cells, ranges, or both. Rather than change these references in my formulas, can I place the references in their own cells so that I can easily change my cell or range references without changing my underlying formulas?

- Each worksheet in a workbook lists monthly sales of a product in cell D1. Is there an easy way to write and copy a formula that lists each month's product sales in one worksheet?

- Suppose I total the values in the A5:A10 range with the SUM(A5:A10) formula. If I insert a blank row somewhere between rows 5 and 10, my formula updates automatically to SUM(A5:A11). How can I write a formula so that when I insert a blank row between rows 5 and 10, my formula still totals the values in the original range, A5:A10?

- How can I use the *INDIRECT* function in a formula to read the range name portion of a formula in a worksheet?

- My workbook contains sales in each country for each of my company's products. How can I easily pool this data in a single summary worksheet?

- Is there an easy way to list all the worksheets in a workbook?

The *INDIRECT* function is probably one of the most difficult Microsoft Excel functions to master. Knowing how to use the *INDIRECT* function, however, enables you to solve many seemingly unsolvable problems. *Essentially, any reference to a cell within the INDIRECT portion of a formula results in the immediate evaluation of the cell reference to equal the content of the cell.* To illustrate the use of INDIRECT, look at the Indirectsimpleex.xlsx file, which is shown in Figure 22-1.

◢	A	B	C
3		Value	Indirect Reference
4	B4	6	6
5	B5	9	9
6			

FIGURE 22-1 Here is a simple example of the *INDIRECT* function.

In cell C4, enter formula =INDIRECT(A4). Excel returns the value 6 because the reference to A4 is immediately replaced by the text string "B4", and the formula is evaluated as =B4, which yields the value 6. Similarly, entering the =INDIRECT(A5) formula in cell C5 returns the value in cell B5, which is 9.

Answers to this chapter's questions

This section provides the answers to the questions that are listed at the beginning of the chapter.

My worksheet formulas often contain references to cells, ranges, or both. Rather than change these references in my formulas, can I place the references in their own cells so that I can easily change my cell or range references without changing my underlying formulas?

In this example, the data you use is contained in the Sumindirect.xlsx file, shown in Figure 22-2. The B4:H16 cell range lists monthly sales data for six products during a 12-month period.

You currently calculate total sales of each product during months 2–12. An easy way to make this calculation is to copy the SUM(C6:C16) formula from C18 to D18:H18. Suppose, however, that you want to change which months are totaled. For example, you might want total sales for months 3–12. You could change the formula in cell C18 to SUM(C7:C16) and then copy this formula to D18:H18, but using this approach is problematic because you have to copy the formula in C18 to D18:H18 and, without looking at the formulas, nobody knows which rows are being added.

	B	C	D	E	F	G	H
1			Lower	Upper			
2			6	16			
3		C	D	E	F	G	H
4	Month	Prod 1	Prod 2	Prod 3	Prod 4	Prod 5	Prod 6
5	1	28	86	79	31	84	58
6	2	38	7	61	1	20	2
7	3	91	48	73	8	80	14
8	4	33	32	24	77	29	80
9	5	82	70	41	29	57	90
10	6	75	40	15	92	55	91
11	7	52	21	26	45	59	21
12	8	19	6	35	67	40	81
13	9	11	18	68	11	52	78
14	10	90	30	52	32	30	1
15	11	47	86	46	0	38	55
16	12	69	71	75	65	53	52
17							
18	Total	607	429	516	427	513	565

FIGURE 22-2 You can use the *INDIRECT* function to change cell references in formulas without changing the formulas themselves.

The *INDIRECT* function provides another approach. Place the starting and ending rows of your summation in cells D2 and E2. Then, by using the *INDIRECT* function, all you need to do is change the starting and ending row references in D2 and E2, and the sums are updated to include the rows you want. Also, by looking at the values in D2 and E2, you can see at a glance which rows (months) are being added. You just need to copy the SUM(INDIRECT(C$3&$D$2&":"&C$3&$E$2)) formula from C18 to D18:H18.

If you want to see how Excel evaluates a reference to the *INDIRECT* function, use the following trick. Click in part of the formula (for example, C$3) and then press F9. Excel shows you the value of the selected portion of the formula. For example, C$3 evaluates to C. Be sure to press Esc to undo the change. Every cell reference within the *INDIRECT* portion of this formula is evaluated to equal the contents of the cell. C$3 is evaluated as C, $D$2 is evaluated as 6, and $E$2 is evaluated as 16. With the ampersand (&) included as the concatenation symbol, Excel evaluates this formula as SUM(C6:C16), which is exactly what you want. The formula in C18 returns the value 38 + 91 + . . . 69

= 607. In cell D18, the formula evaluates as SUM(D6:D16), which is the result you want. If you want to add up sales during months 4 through 6, you simply enter 8 in D2 and 10 in E2, and then the formula in C18 returns 33 + 82 + 75 = 190. (For information about using the ampersand to concatenate values, see Chapter 5, "Text functions.")

Each worksheet in a workbook lists monthly sales of a product in cell D1. Is there an easy way to write and copy a formula that lists each month's product sales in one worksheet?

The Indirectmultisheet.xlsx file (see Figure 22-3) contains seven worksheets. In each worksheet, cell D1 contains data about the sales of a product during a particular month. Suppose Sheet 1 contains Month 1 sales, Sheet 2 contains Month 2 sales, and so on. For example, sales in Month 1 equals 1, in Month 2 it equals 4, and so on.

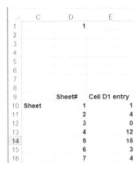

FIGURE 22-3 This figure shows monthly sales (months 1–7) of a product listed by using the *INDIRECT* function.

Now suppose you want to compile a list of each month's sales into one worksheet. A tedious approach would be to list Month 1 sales with the =Sheet1!D1 formula, Month 2 sales with the =Sheet2!D1 formula, and so on until you list Month 7 sales with the =Sheet7!D1 formula. If you have 100 months of data, this approach is time consuming and error prone. A much more elegant approach is to list Month 1 sales in cell E10 of Sheet1 with the INDIRECT($C$10&D10&"!D1") formula. Excel evaluates $C$10 as "Sheet", D10 as "1", and "!D1" as the text string "!D1". The whole formula is evaluated as =Sheet1!D1, which yields Month 1 sales, located in cell D1 of Sheet1. Copying this formula to the E11:E16 range lists the entries in cell D1 of Sheet 2 through Sheet 7. When the formula in cell E10 is copied to cell E11, the reference to D10 changes to D11, and cell E11 returns the value located at Sheet2!D1.

Suppose I total the values in the A5:A10 range with the SUM(A5:A10) formula. If I insert a blank row somewhere between rows 5 and 10, my formula updates automatically to SUM(A5:A11). How can I write a formula so that when I insert a blank row between rows 5 and 10, my formula still totals the values in the original range, A5:A10?

The SUM(A5:A10) worksheet in the Indirectinsertrow.xlsx file (shown in Figure 22-4) illustrates several ways to total the numbers in cell range A5:A10. In cell A12, you can enter the traditional SUM(A5:A10) formula, which yields 6+7+8+9+1+2=33.

Similarly, the SUM($A$5:$A$10) formula in cell E9 yields a value of *33*. However, if you insert a row between rows 5 and 10, both formulas attempt to total the cells in the A5:A11 range.

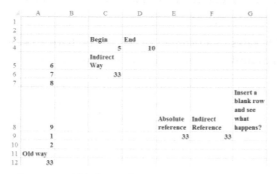

FIGURE 22-4 This figure shows several ways to sum the values in the A5:A10 cell range.

With the *INDIRECT* function, you have at least two ways to total the values in the A5:A10 range. Enter the SUM(INDIRECT("A5:A10")) formula in cell F9. Because Excel treats INDIRECT("A5:A10") as the text string "A5:A10", if you insert a row in the worksheet, this formula still totals the entries in the A5:A10 cell range.

Another way to use the *INDIRECT* function to total the entries in the A5:A10 range is the SUM(INDIRECT("A"&C4&":A"&D4)) formula, which is the formula entered in cell C6. Excel treats the reference to C4 as a 5 and the reference to D4 as a 10, so this formula becomes SUM(A5:A10). Inserting a blank row between row 5 and row 10 has no effect on this formula because the reference to C4 is still treated as a 5, and the reference to D4 is still treated as a 10. In Figure 22-5, you can see the sums calculated by the four formulas after a blank row is inserted below row 7. You can find this data on the Row Inserted worksheet in the Indirectinsertrow.xlsx file.

As you can see, the classic SUM formulas, which do not use the *INDIRECT* function, have changed to add up the entries in the A5:A11 range, so these formulas still yield a value of *33*. The two SUM formulas that do use the *INDIRECT* function continue to add up the entries in the A5:A10 range, so the value of *2* (now in cell A11) is no longer included in the calculated sum. The SUM formulas that use the *INDIRECT* function yield a value of *31*.

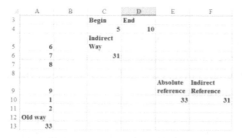

FIGURE 22-5 This figure shows the results of SUM formulas after inserting a blank row in the original range.

How can I use the *INDIRECT* function in a formula to read the range name portion of a formula in a worksheet?

Suppose you have named several ranges in a worksheet to correspond to quarterly product sales. (See Figure 22-6 and the Indirectrange.xlsx file.) For example, the D4:E6 range (named Quarter1) contains fictitious first-quarter sales of various Microsoft products.

	D	E	F	G	H	I	J
3	Quarter1						
4	Office	63					
5	Windows	66					
6	Xbox	70					
7							
8	Quarter2						
9	Office	93					
10	Windows	90					
11	Xbox	99					
12							
13	Quarter3						
14	Office	77					
15	Windows	58					
16	Xbox	60			Office	Windows	Xbox
17				Quarter1	63	66	70
18	Quarter4			Quarter2	93	90	99
19	Office	97		Quarter3	77	58	60
20	Windows	56		Quarter4	97	56	95
21	Xbox	95					

FIGURE 22-6 Use the *INDIRECT* function to create a reference to a range name within a formula.

It would be great to write a formula that can easily be copied and that then yields the sales of each product in each quarter in a single rectangular range of the worksheet, as shown in H17:J20. You would think you could enter the =VLOOKUP(H$16,$G17,2,FALSE) formula in cell H17 and then copy this formula to the H17:J20 range. Unfortunately, Excel does not recognize $G17 as referring to the Quarter1 range name. Rather, Excel just thinks $G17 is the text string "Quarter1". The formula, therefore, returns an #NA error. To remedy this problem, simply enter the =VLOOKUP(H$16,INDIRECT($G17),2,FALSE) formula in cell H17 and then copy this formula to the H17:J20 range. This works perfectly! INDIRECT($G17) is evaluated as Quarter1 and is now recognized as a range name. You have now easily generated sales data of all products during all four quarters.

My workbook contains sales in each country for each of my company's products. How can I easily pool this data in a single summary worksheet?

Cells E7:E9 of the Indirectconsolidate.xlsx file contain sales of cars, trucks, and planes on each continent. Each continent has its own worksheet. How can you summarize this data in a single sheet?

In the Summary worksheet, create the summary shown in Figure 22-7.

	C	D	E	F	G	H	I
4							
5			=LA!E7				
6			LA	NA	Asia	Africa	Europe
7	E7	Cars	100	200	500	100	80
8	E8	Trucks	150	150	400	50	120
9	E9	Planes	200	100	200	25	100

FIGURE 22-7 Use the *INDIRECT* function to create a summary of product sales.

Copy the INDIRECT(E$6&"!"&$C7) formula from cell E7 to the E7:I9 range. This formula creates the =LA!E7 formula, which calculates car sales in Latin America. Copying this formula picks off the sales for each type of product on each continent.

In the Another Summary worksheet (see Figure 22-7), you can create the same table in a slightly different manner; you can automate the generation of the cell addresses from which to pull car, truck, and plane sales by copying the ADDRESS(ROW(),COLUMN()+2) formula from C7 to C8:C9. This generates column E in the cell address and then rows 8 and 9. The *ROW()* function entered in a cell returns the cell's row number, and the *COLUMN()* function entered by itself in a cell returns the column number of the current cell (in this case, 3). When entered as part of the third argument of the *ADDRESS* function, the term COLUMN()+2 effectively returns the column label for the cell two columns to the right of the current cell (in this case, column E). Then you can copy the INDIRECT(E$6&"!"&$C7) formula from cell E7 to the E7:I9 range.

Is there an easy way to list all the worksheets in a workbook?

In the previous example, it was easy to list the worksheet names. Suppose you had a workbook with 100 or more worksheets. If you want to unleash the full power of the *INDIRECT* function to pull data from a subset of these worksheets, you need an efficient method for listing the name of each worksheet in a workbook. To list all worksheet names in a workbook efficiently, proceed as follows. (See workbook Worksheetnames.xlsm and Figure 22-8 and Figure 22-9.)

1. As shown in Figure 22-8, on the **Formulas** tab, select **Define Names**; in the **New Name** dialog box, create a range name. Call the range Worksheets with the =GET.WORKBOOK(1) formula.

   GET.WORKBOOK(1) is a macro, so the file suffix must be .xlsm.

2. Select a horizontal array containing as many rows as your workbook has worksheets, although in this example, it is easy to see that there are only three worksheets. If you do not know the number of worksheets in a workbook, you can use the Excel 2013 *SHEETS()* function. In cell H13, the *SHEETS()* function returns the number of worksheets in a workbook (in this case, 3).

   By the way, the new Excel 2013 SHEET() formula enters the number of the current worksheet in the workbook. If you entered =SHEET() anywhere in the Bob worksheet, the formula would enter 1; anywhere in the Allen worksheet, 2; anywhere in the Jill worksheet, 3.

3. In the left corner of the selected range (in this case, H15), type =Worksheet and press Ctrl+Shift+Enter.

   The Worksheet range name acts as an array formula (see Chapter 87, "Using array functions," for more discussion of array formulas), so you must press Ctrl+Shift+Enter for the formula to work. In the H15:J15 cell range, you now see the workbook name enclosed in square brackets followed by the worksheet names, listed in the order of the worksheets.

To return each worksheet name to a separate cell, just use the *RIGHT* and *FIND* functions from Chapter 5 to extract each worksheet name by pulling out all characters to the right of the square bracket. Copy the =RIGHT(I15,LEN(I15)-FIND("]",I15,1)) formula from H16 to I16:J16. You now see the worksheet names listed in the H16:J16 range. However, if the worksheet names change, the H15:J15 range remains unchanged. If you want the worksheet names to update after they are changed, you must delete the contents of H15:J15 and reenter the Worksheet array formula.

FIGURE 22-8 Create a range name that can be used to extract worksheet names.

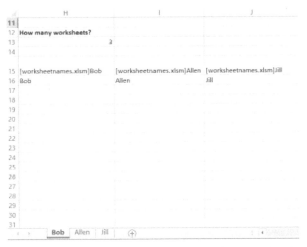

FIGURE 22-9 Worksheet names are extracted in Row 16 and number of sheets is pulled, using the *SHEET()* function.

Problems

1. The *ADDRESS* function yields the actual cell address associated with a row and column. For example, the ADDRESS(3,4) formula yields $D$3. What result would be obtained if you entered formula =INDIRECT(ADDRESS(3,4))?

2. The P23_2.xlsx workbook contains data for the sales of five products in four regions (East, West, North, and South). Use the *INDIRECT* function to create formulas that enable you to calculate the total sales of any combination of consecutively numbered products easily, such as Product 1 through Product 3, Product 2 through Product 5, and so on.

3. The P23_3.xlsx file contains six worksheets. Sheet 1 contains Month 1 sales for Product 1 through Product 4. These sales are always listed in the E5:H5 range. Use the *INDIRECT* function to tabulate the sales of each product efficiently by month in a separate worksheet.

4. Write a formula that totals the entries in the G2:K2 cell range even if you insert one or more columns between columns G and K.

5. The Marketbasketdata.xlsx file contains sales of various items. For each row, a 1 in columns B through K indicates a purchased item, whereas a 0 marks an item that was not purchased. In the Day Week column, a 1 means the transaction was on a Monday, a 2 means the transaction was on a Tuesday, and so on. For each item listed in K9:K14, calculate the percentage of transactions in which the item was purchased. In addition, calculate the fraction of transactions taking place on each day.

6. The Verizonindirectdata.xlsx file contains each employee's hours of work and employee rating for January–May. Set up a consolidation sheet that enables you to choose any person and then report that person's hours of work during each month along with her overall rating for the month.

CHAPTER 23

Conditional formatting

Questions answered in this chapter:

■ How can I visually indicate whether recent temperature data is consistent with global warming?

■ How does the Highlight Cells conditional formatting feature work?

■ How can I check or customize my rules?

■ How do data bars work?

■ How does Excel 2013 treat negative data bars?

■ How do color scales work?

■ How do icon sets work?

■ How can I color code monthly stock returns so that every good month is indicated in one color and every bad month in another?

■ Given quarterly corporate revenues, how can I indicate quarters in which revenues increased over the previous quarter in one color and quarters in which revenues decreased from the previous quarter in another color?

■ Given a list of dates, how can I indicate weekend dates in a specific color?

■ Our basketball coach has given each player a rating between 1 and 10 based on the player's ability to play guard, forward, or center. Can I set up a worksheet that visually indicates the ability of each player to play the position to which she's assigned?

■ What does Stop If True in the Manage Rules dialog box do?

■ How can I use the Format Painter to copy a conditional format?

Use conditional formatting to specify formatting for a cell range on the basis of the contents of the cell range. For example, given exam scores for students, you can use conditional formatting to display the names of students in red who have a final average of at least 90. Basically, when you set up conditions to format a range of cells, Microsoft Excel 2013 checks each cell in the range to determine whether any of the conditions you specified (such as exam score >90) is satisfied. Excel applies the format you chose to all the cells that satisfy the condition. If the content of a cell does not satisfy any of the conditions, the formatting of the cell remains unchanged. In Excel 2007, conditional formatting was completely revised and expanded. Excel 2010 added some minor improvements to conditional formatting. In this chapter, you see how to use all the conditional formatting features included in Excel 2013.

To view the conditional formatting options, first select the range you want to format. Then, on the **Home** tab, in the **Styles** group, click the **Conditional Formatting** arrow (see Figure 23-1) to open a menu of conditional formatting options, as shown in Figure 23-2.

FIGURE 23-1 This figure shows the conditional formatting command.

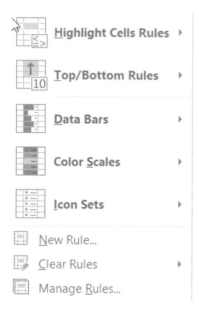

FIGURE 23-2 These are the conditional formatting options.

Here is a short explanation of each option:

- **Highlight Cells Rules** These rules enable you to assign a format to cells whose contents meet one of the following criteria:

  - Are within a specific numerical range

  - Match a specific text string

  - Are within a specific range of dates (relative to the current date)

  - Occur more than once (or only once) in the selected range

- **Top/Bottom Rules**   Use these rules to assign a format to any of the following:

  - *N* largest or smallest values in a range. For example, *N* = 10 will highlight the 10 largest or 10 smallest values in a range.

  - Top or bottom *n* percent of numbers in a range.

  - Numbers above or below the average of all the numbers in a range.

- **Data Bars, Color Scales, and Icon Sets**   Use these formats to identify large, small, or intermediate values in the selected range easily. Larger data bars are associated with larger numbers. With color scales, you might, for example, have smaller values appear in red and larger values in blue with a smooth transition applied as values in the range increase from small to large. With icon sets, you can use as many as five symbols to identify different ranges of values. For example, you might display an arrow pointing up to indicate a large value, pointing to the right to indicate an intermediate value, and pointing down to indicate a small value.

- **New Rule**   Use this rule to create your own formula to determine whether a cell should have a specific format. For example, if a cell exceeds the value of the cell above it, you could apply the color green to the cell. If the cell is the fifth-largest value in its column, you could apply the color red to the cell, and so on.

- **Clear Rules**   Use these rules to delete all conditional formats you have created for a selected range or for the entire worksheet.

- **Manage Rules**   Use these rules to view, edit, and delete conditional formatting rules; create new rules; or change the order in which Excel applies the conditional formatting rules you have set.

Answers to this chapter's questions

This section provides the answers to the questions that are listed at the beginning of the chapter.

How can I visually indicate whether recent temperature data is consistent with global warming?

This question offers a perfect opportunity to apply the Top/Bottom conditional formatting rules. The Globalwarming2011.xlsx file (Figure 23-4 shows a subset of this data) contains the average world temperatures for years 1881 through 2011. If global warming has occurred, you would expect the numbers in recent years to be larger than the numbers in earlier years. To determine whether recent years are warmer, try to highlight the 20 warmest years in red. Select the F5:F135 range containing the temperatures. On the **Home** tab, in the **Styles** group, click **Conditional Formatting** and then select **Top/Bottom Rules**. Select **Top 10 Items** and fill in the dialog box as shown in Figure 23-3.

FIGURE 23-3 Highlight the 20 highest temperatures in red.

Note Opening the drop-down list on the right side of Figure 23-3 displays a list of options, including Custom Format. Selecting this option displays the Format Cells dialog box, in which you create a custom format that is applied when the conditional formatting condition is satisfied.

Now select the G5:G135 range, return to **Top/Bottom Rules**, and select **Top 10%**. Accepting the default selection of 10 highlights the top 10 percent of the temperatures in red and the bottom 10 percent in green. Note that all years in the bottom 10 percent were 1918 or earlier, and all years in the top 10 percent were 1997 or later. Finally, in column H, highlight above-average temperatures in green and below-average temperatures in red. Note that all years earlier than 1936 had below-average temperatures, whereas all years after 1976 had above-average temperatures. Conditional formatting is a powerful tool that can be used to demonstrate that the earth (for whatever reasons) seems to have become warmer recently.

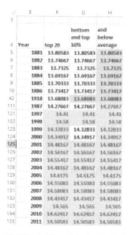

FIGURE 23-4 Use conditional formatting to implement Top/Bottom Rules.

How does the Highlight Cells conditional formatting feature work?

The Highlightcells.xlsx file (see Figure 23-5) demonstrates how the Highlight Cells feature is used. For example, suppose you want to highlight all duplicate names in C2:C11 in red. Simply select the C2:C11 cell range, choose **Conditional Formatting** in the **Styles** group on the **Home** tab, choose **Highlight Cells Rules** and **Duplicate Values**, and then choose **Light Red Fill With Dark Red Text**. Click **OK** to apply the rule so that all names occurring more than once (John and Josh) are highlighted in red.

	C	D	E	F
	duplicates red fill	text containing Eric red fill red text	last 7 days red then yesterday green	
2	John	John	6/1/2006	
3	Eric	Eric	7/18/2013	today()-1
4	James	James	7/14/2013	today()-5
5	John	John	5/15/2007	
6	Erica	Erica	6/14/2006	
7	JR	JR	2/3/2003	
8	Adam	Adam	5/12/2006	
9	Josh	Josh	6/17/2005	
10	Babe	Babe	8/1/2006	
11	Josh	Josh	9/2/2005	

FIGURE 23-5 Use Highlight Cells Rules.

Now suppose you want to highlight in red all cells in the D2:D11 range that contain the text "Eric". Select the D2:D11 cell range, click **Conditional Formatting**, choose **Highlight Cells Rules**, and then select **Text That Contains**. Type Eric in the left box and choose **Light Red Fill With Dark Red Text** on the right. As shown in Figure 23-5, both Eric and Erica are highlighted. (Erica contains the "Eric" text string.)

Suppose you have a list of dates (such as in E2:E11), and you want to highlight any cell that contains yesterday's date in green and any other date during the past seven days in red. (See the Right Way worksheet in the Highlightcells.xlsx file.) Assume (as in Figure 23-5) that the current date is July 19, 2013. Note that cell E3 contains the =TODAY()–1 formula, so cell E3 always displays yesterday's date. Cell E4 contains the =TODAY()–5 formula.

Begin by selecting the cell range you want to format (E2:E11). Select **A Date Occurring** and then select **Yesterday** with **Green Fill With Dark Green Text**. Click **Conditional Formatting** and **Highlight Cells Rules** and again choose **A Date Occurring**. In the **A Date Occurring** dialog box, select **In The Last 7 Days** and **Light Red Fill With Dark Red Text**. Formatting rules created later have precedence over rules created earlier (unless you change the order of precedence, as explained in the next section of this chapter). This explains why 7/18/2013 is formatted in red rather than in green.

How can I check or customize my rules?

After creating conditional formatting rules, you can view your rules by choosing **Manage Rules** on the **Conditional Formatting** menu. For example, select the dates in E2:E11, click **Conditional Formatting**, and choose **Manage Rules**; you see the rules displayed in Figure 23-6. You can see that the Last 7 Days formatting rule will be applied before the Yesterday formatting rule. This is because the format placed in a cell is based on the first matched rule.

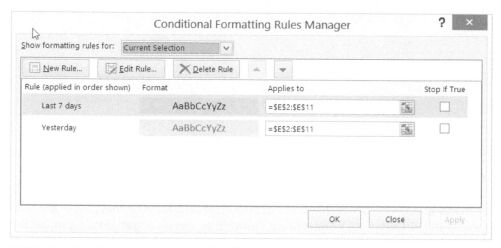

FIGURE 23-6 This figure shows the Conditional Formatting Rules Manager dialog box.

In the Conditional Formatting Rules Manager dialog box, you can do the following:

- Create a rule by clicking the **New Rule** button.

- Edit or change a rule by clicking the **Edit Rule** button.

- Delete a rule by selecting it and then clicking the **Delete Rule** button.

- Change the order of precedence by selecting a rule and then clicking the up arrow or down arrow.

To illustrate the use of the Conditional Formatting Rules Manager dialog box, copy the previous worksheet (right-click the worksheet tab, click **Move Or Copy**, and then select the **Create A Copy** check box) to the Right Way worksheet of the Highlightcells.xlsx file. Select the **Yesterday** rule and click the up arrow. The Yesterday rule now has higher precedence than the Last 7 Days rule, so E3 will be formatted green and not red. Figure 23-7 shows how the Conditional Formatting Rules Manager dialog box looks, and Figure 23-8 shows that cell E3 is green and cell E4 is red as you wanted.

FIGURE 23-7 Now Yesterday has a higher priority than Last 7 Days.

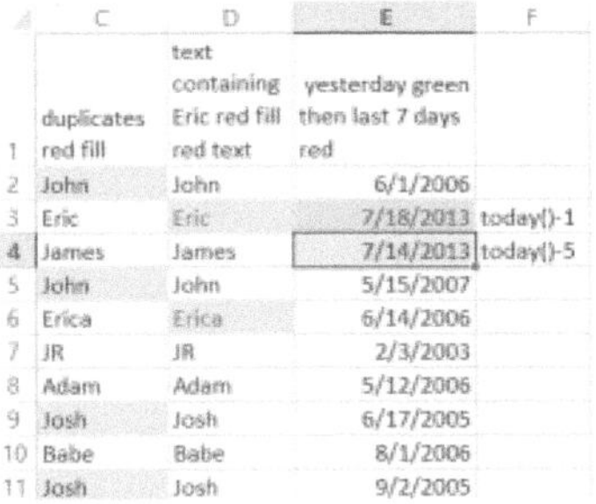

	C	D	E	F
1	duplicates red fill	text containing Eric red fill red text	yesterday green then last 7 days red	
2	John	John	6/1/2006	
3	Eric	Eric	7/18/2013	today()-1
4	James	James	7/14/2013	today()-5
5	John	John	5/15/2007	
6	Erica	Erica	6/14/2006	
7	JR	JR	2/3/2003	
8	Adam	Adam	5/12/2006	
9	Josh	Josh	6/17/2005	
10	Babe	Babe	8/1/2006	
11	Josh	Josh	9/2/2005	

FIGURE 23-8 After you change the precedence of rules, yesterday is now formatted in green.

How do data bars work?

When you have a long list of numbers, it's nice to have a visual indicator that enables you to identify large and small numbers easily. Data bars, color scales, and icon sets (all introduced in Excel 2007) are perfect tools for displaying differences in a list of numbers.

Figure 23-9 (see the Databars.xlsx file) shows the use of data bars. Begin by applying the default data bars to the data in D6:D15. Select the data in D6:D15, click **Conditional Formatting**, and then choose **Data Bars**. Select blue data bars and choose **Gradient Fill** to create the format shown in column D of Figure 23-9. Cells containing larger numbers contain longer blue bars. The default option is to associate the shortest data bar with the smallest number in the selected range and the longest data bar with the largest number. As you can see in column D, the size of the data bars is directly proportional to the data value; that is, the data bar for 4 is twice as large as the data bar for 2, and so on.

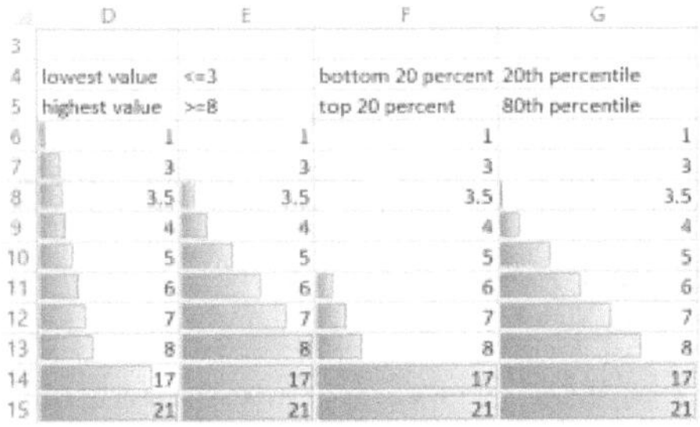

	D	E	F	G
3				
4	lowest value	<=3	bottom 20 percent	20th percentile
5	highest value	>=8	top 20 percent	80th percentile
6	1	1	1	1
7	3	3	3	3
8	3.5	3.5	3.5	3.5
9	4	4	4	4
10	5	5	5	5
11	6	6	6	6
12	7	7	7	7
13	8	8	8	8
14	17	17	17	17
15	21	21	21	21

FIGURE 23-9 Visually distinguish numeric values by using data bars.

If, after clicking **Data Bars**, you choose **More Rules**, the **New Formatting Rule** dialog box shown in Figure 23-10 opens. (You can also display this dialog box by choosing **Manage Rules** and **Edit Rule** or by double-clicking a rule.) In this dialog box, you can change the criteria used to assign no data bar and the longest data bars to cells. In E6:E15, assign no data bar to numbers less than or equal to 3 and the longest bar to any number greater than or equal to 8. As shown in Figure 23-9, all numbers in column E that are less than or equal to 3 have no data bar, all numbers that are greater than or equal to 8 have the longest bar, and the numbers between 3 and 8 have graduated bars. Note that in the **Edit Formatting Rule** dialog box, you can select the **Show Bar Only** check box to display only the color bar and not the cell value in the conditionally formatted cells.

FIGURE 23-10 You can customize your data bars by using this dialog box.

Next, in column F, assign no bar to numbers in the bottom 20 percent of the F6:F15 range and the longest bar to numbers in the top 20 percent. In other words, all numbers $< = 1 + .2(21 - 1) = 5$ have no data bar, and all numbers $> = 1 + .8(21 - 1) = 17$ have the longest data bar. Figure 23-9 shows that in column F, the first five numbers have no data bar, and the numbers 17 and 21 have the longest data bar.

In the G6:G13 cell range, associate no data bar with all numbers at or below the twentieth percentile of the data (3) and associate the longest data bar with all numbers at or above the eightieth percentile of the data (17). From the **Bar Direction** list, you can specify whether your data bars begin at the right or left border of the cell.

Excel 2013 allows solid shading for data bars and enables you to orient data bars associated with negative values so that they run in a direction opposite to positive values. After selecting **Negative Values** and **Axis** from the **Edit the Rule Description** dialog box, you can move the axis from the normal position in the center of the cell or make the negative data bars open to the left (the default) or to the right. The Negativedatabars.xlsx file and Figure 23-11 show how solid data bars appear for a data set containing negative numbers. The last two columns in Figure 23-11 use the Automatic Axis setting, which allocates more space to the positive entries because they are larger in magnitude than the negative values.

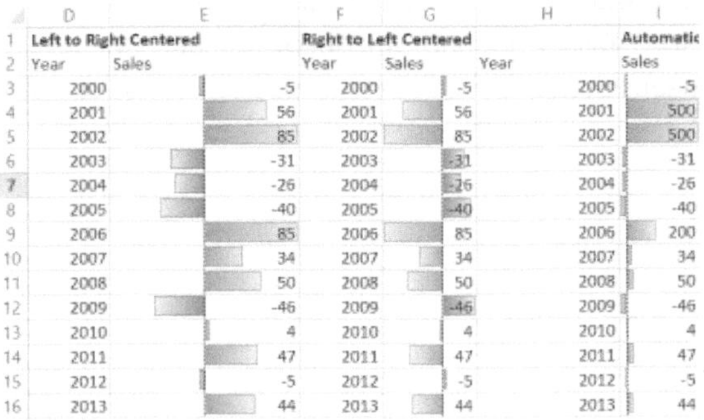

	D	E	F	G	H	I
1	Left to Right Centered		Right to Left Centered			Automatic
2	Year	Sales	Year	Sales	Year	Sales
3	2000	-5	2000	-5	2000	-5
4	2001	56	2001	56	2001	500
5	2002	85	2002	85	2002	500
6	2003	-31	2003	-31	2003	-31
7	2004	-26	2004	-26	2004	-26
8	2005	-40	2005	-40	2005	-40
9	2006	85	2006	85	2006	200
10	2007	34	2007	34	2007	34
11	2008	50	2008	50	2008	50
12	2009	-46	2009	-46	2009	-46
13	2010	4	2010	4	2010	4
14	2011	47	2011	47	2011	47
15	2012	-5	2012	-5	2012	-5
16	2013	44	2013	44	2013	44

FIGURE 23-11 This figure shows data bars for negative values with both solid and gradient shading.

How do color scales work?

Use color scales to summarize some data sets. Like Highlight Cells Rules, a color scale uses cell shading to display the differences in cell values. This section describes an example of a three-color scale. (The Colorscaleinvestment.xlsx file and Figure 23-12 illustrate the use of a three-color scale. Note rows 19–75 are hidden; to display them, select rows 18 and 76, right-click the selection, and then click **Unhide**.) Select the annual returns on Stocks, T-Bills, and T-Bonds in cells B8:D89. Choose **Conditional Formatting**, **Color Scales**, and then **More Rules** to display the **Edit Formatting Rule** dialog box, which is filled in as shown in Figure 23-13.

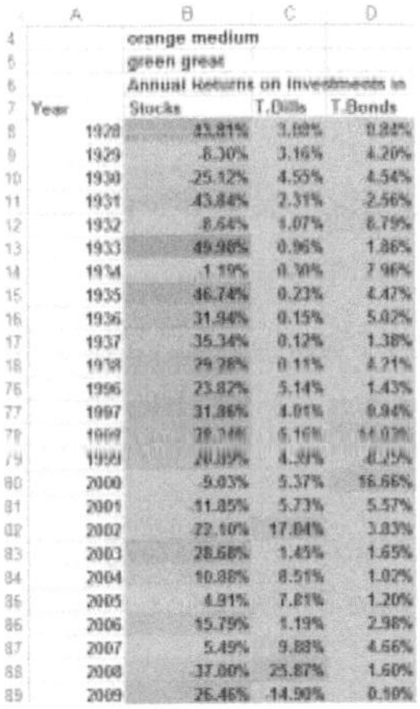

	A	B	C	D
4		orange medium		
5		green great		
6		Annual Returns on Investments in		
7	Year	Stocks	T.Bills	T.Bonds
8	1928	43.81%	3.08%	0.84%
9	1929	-8.30%	3.16%	4.20%
10	1930	-25.12%	4.55%	4.54%
11	1931	-43.84%	2.31%	-2.56%
12	1932	-8.64%	1.07%	8.79%
13	1933	49.98%	0.96%	1.86%
14	1934	-1.19%	0.30%	7.96%
15	1935	46.74%	0.23%	4.47%
16	1936	31.94%	0.15%	5.02%
17	1937	-35.34%	0.12%	1.38%
18	1938	29.28%	0.11%	4.21%
76	1996	23.82%	5.14%	1.43%
77	1997	31.86%	4.91%	9.94%
78	1998	28.34%	5.16%	14.92%
79	1999	20.89%	4.39%	-8.25%
80	2000	-9.03%	5.37%	16.66%
81	2001	-11.85%	5.73%	5.57%
82	2002	-22.10%	17.84%	3.83%
83	2003	28.68%	1.45%	1.65%
84	2004	10.88%	8.51%	1.02%
85	2005	4.91%	7.81%	1.20%
86	2006	15.79%	1.19%	2.98%
87	2007	5.49%	9.88%	4.66%
88	2008	-37.00%	25.87%	1.60%
89	2009	26.46%	-14.90%	0.10%

FIGURE 23-12 This figure shows three-color scales.

Choose the color red to indicate the lowest return, green to indicate the highest return, and orange to indicate the return at the midpoint. Amazingly, Excel makes small changes to the color shading of each cell based on the value in the cell. In column B of Figure 23-12, the lowest return is shaded red. Note that 1931 and 2008 (as we all know) were very poor years for stocks. As the returns approach the fiftieth percentile, the cell color gradually changes to yellow. Then, as the returns increase from the fiftieth percentile toward the largest return, the cell color changes from yellow to green. Most of the green and red cells are associated with stocks because annual stock returns are more variable than bond or T-bill returns. This variability causes large and small stock returns to occur quite frequently. Virtually all annual returns for T-Bills or T-Bonds are yellow because the low variability of annual returns on these investments means that intermediate returns occur most of the time.

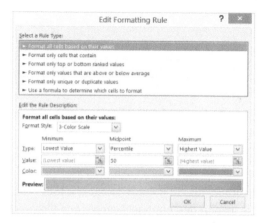

FIGURE 23-13 Customize a three-color scale.

Some two-color scales were created in the Scalesiconsdatabars.xlsx file shown in Figure 23-14. To do this, select the range of cells; click **Conditional Formatting** and choose **Color Scales**. You can select the color combination you want from the given list or create your own by choosing **More Rules**.

You can choose a two-color scale that indicates lower values in white and higher values in dark blue.

- In the D19:D28 cell range, choose to make the lowest value white and the highest value blue. As numbers increase, the cell shading becomes darker.

- In the E19:E28 range, choose to make values less than or equal to 3 white and values greater than or equal to 8 blue. For numbers between 3 and 8, as numbers increase, the cell shading becomes darker.

- In the F19:F28 range, choose to make values in the bottom 20 percent of the range white and numbers in the top 20 percent blue. For numbers in the middle 60 percent, cell shading becomes darker as numbers increase.

	D	E	F
16	Color Scales		
17	lowest value	<=3	20th percentile
18	highest value	>=8	80th percentile
19	1	1	1
20	2	2	1
21	3	3	2
22	4	4	2
23	5	5	4
24	6	6	5
25	7	7	5
26	8	8	7
27	9	9	9
28	10	10	10

FIGURE 23-14 This figure shows two-color scales.

How do icon sets work?

You can also display numerical differences by using icon sets. (See Figure 23-15 and the Scalesiconsdatabars.xlsx file.) An icon set consists of three to five symbols. You define criteria to associate an icon with each value in a cell range. For example, you might use a down arrow for small numbers, an up arrow for large numbers, and a horizontal arrow for intermediate values. The E32:F41 cell range contains two illustrations of the use of icon sets. For each column, you can use the red down arrow, the yellow horizontal arrow, and the green up arrow, for instance.

	D	E	F	
30	down arrow	<=3		20th percentile
31	up arrow	>=8		80th percentile
32		⬇	1 ⬇	1
33		⬇	2 ⬇	1
34		⬇	3 ➡	2
35		➡	4 ➡	2
36		➡	5 ➡	3
37		➡	6 ➡	5
38		➡	7 ➡	5
39		⬆	8 ➡	7
40		⬆	9 ⬆	8
41		⬆	10 ⬆	10

FIGURE 23-15 This figure shows how icon sets with arrows are used to summarize data.

You can assign icons to a range of numerical values as follows:

1. After selecting the numbers in E32:E41, choose **Conditional Formatting** and **Icon Sets**; choose **More Rules** and the **3 Arrows (Colored)** icon set from the **Icon Styles** list. In column E, you want numbers less than 4 to display a down arrow, numbers from 4 to 8 to display a horizontal arrow, and numbers 8 or larger to display an up arrow. To accomplish this goal, set the options in the **Edit Formatting Rule** dialog box as shown in Figure 23-16.

FIGURE 23-16 Assign icons to numerical values.

2. In a similar fashion, set up a formatting rule for F31:F42 so that up arrows are placed in cells containing numbers in the eightieth percentile or above of all values (>=8), and down

arrows are placed in cells containing numbers in the bottom 20 percent of all values (<=1). Figure 23-17 displays the configured formatting settings.

FIGURE 23-17 Assign icons to percentile values.

Optional settings include Reverse Icon Order, which associates the icons on the left with small numbers and the icons on the right with larger numbers, and Show Icon Only, which hides the contents of the cell. In Excel 2013, you can hide a subset of icons. You can also customize icon sets. In the Customize Icons worksheet in the Historicalinvest.xlsx file, you can use three icons to summarize investment returns. The top third of the returns appear with a gray up arrow; the bottom third of the returns contain a red down arrow. You can hide the flat arrow icon for the middle third of the returns. Figure 23-18 shows the resulting icons, and Figure 23-19 shows the dialog box (accessed from Manage Rules) that creates this formatting. You can customize the three-gray-arrow icon set by replacing the gray down arrow with a red arrow.

	A	B	C	D
6		Annual Returns on Investments in		
7	Year	Stocks	T.Bills	T.Bonds
8		1928 ⬆ 43.81%	3.08% ⬇	0.84%
9		1929 ⬇ -8.30%	3.16%	4.20%
10		1930 ⬇ -25.12%	4.55%	4.54%
11		1931 ⬇ -43.84%	2.31% ⬇	-2.56%
12		1932 ⬇ -8.64% ⬇	1.07% ⬆	8.79%
13		1933 ⬆ 49.98% ⬇	0.96% ⬇	1.86%
14		1934 ⬇ -1.19% ⬇	0.30% ⬆	7.96%
15		1935 ⬆ 46.74% ⬇	0.23%	4.47%
80		2000 ⬇ -9.03%	5.37% ⬆	16.66%
81		2001 ⬇ -11.85%	5.73%	5.57%
82		2002 ⬇ -22.10% ⬆ 17.84%		3.83%
83		2003 ⬆ 28.68% ⬇	1.45%	1.65%
84		2004 ⬆ 10.88% ⬆	8.51% ⬇	1.02%
85		2005 4.91%	7.81% ⬇	1.20%
86		2006 ⬆ 15.79% ⬇	1.19%	2.98%
87		2007 5.49% ⬆	9.88%	4.66%
88		2008 ⬇ -37.00% ⬆ 25.87%		1.60%
89		2009 ⬆ 26.46% ⬇ -14.90% ⬇		0.10%

FIGURE 23-18 This figure shows a customized icon set with a hidden icon.

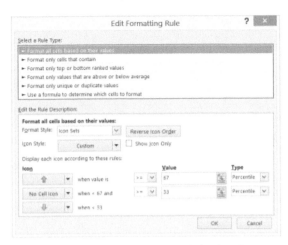

Edit Formatting Rule

Select a Rule Type:

► Format all cells based on their values
► Format only cells that contain
► Format only top or bottom ranked values
► Format only values that are above or below average
► Format only unique or duplicate values
► Use a formula to determine which cells to format

Edit the Rule Description:

Format all cells based on their values:

Format Style: Icon Sets   Reverse Icon Order

Icon Style: Custom   ☐ Show Icon Only

Display each icon according to these rules:

Icon		Value	Type
⬆	when value is >=	67	Percentile
No Cell Icon	when < 67 and >=	33	Percentile
⬇	when < 33		

OK   Cancel

FIGURE 23-19 This figure shows the dialog box for customizing and hiding icons.

How can I color-code monthly stock returns so that every good month is indicated in one color and every bad month in another?

The Sandp.xlsx file, shown in Figure 23-20, contains monthly values and returns on the Standard & Poor's stock index. Suppose that you want to highlight each month in green in which the S&P index went up by more than 3 percent and highlight each month in red in which it went down more than 3 percent.

Begin by moving to cell C10 (the first month containing an S&P return) and selecting all monthly returns by pressing Ctrl+Shift+down arrow. Choose **Conditional Formatting**, **Manage Rules**, and **New Rule** and select **Format Only Cells That Contain**. Fill in the dialog box as shown in Figure 23-21. You can tell Excel to format cells in the selected range that are >0.03 and, after clicking **Format**, select the format to use (a green fill).

Notice that the lists for fonts and font size aren't available, so your choice of formatting can't change these attributes. You can use the **Fill** tab to shade cells in a color you choose and use the **Borders** tab to create a border for cells that satisfy your conditional criteria. After clicking **OK** in the **Format Cells** dialog box, you return to the **Conditional Formatting** dialog box. You can now select **New Rule** again and, in a similar fashion, set things up so that all cells containing numbers that are less than −0.03 have a red fill. (See Figure 23-22.)

When you click **OK**, all months with an S&P return that's greater than 3 percent (see cell C23, for example) are displayed in green, and all months with an S&P return of less than −3 percent (see cell C18) are displayed in red. Cells in which the monthly returns don't meet either of these conditions maintain their original formatting.

	A	B	C	D
6		S&P		
7		Comp.		
8	Date	P	Change	
9	1871.01	4.44		
10	1871.02	4.5	0.01351	
11	1871.03	4.61	0.02444	
12	1871.04	4.74	0.0282	
13	1871.05	4.86	0.02532	
14	1871.06	4.82	-0.0082	
15	1871.07	4.73	-0.0187	
16	1871.08	4.79	0.01268	
17	1871.09	4.84	0.01044	
18	1871.1	4.59	-0.0517	
19	1871.11	4.64	0.01089	
20	1871.12	4.74	0.02155	
21	1872.01	4.86	0.02532	
22	1872.02	4.88	0.00412	
23	1872.03	5.04	0.03279	
24	1872.04	5.18	0.02778	
25	1872.05	5.18	0	
26	1872.06	5.13	-0.0097	

FIGURE 23-20 Conditional formatting highlights returns in the S&P stock index.

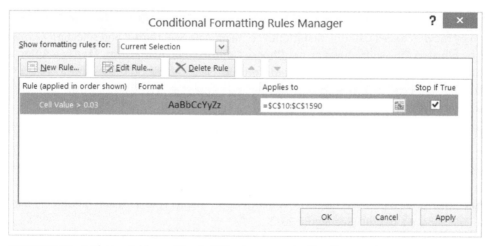

FIGURE 23-21 Apply special formatting to S&P returns greater than 3 percent.

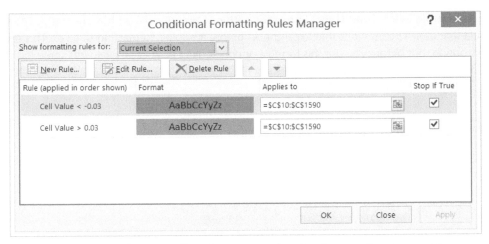

FIGURE 23-22 Color stock returns of less than 3 percent in red and greater than 3 percent in green.

Here are some useful tips concerning conditional formatting:

- To delete conditional formatting (or any format) applied to a range of cells, simply select the range of cells, click **Conditional Formatting**, choose **Clear Rules**, and then choose **Clear Rules From Selected Cells**.

- To select all the cells in a worksheet to which conditional formatting applies, press F5 to open the Go To dialog box. In the dialog box, click **Special**, select **Conditional Formats**, and then click **OK**.

- If you want to edit a conditional formatting rule, choose **Manage Rules** and then double-click the rule or click **Edit Rules**.

- You can delete a specific conditional formatting rule by choosing **Manage Rules**, selecting the rule, and then choosing **Delete Rule**.

Notice that after both rules are defined, the red formatting rule is listed first (because it was created more recently than the green formatting rule). In the Conditional Formatting Rules Manager dialog box, rules are listed in order of precedence. In this example, it does not matter which rule is listed first because no cell can satisfy the criteria for both rules. If rules conflict, however, the rule listed first takes precedence. To change the order of conditional formatting rules, select the rule and click the up arrow to move the rule up in precedence or the down arrow to move the rule down in precedence.

Given quarterly corporate revenues, how can I indicate quarters in which revenues increased over the previous quarter in one color and quarters in which revenues decreased from the previous quarter in another color?

The Amazon.xlsx file contains quarterly revenues (in millions) for Amazon.com from 1995 through 2009. (See Figure 23-23.) You want to highlight quarters in which revenues increased over the previous quarter in green and highlight quarters in which revenues decreased over the previous quarter in red.

Use A Formula in the **Conditional Formatting Rules Manager** dialog box enables you to specify a formula that defines conditions that Excel checks before it applies formatting to a cell. This section uses this option, but before you use this formula option, look at how Excel evaluates some logical functions. The work is in the Logicalexamples.xlsx file.

	B	C	D	E
4		FiscalYear	FiscalQuarter	Revenue
5		1995	4	0.511
6		1996	1	0.875
7		1996	2	2.230
8		1996	3	4.173
9		1996	4	8.468
10		1997	1	16.005
11		1997	2	27.855
12		1997	3	37.887
13		1997	4	66.040
14		1998	1	87.361
15		1998	2	115.982
16		1998	3	153.649
17		1998	4	252.893
18		1999	1	293.643
19		1999	2	314.376
20		1999	3	355.778
21		1999	4	676.042
22		2000	1	573.889
23		2000	2	577.876
24		2000	3	637.858
25		2000	4	972.360
26		2001	1	700.356

FIGURE 23-23 Highlight increased sales in green and decreased sales in red.

What happens when you type a formula such as =B3<2 in cell B4? If the value in B3 is a number smaller than *2*, Excel returns the value *True* in cell B4; otherwise, Excel returns *False*. You can refer to the Logicalexamples.xlsx file, shown in Figure 23-24, for other examples like this, including combinations of *AND*, *OR*, and *NOT* in formulas.

- In cell B6, the =OR(B3<3,C3>5) formula returns the value *True* if either of the conditions, B3<3 or C3>5, is true. Because the value of C3 is greater than *5*, Excel returns *True*.

- In cell B7, the =AND(B3=3,C3>5) formula returns *True* if B3=3 and C3>5. Because B3 is not equal to 3, Excel returns *False*. In cell B8, however, the =AND(B3>3,C3>5) formula returns *True* because B3>3 and C3>5 are both true.

- In cell B9, the =NOT(B3<2) formula returns *True* because B3<2 would return *False*, and a not-false value becomes *True*.

	A	B	C
2		**Logical functions**	
3		4	6
4	B3<2	FALSE	
5	B3>3	TRUE	
6	OR(B3<3,C3>5)	TRUE	
7	AND(B3=3,C3>5)	FALSE	
8	AND(B3>3,C3>5)	TRUE	
9	NOT(B3<2)	TRUE	

FIGURE 23-24 This figure shows logical functions.

Now look at how Use A Formula enables you to create a conditional format in a range of cells. Begin by selecting the range of cells to which you want to apply a conditional format. Click **Conditional Formatting** and choose **Manage Rules** to open the **Conditional Formatting Rules Manager** dialog box. Choose **New Rule** and then select **Use A Formula To Determine Which Cells To Format** (the last option, also called the *formula option*). To use the formula option, you enter a formula (the formula must start with an equals sign) that is true if and only if you want the cell in the upper left corner to be assigned the chosen format. Your logical formula can be copied like an ordinary formula to the remainder of the selected range, so use dollar signs ($) judiciously to ensure that for each cell of the selected range the formula will be true if and only if you want your format to apply to the cell. Choose **Format** and then enter the formatting you want. Click **OK**. After clicking **OK** in the **Conditional Formatting** dialog box, your formula and formatting are copied to the whole cell range. The formatting is applied to any cell in the selected range that satisfies the condition defined in the formula.

Now return to the Amazon.xlsx file, and you will highlight in green the quarters in which revenues increase. Select the E6:E61 range (there is no prior quarter to which you can compare the revenue figure in cell E5) and then instruct Excel to highlight a cell's value in green if it is larger than the cell's value above it. Figure 23-25 shows how to set up the rule.

If you enter =E6>E5 by pointing to the appropriate cells, be sure you remove the $ signs from the formula in the Conditional Formatting dialog box, or the formula won't be copied. Probably the easiest way to insert or delete dollar signs is to use the F4 key. When you highlight a cell reference such as A3, pressing F4 includes or deletes dollar signs in the following order: A3, $A$3, A$3, $A3. Thus, if you start with $A$3, pressing F4 changes the cell reference to A$3. The formula in this example ensures that cell E6 is colored green if and only if sales in that quarter exceed the previous quarter. After clicking OK, you'll find that all quarters in which revenue increased are colored green. In cell E7, for example, the formula was copied in the usual way, becoming =E7>E6.

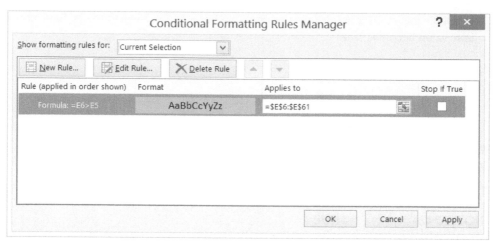

FIGURE 23-25 This figure shows conditional formatting settings that will display in green the quarters in which revenue increased.

To add the condition for formatting cells in which revenue decreased, select the E6:E61 range again, open the **Conditional Formatting Rules Manager** dialog box, choose **New Rule**, and then select **Use A Formula To Determine Which Cells To Format**. Enter the =E6<E5 formula and then click **Format**. On the **Fill** tab, change the fill color to red and then click **OK** twice. The **Conditional Formatting Rules Manager** dialog box opens, as shown in Figure 23-26.

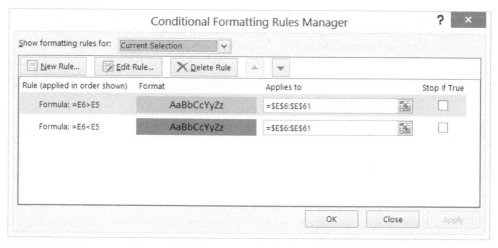

FIGURE 23-26 These conditions will display quarters in which revenue increased in green and quarters in which revenue decreased in red.

You can use the formula option with color scales, data bars, and icon sets. Select the option when setting the criteria for your color scale, data bars, or icon sets.

Given a list of dates, how can I indicate weekend dates in a specific color?

The Weekendformatting.xlsx file (see Figure 23-27) contains several dates. You want to highlight all Saturdays and Sundays in red. To do this, copy the WEEKDAY(C6,2) formula from cell D6 to D7:D69. Choosing Type=2 for the *WEEKDAY* function returns a 1 for each Monday, a 2 for each Tuesday, and so on, so that the function returns a 6 for each Saturday and a 7 for each Sunday.

	C	D	E	F
3		Monday = 1 Tuesday = 2 ,etc.		
4				
5	Date	Weekday		
6	2/8/2003	6		
7	1/2/2007	2		
8	1/2/2005	7		
9	10/25/2005	2		
10	10/10/2004	7		
11	10/13/2006	5		
12	9/26/2006	2		
13	9/25/2006	1		
14	11/1/2005	2		
15	11/29/2006	3		
16	2/16/2005	3		
17	7/27/2007	5		
18	3/24/2004	3		
19	10/6/2008	1		
20	4/11/2007	3		
21	2/3/2004	2		
22	1/22/2009	4		
23	10/29/2006	7		
24	6/9/2005	4		
25	8/16/2008	6		

FIGURE 23-27 Use the *WEEKDAY* function to highlight weekend days in red.

Select the D6:D69 range, click **Conditional Formatting**, and then choose **Manage Rules**. Click **New Rule** and the formula option and fill in the dialog box as shown in Figure 23-28.

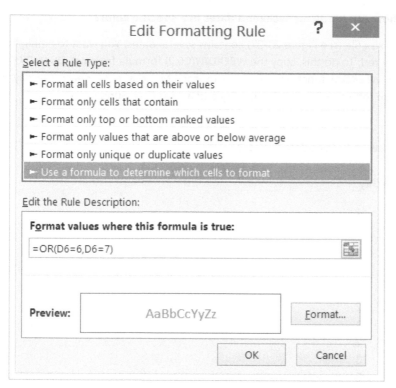

FIGURE 23-28 Use the Edit Formatting Rule dialog box setup to display weekend days in red.

After you click **OK**, each date whose weekday is equal to 6 (for Saturday) or 7 (for Sunday) is colored red. The =OR(D6=6,D6=7) formula implies that a cell entry of 6 or 7 will activate the red font color. You could have also used **Format Only Cells That Contain** and >=6 or >5 to obtain the same formatting.

Our basketball coach has given each player a rating between 1 and 10 based on the player's ability to play guard, forward, or center. Can I set up a worksheet that visually indicates the ability of each player to play the position to which she's assigned?

The Basketball.xlsx file, shown in Figure 23-29, contains ratings given to 20 players for each position and the position (1=Guard, 2=Forward, 3=Center) played by each player. The goal here is to fill with red the cell containing the rating for each player for the position to which she's assigned.

	A	B	C	D	E	F
1			1	2	3	
2	Position played	Player	Guard rating	Forward rating	Center rating	
3	1	1	1	9	2	1=Guard
4	1	2	4	3	9	2=Forward
5	2	3	7	3	7	3=Center
6	2	4	9	8	8	
7	2	5	5	8	9	
8	3	6	2	7	2	
9	3	7	7	6	6	
10	3	8	4	4	3	
11	3	9	3	8	10	
12	3	10	6	1	4	
13	2	11	6	7	5	
14	2	12	2	6	5	
15	2	13	8	6	9	
16	1	14	1	1	3	
17	1	15	3	6	8	
18	2	16	4	10	1	
19	2	17	8	5	1	
20	2	18	1	7	7	
21	3	19	9	2	7	
22	3	20	10	3	10	
23						

FIGURE 23-29 This worksheet rates each player's ability to play a position.

Begin by selecting the C3:E22 range, which contains the players' ratings. Click **Conditional Formatting** and choose **Manage Rules**. Choose **New Rule** and then choose the formula option. Now fill in the dialog box as shown Figure 23-30.

The =$A3=C$1 formula compares the player's assigned position to the column heading (1, 2, or 3) in row 1. If the player's assigned position is set to 1 (Guard), her rating in column C, which is her guard rating, appears in red. Similarly, if the player's assigned position is set to 2, her forward rating in column D appears in red. Finally, if the assigned position is set to 3, her center rating in column E appears in red. Note that if you do not include the dollar sign with the A and the 1 in the formula, it will not copy down and across correctly.

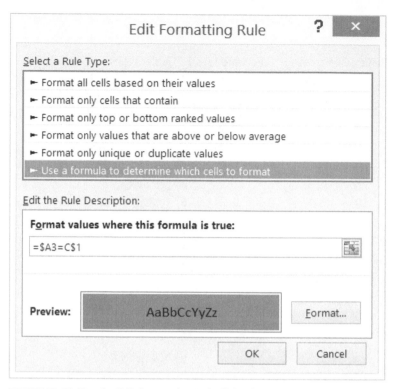

FIGURE 23-30 Use the Edit Formatting Rule dialog box setup to show player ratings in red fill.

Note also that Excel 2013 allows conditional formats created with formulas to reference data in other worksheets.

What does the Stop If True option in the Manage Rules dialog box do?

Suppose that Stop If True is selected for a rule. If a cell satisfies this rule, all lower precedent rules are ignored. Use the Income.xlsx file to illustrate the use of Stop If True. This file shows median income for each US state for years between 1984 and 2010. Suppose (as shown in Figure 23-31) that you want to have up arrows show for the 10 states that have the highest 2010 median income and no icons to appear for any other states. The key is to make the first rule **No Format** for the states with the 40 lowest median incomes and then to select **Stop If True**. Then create the desired icon set.

The settings that hide the arrows for the 40 states with the lowest 40 median 2010 incomes are shown in Figure 23-32.

	State	2010 Median income
6	Alabama	40,976
7	Alaska	⬆ 58,198
8	Arizona	47,279
9	Arkansas	38,571
10	California	54,459
11	Colorado	⬆ 60,442
12	Connecticut	⬆ 66,452
13	Delaware	55,269
14	Florida	44,243
15	Georgia	44,108
16	Hawaii	⬆ 58,507
17	Idaho	47,014
18	Illinois	50,761
19	Indiana	46,322
20	Iowa	49,177
21	Kansas	46,229
22	Kentucky	41,236
23	Louisiana	39,443
24	Maine	48,133
25	Maryland	⬆ 64,025
26	Massachusetts	⬆ 61,333
27	Michigan	46,441

FIGURE 23-31 Use up arrows to highlight the 10 states with largest median income.

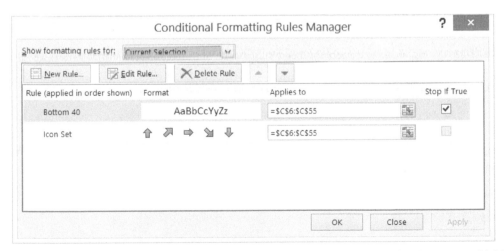

FIGURE 23-32 This figure shows the settings that ensure that only the top 10 median incomes are highlighted with up arrows.

The settings for the second rule are shown in Figure 23-33. Note that the top 20 percent of states involves .2 * 50 = 10 states. The remaining settings are of no importance.

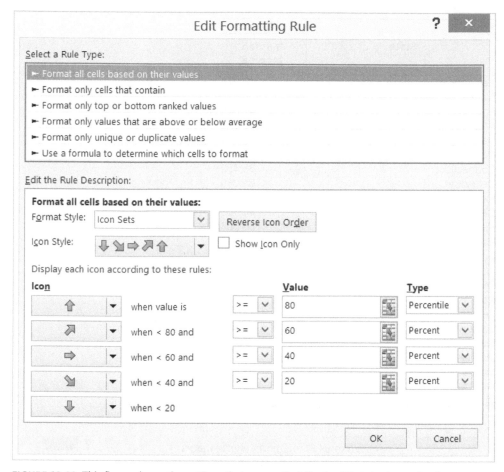

FIGURE 23-33 This figure shows the settings that ensure that the top 10 states in median income get an up arrow.

How can I use the Format Painter to copy a conditional format?

The Format Painter icon (see the paintbrush shown in Figure 23-34) enables you to paint the format (including conditional formats) from any cell or group of cells to any group of cells. Select the cell or group of cells with the format you want to copy and click the Format Painter icon. Use the paintbrush to select the cells where you want the format copied.

FIGURE 23-34 This figure shows the Format Painter icon.

If you want to copy a format to a range that includes nonadjacent cells, double-click the Format Painter and select all the cells where you want the format copied. To turn off the Format Painter, click the Format Painter icon.

Problems

1. Using the data in the Sandp.xlsx file, use conditional formatting in the following situations:

   - Format in bold each month in which the value of the S&P index increased and underline each month in which the value of the S&P index decreased.

   - Highlight in green each month in which the S&P index changed by a maximum of 2 percent.

   - Highlight the largest S&P index value in red and the smallest in purple.

2. Using the data in the Toysrusformat.xlsx file, highlight all fourth-quarter revenues in blue and first-quarter revenues in red.

3. The Test.xlsx file contains exam scores for students. The top 10 students receive an A, the next 20 students receive a B, and all other students receive a C. Highlight the A grades in red, the B grades in green, and the C grades in blue. Hint: The *LARGE(D4:D63,10)* function gives you the tenth-highest grade on the test.

4. In the Weekendformatting.xlsx file, highlight all weekdays in red. Highlight in blue all days that occur in the first 10 days of the month.

5. Suppose each worker in the Microsoft finance department has been assigned to one of four groups. The supervisor of each group has rated each worker on a 0–10 scale, and each worker has rated his satisfaction with each of the four groups. (See the Satissuper.xlsx file.) Based on the group to which each worker is assigned, highlight the supervisor rating and the worker satisfaction rating for each worker.

6. The Varianceanalysis.xlsx file contains monthly profit forecasts and monthly actual sales. The sales variance for a month equals:

$$\frac{actualsales - predictedsales}{predictedsales}$$

   Highlight in red all months with a favorable variance of at least 20 percent and highlight in green all months with an unfavorable variance of more than 20 percent.

7. For your drug cost example from Chapter 21, "The OFFSET function," format the worksheet so that all Phase 1 costs are displayed in red, all Phase 2 costs are displayed in green, and all Phase 3 costs are displayed in purple.

8. The Names.xlsx file contains a list of names. Highlight all duplicates in green and all names containing Ja in red.

9. The Duedates.xlsx file contains due dates for various invoices. Highlight in red all invoices due by the end of the next month.

10. In the Historicalinvest.xlsx file, set up conditional formatting with three icons so that 10 percent of returns have an up arrow, 10 percent have a down arrow, and 80 percent have a horizontal arrow.

11. The Nbasalaries.xlsx file contains salaries of NBA players in millions of dollars. Set up data bars to summarize this data. Players making less than $1 million should have the shortest data bar, and players making more than $15 million should have the longest data bar.

12. Set up a three-color scale to summarize the NBA salary data. Change the color of the bottom 10 percent of all salaries to green and the top 10 percent to red.

13. Use five icons to summarize the NBA player data. Create break points for icons at $3 million, $6 million, $9 million, and $12 million.

14. How could you set things up so that no icons are shown for players who have salaries between $7 million and $8 million? Hint: Use Stop If True.

15. The Fractiondefective.xlsx file contains the percentage of defective units produced daily. A day's production is considered acceptable if 2 percent or less of the items produced are defective. Highlight all acceptable days with a green flag. In another worksheet, highlight all acceptable days with a red flag. Hint: Use Stop If True to ensure that no icon occurs in any cell containing a number greater than 2.

16. Summarize the global warming data with a three-color scale. Lower temperatures should be blue, intermediate temperatures should be yellow, and higher temperatures should be red.

17. Suppose you are saving for your child's college fund. You will contribute the same amount of money to the fund at the end of each year. Your goal is to end up with $100,000. For annual investment returns ranging from 4 percent to 15 percent and number of years investing varying from 5 to 15 years, determine your required annual contribution. Suppose you can save $10,000 per year. Use conditional formatting to highlight the minimum number of years needed for each annual return rate to accumulate $100,000.

18. The Amazon.xlsx file contains quarterly revenues for Amazon.com. Use conditional formatting to ensure that sales during each quarter are highlighted in a different color.

19. Set up conditional formatting that colors the A1:H8 cell range like a checkerboard, with alternating white and black coloring. Hint: The ROW() function gives the row number of a cell, and the COLUMN() function gives the column number of a cell.

20. When students take Vivian's accounting exam, they are told to enter their email alias on a Scantron. Often, they make a mistake. Vivian has a list of the actual email aliases for the students in the class. She would like to highlight in yellow the email aliases students enter that are not true aliases. This will help her correct them easily. The Scantrons.xlsx file contains the necessary data. Help Vivian out!

21. The Top5.xlsx file contains the revenues each year of 50 companies. For each year, highlight the companies that have the five largest revenues. Hint: The *LARGE(B1:B50,5)* function would return the fifth largest number in the B1:B50 range.

22. The Threetimes.xlsx file contains a list of names. Highlight in red each name that appears at least three times.

23. The GNP.xlsx file contains quarterly US gross national product. Take advantage of the fact that data bars handle negative values to summarize quarterly GNP percentage growth rates.

24. Using the data in the Globalwarming2011temp.xlsx file, highlight the years (not the temperatures) in which the temperature is above average.

25. The Accountsums.xlsx file (see Figure 23-35) shows weekly salaries in thousands of dollars (listed in chronological order) paid to several top-notch consultants. For example, during the first week, Britney made $91,000 and, during the last week, made $57,000:

   - Use the Formula option to highlight each person's name in yellow.

   - Use the Formula option to highlight each person's first week of salary in orange.

▲	A	B	C	D
4		Britney		
5			91	
6			79	
7			81	
8			67	
9			59	
10			93	
11			94	
12			91	
13			86	
14			82	
15			93	
16			76	
17			71	
18			94	
19			57	
20		Lindsay		
21			95	
22			71	

FIGURE 23-35 This figure shows the data for Problem 25.

26. The Shading.xlsx file contains 27 quarters of sales:

- Shade alternate rows in green and yellow.

- Alternately shade four rows in green, four rows in yellow, and so on.

CHAPTER 24

Sorting in Excel

Questions answered in this chapter:

- How can I sort sales transaction data so that transactions are sorted first by salesperson and then by product, by units sold, and in chronological order from oldest to most recent?

- I have always wanted to sort my data based on cell color or font color. Is this possible in Excel 2013?

- I love the great icon sets described in Chapter 23, "Conditional formatting." Can I sort my data based on the icon in the cell?

- My worksheet includes a column containing the month in which each sale occurred. When I sort by this column, I get either April (first month alphabetically) or October (last month alphabetically) on top. How can I sort by this column so that the months are chronologically sorted, that is, January transactions on top, followed by February and the following months?

- Can I sort data without using the Sort dialog box?

Almost every user of Microsoft Excel has at one time or another sorted columns of data alphabetically or by numerical value. Look at some examples of how powerful sorting is in Excel 2013.

Answers to this chapter's questions

This section provides the answers to the questions that are listed at the beginning of the chapter.

How can I sort sales transaction data so that transactions are sorted first by salesperson and then by product, by units sold, and in chronological order from oldest to most recent?

JAC is a small company that sells makeup. The Makeup worksheet in the Makeupsorttemp.xlsx file in the Templates folder for this chapter (see Figure 24-1) contains the following sales transaction information:

- Transaction number

- Name of salesperson

- Date of transaction

- Product sold

- Units sold

- Dollars received

- Location of transaction

Q16	▾	: ✕ ✓ ƒ×				

	E	F	G	H	I	J	K
3	Trans Number	Name	Date	Product	Units	Dollars	Location
4	1	Betsy	4/1/2004	lip gloss	45	$ 137.20	south
5	2	Hallagan	3/10/2004	foundatior	50	$ 152.01	midwest
6	3	Ashley	2/25/2005	lipstick	9	$ 28.72	midwest
7	4	Hallagan	5/22/2006	lip gloss	55	$ 167.08	west
8	5	Zaret	6/17/2004	lip gloss	43	$ 130.60	midwest
9	6	Colleen	11/27/2005	eye liner	58	$ 175.99	midwest
10	7	Cristina	3/21/2004	eye liner	8	$ 25.80	midwest
11	8	Colleen	12/17/2006	lip gloss	72	$ 217.84	midwest
12	9	Ashley	7/5/2006	eye liner	75	$ 226.64	south
13	10	Betsy	8/7/2006	lip gloss	24	$ 73.50	east
14	11	Ashley	11/29/2004	mascara	43	$ 130.84	east
15	12	Ashley	11/18/2004	lip gloss	23	$ 71.03	west

FIGURE 24-1 This figure shows the sales transaction data before sorting.

You want to sort the data so that:

- Transactions are listed alphabetically by salesperson. You want to sort in the usual A-to-Z order so that all of Ashley's transactions are first and all of Zaret's transactions are last.

- Each person's transactions are sorted alphabetically by product. Thus, Ashley's eyeliner transactions will be followed by Ashley's foundation transactions and so on.

- For each salesperson and product, transactions are listed by number of units sold (in descending order).

- If a salesperson makes two or more sales of the same product for the same number of units, transactions are listed in chronological order.

In versions of Excel before Excel 2007, it was difficult to sort by more than three criteria. Now Excel enables you to apply up to 64 criteria in one sort. To sort the sales data, you need to select the data (cell range E3:K1894) first. Two easy ways to select these data are as follows:

- Position the cursor in the upper-left corner of the data (cell E3) and then press Ctrl+Shift+right arrow followed by Ctrl+Shift+down arrow.

- Position the cursor anywhere in the cell range and press Ctrl+Shift+*.

On the **Data** tab, in the **Sort & Filter** group, choose **Sort** to open the **Sort** dialog box shown in Figure 24-2.

FIGURE 24-2 The Sort dialog box is not yet filled in.

Because row 3 contains headings for the data columns, select the **My Data Has Headers** check box. Select the following four criteria in the order shown:

1. Sort by the Name column so that values (this means cell contents) are in A-to-Z order.

2. Sort by the Product column so that values are in A-to-Z order.

3. Sort by the Units column so that values are in order from largest to smallest.

4. Sort by the Date column so that values are in chronological order from oldest to newest.

The dialog box now looks like Figure 24-3.

FIGURE 24-3 The Sort dialog box is set up for the sales sorting example.

The result of your sort is shown in Figure 24-4.

	E	F	G	H	I	J	K
3	Trans Number	Name	Date	Product	Units	Dollars	Location
4	785	Ashley	4/10/2005	eye liner	92	$ 278.34	east
5	1879	Ashley	8/18/2006	eye liner	90	$ 271.85	midwest
6	1685	Ashley	11/5/2005	eye liner	88	$ 265.96	south
7	1737	Ashley	3/28/2006	eye liner	88	$ 265.53	east
8	1579	Ashley	6/6/2004	eye liner	87	$ 262.85	east
9	1748	Ashley	5/4/2004	eye liner	85	$ 256.45	east
10	999	Ashley	10/14/2005	eye liner	82	$ 248.12	west
11	449	Ashley	6/6/2004	eye liner	81	$ 244.97	east
12	503	Ashley	7/7/2005	eye liner	81	$ 245.19	west
13	356	Ashley	8/29/2006	eye liner	76	$ 229.58	east
14	9	Ashley	7/5/2006	eye liner	75	$ 226.64	south
15	84	Ashley	10/1/2006	eye liner	73	$ 221.48	west
16	1552	Ashley	1/26/2004	eye liner	72	$ 218.33	south
17	1201	Ashley	12/17/2006	eye liner	66	$ 199.89	south
18	465	Ashley	6/13/2006	eye liner	58	$ 176.27	south
19	124	Ashley	1/10/2006	eye liner	57	$ 173.36	west
20	1653	Ashley	5/4/2004	eye liner	56	$ 170.25	east
21	1428	Ashley	12/6/2006	eye liner	53	$ 160.85	midwest
22	1470	Ashley	10/3/2005	eye liner	51	$ 155.05	west

FIGURE 24-4 This figure shows the sorted sales transaction data.

Note that all of Ashley's transactions are listed first, with eyeliner followed by foundation and so on. Eyeliner transactions are listed from the largest number of units sold to the smallest. In the case of a tie (see rows 6 and 7), the transactions are listed in chronological order.

Using the **Sort** dialog box, you can easily add sort criteria (Add Level), delete sort criteria (Delete Level), copy the settings that define a level of the sort (Copy Level), or specify whether your data has headers. By selecting **Options**, you can make the sort operation case sensitive or even sort data for which each data item is listed in a different column (instead of the more common situation in which each case is in a different row).

I have always wanted to sort my data based on cell color or font color. Is this possible in Excel 2013?

In Excel 2013, sorting on cell or font color is simple. Consider the Makeup worksheet in the Makeupsorttemp.xlsx file. Several names in column F are highlighted in different colors. For example, Cici in cell F620 is highlighted in red, and Colleen in cell F833 is highlighted in yellow. Suppose you want names with green fill on top, followed by yellow and then by red, with the rest of the rows on the bottom. To sort the **Name** column by color, simply select the range you want to sort (E3:K1894), click **Sort**, and choose **Add Level**. Select the **Name** column, click the **Sort On** setting, and select **Cell Color**. (Selecting **Font Color** sorts by font color.) For the first level, select green from the **Order** list, select yellow for the second level, and select red for the third level. The completed dialog box is shown in Figure 24-5. The resulting sort is shown in the Colors worksheet of the Makeupsort.xlsx file in the Practice Files folder for this chapter and in Figure 24-6.

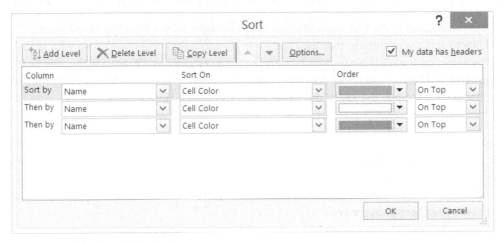

FIGURE 24-5 The Sort dialog box is set up to sort by color.

	Trans Number	Name	Date	Product	Units	Dollars	Location
3	Trans Number	Name	Date	Product	Units	Dollars	Location
4	105	Cristina	9/13/2004	lipstick	51	$ 155.30	midwest
5	165	Hallagan	12/19/2005	foundatio	25	$ 76.99	east
6	86	Jen	8/9/2005	eye liner	-2	$ (4.24)	east
7	23	Colleen	2/1/2006	mascara	25	$ 77.31	midwest
8	14	Hallagan	1/1/2005	eye liner	18	$ 56.47	south
9	33	Cici	6/17/2004	mascara	41	$ 125.27	west
10	785	Ashley	4/10/2005	eye liner	92	$ 278.34	east
11	1879	Ashley	8/18/2006	eye liner	90	$ 271.85	midwest
12	1685	Ashley	11/5/2005	eye liner	88	$ 265.96	south
13	1737	Ashley	3/28/2006	eye liner	88	$ 265.53	east
14	1579	Ashley	6/6/2004	eye liner	87	$ 262.85	east
15	1748	Ashley	5/4/2004	eye liner	85	$ 256.45	east

FIGURE 24-6 This figure shows the results of sorting by color.

I love the great icon sets described in Chapter 23. Can I sort my data based on the icon in the cell?

To sort by icon, select **Cell Icon** from the **Sort On** list in the **Sort** dialog box. In the **Order** list, choose the icon you want on top for the first level and so on.

My worksheet includes a column containing the month in which each sale occurred. When I sort by this column, I get either April (first month alphabetically) or October (last month alphabetically) on top. How can I sort by this column so that the months are chronologically sorted, that is, January transactions on top, followed by February and the following months?

The Dates worksheet in the Makeupsorttemp.xlsx file contains a list of months. (See Figure 24-7.) You would like to sort the months so that they appear in chronological order beginning with January. Begin by selecting the D6:D15 range and sorting column D by values. When selecting the order, select **Custom List** and then select the option, beginning with January, February, March. Note that you could also have sorted by the day of the week. The completed dialog box is shown in Figure 24-8, with the resulting sort shown in Figure 24-9.

Note that in the **Custom Lists** dialog box, you can create a custom sort order list. Select New List; under List Entries, type the entries in the order you want to sort by and then click **Add**. Your new list is now included as a menu selection. For example, if you enter Jack, John, and Alan in List Entries (on different lines or separated by commas), all entries with Jack would be listed first, followed by John listings, with Alan listings at the end.

	D
5	Month
6	Feb
7	Feb
8	Jan
9	Aug
10	Mar
11	Apr
12	May
13	Jan
14	Feb
15	Feb

FIGURE 24-7 This figure shows the months to be sorted.

FIGURE 24-8 The Sort dialog box is set up to sort by month.

	D
6	**Month**
7	**Jan**
8	**Jan**
9	**Feb**
10	**Feb**
11	**Feb**
12	**Feb**
13	**Mar**
14	**Apr**
15	**May**
16	**Aug**

FIGURE 24-9 The months are sorted in chronological order.

Can I sort data without using the Sort dialog box?

Sometimes sorting data without using the Sort dialog box is more convenient. To illustrate how this is done, suppose again that you want to sort the sales transaction data in the Makeup worksheet in the Makeupsort.xlsx file so that transactions are sorted first by salesperson and then by product, by units sold, and, finally, in chronological order from the oldest to the most recent. To begin, select the least important column to sort on first, which is the date column (G3:G1894). Next, in the **Sort & Filter** group on the **Data** tab, click the **Sort A To Z** button (see Figure 25-10) and, with **Expand The Selection** selected, click **Sort** so that all the columns are sorted. The Sort A To Z button sorts numerical data so that the smallest numbers or oldest dates are on top and sorts text so that A precedes B and so on.

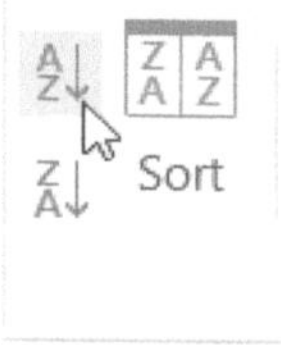

FIGURE 24-10 The Sort icon can be used to sort without the Sort dialog box.

The Sort Z To A button sorts numerical data so that the largest numbers or most recent dates are on top and sorts text data so that Z precedes Y.

Next, sort by the second least important column (Units) Z To A because you want larger sales on top. Then sort from A to Z by Product, and, finally, from A to Z by salesperson. These steps achieve the same results as shown in Figure 24-4.

Problems

1. In the Makeupsort.xlsx file, sort the sales data alphabetically by location and then by product type, name, date of sale, and units sold.

2. The Sortday.xlsx file contains hours worked on different days of the week. Sort the data so that Monday data is followed by Tuesday data and so on.

3. The Sorticons.xlsx file contains annual investment returns with an up arrow used to indicate good years, a horizontal arrow used to indicate average years, and a red down arrow used to indicate bad years. Sort the data by the icons in the Stock column with up arrows on top, followed by horizontal arrows and then red down arrows.

4. The Makeupsortfont.xlsx file contains your makeup data with certain dates shown in blue, red, or brown font. Sort the data so that brown dates are on top, followed by red dates and then blue dates.

Tables

Questions answered in this chapter:

- I have entered the number of units sold and total revenue for each salesperson in a worksheet, and I can easily compute average price for each salesperson. How can I create a nice format that is automatically copied if I enter new data? In addition, is there an easy way to copy my formulas automatically when new data is added?

- I have entered several years of natural gas prices in my worksheet, and I created a nice line chart displaying the monthly variation in prices. Can I set things up so that when I add new gas price data, my chart automatically updates?

- For each sales transaction, I have the salesperson, date, product, location, and size of the transaction. Can I easily summarize, for example, total lipstick sales by Jen or Colleen in the East?

- How do Table Slicers (new to Excel 2013) help us slice and dice data in an Excel table?

- How can I easily refer to portions of a table in other parts of my workbook?

- Do conditional formats automatically apply to new data added to a table?

When most of us use Microsoft Excel, we often enter new data. Then we manually update our formulas, formats, and charts. What a drag! Now the Excel 2013 Table capabilities make this drudgery a thing of the past.

Answers to this chapter's questions

This section provides the answers to the questions that are listed at the beginning of the chapter.

I have entered the number of units sold and total revenue for each salesperson in a worksheet, and I can easily compute average price for each salesperson. How can I create a nice format that is automatically copied if I enter new data? In addition, is there an easy way to copy my formulas automatically when new data is added?

The Tableexampletemp.xlsx file in the Templates folder for this chapter (see Figure 25-1) contains units sold and revenue data for each of six salespersons. You know that new data will be added beginning in row 12 and, in column H, you would like to calculate the average price (Units/Revenue) generated by each salesperson. You would like to create an attractive format for the data and have the formula for average price copied automatically as new data is added.

	E	F	G
4			
5	Name	Units	Revenue
6	John	814	39886
7	Adam	594	26136
8	Dixie	528	13200
9	Tad	806	20956
10	Erica	826	27258
11	Gabrielle	779	28044

FIGURE 25-1 This figure shows the data for creating a table.

By creating a table, your formulas and formatting can be automatically updated when you add data. Begin by selecting the current range of data and headers (E5:G11). Click **Table** on the **Insert** tab or press Ctrl+T. After ensuring that the **My Table Has Headers** box is selected, you will see that the table range (E5:G11) is formatted beautifully. This formatting will continue automatically whenever new data is entered in the table. When you are working in a table, many styles and options are available on the **Table Tools Design** tab. (See Figure 25-2.) This tab is visible only when the active cell is within a table. You can select a formatting style that will be applied to the current table data and to any new data that is added to the table.

Note that the column headings have arrows, as you can see in Figure 25-3. These arrows serve as functionality you can use to sort or filter the table (more on filtering when how to summarize easily, for example, total lipstick sales by Jen or Colleen in the East is discussed later in this chapter).

FIGURE 25-2 This figure shows the table design options.

	E	F	G
5	Name ▾	Units ▾	Revenue ▾
6	John	814	39886
7	Adam	594	26136
8	Dixie	528	13200
9	Tad	806	20956
10	Erica	826	27258
11	Gabrielle	779	28044

FIGURE 25-3 This is a table formatted with filters.

The cells in the selected table (excluding the headers) are given the name Table1 by default. The name has been changed to Sales in the Properties group on the Design tab. If you click the **Formulas** tab and then choose **Name Manager**, you can see that the E6:G12 range is named Sales. The beauty of this range name (and the table) is that the range dynamically expands to include new rows added to the bottom of the table and new columns added to the right of the table. In Chapter 21, "The OFFSET function," you used the *OFFSET* function to create a dynamic range, but the new table capabilities make creation of a dynamic range easy.

Suppose that in D15 you want to compute total revenue. Begin by typing =SUM(S; Microsoft Excel offers you the option to complete the entry automatically with the Sales table range. Implement AutoComplete by double-clicking the range name. You can also implement AutoComplete by moving the cursor to Sales and pressing the Tab key. Then, when you see =SUM(Sales and type an opening bracket ([ ), Formula AutoComplete offers the option to complete the formula with column headings from the Sales table. (See Figure 25-4.) You can complete your formula as =SUM(Sales[Revenue]) and calculate total revenue as $155,480. (See Figure 25-5.) (You will see an example of selecting the entries in the **AutoComplete** box that begin with number signs [#] when table structure is discussed later in this chapter.)

FIGURE 25-4 Here are AutoComplete options for a table.

If new rows of data are added, the data in these rows is automatically accounted for in the formula. To illustrate this idea, you can add new data in row 12: Amanda sold 400 units for $5,000. As shown in Figure 25-6, the total revenue has increased by $5,000 to $160,480.

The formatting has been extended to row 12 as well, and the total revenue formula has been updated to include Amanda's data. Even if data is added within the table (instead of at the bottom), everything will be updated in a consistent fashion.

	D		E	F	G
5			Name ▾	Units ▾	Revenue ▾
6			John	814	39886
7			Adam	594	26136
8			Dixie	528	13200
9			Tad	806	20956
10			Erica	826	27258
11			Gabrielle	779	28044
12					
13					
14	Revenue				
15		155480			
16					
17	=SUM(sales[Revenue])				
18					

FIGURE 25-5 This figure shows total revenue for original data.

	C	D	E	F	G
5			Name ▾	Units ▾	Revenue ▾
6			John	814	39886
7			Adam	594	26136
8			Dixie	528	13200
9			Tad	806	20956
10			Erica	826	27258
11			Gabrielle	779	28044
12			Amanda	400	5000
13					
14					
15	revenue	160480			

FIGURE 25-6 New data is added to the table in row 12.

Now suppose that you want to compute the price per unit earned by each salesperson in column H. Type Unit Price in H5 as the column heading and, while in cell H6, point to cell G6. The formula is now [@Revenue]. Type a slash (/) and point to cell F6 and press Enter. An amazing thing happens. Excel automatically copies the formula down to the bottom of the table in cell H12, as shown in Figure 25-7. If you open any cell in column H, the formula appears as [@Revenue]/[@Units]. Of course, =[@Revenue]/[@Units] is a lot easier to understand than =G6/F6. This formula can be interpreted as dividing whatever is in the current row in the Revenue column by whatever is in the current row in the

Units column. If you now add new data to the first three columns of the table, your price formula will automatically copy down.

	C	D	E	F	G	H
5			Name ▼	Units ▼	Revenue ▼	Unit price ▼
6			John	814	39886	49
7			Adam	594	26136	44
8			Dixie	528	13200	25
9			Tad	806	20956	26
10			Erica	826	27258	33
11			Gabrielle	779	28044	36
12			Amanda	400	5000	12.5
13						
14						
15	revenue	160480				

FIGURE 25-7 The Table feature causes the unit price formula to AutoCopy.

If you click anywhere in a table, the **Table Tools** contextual tab appears on the ribbon and offers choices, including the following:

- **Change Table Name**   Can be used to rename a table, such as changing the name from Table1 (the default) to Sales.

- **Convert to Range**   Converts the table range to normal cells and removes the table structure.

- **Resize Table**   Adds or subtracts rows and/or columns to the defined table range.

- **Remove Duplicates**   Removes rows that contain duplicates. For example, selecting only the Name column in the **Remove Duplicates** dialog box ensures that a name will not occur more than once. Selecting both the Name and Units columns ensures that no rows in the table will match both Name and Units and or other column names.

- **Header Row**   If selected, displays the header row. If cleared, the header row is not displayed.

- **Total Row**   Total Row is discussed when table structure is explained later in this chapter.

- **First Column**   If selected, applies a special format to the first column of the table.

- **Last Column**   If selected, assigns a special format to the last column of the table.

- **Banded Rows**   If selected, gives the even-numbered rows in the table a different format than odd-numbered rows.

- **Banded Columns**   If selected, gives odd-numbered columns in the table a different format than even-numbered columns.

- **Table Styles** Can be selected from any of the table formats shown in this group. If the table expands or contracts, the format will be consistently applied.

I have entered several years of natural gas prices in my worksheet, and I created a nice line chart displaying the monthly variation in prices. Can I set things up so that when I add new gas price data, my chart automatically updates?

In the Gasprices507.xlsx file, the Original worksheet contains natural gas prices per thousand feet from July 2002 through December 2004. (See Figure 25-8.) As previously described, you can select B4:C34 (containing months and prices) and press Ctrl+T to create a table from this range, and then you can create a line graph to display this data by choosing **Line** in the **Charts** group on the **Insert** tab and selecting the fourth type of line graph. The line graph already created is shown in Figure 25-9.

	A	B	C
4		month	gas price
5		Jul-02	3.278
6		Aug-02	2.976
7		Sep-02	3.288
8		Oct-02	3.686
9		Nov-02	4.126
10		Dec-02	4.140
11		Jan-03	4.988
12		Feb-03	5.660
13		Mar-03	9.133
14		Apr-03	5.146
15		May-03	5.123
16		Jun-03	5.945
17		Jul-03	5.291
18		Aug-03	4.693
19		Sep-03	4.927
20		Oct-03	4.430
21		Nov-03	4.459
22		Dec-03	4.860
23		Jan-04	6.150
24		Feb-04	5.775
25		Mar-04	5.150
26		Apr-04	5.365
27		May-04	5.935
28		Jun-04	6.680
29		Jul-04	6.141
30		Aug-04	6.048
31		Sep-04	5.082
32		Oct-04	5.723
33		Nov-04	7.626
34		Dec-04	7.976

FIGURE 25-8 Here is the gas price data for 2002–2004.

Next, you can copy this worksheet (by right-clicking the worksheet name, choosing **Move Or Copy Sheet**, and then selecting **Make A Copy**) and add gas prices through July 2006. (The data now extends to row 53.) The new worksheet is named New Data. Note that the line graph in this worksheet automatically updates to include the new data. (See Figure 25-10.)

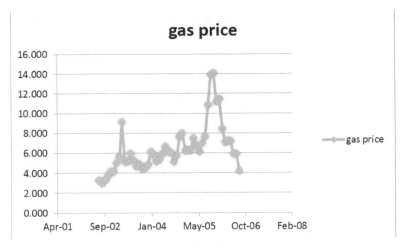

FIGURE 25-9 Gas price line graph: 2002–2004 data.

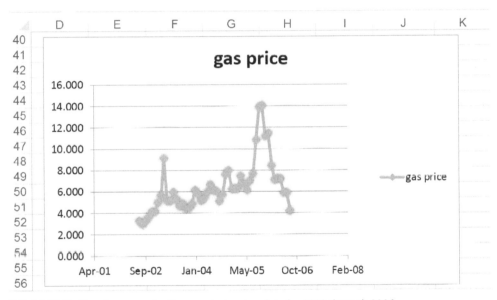

FIGURE 25-10 Here is a gas price line graph showing data for 2002 through 2006.

This example illustrates that if you base your chart on a table, new data will automatically be included in the chart.

For each sales transaction, I have the salesperson, date, product, location, and size of the transaction. Can I easily summarize, for example, total lipstick sales by Jen or Colleen in the East?

The Tablemakeuptemp.xlsx file from the template folder contains sales transactions. (See Figure 25-11.) For each transaction, you have the following information: transaction number, name, date, product, location, dollars, and units sold. If you format this data as a table, you can add a total row for the Units and Dollars columns and then use the filter arrows to make the total row include the subset of transactions you want. To begin, place the cursor anywhere within the data and create a table by pressing Ctrl+T. Note that if you scroll through the table, the header row remains visible. With the cursor in the table, select the **Total Row** check box in the **Table Style Options** group on the **Design** tab. By default, Excel enters the total number of rows in the table in cell K1895, which you can delete. After first selecting the cell in which the arrows appear, click the arrows to the right of cells I1895 and J1895 and then click **Sum**. This totals all entries in the table's Units and Dollars columns. Thus, the total revenue is currently $239,912.67, and 78,707 units were sold. (See Figure 25-12 and the Tablemakeuptotals.xlsx file.)

	E	F	G	H	I	J	K
3	Trans Number	Name	Date	Product	Units	Dollars	Location
4	1	Betsy	38078	lip gloss	45	137.2045583	south
5	2	Hallagan	38056	foundation	50	152.0073031	midwest
6	3	Ashley	38408	lipstick	9	28.71948312	midwest
7	4	Hallagan	38859	lip gloss	55	167.0753225	west
8	5	Zaret	38155	lip gloss	43	130.6028724	midwest
9	6	Colleen	38683	eye liner	58	175.9909741	midwest
10	7	Cristina	38067	eye liner	8	25.80069218	midwest
11	8	Colleen	39068	lip gloss	72	217.8396539	midwest
12	9	Ashley	38903	eye liner	75	226.6423269	south
13	10	Betsy	38936	lip gloss	24	73.50234217	east
14	11	Ashley	38320	mascara	43	130.8353684	east
15	12	Ashley	38309	lip gloss	23	71.03436769	west
16	13	Emilee	38595	lip gloss	49	149.5927969	west
17	14	Hallagan	38353	eye liner	18	56.47199923	south
18	15	Zaret	38980	foundation	-8	-21.99304472	east
19	16	Emilee	38089	mascara	45	137.3903759	east

FIGURE 25-11 This table shows makeup sales data.

	E	F	G	H	I	J	K
1893	1899	Hallagan	39024	eye liner	28	85.65682953	south
1894	1900	Cristina	38881	eye liner	54	164.4873342	midwest
1895	Total				78707	239912.6741	

FIGURE 25-12 This figure shows the total revenue and units sold.

To make the totals reflect only lipstick sales in the East by either Ashley or Hallagan, click the arrow in F3 (to the right of the Name header). Clear the **Select All** check box so that no names are selected, select the check boxes for Ashley and Hallagan (see Figure 25-13), and click **OK**. Next, click the Product arrow, select the **Lipstick** check box, and then click the **Location** arrow and select the **East** check box. You now see all the data fitting the filtering criteria in Figure 25-14 and in the Slicers worksheet of the Tablemakeuptotals.xlsx file. You'll see that Ashley and Hallagan sold 564 units of lipstick in the East for a total of $1,716.56. This table filtering feature makes it easy to compute totals for any subset of rows in an Excel worksheet. If you want, you can also copy the rows involving Colleen or Jen selling lipstick in the East and paste them elsewhere.

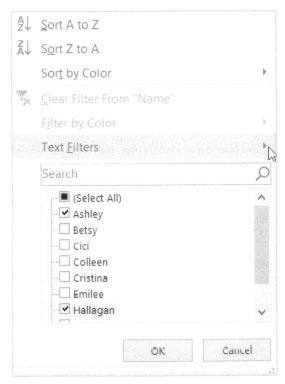

FIGURE 25-13 Filter on names from the table.

	E	F	G	H	I	J	K
3	**Trans Number** ▼	**Name** ⤓	**Date** ▼	**Product** ⤓	**Units** ▼	**Dollars** ▼	**Location** ⤓
282	288	Ashley	38606	lipstick	-8	-21.9125458	east
565	571	Hallagan	38925	lipstick	60	182.2924607	east
670	676	Hallagan	38023	lipstick	8	25.63945706	east
702	708	Ashley	38375	lipstick	71	215.1433462	east
968	974	Ashley	39002	lipstick	72	218.0571538	east
1142	1148	Ashley	38727	lipstick	42	127.8685805	east
1173	1179	Ashley	38452	lipstick	70	211.6914545	east
1186	1192	Hallagan	38023	lipstick	40	122.5516179	east
1282	1288	Ashley	38320	lipstick	84	254.1193721	east
1332	1338	Ashley	38969	lipstick	50	152.3101916	east
1423	1429	Hallagan	38441	lipstick	24	73.61606446	east
1469	1475	Ashley	38705	lipstick	51	155.1847283	east
1895	**Total**				564	1716.561881	

FIGURE 25-14 Subtotals are filtered for units and revenue.

How do Table slicers (new to Excel 2013) help us slice and dice data in an Excel table?

In Excel 2010, slicers were introduced to simplify the filtering of PivotTables. (See Chapter 43, "Using PivotTables and Slicers to describe data," for details.) In Excel 2013, slicers can now be used to filter tables. The advantage of slicers is that you can easily see the filter options and selection. To create filters for your Makeup example, place your cursor inside the table and, on the **Insert** tab, select **Slicers** from the **Filters** group. To create slicers for Name, Product, and Location, select them as shown in Figure 25-15.

The slicers are shown in Figure 25-16. In a slicer, you can filter on multiple items by using the Shift key to select adjacent items or the Control key to select nonadjacent items.

Your slicers in Figure 25-16 filter on all sales involving Ashley and Hallagan selling lipstick in the East. Note that the Totals row and visible rows are identical to Figure 25-14. To remove all filters, click the filter icon located at the right corner of the slicer.

You can resize a slicer by selecting it and dragging the edges or corners. When you select a slicer, you can configure it by using the **Slicer Tools Options** tab on the ribbon. On this tab, you can modify many features of the slicer, including the slicer style, slicer name, the number of columns, and the slicer's size.

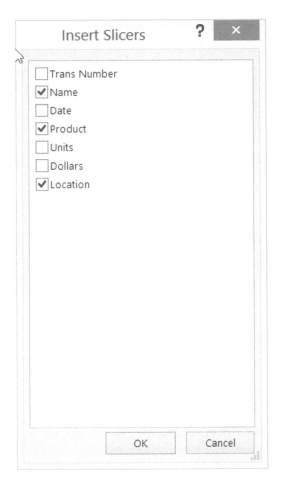

FIGURE 25-15 Create slicers for Name, Product, and Location.

	Trans Number	Name	Date	Product	Units	Dollars	Location
282	288	Ashley	38606	lipstick	-8	-21.9125458	east
565	571	Hallagan	38925	lipstick	60	182.2924607	east
670	676	Hallagan	38023	lipstick	8	25.63945706	east
702	708	Ashley	38375	lipstick	71	215.1433462	east
968	974	Ashley	39002	lipstick	72	218.0571538	east
1142	1148	Ashley	38727	lipstick	42	127.8685805	east
1173	1179	Ashley	38452	lipstick	70	211.6914545	east
1186	1192	Hallagan	38023	lipstick	40	122.5516179	east
1282	1288	Ashley	38320	lipstick	84	254.1193721	east
1332	1338	Ashley	38969	lipstick	50	152.3101916	east
1423	1429	Hallagan	38441	lipstick	24	73.61606446	east
1469	1475	Ashley	38705	lipstick	51	155.1847283	east
1895	Total				564	1716.561881	
1896							

Name: Ashley, Betsy, Cici, Colleen, Cristina, Emilee, Hallagan, Jen

Product: eye liner, foundation, lip gloss, lipstick, mascara

Location: east, midwest, south, west

FIGURE 25-16 Use slicers to filter a table.

How can I easily refer to portions of a table in other parts of my workbook?

The Tablestructure.xlsx file shows many examples of how you can refer to parts of a table when you are working outside the table's range. These references are often called *structured references*. (See Figure 25-17.) When you enter a table name in a formula followed by an opening bracket ([), AutoComplete makes the column names and the following table specifics available for selection:

- **Table Name**   All cells in the table, excluding the header and total rows.

- **#All**   All cells in the table, including the total row (if any).

- **#Data**   All cells in the table except for the first row and the total row.

- **#Headers**   Just the header row.

- **#Totals**   Just the total row. If there is no total row, this returns an empty cell range.

- **#This Row**   All table entries in the current row.

A column reference includes all cells in a table column, excluding the header and total row entries (if any).

Here are some examples of how table specifiers can be used in formulas:

- In cell B8, the =SUM(Table1[@]) formula sums the entries in row 8 (41+28+49+40).

- In cell C15, the =COUNTA(Table1[#All]) formula yields 55 because the table contains 55 entries.

- In cell C16, the =COUNTA([Table1]) formula yields 45 because the header and total rows are not counted. In cell C17, the =COUNTA(Table[#data]) formula yields 45 because the D5:H13 cell range is referenced.

- In cell C18, the =COUNTA(Table1[#Headers]) formula yields 5 because only the header row (D4:H4) is referenced.

- In cell C19, the =SUM(Table1[Q1]) formula yields 367 because the formula sums the entries in E5:E13.

- In cell C20, the =SUM(Table1[#Totals]) formula sums up all entries in the total row and yields 1,340, which is the total sum of all table entries.

- In cell C21, the =SUM(Table1[[#Data],[Q1]:[Q3]]) formula sums up all data entries that are in columns Q1:Q3, inclusive (cells E5:G13). Thus, column names separated by a colon include all data entries between and including the column name before the colon and the column name after the colon.

Of course, all these formulas are automatically updated if new data is added to the table.

	A	B	C	D	E	F	G	H
4				Product	Q1	Q2	Q3	Q4
5				food1	37	42	24	32
6				mag1	20	23	24	41
7				drug1	47	34	41	28
8		158		drug2	41	28	49	40
9				food2	44	22	46	50
10	=SUM(Table1[@])			drug1	39	25	38	29
11				mag2	26	35	31	30
12				food4	48	49	50	50
13				mag3	65	34	35	43
14				Total	367	292	338	343
15			55	=COUNTA(Table1[#All])				
16			45	=COUNTA(Table1)				
17			45	=COUNTA(Table1[#Data])				
18			5	=COUNTA(Table1[#Headers])				
19			367	=SUM(Table1[Q1])				
20			1340	=SUM(Table1[#Totals])				
21			997	=SUM(Table1[[#Data],[Q1]:[Q3]])				

FIGURE 25-17 This table shows structured references.

Do conditional formats automatically apply to new data added to a table?

Yes, conditional formats automatically include new table data. (See Figure 25-18.) To illustrate, a conditional format was placed in worksheet Original of file Tablestructure.xlsx to highlight the three largest Q1 sales in column E. Entries in rows 7, 12, and 13 were highlighted. In worksheet Add Biggersale, the entry 90 was added in cell E14. This becomes the largest entry in the column and is immediately highlighted. Cell E7 is no longer highlighted because it is no longer one of the three largest numbers in column E of the table.

	D	E	F	G	H
4	Product	Q1	Q2	Q3	Q4
5	food1	37	42	24	32
6	mag1	20	23	24	41
7	drug1	47	34	41	28
8	drug2	41	28	49	40
9	food2	44	22	46	50
10	drug1	39	25	38	29
11	mag2	26	35	31	30
12	food4	48	49	50	50
13	mag3	65	34	35	43
14	drug3	90	45	34	23

FIGURE 25-18 Conditional formatting extends automatically to new table data.

Problems

1. The Singers.xlsx file contains a list of songs sung by different singers as well as the length of each song. Set up your worksheet to compute the total number of songs sung by Eminem and the average length of each song. If new data is added, your formulas should automatically update.

2. In the Tableexample.xlsx file, set things up so that each salesperson's rank according to total revenue and units sold is included in the worksheet. If new data is included, your ranks should automatically update. You might find it convenient to use the *RANK.EQ* function. The syntax of the *RANK* function is =RANK.EQ(number,array,0). This function yields the rank of a number in a range array; rank=1 is the largest number.

3. The Lookupdata.xlsx file contains product codes and prices. Set up the worksheet so that you can enter a product code, and your worksheet will return the product price. When new products are introduced, your formula should still work.

4. The Productlookup.xlsx file contains the product sales made each day of the week. Set up a formula that returns the sale of any product on any given day. If new products are added to the data, your formula should be able to include sales for those products.

5. The Tablepie.xlsx file contains sales information for different products sold in a small general store. You want to set up a pie chart to summarize this data. If new product categories are added, the pie chart should automatically include the new data.

6. The Tablexnpvdata.xlsx file lists cash flows received by a small business. Set up a formula to compute (as of January 5, 2007) the net present value (NPV) of all cash flows. Assume an annual discount rate of 10 percent. If new cash flows are entered, your formula should automatically include them.

7. The Nikedata.xlsx file contains quarterly sales revenues for Nike. Create a graph of Nike sales that automatically includes new sales revenue data.

8. For the data in file Tablemakeuptemp.xlsx, determine total units and revenue for all lip gloss or lipstick sold by Jen or Ashley in the South or East.

9. The Closest.xlsx file contains people's names and salaries. Set up a worksheet that takes any number and finds the person whose salary is closest to that number. Your worksheet should accomplish this goal even if new names are added or existing names are deleted from the list.

10. The Adagency.xlsx file contains salaries and ages for employees of an ad agency. Set up a spreadsheet that will compute the average salary and age of the agency's employees. Your calculations should automatically update if the agency hires or fires workers.

CHAPTER 26

Spinner buttons, scroll bars, option buttons, check boxes, combo boxes, and group list boxes

Questions answered in this chapter:

- I need to run a sensitivity analysis that has many key inputs, such as Year 1 sales, annual sales growth, Year 1 price, and unit cost. How can I quickly vary these inputs and see the effect of the variation on the calculation of net present value, for example?

- How can I set up a simple check box that toggles conditional formatting on and off?

- How can I set up my worksheet so that my supply-chain personnel can click a button to choose whether we charge a high, low, or medium price for a product?

- How can I create an easy way for a user of my worksheet to enter a day of the week without having to type any text?

User forms enable people who use Microsoft Excel 2013 to add a variety of useful controls to a worksheet. In this chapter, you'll see how easy it is to use spinner buttons, scroll bars, check boxes, option buttons, combo boxes, and list boxes. To access Excel user forms, click the **Developer** tab on the ribbon and choose **Insert** in the **Controls** group to display the forms controls (not to be confused with ActiveX controls, which are usually used within the Microsoft Visual Basic for Applications [VBA] programming language).

 Note To display the **Developer** tab, click the **File** tab and then choose **Options**. Choose **Customize Ribbon** and then select **Developer** in the **Main Tabs** list.

The user forms discussed in this chapter are shown in Figures 26-1 through 26-6. (See also the Controls.xlsx file in the Practice files folder for this chapter.)

FIGURE 26-1 This is the spinner button.

FIGURE 26-2 This is the scroll bar.

FIGURE 26-3 This is a check box.

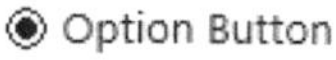

◉ Option Button

FIGURE 26-4 This is an option button.

FIGURE 26-5 This is a combo box.

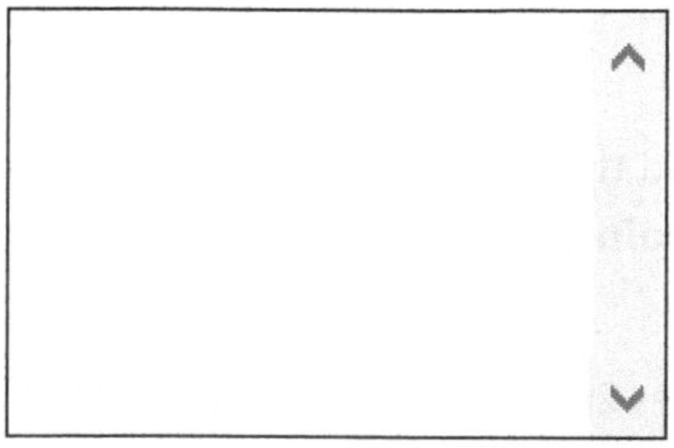

FIGURE 26-6 This is a list box.

Answers to this chapter's questions

This section provides the answers to the questions that are listed at the beginning of the chapter.

First, see how to use spinner buttons and scroll bars.

As discussed in Chapter 18, "Using the Scenario Manager for sensitivity analysis," you use the Scenario Manager to change a group of input cells to see how various outputs change. Unfortunately, the Scenario Manager requires you to enter each scenario individually, which makes creating more than a few scenarios difficult. For example, suppose you believe that four key inputs to the car net present value (NPV) model are Year 1 sales, Sales growth, Year 1 price, and Year 1 cost. (See the NPVspinners.xlsx file.) You'd like to see how NPV changes as the inputs change in the following ranges:

Input	Low value	High value
Year 1 sales	$5,000	$30,000
Annual sales growth	0%	50%
Year 1 price	$6	$20
Year 1 cost	$2	$15

Using the Scenario Manager to generate the scenarios in which the input cells vary within the given ranges would be very time-consuming. By using *spinner buttons*, however, a user can quickly generate a host of scenarios that vary each input between its low and high value. A spinner button is a control that is linked to a specific cell. As you click the up or down arrow on the spinner button, the value of the linked cell changes. You can see how formulas of interest (such as one that calculates a car's NPV) change in response to changes in the inputs.

I need to run a sensitivity analysis that has many key inputs, such as Year 1 sales, annual sales growth, Year 1 price, and Year 1 unit cost. How can I quickly vary these inputs and see the effect of the variation on the calculation of net present value, for example?

Here's how to create spinner buttons by which you can vary Year 1 sales, sales growth, Year 1 price, and Year1 cost within the ranges you want. The Original Model worksheet (see the NPVspinnerstemp.xlsx file in the Templates folder) is shown in Figure 26-7.

	A	B	C	D	E	F
1		taxrate	0.4			
2		Year1sales	10000		-	
3		Sales growth	0.48		48	
4		Year1price	$ 9.00			
5		Year1cost	$ 6.00			
6		intrate	0.15			
7		costgrowth	0.05			
8		pricegrowth	0.03			
9	Year	1	2	3	4	5
10	Unit Sales	10000	14800	21904	32417.92	47978.5216
11	unit price	$ 9.00	$ 9.27	$ 9.55	$ 9.83	$ 10.13
12	unit cost	$ 6.00	$ 6.30	$ 6.62	$ 6.95	$ 7.29
13	Revenues	$ 90,000.00	$ 137,196.00	$ 209,141.58	$ 318,815.43	$ 486,002.24
14	Costs	$ 60,000.00	$ 93,240.00	$ 144,894.96	$ 225,166.77	$ 349,909.16
15	Before Tax Profits	$ 30,000.00	$ 43,956.00	$ 64,246.62	$ 93,648.66	$ 136,093.08
16	Tax	$ 12,000.00	$ 17,582.40	$ 25,698.65	$ 37,459.46	$ 54,437.23
17	Aftertax Profits	$ 18,000.00	$ 26,373.60	$ 38,547.97	$ 56,189.20	$ 81,655.85
18						
19	NPV	$133,664.07				

FIGURE 26-7 This figure shows the Original Model worksheet without any spinner buttons.

To create the spinner buttons, select the rows in which you want to insert spinner buttons (in this example, rows 2–5) and then increase the height of the rows by right-clicking and selecting **Format**, **Row**, and **Height**. A row height of 27 is usually enough to accommodate the spinner button arrows. Alternatively, hold down the Alt key while you draw the control so that it fits the cell.

Display the **User Forms** menu by clicking **Insert** in the **Controls** group on the **Developer** tab. Click the spinner button form control (shown in Figure 26-1) and drag it to where you want it to appear in your worksheet (cell D2). You see a plus sign (+). Pressing the left mouse button anchors the spinner button where you want it, and you can draw the shape for the spinner button. To change the shape of a form control or to move the control, place the cursor on the control and hold down the Ctrl key. When the pointer turns into a four-headed arrow, drag the control to move it. When the pointer appears as a two-headed arrow, you can drag the control to resize it.

A spinner button now appears in cell D2. After configuring the spinner button, you can use it to change the value of Year1 sales. Right-click the spinner button and, on the shortcut menu, click **Copy**. Right-click cell D3 and then click **Paste**. Also, paste the spinner button into cells D4 and D5. You should now see four spinner buttons as shown in Figure 26-8.

▲	A	B	C	D
1		**taxrate**	0.4	
2		**Year1sales**	10000	
3		**Sales growth**	0.48	
4		**Year1price**	$ 9.00	
5		**Year1cost**	$ 6.00	

FIGURE 26-8 Spinner buttons are placed in worksheet cells.

Now you need to link each spinner button to an input cell. To link the spinner button in D2 to cell C2, right-click the spinner button in cell D2 and then click **Format Control**. Fill in the **Format Control** dialog box as shown in Figure 26-9.

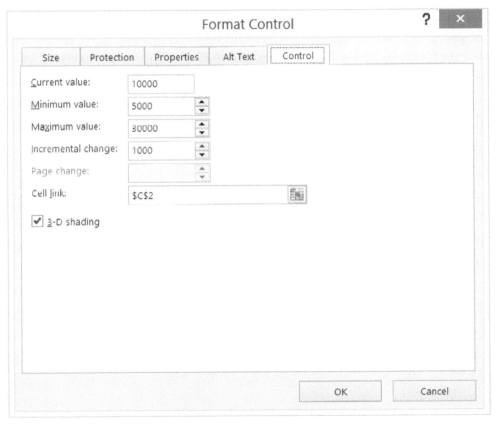

FIGURE 26-9 Use the Format Control dialog box to link Year1sales to a spinner button.

The current value is not important. The rest of the settings tell Excel that this spinner button is linked to the values in cell C2 (Year1sales); that each click of the up arrow will increase the value in C2 by 1,000; and that each click of the down arrow will decrease the value in C2 by 1,000. When the value in C2 reaches 30,000, clicking the up arrow will not increase it; when the value in C2 reaches 5,000, clicking the down arrow will not decrease the value.

Use the **Format Control** dialog box to link the spinner button in D4 to Year1price (cell C4). For the current value, 9 was used. The minimum value is 6, the maximum value is 20, and the incremental change is 1. Clicking the spinner button arrows in cell D4 varies the Year1price between $6 and $20 in $1 increments.

To link the spinner button in cell D5 to Year1 cost (cell D5), 6 was used for the current value, 2 for the minimum value, 15 for the maximum value, and 1 as the incremental change. Clicking the spinner button arrows in cell D5 changes Year1 cost from $2 to $15 in $1 increments.

Linking the spinner button in cell D3 to Sales growth is trickier. You want the spinner button control to change sales growth to 0 percent, 1 percent, . . . 50 percent. The problem is that the minimum increment a spinner button value can change is 1. Therefore, you need to link this spinner button to a dummy value in cell E3 and place the E3/100 formula in cell C3. Now, as cell E3 varies from 1 to 50, sales growth varies between 1 percent and 50 percent. Figure 26-10 shows how to link this spinner button to cell E3. Remember that sales growth in cell C3 is simply the number in cell E3 divided by 100.

By the way, if the cursor is within the control and you hold down the Control key, you can easily use the handles to resize a control.

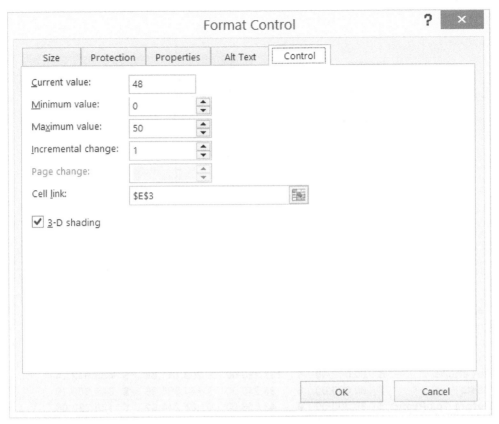

FIGURE 26-10 These are the Format Control dialog box settings that link the spinner button in cell D3 to cell E3.

By clicking a spinner button arrow, you can easily see how changing a single input cell—given the values for the other inputs listed in the worksheet—changes the car's NPV. To see the effect of the changes, you can select cell F9, click **Freeze Panes** on the **View** menu, and then click **Freeze Panes** again. This command freezes the data above row 9 and to the left of column F. You can now use the scroll bars on the right of the window to arrange it as you see it in Figure 26-11.

| H19 | ▾ | : | × | ✓ | fx | | |

◢	A	B	C	D	F
1		taxrate	0.4		
2		Year1sales	10000		
3		Sales growth	0.48		
4		Year1price	$ 9.00		
5		Year1cost	$ 6.00		
6		intrate	0.15		
7		costgrowth	0.05		
8		pricegrowth	0.03		
9	Year	1	2	3	5
10	Unit Sales	10000	14800	21904	47978.5216
11	unit price	$ 9.00	$ 9.27	$ 9.55	$ 10.13
12	unit cost	$ 6.00	$ 6.30	$ 6.62	$ 7.29
13	Revenues	$ 90,000.00	$ 137,196.00	$ 209,141.58	$ 486,002.24
14	Costs	$ 60,000.00	$ 93,240.00	$ 144,894.96	$ 349,909.16
15	Before Tax Profits	$ 30,000.00	$ 43,956.00	$ 64,246.62	$ 136,093.08
16	Tax	$ 12,000.00	$ 17,582.40	$ 25,698.65	$ 54,437.23
17	Aftertax Profits	$ 18,000.00	$ 26,373.60	$ 38,547.97	$ 81,655.85
18					
19	NPV	$133,664.07			

FIGURE 26-11 You can freeze panes to see the results of calculations in other parts of a worksheet.

Given the values of the other inputs, clicking the sales growth spinner button arrows shows that a 1 percent increase in sales growth is worth about $2,000. (To return the worksheet to its normal state, click **Freeze Panes** on the **View** menu, followed by **Unfreeze Panes**.)

The scroll bar control is very similar to the spinner button. The main difference is that by moving the cursor over the gray area in the middle of the scroll bar, you can cause the linked cell to change in value continuously. By selecting **Format Control** on the shortcut menu and changing the value under **Page Change** in the **Format Control** dialog box, you can control the speed with which the linked cell changes.

How can I set up a simple check box that toggles conditional formatting on and off?

A check box is a form of control that specifies a value of *True* in a cell when the box is selected and *False* when the box is cleared. Check boxes can be used to create toggle switches that turn a particular feature on or off. As an example, see how to use a check box to turn the conditional formatting feature on or off.

Suppose a worksheet contains monthly sales, and you want to color the five largest sales in green and the five smallest sales in red. (See the Checkbox.xlsx file.) You enter the =LARGE(Sales,5) formula in cell G4, which computes the fifth-largest sales value. In cell H4, you compute the fifth-smallest sales value with the =SMALL(Sales,5) formula. (See Figure 26-12.)

	D	E	F	G	H	I
1			TRUE			
2						
3	Sales			5th largest	5th smallest	
4	1010			1050	584	
5	619					
6	524					
7	1114					
8	619					
9	1097			☑ TURN FORMATTING ON OR OFF		
10	627					
11	578					
12	947					
13	1020					
14	1046					
15	678					
16	510					
17	674					
18	756					
19	665					
20	609					
21	556					
22	959					

FIGURE 26-12 Use a check box to turn conditional formatting on and off.

Next, you create a check box and configure it to enter *True* or *False* in cell F1. On the **Developer** tab, click **Insert** and select the check box (see Figure 26-3) from the **Forms Controls** palette. Drag the check box to cell G9 and change its text to read **Turn Formatting On Or Off**. Right-click the check box, click **Format Control**, and fill in the dialog box as shown in Figure 26-13.

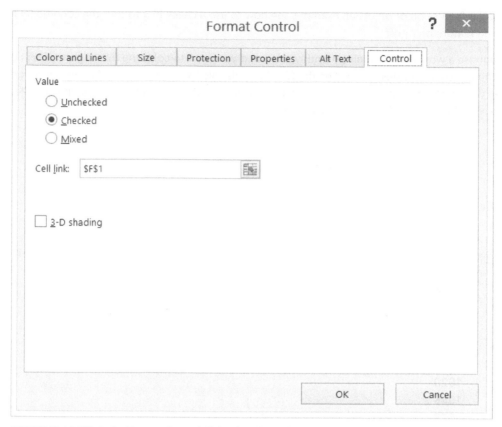

FIGURE 26-13 This is the Format Control dialog box for a check box.

Now, whenever you select the check box, True is placed in F1, and whenever you clear the check box, False is placed in cell F1.

After selecting the D4:D29 cell range, click **Conditional Formatting** in the **Styles** group on the **Home** tab and then click **New Rule**. Enter the formulas shown in Figure 26-14 and Figure 26-15 to color the top five sales green and the bottom five sales red. Note that the AND($F$1) portion of the formula ensures that the formatting can be applied if cell F1 is *True*. The check box determines whether cell F1 is *True* or *False*, so if the check box is not selected, the cells will not turn green or red.

If you want, you can select cell F1 and change the font color to white to hide True and False.

FIGURE 26-14 This figure shows the format to turn the five largest cells green.

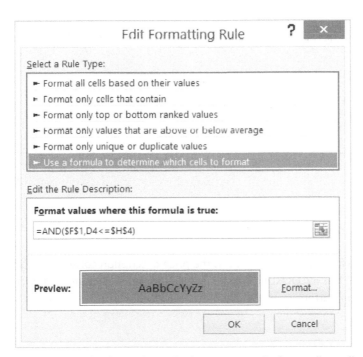

FIGURE 26-15 This figure shows the format to turn the five smallest cells red.

How can I set up my worksheet so that my supply-chain personnel can click a button to choose whether we charge a high, low, or medium price for a product?

Suppose that you can charge one of three prices for a product: high, medium, or low. These prices are listed in cells B7:B9 of the Optionbuttons.xlsx file. You could easily use a lookup table to print the price if a user typed in High, Medium, or Low. It's better design, however, if the user can select an option button that says High Price, Medium Price, or Low Price, and a formula automatically computes the price. (See Figure 26-16.)

To use option buttons, you first draw a group box (see Figure 26-5) after choosing this control from the **User Forms** menu. Then you drag an option button for each choice into the group box. Because you have three price levels, you need to drag three option buttons into the group box. Right-click any option button and then use the **Format Control** command to link any one of the option buttons to a cell. The first option button was linked to cell E4. All the option buttons in the group box are now linked to the same cell. Selecting the first option button enters a 1 in cell E4, selecting the second option button enters a 2 in cell E4, and selecting the third option button enters a 3 in cell E4.

	A	B	C	D	E	F
4						3
5				2		
6					Price level	Price
7	High	$ 8.00			Low	$ 3.00
8	Medium	$ 6.00				
9	Low	$ 3.00				
10						
11						
12						
13						
14	Select price					
15	○ High price					
16						
17	○ Medium price					
18						
19	◉ Low price					
20						
21						

FIGURE 26-16 Use option buttons to select product price.

Entering the =INDEX(A7:A9,E4,1) formula in cell E7 returns the price description corresponding to the selected option button. In cell F7, the =VLOOKUP(E7,A7:B9,2,FALSE) formula computes the price corresponding to the selected option button.

How can I create an easy way for a user of my spreadsheet to select a day of the week without having to type any text?

The Combobox.xlsx file shows how to create a combo box or a list box (see Figure 26-17) a user can click to select an item easily from a list. (Data validation also makes it easy to create drop-down boxes; see Chapter 40, "Validating data.") The goal here is to compute the number of hours an employee worked on a given day. The hours worked each day are listed in cells G9:G15. You can use a combo box or list box to select an entry from a list. If the combo box or list box is linked to a cell (by Format Control), a 1 is placed in the linked cell if the first entry in the box is selected; if the second entry in the list is selected, a 2 is entered in the linked cell and so on. To set up the worksheet, click the **Developer** tab, choose **Insert**, and then drag a combo box from the **Form Controls** menu to C5 and a list box to D16. Right-click the combo box and choose **Format Control**. Select the F9:F15 input range (which contains days of the week) and link cell A8. Now right-click the list box and select **Format Control**. Select the F9:F15 input range and link cell A13. After these steps, if you select Tuesday from the combo box and Friday from the list box, for example, you see a 2 in A8 and a 5 in A13.

In cell F3, the =INDEX(F9:F15,A8,1) formula lists the day of the week corresponding to the combo box selection. In cell G3, the =VLOOKUP(F3,$F$9:$G$15,2,False) formula locates the number of hours worked for the day selected in the combo box. In a similar fashion, the formulas in F4 and G4 list the day of the week and hours worked for the day selected in the list box.

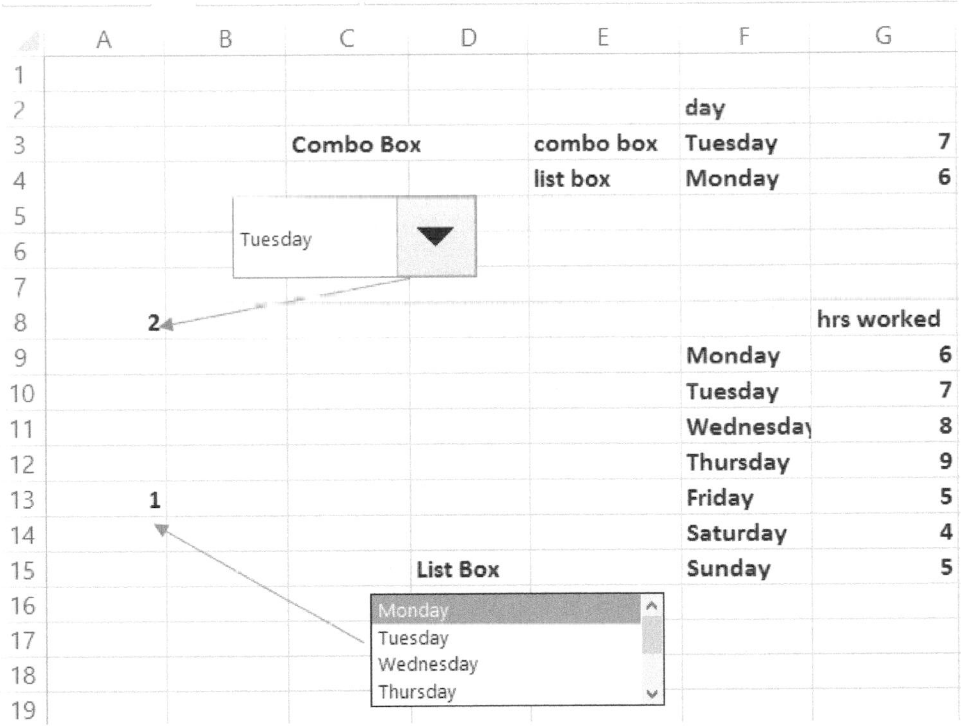

FIGURE 26-17 Use combo boxes and list boxes to select the day of the week.

Problems

1. Add a spinner button for the car NPV example that enables you to vary the tax rate between 30 percent and 50 percent.

2. Add a spinner button for the car NPV example that enables you to vary the interest rate between 5 percent and 20 percent.

3. The Format Control dialog box allows a minimum value of 0. Despite this limitation, can you figure out a way to use a spinner button to vary sales growth between –10 percent and 20 percent?

4. Using the lemonade example in Chapter 16, "Sensitivity analysis with data tables," create spinner buttons that allow the inputs to vary within the following ranges:

Input	Low value	High value
Price	$2.00	$5.00
Unit cost	$0.20	$1.00
Fixed cost	$20,000.00	$100,000.00

Using the mortgage payment example in Chapter 17, "The Goal Seek command," create spinner buttons that allow inputs to vary within the following ranges:

Input	Low value	High value
Amount borrowed	$270,000	$800,000
Number of months of payments	120	360
Annual interest rate	4%	10%

For the weekend example used in Chapter 23, "Conditional formatting," set up a check box that turns conditional formatting on or off.

5. In the financial formulas described in Chapter 9, "More Excel financial functions," you used a last argument of 1 to indicate end-of-month cash flows and 0 to indicate beginning-of-month cash flows. Excel recognizes True as equivalent to a 1 and False as equivalent to 0. Set up a worksheet in which a user can enter the number of months of a loan, principal, and annual interest rate to find the monthly payment. Then use a check box to select whether the payments are at the beginning or end of the month.

6. Using the data for Problem 15 in Chapter 21, "The *OFFSET* function," create a spinner to graph the last few months of sales (ranging from 3 to 8 months).

7. The Suppliers.xlsx file contains the unit price you pay to each of your suppliers and the units purchased. Create a list box by which to pick the supplier and return the unit price and units purchased.

CHAPTER 27

The analytics revolution

Questions answered in this chapter:

- What is analytics?

- What is predictive analytics?

- What is prescriptive analytics?

- Why has analytics increased in importance?

- How important is analytics to your organization?

- What do you need to know to do analytics?

- What difficulties can occur when undertaking an analytics implementation?

- What trends will affect future developments in analytics?

Answers to this chapter's questions

This section provides the answers to the questions that are listed at the beginning of the chapter.

What is analytics?

Analytics·is the practice of using data to help make decisions that meet the organization's objectives better. Typical objectives include maximizing profit, minimizing cost, reducing financial risk, improving health care and educational outcomes, reducing crime, and other considerations. Of course, the use of data to make decisions is not a recent phenomenon. For example, the Greek philosopher Thales used options (see Chapter 77, "Pricing Stock Options") to increase profits and decrease the risk incurred by renting out olive presses. The term *analytics* became popular after the 2007 publication of Thomas Davenport's book, *Competing on Analytics* (Boston: Harvard Business School Press, 2007).

What is predictive analytics?

Predictive analytics is simply using data to make accurate predictions about quantities of interest. Some examples include:

- Predicting the outcome of presidential elections (see Chapter 58, "Incorporating qualitative factors into multiple regression").

- Predicting the outcome of NFL games (see Chapter 34, "Using Solver to rate sports teams").

- Determining how placement of a product in a store determines product sales (see Chapter 60, "Analysis of variance: One-way ANOVA").

- Determining how course of treatment affects chance of survival from cancer.

- Determining how the marketing mix (advertising, price cuts, putting product on display) affects daily sales of 3M Scotch tape. This is difficult because seasonality also affects sales, and the prediction model must adjust for the effect of seasonality on sales.

- What is the chance of each team to win the NCAA tournament? (See Chapter 76, "Fun and games: Simulating gambling and sporting event probabilities.")

- Chapters 34 and 76 and Chapters 53–64 cover topics in predictive analytics.

What is prescriptive analytics?

Prescriptive analytics involves using mathematical models, usually data driven, to help make decisions that maximize or minimize an appropriate objective. Some examples include:

- What product price maximizes profit? (See Chapters 83–86.)

- What product mix maximizes Eli Lilly's monthly profit? (See Chapter 29, "Using Solver to determine the optimal product mix.")

- How can I schedule my workforce to minimize operating costs? (See Chapter 30, "Using Solver to schedule your workforce.")

- How can a company minimize the cost of shipping products from plants to customers? (See Chapter 31, "Using Solver to solve transportation or distribution problems.")

- How can an organization choose projects that maximize corporate objectives subject to limited resources? For example, given limited capital and programmers, how can Microsoft maximize the profitability generated from new products? How can your local school board use limited funds to maximize the high school graduation rate? These topics are discussed in Chapter 32, "Using Solver for capital budgeting."

- How much money do I need to save each year to have enough money for retirement? (See Chapter 33, "Using Solver for financial planning.")

- How can bookies set point spreads that ensure that they earn a profit? (See Chapter 34.)

- Where should warehouses be located to minimize the distance shipments must travel? (See Chapter 35, "Warehouse location and the GRG Multistart and Evolutionary Solver engines.")

- How should workers be assigned to jobs to make both bosses and employees happy? (See Chapter 36, "Penalties and the Evolutionary Solver.")

- In what order should your UPS driver drop off packages to minimize the time needed to deliver all packages? (See Chapter 37, "The traveling salesperson problem.")

- How many Valentine's Day cards should Hallmark print to maximize expected profit? (See Chapter 73.)

- What should a company bid on a construction project to maximize its expected profit? (See Chapter 74, "Calculating an optimal bid.")

- What asset allocation minimizes the risk needed to obtain a desired expected return? (See Chapter 75, "Simulating stock prices and asset allocation modeling.")

Why has analytics increased in importance?

Analytics has recently become more important for several reasons. First, much more useful data is available. For example, FACTUAL is a start-up company that is trying to collect *all* data that might be useful; it has a database containing the location of all US gas stations and nutritional information on all items sold by a grocery chain. New sources of useful data are being generated at a rapidly increasing rate. For example, starting with the 2013–2014 season, all NBA arenas will have cameras that track the location of each player and the ball every second during the game.

In addition to more data being available, computers and programs are getting faster all the time, making it easier to handle big data sets. For example, PowerPivot (see Chapter 45, "PowerPivot") makes it easy to create business intelligence (BI) reports based on hundreds of millions of rows of data. Software that is not Microsoft Excel–based, such as SAS and HADOOP, make it relatively easy to process and analyze huge data sets.

How important is analytics to your organization?

The importance of analytics to an organization depends on the benefits gained from an analytics approach balanced against the costs of implementation. For example, do the benefits obtained from evaluating teachers through analytics outweigh the costs?

Looking at the use of analytics in professional sports sheds a lot of light on the importance of analytics. In baseball (think Moneyball), much readily available data can be used to evaluate baseball players. This data is relatively easy to analyze, so almost every major league team has an analytics department. In the past, few NBA teams had analytics departments. At the 2013 Sloan Conference on Sports Analytics, only one team (the Lakers, and we know how they performed—poorly) was not represented. However, not that many NFL teams have analytics departments, perhaps because many important problems in football analytics are difficult to solve. For example, in baseball and basketball, it is not that difficult to estimate a fair value for a player. In football, this is much more difficult. How can we estimate the value of a great pass blocker when there are few available statistics measuring the performance of offensive linemen?

What do you need to know to do analytics?

Many universities are developing undergraduate, graduate, and online programs to certify analytics professionals. Analogous to the Certified Public Accountant (CPA) exam, INFORMS (Institute for Operations Research and Management Science) introduced an exam in 2013 to certify people as certified analytics professionals. At a minimum, the analytics professional should have knowledge of the following topics:

- How to manipulate data in any form. This includes manipulation of nonquantitative data such as tweets on Twitter.

- How to bring disparate data sets together so they can be used in an analytics study. For example, a fast food restaurant might want to reduce employee turnover. This would require what was known about each employee (education, age, test scores, and other statistics) as well as the employee's performance history. Then a model could be developed that predicts employee turnover based on what was known when the employee was hired. Unfortunately, at many firms, data on employee hires and employee performance resides in separate databases that do not talk to one another.

- Good skills to analyze and manipulate data in Excel.

- How to analyze big data sets by using a statistical package such as R, SPSS, or SAS.

- Knowledge of statistics, including all forms of predictive analytics and classification algorithms. For example, how can a person be classified as a likely candidate for a heart attack?

- Knowing how simulation can model uncertain situations such as the future value of your 401k portfolio or the queue at the hospital emergency room.

- Using optimization to find the best way to do something. For example, what space allocation to different products maximizes a department store's profits?

What difficulties can occur when undertaking an analytics implementation?

Several problems can arise during an analytics implementation:

- Often, it is difficult to agree on the right metric to evaluate success. For example, until Saber metrics guru Bill James came along, everyone thought fielders should be evaluated based on fielding percentage, which is the fraction of balls hit near a fielder that are successfully fielded. Clearly, this metric does not account for the fact that a slow-footed shortstop allows many balls to go to the outfield and turn into hits. Bill James created range factor, which is a much better measure of fielding performance. For a shortstop, for example, range factor is put-outs + assists per inning for the player, divided by average putouts + assists per inning for all shortstops. A range factor exceeding 1 indicates that a player gets to many balls the average shortstop misses. Ozzie Smith is generally considered one of the greatest fielding shortstops of all time. His career fielding percentage of .966 is not great, but during his best years, his range factor was superb. Of course, Ozzie played on artificial turf, and this makes his range factor even more amazing. The moral is not to hesitate to question metrics that you think are not reflective of your organization's actual performance.

- As previously mentioned, often data sources needed for an analytics project do not talk to each other. For example, a software company wanted to predict future revenues. It knew that future revenues depended on trial versions that had been sent to potential customers and personal sales calls on potential customers. Unfortunately, the sales data and the customer data were in different databases that did not communicate, so the project suffered a huge and unnecessary delay.

- In a predictive analytics study, analysts often do not know what data is needed to make better decisions. I suggest working backward. After determining what you want to forecast, think about the variables that might help you predict the variable of interest. Here are some examples of situations in which a new set of data needed to be created to complete an analytics project:

  - Noted sports analytics personality Jeff Sagarin and the author wanted to determine a method to evaluate the defensive ability of NBA players. Because the NBA box score includes few defensive (steals and blocks) statistics, a new set of data was needed. We reasoned that a good defensive player would cause his team to give up few points when he was in the game, and his absence would cause this team to give up more points when the player was out. We created a data set listed for all minutes the players were on the court and the number of points given up. Using this data, we could identify the defensive contributions of great defenders such as Ron Artest, Kevin Garnett, and Marc Gasol.

  - United Health wanted to reduce health care costs incurred by its employees. It determined that it needed to know whether employees were being treated for conditions that could cause high future health care costs. Diabetes causes large future health care costs (and horrible problems). United Health paid employees $450 to be screened for diabetes and other conditions. An amazing 30 percent of employees were diabetic or pre-diabetic and did not know it. Treating those patients enabled United Health to keep health costs flat and improve future quality of life for its employees.

What trends will affect future developments in analytics?

Faster computers and better algorithms for analyzing data and performing optimizations virtually ensure that analytics will become more important in the future. Improvements in visualization will make it easier for the novice analyst to spot patterns in complex data. Chapter 46, "Power View," discusses the exciting capability of Excel 2013 Power View to create beautiful, insightful visualizations. In Chapter 52, "Charting tricks," you learn many exciting charting tricks that help you create charts that lead to better understanding of data.

Probably the most important trend in analytics in the near future is that many analytics applications will be available anywhere, anytime on mobile devices. For example, in 2011, San Ramon, California, developed a smartphone application that signed up people who know cardiopulmonary resuscitation (CPR) so they could perform CPR on a person near them who needs it. When a 911 call arrives and an ambulance cannot get there in time, a text message is sent to any registered person, giving the location of the stricken person. This enables the ill person to receive CPR much more quickly.

Another trend in analytics will be an increase in real-time predictions that lead to action in real time. For example, if predictions indicate a Target store will run out of Pepsi by 11 A.M., the analytics application will know the location of all Pepsi trucks, and a message will be sent to the truck, telling the driver to restock Pepsi by 11 A.M.

CHAPTER 28

Introducing optimization with Excel Solver

In many situations, you want to find the best way to do something. More formally, you want to find the values of certain cells in a worksheet that *optimize* (maximize or minimize) a certain objective. Microsoft Excel Solver helps you answer optimization problems such as the following ones:

- How can a large drug company determine the monthly product mix that maximizes corporate profitability at its Indianapolis plant?

- If Microsoft produces Xbox consoles at three locations, how can it minimize the cost of meeting demand for them?

- What price for Xbox consoles and games will maximize profit from Xbox sales for Microsoft?

- Microsoft would like to undertake 20 strategic initiatives that will tie up money and skilled programmers for the next five years. It does not have enough resources for all 20 projects; which ones should it undertake?

- How do bookmakers find the best set of ratings to set accurate point spreads for NFL teams?

- How should I allocate my retirement portfolio among high-tech stocks, value stocks, bonds, cash, and gold?

An optimization model has three parts: the target cell, the changing cells, and the constraints. The *target cell* represents the objective or goal. You want to minimize or maximize the amount in the target cell. In the question about a drug company's product mix given earlier, the plant manager would presumably want to maximize the profitability of the plant during each month. The cell that measures profitability would be the target cell. The target cells for each situation described at the beginning of the chapter are listed in Table 28-1.

Keep in mind, however, that in some situations, you might have multiple target cells. For example, Microsoft might have a secondary goal to maximize Xbox market share.

TABLE 28-1 List of target cells

Model	Maximize or minimize	Target cell
Drug company product mix	Maximize	Monthly profit
Xbox shipping	Minimize	Distribution costs
Xbox pricing	Maximize	Profit from Xbox consoles and games
Microsoft project initiatives	Maximize	Net present value (NPV) contributed by selected projects
NFL ratings	Minimize	Difference between scores predicted by ratings and actual game scores
Retirement portfolio	Minimize	Risk factor of portfolio

Changing cells are the worksheet cells that you can change or adjust to optimize the target cell. In the drug company example, the plant manager can adjust the amount produced for each product during a month. The cells in which these amounts are recorded are the changing cells in this model. Table 28-2 lists the appropriate changing cell definitions for the models described at the beginning of the chapter, and Table 28-3 lists the problem constraints.

TABLE 28-2 List of changing cells

Model	Changing cells
Drug company product mix	Amount of each product produced during the month
Xbox shipping	Amount produced at each plant each month that is shipped to each customer
Xbox pricing	Console and game prices
Microsoft program initiatives	Which projects are selected
NFL ratings	Team ratings
Retirement portfolio	Fraction of money invested in each asset class

TABLE 28-3 List of problem constraints

Model	Constraints
Drug company product mix	Product mix uses no more resources than are available Do not produce more of a product than can be sold
Xbox shipping	Do not ship more units each month from a plant than plant capacity Make sure that each customer receives the number of Xbox consoles that it needs
Xbox pricing	Prices can't be too far out of line with competitors' prices
Microsoft project initiatives	Projects selected can't use more money or skilled programmers than are available
NFL ratings	None
Retirement portfolio	Invest all our money somewhere (cash is a possibility) Obtain an expected return of at least 10 percent on our investments

The best way to understand how to use Solver is by looking at some detailed examples. In later chapters, you learn how to use Solver to address each of the situations described in this chapter as well as several other important business problems.

To activate Solver, click the **File** tab, choose **Options**, and then click **Add-Ins**. In the **Manage** box at the bottom of the dialog box, select **Excel Add-Ins** and click **Go**. Select the **Solver Add-In** check box in the **Add-Ins** dialog box and click **OK**. After Solver is activated, you can run Solver by clicking **Solver** in the **Analysis** group on the **Data** tab. Figure 28-1 shows the **Solver Parameters** dialog box. In the next few chapters, you see how to use this dialog box to configure the target cell, changing cells, and constraints for a Solver model.

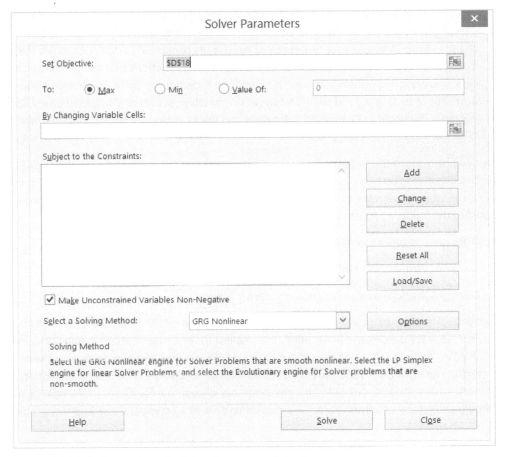

FIGURE 28-1 This figure shows the Solver Parameters dialog box.

Beginning with Excel 2010, Solver has been greatly revamped and improved. The primary change is the presence of the Select A Solving Method list. From this list, you must select the appropriate solution engine for your optimization problem:

- The Simplex LP engine solves linear optimization problems. As you will see in Chapters 29–32, a linear optimization problem is one in which the target cell and constraints are all created by adding terms of the (changing cell)*(constant) form.

- The GRG nonlinear engine solves optimization problems in which the target cell or some of the constraints are not linear and are computed by using common mathematical operations such as multiplying or dividing changing cells, raising changing cells to a power, exponential or trigonometric functions involving changing cells, and so on. The GRG engine includes a powerful Multistart option that enables you to solve many problems that were solved incorrectly with previous versions of Excel. Chapters 33 through 35 discuss the GRG nonlinear engine.

- The Evolutionary Solver engine is used when your target cell or constraints contain non-smooth functions that reference changing cells. A nonsmooth function is one whose slope abruptly changes. For example, when $x = 0$, the slope of the absolute value of x abruptly changes from -1 to 1. If your target cell or constraints contain *IF, SUMIF, COUNTIF, SUMIFS, COUNTIFS, AVERAGEIF, AVERAGEIFS, ABS, MAX,* or *MIN* functions that reference the changing cells, you are using nonsmooth functions, and the Evolutionary Solver engine probably has the best shot at finding a good solution to your optimization problem. The Evolutionary Solver engine is discussed in Chapter 36, "Penalties and the Evolutionary Solver," and Chapter 37, "The traveling salesperson problem."

After you have input the target cell, changing cells, and constraints, what does Solver do? To answer this question, you need some background in Solver terminology. Any specification of the changing cells that satisfies the model's constraints is a *feasible solution*. For instance, any product mix that satisfies the following three conditions would be a feasible solution:

- Does not use more raw material or labor than is available.

- Does not produce more of each product than is demanded.

- Does not produce a negative amount of any product.

Essentially, Solver searches all feasible solutions and finds the one that has the best target cell value (the largest value for maximum optimization, the smallest for minimum optimization). Such a solution is called an *optimal solution*. As you'll see in Chapter 29, "Using Solver to determine the optimal product mix," some Solver models have no optimal solution, and some have a unique solution. Other Solver models have multiple (actually, an infinite number of) optimal solutions. In the next chapter, you'll begin your study of Solver examples by examining the drug company product mix problem.

Problems

For each situation described, identify the target cell, changing cells, and constraints:

1. I am borrowing $100,000 for a 15-year mortgage. The annual rate of interest is 8 percent. How can I determine my monthly mortgage payment?

2. How should an auto company allocate its advertising budget between different advertising formats?

3. How should cities transport students to more distant schools to obtain racial balance?

4. If a city has only one hospital, where should it be located?

5. How should a drug company allocate its sales force's efforts among its products?

6. A drug company has allocated $2 billion to purchasing biotech companies. Which companies should it buy?

7. The tax rate charged to a drug company depends on the country in which a product is produced. How can a drug company determine where each drug should be made?

Using Solver to determine the optimal product mix

Questions answered in this chapter:

- How can I determine the monthly product mix that maximizes profitability?

- Does a Solver model always have a solution?

- What does it mean if a Solver model yields the Set Values Do Not Converge result?

Answers to this chapter's questions

This section provides the answers to the questions that are listed at the beginning of the chapter.

How can I determine the monthly product mix that maximizes profitability?

Companies often need to determine the quantity of each product to produce on a monthly basis. In its simplest form, the product mix problem involves how to determine the amount of each product that should be produced during a month to maximize profits. Product mix must usually adhere to the following constraints:

- Product mix can't use more resources than are available.

- Because demand for each product is limited, you don't want to produce more of it during a month than demand dictates because the excess production is wasted (for example, a perishable drug).

Now, solve the following example of the product mix problem. You can find a feasible solution to this problem in the Feasible Solution worksheet of the Prodmix.xlsx file, shown in Figure 29-1. Trial values for the amount produced of each drug have been entered in row 2.

	B	C	D	E	F	G	H	I
1								
2		Pounds made	150	160	170	180	190	200
3	Available	Product	1	2	3	4	5	6
4	4500	Labor	6	5	4	3	2.5	1.5
5	1600	Raw Material	3.2	2.6	1.5	0.8	0.7	0.3
6		Unit price	$ 12.50	$ 11.00	$ 9.00	$ 7.00	$ 6.00	$ 3.00
7		Variable cost	$ 6.50	$ 5.70	$ 3.60	$ 2.80	$ 2.20	$ 1.20
8		Demand	960	928	1041	977	1084	1055
9		Unit profit cont.	$ 6.00	$ 5.30	$ 5.40	$ 4.20	$ 3.80	$ 1.80
10								
11								
12		Profit	$ 4,504.00					
13					Available			
14		Labor Used	3695 <=		4500			
15		Raw Material Used	1488 <=		1600			

FIGURE 29-1 This figure shows a feasible product mix.

You work for a drug company that produces six products at its plant. Production of each product requires labor and raw material. Row 4 in Figure 29-1 shows the hours of labor needed to produce a pound of each product, and row 5 shows the pounds of raw material needed to produce a pound of each product. For example, producing a pound of Product 1 requires six hours of labor and 3.2 pounds of raw material. For each drug, the price per pound is given in row 6, the unit cost per pound is given in row 7, and the profit contribution per pound is given in row 9. For example, Product 2 sells for $11.00 per pound, incurs a unit cost of $5.70 per pound, and contributes $5.30 profit per pound. The month's demand for each drug is given in row 8. For example, demand for Product 3 is 1,041 pounds. This month, 4,500 hours of labor and 1,600 pounds of raw material are available. How can this company maximize its monthly profit?

If you knew nothing about Solver, you might attack this problem by constructing a worksheet to track profit and resource usage associated with the product mix. Then you could use trial and error to vary the product mix to optimize profit without using more labor or raw material than is available or producing any drug in excess of demand. You use Solver in this process only at the trial-and-error stage. Essentially, Solver is an optimization engine that flawlessly performs the trial-and-error search.

A key to solving the product mix problem is to compute the resource usage and profit associated with any given product mix efficiently. An important tool that you can use to make this computation is the *SUMPRODUCT* function. It multiplies corresponding values in cell ranges and returns the sum of those values. Each cell range used in a *SUMPRODUCT* evaluation must have the same dimensions, so you can use *SUMPRODUCT* with two rows or two columns but not with one column and one row.

As an example of how you can use the *SUMPRODUCT* function in the product mix example, compute resource usage. Labor usage is calculated by the following formula:

```
(Labor used per pound of drug 1)*(Drug 1 pounds produced)+(Labor used per pound of drug 2)
    *(Drug 2 pounds produced)+...(Labor used per pound of drug 6)*(Drug 6 pounds produced)
```

You could compute labor usage in a more tedious fashion as D2*D4+E2*E4+F2*F4+G2*G4+ H2*H4+I2*I4. Similarly, raw material usage could be computed as D2*D5+E2*E5+F2*F5+G2*G5+ H2*H5+I2*I5. However, entering these formulas in a worksheet for six products is time-consuming. Imagine how long it would take if you were working with a company that produced, for example, 50 products at its plant. A much easier way to compute labor and raw material usage is to copy the SUMPRODUCT($D$2:$I$2,D4:I4) formula from D14 to D15. This formula computes D2*D4+E2*E4+F2 *F4+G2*G4+H2*H4+I2*I4 (which is the labor usage) but is much easier to enter. Use the $ sign with the D2:I2 range so that when you copy the formula, you still capture the product mix from row 2. The formula in cell D15 computes raw material usage.

In a similar fashion, profit is determined by the following formula:

```
(Drug 1 profit per pound)*(Drug 1 pounds produced)+(Drug 2 profit per pound)
    *(Drug 2 pounds produced)+...(Drug 6 profit per pound)*(Drug 6 pounds produced)
```

Profit is easily computed in cell D12 with the SUMPRODUCT(D9:I9,$D$2:$I$2) formula.

You now can identify the three components of the product mix Solver model:

- **Target cell**   The goal is to maximize profit (computed in cell D12).

- **Changing cells**   The number of pounds produced of each product is listed in the D2:I2 cell range.

- **Constraints**   You have the following constraints:

  - Do not use more labor or raw material than is available. That is, the values in cells D14:D15 (the resources used) must be less than or equal to the values in cells F14:F15 (the available resources).

  - Do not produce more of a drug than is in demand. That is, the values in the D2:I2 cells (pounds produced of each drug) must be less than or equal to the demand for each drug (listed in cells D8:I8).

  - You can't produce a negative amount of any drug.

This chapter shows you how to enter the target cell, changing cells, and constraints into Solver. Then all you need to do is click the Solve button to find a profit-maximizing product mix.

To begin, click the **Data** tab and, in the **Analysis** group, click **Solver**.

> **Note** As explained in Chapter 28, "Introducing optimization with Excel Solver," Solver is activated by clicking the **File** tab and then choosing **Options** and **Add-Ins**. In the **Manage** list, click **Excel Add-ins** and click **Go**. Select the **Solver Add-In** check box and then click **OK**.

The **Solver Parameters** dialog box opens, as shown in Figure 29-2.

FIGURE 29-2 This figure shows the Solver Parameters dialog box.

Click the **Set Objective** box and then select the profit cell (cell D12). Click the **By Changing Variable Cells** box and then point to the D2:I2 range, which contains the pounds produced of each drug. The dialog box should now look like Figure 29-3.

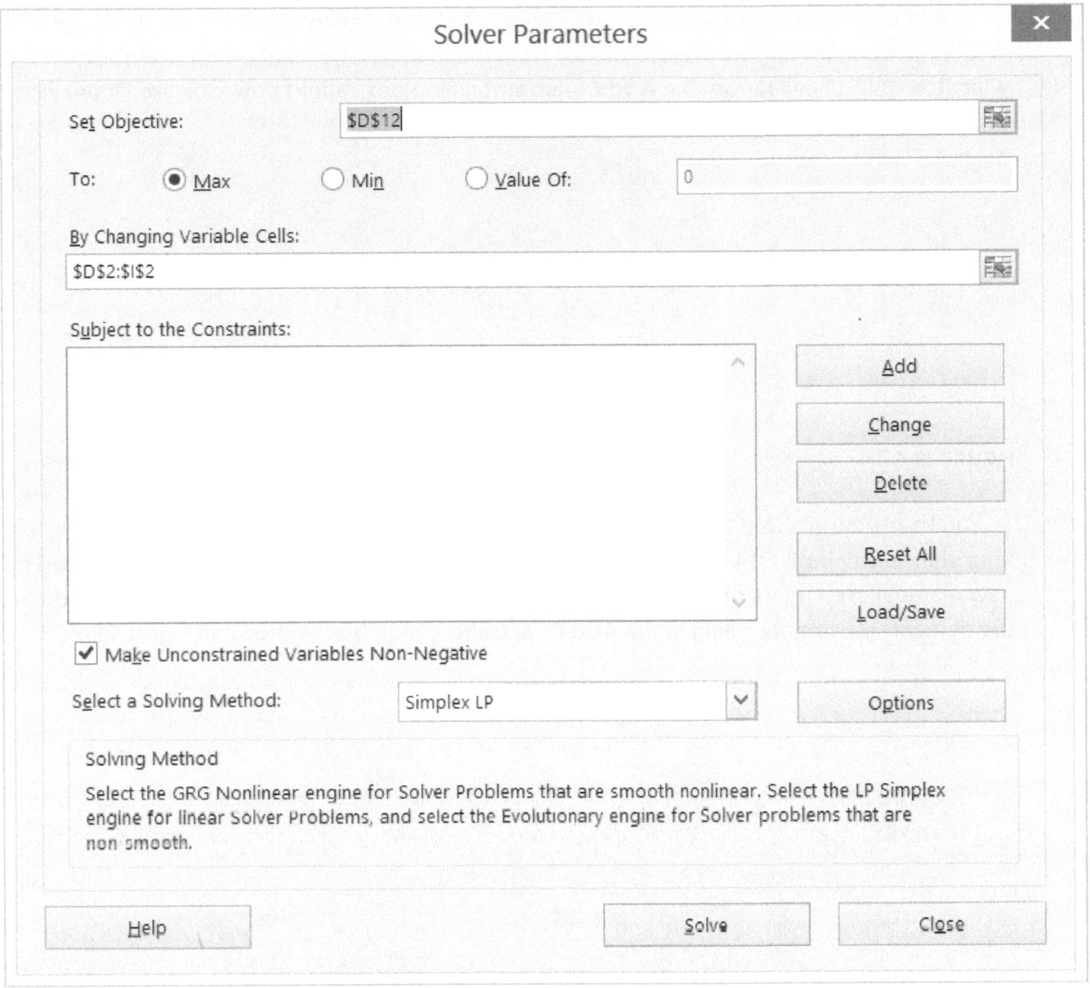

FIGURE 29-3 This figure shows the Solver Parameters dialog box with target cell and changing cells defined.

You're now ready to add constraints to the model. Click the **Add** button. The **Add Constraint** dialog box opens, as shown in Figure 29-4.

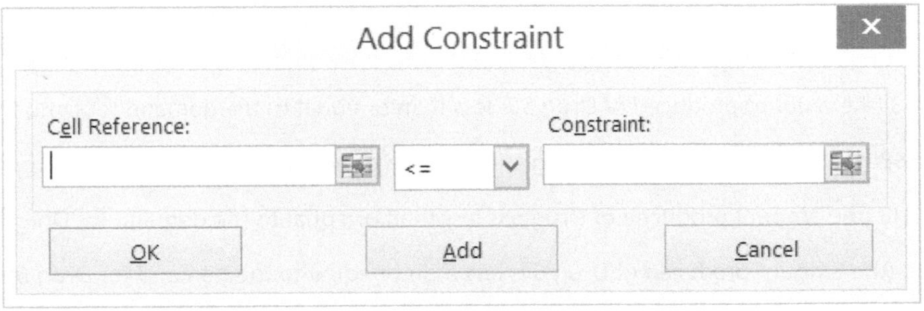

FIGURE 29-4 This figure shows the Add Constraint dialog box.

To add the resource usage constraints, click the **Cell Reference** box and then select the D14:D15 range. After confirming the selection of <= from the middle list, click the **Constraint** box and then select the F14:F15 cell range. The **Add Constraint** dialog box should now look like Figure 29-5.

FIGURE 29-5 This figure shows the Add Constraint dialog box with the resource usage constraints entered.

You have now ensured that when Solver tries different values for the changing cells, only combinations that satisfy both D14<=F14 (labor used is less than or equal to labor available) and D15<=F15 (raw material used is less than or equal to raw material available) are considered. Click **Add** to enter the demand constraints, filling in the **Add Constraint** dialog box as shown in Figure 29-6.

FIGURE 29-6 This figure shows the Add Constraint dialog box with the demand constraints entered.

Adding these constraints ensures that when Solver tries different combinations for the changing cell values, only combinations that satisfy the following parameters are considered:

- D2<=D8 (the amount produced of Drug 1 is less than or equal to the demand for Drug 1)

- E2<=E8 (the amount produced of Drug 2 is less than or equal to the demand for Drug 2)

- F2<=F8 (the amount produced of Drug 3 is less than or equal to the demand for Drug 3)

- G2<=G8 (the amount produced of Drug 4 is less than or equal to the demand for Drug 4)

- H2<=H8 (the amount produced of Drug 5 is less than or equal to the demand for Drug 5)

- I2<=I8 (the amount produced of Drug 6 is less than or equal to the demand for Drug 6)

Click **OK** in the **Add Constraint** dialog box. The **Solver Parameters** dialog box should look like Figure 29-7.

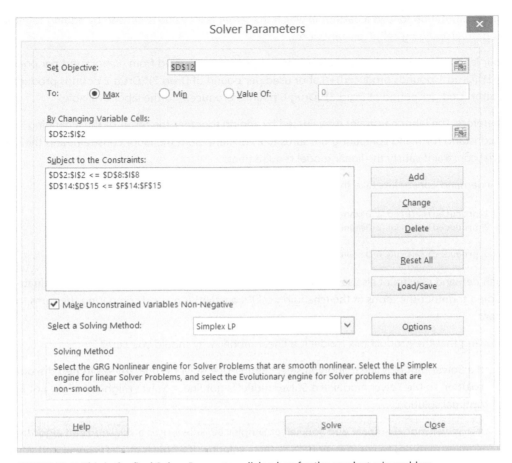

FIGURE 29-7 This is the final Solver Parameters dialog box for the product mix problem.

Selecting the **Make Unconstrained Variables Non-Negative** check box ensures that all the changing cells are forced to be greater than or equal to 0.

Next, choose Simplex LP from the Select A Solving Method list. You choose the Simplex LP engine because the product mix problem is a special type of Solver problem called a *linear* model. Essentially, a Solver model is linear under the following conditions:

- The target cell is computed by adding together the terms of the (changing cell)*(constant) form.

- Each constraint satisfies the *linear model requirement*. This means that each constraint is evaluated by adding together the terms of the (changing cell)*(constant) form and comparing the sums to a constant.

Why is this Solver problem linear? Your target cell (profit) is computed as follows:

```
(Drug 1 profit per pound)*(Drug 1 pounds produced)+(Drug 2 profit per pound)
  *(Drug 2 pounds produced)+...(Drug 6 profit per pound)*(Drug 6 pounds produced)
```

This computation follows a pattern in which the target cell's value is derived by adding together terms of the (changing cell)*(constant) form.

Your labor constraint is evaluated by comparing the value derived from (Labor used per pound of Drug 1)*(Drug 1 pounds produced)+(Labor used per pound of Drug 2)*(Drug 2 pounds produced)+ . . . (Labor used per pound of Drug 6)*(Drug 6 pounds produced) to the labor available.

Therefore, the labor constraint is evaluated by adding together the terms of the (changing cell)*(constant) form and comparing the sums to a constant. Both the labor constraint and the raw material constraint satisfy the linear model requirement.

The demand constraints take the following form:

```
(Drug 1 produced)<=(Drug 1 Demand)
(Drug 2 produced)<=(Drug 2 Demand)
...
(Drug 6 produced)<=(Drug 6 Demand)
```

Each demand constraint also satisfies the linear model requirement because each is evaluated by adding together the terms of the (changing cell)*(constant) form and comparing the sums to a constant.

Knowing that the product mix model is a linear model, why should you care?

- If a Solver model is linear and you select Simplex LP, Solver is guaranteed to find the optimal solution to the Solver model. If a Solver model is not linear, Solver might or might not find the optimal solution.

- If a Solver model is linear and you select Simplex LP, Solver uses a very efficient algorithm (the simplex method) to find the model's optimal solution. If a Solver model is linear and you do not select Simplex LP, Solver uses a very inefficient algorithm (the GRG2 method) and might have difficulty finding the model's optimal solution.

After you click **Solve**, Solver calculates an optimal solution (if one exists) for the product mix model. As stated in Chapter 28, an optimal solution to the product mix model would be a set of changing cell values (pounds produced of each drug) that maximizes profit over the set of all feasible solutions. Again, a feasible solution is a set of changing cell values satisfying all constraints. The changing cell values shown in Figure 29-8 are a feasible solution because all production levels are nonnegative, production levels do not exceed demand, and resource usage does not exceed available resources.

	C	D	E	F	G	H	I
1							
2	Pounds made	150	160	170	180	190	200
3	Product	1	2	3	4	5	6
4	Labor	6	5	4	3	2.5	1.5
5	Raw Material	3.2	2.6	1.5	0.8	0.7	0.3
6	Unit price	$ 12.50	$ 11.00	$ 9.00	$ 7.00	$ 6.00	$ 3.00
7	Variable cost	$ 6.50	$ 5.70	$ 3.60	$ 2.80	$ 2.20	$ 1.20
8	Demand	960	928	1041	977	1084	1055
9	Unit profit cont.	$ 6.00	$ 5.30	$ 5.40	$ 4.20	$ 3.80	$ 1.80
10							
11							
12	Profit	$ 4,504.00					
13			Available				
14	Labor Used	3695 <=	4500				
15	Raw Material Used	1488 <=	1600				

FIGURE 29-8 A feasible solution to the product mix problem fits within constraints.

The changing cell values shown in Figure 29-9 represent an *infeasible solution* for the following reasons:

- You produce more of Drug 5 than the demand for it.

- You use more labor than is available.

- You use more raw material than is available.

B	C	D	E	F	G	H	I
	Pounds made	300	0	0	0	1085	1000
Available	Product	1	2	3	4	5	6
4500	Labor	6	5	4	3	2.5	1.5
1600	Raw Material	3.2	2.6	1.5	0.8	0.7	0.3
	Unit price	$ 12.50	$ 11.00	$ 9.00	$ 7.00	$ 6.00	$ 3.00
	Variable cost	$ 6.50	$ 5.70	$ 3.60	$ 2.80	$ 2.20	$ 1.20
	Demand	960	928	1041	977	1084	1055
	Unit profit cont.	$ 6.00	$ 5.30	$ 5.40	$ 4.20	$ 3.80	$ 1.80
	Profit	$ 7,723.00					
			Available				
	Labor Used	6012.5 <=	4500				
	Raw Material Used	2019.5 <=	1600				

FIGURE 29-9 An infeasible solution to the product mix problem doesn't fit within the defined constraints.

	B	C	D	E	F	G	H	I
2		Pounds made	0	0	0	596.6667	1084	0
3	Available	Product	1	2	3	4	5	6
4	4500	Labor	6	5	4	3	2.5	1.5
5	1600	Raw Material	3.2	2.6	1.5	0.8	0.7	0.3
6		Unit price	$ 12.50	$ 11.00	$ 9.00	$ 7.00	$ 6.00	$ 3.00
7		Variable cost	$ 6.50	$ 5.70	$ 3.60	$ 2.80	$ 2.20	$ 1.20
8		Demand	960	928	1041	977	1084	1055
9		Unit profit cont.	$ 6.00	$ 5.30	$ 5.40	$ 4.20	$ 3.80	$ 1.80
10								
11								
12		Profit	$ 6,625.20					
13					Available			
14		Labor Used	4500 <=		4500			
15		Raw Material Used	1236.13333 <=		1600			

FIGURE 29-10 This is the optimal solution to the product mix problem.

Your drug company can maximize its monthly profit at a level of $6,625.20 by producing 596.67 pounds of Drug 4; 1,084 pounds of Drug 5; and none of the other drugs. You can't determine whether you can achieve the maximum profit of $6,625.20 in other ways. All you can be sure of is that with your limited resources and demand, you cannot make more than $6,625.20 this month.

Does a Solver model always have a solution?

Suppose that demand for each product *must* be met. (See the No Feasible Solution worksheet in the Prodmix.xlsx file.) You then have to change your demand constraints from D2:I2<=D8:I8 to D2:I2>=D8:I8. To do this, open **Solver**, select the D2:I2<=D8:I8 constraint, and then click **Change**. The **Change Constraint** dialog box, shown in Figure 29-11, opens.

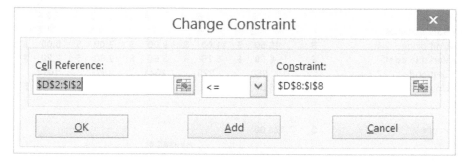

FIGURE 29-11 This is the Change Constraint dialog box.

As shown in Figure 29-12, select >= and then click **OK**. You've now ensured that Solver will consider changing only cell values that meet all demands. When you click **Solve**, you'll see the message, "Solver could not find a feasible solution." This message does not mean that you made a mistake in your model but, rather, that with limited resources, you can't meet demand for all products. Solver is simply telling you that if you want to meet demand for each product, you need to add more labor, more raw material, or both.

FIGURE 29-12 Demand constraint now ensures that demand is met.

What does it mean if a Solver model yields the Set Values Do Not Converge result?

What happens if you allow unlimited demand for each product and negative quantities to be produced of each drug? (You can see this Solver problem on the Set Values Do Not Converge worksheet in the Prodmix.xlsx file.) To find the optimal solution for this situation, open **Solver** and clear the **Make Unconstrained Variables Non-Negative** check box. In the **Solver Parameters** dialog box, select the D2:I2<=D8:I8 demand constraint and then click **Delete** to remove the constraint. When you click **Solve**, Solver returns the Set Cell Values Do Not Converge message. This message means that if the target cell is to be maximized (as in this example), there are feasible solutions with arbitrarily large target cell values. For example, if you wanted to make a billion dollars in profit, Solver could find a feasible solution to make that level of profit (see Problem 7). (If the target cell is to be minimized, the Set Cell Values Do Not Converge message means there are feasible solutions with arbitrarily small target cell values.) In this situation, by allowing negative production of a drug, you create resources that can be used to produce arbitrarily large amounts of other drugs. Given your unlimited demand, you can make unlimited profit. In a real situation, you can't make an infinite amount of money. In short, if you see Set Values Do Not Converge, your model does have an error.

Problems

1. Suppose your drug company can purchase up to 500 hours of labor at $1 more per hour than current labor costs. How can it maximize profit?

2. At a chip manufacturing plant, four technicians (A, B, C, and D) produce three products (Products 1, 2, and 3). This month, the chip manufacturer can sell 80 units of Product 1, 50 units of Product 2, and, at most, 50 units of Product 3. Technician A can make only Products 1 and 3. Technician B can make only Products 1 and 2. Technician C can make only Product 3. Technician D can make only Product 2. For each unit produced, the products contribute the

following profit: Product 1, $6; Product 2, $7; and Product 3, $10. The time (in hours) each technician needs to manufacture a product is as follows:

Product	Technician A	Technician B	Technician C	Technician D
1	2	2.5	Cannot do	Cannot do
2	Cannot do	3	Cannot do	3.5
3	3	Cannot do	4	Cannot do

Each technician can work up to 120 hours per month. How can the chip manufacturer maximize its monthly profit? Assume a fractional number of units can be produced.

3. A computer manufacturing plant produces mice, keyboards, and video game joysticks. The per-unit profit, per-unit labor usage, monthly demand, and per-unit machine-time usage are given in the following table:

	Mice	Keyboards	Joysticks
Profit/unit	$8	$11	$9
Labor usage/unit	.2 hour	.3 hour	.24 hour
Machine time/unit	.04 hour	.055 hour	.04 hour
Monthly demand	15,000	29,000	11,000

Each month, a total of 13,000 labor hours and 3,000 hours of machine time are available. How can the manufacturer maximize its monthly profit contribution from the plant?

4. Resolve your drug example, assuming that a minimum demand of 200 units for each drug must be met.

5. Jason makes diamond bracelets, necklaces, and earrings. He wants to work a maximum of 160 hours per month. He has 800 ounces of diamonds. The profit, labor time, and ounces of diamonds required to produce each product are as follows. If demand for each product is unlimited, how can Jason maximize his profit?

Product	Unit profit	Labor hours per unit	Ounces of diamonds per unit
Bracelet	$300	.35	1.2
Necklace	$200	.15	.75
Earrings	$100	.05	.5

In your product mix example, suppose that whenever you sell more than 400 pounds of any product, you must give a $1 per pound discount on each pound above 400 sold. How does this change the answer to the problem?

6. If demand is unlimited and negative production is allowed, find a feasible solution that earns a billion dollars.

7. Assuming unlimited demand and unlimited resources, find a feasible solution that earns $1 billion in profit.

CHAPTER 30

Using Solver to schedule your workforce

Question answered in this chapter:

- How can I schedule my workforce efficiently to meet labor demands?

Many organizations (such as banks, restaurants, and postal service companies) know what their labor requirements are at different times of the day, and they need a method to schedule their workforce efficiently. You can use Solver to solve workforce scheduling problems easily.

Answer to this chapter's question

This section provides the answer to the question that is listed at the beginning of the chapter.

How can I schedule my workforce efficiently to meet labor demands?

Bank 24 processes checks seven days a week. The number of workers needed each day to process checks is shown in row 14 of the Bank24.xlsx file, which appears in Figure 30-1. For example, 13 workers are needed on Tuesday, 15 workers are needed on Wednesday, and so on. All bank employees work five consecutive days. What is the minimum number of employees Bank 24 can have and still meet its labor requirements?

	A	B	C	D	E	F	G	H	I	J
2	Total				There are multiple solutions all of which use 20 workers.					
3	20		Working?							
4	Number starting	Day worker starts	Monday	Tuesday	Wednesday	Thursday	Friday	Saturday	Sunday	
5	1	Monday	1	1	1	1	1	0	0	
6	3	Tuesday	0	1	1	1	1	1	0	
7	0	Wednesday	0	0	1	1	1	1	1	
8	4	Thursday	1	0	0	1	1	1	1	
9	1	Friday	1	1	0	0	1	1	1	
10	2	Saturday	1	1	1	0	0	1	1	
11	9	Sunday	1	1	1	0	0	0	1	
12		Number working	17	16	15	17	9	10	16	
13			>=	>=	>=	>=	>=	>=	>=	
14		Number needed	17	13	15	17	9	9	12	

FIGURE 30-1 This figure shows the data you'll use to work through the bank workforce scheduling problem.

- **Target cell** Minimize total number of employees.

- **Changing cells** Number of employees who start work (the first of five consecutive days) each day of the week. Each changing cell must be a nonnegative integer.

- **Constraints** For each day of the week, the number of employees who are working must be greater than or equal to the number of employees required—(Number of employees working)>=(Needed employees).

To set up the model for this problem, you need to track the number of employees working each day. Begin by entering trial values in the A5:A11 cell range for the number of employees who start their five-day shift each day. For example, in A5, 1 is entered, indicating that 1 employee begins work on Monday and works Monday through Friday. Each day's required workers are entered in the C14:I14 range.

To track the number of employees working each day, a 1 or a 0 is entered in each cell in the C5:I11 range. The value *1* indicates that the employees who started working on the day designated in the cell's row are working on the day associated with the cell's column. For example, the 1 in cell G5 indicates that employees who started working on Monday are working on Friday; the 0 in cell H5 indicates that the employees who started working on Monday are not working on Saturday.

By copying the =*SUMPRODUCT($A$5:$A$11,C5:C11)* formula from C12 to D12:I12, you can compute the number of employees working each day. For example, in cell C12, this formula evaluates to =A5+A8+A9+A10+A11, which equals (Number starting on Monday) + (Number starting on Thursday) + (Number starting on Friday) + (Number starting on Saturday) + (Number starting on Sunday). This total is indeed the number of people working on Monday.

After computing the total number of employees in cell A3 with the =SUM(A5:A11) formula, you can enter a model in Solver as shown in Figure 30-2.

In the target cell (A3), you want to minimize the number of total employees. The C12:I12>=C14:I14 constraint ensures that the number of employees working each day is at least as large as the number needed each day. The A5:A11=integer constraint ensures that the number of employees beginning work each day is an integer. To add this constraint, click **Add** in the **Solver Parameters** dialog box and fill in the **Add Constraint** dialog box as shown in Figure 30-3.

Note that this model is linear because the target cell is created by adding together changing cells, and the constraint is created by comparing the result obtained by adding together the product of each changing cell times a constant (either 1 or 0) to the required number of workers. Therefore, you select the Simplex LP engine. Because you cannot start a negative number of workers on a day, select **Make Unconstrained Variables Non-Negative**. After clicking **Solve**, you find the optimal solution that was shown earlier, in Figure 30-1.

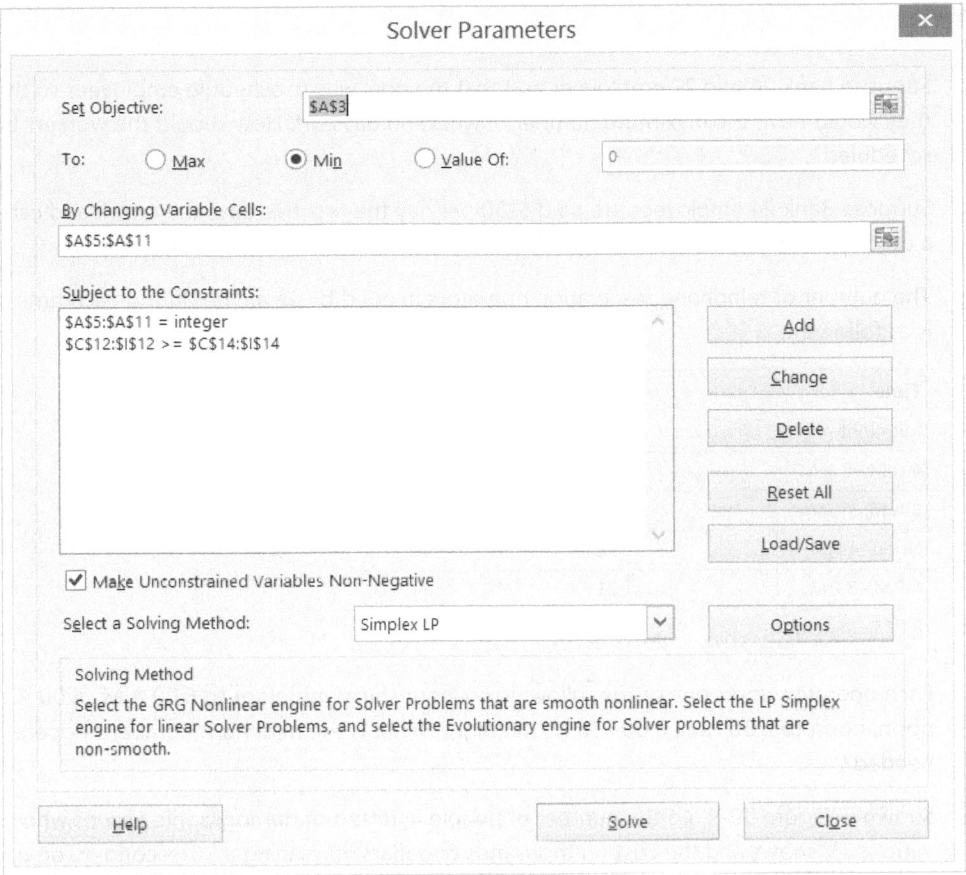

FIGURE 30-2 The Solver Parameters dialog box is filled in to solve the workforce problem.

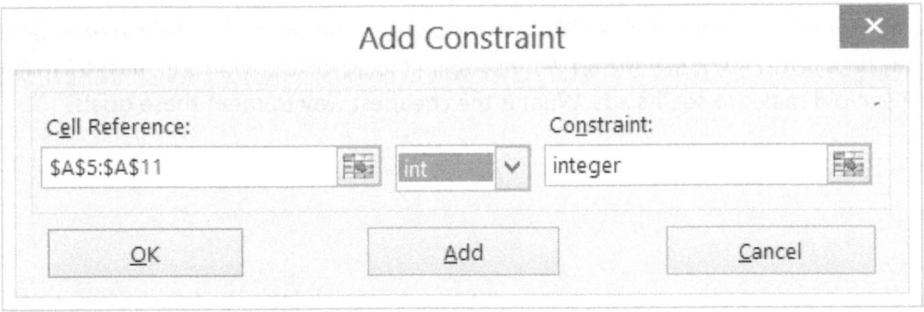

FIGURE 30-3 This constraint defines the number of workers who start each day as an integer.

A total of 20 employees is needed. One employee starts on Monday, three start on Tuesday, four start on Thursday, one starts on Friday, two start on Saturday, and nine start on Sunday. Note that this model actually has multiple optimal solutions that use 20 workers. If you run Solver again, you might very well find one of these alternative optimal solutions.

Problems

1. Suppose Bank 24 had 22 employees and that the goal was to schedule employees so that they would have the maximum number of weekend days off. How should the workers be scheduled?

2. Suppose Bank 24 employees are paid $150 per day the first five days they work and can work a day of overtime at a cost of $350. How should the bank schedule its employees?

3. The number of telephone reservation operators needed by an airline during each time of day is as follows:

Time	Operators needed
Midnight–4 A.M.	12
4 A.M.–8 A.M.	16
8 A.M.–noon	22
Noon–4 P.M.	30
4 P.M.–8 P.M.	31
8 P.M.–midnight	22

Each operator works one of the following six-hour shifts: midnight to 6:00 A.M., 6:00 A.M. to noon, noon to 6:00 P.M., 6:00 P.M. to midnight. What is the minimum number of operators needed?

4. Shown in Figure 30-4 are the number of people in different demographic groups who watch various TV shows and the cost (in thousands of dollars) of placing a 30-second ad on each show. For example, it costs $160,000 to place a 30-second ad on *Friends*. The show is watched by 6 million males between the ages of 18 and 35, 3 million males between 36 and 55, 1 million males over 55, 9 million females between 18 and 35, 4 million females between 36 and 55, and 2 million females over 55. The data also includes the number of people in each group (in millions) that you want to see the ad. For example, the advertiser wants at least 60 million 18 to 35-year-old males to see its ads. What is the cheapest way to meet these goals?

	D	E	F	G	H	I	J
4	needed	60	60	28	60	60	28
5	Show	M 18-35	M 36-55	M >55	W 18-35	W 36-55	W >55
6	Friends	6	3	1	9	4	2
7	MNF	6	5	3	1	1	1
8	Malcolm	5	2	0	4	2	0
9	Sports Center	0.5	0.5	0.3	0.1	0.1	0
10	MTV	0.7	0.2	0	0.9	0.1	0
11	Lifetime	0.1	0.1	0	0.6	1.3	0.4
12	CNN	0.1	0.2	0.3	0.1	0.2	0.3
13	Jag	1	2	4	1	3	4

FIGURE 30-4 This figure shows the data for problem 4.

5. The Pine Valley Credit Union is trying to schedule bank tellers. The credit union is open from 8 A.M. to 6 P.M. and needs the following number of tellers each hour:

Needed	Time
4	8–9
8	9–10
6	10–11
4	11–12
9	12–1
8	1 2
5	2–3
4	3–4
4	4–5
5	5–6

Full-time tellers can work from 8 A.M. to 5 P.M. (with a 12 to 1 P.M. lunch hour) or from 9 A.M. to 6 P.M. (with a 1 P.M. to 2 P.M. lunch hour).

Part-time tellers work from 10 A.M. to 2 P.M. Full-time tellers receive $300 per day, and part-time tellers $60 per day. At most, four part-time tellers can be hired. How can the credit union minimize its daily teller salary cost?

CHAPTER 31

Using Solver to solve transportation or distribution problems

Question answered in this chapter:

- How can a drug company determine at which location it should produce drugs and from which location it should ship drugs to customers?

Many companies manufacture products at different locations (often called *supply points*) and ship their products to customers (often called *demand points*). A natural question is, "What is the least expensive way to produce and ship products to customers and still meet demand?" This type of problem is called a *transportation problem*. A transportation problem can be set up as a linear Solver model with the following specifications:

- **Target cell**   Minimize total production and shipping cost.

- **Changing cells**   This is the amount produced at each supply point that is shipped to each demand point.

- **Constraints**   The amount shipped from each supply point can't exceed plant capacity. Each demand point must receive its required demand. In addition, each changing cell must be nonnegative.

Answer to this chapter's question

This section provides the answer to the question that is listed at the beginning of the chapter.

How can a drug company determine at which location it should produce drugs and from which location it should ship drugs to customers?

You can follow along with this problem by looking at the Transport.xlsx file. Suppose a company produces a certain drug at its Los Angeles, Atlanta, and New York facilities. Each month, the Los Angeles plant can produce up to 10,000 pounds of the drug. Atlanta can produce up to 12,000 pounds, and New York can produce up to 14,000 pounds. The company must ship the number of pounds listed in cells B2:E2 each month to the four regions of the United States—East, Midwest, South, and West—as shown in Figure 31-1. For example, the West region must receive at least 13,000 pounds of the drug each month. The cost per pound of producing a drug at each plant and shipping the drug to each region of the country is given in cells B4:E6. For example, it costs $3.50 to produce one pound of the drug in Los Angeles and ship it to the Midwest region. What is the cheapest way to deliver the quantity of the drug each region needs?

	A	B	C	D	E	F	G	H
1								
2	DEMAND	9000	6000	6000	13000			
3		EAST	MIDWEST	SOUTH	WEST	CAPACITY		
4	LA	$ 5.00	$ 3.50	$ 4.20	$ 2.20	10000		
5	ATLANTA	$ 3.20	$ 2.60	$ 1.80	$ 4.80	12000		
6	NEW YORK CITY	$ 2.50	$ 3.10	$ 3.30	$ 5.40	14000		
7								
8	Shipments							
9		EAST	MIDWEST	SOUTH	WEST	Sent		Capacity
10	LA	0	0	0	10000	10000	<=	10000
11	ATLANTA	0	3000	6000	3000	12000	<=	12000
12	NEW YORK CITY	9000	3000	0	0	12000	<=	14000
13	Received	9000	6000	6000	13000			
14		>=	>=	>=	>=			
15	Demand	9000	6000	6000	13000			
16								
17								
18	Total Cost	$86,800.00						

FIGURE 31-1 This is data for a transportation problem.

To express the target cell, you need to track total shipping cost. After entering trial values in the B10:E12 cell range for shipments from each supply point to each region, you can compute total shipping cost as follows:

```
(Amount sent from LA to East)*(Cost per pound of sending drug from LA to East)
  +(Amount sent from LA to Midwest)*(Cost per pound of sending drug from LA to Midwest)
  +(Amount sent from LA to South)*(Cost per pound of sending drug from LA to South)
  +(Amount sent from LA to West)*(Cost per pound of sending drug from LA to West)
  +...(Amount sent from New York City to West)
  *(Cost per pound of sending drug from New York City to West)
```

The *SUMPRODUCT* function can multiply corresponding elements in two rectangles (as long as the rectangles are the same size) and add the products together. The B4:E6 cell range has been named Costs and the changing cells range (B10:E12) Shipped. Therefore, total shipping and production cost is computed in cell B18 with the SUMPRODUCT(costs,shipped) formula.

To express the problem's constraints, first compute the total shipped from each supply point. By entering the SUM(B10:E10) formula in cell F10, you can compute the total number of pounds shipped from Los Angeles as (LA shipped to East) + (LA shipped to Midwest) + (LA shipped to South) + (LA shipped to West). Copying this formula to F11:F12 computes the total shipped from Atlanta and

New York City. Later, you'll add a constraint (called a *supply constraint*) that ensures that the amount shipped from each location does not exceed the plant's capacity.

Next, compute the total received by each demand point. Begin by entering the SUM(B10:B12) formula in cell B13. This formula computes the total number of pounds received in the East as (Pounds shipped from LA to East) + (Pounds shipped from Atlanta to East) + (Pounds shipped from New York City to East). By copying this formula from B13 to C13:E13, you compute the pounds of the drug received by the Midwest, South, and West regions. Later, you'll add a constraint (called a *demand constraint*) that ensures that each region receives the amount of the drug it requires.

Open the **Solver Parameters** dialog box (click **Solver** in the **Analysis** group on the **Data** tab) and fill it in as shown in Figure 31-2.

FIGURE 31-2 Solver is set up to solve your transportation problem.

You want to minimize total shipping cost (computed in cell B18). The changing cells are the number of pounds shipped from each plant to each region of the country. (These amounts are listed in the range named Shipped, consisting of cells B10:E12.) The F10:F12<=H10:H12 constraint (the supply constraint) ensures that the amount sent from each plant does not exceed its capacity. The

B13:E13>=B15:E15 constraint (the demand constraint) ensures that each region receives at least the amount of the drug it needs.

This model is a linear Solver model because the target cell is created by adding together the terms of the form (changing cell)*(constant), and both your supply and demand constraints are created by comparing the sum of changing cells to a constant. Because the model is linear, choose the Simplex LP engine. Clearly, shipments must be nonnegative, so select the **Make Unconstrained Variables Non-Negative** check box.

After clicking **Solve** in the **Solver Parameters** dialog box, you are presented with the optimal solution shown earlier, in Figure 31-1. The minimum cost of meeting customer demand is $86,800. This minimum cost can be achieved if the company uses the following production and shipping schedule:

- Ship 10,000 pounds from Los Angeles to the West region.

- Ship 3,000 pounds from Atlanta to the West region and the same amount from Atlanta to the Midwest region. Ship 6,000 pounds from Atlanta to the South region.

- Ship 9,000 pounds from New York City to the East region and 3,000 pounds from New York City to the Midwest region.

Problems

1. The following table gives the distances between Boston, Chicago, Dallas, Los Angeles, and Miami. Each city requires 40,000 kilowatt hours (kWh) of power, and Chicago, Dallas, and Miami are capable of producing 70,000 kWh. Assume that shipping 1,000 kWh over 100 miles costs $4. From where should power be sent to minimize the cost of meeting each city's demand?

	Boston	Chicago	Dallas	Los Angeles	Miami
Chicago	983	0	1205	2112	1390
Dallas	1815	1205	0	801	1332
Miami	1539	1390	1332	2757	0

2. Resolve this chapter's example assuming that demand in the West region increases to 13,000.

3. Your company produces and sells drugs at several locations. The decision of where to produce goods for each sales location can have a huge impact on profitability. The model here is similar to the model used in this chapter to determine where drugs should be produced. Use the following assumptions:

- You produce drugs at six locations and sell to customers in six areas.

- The tax rate and variable production cost depend on where the drug is produced. For example, any units produced at Location 3 cost $6 per unit to produce; profits from these goods are taxed at 20 percent.

- The sales price of each drug depends on where the drug is sold. For example, each product sold in Location 2 is sold for $40:

Production location	1	2	3	4	5	6
Sales price	$45	$40	$38	$36	$39	$34
Tax rate	31%	40%	20%	40%	35%	18%
Variable production cost	$8	$7	$6	$9	$7	$7

- Each of the six plants can produce up to 6 million units per year.

- The annual demand (in millions) for your product in each location is as follows:

Sales location	1	2	3	4	5	6
Demand	1	2	3	4	5	6

- The unit shipping cost depends on the plant where the product is produced and where the product is sold:

	Sold 1	Sold 2	Sold 3	Sold 4	Sold 5	Sold 6
Plant 1	$3	$4	$5	$6	$7	$8
Plant 2	$5	$2	$6	$9	$10	$11
Plant 3	$4	$3	$1	$6	$8	$6
Plant 4	$5	$5	$7	$2	$5	$5
Plant 5	$6	$9	$6	$5	$3	$7
Plant 6	$7	$7	$8	$9	$10	$4

For example, if you produce a unit at Plant 1 and sell it in Location 3, it costs $5 to ship it.

How can you maximize after-tax profit with your limited production capacity?

4. Suppose that each day, northern, central, and southern California each uses 100 billion gallons of water. Also, assume that northern California and central California have 120 billion gallons of water available, whereas southern California has 40 billion gallons of water available. The cost of shipping 1 billion gallons of water between the three regions is as follows:

	Northern	Central	Southern
Northern	$5,000	$7,000	$10,000
Central	$7,000	$5,000	$6,000
Southern	$10,000	$6,000	$5,000

You will not be able to meet all demand for water, so assume that each billion gallons of unmet demand incurs the following shortage costs:

	Northern	Central	Southern
Shortage cost/billion gallons short	$6,000	$5,500	$9,000

How should California's water be distributed to minimize the sum of shipping and shortage costs?

CHAPTER 32

Using Solver for capital budgeting

Question answered in this chapter:

- How can a company use Solver to determine which projects it should undertake?

Each year, a company such as Eli Lilly needs to determine which drugs to develop; a company such as Microsoft, which software programs to develop; a company such as Proctor & Gamble, which new consumer products to develop. Solver can help a company make these decisions.

Answer to this chapter's question

This section provides the answer to the question that is listed at the beginning of the chapter.

How can a company use Solver to determine which projects it should undertake?

Most corporations want to undertake projects that contribute the greatest net present value (NPV), subject to limited resources (usually capital and labor). Say that a software development company is trying to determine which of 20 software projects it should undertake. The NPV (in millions of dollars) contributed by each project as well as the capital (in millions of dollars) and the number of programmers needed during each of the next three years is given on the Basic Model worksheet in the Capbudget.xlsx file, shown in Figure 32-1. For example, Project 2 yields $908 million. It requires $151 million during Year 1, $269 million during Year 2, and $248 million during Year 3. Project 2 requires 139 programmers during Year 1, 86 programmers during Year 2, and 83 programmers during Year 3. Cells E4:G4 show the capital (in millions of dollars) available during each of the three years, and cells H4:J4 indicate how many programmers are available. For example, during Year 1, up to $2.5 billion in capital and 900 programmers are available.

	A	B	C	D	E	F	G	H	I	J
1		Total NPV								
2		9293		Used	2460	2684	2742	876	895	702
3				<=	<=	<=	<=	<=	<=	<=
4				Available	2500	2800	2900	900	900	900
5	Do IT?		NPV		Cost Year 1	Cost Year 2	Cost Year 3	Labor Year 1	Labor Year 2	Labor Year 3
6		0 Project 1	928		398	180	368	111	108	123
7		1 Project 2	908		151	269	248	139	86	83
8		1 Project 3	801		129	189	308	56	61	23
9		0 Project 4	543		275	218	220	54	70	59
10		0 Project 5	944		291	252	228	123	141	70
11		1 Project 6	848		80	283	285	119	84	37
12		1 Project 7	545		203	220	77	54	44	42
13		1 Project 8	808		150	113	143	67	101	43
14		1 Project 9	638		282	141	160	37	55	64
15		1 Project 10	841		214	254	355	130	72	62
16		0 Project 11	664		224	271	130	51	79	58
17		0 Project 12	546		225	150	33	35	107	63
18		0 Project 13	699		101	218	272	43	90	71
19		1 Project 14	599		255	202	70	3	75	83
20		1 Project 15	903		228	351	240	60	93	80
21		1 Project 16	859		303	173	431	60	90	41
22		0 Project 17	748		133	427	220	59	40	39
23		0 Project 18	668		197	98	214	95	96	74
24		1 Project 19	888		313	278	291	66	75	74
25		1 Project 20	655		152	211	134	85	59	70

FIGURE 32-1 This is data you will use with Solver to determine which projects to undertake.

The company must decide whether it should undertake each project. Assume that the company can't undertake a fraction of a software project; if 0.5 of the needed resources is allocated, for example, the company would have a nonworking program that would bring in $0 revenue!

The trick in modeling situations in which you either do or don't do something is to use *binary changing cells*. A binary changing cell always equals 0 or 1. When a binary changing cell that corresponds to a project equals 1, you do the project. If a binary changing cell that corresponds to a project equals 0, you don't do the project. You set up Solver to use a range of binary changing cells by adding a constraint; select the changing cells you want to use and then choose **Bin** from the list in the **Add Constraint** dialog box.

With this background, you're ready to solve the software project selection problem. As with any Solver model, you should begin by identifying the target cell, the changing cells, and the constraints:

- **Target cell**   Maximize the NPV generated by selected projects.

- **Changing cells**   Look for a 0 or 1 binary changing cell for each project. Locate these cells in the A6:A25 range (named the doit range). For example, a 1 in cell A6 indicates that you undertake Project 1; a 0 in cell A6 indicates that you don't undertake Project 1.

- **Constraints**   You need to ensure that for each Year t (t = 1, 2, 3), Year t capital used is less than or equal to Year t capital available, and Year t labor used is less than or equal to Year t labor available.

As you can see, the worksheet must compute the NPV, the capital used annually, and the programmers used each year for any selection of projects. In cell B2, use the SUMPRODUCT(doit,NPV) formula to compute the total NPV generated by selected projects. (The NPV range name refers to the C6:C25 range.) For every project with a 1 in column A, this formula picks up the NPV of the project, and for every project with a 0 in column A, this formula does not pick up the NPV of the project. Therefore, you can compute the NPV of all projects, and the target cell is linear because it is computed by summing terms that follow the (changing cell)*(constant) form. In a similar fashion, compute the capital used each year and the labor used each year by copying the *SUMPRODUCT(doit,E6:E25)* formula from E2 to F2:J2.

Now fill in the **Solver Parameters** dialog box as shown in Figure 32-2.

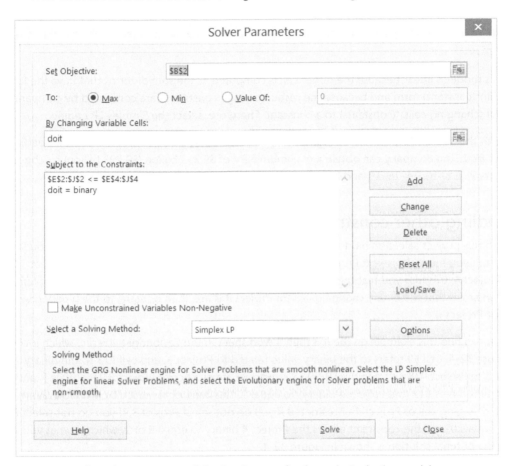

FIGURE 32-2 The Solver Parameters dialog box is set up for the project selection model.

The goal is to maximize the NPV of selected projects (cell B2). The changing cells (the range named doit) are the binary changing cells for each project. The E2:J2<=E4:J4 constraint ensures that during each year, the capital and labor used are less than or equal to the capital and labor available. To add the constraint that makes the changing cells binary, click **Add** in the **Solver Parameters** dialog box and then select **Bin** from the list in the middle of the **Add Constraint** dialog box. The **Add Constraint** dialog box should appear as shown in Figure 32-3.

FIGURE 32-3 Use Bin in the Add Constraint dialog box to set up binary changing cells—cells that display either a 0 or a 1.

This model is linear because the target cell is computed as the sum of terms that have the (changing cell)*(constant) form and because the resource usage constraints are computed by comparing the sum of (changing cells)*(constants) to a constant. Therefore, select the Simplex LP engine.

With the **Solver Parameters** dialog box filled in, click **Solve** and get the results shown earlier, in Figure 32-1. The company can obtain a maximum NPV of $9,293 billion ($9.293 billion) by choosing Projects 2, 3, 6–10, 14–16, 19, and 20.

Handling other constraints

Sometimes project selection models have other constraints. For example, suppose that if you select Project 3, you must also select Project 4. Because the current optimal solution selects Project 3 but not Project 4, this tells you that the current solution can't remain optimal. To solve this problem, add the constraint that the binary changing cell for Project 3 is less than or equal to the binary changing cell for Project 4.

You can find this example on the If 3 then 4 worksheet in the Capbudget.xlsx file, which is shown in Figure 32-4. Cell L9 refers to the binary value related to Project 3, and cell L12 to the binary value related to Project 4. By adding the L9<=L12 constraint, if you choose Project 3, L9 equals 1, and this constraint forces L12 (the Project 4 binary) to equal 1. This constraint must also leave the binary value in the changing cell of Project 4 unrestricted if you do not select Project 3. If you do not select Project 3, L9 equals 0, and the constraint allows the Project 4 binary to equal 0 or 1, which is what you want. The new optimal solution is shown in Figure 32-4.

Now suppose that you can do only four projects from among Projects 1 through 10. (See the At Most 4 Of P1–P10 worksheet, shown in Figure 32-5.) In cell L8, you compute the sum of the binary values associated with Projects 1 through 10 with the *SUM(A6:A15)* formula. Then add the L8<=L10 constraint, which ensures that at most, 4 of the first 10 projects are selected. The new optimal solution is shown in Figure 32-5. The NPV has dropped to $9.014 billion.

	Total NPV										
	9157		Used	2444	2760	2837	866	895	659		
				<=	<=	<=	<=	<=	<=		
			Available	2500	2800	2900	900	900	900		
Do IT?		NPV		Cost Year 1	Cost Year 2	Cost Year 3	Labor Year 1	Labor Year 2	Labor Year 3		
0	Project 1	928		398	180	368	111	108	123		
1	Project 2	908		151	269	248	139	86	83		
1	Project 3	801		129	189	308	56	61	23	Proj 3	
1	Project 4	543		275	218	220	54	70	59		1
0	Project 5	944		291	252	228	123	141	70	<=	
1	Project 6	848		80	283	285	119	84	37	Proj 4	
1	Project 7	545		203	220	77	54	44	42		1
1	Project 8	808		150	113	143	67	101	43		
1	Project 9	638		282	141	160	37	55	64		
0	Project 10	841		214	254	355	130	72	62		
0	Project 11	664		224	271	130	51	79	58		
0	Project 12	546		225	150	33	35	107	63		
0	Project 13	699		101	218	272	43	90	71		
0	Project 14	599		255	202	70	3	75	83		
1	Project 15	903		228	351	240	60	93	80		
1	Project 16	859		303	173	431	60	90	41		
1	Project 17	748		133	427	220	59	40	39		
1	Project 18	668		197	98	214	95	96	74		
1	Project 19	888		313	278	291	66	75	74		
0	Project 20	655		152	211	134	85	59	70		

FIGURE 32-4 This is the new optimal solution for If Project 3's selection requires we do Project 4.

M27

	Total NPV										
	9014		Used	2378	2734	2755	770	896	702		
				<=	<=	<=	<=	<=	<=		
			Available	2500	2800	2900	900	900	900		
Do IT?		NPV		Cost Year 1	Cost Year 2	Cost Year 3	Labor Year 1	Labor Year 2	Labor Year 3		
0	Project 1	928		398	180	368	111	108	123	At most 4 of Projects 1-10	
0	Project 2	908		151	269	248	139	86	83		
1	Project 3	801		129	189	308	56	61	23		4
0	Project 4	543		275	218	220	54	70	59	<=	
0	Project 5	944		291	252	228	123	141	70		4
0	Project 6	848		80	283	285	119	84	37		
1	Project 7	545		203	220	77	54	44	42		
1	Project 8	808		150	113	143	67	101	43		
0	Project 9	638		282	141	160	37	55	64		
1	Project 10	841		214	254	355	130	72	62		
1	Project 16	859		303	173	431	60	90	41		
1	Project 17	748		133	427	220	59	40	39		
1	Project 18	668		197	98	214	95	96	74		
1	Project 19	888		313	278	291	66	75	74		
1	Project 20	655		152	211	134	85	59	70		

FIGURE 32-5 Optimal solution when only 4 of Projects 1–10 can be selected.

Solving binary and integer programming problems

Linear Solver models in which some or all changing cells are required to be binary or an integer are usually harder to solve than linear models in which all changing cells are allowed to be fractions. For this reason, analysts are often satisfied with a near-optimal solution to a binary or integer programming problem. If your Solver model runs for a long time, you might want to consider adjusting the Integer Optimality (formerly called Tolerance) setting in the Solver Options dialog box. (See Figure 32-6.) For example, a Tolerance setting of .5 means that Solver will stop the first time it finds a feasible solution that is within 0.5 percent of the theoretical optimal target cell value. (The theoretical optimal target cell value is the optimal target value found when the binary and integer constraints are omitted.) Often you'll be faced with a choice between finding an answer within 10 percent of opti-mal in 10 minutes or finding an optimal solution in two weeks of computer time! The default Integer Optimality value is 5%, which means that Solver stops when it finds a target cell value within 5 per-cent of the theoretical optimal target cell value. When the software development example was first solved, the Integer Optimality was set to 5% and found an optimal target cell value of 9269. When the Integer Optimality value was changed to 0.50%, a better target cell value (9293) was obtained.

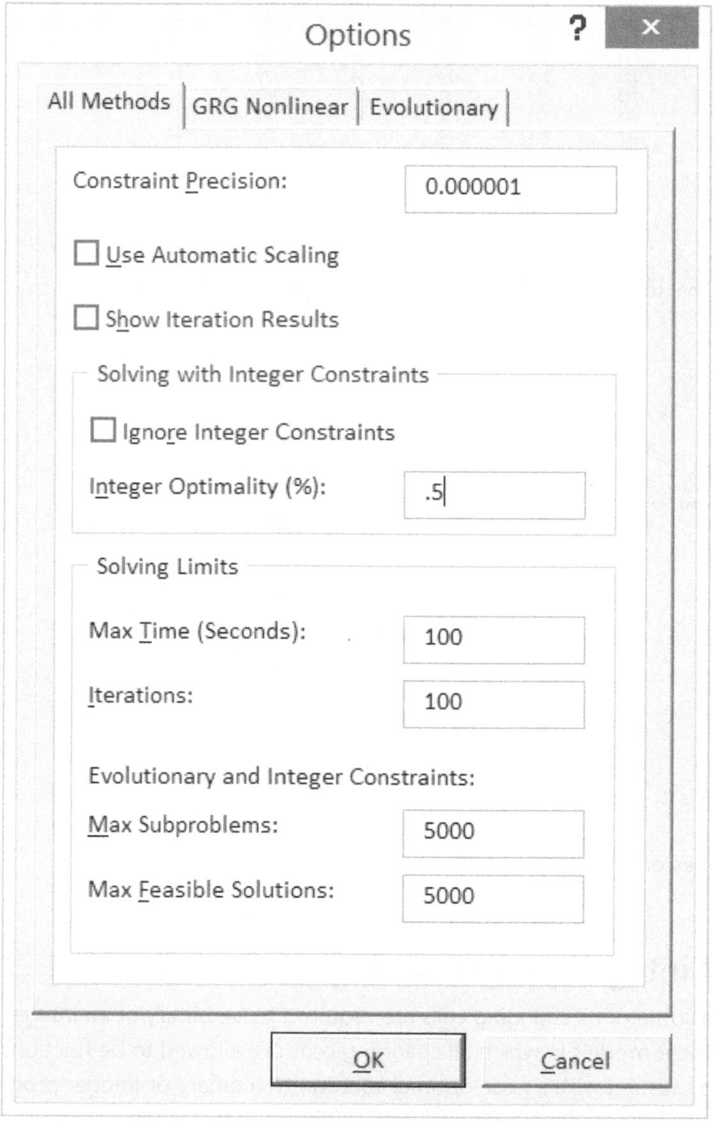

FIGURE 32-6 This figure shows adjustment of the Integer Optimality option.

Problems

1. A company has nine projects under consideration. The NPV added by each project and the capital required for each project during the next two years is shown in the following table. (All numbers are in millions.) For example, Project 1 will add $14 million in NPV and require expenditures of $12 million during Year 1 and $3 million during Year 2. During Year 1, $50 million in capital is available for projects, and $20 million is available during Year 2:

	NPV	Year 1 expenditure	Year 2 expenditure
Project 1	14	12	3
Project 2	17	54	7
Project 3	17	6	6
Project 4	15	6	2
Project 5	40	32	35
Project 6	12	6	6
Project 7	14	48	4
Project 8	10	36	3
Project 9	12	18	3

   - If you can't undertake a fraction of a project but must undertake either all or none of it, how can you maximize NPV?

   - Suppose that if Project 4 is undertaken, Project 5 must be undertaken. How can you maximize NPV?

2. A publishing company is trying to determine which of 36 books it should publish this year. The Pressdata.xlsx file gives the following information about each book:

   - Projected revenue and development costs (in thousands of dollars)

   - Pages in each book

   - Whether the book is geared toward an audience of software developers (indicated by a 1 in column E)

   The company can publish books with a total of up to 8,500 pages this year and must publish at least four books geared toward software developers. How can the company maximize its profit?

3. In the SEND + MORE = MONEY equation, each letter represents a different digit from 0–9. Which digit is associated with each letter?

4. Jill is trying to determine her class schedule for the next semester. A semester consists of two seven-week half semesters. Jill must take four courses during each half semester. There are five time slots during each semester. Of course, Jill cannot take the same course twice. Jill has associated a value with each course and time slot. This data is in the Classdata.xlsx file. For example, course 1 during time slot 5 in semester 1 has a value of 5. Which courses should Jill take during each semester to maximize her total value from the semester's courses?

5. Use conditional formatting to highlight in yellow fill each row corresponding to a selected project.

6. Use Solver to determine the minimum number of coins needed to make change for 92 cents.

CHAPTER 33

Using Solver for financial planning

Questions answered in this chapter:

- Can I use Solver to verify the accuracy of the Excel *PMT* function or to determine mortgage payments for a variable interest rate?

- Can I use Solver to determine how much money I need to save for retirement?

Solver can be a powerful tool for analyzing financial planning problems. In many of these types of problems, a quantity such as the unpaid balance on a loan or the amount of money needed for retirement changes over time. For example, consider a situation in which you borrow money. Because only the noninterest portion of each monthly payment reduces the unpaid loan balance, you know that the following equation (Equation 1) is true:

```
(Unpaid loan balance at end of period t) = (Unpaid loan balance at beginning of period t)
    - [(Month t payment) - (Month t interest paid)]
```

Now suppose that you are saving for retirement. Until you retire, you deposit at the beginning of each period (say *periods* equal *years*) an amount of money in your retirement account, and during the year, your retirement fund is invested and receives a return of some percentage. During retirement, you withdraw money at the beginning of each year, and your retirement fund still receives an investment return. You know that the following equation (Equation 2) describes the relationship among contributions, withdrawals, and return:

```
(Retirement savings at end of Year t+1) = (Retirement savings at end of Year t + retirement
    contribution at beginning of Year t+1 - Year t+1 retirement withdrawal)
    *(Investment return earned during Year t+1)
```

Combining basic relationships such as these with Solver enables you to answer a myriad of interesting financial planning problems.

Answers to this chapter's questions

This section provides the answers to the questions that are listed at the beginning of the chapter.

Can I use Solver to verify the accuracy of the Excel *PMT* function or to determine mortgage payments for a variable interest rate?

Recall that in Chapter 9, "More Excel financial functions," you found the monthly payment (assuming payments occur at the end of a month) on a 10-month loan for $8,000 at an annual interest rate of 10 percent to be $1,037.03. Could you have used Solver to determine your monthly payment? You'll find the answer in the PMT By Solver worksheet in the Finmathsolver.xlsx file, which is shown in Figure 33-1.

	A	B	C	D	E
1			rate	0.00667	
2					
3		From PMT function	$1,037.03		
4	Month	Beginning Balance	Payment	Interest Owed	Ending Balance
5	1	$ 10,000.00	$ 1,037.03	$ 66.67	$ 9,029.63
6	2	$ 9,029.63	$ 1,037.03	$ 60.20	$ 8,052.80
7	3	$ 8,052.80	$ 1,037.03	$ 53.69	$ 7,069.45
8	4	$ 7,069.45	$ 1,037.03	$ 47.13	$ 6,079.55
9	5	$ 6,079.55	$ 1,037.03	$ 40.53	$ 5,083.05
10	6	$ 5,083.05	$ 1,037.03	$ 33.89	$ 4,079.90
11	7	$ 4,079.90	$ 1,037.03	$ 27.20	$ 3,070.07
12	8	$ 3,070.07	$ 1,037.03	$ 20.47	$ 2,053.51
13	9	$ 2,053.51	$ 1,037.03	$ 13.69	$ 1,030.16
14	10	$ 1,030.16	$ 1,037.03	$ 6.87	$ 0.00

FIGURE 33-1 This is the Solver model for calculating the monthly payment for a loan.

The key to this model is to use Equation 1 (shown earlier in the chapter) to track the monthly beginning balance. The Solver target cell is to minimize the monthly payment. The changing cell is the monthly payment. The only constraint is that the ending balance in Month 10 equals 0.

Enter the beginning balance in cell B5. You can enter a trial monthly payment in cell C5 and then copy the monthly payment to the C6:C14 range. Because you assume that the payments occur at the end of each month, interest is incurred on the balance at the beginning of the month. The monthly interest rate (cell C1 is named Rate) is computed in D1 by dividing the annual rate of 0.08 by 12. The interest paid each month is computed by copying the rate*B5 formula from cell D5 to D6:D14. Each month, this formula computes the interest as .006666*(month's beginning balance). By copying the (B5–(Payment–D5)) formula from cell E5 to E6:E14, you use Equation 1 to compute each month's ending balance. Because (Month t+1 beginning balance) = (Month t ending balance), each month's beginning balance is computed by copying the =E5 formula from cell B6 to B7:B14.

You are now ready to use Solver to determine the monthly payment. To see how you've set up the Solver Parameters dialog box, take a look at Figure 33-2.

FIGURE 33-2 The Solver Parameters dialog box is set up to determine mortgage payments.

The goal is to minimize the monthly payment (cell C5). Note that the changing cell is the same as the target cell. The only constraint is that the ending balance for Month 10 must equal 0. Adding this constraint ensures that the loan is paid off. After you choose the Simplex LP engine and select the nonnegative variables option, Solver calculates a payment of $1,037.03, which matches the amount calculated by the Excel *PMT* function.

This model is linear because the target cell equals the changing cell, and the constraint is created by adding multiples of changing cells.

It should be mentioned that when Solver models involve very large or very small numbers, Solver sometimes thinks models that *are* linear are *not* linear. To avoid this problem, it is good practice to select **Use Automatic Scaling** in the **Options** dialog box. This should ensure that Solver properly recognizes linear models as being linear.

Can I use Solver to determine how much money I need to save for retirement?

By using Equation 2 (shown earlier in the chapter), you can easily determine how much money a person needs to save for retirement. Here's an example.

You are planning for your retirement, and at the beginning of this year and each of the next 39 years, you will contribute some money to your retirement fund. Each year, you plan to increase your retirement contribution by $500. When you retire in 40 years, you plan to withdraw (at the beginning of each year) $100,000 per year for 20 years. You make the following assumptions about the yields for your retirement investment portfolio:

- During the first 20 years of your investing, the investments will earn 10 percent per year.

- During all other years, your investments will earn 5 percent per year.

You assume that all contributions and withdrawals occur at the beginning of the year. Given these assumptions, what is the least amount of money you can contribute this year and still have enough to make your retirement withdrawals?

You can find the solution to this question on the Retire worksheet in the Finmathsolver.xlsx file, shown in Figure 33-3. Note that many rows are hidden in the model.

This worksheet simply tracks your retirement balance during each of the next 60 years. Each year, you earn the indicated interest rate on the retirement balance. Begin by entering a trial value for the Year 1 payment in cell C6. Copying the C6+500 formula from cell C7 to C8:C45 ensures that the retirement contribution increases by $500 per year during Years 2 through 40. Enter in column D the assumed return on your investments for each of the next 60 years. In cells E46:E65, enter the annual $100,000 withdrawal for Years 41 through 60. Copying the (B6+C6–E6)*(1+D6) formula from F6 to F7:F65 uses Equation 2 to compute each year's ending retirement account balance. Copying the =F6 formula from cell B7 to B8:B65 computes the beginning balance for Years 2 through 60. Of course, the Year 1 initial balance is 0. Note that the 6.8704E-07 value in cell F65 is approximately 0, with the difference the result of a rounding error.

	A	B	C	D	E	F
5	Year	Initial balance	Contribution	Return	Withdrawal	Ending Balance
6	1	$0.00	$ 1,387.87	10%	$0.00	$1,526.65
7	2	$1,526.65	$ 1,887.87	10%	$0.00	$3,755.98
8	3	$3,755.98	$ 2,387.87	10%	$0.00	$6,758.23
44	39	$1,146,596.10	$ 20,387.87	5%	$0.00	$1,225,333.17
45	40	$1,225,333.17	$ 20,887.87	5%	$0.00	$1,308,532.09
46	41	$1,308,532.09		5%	$100,000.00	$1,268,958.69
47	42	$1,268,958.69		5%	$100,000.00	$1,227,406.62
62	57	$372,324.80		5%	$100,000.00	$285,941.04
63	58	$285,941.04		5%	$100,000.00	$195,238.10
64	59	$195,238.10		5%	$100,000.00	$100,000.00
65	60	$100,000.00		5%	$100,000.00	$0.00

FIGURE 33-3 Here is retirement planning data that can be set up for analysis with Solver.

The **Solver Parameters** dialog box for this model is shown in Figure 33-4. You want to minimize your Year 1 contribution (cell C6). The changing cell is also your Year 1 contribution (cell C6). Ensure that you never run out of money during retirement by adding the F46:F65>=0 constraint so that the ending balance for Years 41 through 60 is nonnegative.

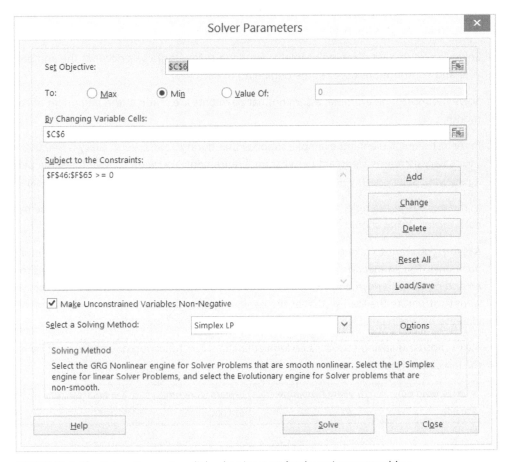

FIGURE 33-4 The Solver Parameters dialog box is set up for the retirement problem.

After choosing the Simplex LP engine and selecting **Make Unconstrained Variables Non-Negative** in the **Solver Parameters** dialog box, click **Solve** in the **Solver Parameters** dialog box; you find that the first year's contribution should equal $1,387.87.

This model is linear because the target cell equals the changing cell, and the constraint is created by adding multiples of changing cells. Note that because the return on the investments is not the same each year, there is no easy way to use Excel financial functions to solve this problem. Solver provides a general framework that can be used to analyze financial planning problems when mortgage rates or investment returns are not constant.

Problems

1. I am borrowing $15,000 to buy a new car. I will make 60 end-of-month payments. The annual interest rate on the loan is 10 percent. The car dealer is a friend of mine, and he will allow me to make the monthly payment for Months 1–30 equal to one-half the payment for Months 31 through 60. What is the payment during each month?

2. Solve the retirement planning problem, assuming that withdrawals occur at the end of each year and contributions occur at the beginning of each year.

3. Solve the mortgage example, assuming that payments are made at the beginning of each month.

4. In the retirement-planning example, suppose that during Year 1, your salary is $40,000 and your salary increases 5 percent per year until retirement. You want to save the same percentage of your salary each year you work. What percentage of your salary should you save?

5. In the mortgage example, suppose that you want your monthly payment to increase by $50 each month. What should each month's payment be?

6. Assume you want to take out a $300,000 loan on a 20-year mortgage with end-of-month payments. The annual rate of interest is 6 percent. Twenty years from now, you need to make an ending balloon payment of $40,000. Because you expect your income to increase, you want to structure the loan so that at the beginning of each year, your monthly payments increase by 2 percent. Determine the amount of each year's monthly payment.

7. Blair's mother is saving for Blair's college education. The following payments must be made at the indicated times:

4 years from now	5 years from now	6 years from now	7 years from now
$24,000	$26,000	$28,000	$30,000

The following investments are available:

- Today, one year from now, two years from now, three years from now, and four years from now, she can invest money for one year and receive a 6 percent return.

- Today, two years from now, and four years from now, she can invest money for two years and receive a 14 percent return.

- Three years from now, she can invest money for three years and receive an 18 percent return.

- Today, she can invest money for seven years and receive a 65 percent return.

What is the minimum amount that Blair's mother needs to commit today to Blair's college education that ensures that she can pay her college bills?

8. I owe $10,000 on one credit card that charges 18 percent annual interest and $5,000 on another credit card that charges 12 percent annual interest. Interest for the month is based on the month's beginning balance. I can afford to make total payments of $2,000 per month, and the minimum monthly payment on each card is 10 percent of the card's unpaid balance at the beginning of the month. My goal is to pay off both cards in two years. What is the minimum amount of interest I need to pay?

CHAPTER 34

Using Solver to rate sports teams

Question answered in this chapter:

- Can I use Excel to set NFL point spreads?

Many of us follow basketball, football, hockey, or baseball. Oddsmakers set point spreads on games in all these sports and others. For example, the bookmakers' best guess was that the Indianapolis Colts would win the 2010 Super Bowl by 7 points. Instead, the New Orleans Saints won the game. In this chapter, you see that Solver predicted that the Saints were the better team and should have been favored. Now see how Solver can estimate the relative ability of NFL teams accurately.

Using a simple Solver model, you can generate reasonable point spreads for games based on the scores of the 2009 season. The work is in file Nfl2009april2010.xlsx, shown in Figure 34-1. You use the score of each game of the 2009 NFL season as input data. The changing cell for the Solver model is a rating for each team and the size of the home field advantage. For example, if the Indianapolis Colts have a rating of +5 and the New York Jets have a rating of +7, the Jets are considered two points better than the Colts.

With regard to the home-field edge, in most years, college and professional football teams, as well as professional basketball teams, tend to win by an average of three points (whereas home college basketball teams tend to win by an average of five points). In your model, however, you will define the home edge as a changing cell and have Solver estimate the home edge. You can define the outcome of an NFL game to be the number of points by which the home team outscores the visitors and predict the outcome of each game by using the following equation (Equation 1):

(Predicted points by which home team outscores visitors) = (Home edge)+(Home team rating)−(Away Team rating)

For example, if the home-field edge equals three points, when the Colts host the Jets, the Colts will be a one-point favorite (3 + 5 − 7). If the Jets host the Colts, the Jets will be a five-point favorite (3 + 7 − 5). (The Tampa Bay–New England game was played in London, so there is no home edge for this game.)

What target cell will yield reliable ratings? The goal is to find the set of values for team ratings and home-field advantage that best predicts the outcome of all games. In short, you want the prediction for each game to be as close as possible to the outcome of each game. This suggests that you want to minimize the sum over all games of (*Actual outcome*) − (*Predicted outcome*). However, the problem with using this target is that positive and negative prediction errors cancel each other out. For example, if you over-predict the home-team margin by 50 points in one game and under-predict the home-team margin by 50 points in another game, the target cell would yield a value of 0, indicating perfect accuracy, when in fact you were off by 50 points a game. You can remedy this problem by minimizing the sum over all games by using the [(*Actual Outcome*) – (*Predicted Outcome*)]^2 formula. Now positive and negative errors will not cancel each other out.

Answer to this chapter's question

This section provides the answer to the question that is listed at the beginning of the chapter.

Can I use Excel to set NFL point spreads?

See now how to determine accurate ratings for NFL teams by using the scores from the 2009 regular season. You can find the data for this problem in the Nfl2009april2010.xlsx file, which is shown in Figure 34-1.

	B	C	D	E	F	G	H	I	J	K
2										SSE
3										43108
4				Week Home	Away	Home Points	Away Points	Home margin	Prediction	Squared Error
5				1 Pittsburgh Steelers	Tennessee Titans	13	10	3	6.722344	13.856
6				1 Atlanta Falcons	Miami Dolphins	19	7	12	5.637121	40.486
7	home			1 Seattle Seahawks	St. Louis Rams	28	0	28	10.3964	309.89
8		2.260510793		1 New York Giants	Washington Redskins	23	17	6	6.910514	0.829
9				1 Baltimore Ravens	Kansas City Chiefs	38	24	14	18.15126	17.233
10	mean	-6E-10		1 Houston Texans	New York Jets	7	24	-17	-4.35591	159.87
11	Team	rating		1 New Orleans Saints	Detroit Lions	45	27	18	27.40592	88.471
12	Pittsburgh Steelers	1.682		1 Tampa Bay Buccaneers	Dallas Cowboys	21	34	-13	-10.4081	6.7179
13	Atlanta Falcons	5.046		1 Arizona Cardinals	San Francisco 49ers	16	20	-4	1.925441	35.111
14	Seattle Seahawks	-9.301		1 Carolina Panthers	Philadelphia Eagles	10	38	-28	0.172907	793.71
15	New York Giants	0.103		1 Green Bay Packers	Chicago Bears	21	15	6	13.51688	56.503
16	Baltimore Ravens	7.465		1 Cincinnati Bengals	Denver Broncos	7	12	-5	2.606708	57.862
17	Houston Texans	1.946		1 Cleveland Browns	Minnesota Vikings	20	34	-14	-13.2951	0.4969
18	New Orleans Saints	10.77		1 Indianapolis Colts	Jacksonville Jaguars	14	12	2	14.6823	160.84
19	Tampa Bay Buccaneers	-5.5		1 Oakland Raiders	San Diego Chargers	20	24	-4	-14.6496	113.41
20	Arizona Cardinals	-0.281		1 New England Patriots	Buffalo Bills	25	24	1	15.16782	200.73
21	Carolina Panthers	3.92		2 Tennessee Titans	Houston Texans	31	34	-3	-2.46553	0.2857
22	Green Bay Packers	7.371		2 Kansas City Chiefs	Oakland Raiders	10	13	-3	4.101831	50.436

FIGURE 34-1 This is the data rating NFL teams that you'll use with Solver.

To begin, place a trial home-field advantage value in cell B8.

Starting in row 5, columns E and F contain the home and away teams for each game. For example, the first game (listed in row 5) is Tennessee playing at Pittsburgh. Column G contains the home team's score, and column H contains the visiting team's score. As you can see, the Steelers beat the Titans 13–10. You can now compute the outcome of each game (the number of points by which the home team beats the visiting team) by entering the =G5–H5 formula in cell I5. By pointing to the lower-right portion of this cell and double-clicking, you can copy this formula down to the last regular season game, which appears in row 260. (By the way, an easy way to select all the data is to press Ctrl+Shift+down arrow. This key combination takes you to the last row filled with data—row 260 in this case.)

In column J, use Equation 1 to generate the prediction for each game. The prediction for the first game is computed in cell J5 as follows:

=$B$8+VLOOKUP(E5,$B$12:$C$43,2,FALSE)-VLOOKUP(F5,$B$12:$C$43,2,FALSE)

This formula creates a prediction for the first game by adding the home edge to the home-team rating and then subtracting the visiting-team rating. (Note that in row 103, the term $B$8 is deleted from the formula because there was no home edge in the New England–Tampa Bay game.) The term VLOOKUP(E5,$B$12:$C$43,2,FALSE) locates the home-team rating, and VLOOKUP(F5,$B$12:$C$43,2,FALSE) looks up the visiting team's rating. (For more information about using lookup functions, see Chapter 2, "Lookup functions.") In column K, compute the squared error (*actual score – predicted score*)^2 for each game. Your squared error for the first game is computed in cell K5 with the =(I5 – J5)^2 formula. After selecting the I5:K5 cell range, you can double-click and copy the formulas down to row 260.

Next, compute the target cell in cell K3 by summing all the squared errors with the SUM(J5:J260) formula.

Tip You can enter a formula for a large column of numbers such as this by typing **=SUM(** and then selecting the first cell in the range you want to add together. Press Ctrl+Shift+down arrow to enter the range from the cell you selected to the bottom row in the column and then add the closing parenthesis.

It is convenient to make the average team rating equal to 0. A team with a positive rating is better than average and a team with a negative rating is worse than average. Compute the average team rating in cell C10 with the AVERAGE(C12:C43) formula.

You can now fill in the **Solver Parameters** dialog box as shown in Figure 34-2.

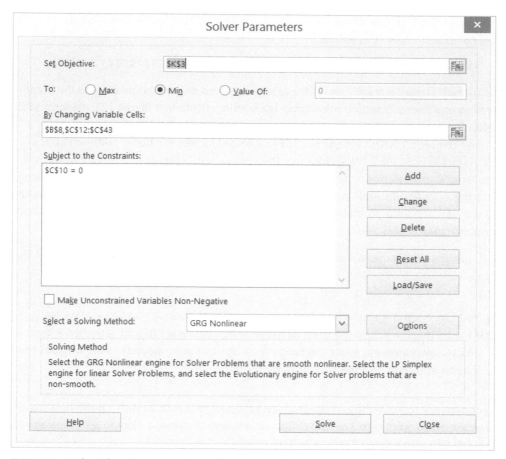

FIGURE 34-2 The Solver Parameters dialog box is set up for NFL ratings.

Minimize the sum of the squared prediction errors for all games (computed in cell K3) by changing each team's rating (listed in cells C12:C43) and the home advantage (cell B8). The C10=0 constraint ensures that the average team rating is 0. From Figure 34-1, you can see that the home team has an advantage of 2.26 points over the visiting team. The 15 highest-rated teams are shown in Figure 34-3. Remember that the ratings listed in cell range E3:E34 are computed by Solver. In the template file, you can start with any numbers in these cells, and Solver will still find the best ratings.

Rank	Team	rating
1	New England Patriots	11.0695
2	New Orleans Saints	10.7697
3	New York Jets	8.56256
4	Baltimore Ravens	7.4648
5	Green Bay Packers	7.37132
6	Minnesota Vikings	7.16877
7	Dallas Cowboys	7.16853
8	San Diego Chargers	6.6428
9	Philadelphia Eagles	6.00733
10	Indianapolis Colts	5.91202
11	Atlanta Falcons	5.04647
12	Carolina Panthers	3.91973
13	Houston Texans	1.94614
14	Pittsburgh Steelers	1.68193
15	Miami Dolphins	1.66985

FIGURE 34-3 These are the top 15 teams for the NFL 2009 season.

These ratings have the Saints around 5 points better than the Colts, so this model would have predicted (before the playoffs) that the Saints would beat the Colts by 5 points.

Why is your model not a linear Solver model?

This model is not linear because the target cell adds together terms of the (Home Team Rating + Home-Field Edge − Visiting Team Rating)^2 form. Recall that for a Solver model to be linear, the target cell must be created by adding together terms with the (changing cell)*(constant) form. This relationship doesn't exist in this case, so the model is not linear. Solver does obtain the correct answer, however, for any sports-rating model in which the target cell minimizes the sum of squared errors. Note that the GRG nonlinear engine was chosen because this model is not linear and did not involve nonmathematical functions such as IF statements. I did not select Make Unconstrained Variables Non-Negative because to have the team ratings average 0, you must allow some of the team ratings to be negative.

Note Recently, I found that the GRG Solver engine works poorly when automatic scaling is checked. I recommend opening the **Options** dialog box and clearing **Use Automatic Scaling**.

Problems

1-4. The Nfl0x.xlsx (x = 1, 2, 3, 4) files contain scores for every regular season game during the 200x NFL season. Rate the teams for each season. During each season, which teams would you forecast to have made the Super Bowl?

5. For the 2004 season, devise a method to predict the actual score of each game. Hint: Give each team an offensive rating and a defensive rating. Who had the best offense? Who had the best defense?

6. True or false? An NFL team could lose every game and be an above-average team.

7. The Nba01_02.xlsx file contains scores for every game during the 2001–2002 NBA season. Rate the teams.

8. The Nba02_03.xlsx file contains scores for every regular season game during the 2002–2003 NBA season. Rate the teams.

9. The Worldball.xlsx file contains all scores from the 2006 World Basketball Championships. Rate the teams. Who were the best three teams?

10. This method of rating teams works fine for football and basketball. What problems arise if you apply these methods to hockey or baseball?

11. The NFL2012data.xlsx file contains scores of all NFL 2012 regular season games. Rate the teams. Even though the Colts were 10–6, your ratings have the Colts as a well-below-average team. Can you explain this anomaly?

CHAPTER 35

Warehouse location and the GRG Multistart and Evolutionary Solver engines

Questions answered in this chapter:

- Where in the United States should an Internet shipping company locate a single warehouse to minimize the total distance that packages are shipped?

- Where in the United States should an Internet shipping company locate two warehouses to minimize the total distance that packages are shipped?

In Microsoft Excel 2013, Solver has been blessed with many new exciting capabilities. This chapter (and Chapter 36, "Penalties and the Evolutionary Solver," and Chapter 37, "The traveling salesperson problem") explains how these algorithms can help you solve many important optimization problems.

Understanding the GRG Multistart and Evolutionary Solver engines

As was pointed out in Chapter 28, "Introducing optimization with Excel Solver," the Excel 2013 Solver uses three engines to solve optimization problems: Simplex LP, GRG Nonlinear, and Evolutionary. The following sections provide more details about how the latter two of these engines are used to solve optimization problems.

How does Solver solve linear Solver problems?

As was pointed out in Chapters 28 through 33, a Solver model is linear if all references to changing cells in the target cells and constraints are created by adding together terms of the (changing cells)*(constants) form. For linear models, you should always select the Simplex LP engine, which is designed to find solutions to linear Solver models efficiently. The Excel 2013 Solver can handle problems with up to 200 changing cells and 100 constraints. Versions of Solver that can handle larger problems are available from the Solver.com website.

How does the GRG Nonlinear engine solve nonlinear optimization models?

If your target cell, any of your constraints, or both contain references to changing cells that are not of the (changing cell)*(constant) form, you have a nonlinear model. If x and y are changing cells, references such as the following in the target cell, any constraints, or both make your model nonlinear:

- x^2

- xy

- $\sin x$

- e^x

- xe^{2y}

If your nonlinear formulas involve ordinary math operators such as the previous examples, proper use of the GRG Nonlinear engine should quickly find the optimal solution to your Solver model. To illustrate how the GRG Nonlinear engine works, suppose you want to maximize $-x^2 + 4x + 2$. This function is graphed in Figure 35-1.

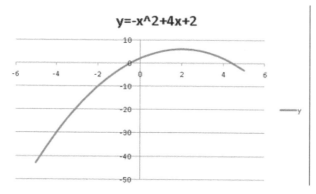

FIGURE 35-1 This is how the GRG Nonlinear engine maximizes a function.

You can see that this function is maximized for $x = 2$. Notice also that for $x = 2$, the function has a slope of 0. The GRG Nonlinear engine solves this problem by trying to find a point at which the slope of the function is 0. Similarly, if you want to minimize $y = x^2$, the GRG Nonlinear engine solves this problem by determining that the slope of this function is 0 for $x = 0$. See Figure 35-2.

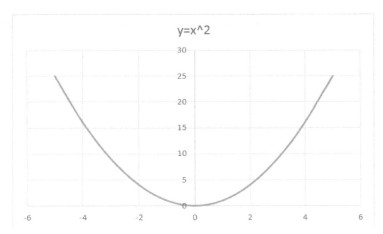

FIGURE 35-2 This is how the GRG Nonlinear engine minimizes a function.

Unfortunately, many functions cannot be maximized simply by locating a point where the function's slope equals 0. For example, suppose you want to maximize the function shown in Figure 35-3, when x ranges between –5 and +10.

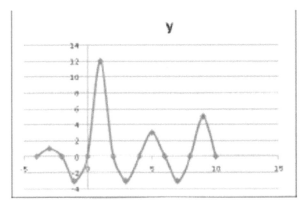

FIGURE 35-3 This is maximizing a function with multiple peaks.

You can see that this function has more than one peak. If you start with a value of x near 1, you will find the right solution to the (x = 1) problem. If you start near another peak—say near x = 5—you will find a solution of x = 5, which is incorrect. Because in most problems (especially those with more than one changing cell) you do not know a good starting point, it appears you have a major hurdle to clear. Fortunately, Excel 2013 has a Multistart option. You can select **Multistart** after choosing **Options** and then clicking the **GRG Nonlinear** tab. When the Multistart option is selected, Excel chooses many starting solutions and finds the best answer after beginning with these starting points. This approach usually resolves the multiple peak and valley problem.

By the way, pressing Esc stops Solver. Also, keep in mind that GRG Multistart works best when you place reasonable upper and lower bounds on your changing cells. (For example, you do not specify changing cell<=100 million.)

The GRG engine also runs into trouble if the target cell, constraints, or both use nonsmooth functions such as *MAX, MIN, ABS, IF, SUMIF, COUNTIF, SUMIFS, COUNTIFS*, and others that involve changing cells. These functions create points where there is no uniquely defined slope because the slope changes abruptly. For example, suppose an optimization problem requires you to model the value of a European call option with a $40 exercise price. This call option enables you to buy the stock for $40. If the stock price is *s* at expiration of the option, then the value of the call option may be computed with the max(0,s-40) or IF(s>40,s-40,0) formula relationship graphed in Figure 35-4. It is clear that when *s* = 40, the option value has no slope, so the GRG engine would break down.

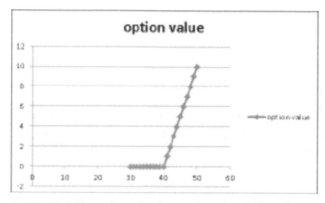

FIGURE 35-4 The option value has no slope for a $40 stock price.

As Figure 35-5 shows, Solver models that include the absolute value function (recall that the absolute value of a number is just the distance of the number from 0) will have no slope for *x* = 0. In Excel, the *ABS(x)* function returns the absolute value of a number *x*.

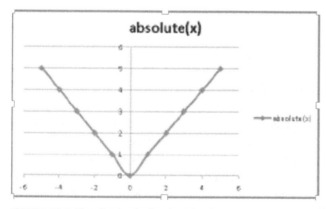

FIGURE 35-5 The absolute value function has no slope for *x* = 0.

Optimization problems in which the target cell, any of the constraints, or both have no slope for any changing cell values are called *nonsmooth* optimization problems. Even GRG Multistart has difficulty with these types of problems. In these situations, you should apply the Solver Evolutionary engine. For nonlinear Solver models, Solver is limited to 100 changing cells and 100 constraints.

How does the Evolutionary Solver engine tackle nonsmooth optimization problems?

Evolutionary Solver in Excel 2013 is based on genetic algorithms, a concept discovered by John Holland, a computer science professor at the University of Michigan. To use the Evolutionary Solver, begin by taking 50 to 100 points in the problem's feasible region (that is, the set of points that meet the constraints). This set of points is called the *population*. Then, the target cell is evaluated for each point. Using the idea of survival of the fittest from the theory of evolution, you change the points in the population in a way that increases the likelihood that future population members are located near previous population members that have a good target cell value. Because this approach is based on target cell values and not on slopes, multiple peaks and valleys pose no problem. Also, functions that do not have slopes (the so-called nonsmooth functions) also become a less important issue. The Evolutionary Solver engine (like GRG Multistart) also works best when reasonable upper and lower bounds are placed on your changing cells. After you select the Evolutionary Solver engine, it's best to choose **Options**, click the **Evolutionary** tab, and change the mutation rate to .5. Also, select the **Required Bounds On Variables** check box and increase the maximum time without improvement to 3,600 seconds. Increasing the mutation rate decreases the likelihood that the Solver gets stuck near a poor solution. Increasing the maximum time without improvement to 3,600 seconds enables the Solver to run until it fails to improve the target cell for 3,600 seconds. That way, the Solver keeps running if you leave your computer.

Now, use Solver to solve two interesting facility location problems.

Answers to this chapter's questions

This section provides the answers to the questions that are listed at the beginning of the chapter.

Where in the United States should an Internet shipping company locate a single warehouse to minimize the total distance that packages are shipped?

The number of shipments (in thousands) made each year to various cities is shown in Figure 35-6. (See the One warehouse worksheet in the Warehouseloc.xlsx file.)

	A	B	C	D	E	F	G	H	I
1									
2									
3						Lat	Long		Mean
4					1	36.813439	92.48191		1125.827
5							Total	252185.2	
6		City	Lat	Long	Shipments	Distance	Shipped* Dist		
7		New York	40.7	73.9	15	1309.8969	19648.45		
8		Boston	42.3	71	8	1529.8326	12238.66		
9		Philadelphia	40	75.1	10	1219.3395	12193.39		
10		Charlotte	35.2	80.8	6	813.70342	4882.221		
11		Atlanta	33.8	84.4	11	595.15484	6546.703		
12		New Orleans	30	89.9	8	502.75019	4022.002		
13		Miami	25.8	80.2	13	1138.2724	14797.54		
14		Dallas	32.8	96.8	10	406.77005	4067.701		
15		Houston	29.8	95.4	12	524.14383	6289.726		
16		Chicago	41.8	87.7	14	476.71185	6673.966		
17		Detroit	42.4	83.1	11	753.42785	8287.706		
18		Cleveland	41.5	81.7	8	811.19304	6489.544		
19		Indy	39.8	86.1	7	486.18479	3403.294		
20		Denver	39.8	105	8	881.28021	7050.242		
21		Minneapolis	45	93.3	9	567.68613	5109.175		
22		Phoenix	33.5	112	11	1372.8197	15101.02		
23		Salt Lake City	40.8	112	10	1367.7932	13677.93		
24		LA	34.1	118	18	1798.1222	32366.2		
25		SF	37.8	123	12	2079.2628	24951.15		
26		SD	32.8	117	10	1721.0736	17210.74		
27		Seattle	41.6	122	13	2090.6012	27177.82		

FIGURE 35-6 Here is data for the single warehouse problem.

A key to this model is the following formula, which gives the approximate distance between two US cities having a latitude and longitude given by (Lat1, Long1) and (Lat2, Long2).

$$Distance = 69 * \sqrt{(Lat1 - Lat2)^2 + (Long1 - Long2)^2}$$

To begin, enter trial values in cells F4:G4 for the latitude and longitude of the warehouse. Next, by copying the 69*SQRT((C7-$F$4)^2+(D7-$G$4)^2) formula from F7 to F8:F27, you compute the approximate distance of each city from the warehouse. Next, copying the E7*F7 formula from G7 to G8:G27 computes the distance traveled by the shipments to each city. In cell H5, the SUM(G7:G27) formula computes the total distance traveled by all shipments. Your target cell is to minimize H5 by changing F4:G4. After you select the GRG Nonlinear engine, the **Solver Parameters** dialog box appears, as in Figure 35-7.

After you click **Solve**, you'll find that the warehouse should be located at 36.81 degrees latitude and 92.48 degrees longitude, which is near Springfield, Missouri. (See Figure 35-6.)

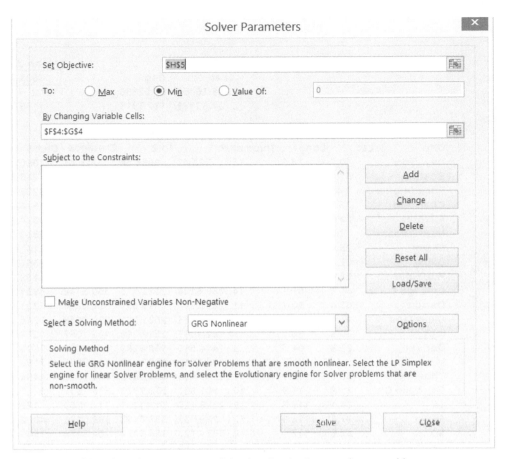

FIGURE 35-7 This is the Solver Parameters dialog box for the One warehouse problem.

Where in the United States should an Internet shipping company locate two warehouses to minimize the total distance that packages are shipped?

The work for this problem is in the Two warehouses worksheet in the Warehouseloc.xlsx file, shown in Figure 35-8.

To begin, enter trial latitudes and longitudes for the warehouses in F4:G5. Next, copy the 69*SQRT((C7-$F$4)^2+(D7-$G$4)^2) formula from F7 to F8:F27 to compute the distance of each city from Warehouse 1. By copying the 69*SQRT((C7-$F$5)^2+(D7-$G$5)^2) formula from G7 to G8:G27, you compute the distance from each city to Warehouse 2. Because the shipments from each city will be sent from the *closer* warehouse, you now compute the distance of each city to the closer warehouse by copying the MIN(F7,G7) formula from H7 to H8:H27. In I7:I27, you compute the distance traveled by each city's shipments by copying the H7*E7 formula from I7 to I8:I27. In cell I5, you compute the total distance traveled by shipments with the SUM(I7:I27) formula.

	A	B	C	D	E	F	G	H	I
1									
2									Mean distance
3						Lat	Long		501.811289
4					1	38.16405	84.02896		Total
5					2	34.93189	117.7916		119676.4655
6		City	Lat	Long	Shipmen	Distance to 1	Distance to 2	Min Distance	Dist*Shipped
7		New York	40.7	73.9	15	720.47	3054.56	720.47	10807.05051
8		Boston	42.3	71	8	943.2073	3268.403	943.2073	7545.658519
9		Philadelphia	40	75.1	10	628.9874	2966.405	628.9874	6289.873795
10		Charlotte	35.2	80.8	6	302.4357	2552.487	302.4357	1814.614483
11		Atlanta	33.8	84.4	11	302.206	2305.344	302.206	3324.265857
12		New Orleans	30	89.9	8	693.8561	1954.375	693.8561	5550.848907
13		Miami	25.8	80.2	13	893.0923	2669.257	893.0923	11610.19974
14		Dallas	32.8	96.8	10	955.7745	1455.871	955.7745	9557.744684
15		Houston	29.8	95.4	12	973.9953	1585.079	973.9953	11687.94305
16		Chicago	41.8	87.7	14	356.5146	2129.715	356.5146	4991.204988
17		Detroit	42.4	83.1	11	299.2264	2448.557	299.2264	3291.490274
18		Cleveland	41.5	81.7	8	280.7258	2531.222	280.7258	2245.806491
19		Indy	39.8	86.1	7	182.1067	2212.369	182.1067	1274.747093
20		Denver	39.8	104.9	8	1444.519	950.8286	950.8286	7606.628829
21		Minneapolis	45	93.3	9	794.7959	1827.139	794.7959	7153.163389
22		Phoenix	33.5	112.1	11	1963.455	404.9579	404.9579	4454.537037
23		Salt Lake Cit	40.8	111.9	10	1931.683	573.7616	573.7616	5737.616195
24		LA	34.1	118.4	18	2388.123	71.11337	71.11337	1280.04075
25		SF	37.8	122.6	12	2661.52	386.3183	386.3183	4635.819785
26		SD	32.8	117.1	10	2311.723	154.6474	154.6474	1546.474352
27		Seattle	41.6	122.4	13	2658.195	559.2874	559.2874	7270.736808

FIGURE 35-8 This figure shows a model for locating two warehouses.

You're now ready to use Solver to determine the optimal warehouse locations. The setup for the Solver Parameters dialog box is shown in Figure 35-9.

Begin by selecting the GRG Nonlinear engine and then use the poor solution, which places each warehouse at 0 latitude and longitude. This solution is poor for two reasons: It locates the warehouses in Africa and it puts two warehouses in the same place. After running Solver, you find that Solver recommends locating both warehouses in the same place. Of course, this is a suboptimal solution. The problem is twofold: The *MIN* function creates situations with no slopes, and perhaps your target cell, as a function of the four changing cells, has multiple peaks and valleys. If your target cell has multiple peaks and valleys (in four dimensions), perhaps your poor starting solution is not near the lowest valley, which is the true optimal solution. When you suspect multiple peaks and valleys exist, it is a good idea to use GRG Multistart, which tries multiple starting points and finds the best answer from each. Most of the time, the best of the best Multistart finds will be the optimal solution to the problem. To use Multistart, place upper and lower bounds on the changing cells. For the bounds on latitude changing cells, you could select 0 and 90 degrees. This ensures that the warehouse is north of the equator. For the bounds on longitude changing cells, choose 0 and 150, which ensures that your location is west of Greenwich, England, and east of Anchorage, Alaska.

FIGURE 35-9 Solver is set up for locating two warehouses.

After running the GRG Multistart engine, you find the total distance traveled was 119,676 miles, and the average distance traveled per shipment is 502 miles. The locations of the warehouses are shown in cells F4:G5 of Figure 35-8. Warehouse 1 is located near Lexington, Kentucky; Warehouse 2 is located near Lancaster, California.

To confirm that Solver found the optimal solution, run the Evolutionary Solver engine. You find no improvement in the optimal solution.

Suppose you had set an upper bound for longitude of 110 degrees. After running Solver, you would have found that Solver recommends a longitude near 110 degrees. If you place bounds on a changing cell and the Solver forces the changing cell to assume a value near a bound, you should relax the bound.

Problems

1. Find the optimal solution to the warehouse problem if three warehouses are allowed.

2. Suppose you want to locate a single restroom so that company employees have to travel the smallest possible distance per day when going to the bathroom. Employees work in four locations within the plant as described in the following table:

X	Y	Number of employees
5	20	6
50	50	12
25	75	23
80	30	15

Assume that employees always walk in a north–south or east–west direction when going to and from the restroom. Where should the restroom be located? Solve Problem 2 if the company wants to locate two restrooms.

CHAPTER 36

Penalties and the Evolutionary Solver

Questions answered in this chapter:

- What are the keys to using the Evolutionary Solver successfully?

- How can I use the Evolutionary Solver to assign 80 workers in Microsoft Finance to a job in one of four workgroups?

Answers to this chapter's questions

This section provides the answers to the questions that are listed at the beginning of the chapter.

What are the keys to using the Evolutionary Solver successfully?

Previously, this book stated that the Evolutionary Solver should be used to find solutions to optimization problems in which the target cell, changing cells, or both involve nonsmooth functions such as *IF*, *ABS*, *MAX*, *MIN*, *COUNTIF*, *COUNTIFS*, *SUMIF*, *SUMIFS*, *AVERAGEIF*, and *AVERAGEIFS*. Before solving a problem with the Evolutionary Solver, you should do the following in the **Solver Parameters** dialog box:

- Click **Options**, select the **Evolutionary** tab, and increase **Mutation Rate** to .50. Increasing the mutation rate enables the Solver to jump around in the set of possible solutions and avoid being stuck in a portion of the set of possible solutions that does not contain a good solution to the Solver model.

- Change **Maximum Time Without Improvement** to 3,600 seconds. Increasing Maximum Time Without Improvement ensures that if you leave your PC, Microsoft Excel will keep looking for a solution for 3,600 seconds. You can stop the Solver at any time by pressing the Esc key.

- Place reasonable lower and upper bounds on your changing cells. Placing bounds on the changing cells reduces the size of the region in which Solver searches for an optimal solution. This can greatly speed Solver's progress toward an optimal solution. The user can change many other Evolutionary Solver settings, but Mutation Rate and Maximum Time Without Improvement have been found to be the only settings that have a significant impact on the solution process.

Everything in life has an upside and a downside, and the Evolutionary Solver is no exception. The upside of the Evolutionary Solver is that it handles nonsmooth functions well. The downside is that constraints that are not linear functions of the changing cells are not handled very well. To handle most constraints with the Evolutionary Solver, you should penalize the target cell to make violation of a constraint a bad thing. Then the survival of the fittest will do away with any constraint violation. The chapter's next question shows how to use penalties with the Evolutionary Solver.

How can I use the Evolutionary Solver to assign 80 workers in Microsoft Finance to a job in one of four workgroups?

You need to assign 80 employees to four workgroups. The head of each workgroup has rated each employee's competence on a 0 to 10 scale (10 equals most competent). Each employee has rated his satisfaction with each job assignment (again on a 0 to 10 scale). For example, Worker 1 has been given a 9 rating from the leader of Workgroup 1, and Worker 1 gives Workgroup 4 a rating of 7.

The work for this question is in the Assign.xlsx file. (See Figure 36-1.) You want to assign between 18 and 22 people to each workgroup. You consider job competence to be twice as important as employee satisfaction. How can you assign employees to workgroups to maximize total satisfaction and ensure that each division has the required number of employees?

		Qual				Sat				576	499			
Division	Worker	1	2	3	4	1	2	3	4	Quality	Satisfaction			
4	1	9	8	6	8	1	2	6	7	8	7			
1	2	10	0	5	6	9	6	7	4	10	9			
3	3	5	8	10	5	1	7	7	3	10	7	Group	#assigned	penalty
1	4	4	0	5	2	9	1	0	3	4	9	1	19	0
2	5	9	10	4	5	9	8	8	3	10	8	2	18	0
3	6	5	2	7	3	2	8	1	5	7	1	3	22	0
1	7	8	3	1	2	1	8	2	2	8	1	4	21	0
3	8	2	2	9	2	8	3	1	6	9	1		Total pen	0
1	9	8	7	6	3	4	3	4	1	8	4			
4	10	7	0	1	8	4	1	5	4	8	4		Total	1651
3	11	8	1	6	6	2	0	9	3	6	9			
2	12	0	7	1	2	5	2	1	1	7	2			
1	13	9	0	5	4	3	0	7	8	9	3			
4	14	9	2	2	7	1	1	2	10	7	10			
3	15	1	3	8	4	9	8	6	8	8	6			
1	16	9	6	4	5	5	7	8	8	9	5			
1	17	8	0	5	0	5	7	2	4	8	5			
2	18	6	7	6	3	2	4	1	6	7	4			
3	19	3	4	5	4	8	7	6	6	5	6			

FIGURE 36-1 This is the data for the job assignment problem.

In cells A3:A82, enter trial assignments of workers to workgroups. Assigning each worker to Workgroup 1, for example, is an acceptable starting solution. Copying the HLOOKUP(A3,Qual,B3+1) formula from K3 to K3:K82 enables you to look up each employee's qualifications for her assigned job. Note that Qual refers to the C2:F82 range. Next, copying the HLOOKUP(A3,Satis,B3+1) formula from L3 to L3:L82 enables you to look up the employee's satisfaction with her assigned job. Satis is the range name for G2:J82.

To deal with the fact that each division needs between 18 and 22 employees, you need to count how many employees have been assigned to each workgroup. You can do this in cells N6:N9 by copying the COUNTIF($A$3:$A$82,M6) formula from N6 to N7:N9. Next, in cells O6:O9, determine whether a workgroup has the incorrect number of employees by copying the IF(OR(N6<18,N6>22),1,0) formula from O6 to O7:O9.

Now you'll see how to work on computing the target cell. In K1:L1, you compute total competence and total job quality by copying the SUM(K3:K82) formula from K1 to K1:L1. To ensure that each workgroup will have between 18 and 22 workers, you can penalize the target cell. Choose a penalty of 1,000 for each workgroup that has fewer than 18 or more than 22 workers. There is no hard and fast rule to help you determine an appropriate penalty. In this situation, the average rating is 5. This yields a target cell of 2*400 + 400 = 1,200. Therefore, it seems likely that putting the wrong number of people in any division would not benefit the target cell by more than 1,000, so survival of the fittest will kill off any solution for which a workgroup has too many or too few workers. The appropriate penalty should not be too large (100,000) because it sometimes makes the Solver ignore the real problem. If the penalty is too small, the Solver will not achieve the goal you've set.

In cell O10, compute the total number of divisions that do not have the correct number of workers with the SUM(O6:O9) formula. Now you are finally ready to compute the target cell in cell O12 by adding twice the total competence to the total job satisfaction and subtracting a penalty of 1,000 for each group that does not have the correct number of employees. Your final target cell is computed with the 2*K1+L1–1000*O10 formula.

You now can create the Solver model for this problem. You need to use the Evolutionary Solver because the COUNTIF and IF functions are nonsmooth functions of the changing cells. The model is shown in Figure 36-2.

Maximize the weighted sum of workgroup and employee satisfaction less the penalty for an incorrect number of workers in a workgroup (cell O12) and then constrain each worker's assignment to be 1, 2, 3, or 4. The solution is shown in Figure 36-1. Each group has the right number of workers; average employee competence is 7.2, and average employee satisfaction is 6.3. Over all 80 workers, the average of their competence ratings is 4.4, and the overall average for satisfaction ratings is 5, so conditions have improved quite a lot over a random assignment.

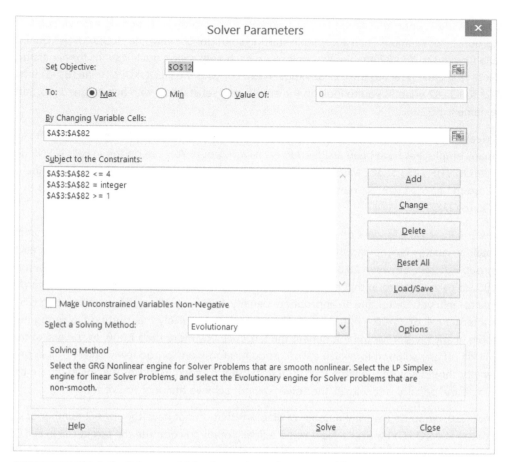

FIGURE 36-2 This is the Solver model for the worker assignment problem.

If you had tried the GRG Nonlinear engine (even with Multistart), the Solver would not have found the optimal solution because the model includes nonsmooth functions. Another tip about using the Evolutionary Solver is to use as few changing cells as possible, and you will usually be rewarded by Solver taking less time to find an optimal solution.

Using conditional formatting to highlight each employee's ratings

You can use the conditional formatting feature to highlight in yellow each employee's actual competence and satisfaction (based on his assignment). At cell C3, select the C3:J82 cell range. Select **New Rule** from **Conditional Formatting** on the **Home** tab, select **Use A Formula To Determine Which Cells To Format**, and fill in the dialog box as shown in Figure 36-3.

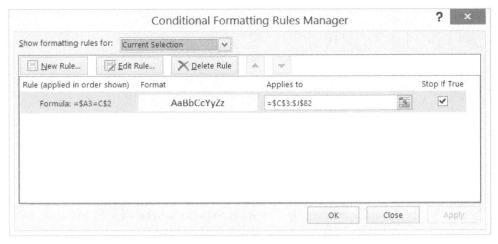

FIGURE 36-3 Use conditional formatting to highlight worker quality and satisfaction.

This formula enters a yellow format in cell C3 if and only if the first worker is assigned to Workgroup 1. Excel copies this formula across and down so that each worker's quality and satisfaction ratings are highlighted only for the workgroup to which each employee is assigned.

Problems

1. Use the Evolutionary Solver to solve Problem 4 in Chapter 32, "Using Solver for capital budgeting."

2. Solve the two-warehouse problems in Chapter 35, "Warehouse location and the GRG Multistart and Evolutionary Solver engines," assuming that each warehouse can ship, at most, 120,000 units.

3. In the fictional state of Politicians Care about U.S., there are eight congressional districts. Each of 15 cities must be assigned to a congressional district, and each district must be assigned between 150,000 and 250,000 voters. The makeup of each district is given in the following table. Assign the cities to districts to maximize the number of districts won by the Democrats:

City	Rep	Dem
1	80	34
2	43	61
3	40	44
4	20	24
5	40	114
6	40	64
7	70	34
8	50	44

9	70	54
10	70	64
11	80	45
12	40	50
13	50	60
14	60	65
15	50	70

4. Solve the assignment of workers example, assuming that worker satisfaction is twice as important as the bosses' ratings.

5. Cook County General is attempting to develop the work schedule for its 20 nurses. Each nurse will work four consecutive days and is assigned to one of the following schedules:

Schedule	Days worked
1	Monday–Thursday
2	Tuesday–Friday
3	Wednesday–Saturday
4	Thursday–Sunday
5	Friday–Monday
6	Saturday–Tuesday
7	Sunday–Wednesday

Each nurse will be assigned for the week to either the ICU or a patient ward. Each nurse's satisfaction with her assignment is given in the Nursejackiedata.xlsx file. For example, if Nurse 5 is assigned to the ICU, Nurse 5 gives a perfect 10 rating to work schedule 3.

Each day, the ICU needs six nurses, and the patient wards need five nurses. Schedule the nurses to maximize their satisfaction and meet hospital needs.

You will need to know which schedules satisfy nurse demand for different days. For example, nurses starting on Monday, Friday, Saturday, and Sunday will work on Monday.

CHAPTER 37

The traveling salesperson problem

Questions answered in this chapter:

- How can I use Excel to solve sequencing problems?

- How can I use Excel to solve a traveling salesperson problem (TSP)?

Answers to this chapter's questions

This section provides the answers to the questions that are listed at the beginning of the chapter.

How can I use Excel to solve sequencing problems?

Many business problems involve the choice of an optimal sequence. Here are two examples:

- In what order should a print shop work on 10 jobs to minimize the total time by which jobs fail to meet their due dates? Problems of this type are called job shop scheduling problems.

- A salesperson lives in Boston and wants to visit 10 other cities before returning home. In which order should he visit the cities to minimize the total distance he travels? This is an example of the classic TSP.

Here are two other examples of a TSP:

- A delivery driver needs to make 20 stops today. In which order should she deliver packages to minimize her time on the road?

- A robot must drill 10 holes to produce a single printed circuit board. Which order of drilling the holes minimizes the total time needed to produce a circuit board?

The Microsoft Excel 2013 Solver makes tackling sequencing problems very easy. Simply choose Evolutionary Solver, select your changing cells, and define All Different constraints. Configuring constraints with All Different ensures that if you have 10 changing cells, Excel will assign the values of 1, 2, . . . 10 to the changing cells, with each value occurring exactly once. In general, if you select a range of n changing cells to be different, Excel ensures that the changing cells assume the values of 1, 2, . . . , n, with each possible value occurring exactly once. See how to use Dif to solve a traveling salesperson problem easily.

How can I use Excel to solve a traveling salesperson problem (TSP)?

Solve the following problem.

Willie Lowman is a salesman who lives in Boston. He needs to visit each of the cities listed in Figure 37-1 and then return to Boston. In what order should Willie visit the cities to minimize the total distance he travels? Your work is in file Tsp.xlsx.

	E	F	G	H	I	J	K	L	M	N	O	P	Q
3			Boston	Chicago	Dallas	Denver	LA	Miami	NY	Phoenix	Pittsburgh	SF	Seattle
4		1 Boston	0	983	1815	1991	3036	1539	213	2664	792	2385	2612
5		2 Chicago	983	0	1205	1050	2112	1390	840	1729	457	2212	2052
6		3 Dallas	1815	1205	0	801	1425	1332	1604	1027	1237	1765	2404
7		4 Denver	1991	1050	801	0	1174	1332	1780	836	1411	1765	1373
8		5 LA	3036	2112	1425	1174	0	2757	2825	398	2456	403	1909
9		6 Miami	1539	1390	1332	1332	2757	0	1258	2359	1250	3097	3389
10		7 NY	213	840	1604	1780	2825	1258	0	2442	386	3036	2900
11		8 Phoenix	2664	1729	1027	836	398	2359	2442	0	2073	800	1482
12		9 Pittsburgh	792	457	1237	1411	2456	1250	386	2073	0	2653	2517
13		10 SF	2385	2212	1765	1765	403	3097	3036	800	2653	0	817
14		11 Seattle	2612	2052	2404	1373	1909	3389	2900	1482	2517	817	0
15		Order	Distance	City									
16	1	8	398	Phoenix									
17	2	3	1027	Dallas									
18	3	6	1332	Miami									
19	4	1	1539	Boston									
20	5	7	213	NY									
21	6	9	386	Pittsburgh									
22	7	2	457	Chicago									
23	8	4	1050	Denver									
24	9	11	1373	Seattle									
25	10	10	817	SF									
26	11	5	403	LA									
27		Total	8995										

FIGURE 37-1 Here is data for the TSP.

To model this problem in a spreadsheet, you should note that any ordering or permutation of the numbers 1 through 11 represents an order for visiting cities. For example, the order of 2-4-6-8-10-1-3-5-7-9-11 can be viewed as traveling from Boston (City 1) to Dallas (City 3), to LA (City 5), and finally to SF (City 10) before returning to Boston. Because the order is viewed from the location of City 1, there are 10! = 10 × 9 × 8 × 7 × 6 . . . × 2 × 1 = 3,628,800 possible orderings for Willie to consider.

To begin, you need to determine the total distance traveled for any given order for visiting the cities. The *INDEX* function is perfect for this situation. Recall from Chapter 3, "The *INDEX* function," that the syntax of the *INDEX* function is INDEX(Range,row#,column#). Excel looks in the range of cells named Range and picks out the entry specified in row# and column#. In this case, you can use the *INDEX* function to find the total distance traveled in visiting all cities.

Begin by entering an order of the integers 1 through 11 in the F16:F26 range. Next, name the G4:Q14 range **distances** and enter the INDEX(distances,F26,F16) formula in cell G16. This formula determines the distance between the last city listed (in F26) and the first city listed (in F16). Enter the

INDEX(Distances,F16,F17) formula in cell G17 and copy it to the G18:G26 range. In G17, the formula computes the distance between the first and second city listed, the second and third city, and so on. Now you can compute the target cell (total distance traveled) in cell G27 with the SUM(G16:G26) formula.

At this point, you're ready to invoke the Evolutionary Solver. Minimize cell G27, click **Add Constraint**, and select the F16:F26 range. Select **Dif** for **All Different**. This ensures that the Solver always keeps the changing cells in the selected range, assuming the values 1, 2, up to 11. Each value will occur exactly once. The Solver Parameters dialog box is shown in Figure 37-2. Before running Solver, increase the mutation rate to .5.

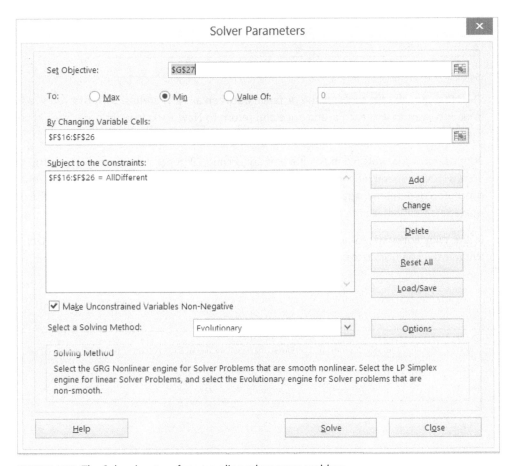

FIGURE 37-2 The Solver is set up for a traveling salesperson problem.

The minimum possible distance to travel is 8,995 miles. To see the order in which the cities are visited, begin in the row with a 1 (corresponding to Willie's home, Boston) and follow the cities in the listed sequence. The cities are visited in the following order: Boston–NY–Pittsburgh–Chicago–Denver–Seattle–San Francisco–Los Angeles–Phoenix–Dallas–Miami–Boston. Many other sequences for visiting the cities also yield the minimum total travel distance of 8,995 miles.

Problems

1. A small job shop needs to schedule six jobs. The due date and days needed to complete each job are given in the following table. In what order should the jobs be scheduled to minimize the total days the jobs are late?

Job	Processing time	Due date (measured from today)
1	9	32
2	7	29
3	8	22
4	18	21
5	9	37
6	6	28

2. The Nbamiles.xlsx file contains the distance between all NBA arenas. Suppose you live in New York and want to visit each arena once and return to New York. In what order should you visit the cities to minimize total distance traveled?

3. Suppose now that you live in Atlanta and are driving 29 general managers on this trip to NBA arenas. Each general manager wants to return to his home. Each time you visit an arena, you drop off a general manager at his home arena. In what order should you drop off the general managers to minimize the total distance traveled by the general managers?

4. In the Willy Lowman problem, suppose you must visit New York immediately after Denver. What is the solution to the problem?

CHAPTER 38

Importing data from a text file or document

Question answered in this chapter:

- How can I import data from a text file into Excel so that I can analyze it?

Jeff Sagarin, the creator of the USA Today basketball and football ratings, and I have developed a system to rate NBA players that several NBA teams have used, including the Dallas Mavericks and New York Knicks. Every day during the season, Jeff's FORTRAN program produces a multitude of information, including ratings for each Dallas Maverick lineup during each game. Jeff's program produces this information in the form of a text file. In this chapter, you see how you can import a text file into Microsoft Excel to use it for data analysis.

Answer to this chapter's question

This section provides the answer to the question that is listed at the beginning of the chapter.

How can I import data from a text file into Excel so that I can analyze it?

You will likely often receive data in a Microsoft Word document or in a text (.txt) file that you need to import into Excel for analysis. To import a Word document into Excel, you should first save it as a text file. You can then use the Text Import Wizard to import the file. With the Text Import Wizard, you can break data in a text file into columns by using one of the following approaches:

- If you choose the fixed-width option, Excel guesses where the data should be broken into columns. You can easily modify the Excel assumptions.

- If you choose the delimited option, you pick delimeter characters (common choices are a comma, a space, or a plus sign), and Excel breaks the data into columns wherever it encounters the character(s) you choose.

As an example, the Lineupsch38.docx file (a sample of the data is shown in the following block) contains the length of time each lineup played for Dallas in several games during the 2002–2003 season. The file also contains the rating of the lineup. For example, the first two lines tell you that against Sacramento, the lineup of Bell, Finley, LaFrentz, Nash, and Nowitzki were on the court together for

9.05 minutes and that the lineup played at a level of 19.79 points (per 48 minutes), worse than an average NBA lineup.

```
Bell     Finley   LaFrentz Nash     Nowitzki   - 19.79   695# 9.05m SAC DAL* Finley   Nash
Nowitzki Van Exel Williams  - 11.63  695# 8.86m SAC DAL* Finley   LaFrentz Nash     Nowitzki
Van Exel  102.98   695# 4.44m SAC DAL* Bradley   Finley   Nash   Nowitzki Van Exel  - 44.26
695# 4.38m SAC DAL* Bradley   Nash    Nowitzki Van Exel Williams   9.71   695# 3.05m SAC DAL*
Bell    Finley   LaFrentz Nowitzki Van Exel - 121.50   695# 2.73m SAC DAL* Bell    LaFrentz
Nowitzki Van Exel Williams   39.35   695# 2.70m SAC DAL* Bradley   Finley   Nowitzki Van Exel
Williams   86.87   695# 2.45m SAC DAL* Bradley   Nash    Van Exel Williams Rigaudeau  - 54.55
695# 2.32m SAC DAL*
```

You'd like to import this lineup information into Excel so that, for each lineup, the following information would be listed in different columns:

- Each player's name

- Minutes played by the lineup

- Rating of the lineup

The player named Van Exel (full name Nick Van Exel) raises a problem. If you choose the delimited option and use a space character to break the data into columns, Van Exel will occupy two columns. For lineups that include Van Exel, the numerical data will be located in a different column than the column in which the data is located for lineups that don't include Van Exel. To remedy this problem, use the Replace command in Word to change each occurrence of Van Exel to Exel. Now, when Excel breaks up the data where a space occurs, Van Exel will require only one column. The first few rows of your data now look like the following.

```
Bell     Finley   LaFrentz Nash     Nowitzki   - 19.79   695# 9.05m SAC DAL* Finley   Nash
Nowitzki Exel   Williams  - 11.63  695# 8.86m SAC DAL* Finley   LaFrentz Nash     Nowitzki
Exel    102.98   69 5# 4.44m SAC DAL* Bradley   Finley   Nash   Nowitzki Exel   - 44.26   695#
4.38m SAC DAL* Bradley   Nash    Nowitzki Exel   Williams   9.71   69 5# 3.05m SAC DAL* Bell
Finley   LaFrentz Nowitzki Exel   - 121.50   695# 2.73m SAC DAL* Bell    LaFrentz Nowitzki
Exel   Williams   39.35   69 5# 2.70m SAC DAL* Bradley   Finley   Nowitzki Exel   Williams
86.87   69 5# 2.45m SAC DAL* Bradley   Nash    Exel   Williams Rigaudeau  - 54.55   695# 2.32m
SAC DAL*
```

Of course, your approach would fail if another player had the last name Exel. If that were the case, you could replace Van Exel with Exel1.

The trick to importing data from a Word or text file into Excel is to use the Excel Text Import Wizard. As mentioned earlier, you first need to save the Word file (Lineupsch38.docx in this example) as a text file. To do this, open the file in Word, click the **File** tab, click **Save As**, and then select **Plain Text** in the **Save As Type** list. In the **File Conversion** dialog box, select **Windows (Default)** and then click **OK**. Your file should now be saved with the Lineupsch38.txt name. Close the Word document.

In Excel, open the Lineupsch38.txt file. To see the text files in the Open window, you need to change the file type drop-down list (located to the right of the File name box) to **Text Files**. When the file opens, you see step 1 of the Text Import Wizard, which is shown in Figure 38-1.

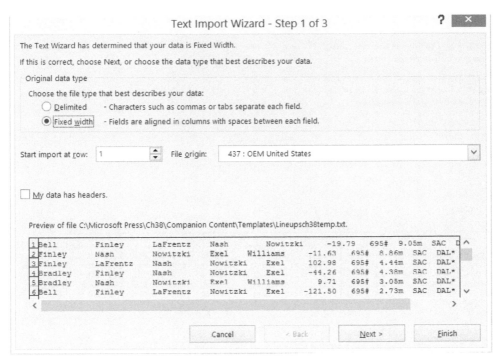

FIGURE 38-1 This figure shows step 1 of the Text Import Wizard.

Clearly, in this case, you want to select **Delimited** and break the data at each space. However, suppose you choose **Fixed Width**. Then step 2 of the Text Import Wizard appears, shown in Figure 38-2. As you can see, you can create, move, or delete a break point. For many data import operations, changing column breaks can be a hit-or-miss adventure.

If you select Delimited in step 1, you see the second step of the Text Import Wizard that's shown in Figure 38-3. Tab is selected by default, and keeping Tab selected is recommended because many Excel add-ins do not work properly if Tab is cleared. Select **Space** as the delimiter. Selecting **Treat Consecutive Delimiters As One** ensures that consecutive spaces result in only a single column break.

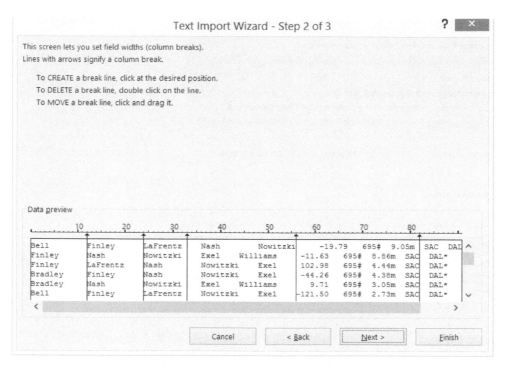

FIGURE 38-2 Step 2 of the Text Import Wizard appears after selecting Fixed Width.

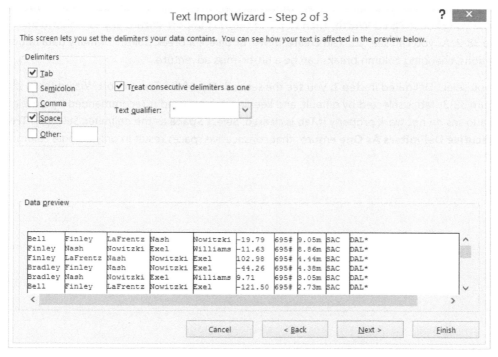

FIGURE 38-3 This figure shows step 2 of the Text Import Wizard after selecting Delimited.

When you click **Next**, you're sent to the third step in the wizard, which is shown in Figure 38-4. You can configure the column data format for a selected column. By selecting **General** as the format, you direct Excel to treat numerical data as numbers and other values as text.

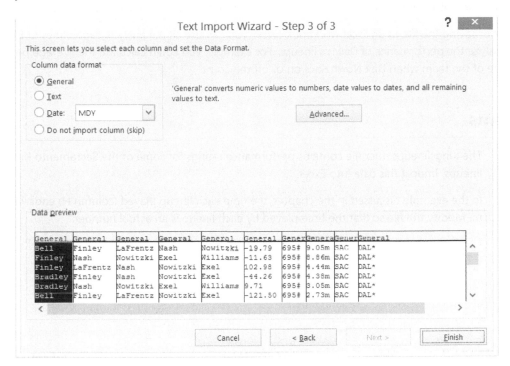

FIGURE 38-4 This figure shows step 3 of the wizard, in which you can select a format to apply to the data you're importing.

When you click **Finish**, the wizard imports the data into Excel, as shown in Figure 38-5.

	A	B	C	D	E	F	G	H	I	J
1	Bell	Finley	LaFrentz	Nash	Nowitzki	-19.79	695#	9.05m	SAC	DAL*
2	Finley	Nash	Nowitzki	Excel	Williams	-11.63	695#	8.86m	SAC	DAL*
3	Finley	LaFrentz	Nash	Nowitzki	Excel	102.98	695#	4.44m	SAC	DAL*
4	Bradley	Finley	Nash	Nowitzki	Excel	-44.26	695#	4.38m	SAC	DAL*
5	Bradley	Nash	Nowitzki	Excel	Williams	9.71	695#	3.05m	SAC	DAL*
6	Bell	Finley	LaFrentz	Nowitzki	Excel	-121.5	695#	2.73m	SAC	DAL*
7	Bell	LaFrentz	Nowitzki	Excel	Williams	39.35	695#	2.70m	SAC	DAL*
8	Bradley	Finley	Nowitzki	Excel	Williams	86.87	695#	2.45m	SAC	DAL*
9	Bradley	Nash	Excel	Williams	Rigaudeau	-54.55	695#	2.32m	SAC	DAL*
10	Finley	LaFrentz	Excel	Williams	Rigaudeau	-26.4	695#	1.73m	SAC	DAL*
11	Bradley	Finley	Nash	Nowitzki	Williams	91.89	695#	1.70m	SAC	DAL*
12	Bell	Finley	Nash	Nowitzki	Excel	34.18	695#	1.05m	SAC	DAL*
13	LaFrentz	Nash	Nowitzki	Excel	Williams	-50.9	695#	1.02m	SAC	DAL*
14	Bell	Bradley	Finley	Nash	Nowitzki	1.42	695#	1.00m	SAC	DAL*
15	Bradley	Finley	Excel	Williams	Rigaudeau	46.75	695#	0.93m	SAC	DAL*
16	Bell	Bradley	Nowitzki	Excel	Williams	-314.43	695#	0.60m	SAC	DAL*

FIGURE 38-5 Here is the Excel file with lineup information.

Each player is listed in a separate column (columns A–E); column F contains the rating of each lineup, column G contains the game number, column H contains the minutes played by each lineup, and columns I and J list the two teams playing in the game. Of course, if you want, you could globally replace Exel with Van Exel, so the player's proper name was restored to the data.

After saving the file as an Excel workbook (.xlsx), you can use all the analytic capabilities of Excel to analyze the performance of Dallas's lineups. For example, you could calculate the average performance of the team when Dirk Nowitzki is on or off the court.

Problems

1. The Kingslineups.docx file contains performance ratings for some of the Sacramento Kings lineups. Import this data into Excel.

2. In the example discussed in the chapter, the time each lineup played (column H) ends with an m. Modify the file so that the time played by each lineup is an actual number.

CHAPTER 39

Importing data from the Internet

Question answered in this chapter:

■ How can I easily download sports statistics into Excel?

We all know that the World Wide Web contains useful data on just about everything. However, you can't really do any sort of analysis of this data while it's on the web. You need to import the data into Microsoft Excel, which you can do very easily, providing the data is defined inside an HTML table. In an Excel workbook, on the **Data** tab, in the **Get External Data** group, click **From Web**. When the **New Web Query** dialog box appears, paste the URL of the webpage into it and then click **Go**. The webpage appears in preview, and you can select the HTML table you want to import. The answer to this chapter's question shows you how to implement this simple procedure.

Answer to this chapter's question

This section provides the answer to the question that is listed at the beginning of the chapter.

How can I easily download sports statistics into Excel?

The *http://www.pro-football-reference.com/players/M/MannPe00/gamelog/* URL leads you to a game-by-game log of Peyton Manning's NFL statistics. A subset of this data imported into Excel is shown in Figure 39-1. Your work for this example is in file Peyton.xlsx.

To import the data into Excel, copy the URL and then open a blank worksheet. Now click the **Data** tab on the ribbon and, in the **Get External Data** group, click **From Web**. When the **New Web Query** dialog box appears, press Ctrl+V to paste the URL into the address box and then click **Go**. The **New Web Query** dialog box displays the data shown in Figure 39-2. (If you receive script errors, click **No** to dismiss the warnings and stop running scripts. It will not affect the import process.)

	Date	Age	Tm		Opp	Result	GS	Cmp	Att	Cmp%	Yds	TD	Int	Rate	Y/A	AY/A	Att		Yds	Y/A	TD
236	Date	Age	Tm		Opp	Result	GS	Cmp	Att	Cmp%	Yds	TD	Int	Rate	Y/A	AY/A	Att		Yds	Y/A	TD
237	9/9/2012	36-169	DEN		PIT	W 31-19	*	19	26	73.08%	253	2	0	129.2	9.73	11.27	4		3	0.75	0
238	9/17/2012	36-177	DEN	@	ATL	L 21-27	*	24	37	64.86%	241	1	3	58.5	6.51	3.41	1		-1	-1	0
239	9/23/2012	36-183	DEN		HOU	L 25-31	*	26	52	50.00%	330	2	0	83	6.35	7.12	0		0		0
240	9/30/2012	36-190	DEN		OAK	W 37-6	*	30	38	78.95%	338	3	0	130	8.89	10.47	1		-1	-1	0
241	10/7/2012	36-197	DEN	@	NWE	L 21-31	*	31	44	70.45%	337	3	0	115.4	7.66	9.02	2		9	4.5	0
242	10/15/2012	36-205	DEN	@	SDG	W 35-24	*	24	30	80.00%	309	3	1	129	10.3	10.8	3		-3	-1	0
243	10/28/2012	36-218	DEN		NOR	W 34-14	*	22	30	73.33%	305	3	0	138.9	10.17	12.17	1		4	4	0
244	11/4/2012	36-225	DEN	@	CIN	W 31-23	*	27	35	77.14%	291	3	2	105.8	8.31	7.46	2		-2	-1	0
245	11/11/2012	36-232	DEN	@	CAR	W 36-14	*	27	38	71.05%	301	1	0	103.1	7.92	8.45	3		4	1.33	0
246	11/18/2012	36-239	DEN		SDG	W 30-23	*	25	42	59.52%	270	3	1	92.4	6.43	6.79	0		0		0
247	11/25/2012	36-246	DEN	@	KAN	W 17-9	*	22	37	59.46%	285	2	1	90.5	7.7	7.57	1		1	1	0
248	12/2/2012	36-253	DEN		TAM	W 31-23	*	27	38	71.05%	242	3	1	103.2	6.37	6.76	2		-5	-2.5	0
249	12/6/2012	36-257	DEN	@	OAK	W 26-13	*	26	36	72.22%	310	1	1	95.8	8.61	7.92	3		-3	-1	0
250	12/16/2012	36-267	DEN	@	BAL	W 34-17	*	17	28	60.71%	204	1	0	94.9	7.29	8	0		0		0
251	12/23/2012	36-274	DEN		CLE	W 34-12	*	30	43	69.77%	339	3	1	106.6	7.88	8.23	0		0		0
252	12/30/2012	36-281	DEN		KAN	W 38-3	*	23	29	79.31%	304	3	0	144.8	10.48	12.55	0		0		0
253						Passing												Rushing			
254	Date	Age	Tm		Opp	Result	GS	Cmp	Att	Cmp%	Yds	TD	Int	Rate	Y/A	AY/A	Att		Yds	Y/A	TD
255	9/5/2013	37-165	DEN		BAL	W 49-27	*	27	42	64.29%	462	7	0	141.1	11	14.33	2		-2	-1	0
256	225 Games							5109	7835	65.21%	59949	443	209	96	7.65	7.58	371		726	1.96	17

FIGURE 39-1 This figure shows Peyton Manning's game-by-game quarterback (QB) statistics.

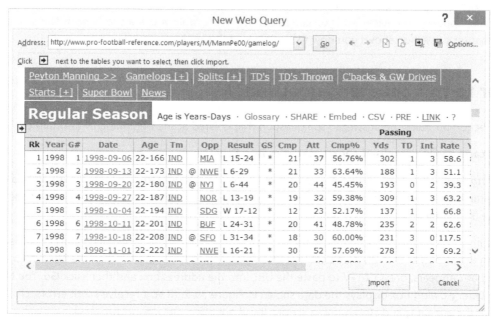

FIGURE 39-2 Here is the New Web Query dialog box after choosing a URL.

Click the arrow that points to the data you want to download (choose to import just Manning's regular season statistics) and **Import**. (Each arrow represents an HTML table within the webpage.) In this case, you would click the arrow above **Rk**. The arrow changes to a check mark. After clicking **Import**, you see the **Import Data** dialog box, in which you indicate to Excel where you want to place the data. Choose cell B2 of the current worksheet for this example. After clicking **OK**, the analysts' ratings are imported into the worksheet. (See Figure 39-1.) Note that the numbers and labels are beautifully separated into different cells. If you right-click within the data and select **Refresh**, Excel goes out to the web and pulls the most recent data. Therefore, if you click Refresh every Tuesday during the NFL season, Manning's latest game stats will be added to your worksheet.

You can easily set your query to be refreshed or updated in any fashion you want. Just right-click anywhere in the query results, select **Data Range Properties**, and change the **Refresh Control** settings. As shown in Figure 39-3, the query was specified to be automatically refreshed whenever the file is opened.

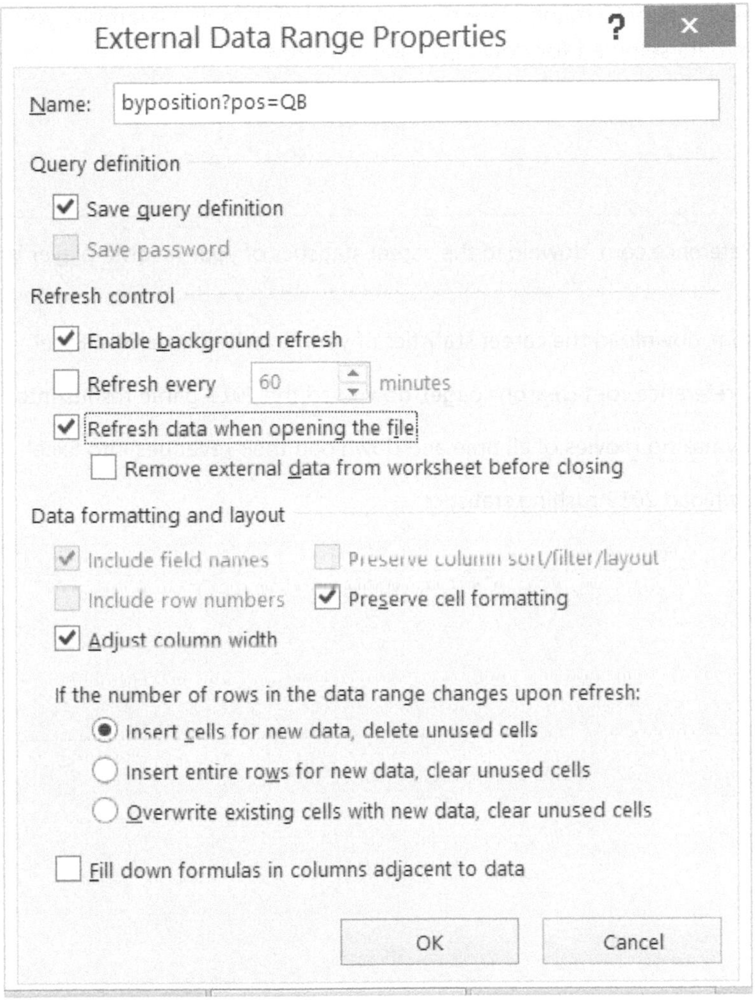

FIGURE 39-3 Refresh settings for the web query.

To edit this query, right-click anywhere within the query output and select **Edit Query**. By clicking the **Options** button shown in the upper-right of Figure 39-2, you can control the formatting of your query results.

If you are using Internet Explorer, you can also create a web query from an HTML table by right-clicking inside the table and selecting **Export To Microsoft Excel**. The data is automatically imported into a new workbook starting in cell A1.

> **Note** If you have Office 2013 Pro Plus or higher, you can download Microsoft Power Query for Excel from *http://office.microsoft.com/en-us/excel/download-microsoft-power-query-for-excel-FX104018616.aspx*. Power Query provides many superb tools for downloading data from the web and makes it easy to manipulate the downloaded data. For example, you can control the columns of data selected for download and filter rows.

Problems

1. From Basketball-Reference.com, download the career statistics of your favorite player into Excel.

2. From Fangraphs.com, download the career statistics of your favorite player into Excel.

3. From Pro-football-reference.com (seasons page), download the 2012 game results into Excel.

4. Find the top moneymaking movies of all time and download their revenues into Excel.

5. From NFL.com, download 2012 rushing statistics.

CHAPTER 40

Validating data

Questions answered in this chapter:

- I'm entering scores from professional basketball games into Excel. I know that a team scores from 50 to 200 points per game. I once entered 1,000 points instead of 100 points, which messed up my analysis. Is there a way Excel can prevent me from making this type of error?

- I'm entering the date and amount of my business expenses for a new year. Early in the year, I often enter the previous year in the Date field by mistake. Can I set up Excel to prevent me from making this type of error?

- I'm entering a long list of numbers. Can Excel warn me if I enter a nonnumeric value?

- My assistant needs to enter state abbreviations when she enters dozens and dozens of sales transactions. Can we set up a list of state abbreviations to minimize the chance that she'll enter an incorrect abbreviation?

A lot of our work often involves mind-numbing data entry. When you're entering a lot of information in Microsoft Excel, it's easy to make an error. The data validation feature in Excel 2013 can greatly lessen the chances that you'll commit a costly error. To set up data validation, you begin by selecting the cell range that you want to apply data validation to. Choose **Data Validation** on the **Data** tab and then specify the criteria (as you'll see in this chapter's examples) that Excel uses to flag any invalid data that's entered.

Answers to this chapter's questions

This section provides the answers to the questions that are listed at the beginning of the chapter.

I'm entering scores from professional basketball games into Excel. I know that a team scores from 50 to 200 points per game. I once entered 1,000 points instead of 100 points, which messed up my analysis. Is there a way Excel can prevent me from making this type of error?

Suppose that you'll enter the number of points scored by the home team in cells A2:A11, and, you'll enter the number of points scored by the visiting team in cells B2:B11. (You'll find the work to solve this problem in the Nbadvl.xlsx file.) You want to ensure that each value entered in the A2:B11 range is a whole number from 50 through 200.

Begin by selecting the A2:B11 range and then choose **Data Validation** on the **Data** tab. Select the **Settings** tab, select **Whole Number** from the **Allow** list, and then fill in the **Data Validation** dialog box as shown in Figure 40-1.

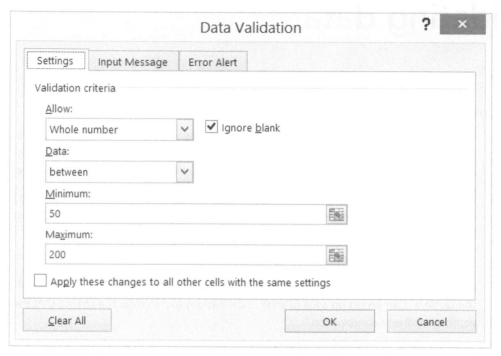

FIGURE 40-1 Use the Settings tab in the Data Validation dialog box to set up data validation criteria.

The Excel default response to invalid data (called an *error alert*) is a message stating, "The value entered is not valid. A user has restricted values that can be entered into the cell." You can use the **Error Alert** tab in the **Data Validation** dialog box (see Figure 40-2) to change the nature of the error alert, including the icon, the title for the message box, and the text of the message itself.

On the Input Message tab, you can create a prompt or alert that informs a user about the type of data that can be safely entered. The message is displayed as a tooltip in the selected cell. For example, you can enter an error alert that states, "Please enter a whole number between 50 and 200." After typing a number that violates that criterion, say 34, in cell E5, you would then see the message shown in Figure 40-3.

FIGURE 40-2 This figure shows Error Alert tab options in the Data Validation dialog box.

FIGURE 40-3 Error alert for the basketball data validation example.

I'm entering the date and amount of my business expenses for a new year. Early in the year, I often enter the previous year in the date field by mistake. Can I set up Excel to prevent me from making this type of error?

Suppose it is early in 2013, and you are entering the date in the A2:A20 cell range. (See the Datedv.xlsx file.) Select the A2:A20 range and then choose **Data Validation** on the **Data** tab. Fill in the **Settings** tab of the **Data Validation** dialog box as shown in Figure 40-4. Then you will not be allowed to enter any date earlier than 1/1/2013.

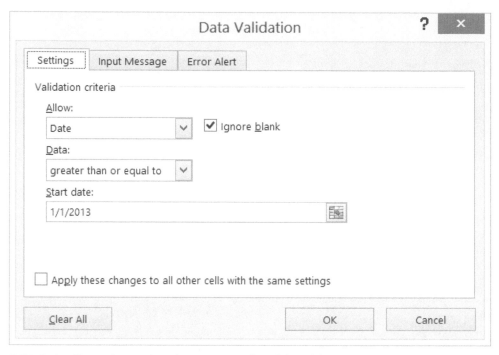

FIGURE 40-4 Use settings such as these to ensure the validity of dates you enter.

If you enter a date in this range that occurs earlier than January 1, 2013, you'll be warned about the error. For example, entering 1/15/2012 in cell A3 brings up the error alert you define.

I'm entering a long list of numbers. Can Excel warn me if I enter a nonnumeric value?

To unleash the full power of data validation, you can use the Custom settings. When you select **Custom** in the **Allow** list on the **Settings** tab of the **Data Validation** dialog box (see Figure 40-5), you use a formula to define valid data. A formula you enter for data validation works the same as a formula used for conditional formatting, which is described in Chapter 23, "Conditional formatting." You enter a formula that is true if and only if the content of the first cell in the selected range is valid. When you click **OK** in the **Data Validation** dialog box, the formula is copied to the validation formula of the remaining cells in the range. When you enter a value in a cell in the selected range, Excel displays an error alert if the formula you entered returns False.

To illustrate the use of the Custom setting, suppose that you want to ensure that each entry in the B2:B20 cell range is a number. (See the Numberdv.xlsx file.) The key to solving this problem is using the Excel *ISNUMBER* function. The *ISNUMBER* function returns True if the function refers to a cell that contains numeric data. The function returns False if the function refers to a cell that contains a nonnumeric value. To ensure that entering a nonnumeric entry in B2:B20 will create an error, proceed as follows.

With the cursor in cell B2, select the B2:B20 cell range. Click the **Data** tab, click **Data Validation** in the **Data Tools** group, and then fill in the **Settings** tab of the **Data Validation** dialog box as shown in Figure 40-5.

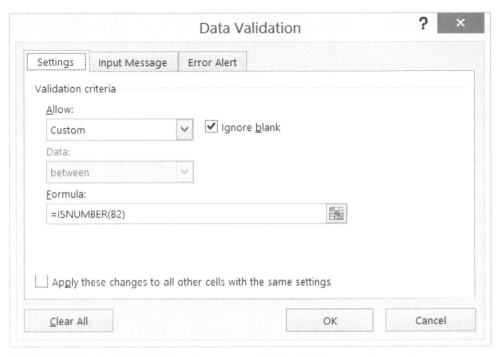

FIGURE 40-5 Use the *ISNUMBER* function to ensure that the data in a range is numeric.

After clicking **OK**, you'll receive an error prompt if you try to enter any nonnumeric value in B2:B20. For example, if you type **John** in cell B3, you receive an error alert.

If you click Data Validation while working in cell B3, the formula shown in Figure 40-5 is displayed as =ISNUMBER(B3). This demonstrates that the formula entered in cell B2 is copied in the correct fashion. Entering **John** in cell B3 causes =ISNUMBER(B3) to return False, so you receive the error alert.

My assistant needs to enter state abbreviations when she enters dozens and dozens of sales transactions. Can we set up a list of state abbreviations to minimize the chance that she'll enter an incorrect abbreviation?

The key to this data validation problem is to use the List validation criteria. Begin by entering a list of state abbreviations. See the Statedv.xlsx file. In this example, use the I6:I55 range and name the range **abbrev**. Next, select the range in which you'll enter state abbreviations. (The example uses D5:D156.) After clicking **Data Validation** on the **Data** tab, fill in the **Data Validation** dialog box as shown in Figure 40-6.

Now, whenever you select a cell in the D5:D156 range, clicking the drop-down arrow displays a list of state abbreviations, as shown in Figure 40-7. Only abbreviations that appear on the list are valid values in this range. If you do not use the drop-down list and instead type a state abbreviation, you'll receive an error message if you enter an incorrect abbreviation (such as ALK for Alaska).

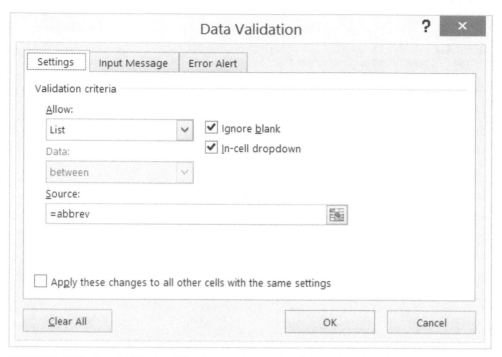

FIGURE 40-6 The Data Validation dialog box can be used to define a list of valid values.

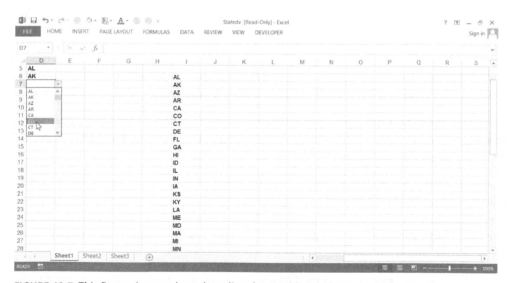

FIGURE 40-7 This figure shows a drop-down list of state abbreviations.

Remarks

Following is some more information you will find useful as you explore the abilities of Excel to help you solve problems and validate data:

- If you press F5, click **Special** in the **Go To** dialog box, and then select **Data Validation**, Excel selects all cells with data validation settings. You can also use the **Go To Special** dialog box to select all cells containing data validation.

- In versions of Excel prior to Excel 2010, if you wanted to use a data validation drop-down list based on a data source list in a different worksheet, you needed to name the list (as this chapter's example was) for the drop-down list to work. Since Excel 2010, this limitation has been removed.

- If you use the dynamic-range technique described in Chapter 21, "The *OFFSET* function," changes you make (adding or deleting items) to the data source list are automatically reflected in the drop-down list. (See Problem 10 in this chapter.) Also, if you name the data source list as an Excel table (see Chapter 25, "Tables"), changes in the data source are reflected in the drop-down list as long as you point to the list range and do not try to type the table name.

- Suppose you want to use a drop-down list to select a company you sell candy bars to. You want another drop-down list that you can use to select the list of candy bars you sell at the selected store. The problem is that the same set of candy bars might not be sold at each store. How do you create such a nested (often referred to as a cascading selection) list selection? Suppose the stores are Target and CVS; suppose you assign a range name of Target to the list of candy bars sold at Target and a range name of CVS to the list of candy bars sold at CVS. If the drop-down list for store selection is in, for example, A20, you could create the appropriate drop-down list in cell B20 by clicking **Data Validation** and filling in the =INDIRECT(A20) formula for the list selected. As discussed in Chapter 22, "The *INDIRECT* function," if A20 contains CVS, the list will key off the CVS range that contains all candy bars sold at CVS, and so on. See Problem 11 in this chapter.

- To clear data validation from a range, select the range, choose **Data Validation** on the **Data** tab, and then select **Clear All**.

- If you have a long list, you probably want to invoke the Excel AutoComplete feature. If you start the range for your drop-down list in the cell below the end of the list (no blank cells allowed), AutoComplete will work. See the Fruitlist.xlsx file.

- You can also use data validation to set up criteria based on the length of text in a cell (see Problem 4 in this chapter) or the time of day (see Problem 15, also in this chapter).

Problems

1. You are entering nonnegative whole numbers in the C1:C20 cell range. Enter a data validation setting that ensures that each entry is a nonnegative whole number.

2. You are entering the dates of transactions in the C1:C15 cell range that occurred during July 2004. Enter a data validation setting that ensures that each date entered occurs in July 2004.

3. With the List option in the group of data validation settings, you can generate an error message if a value that is not included in a list is entered in the cell range you're validating. Suppose you're entering employee first names in the A1:A10 cell range. The only employees of the company are Jen, Greg, Vivian, Jon, and John. Use the List option to ensure that no one misspells a first name.

4. With the Text Length option in the group of data validation settings, you can generate an error alert when the number of characters in a cell does not match the number you define. Use Text Length to ensure that each cell in the C1:C10 range will contain at most five characters (including blanks).

5. You are entering employee names in the A1:A10 cell range. Use data validation to ensure that no employee's name is entered more than twice. (Hint: Use the Custom setting and the *COUNTIF* function.)

6. You are entering product ID codes in the A1:A15 cell range. Product ID codes must always end with the characters xyz. Use data validation to ensure that each product ID code entered ends with xyz. (Hint: Use the Custom setting and the *RIGHT* function.)

7. Suppose you want every entry in the B2:B15 cell range to contain text and not a numerical value. Use data validation to ensure that entering a numerical value returns an error. (Hint: Use the *ISTEXT* function.)

8. Set up a data validation procedure that ensures that all numbers typed in column E will contain exactly two decimal places. (Hint: Use the *LEN* and *FIND* functions.)

9. The Latitude.xlsx file contains a formula to compute the distance between two cities, using their latitude and longitude. The file also contains the latitude and longitude of various US cities. Set up a drop-down list so that when you select a city in cell P2 and another city in cell Q2, the distance between the cities is computed in Q10.

10. Ensure that if new cities are added to the list of cities in Problem 9, the drop-down list will include the new cities.

11. The Candybardata.xlsx file contains a list of stores where you sell candy bars. The worksheet also contains the types of candy bars you sell at each store and the price charged for each candy bar. Set up your worksheet so that users can enter or select both the store and a candy bar from a drop-down list and have the price show up in D19:

   - Enable users to select a store from the drop-down list in B19.

   - Set up a drop-down list in C13 to let users choose a type of candy bar from a list containing only those candy bars sold at a selected store. (Hint: Use the *INDIRECT* function when defining the list.)

   - If you change the store in B19, C19 might temporarily not list a candy bar sold at the newly selected store. Ensure that in C19, your worksheet says Make Selection Above if this is the case. For example, if B19 says CVS and C13 says Gumballs, C19 should say Make Selection Above.

12. You have a $100,000 expense budget. In column A, you will enter expenses as they are incurred. Set up a data validation criterion that ensures that the total expenses listed in column E do not exceed your budget.

13. Set up a data validation criterion that ensures that a column of numbers is entered in descending order.

14. Set up data validation criteria that ensure that a person can only enter dates that are on Monday through Friday. (Hint: The *WEEKDAY* function returns a 1 for Sunday, a 2 for Monday, and so on.)

15. Set up data validation criteria that ensure that the time entered in the A1:A20 cell range will be a morning time.

CHAPTER 41

Summarizing data by using histograms

Questions answered in this chapter:

- People often say that a picture is worth a thousand words. Can I use Excel to create a picture (called a histogram) that summarizes the values in a data set?

- What are some common shapes of histograms?

- What can I learn by comparing histograms from different data sets?

The ability to summarize a large data set is important. The three tools used most often to summarize data in Microsoft Excel are *histograms*, *descriptive statistics*, and *PivotTables*. This chapter discusses the use of histograms for summarizing data. It covers descriptive statistics in Chapter 42, "Summarizing data by using descriptive statistics," and PivotTables in Chapter 43, "Using PivotTables and slicers to describe data."

Answers to this chapter's questions

This section provides the answers to the questions that are listed at the beginning of the chapter.

People often say that a picture is worth a thousand words. Can I use Excel to create a picture (called a histogram) that summarizes the values in a data set?

A histogram is a commonly used tool to summarize data. Essentially, a histogram tells you how many observations (another term for *data points*) fall in various ranges of values. For example, a histogram created from monthly Cisco stock returns might show how many monthly returns Cisco had from 0 percent through 10 percent, 11 percent through 20 percent, and so on. The ranges in which you group data are referred to as *bin ranges*.

Look at how to construct and interpret histograms that summarize the values of monthly returns for Cisco and GM stock in years 1990–2000. You'll find this data (and returns for other stocks) in the Stock.xlsx file. Figure 41-1 shows a subset of the data (in the Stockprices worksheet). During March 1990, for example, Cisco stock increased in value by 1.1 percent.

	A	B	C	D	E	F
48						
49				min	-0.240	-0.203
50				max	0.277	0.339
51	Date	Microsoft	GE	Intel	GM	CSCO
52	3/30/1990	0.122	0.040	0.037	0.022	0.011
53	4/30/1990	0.047	-0.004	-0.054	-0.035	0.011
54	5/31/1990	0.259	0.084	0.222	0.116	0.042
55	6/29/1990	0.041	0.005	-0.026	-0.021	0.071
56	7/31/1990	-0.125	0.034	-0.053	-0.021	-0.038
57	8/31/1990	-0.075	-0.134	-0.250	-0.131	-0.029
58	9/28/1990	0.024	-0.113	-0.004	-0.088	-0.091
59	10/31/1990	0.012	-0.046	0.008	0.014	0.311
60	11/30/1990	0.133	0.053	0.119	0.014	0.339
61	12/31/1990	0.042	0.057	0.027	-0.058	0.136
62	1/31/1991	0.304	0.115	0.188	0.055	0.304
63	2/28/1991	0.057	0.070	0.044	0.101	-0.043
64	3/28/1991	0.023	0.024	-0.021	-0.044	-0.129
65	4/30/1991	-0.067	0.016	0.053	-0.053	0.221
66	5/31/1991	0.109	0.099	0.132	0.217	0.084
67	6/28/1991	-0.069	-0.042	-0.166	-0.055	-0.054

FIGURE 41-1 This figure shows monthly stock returns.

When constructing histograms with Excel, you can let Excel define the bin ranges, or you can define the bin ranges yourself. If Excel defines the bin ranges, you could end up with weird-looking bin ranges, such as −12.53 percent to 4.52 percent. For this reason, you might prefer to define the ranges yourself.

A good way to start defining bin ranges for a histogram (you can think of defining bin ranges as setting boundaries) is to divide the range of values (between the smallest and largest) into 8 to 15 equally spaced categories. All the monthly returns for Cisco are from −30 percent through 40 percent, so choose bin range boundaries of −30 percent, −20 percent, −10 percent, 0 percent, and so on up to 40 percent.

To create bin ranges, enter CSCO, .4, .3, .2, ... , −.2, −.3 (the boundaries of the bin ranges) in cells H54:H62. Next, on the **Data** tab on the ribbon, in the **Analysis** group, click **Data Analysis** to open the **Data Analysis** dialog box; it lists the functions of the Analysis ToolPak, which contains many of the statistical capabilities in Excel.

Note If the Data Analysis command doesn't appear on the Data tab, click the **File** tab, choose **Options**, and then select **Add-Ins**. In the **Manage** box, click **Excel Add-Ins** and then click **Go**. In the **Add-Ins** dialog box, select **Analysis ToolPak** (the first choice, not Analysis ToolPak VBA) and then click **OK**. Now you can access the *Analysis ToolPak* functions by clicking **Data Analysis** in the **Analysis** group on the **Data** tab.

By clicking **Histogram** in the **Data Analysis** dialog box, you open the **Histogram** dialog box (with all inputs blank) shown in Figure 41-2.

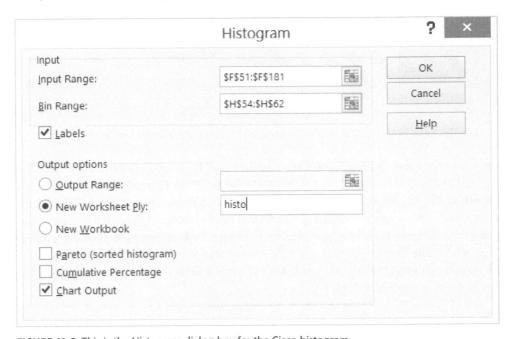

FIGURE 41-2 This is the Histogram dialog box for the Cisco histogram.

Here's how to fill in the dialog box as it's shown in Figure 41-2:

■ Select the input range (F51:F181). (To select the F51:F181 range, you can select cell F51 and then press Ctrl+Shift+down arrow. This takes you to the bottom of the column.) This range includes all the data you want to use to create the histogram. Include the CSCO label from cell F51 because when you do not include a label in the first row, the *x*-axis of the histogram is often labeled with a number, which can be confusing.

■ The bin range (H54:H62) includes the boundaries of the bin ranges. Excel creates bins of −30 percent through −20 percent, −20 percent through −10 percent, and so on up to 30–40 percent.

■ Select **Labels** because the first rows of both the bin range and the input range contain labels.

- Choose to create the histogram in a new worksheet (name it **histo**).

- Select **Chart Output**, or Excel will not create a histogram.

Click **OK** in the **Histogram** dialog box. The Cisco histogram will look like the one shown in Figure 41-3.

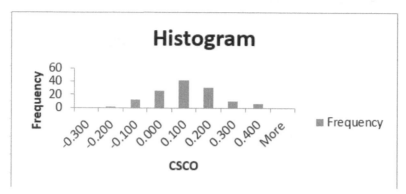

FIGURE 41-3 This Cisco histogram was created by using an Excel *Analysis ToolPak* function.

When you create the histogram, you'll see gaps between the bars. To remove these gaps, right-click any bar on the graph and choose **Format Data Series**. In the **Format Data Series** pane, drag **Gap Width** to 0%. You might also see that a label does not appear for each bar. If all the labels do not appear, select the graph and drag any handle that has two arrows to widen the graph. You can also reduce the font size to make a label appear. To reduce the font size, right-click the graph axis and then right-click **Font**. Change the font size to 5. You can also change the title of the chart by selecting the text and entering the title you want. After you make some of these changes, the histogram appears as it's shown in Figure 41-4.

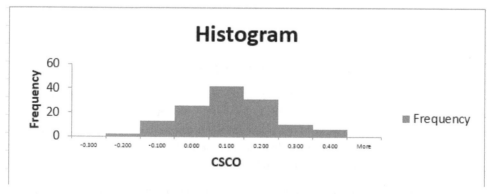

FIGURE 41-4 You can change the format of different elements in the chart.

Notice that Cisco returns are most likely between 0 and 10 percent per month, and the height of the bars drops off as the graph moves away from the tallest bar. When you create the histogram, you also obtain the bin-range frequency summary shown in Figure 41-5.

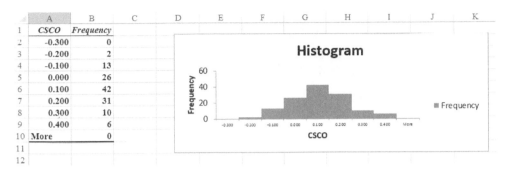

FIGURE 41-5 These are Cisco bin-range frequencies.

From the bin-range frequencies, you can learn, for example, that for two months, Cisco's return was greater than –30 percent and less than or equal to –20 percent; for 13 months, the monthly return was greater than –20 percent and less than or equal to –10 percent.

What are some common shapes of histograms?

For most data sets, a histogram created from the data will be classified as one of the following:

- Symmetric

- Skewed right (positively skewed)

- Skewed left (negatively skewed)

- Multiple peaks

The following list looks at each type in more detail. See the Skewexamples.xlsx file:

- **Symmetric distribution**   A histogram is symmetric if it has a single peak and looks approximately the same to the left of the peak as to the right of the peak. Test scores (such as IQ tests) are often symmetric. For example, the histograms of IQs (see cell W42) might look like Figure 41-6. Notice that the height of the bars one bar away from the peak bar are approximately the same, the height of the bars two bars away from the peak bar are approximately the same, and so on. The bar labeled 105 represents all people with an IQ greater than 95 and less than or equal to 105, the bar labeled 65 represents all people having an IQ less than or equal to 65, and so on. Also note that Cisco monthly returns are approximately symmetric.

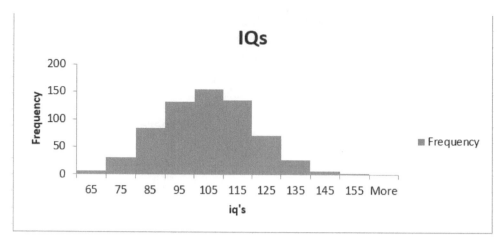

FIGURE 41-6 This is a symmetric histogram.

- **Skewed right (positively skewed)**   A histogram is skewed right (positively skewed) if it has a single peak and the values of the data set extend much farther to the right of the peak than to the left of the peak. Many economic data sets (such as family or individual income) exhibit a positive skew. Figure 41-7 (see cell T24) shows an example of a positively skewed histogram created from a sample of family incomes.

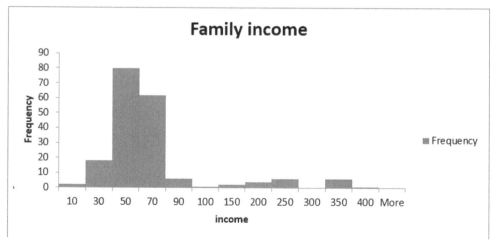

FIGURE 41-7 A positively skewed histogram was created from data about family income.

- **Skewed left (negatively skewed)**   A histogram is skewed left (negatively skewed) if it has a single peak and the values of the data set extend much farther to the left of the peak than to the right of the peak. Days from conception to birth are negatively skewed. An example is shown in cell Q7 of Figure 41-8. The height of each bar represents the number of women whose time from conception to birth fell in the given bin range. For example, two women gave birth fewer than 180 days after conception.

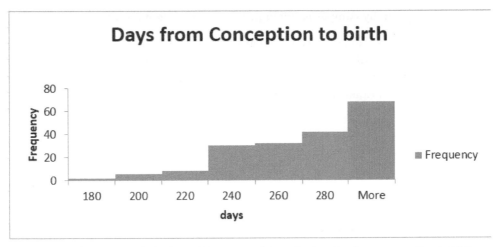

FIGURE 41-8 This is a negatively skewed histogram of data plotting days from conception to birth.

- **Multiple peaks** When a histogram exhibits multiple peaks, it usually means that data from two or more populations are being graphed together. For example, suppose the diameter of elevator rails produced by two machines yields the histogram shown in Figure 41-9. See cell Q11 of the Twinpeaks.xlsx file.

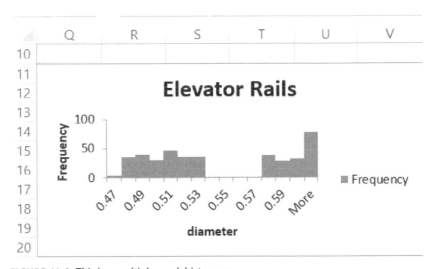

FIGURE 41-9 This is a multiple-peak histogram.

In this histogram, the data clusters into two groups. In all likelihood, each group of data corresponds to the elevator rails produced by one of the machines. If you assume that the diameter you want for an elevator rail is .55 inches, you can conclude that one machine is producing elevator rails that are too narrow, whereas the other machine is producing elevator rails that are too wide. You should follow up with your interpretation of this histogram by constructing a histogram charting the elevator rails produced by each machine. This example shows why histograms are a powerful tool in quality control.

What can I learn by comparing histograms from different data sets?

Analysts are often asked to compare different data sets. For example, you might be asked how the monthly returns on GM and Cisco stock differ. To answer a question such as this, you can construct a histogram for GM by using the same bin ranges as for Cisco and then place one histogram above the other, as shown in Figure 41-10. See the Histograms worksheet in the Stock.xlsx file.

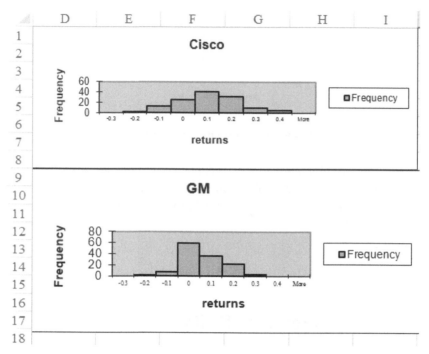

FIGURE 41-10 This figure shows the use of histograms that include the same bin ranges to compare different data sets.

By comparing these two histograms, you can draw two important conclusions:

- Typically, Cisco performed better than GM. You know this because the highest bar for Cisco is one bar to the right of the highest bar for GM. Also, the Cisco bars extend farther to the right than the GM bars.

- Cisco had more variability, or spread about the mean, than GM. Note that GM's peak bar contains 59 months, whereas Cisco's peak bar contains only 41 months. This shows that for Cisco, more of the returns are outside the bin that represents the most likely Cisco return. Cisco returns are more spread out than GM returns.

In Chapter 42, you look at more details about the differences between the monthly returns on Cisco and GM.

Problems

1. Use the data in Stock.xlsx to construct histograms for monthly returns for GE and Intel.

2. Use the data in Historicalinvest2009.xlsx to create histograms for annual returns on stocks and bonds. Then compare the annual returns on these stocks and bonds.

3. You are given (in the Deming.xlsx file) the measured diameter (in inches) for 500 rods produced by Rodco, as reported by the production foreman. A rod is considered acceptable if it is at least 1 inch in diameter. In the past, the diameter of the rods produced by Rodco has followed a symmetric histogram:

    *   Construct a histogram of these measurements.

    *   Comment on any unusual aspects of the histogram.

    Can you guess what might have caused any unusual aspects of the histogram? (Hint: One of quality-guru Edwards Deming's 14 points is to "Drive out fear.")

4. The Unemployment.xlsx file contains monthly US unemployment rates. Create a histogram. Are unemployment rates symmetric or skewed?

5. The Teams.xlsx file contains runs scored by Major League Baseball teams during a season. Create a histogram. Are runs scored symmetric or skewed?

6. The NFLpoints.xlsx file contains points scored by NFL teams during a season. Create a histogram. Are points scored symmetric or skewed?

CHAPTER 42

Summarizing data by using descriptive statistics

Questions answered in this chapter:

- What defines a typical value for a data set?

- How can I measure how much a data set spreads from its typical value?

- Together, what do the mean and standard deviation of a data set tell me about the data?

- How can I use descriptive statistics to compare data sets?

- For a given data point, can I easily find its percentile ranking within the data set? For example, how can I find the ninetieth percentile of a data set?

- How can I easily find the second largest or second smallest number in a data set?

- How can I rank numbers in a data set?

- What is the trimmed mean of a data set?

- When I select a range of cells, is there an easy way to get a variety of statistics that describe the data in those cells?

- Why do financial analysts often use the geometric mean to summarize the average return on a stock?

Chapter 41, "Summarizing data by using histograms," showed how you can describe data sets by using histograms. In this chapter, you see how to describe a data set by using particular characteristics of the data such as the mean, median, standard deviation, and variance—measures that Microsoft Excel 2013 groups as *descriptive statistics*. You can obtain the descriptive statistics for a set of data by clicking **Data Analysis** in the **Analysis** group on the **Data** tab and then selecting **Descriptive Statistics**. After you enter the relevant data and click **OK**, all the descriptive statistics of your data are displayed. If you do not see **Data Analysis** on the **Data** tab, install the **Data Analysis** add-in by following the instructions given in Chapter 41.

Answers to this chapter's questions

This section provides the answers to the questions that are listed at the beginning of the chapter.

What defines a typical value for a data set?

To illustrate the use of descriptive statistics, return to the Cisco and GM monthly stock return data in the Stock.xlsx file. To create a set of descriptive statistics for this data, click **Data Analysis** on the **Analysis** tab and then select **Descriptive Statistics**. Fill in the **Descriptive Statistics** dialog box as shown in Figure 42-1.

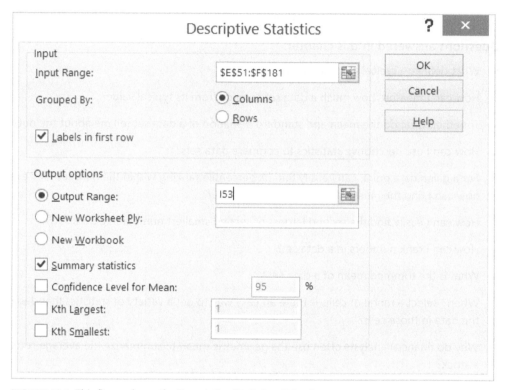

FIGURE 42-1 This figure shows the Descriptive Statistics dialog box.

The input range is the monthly Cisco and GM returns, located in the E51:F181 range (including the labels in row 51). The remainder of the Descriptive Statistics dialog box has been filled in as shown in Figure 42-1 for the following reasons:

- Columns was selected in the Grouped By options because each data set is listed in a different column.

- Labels In First Row was selected because the first row of the data range contains labels and not data.

- Cell I53 of the current worksheet was selected as the first cell in the output range.

- Summary Statistics was selected to ensure that the most commonly used descriptive statistics measures for both GM and Cisco monthly returns were displayed.

When you click OK, Excel calculates the descriptive statistics, as shown in Figure 42-2.

	I	J	K	L
53	*GM*		*CSCO*	
54				
55	Mean	0.009	Mean	0.056
56	Standard Error	0.008	Standard Error	0.011
57	Median	-0.005	Median	0.050
58	Mode	#N/A	Mode	0.051
59	Standard Deviation	0.090	Standard Deviation	0.122
60	Sample Variance	0.008	Sample Variance	0.015
61	Kurtosis	0.475	Kurtosis	-0.320
62	Skewness	0.224	Skewness	0.105
63	Range	0.517	Range	0.541
64	Minimum	-0.240	Minimum	-0.203
65	Maximum	0.277	Maximum	0.339
66	Sum	1.206	Sum	7.224
67	Count	130.000	Count	130.000

FIGURE 42-2 This figure shows the descriptive statistics results for Cisco and GM stocks.

Now, interpret the descriptive statistics that define a typical value (or a central location) for Cisco's monthly stock returns. The Descriptive Statistics output contains three measures of central location: mean (or average), median, and mode:

- **Mean** The mean of a data set is written as x and is simply the average of all observations in the sample. If the data values were $x_1, x_2, \ldots, x_n$ the following equation calculates the mean:

$$\bar{x} = \frac{1}{n} \sum_{i=1}^{i=n} x_i$$

Here, n equals the number of observations in the sample, and xi is the ith observation in the sample. You find that Cisco's mean monthly return is 5.6 percent per month.

It is always true that the sum of the deviations of all values from the mean equals 0. Thus, you can think of a data set's mean as a balancing point for the data. Of course, without using the Descriptive Statistics option, you can obtain a sample's mean in Excel by applying the *AVERAGE* function to the appropriate cell range.

- **Median**   The median of a sample is the middle observation when the data is listed from smallest to largest. If a sample contains an odd number of observations, the median is the observation that has as many observations below it as above it. Thus, for a sample of nine, the median would be the fifth smallest (or fifth largest) observation. When a sample includes an even number of observations, you can simply average the two middle observations. Essentially, the median is the fiftieth percentile of the data. For example, the median monthly return on Cisco is 5 percent. You could also obtain this information by using the *MEDIAN* function.

- **Mode**   The mode is the most frequently occurring value in the sample. If no value occurs more than once, the mode does not exist. For GM, no monthly return occurred more than once for years 1990–2000, so the mode does not exist. For Cisco, the mode was approximately 5.14 percent. In versions of Excel prior to Excel 2010, you could also use the *MODE* function to compute the mode. If no data value occurred more than once, the *MODE* function returned #NA.

The problem is that a data set can have more than one mode, and the *MODE* function simply returned the first mode it found. For this reason, Excel 2010 introduced two functions: *MODE. SNGL* and *MODE.MULT*. (See the file Modefunctions.xlsx.)

MODE.SNGL performs exactly as the *MODE* function performed in earlier Excel versions. Earlier versions of Excel, however, do not recognize the *MODE.SNGL* function.

MODE.MULT is an array function. You'll learn more about array functions in Chapter 87, "Array functions and formulas." To use the *MODE.MULT* function (or any other array function) you must first select the range of cells where the function will return values. Next, enter the function or formula. Finally, do not just press Enter; you must hold down the Ctrl key followed by the Shift key and then press Enter. The problem with the *MODE.MULT* function is that you do not know in advance how many modes a data set has, so you do not know the correct size of the range that you need to select.

The Modefunctions.xlsx file (see Figure 42-3) shows the use of all three functions involving modes.

	C	D	E	F	G
3		**3 and 5 are both modes**			
4					
5		3			
6		4			
7		5			
8		3			
9		2			
10		1			
11		5			
12					
13				3 =MODE(D5:D11)	
14	3 cells selected			3 =MODE.SNGL(d5:d11)	
15	Mode.Mult				
16	**3**			**3** Mode.Mult	
17	**5**			**5** two cells selected	
18	**#N/A**				
19			Mode.mult one cell selected		
20			**3**		

FIGURE 42-3 This figure shows examples of Excel *MODE* functions.

The mode is rarely used as a measure of central location. It is interesting to note, however, that for a symmetric data set, the mean, median, and mode are equal.

A natural question is whether the mean or median is a better measure of central location. Essentially, the mean is the best measure of central location if the data set does not exhibit an excessive skew. Otherwise, you should use the median as the measure of central location. If a data set is highly skewed, extreme values distort the mean. In this case, the median is a better measure of a typical data set value. For example, the US government reports median family income instead of mean family income because family income is highly positively skewed.

The skewness measure the Descriptive Statistics output reports indicates whether a data set is highly skewed:

- A skew greater than +1 indicates a high degree of positive skew.

- A skew less than –1 indicates a high degree of negative skew.

- A skew between –1 and +1, inclusive, indicates a relatively symmetric data set.

Thus, monthly returns of GM and Cisco exhibit a slight degree of positive skewness. Because the skewness measure for each data set is less than +1, the mean is a better measure of a typical return than the median. You can also use the *SKEW* function to compute the skew of a data set.

- **Kurtosis** Kurtosis, which sounds like a disease, is not a very important measure. Kurtosis near 0 means a data set exhibits peakedness close to the normal (or standard bell-shaped) curve. (The normal curve is discussed in Chapter 69, "The normal random variable.") Positive kurtosis means that a data set is more peaked than a normal random variable, whereas negative kurtosis means that data is less peaked than a normal random variable. GM monthly returns are more peaked than a normal curve, whereas Cisco monthly returns are less peaked than a normal curve.

How can I measure how much a data set spreads from its typical value?

Consider two investments that each yield an average of 20 percent per year. Before deciding which investment you prefer, you'd like to know about the spread, or riskiness, of the investment. The most important measures of the spread (or dispersion) of a data set from its mean are sample variance, sample standard deviation, and range.

- **Sample variance and sample standard deviation** The sample variance s^2 is defined by the following formula:

$$s^2 = \frac{1}{n-1} \sum_{i-1}^{i-n} (x_i - \overline{x})^2$$

You can think of the sample variance as the average squared deviation of the data from its mean. Intuitively, it seems that you should divide by n to compute a true average squared deviation, but for technical reasons, you need to divide by $n - 1$.

Dividing the sum of the squared deviations by $n - 1$ ensures that the sample variance is an unbiased measure of the true variance of the population from which the sampled data is drawn.

The sample standard deviation s is just the square root of s^2.

Here is an example of these computations for the three numbers 1, 3, and 5:

$$s^2 = \frac{1}{3-1} [(1-3)^2 + (3-3)^2 + (5-3)^2] = 4$$

You find that:

$$s = \sqrt{4} = 2$$

In the stock example, the sample standard deviation of monthly returns for Cisco is 12.2 percent with a sample variance of 0.015%^{2}. Naturally, %^{2} is hard to interpret, so you usually look at the sample standard deviation. For GM, the sample standard deviation is 8.97 percent.

In previous versions of Excel, the sample variance of a data set was computed with the *VAR* function, and the sample standard deviation was computed with the *STDEV* function. You can still use these functions in Excel 2010, but Excel 2010 has added the equivalent functions, *VAR.S* and *STDEV.S*. (The S stands for *sample*.) The new functions, *VAR.P* and *STDEV.P*, compute the population variance and population standard deviation. To compute a population variance or standard deviation, simply replace $n - 1$ in the denominator of the definition of s^2 by n.

- **Range** The range of a data set is the largest number in the data set minus the smallest number. Here, the range in the monthly Cisco returns is equal to 54 percent, and the range for GM monthly returns is 52 percent.

Together, what do the mean and standard deviation of a data set tell me about the data?

Assuming that a histogram can be described by a symmetric histogram, the rule of thumb says the following:

- Approximately 68 percent of all observations are between $x - s$ and $x + s$.

- Approximately 95 percent of all observations are between $x - 2s$ and $x + 2s$.

- Approximately 99.7 percent of all observations are between $x - 3s$ and $x + 3s$.

In Chapter 69, you will see that the 68 percent, 95 percent and 99.7 percent are derived from the Gaussian, or normal random variable.

For example, you would expect that approximately 95 percent of all Cisco monthly returns are from −19 percent through 30 percent, as shown here:

Mean − 2s = .056 − 2 × (.122) = −19% and Mean + 2s = .056 + 2 × (.122) = 30%

Any observation more than two standard deviations away from the mean is called an *outlier*. For the Cisco data, 9 of 130 observations (or roughly 7 percent of all returns) are outliers. In general, the rule of thumb is less accurate for highly skewed data sets but is usually very accurate for relatively symmetric data sets, even if the data does not come from a normal population.

Many valuable insights can be obtained by finding causes of outliers. Companies should try to ensure that the causes of good outliers occur more frequently and the causes of bad outliers occur less frequently.

Using conditional formatting to highlight outliers

You'll find that it is often useful to highlight all outliers in a data set. An example is shown in Figure 42-4. (See the Stockprices worksheet in the Stock.xlsx file.)

	C	D	E	F
49		min	-0.240	-0.203
50		max	0.277	0.339
51	GE	INTC	GM	CSCO
52	0.040485829	0.037	0.022	0.011
53	-0.003891051	-0.054	-0.035	0.011
54	0.083515622	0.222	0.116	0.042
55	0.005444646	-0.026	-0.021	0.071
56	0.034296028	-0.053	-0.021	-0.038
57	-0.13438046	-0.250	-0.131	-0.029
58	-0.113387093	-0.004	-0.088	-0.091
59	-0.04587156	0.008	0.014	0.311
60	0.052884616	0.119	0.014	0.339
61	0.057260275	0.027	-0.058	0.136
62	0.115468413	0.188	0.055	0.304
63	0.070468754	0.044	0.101	-0.043

FIGURE 42-4 Outliers for Cisco are highlighted with conditional formatting.

For example, to highlight the outliers for the Cisco data, you first compute the lower cutoff for an outlier (*mean* − 2*s*) in cell J69 and the upper cutoff for an outlier (*mean* + 2*s*) in cell J70. Next, select the entire range of Cisco returns (cells F52:F181). Then, at the first cell in the (F52) range, select **Conditional Formatting** on the **Home** tab and select **New Rule**. In the **Edit Formatting Rule** dialog box, select **Use A Formula To Determine Which Cells To Format** and then fill in the rest of the dialog box as shown in Figure 42-5.

This condition ensures that if cell F52 is more than 2*s* above or below the mean monthly Cisco return, the format you select (a red font color in this case) will be applied to cell F52. This formatting condition is automatically copied to the selected range, and all outliers show up in red.

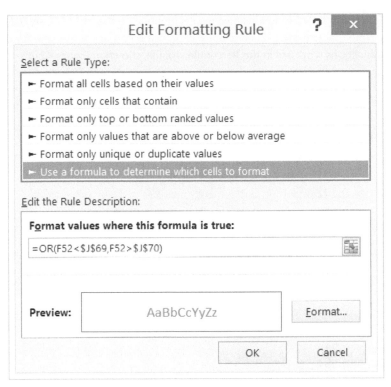

FIGURE 42-5 This figure shows the conditional formatting rules to select outliers, as shown in the Edit Formatting Rule dialog box.

How can I use descriptive statistics to compare data sets?

You can use descriptive statistics to summarize the differences between data sets, for example, between Cisco and GM monthly returns. Looking at the shape and the measures and spread of a typical value, you can conclude the following:

- Typically (looking at either the mean or the median), Cisco monthly returns are higher than GM.

- Cisco monthly returns are more variable (looking at standard deviation, variance, and range) than monthly GM returns.

- Both Cisco and GM monthly returns exhibit slightly positive skews. GM monthly returns are more peaked than a normal curve, whereas Cisco monthly returns are less peaked than a normal curve.

For a given data point, can I easily find its percentile ranking within the data set? For example, how can I find the ninetieth percentile of a data set?

Before Excel 2010, the *PERCENTILE* and *PERCENTRANK* functions were useful when you wanted to determine an observation's relative position in a data set. Four new related functions were added in Excel 2010: *PERCENTILE.INC*, *PERCENTILE.EXC*, *PERCENTRANK.INC*, and *PERCENTRANK.EXC*. The

PERCENTILE.INC and *PERCENTRANK.INC* functions give results identical to the old *PERCENTILE* and *PERCENTRANK* functions. Note that previous versions of Excel do not recognize these new functions. Examples of how all these functions work are in the Percentile.xlsx file, shown in Figure 42-6.

	C	D	E	F	G	H
2		RANK	RANK			
3	Data	EXC	INC			
4	10	0.062	0	Percentile	EXC	INC
5	20	0.125	0.071	0.1	16	24
6	30	0.187	0.142	0.2	32	38
7	40	0.25	0.214	0.3	48	52
8	50	0.312	0.285	0.4	64	66
9	60	0.375	0.357	0.5	80	80
10	70	0.437	0.428	0.6	96	94
11	80	0.5	0.5	0.7	112	108
12	90	0.562	0.571	0.8	128	122
13	100	0.625	0.642	0.9	204	136
14	110	0.687	0.714			
15	120	0.75	0.785			
16	130	0.812	0.857			
17	140	0.875	0.928			
18	300	0.937	1			

FIGURE 42-6 This figure shows examples of *PERCENTILE* and *PERCENTRANK* functions.

The *PERCENTILE*, *PERCENTILE.INC*, and *PERCENTILE.EXC* functions return the percentile of a data set that you specify. The syntax of these functions is of the PERCENTILE.INC(*data,k*) form, which returns the *k*th percentile of the information in the cell range specified by *data*.

Consider a data set consisting of *n* pieces of data. The old *PERCENTILE* and the new *PERCENTILE.INC* functions returned the *p*th percentile (0<p<1) as the $1 + (n - 1)p$ ranked item in the data set. For example, in H13, the PERCENTILE.INC(C4:C18,F13) formula computes the ninetieth percentile of the data in C4:C18 as $1 + (15 - 1).9$, which equals the 13.6 ranked item. That is, assuming the data is sorted in ascending order, Excel computes a number 60 percent of the way between the thirteenth data point (130) and the fourteenth data point (140). This yields 136.

The *PERCENTILE.EXC* function computes the *k*th percentile as the $(n + 1)p$ ranked item in the data set. *PERCENTILE.EXC* computes the ninetieth percentile of the data as $(15 + 1)(.9)$, which is the 14.4 ranked item. That is, the ninetieth percentile (assuming again data is sorted in ascending order) is computed to be 40 percent of the way between the fourteenth data point (140) and the fifteenth data point (300). This yields $(.60)(140) + (.40)(300) = 204$. You can see that the two functions return drastically different answers. If you consider the data to have been drawn by sampling from a large set of data, you might assume that given the data you've seen, there is much more than a 10 percent chance that a piece of data would be more than 136. After all, two of the 15 data points are more than 130, so it does not seem reasonable to say that the ninetieth percentile of the data is only 136. Therefore, saying the ninetieth percentile is 204 seems more reasonable. Using the *.EXC* function instead of the *.INC* function is strongly recommended. Note that the *.EXC* function does not compute a percentile for 0 and 1. The *.EXC* stands for the fact that the *PERCENTILE.EXC* function excludes the zero and one hundredth percentiles.

The *PERCENTRANK*, *PERCENTRANK.INC*, and *PERCENTRANK.EXC* functions return the ranking of an observation relative to all values in a data set. The syntax of the *PERCENTRANK.EXC* function, for example, is PERCENTRANK.EXC(*data,value*). The *PERCENTRANK* and *PERCENTRANK.INC* functions both calculate the percentile rank of the *k*th smallest number in the data set as $(k - 1)/(n-1)$. Thus, as shown in cell E4, the *PERCENTILE* or *PERCENTILE.INC* function yields a rank of 0 for 10 because $k = 1$ for this data point. The *PERCENTRANK.EXC* function computes the rank of the *k*th smallest data point as $k/(n + 1)$. In cell D4, the *PERCENTRANK.EXC* function returns a rank of $1/16 = .0625$. A percentile ranking of 6.25 percent seems more realistic than a ranking of 0 percent because there is little reason to think that a value of 10 is the smallest data point in a larger data set from which this data was sampled.

Note The *PERCENTILE* and *PERCENTRANK* functions are easily confused. To simplify, *PERCENTILE* yields a value of the data, whereas *PERCENTRANK* yields a percentage.

How can I easily find the second largest or second smallest number in a data set?

The =LARGE(range,k) formula returns the *k*th largest number in a cell range. The =SMALL(range,k) formula returns the *k*th smallest number in a cell range. For example, in the Trimmean.xlsx file, in cell F1, the =LARGE(C4:C62,2) formula returns the second largest number in the C4:C62 (99) cell range, whereas in cell F2, the =SMALL(C4:C62,2) formula returns the second smallest number in the C4:C62 (80) cell range. (See Figure 42-7.)

	C	D	E	F	G	H
1					2nd highest score	99
2					2nd lowest score	80
3	Scores	Rank(ties)	Average Rank		10% trimmed mean	90.04
4	93	20	21.5		5% trimmed mean	90.02
5	84	48	49			
6	88	38	39			
7	100	1	1			
8	86	45	45.5			
9	86	45	45.5		93 is 20th-23rd	
10	95	12	14		94 17th-19th	
11	92	24	24.5			
12	88	38	39			
13	94	17	18			
14	97	5	6.5			
15	91	26	27			
16	92	24	24.5			
17	95	12	14			
18	93	20	21.5			
19	80	56	57.5			

FIGURE 42-7 This figure shows examples of the *LARGE* and *SMALL* functions, the *RANK* and *RANK.AVG* functions, and trimmed mean.

How can I rank numbers in a data set?

In previous versions of Excel, you used the *RANK* function to rank numbers in a data set. The syntax of the *RANK* function is RANK(*number,array,*0). Excel 2010 introduced a function, *RANK.EQ*, that returns results identical to the *RANK* function. This formula yields the rank of a number in a given array, where the largest number in the array is assigned rank *1*, the second largest number is rank *2*, and so on. The RANK(*number,array,*1) or RANK.EQ(*number,array,*1) syntax results in assigning a rank of *1* to the smallest number in the array, a rank of *2* to the second smallest number, and so on. In the Trimmean.xlsx file (see Figure 42-7), copying the RANK.EQ(C4,$C$4,$C$62,0) formula from cell D4 to D5:D62 returns the rank of each test score. For example, the score of 100 in cell C7 is the highest score, whereas the scores of 98 in cells C21 and C22 tied for third highest. Note that the *RANK* function returned a 3 for both scores of 98.

The Excel *RANK.AVG* function has the same syntax as the other *RANK* functions, but in the case of ties, *RANK.AVG* returns the average rank for all tied data points. For example, because the two scores of 98 ranked third and fourth, *RANK.AVG* returns 3.5 for each. The average ranks were generated by copying the RANK.AVG(C4,$C$4:$C$62,0) formula from E4 to E5:E62.

What is the trimmed mean of a data set?

Extreme skewness in a data set can distort the mean of the data set. In these situations, people usually use median as a measure of the data set's typical value. The median, however, is unaffected by many changes in the data. For example, compare the following two data sets:

Set 1: –5, –3, 0, 1, 3, 5, 7, 9, 11, 13, 15

Set 2: –20, –18, –15, –10, –8, 5, 6, 7, 8, 9, 10

These data sets have the same median (5), but the second data set should have a lower typical value than the first. The Excel *TRIMMEAN* function is less distorted by extreme values than the *AVERAGE* function, but it is more influenced by extreme values than the median. The =TRIMMEAN(range,percent) formula computes the mean of a data set after deleting the data points at the top percent divided by 2 and bottom percent divided by 2. Before Excel determines the number of data points to remove, it rounds down the number of excluded points to the nearest multiple of 2. For example, applying the *TRIMMEAN* function with percent=10% converts the mean after deleting the top 5 percent and bottom 5 percent of the data. In cell F3 of the Trimmean.xlsx file, the =TRIMMEAN(C4:C62,.10) formula computes the mean of the scores in C4:C62 after deleting the two highest and two lowest scores. Four observations are deleted because 0.1*59 = 5.9 rounds down to four. (The result is 90.04.) In cell F4, the =TRIMMEAN(C4:C62,.05) formula computes (90.02) the mean of the scores in C4:C62 after deleting the top and bottom scores. Two observations are removed because 0.05*59 = 2.95 rounds down to two. (See Figure 42-7.)

When I select a range of cells, is there an easy way to get a variety of statistics that describes the data in those cells?

To see the solution to this question, select the C4:C36 cell range in the Trimmean.xlsx file. In the lower-right corner of your screen, the Excel status bar displays a cornucopia of statistics describing the numbers in the selected cell range. (See Figure 42-8.) For example, for the C4:C36 cell range, the mean is 90.39, there are 33 numbers, the smallest value is 80, and the largest value is 100. If you right-click the status bar, you can change the displayed set of statistics.

AVERAGE: 90.39393939   COUNT: 33   SUM: 2983

FIGURE 42-8 This figure shows the statistics on the status bar.

Why do financial analysts often use the geometric mean to summarize the average return on a stock?

The Geommean.xlsx file contains the annual returns of two fictitious stocks. (See Figure 42-9.)

Cell C9 indicates that the average annual return on Stock 1 is 5 percent, and the average annual return on Stock 2 is 10 percent. This would seem to indicate that Stock 2 is a better investment. If you think about it, however, what will probably happen with Stock 2 is that one year you will lose 50 percent and the next gain 70 percent. This means that every two years, $1.00 becomes 1(1.7)(.5) = .85. Because Stock 1 never loses money, you know that it is clearly the better investment. Using the geometric mean as a measure of average annual return helps to conclude correctly that Stock 1 is the better investment. The geometric mean of n numbers is simply the nth root of the product of the numbers. For example, the geometric mean of 1 and 4 is the square root of 4 (2), whereas the geometric mean of 1, 2, and 4 is the cube root of 8 (also 2). To use the geometric mean to calculate an average annual return on an investment, you add 1 to each annual return and take the geometric mean of the resulting numbers. Then subtract 1 from this result to obtain an estimate of the stock's average annual return.

	B	C	D
1			
2			
3			
4		**Stock 1**	**Stock 2**
5	**Year 1**	0.05	-0.5
6	**Year 2**	0.05	0.7
7	**Year 3**	0.05	-0.5
8	**Year 4**	0.05	0.7
9	**Average**	0.05	0.1
10			
11		**1+return**	
12		1.05	0.5
13		1.05	1.7
14		1.05	0.5
15		1.05	1.7
16	**geometric means**	0.05	-0.07805

FIGURE 42-9 This figure shows the geometric mean.

The =GEOMMEAN(range) formula finds the geometric mean of numbers in a range. So, to estimate the average annual return on each stock, you proceed as follows:

1. Compute 1 + each annual return by copying the =1+C5 formula from C12 to C12:D15.

2. Copy the =GEOMEAN(C12:C15)–1 formula from C16 to D16.

The annual average return on Stock 1 is estimated to be 5 percent, and the annual average return on Stock 2 is –7.8 percent. Note that if Stock 2 yields the mean return of –7.8 percent during two consecutive years, $1 becomes 1(1 –.078)2 = .85, which agrees with common sense.

Problems

1. Use the data in the Stock.xlsx file to generate descriptive statistics for Intel and GE stock.

2. Use your answer to Problem 1 to compare the monthly returns on Intel and GE stock.

3. City Power & Light produces voltage-regulating equipment in New York and ships the equipment to Chicago. A voltage regulator is considered acceptable if it can hold a voltage of 25 to 75 volts. The voltage held by each unit is measured in New York before each unit is shipped. The voltage is measured again when the unit arrives in Chicago. A sample of voltage measurements from each city is given in the Citypower.xlsx file:

- Using descriptive statistics, comment on what you have learned about the voltage units hold before and after shipment.

- What percentage of units is acceptable before and after shipping?

- Do you have any suggestions about how to improve the quality of City Power & Light's regulators?

- Ten percent of all New York regulators have a voltage exceeding what value?

- Five percent of all New York regulators have a voltage less than or equal to what value?

4. In the Decadeincome.xlsx file, you are given a sample of incomes (in thousands of 1980 dollars) for a set of families sampled in 1980 and 1990. Assume that these families are representative of the whole United States. Republicans claim that the country was better off in 1990 than in 1980 because average income increased. Do you agree?

5. Use descriptive statistics to compare the annual returns on stocks, T-bills, and corporate bonds. Use the data contained in the Historicalinvest.xlsx file.

6. In 1970 and 1971, eligibility for the US armed services draft was determined on the basis of a draft lottery number. The number was determined by birth date. A total of 366 balls, one for each possible birth date, were placed in a container and shaken. The first ball selected was given the number 1 in the lottery, the second ball the number 2, and so on. Men whose birthdays corresponded to the lowest numbers were drafted first. The Draftlottery.xlsx file contains the actual results of the 1970 and 1971 drawings. For example, in the 1970 drawing, January 1 received the number 305. Use descriptive statistics to demonstrate that the 1970 draft lottery was not random and the 1971 lottery was random. (Hint: Use the *AVERAGE* and *MEDIAN* functions to compute the mean and median lottery number for each month.)

7. The Jordan.xlsx file gives the starting salaries (hypothetical) of all 1984 geography graduates from the University of North Carolina (UNC). What is your best estimate of a typical starting salary for a geography major? In reality, the major at UNC having the highest average starting salary in 1984 was geography because the great basketball player Michael Jordan was a geography major!

8. Use the *LARGE* or *SMALL* function to sort the annual stock returns in the Historicalinvest.xlsx file. What advantage does this method of sorting have over clicking the Sort button?

9. Compare the mean, median, and trimmed mean (trimming 10 percent of the data) of the annual returns on stocks, T-bills, and corporate bonds given in the Historicalinvest.xlsx file.

10. Use the geometric mean to estimate the mean annual return on stocks, bonds, and T bills in the Historicalinvest.xlsx file.

11. The Dow.xlsx file contains monthly returns on the 30 Dow stocks during the past 20 years. Use this data to determine the three stocks with the largest mean monthly returns.

12. Using the Dow.xlsx data again, determine the three stocks with the most risk or variability.

13. Using the Dow.xlsx data, determine the three stocks with the highest skew.

14. Using the Dow.xlsx data, how do the trimmed-mean returns (trim off 10 percent of the returns) differ from the overall mean returns?

15. The Incomedata.xlsx file contains incomes of a representative sample of Americans in years 1975, 1985, 1995, and 2005. Describe how US personal income has changed over this time period.

16. The Coltsdata.xlsx file contains yards gained by the 2006 Indianapolis Colts on each rushing and passing play. Describe how the outcomes of rushing plays and passing plays differ.

CHAPTER 43

Using PivotTables and slicers to describe data

Questions answered in this chapter:

- What is a PivotTable?

- How can I use a PivotTable to summarize grocery sales at several grocery stores?

- What PivotTable layouts are available in Excel 2013?

- Why is a PivotTable called a PivotTable?

- How can I easily change the format in a PivotTable?

- How can I collapse and expand fields?

- How can I sort and filter PivotTable fields?

- How can I summarize a PivotTable by using a PivotChart?

- How can I use the Report Filter section of the PivotTable?

- How do PivotTable slicers work?

- How can I add blank rows or hide subtotals in a PivotTable?

- How can I apply conditional formatting to a PivotTable?

- How can I update my calculations when I add new data?

- I work for a small travel agency for which I need to mass-mail a travel brochure. My funds are limited, so I want to mail the brochure to people who spend the most money on travel. From information in a random sample of 925 people, I know the gender, the age, and the amount these people spent on travel last year. How can I use this data to determine how gender and age influence a person's travel expenditures? What can I conclude about the type of person to whom I should mail the brochure?

- I'm doing market research about station wagons. I need to determine what factors influence the likelihood that a family will purchase a station wagon. From information in a large sample of families, I know the family size (large or small) and the family income (high or low). How can I determine how family size and income influence the likelihood that a family will purchase a station wagon?

- I work for a manufacturer that sells microchips globally. I'm given monthly actual and predicted sales for Canada, France, and the United States for Chip 1, Chip 2, and Chip 3. I'm also given the variance, or difference, between actual and budgeted revenues. For each month and each combination of country and product, I'd like to display the following data: actual revenue, budgeted revenue, actual variance, actual revenue as a percentage of annual revenue, and variance as a percentage of budgeted revenue. How can I display this information?

- What is a calculated field?

- How can I use a report filter or slicer?

- How can I group items in a PivotTable?

- What is a calculated item?

- What is "drilling down"?

- I often have to use specific data in a PivotTable to determine profit, such as the April sales in France of Chip 1. Unfortunately, this data moves around when new fields are added to my PivotTable. Does Excel have a function that enables me always to extract April's Chip 1 sales in France from the PivotTable?

- How can I use the New Excel 2013 Timeline feature to summarize data during different time periods?

- How can I use a PivotTable to summarize total sales to date during a year?

- How can I use a PivotTable to summarize sales this month compared to the same month a year earlier?

- How can I create a PivotTable based on data in several locations?

- How can I create a PivotTable based on an already created PivotTable?

Answers to this chapter's questions

This section provides the answers to the questions that are listed at the beginning of the chapter.

What is a PivotTable?

In numerous business situations, you need to analyze, or slice and dice, your data to gain important insights. Imagine that you sell different grocery products in different stores at different points in time. You might have hundreds of thousands of data points to track. PivotTables enable you to summarize your data quickly in almost any way imaginable. For example, for your grocery store data, you could use a PivotTable to determine the following quickly:

- Amount spent per year in each store on each product

- Total spending at each store

- Total spending for each year

In a travel agency, as another example, you might slice data so that you can determine whether the average amount spent on travel is influenced by age or gender or by both factors. In analyzing automobile purchases, you'd like to compare the fraction of large families that buy a station wagon to the fraction of small families that purchase a station wagon. For a microchip manufacturer, you'd like to determine total Chip 1 sales in France, for example, during April, and so on. A PivotTable is an incredibly powerful tool that you can use to slice and dice data. The easiest way to understand how a PivotTable works is to walk through some carefully constructed examples, so get started! Begin with an introductory example and then explore many advanced PivotTable features through subsequent examples.

How can I use a PivotTable to summarize grocery sales at several grocery stores?

The Data worksheet in the Groceriespt.xlsx file contains more than 900 rows of sales data. (See Figure 43 1.) Each row contains the number of units sold and revenue of a product at a store as well as the month and year of the sale. The product group (fruit, milk, cereal, or ice cream) is also included. You would like to see a breakdown of sales during each year of each product group and product at each store. You would also like to be able to show this breakdown during any subset of months in a given year (for example, what the sales were from January through June).

	A	B	C	D	E	F	G
1	Year	Month	Store	Group	Product	Units	Revenue
2	2007	August	south	milk	low fat	805	$3,187.80
3	2007	March	south	ice cream	Edies	992	$3,412.48
4	2007	January	east	milk	skim	712	$1,808.48
5	2006	March	north	ice cream	Edies	904	$2,260.00
6	2006	January	south	ice cream	Edies	647	$2,076.87
7	2005	September	west	fruit	plums	739	$1,707.09
8	2006	March	east	milk	low fat	974	$2,181.76
9	2007	June	north	fruit	apples	615	$1,894.20
10	2007	July	west	fruit	cherries	714	$1,856.40
11	2006	May	south	cereal	Special K	703	$1,553.63
12	2005	June	west	ice cream	Edies	528	$2,064.48
13	2006	October	east	cereal	Raisin Bran	644	$1,809.64
14	2005	June	south	fruit	grapes	919	$2,196.41
15	2007	May	west	milk	skim	767	$1,932.84
16	2007	June	west	cereal	Raisin Bran	984	$1,987.68
17	2005	March	south	cereal	Raisin Bran	744	$2,217.12
18	2007	September	east	ice cream	Edies	693	$2,189.88
19	2006	October	east	milk	chocolate	658	$1,895.04
20	2005	November	east	ice cream	Breyers	878	$3,274.94
21	2005	May	south	ice cream	Breyers	848	$3,281.76
22	2007	August	south	milk	low fat	547	$1,247.16

FIGURE 43-1 This is the data for the grocery PivotTable example.

Before creating a PivotTable, you must have headings in the first row of your data. Notice that the grocery data contains headings (Year, Month, Store, Group, Product, Units, and Revenue) in row 2. Place your cursor anywhere in the data and then click **PivotTable** in the **Tables** group on the **Insert** tab. Excel opens the **Create PivotTable** dialog box, shown in Figure 43-2, and makes an assumption about your data range. (In this case, Excel correctly guessed that the data range was A1:G923.) By selecting **Use An External Data Source**, you can also refer to a database as a source for a PivotTable. **Data Model**, new in Excel 2013, is discussed in Chapter 44, "The Data Model."

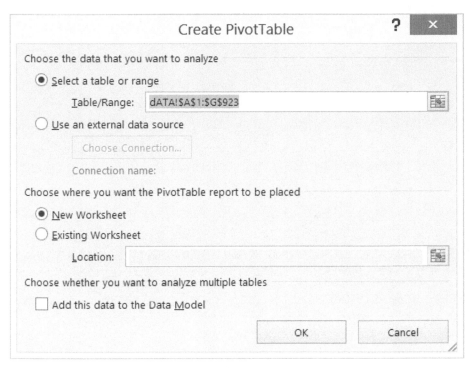

FIGURE 43-2 This is the Create PivotTable dialog box.

After you click **OK**, you see the **PivotTable Fields** list shown in Figure 43-3.

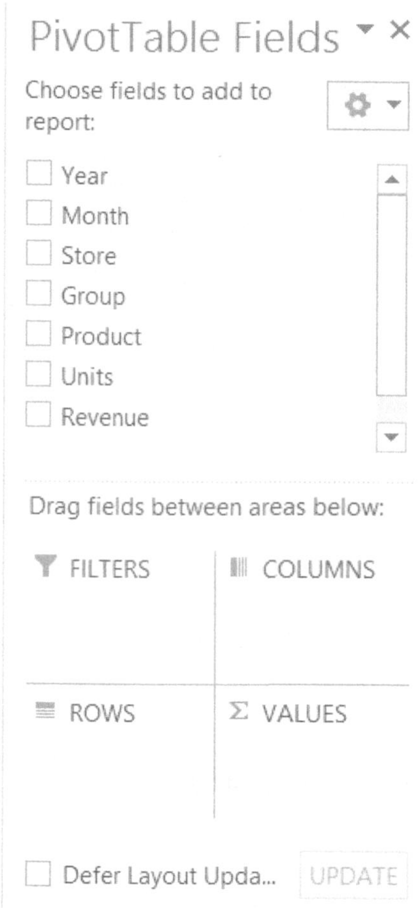

PivotTable Fields ▾ ✕

Choose fields to add to report:

⚙ ▾

☐ Year
☐ Month
☐ Store
☐ Group
☐ Product
☐ Units
☐ Revenue

Drag fields between areas below:

▼ FILTERS   ▥ COLUMNS

☰ ROWS   Σ VALUES

☐ Defer Layout Upda...   UPDATE

FIGURE 43-3 This is the PivotTable Fields list.

You fill in the PivotTable Field list by dragging PivotTable headings, or *fields*, into the boxes, or *zones*. This step is critical to ensuring that the PivotTable summarizes and displays the data in the manner you want. The four zones are as follows:

- **Row Labels**   Fields dragged here are listed on the left side of the table in the order in which they are added to the box. For example, you can drag the Year, Group, Product, and Store fields, in that order, to the **Row Labels** box. This causes Excel to summarize data first by year, then for each product group within a given year, then by product within each group, and, finally, each product by store. At any time, you can drag a field to a different zone or reorder the fields within a zone by dragging a field up or down in a zone or by clicking the arrow to the right of the field label.

- **Column Labels**   Fields dragged here have their values listed across the top row of the PivotTable. To start out this example, you have no fields in the Column Labels zone.

- **Values** Fields dragged here are summarized mathematically in the table. Units and Revenue (in that order) have been dragged to this zone. Excel tries to guess what kind of calculation you want to perform on a field. In this example, Excel guesses that Revenue and Units should be summed, which happens to be correct. If you want to change the method of calculation for a data field to an average, a count, or something else, click the data field and choose **Value Field Settings**. An example of how to use the Value Field Settings command is given later in the chapter. If you select a numeric field from the field list, the field is automatically added to the Values zone and aggregated by using Sum. If you select a nonnumeric field from the field list, the field is automatically placed in the Rows zone.

- **Report Filter** Beginning in Excel 2007, *Report Filter* is the new name for the old Page Field area. For fields dragged to the Report Filter area, you can easily pick any subset of the field values so that the PivotTable shows calculations based only on that subset. In this example, Month was dragged to the Report Filter area. You can easily select any subset of months, for example January to June, and the calculations are based on only those months.

The completed PivotTable Fields is shown in Figure 43-4. The resulting PivotTable is shown in Figure 43-5 and in the All Row Fields worksheet of the Groceriespt.xlsx workbook. In row 5, you can see that 243,228 units were sold for $728,218.68 in 2005.

Tip Here is some advice about navigating between worksheets:

- Control+PageUp key sequence moves you back one worksheet.
- Control+PageDn key sequence moves you forward one worksheet.
- Right-clicking either of the arrows to the left of the first worksheet name brings up a list of worksheet names from which you can move to any worksheet in the workbook.

Note To see the field list, you need to be in a field in the PivotTable. If you do not see the field list, right-click any cell in the PivotTable and select **Show Field List**.

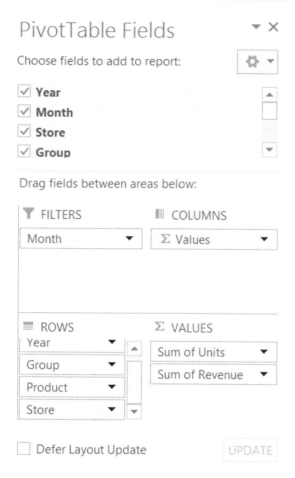

FIGURE 43-4 This is the completed PivotTable Fields list.

	A	B	C
1	Month	(All)	
2			
3		**Values**	
4	**Row Labels**	**Sum of Units**	**Sum of Revenue**
5	⊟ **2005**	**243228**	**728218.68**
6	⊟ **cereal**	**63689**	**192172.93**
7	⊟ Cheerios	11163	32993.1
8	east	1645	5055.8
9	north	1639	4988
10	south	3265	9216.47
11	west	4614	13732.83
12	⊟ Raisin Bran	35797	105793.04
13	east	6226	19500.19
14	north	8458	22822.23
15	south	8989	26069.35
16	west	12124	37401.27
17	⊟ Special K	16729	53386.79
18	east	2289	5998.21
19	north	4172	14956.36
20	south	3366	11339.47
21	west	6902	21092.75
22	⊟ **fruit**	**60047**	**182813.88**
23	⊟ apples	14535	48127.74

FIGURE 43-5 This is the grocery PivotTable in compact form.

What PivotTable layouts are available?

The PivotTable layout shown in Figure 43-5 is called the *compact form*. In the compact form, the row fields are shown one on top of another. To change the layout, first place your cursor anywhere within the table. On the **Design** tab, in the **Layout Group**, click **Report Layout** and choose one of the following: **Show In Compact Form** (see Figure 43-5), **Show In Outline Form** (see Figure 43-6 and the Outline Form worksheet), or **Show In Tabular Form** (Figure 43-7 and the Tabular Form worksheet).

	A	B	C	D	E	F
1	Month	(All)	▾			
2						
3					**Values**	
4	Year ▾	Group ▾	Product ▾	Store ▾	Sum of Units	Sum of Revenue
5		⊟ 2005			**243228**	**728218.68**
6			⊟ cereal		**63689**	**192172.93**
7				⊟ Cheerios	11163	32993.1
8				east	1645	5055.8
9				north	1639	4988
10				south	3265	9216.47
11				west	4614	13732.83
12				⊟ Raisin Bran	35797	105793.04
13				east	6226	19500.19
14				north	8458	22822.23
15				south	8989	26069.35
16				west	12124	37401.27
17				⊟ Special K	16729	53386.79
18				east	2289	5998.21
19				north	4172	14956.36
20				south	3366	11339.47
21				west	6902	21092.75
22			⊟ fruit		**60047**	**182813.88**

FIGURE 43-6 This is the outline form.

	A	B	C	D	E	F
1	Month	(All)	▾			
2						
3					**Values**	
4	Year ▾	Group ▾	Product ▾	Store ▾	Sum of Units	Sum of Revenue
5		⊟ 2005	⊟ cereal	⊟ Cheerios	east	1645	5055.8
6					north	1639	4988
7					south	3265	9216.47
8					west	4614	13732.83
9				Cheerios Total		11163	32993.1
10				⊟ Raisin Bran	east	6226	19500.19
11					north	8458	22822.23
12					south	8989	26069.35
13					west	12124	37401.27
14				Raisin Bran Total		35797	105793.04
15				⊟ Special K	east	2289	5998.21
16					north	4172	14956.36
17					south	3366	11339.47
18					west	6902	21092.75
19				Special K Total		16729	53386.79
20			cereal Total			63689	192172.93
21			⊟ fruit	⊟ apples	east	1229	3972.44

FIGURE 43-7 This is the tabular form.

Why is a PivotTable called a PivotTable?

You can easily pivot fields from a row to a column and vice versa to create a different layout. For example, by dragging the **Year** field to the **Column Labels** box, you create the PivotTable layout shown in Figure 43-8. (See the Years Column worksheet.)

	A	B	C	D	E	F	G	H	I
1	Month	(All)							
2									
3		Column Labels							
4		Sum of Units			Sum of Revenue			Total Sum of Units	Total Sum of Revenue
5	Row Labels	2005	2006	2007	2005	2006	2007		
6	⊟cereal	63689	52489	58671	192172.93	150710	172828.96	174849	515711.89
7	⊟Cheerios	11163	16142	13652	32993.1	46657.49	38617.12	40957	118267.71
8	east	1645	5237	4795	5055.8	13311.86	13938.21	11677	32305.87
9	north	1639	3027	4207	4988	10199.31	11409.85	8873	26597.16
10	south	3265	6424	3064	9216.47	18450.16	8635.3	12753	36301.93
11	west	4614	1454	1586	13732.83	4696.16	4633.76	7654	23062.75
12	⊟Raisin Bran	35797	24056	27715	105793.04	69391.29	81254.09	87568	256438.42
13	east	6226	6021	3905	19500.19	15550.29	12574.91	16152	47625.39
14	north	8458	7505	8366	22822.23	23099.35	25008.01	24329	70929.59
15	south	8989	6015	5329	26069.35	16593.97	16632.9	20333	59296.22
16	west	12124	4515	10115	37401.27	14147.68	27038.27	26754	78587.22
17	⊟Special K	16729	12291	17304	53386.79	34661.22	52957.75	46324	141005.76
18	east	2289	3700	5361	5998.21	9154.5	15712.79	11350	30865.5
19	north	4172	2570	3789	14956.36	8665.32	12736.82	10531	36358.5
20	south	3366	3436	5826	11339.47	9125.62	17647.74	12628	38112.83
21	west	6902	2585	2328	21092.75	7715.78	6860.4	11815	35668.93
22	⊟fruit	60047	53910	61816	182813.88	157192.37	189616.27	175773	529622.52

FIGURE 43-8 The Years field is pivoted to the column field.

How can I easily change the format in a PivotTable?

If you want to change the format of an entire column field, double-click the column heading and click **Number Format** in the **Value Field Settings** dialog box. Apply the format you want. For example, in the Formatted $s worksheet, the Revenue field is formatted as currency by double-clicking the Sum Of Revenue heading and applying a currency format. You can also change the format of a value field by clicking the arrow to the right of the **Value** field in **PivotTable Fields**. Select **Value Field Settings** followed by **Number Format**, and then you can reformat the column as you want it.

From any cell in a PivotTable, you can select the **Design** tab on the ribbon to reveal many PivotTable styles.

How can I collapse and expand fields?

Expanding and collapsing fields (a feature introduced in Excel 2007) is a great advantage in PivotTables. In Figure 43-5, you see minus (−) signs by each year, group, and product. Clicking the minus sign collapses a field and changes the sign to a plus (+) sign. Clicking the plus sign expands the field. For example, if you click the minus sign by cereal in any cell in column A, you find that in each year, cereal is contracted to one row, and the various cereal stores are no longer listed. See Figure 43-9 and the Cerealcollapse worksheet. Clicking the plus sign in cell A6 brings back the detailed or expanded view listing sales for each individual cereal.

	A	B	C
1	Month	(All)	
2			
3		**Values**	
4	**Row Labels**	**Sum of Units**	**Sum of Revenue**
5	⊟ 2005	243228	728218.68
6	⊞ cereal	63689	192172.93
7	⊟ fruit	60047	182813.88
8	⊟ apples	14535	48127.74
9	east	1229	3972.44
10	north	3734	13631.83
11	south	4317	14763.88
12	west	5255	15759.59
13	⊟ cherries	11083	32042.39
14	east	1646	4051.22
15	north	3701	11087.14
16	south	3277	9092.92
17	west	2459	7811.11
18	⊟ grapes	20005	60126.15
19	east	4811	13052.68
20	north	4865	14698.63
21	south	6268	20474.65
22	west	4061	11900.19
23	⊟ plums	14424	42517.6
24	east	2216	7497.52
25	north	1515	5055.55

FIGURE 43-9 The cereal item is collapsed.

You can also expand or contract an entire field. Go to any row containing a member of that field and select **PivotTable Tools Analyze** on the ribbon. In the **Active Field** group, click either the green **Expand Field** button (labeled with a plus sign) or the red **Contract Field** button (labeled with a minus sign). (See Figure 43-10.)

FIGURE 43-10 This shows the Expand Field and Collapse Field button.

For example, suppose you simply want to see only the sales by product group for each year. Pick any cell containing a group's name (for example, A6), select **PivotTable Tools Options** on the ribbon, and click the **Collapse Field** button. You see the result shown in Figure 43-11 (the Groups Collapsed worksheet). Selecting the **Expand Field** button brings you back to the original view.

	A	B	C	D
1	Month	(All) ▼		
2				
3		**Values**		
4	Row Labels ▼	Sum of Units	Sum of Revenue	
5	⊟2005	243228	728218.68	
6	⊞cereal	63689	192172.93	
7	⊞fruit	60047	182813.88	
8	⊞ice cream	56518	174378.59	
9	⊞milk	62974	178853.28	
10	⊟2006	216738	637719.85	
11	⊞cereal	52489	150710	
12	⊞fruit	53910	157192.37	
13	⊞ice cream	56222	167211.04	
14	⊞milk	54117	162606.44	
15	⊟2007	233161	702395.82	
16	⊞cereal	58671	172828.96	
17	⊞fruit	61816	189616.27	
18	⊞ice cream	55693	169327.53	
19	⊞milk	56981	170623.06	
20	Grand Total	693127	2068334.35	

FIGURE 43-11 The Group field is collapsed.

How can I sort and filter PivotTable fields?

In Figure 43-5, the products are listed alphabetically within each group. For example, Cheerios is the first type of cereal listed. If you want the products to be listed in reverse alphabetical order, simply move the cursor to any cell containing a product (for example, A7 containing Cheerios in the All Row Fields worksheet) and click the drop-down arrow to the right of **Row Labels** in A5. You see the list of filtering options shown in Figure 43-12. Selecting **Sort Z To A** as shown in Figure 43-12 would list Special K first for Cereal, whole milk first for Milk, plums for Fruit, and so on.

Initially, your PivotTable displays results first from 2005, then 2006, and then 2007. If you want to see the data for 2007 first, move the cursor to any cell containing a year (for example, A5) and choose **Sort Largest To Smallest** from the available options.

At the bottom of the filtering options dialog box, you can also select any subset of products to be displayed. You might want to clear Select All first and then select the products you want to show.

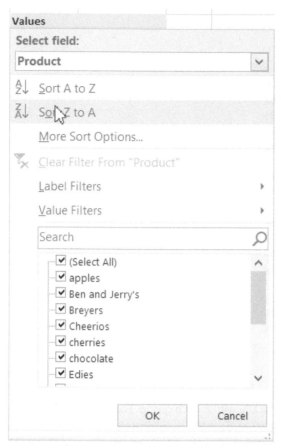

FIGURE 43-12 These are the PivotTable filtering options for the Product field.

For another example of filtering, look at the Data worksheet in the Ptcustomers.xlsx file, shown in Figure 43-13. The worksheet data contains the customer number, the amount paid, and the quarter of the year in which payment was received for each customer transaction. After dragging **Customer** to the **Row Labels** box, **Quarter** to the **Column Labels** box, and **Paid** to the **Values** box, the PivotTable shown in Figure 43-14 is displayed. (See the Ptable worksheet in the Pcustomers.xlsx file.)

	Customer	Paid	Quarter
4	Customer	Paid	Quarter
5	20	8048	4
6	6	7398	4
7	10	5280	2
8	28	3412	3
9	8	3316	1
10	17	821	2
11	4	7024	3
12	20	1379	1
13	27	1924	2
14	23	631	3
15	28	9743	4
16	8	8192	2
17	19	875	1
18	3	9803	4
19	24	7344	3
20	13	6114	1
21	9	6728	4
22	2	4554	1
23	16	8230	4
24	25	1296	1
25	30	4179	1

FIGURE 43-13 The Customer PivotTable data.

	A	B	C	D	E	F
3	Sum of Paid	Column Labels				
4	Row Labels	1	2	3	4	Grand Total
5	1	30965	42039	57790	43417	174211
6	2	96038	121118	59089	45355	321600
7	3	57419	33589	61960	97548	250516
8	4	48947	79352	63052	59520	250871
9	5	57270	86555	69517	33471	246813
10	6	75639	71976	55212	78644	281471
11	7	53130	65768	49064	89018	256980
12	8	33289	74001	45219	43512	196021
13	9	61611	99009	61075	50945	272640
14	10	31785	71213	60417	63835	227250
15	11	59127	35567	62130	107832	264656
16	12	71862	21670	67312	63558	224402
17	13	100626	56058	39500	75109	271293
18	14	74240	63023	36217	77218	250698
19	15	30612	62277	45561	52567	191017
20	16	41870	71490	64909	57120	235389
21	17	61811	85706	46978	40802	235297
22	18	24456	44916	55519	81421	206312
23	19	89591	53157	37558	38247	218553

FIGURE 43-14 This is the Customer PivotTable.

Naturally, you might like to show a list of just your top 10 customers. To obtain this layout, click the **Row Labels** arrow and select **Value Filters**. Choose **Top 10 Items** to obtain the layout shown in Figure 43-15. (See the Top 10 cus worksheet.) Of course, by selecting **Clear Filter**, you can return to the original layout.

	A	B	C	D	E	F
3	**Sum of Paid**	**Column Labels** ▾				
4	**Row Labels** 🔻	**1**	**2**	**3**	**4**	**Grand Total**
5	2	96038	121118	59089	45355	321600
6	6	75639	71976	55212	78644	281471
7	9	61611	99009	61075	50945	272640
8	11	59127	35567	62130	107832	264656
9	13	100626	56058	39500	75109	271293
10	20	68349	104140	35083	69424	276996
11	22	31149	77333	104364	65664	278510
12	23	87124	56387	63290	71953	278754
13	27	45214	89826	56302	71285	262627
14	28	53737	69938	73471	69135	266281
15	**Grand Total**	**678614**	**781352**	**609516**	**705346**	**2774828**

FIGURE 43-15 This figure shows Top 10 customers.

Suppose you simply want to see the top customers that generate 50 percent of your revenue. Select the **Row Labels** filtering icon, select **Value Filters** and **Top 10**, and fill in the dialog box as shown in Figure 43-16.

FIGURE 43-16 Configure the Top 10 Filter dialog box to show customers generating 50 percent of revenue.

The resulting PivotTable is in the Top Half worksheet and shown in Figure 43-17. As you can see, the top 14 customers generate a little more than half of the revenue.

	A	B	C	D	E	F
3	Sum of Paid	Column Labels				
4	Row Labels	1	2	3	4	Grand Total
5	2	96038	121118	59089	45355	321600
6	3	57419	33589	61960	97548	250516
7	4	48947	79352	63052	59520	250871
8	6	75639	71976	55212	78644	281471
9	7	53130	65768	49064	89018	256980
10	9	61611	99009	61075	50945	272640
11	11	59127	35567	62130	107832	264656
12	13	100626	56058	39500	75109	271293
13	14	74240	63023	36217	77218	250698
14	20	68349	104140	35083	69424	276996
15	22	31149	77333	104364	65664	278510
16	23	87124	56387	63290	71953	278754
17	27	45214	89826	56302	71285	262627
18	28	53737	69938	73471	69135	266281
19	**Grand Total**	**912350**	**1023084**	**819809**	**1028650**	**3783893**

FIGURE 43-17 The top customers generate half of the revenues.

Now suppose you want to sort your customers by Quarter 1 revenue. (See the Sorted q1 worksheet.) Right-click anywhere in the Quarter 1 column, point to **Sort**, and then click **Sort Largest To Smallest**. The resulting PivotTable is shown in Figure 43-18. Note that Customer 13 paid the most in Quarter 1, Customer 2 paid the second most, and so on.

	A	B	C	D	E	F
3	**Sum of Paid**	**Column Labels** 🔽				
4	**Row Labels** 🔽	**1**	**2**	**3**	**4**	**Grand Total**
5	13	100626	56058	39500	75109	271293
6	2	96038	121118	59089	45355	321600
7	19	89591	53157	37558	38247	218553
8	23	87124	56387	63290	71953	278754
9	21	77336	37476	51815	57065	223692
10	6	75639	71976	55212	78644	281471
11	14	74240	63023	36217	77218	250698
12	12	71862	21670	67312	63558	224402
13	20	68349	104140	35083	69424	276996
14	17	61811	85706	46978	40802	235297
15	9	61611	99009	61075	50945	272640
16	26	59994	70594	50446	44050	225084
17	30	59599	64192	44335	42944	211070
18	11	59127	35567	62130	107832	264656
19	3	57419	33589	61960	97548	250516
20	5	57270	86555	69517	33471	246813
21	28	53737	69938	73471	69135	266281
22	7	53130	65768	49064	89018	256980

FIGURE 43-18 Customers are sorted on Quarter 1 revenue.

How can I summarize a PivotTable by using a PivotChart?

Excel makes it easy to summarize PivotTables visually by using PivotCharts. The key to laying out the data the way you want it in a PivotChart is to sort data and collapse or expand fields. In the grocery example, suppose you want to summarize the trend over time of each food group's unit sales. (See the Chart 2 worksheet in the Groceriespt.xlsx file.) You should move the **Year** field to the **Row** area and delete **Revenue** from the **Values** area. You also need to collapse the entire **Group** field in the **Row Labels** zone and move **Groups** to the **Column** area. Now you are ready to create a PivotChart. Click anywhere inside the table and select **PivotChart** from the **Analyze** tab. Now pick the chart type you want to create. The fourth **Line Graph** option, which displays the chart shown in Figure 43-19, has been chosen here. The chart shows that milk sales were highest in 2005 and lowest in 2006.

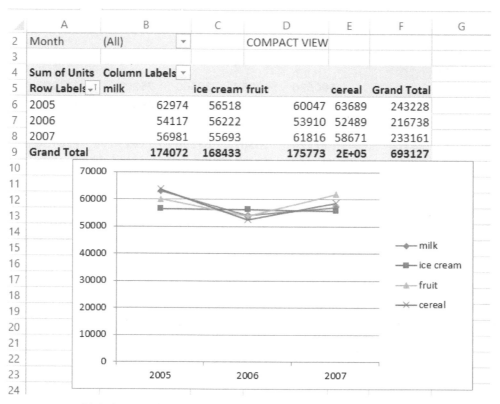

	A	B	C	D	E	F	G
2	Month	(All)	▾		COMPACT VIEW		
3							
4	**Sum of Units**	**Column Labels** ▾					
5	**Row Labels** ▾ᵀ	**milk**	**ice cream**	**fruit**		**cereal**	**Grand Total**
6	2005	62974	56518	60047	63689		243228
7	2006	54117	56222	53910	52489		216738
8	2007	56981	55693	61816	58671		233161
9	**Grand Total**	**174072**	**168433**	**175773**	**2E+05**		**693127**

FIGURE 43-19 This is the PivotChart for the unit group sales trend.

How can I use the Report Filter section of the PivotTable?

Recall that Months was placed in the Report Filter section of the table. To see how to use a report filter, suppose that you want to summarize sales for the months of January to June. By clicking the **Filter** icon in cell B2 of the First 6 months worksheet, you can select **January–June**. This results in the PivotTable shown in Figure 43-20, which summarizes the number of units sold by product, group, and year for the months of January to June.

	A	B	C
2	Month	(Multiple Items) ⊤	
3			
4		Values	
5	Row Labels ⊤	Sum of Units	Sum of Revenue
6	⊟ 2007	115258	346295.58
7	⊟ milk	30069	89222.68
8	⊟ chocolate	4875	14077.99
9	west	2014	5839.06
10	south	736	2141.76
11	north	1437	4136.37
12	east	688	1960.8
13	⊟ low fat	9447	27341.25
14	west	3285	10732.35
15	south	531	1062
16	north	3905	10212.44
17	east	1726	5334.46
18	⊟ skim	10182	30450.57
19	west	2156	6169.53
20	south	2778	8881.2

FIGURE 43-20 A PivotTable summarizing January to June sales.

How do PivotTable slicers work?

The problem with a report filter is that a viewer of the PivotTable shown in Figure 43-20 cannot easily see that the table summarizes January to June sales. The Excel slicer feature (introduced in Excel 2010) neatly solves this problem. To create a slicer for any of the columns of data used to generate your PivotTable, place your cursor anywhere in the PivotTable and then click **Slicer** on the ribbon's **Insert** tab. In the Slicers worksheet of the Groceriespt.xlsx file, Slicer was selected from the Insert menu. The Month and Product fields were selected to create slicers for Month and Product. Using a given slicer, you can select any subset of possible values to be used in creating your table. In the Month slicer, the months January through June were selected (one at a time while holding down the Ctrl key). Nothing was done to the Product slicer, so the data is based on January to June sales. The slicers are shown in Figure 43-21.

You can also add a slicer for a field by right-clicking the field in the **PivotTable Fields** pane and selecting **Add As Slicer**.

▲	A	B	C	D	E	F	G	H
1								
2	Month	(Multiple Ite▼)						
3				Month ▼		Product ▼		
4		Values						
5	Row Labels ▼	Sum of Units	Sum of Revenue	January		apples		
6	⊟ 2007	115258	346295.58	February		Ben and Jerry's		
7	⊟ milk	30069	89222.68	March		Breyers		
8	⊟ chocolat	4875	14077.99	April		Cheerios		
9	west	2014	5839.06	May		cherries		
10	south	736	2141.76	June		chocolate		
11	north	1437	4136.37	July		Edies		
12	east	688	1960.8	August		grapes		
13	⊟ low fat	9447	27341.25					
14	west	3285	10732.35					
15	south	531	1062					
16	north	3905	10212.44					
17	east	1726	5334.46					
18	⊟ skim	10182	30450.57					
19	west	2156	6169.53					

FIGURE 43-21 Here is an example of slicers for the Month and Product fields.

If you select a slicer, on the **Slicer Tools Options** ribbon tab, you see formatting options that enable you to change its appearance. For example, you can change the height and width as well as the number of columns in the slicer. You can also easily resize a slicer by dragging its sides or corners.

How can I add blank rows or hide subtotals in a PivotTable?

If you want to add a blank row between each grouped item, select **PivotTable Tools Design** on the ribbon, click **Blank Rows**, and then click **Insert Blank Line After Each Item**. If you want to hide subtotals or grand totals, select **PivotTable Tools Design** and then select **Subtotals** or **Grand Totals**. After adding blank rows and hiding all totals, you can obtain the table in the Blank rows no totals worksheet of the Grocerypt.xlsx workbook, shown in Figure 43-22. After right-clicking in any PivotTable cell, you can select **PivotTable Options** to open the **PivotTable Options** dialog box.

▲	A	B	C
2	Month	(All) ▼	
3			
4		**Values**	
5	**Row Labels**	↓T Sum of Units	Sum of Revenue
6	⊟ 2007		
7	⊟ milk		
8	⊟ chocolate		
9	west	4379	12668.95
10	south	1545	4528.31
11	north	2322	7579.02
12	east	2184	5791.1
13			
14	⊟ low fat		
15	west	4668	15042.24
16	south	2431	7606.76
17	north	7957	23490.32
18	east	2517	7762.83
19			
20	⊟ skim		
21	west	3571	9951.37
22	south	2778	8881.2
23	north	3594	10792.09
24	east	4839	14609.52
25			

FIGURE 43-22 Here is the grocery PivotTable without totals.

How can I apply conditional formatting to a PivotTable?

Suppose you want to apply data bars to the Units column in the grocery PivotTable. One problem you'll encounter is that subtotals and grand totals will have large data bars and make the other data bars smaller than they should be. It's better to have the data bars apply to all product sales, not the subtotals and grand totals. (See the Cond form worksheet of workbook Groceriespt.xlsx.) To apply the data bars to only the unit sales by product, begin by placing the cursor in any cell containing unit sales for a product (for example, chocolate milk in B8). On the **Home** tab, click **Conditional Formatting** followed by **Data Bars** and then choose **More Rules**. You see the **New Formatting Rule** dialog box shown in Figure 43-23.

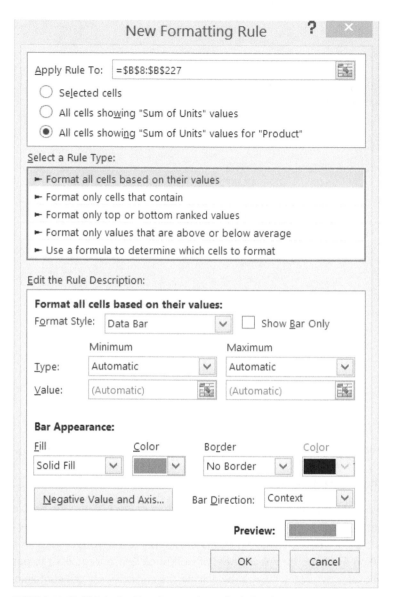

FIGURE 43-23 This is the New Formatting Rule dialog box for using conditional formatting with PivotTables.

By selecting **All Cells Showing "Sum of Units" Values For "Product"** and selecting the $B$8:$B$227 range, you can ensure that data bars apply only to cells listing unit sales for products, as you can see in the Cond form worksheet and Figure 43-24.

	A	B	C
2	Month	(All) ▼	
3			
4		Values	
5	Row Labels ⏷T	Sum of Units	Sum of Revenue
6	⊟2007	233161	702395.82
7	⊟milk	56981	170623.06
8	⊟chocolate	10430	30567.38
9	west	4379	12668.95
10	south	1545	4528.31
11	north	2322	7579.02
12	east	2184	5791.1
13	⊟low fat	17573	53902.15
14	west	4668	15042.24
15	south	2431	7606.76
16	north	7957	23490.32
17	east	2517	7762.83
18	⊟skim	14782	44234.18
19	west	3571	9951.37
20	south	2778	8881.2
21	north	3594	10792.09
22	east	4839	14609.52
23	⊟whole	14196	41919.35
24	west	3252	8311.84
25	south	1562	4495.15

FIGURE 43-24 This figure shows data bars for a PivotTable.

How can I update my calculations when I add new data?

If the data in your original set of rows changes, you can update your PivotTable to include the data changes by right-clicking the table and selecting **Refresh**. You can also select **Refresh** from the **Analyze** tab.

If you want data you add to be automatically included in your PivotTable calculations when you refresh it, you should define your original data set as a table by selecting it with Ctrl+T. (See Chapter 25, "Tables," for more information.)

If you want to change the range of data used to create a PivotTable, you can always select **Change Data Source** on the **Analyze** tab. You can also move the table to a different location by selecting **Move PivotTable**.

I work for a small travel agency for which I need to mass-mail a travel brochure. My funds are limited, so I want to mail the brochure to people who spend the most money on travel. From information in a random sample of 925 people, I know the gender, the age, and the amount these people spent on travel last year. How can I use this data to determine how gender and age influence a person's travel expenditures? What can I conclude about the type of person to whom I should mail the brochure?

To understand this data, you need to break it down as follows:

- Average amount spent on travel by gender

- Average amount spent on travel for each age group

- Average amount spent on travel by gender for each age group

The data is included on the Data worksheet in the Traveldata.xlsx file, and a sample is shown in Figure 43-25. For example, the first person is a 44-year-old male who spent $997 on travel.

	A	B	C
2	Amount Spent on Travel	Age	Gender
3	997	44	M
4	850	39	F
5	997	43	M
6	951	41	M
7	993	50	F
8	781	39	F
9	912	45	F
10	649	59	M
11	1265	25	M
12	680	38	F
13	800	41	F
14	613	32	F
15	993	46	F
16	1059	38	M
17	939	42	F
18	841	44	F
19	828	38	F
20	1004	50	F

FIGURE 43-25 This is travel agency data showing age, gender, and amount spent on travel.

First, get a breakdown of spending by gender. Begin by selecting **Insert PivotTable**. Excel extracts the A2:D927 range. After clicking **OK**, put the cursor in the table so that the field list appears. Next, drag the **Gender** column to the **Row Labels** zone and drag **Amount Spent On Travel** to the **Values** zone. This results in the PivotTable shown in Figure 43-26.

You can tell from the heading, Sum Of Amount Spent On Travel, that you are summarizing the total amount spent on travel, but you actually want the average amount spent on travel by men and women. To calculate these quantities, double-click **Sum Of Amount Spent On Travel** from the PivotTable (not the field list!) and then select **Average** from the **Value Field Settings** dialog box, shown in Figure 43-27.

	A	B
1		
2		
3	Row Labels ▼	Sum of Amount Spent on Travel
4	F	413632
5	M	426387
6	**Grand Total**	**840019**

FIGURE 43-26 This PivotTable summarizes the total travel expenditures by gender.

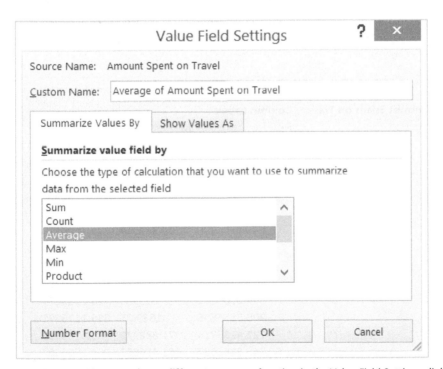

FIGURE 43-27 You can select a different summary function in the Value Field Settings dialog box.

You now see the results, shown in Figure 43-28.

	A	B
1		
2		
3	Row Labels ▾	Average of Amount Spent on Travel
4	F	901.1590414
5	M	914.9935622
6	**Grand Total**	**908.1286486**

FIGURE 43-28 Here are the average travel expenditures by gender.

On average, people spend $908.13 on travel. Women spend an average of $901.16, whereas men spend $914.99. This PivotTable indicates that gender has little influence on the propensity to travel. By clicking the **Row Labels** arrow, you can filter to show just male or female results.

Now you want to see how age influences travel spending. Switch **Gender** to the **Columns** zone of the PivotTable by dragging **Gender** from the **Row Labels** zone to the **Column Labels** zone. To break down spending by age, drag **Age** to the **Row** area. The PivotTable now appears as it's shown in Figure 43-29.

	A	B	C	D
1				
2				
3	Average of Amount Spent on Travel	Column Labels ▾		
4	Row Labels ▾	F	M	Grand Total
5	25	482.3846154	1305.764706	948.9666667
6	26	526.6923077	1281.583333	889.04
7	27	532.5714286	1266.722222	1061.16
8	28	584	1243.666667	960.952381
9	29	564.5	1229.833333	814
10	30	578	1176.666667	877.3333333
11	31	604.3333333	1212.733333	1038.904762
12	32	636.6153846	1160.818182	876.875
13	33	661.6153846	1146.928571	913.2592593
14	34	674.0909091	1128.615385	920.2916667
15	35	705.5555556	1089.25	886.1176471
16	36	722.4285714	1071.888889	859.173913
17	37	746.9166667	1061.416667	904.1666667
18	38	764.25	1051.846154	913.8

FIGURE 43-29 This PivotTable shows the average travel expenditures by age and gender.

Age seems to have little effect on travel expenditures. In fact, this PivotTable is pretty useless in its present state. You need to group data by age to see any trends. To group the results by age, right-click anywhere in the **Age** column and choose **Group**. In the **Grouping** dialog box (shown in Figure 43-30), you can designate the interval by which to define an age group. By using 10-year increments, you obtain the PivotTable shown in Figure 43-31.

On average, 25–34-year-olds spend $935.84 on travel, 55–64-year-olds spend $903.57 on travel, and so on. This information is more useful, but it still indicates that people of all ages tend to spend about the same amount on travel. This view of the data does not help determine whom you should mail your brochure to.

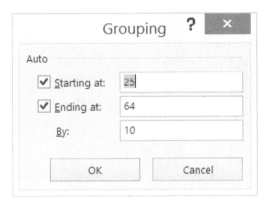

FIGURE 43-30 Use the Group And Show Detail command to group detailed records.

Finally, get a breakdown of average travel spending by age for men and women separately. All you have to do is drag **Gender** to the **Column Labels** zone of the field list, resulting in the PivotTable shown in Figure 43-31. (See the Final Table worksheet.)

	A	B	C	D
1				
2				
3	Average of Amount Spent on Travel	Column Labels ▾		
4	Row Labels ▾	F	M	Grand Total
5	25-34	585.4752475	1221.209677	935.8355556
6	35-44	790.1652174	1004.098214	895.7180617
7	45-54	979.4782609	813.5765766	897.9955752
8	55-64	1179.609375	606.6470588	903.5668016
9	Grand Total	901.1590414	914.9935622	908.1286486

FIGURE 43-31 This is the age and gender breakdown of travel spending.

Now you're cooking! You can see that as age increases, women spend more on travel and men spend less. Now you know who should get the brochure: older women and younger men. As a student once said, "That would be some kind of cruise!"

A graph provides a nice summary of this analysis. Move the cursor inside the PivotTable and, from the **Analyze** tab on the ribbon, select **PivotChart**. A menu of recommended charts appears. The first choice (**Clustered Column**) has been selected. The result is the chart shown in Figure 43-32. If you want to edit the chart further, select **PivotChart Tools**. Then, for example, if you choose **Layout**, you can add titles to the chart and axis and make other changes.

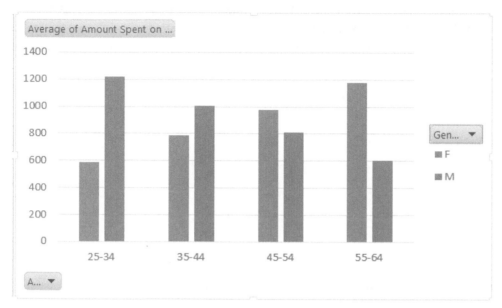

FIGURE 43-32 This is a PivotChart for the age and gender travel expenditure breakdown.

Each age group spends approximately the same on travel, but as age increases, women spend more than men. (If you want to use a different type of chart, you can change the chart type by right-clicking the PivotChart and then choosing **Chart Type**.)

Notice that the bars showing expenditures by males decrease with age, and the bars representing the amount spent by women increase with age. You can see why the PivotTables that showed only gender and age data failed to unmask this pattern. Because half your sample population is men and half is women, you found that the average amount spent by people does not depend on their age. (Notice that the average height of the two bars for each age is approximately the same.) You also found that the average amount spent by men and women was approximately the same. You can see this because, averaged over all ages, the blue and red bars have approximately equal heights. Slicing and dicing the data simultaneously across age and gender does a much better job of showing you the real information.

Note that by clicking the drop-down arrow associated with A, you could filter the graph on Age, and by clicking the drop-down arrow associated with Gen, you could filter the graph based on Gender.

I'm doing market research about station wagons. I need to determine what factors influence the likelihood that a family will purchase a station wagon. From information in a large sample

of families, I know the family size (large or small) and the family income (high or low). How can I determine how family size and income influence the likelihood that a family will purchase a station wagon?

In the Station.xlsx file, you can find the following information:

- Is the family size large or small?

- Is the family's income high or low?

- Did the family buy a station wagon? Yes or No.

A sample of the data is shown in Figure 43-33 (see the Data worksheet). For example, the first family listed is a small, high-income family that did not buy a station wagon.

	A	B	C	D
2		Station Wagon?	Family Size	Salary
3		No	Small	High
4		Yes	Large	High
5		Yes	Large	High
6		Yes	Large	High
7		Yes	Large	High
8		No	Small	High
9		Yes	Large	High
10		Yes	Large	High
11		Yes	Large	Low
12		Yes	Large	High
13		Yes	Large	Low
14		No	Small	Low
15		No	Small	Low
16		No	Small	High
17		Yes	Large	High
18		Yes	Large	High
19		No	Small	High
20		Yes	Large	High

FIGURE 43-33 This is data collected about income, family size, and the purchase of a station wagon.

You want to determine how family size and income influence the likelihood that a family will purchase a station wagon. The trick is to look at how income affects purchases for each family size and how family size affects purchases for each income level.

To begin, choose **Insert Pivot Table** and then select the data (the B2:D345 cell range). Using **PivotTable Fields**, drag **Family Size** to the **Row Labels** area, **Station Wagon** to the **Column Labels** area, and any of the three fields to the **Values** area. The result is the PivotTable shown in Figure 43-34. (See the 1st Table worksheet.) Notice that Excel has chosen to summarize the data appropriately by counting the number of observations in each category. For example, 34 high-salary, large families did not buy a station wagon, whereas 100 high-salary, large families did buy one.

	A	B	C	D
3	**Count of Station Wagon? Column Labels** ▾			
4	**Row Labels** ▾	**No**	**Yes**	**Grand Total**
5	⊟**Large**	48	138	186
6	High	34	100	134
7	Low	14	38	52
8	⊟**Small**	147	10	157
9	High	104	8	112
10	Low	43	2	45
11	**Grand Total**	195	148	343

FIGURE 43-34 This is a summary of station wagon ownership by family size and salary.

You would like to know for each row in the PivotTable the percentage of families that purchased a station wagon. To display the data in this format, right-click any value cell in the PivotTable data and then choose **Value Field Settings**, which opens the **Value Field Settings** dialog box. In the dialog box, click **Show Values As** and then select **% Of Row** in the **Show Data As** list. You now obtain the PivotTable shown in Figure 43-35. (See the 1st Percent Breakdown worksheet.)

	A	B	C	D
1				
2				
3	**Count of Station Wagon?**	**Column Labels** ▾		
4	**Row Labels** ▾	**No**	**Yes**	**Grand Total**
5	⊟**Large**	**25.81%**	**74.19%**	**100.00%**
6	High	25.37%	74.63%	100.00%
7	Low	26.92%	73.08%	100.00%
8	⊟**Small**	**93.63%**	**6.37%**	**100.00%**
9	High	92.86%	7.14%	100.00%
10	Low	95.56%	4.44%	100.00%
11	**Grand Total**	**56.85%**	**43.15%**	**100.00%**

FIGURE 43-35 This is the percentage breakdown of station wagon ownership by income for large and small families.

From Figure 43-35, you learn that for both large and small families, income has little effect on whether the family purchases a station wagon. Now you need to determine how family size affects the propensity to buy a station wagon for high-income and low-income families. To do this, move **Salary** above **Family Size** in the **Row Labels** zone, resulting in the PivotTable shown in Figure 43-36. (See the Final Percent Breakdown worksheet.)

	A	B	C	D
3	**Count of Station Wagon?**	**Column Labels**		
4	**Row Labels**	**No**	**Yes**	**Grand Total**
5	**☐ High**	**56.10%**	**43.90%**	**100.00%**
6	Large	25.37%	74.63%	100.00%
7	Small	92.86%	7.14%	100.00%
8	**☐ Low**	**58.76%**	**41.24%**	**100.00%**
9	Large	26.92%	73.08%	100.00%
10	Small	95.56%	4.44%	100.00%
11	**Grand Total**	**56.85%**	**43.15%**	**100.00%**

FIGURE 43-36 This is the breakdown of station wagon ownership by family size for high and low salaries.

From this table, you learn that for high-income families, a large family is much more likely to buy a station wagon than a small family. Similarly, for low-income families, a large family is also more likely to purchase a wagon than a small family. The bottom line is that family size has a much greater effect on the likelihood that a family will purchase a station wagon than income.

I work for a manufacturer that sells microchips globally. I'm given monthly actual and predicted sales for Canada, France, and the United States for Chip 1, Chip 2, and Chip 3. I'm also given the variance, or difference, between actual and budgeted revenues. For each month and each combination of country and product, I'd like to display the following data: actual revenue, budgeted revenue, actual variance, actual revenue as a percentage of annual revenue, and variance as a percentage of budgeted revenue. How can I display this information?

In this scenario, you are a finance manager for a microchip manufacturer. You sell your products in different countries and regions and at different times. PivotTables can help you summarize your data in a format that's easily understood.

The Ptableexample.xlsx file includes monthly actual and predicted sales during 1997 of Chip 1, Chip 2, and Chip 3 in Canada, France, and the United States. The file also contains the variance, or difference, between actual revenues and budgeted revenues. A sample of the data is shown in Figure 43-37. (See the Data worksheet.) For example, in the United States in January, sales of Chip 1 totaled $4,000, although sales of $5,454 were predicted. This yielded a variance of –$1,454.

	A	B	C	D	E	F
1	Month	Product	Country	Revenue	Budget	Var
2	January	Chip 1	US	4000	5454	-1454
3	January	Chip 1	Canada	3424	5341	-1917
4	January	Chip 1	US	8324	1232	7092
5	January	Chip 1	France	5555	3424	2131
6	January	Chip 1	Canada	5341	8324	-2983
7	January	Chip 1	US	1232	5555	-4323
8	January	Chip 1	France	3424	5341	-1917
9	January	Chip 1	Canada	8324	1232	7092
10	January	Chip 1	US	5555	3424	2131
11	January	Chip 1	France	5341	8324	-2983
12	January	Chip 1	Canada	1232	5555	-4323
13	January	Chip 1	US	3424	5341	-1917
14	January	Chip 1	Canada	8383	5454	2929
15	January	Chip 1	France	8324	1232	7092
16	January	Chip 1	Canada	5555	3424	2131
17	January	Chip 1	US	5341	8324	-2983
18	January	Chip 1	France	1232	5555	-4323
19	January	Chip 1	France	3523	9295	-5772

FIGURE 43-37 Chip data from different countries for different months shows actual, budget, and variance revenues.

For each month and each combination of country and product, you would like to display the following data:

- Actual revenue

- Budgeted revenue

- Actual variance

- Actual revenue as a percentage of annual revenue

- Variance as a percentage of budgeted revenue

To begin, select a cell within the range of data you're working with (remember that the first row must include headings) and then choose **Insert PivotTable**. Excel automatically determines that your data is in the A1:F208 range.

If you drag **Month** to the **Rows** zone, **Country** to the **Columns** zone, and **Revenue** to the **Values** area, for example, you obtain the total revenue each month by country. A field you add to the **Filters** zone (Product, for example) enables you to filter your PivotTable by using values in that field. By adding **Product** to the **Filters** zone, you can view sales of only Chip 1 by month for each country. Given that you want to be able to show data for any combination of country and product, you should add **Month** to the **Rows** zone of the PivotTable and both **Country** and **Product** to the **Filters** zone. Next, drag **Var**, **Revenue**, and **Budget** to the **Values** zone. You have now created the PivotTable that is shown in Figure 43-38. (See the 1st Table worksheet.)

	A	B	C	D
1	Product	(All)		
2	Country	(All)		
3				
4		Values		
5	Row Labels	Sum of Var	Sum of Revenue	Sum of Budget
6	January	-4297	87534	91831
7	February	2843	90377	87534
8	March	-1389	88988	90377
9	April	-2774	84982	87756
10	May	-423	84559	84982
11	June	-548	84011	84559
12	July	2366	86377	84011
13	August	-2843	83534	86377
14	September	1389	84923	83534
15	October	-4318	80605	84923
16	November	3406	84011	80605
17	December	2366	86377	84011
18	Grand Total	-4222	1026278	1030500

FIGURE 43-38 This is a monthly summary of revenue, budget, and variance.

For example, in January, total revenue was $87,534, and total budgeted sales were $91,831, so actual sales fell $4,297 short of the forecast.

You want to determine the percentage of revenue earned during each month. Again, drag **Revenue** from the field list to the **Values** area of the PivotTable. Right-click in this value column and then choose **Value Field Settings**. In the **Value Field Settings** dialog box, click **Show Values As**. In the **Show Values As** list, select **% Of Column** and rename this field as **Sum Of Revenue2**, as shown in Figure 43-39.

You now obtain the PivotTable shown in Figure 43-40. (See the 2nd Table worksheet.) January sales provided 8.53 percent of revenue. Total revenue for the year was $1,026,278.

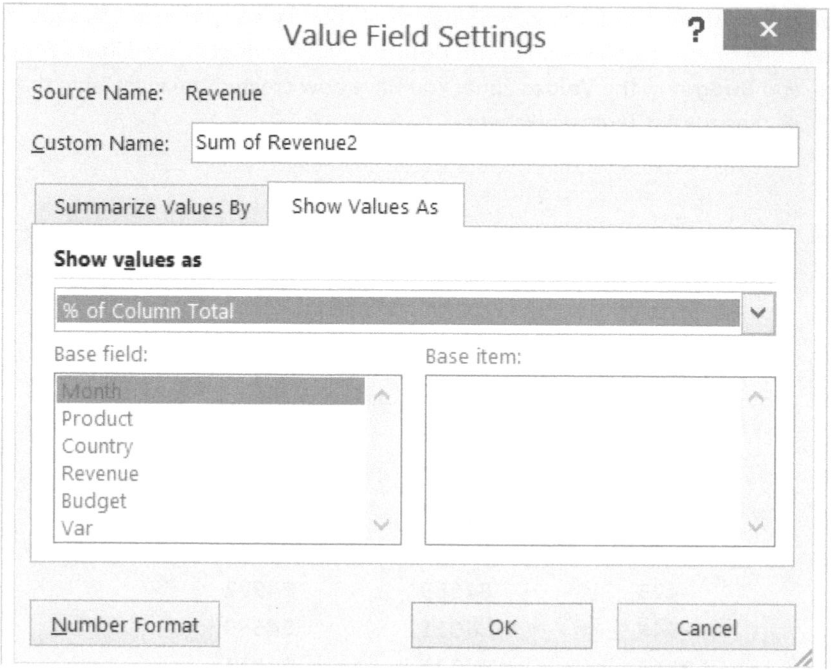

FIGURE 43-39 Create each month's percentage of annual revenue.

	A	B	C	D	E
Product	(All) ▾				
Country	(All) ▾				
		Values			
Row Labels ▾	**Sum of Var**	**Sum of Revenue**	**Sum of Budget**	**Sum of Revenue2**	
January	-4297	87534	91831	8.53%	
February	2843	90377	87534	8.81%	
March	-1389	88988	90377	8.67%	
April	-2774	84982	87756	8.28%	
May	-423	84559	84982	8.24%	
June	-548	84011	84559	8.19%	
July	2366	86377	84011	8.42%	
August	-2843	83534	86377	8.14%	
September	1389	84923	83534	8.27%	
October	-4318	80605	84923	7.85%	
November	3406	84011	80605	8.19%	
December	2366	86377	84011	8.42%	
Grand Total	**-4222**	**1026278**	**1030500**	**100.00%**	

FIGURE 43-40 This is the monthly revenue breakdown.

Instead of using Value Fields Settings to change the display of a data field, you may change the way a Values field is displayed by right-clicking a value cell and selecting **Show Values As**.

What is a calculated field?

Now you want to determine for each month the variance as a percentage of total sales. To do this, you can create a *calculated field*. Select a cell anywhere within the data area of the PivotTable and then choose **Fields Items** and **Sets** from the **Analyze** tab. Choose **Calculated Field** to open the **Insert Calculated Field** dialog box. As shown in Figure 43-41, enter a name for your field and then enter your formula. The formula for this example is =Var/Budget. You can enter the formula yourself or use the list of fields and the **Insert Field** button to add a field to the formula. After clicking **Add** and then **OK**, you see the PivotTable shown in Figure 43-42. (See the Calc Field worksheet of the Ptableexample.xlsx file.)

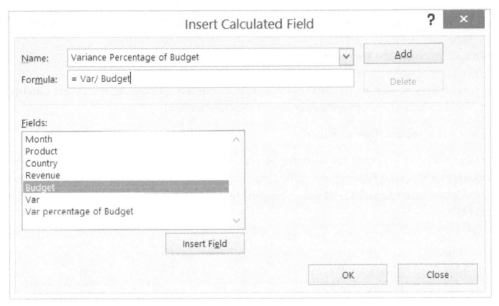

FIGURE 43-41 Create a calculated field.

	A	B	C	D	E	F
1	Product	(All) ▾				
2	Country	(All) ▾				
3						
4		Values				
5	Row Labels ▾	Sum of Var	Sum of Budget	Sum of Revenue	Sum of Revenue2	Sum of Var percentage of Budget
6	January	-4297	91831	87534	8.53%	-0.046792477
7	February	2843	87534	90377	8.81%	0.032478808
8	March	-1389	90377	88988	8.67%	-0.015368954
9	April	-2774	87756	84982	8.28%	-0.031610374
10	May	-423	84982	84559	8.24%	-0.004977525
11	June	-548	84559	84011	8.19%	-0.006480682
12	July	2366	84011	86377	8.42%	0.028162979
13	August	-2843	86377	83534	8.14%	-0.032913854
14	September	1389	83534	84923	8.27%	0.01662796
15	October	-4318	84923	80605	7.85%	-0.050846061
16	November	3406	80605	84011	8.19%	0.042255443
17	December	2366	84011	86377	8.42%	0.028162979
18	Grand Total	-4222	1030500	1026278	100.00%	-0.00409704

FIGURE 43-42 This shows the PivotTable with calculated field for variance percentage.

Thus, in January, sales were 4.7 percent lower than budgeted. By opening the **Insert Calculated Field** dialog box again, you can modify or delete a calculated field.

How can I use a report filter or slicer?

To see sales of Chip 2 in France, for example, you can select the appropriate values from the **Product** and **Country** fields in the **Filters** zone. With Chip 2 and France selected, you would see the PivotTable shown in Figure 43-43. Figure 43-44 shows how to create the same table with slicers (see the Slicers worksheet).

	A	B	C	D	E
1	Product	Chip 2 ▾			
2	Country	France ▾			
3					
4		Values			
5	Row Labels ▾	Sum of Var	Sum of Revenue	Sum of Budget	Sum of Revenue2
6	February	-3846	29108	32954	23.90%
7	May	3318	35363	32045	29.04%
8	August	2769	33432	30663	27.45%
9	November	0	23876	23876	19.61%
10	Grand Total	2241	121779	119538	100.00%

FIGURE 43-43 This figure shows sales of Chip 2 in France.

In the Slicers worksheet, Slicers was used to create the same table. You can click in the PivotTable and select **Slicers** from the **Insert** tab. Create the slicers shown in Figure 43-44 by selecting the **Product** and **Country** fields. Selecting Chip 2 from the **Product** slicer and France from the **Country** slicer yields the relevant computations for all transactions involving Chip 2 in France. As was previously mentioned, you can also create a slicer by right-clicking the field in the **Fields** list.

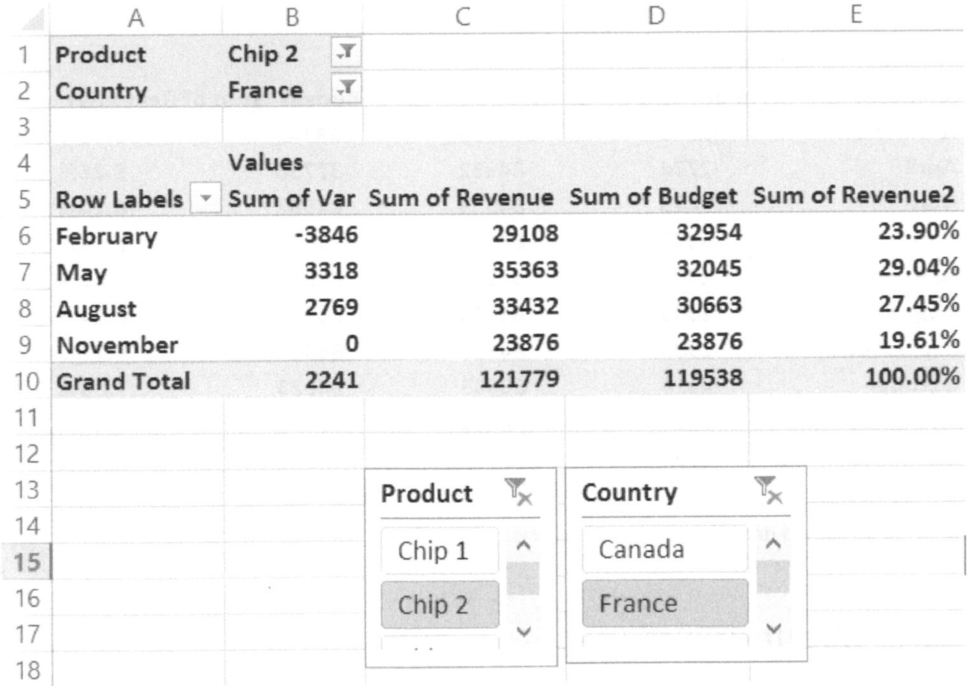

	A	B	C	D	E
1	Product	Chip 2 ⚟			
2	Country	France ⚟			
3					
4		Values			
5	Row Labels ▾	Sum of Var	Sum of Revenue	Sum of Budget	Sum of Revenue2
6	February	-3846	29108	32954	23.90%
7	May	3318	35363	32045	29.04%
8	August	2769	33432	30663	27.45%
9	November	0	23876	23876	19.61%
10	Grand Total	2241	121779	119538	100.00%
11					
12					
13			Product ⚟	Country ⚟	
14					
15			Chip 1 ⌃	Canada ⌃	
16			Chip 2	France	
17			⌄	⌄	
18					

FIGURE 43-44 This figure shows sales of Chip 2 in France with slicers.

How can I group items in a PivotTable?

Often, you want to group headings in a PivotTable. For example, you might want to combine sales for January to March. To create a group, select the items you want to group, right-click the selection, and then choose **Group And Show Detail**, **Group**. After changing the name Group 1 to **Jan-March** and deleting Month from the **Row Labels** section of the **PivotTable** dialog box, you obtain the PivotTable shown in Figure 43-45.

	A	B	C	D	E
1	Product	(All)			
2	Country	(All)			
3					
4		Values			
5	Row Labels	Sum of Var	Sum of Revenue	Sum of Budget	Sum of Revenue2
6	Jan-March	-2843	266899	269742	26.01%
7	April	-2774	84982	87756	8.28%
8	May	-423	84559	84982	8.24%
9	June	-548	84011	84559	8.19%
10	July	2366	86377	84011	8.42%
11	August	-2843	83534	86377	8.14%
12	September	1389	84923	83534	8.27%
13	October	-4318	80605	84923	7.85%
14	November	3406	84011	80605	8.19%
15	December	2366	86377	84011	8.42%
16	Grand Total	-4222	1026278	1030500	100.00%

FIGURE 43-45 Grouping items for January, February, and March.

Remarks about grouping

Following are some further insights about using grouping in Excel:

- You can disband a group by selecting **Group And Show Detail** and then **Ungroup**.

- You can group nonadjacent selections by holding down the Ctrl key while you select nonadjacent rows or columns.

- With numerical values or dates in a row field, you can group by number or dates in arbitrary intervals. For example, you can create groups for age ranges and then find the average income for all 25–34-year-olds.

What is a calculated item?

A calculated item works just like a calculated field except that you are creating one row rather than a column. To create a calculated item, you should select an item in the row area of the PivotTable, not an item in the body of the PivotTable. Then, on the **Analyze** tab, select **Fields Items** and **Sets**, followed by **Calculated Item**.

To illustrate how to create a Calculated Item, look at the Calculateditem.xlsx file. In the worksheet data (see Figure 43-46), you have sales of different car brands. You would like to summarize total sales by the company's country (Japan, Germany, or United States).

	G	H	I
8		Brand	Sales
9		Ford	3
10		Nissan	2
11		Ford	6
12		VW	2
13		VW	4
14		Nissan	4
15		Chrysler	2
16		VW	2
17		BMW	6
18		Honda	2
19		VW	4
20		Honda	5
21		BMW	6
22		Honda	4
23		Ford	5
24		Ford	5
25		Ford	2

FIGURE 43-46 This is the data for creating a calculated field.

To begin, create a PivotTable listing total sales by country (see worksheet PT1). Drag **Brand** to the **Rows** zone and **Sales** to the **Values** zone. You now obtain the PivotTable shown in Figure 43-47.

	A	B
3	Row Labels ⏷	Sum of Sales
4	BMW	359
5	Chrysler	286
6	Ford	277
7	GM	239
8	Honda	283
9	Nissan	219
10	VW	323
11	Japan	502
12	Germany	682
13	US	802
14	**Grand Total**	**3972**

FIGURE 43-47 The PivotTable is summarizing sales by brand.

Before creating a calculated item, it is a good idea to hide the Grand Total by selecting **Grand Totals** from the **Design Tab** and selecting **Off** for **Rows** and **Columns**. Otherwise, after you create the calculated item, the Grand Totals will double-count each car.

To create a calculated item for Japan, put your cursor anywhere in the **Row Labels Column** of the PivotTable and then select **Fields Items** and **Sets** from the **Analyze** tab. After selecting **Calculated Item**, fill in the dialog box as shown in Figure 43-48 and select **OK**.

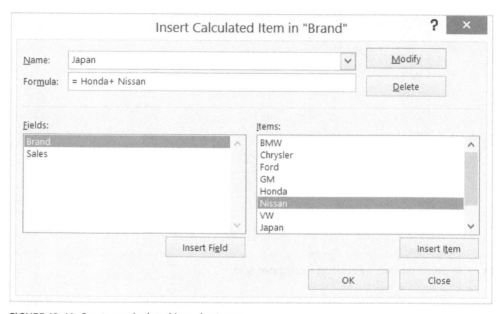

FIGURE 43-48 Create a calculated item for Japan.

This dialog box creates a calculated item for Japan by adding together Honda and Nissan sales. In a similar fashion, you can create calculated fields that summarize sales in Germany and the United States. The resulting PivotTable is in worksheet Calc Item and is shown in Figure 43-49.

If you want to delete a calculated item or calculated field, select **Calculated Item** or **Calculated Field** from **Fields Items** and **Sets**. From the **Name** section of the dialog box, select the field or item you wish to delete and select **Delete**.

	A	B	C
1			
2			
3	**Row Labels** ▾	**Sum of Sales**	
4	BMW	359	
5	Chrysler	286	
6	Ford	277	
7	GM	239	
8	Honda	283	
9	Nissan	219	
10	VW	323	
11	Japan	502	
12	Germany	682	
13	US	802	

FIGURE 43-49 This is a list of calculated items.

If you desire, you may hide the individual brand sales by filtering on the row labels and selecting just Japan, Germany, and United States.

See problem 11 in the "Problems" section of this chapter for an example of creating a calculated item. In the chip manufacturing PivotTable example, you could not create a calculated item because you had multiple copies of the Revenue field.

What is "drilling down"?

"Drilling down" is double-clicking a cell in a PivotTable to display all the detailed data that's summarized in that field. For example, double-clicking any March entry in the microchip scenario displays the data that's related to March sales.

I often have to use specific data in a PivotTable to determine profit, such as the April sales in France of Chip 1. Unfortunately, this data moves around when new fields are added to my PivotTable. Does Excel have a function that enables me always to extract April's Chip 1 sales in France from the PivotTable?

Yes, there is such a function. The *GETPIVOTDATA* function fills the bill. Suppose that you want to extract sales of Chip 1 in France during April from the PivotTable contained in the Data worksheet in the Getpivotdata.xlsx file. (See Figure 43-50.) Entering the GETPIVOTDATA(A4,"April_France_Chip_1_Sum_of_Revenue") formula in cell E2 yields the correct value ($37,600) even if additional products, countries, and months are added to the PivotTable later. You can also determine the resulting revenue by pointing to the cell containing Chip 1 April sales in France (cell D26).

The first argument for this function is in the cell in the upper-left corner of the PivotTable (cell A4). You enclose the PivotTable headings in quotation marks (separated by spaces) that define the entry you want. The last entry must specify the data field, but other headings can be listed in any order.

Thus, the formula here means "For the PivotTable whose upper-left corner is in cell A4, find the Sum of Revenue for Chip 1 in France during April." This formula returns the correct answer even if the sales data for Chip 1 in France in April moves to a different location in the PivotTable.

Row Labels	Values Sum of Var	Sum of Budget	Sum of Revenue	Sum of Revenue2	Sum of Var percentage of Budget
			april chip 1 France total revenue		
			37600		1026278
⊟Group1					
⊟January	-4297	91831	87534	8.53%	-0.046792477
⊟Chip 1	-4297	91831	87534	8.53%	-0.046792477
Canada	2929	29330	32259	3.14%	0.099863621
France	-5772	33171	27399	2.67%	-0.174007416
US	-1454	29330	27876	2.72%	-0.049573815
⊟February	2843	87534	90377	8.81%	0.032478808
⊟Chip 2	2843	87534	90377	8.81%	0.032478808
Canada	3318	32045	35363	3.45%	0.103541894
France	-3846	32954	29108	2.84%	-0.116708139
US	3371	22535	25906	2.52%	0.149589527
⊟March	-1389	90377	88988	8.67%	-0.015368954
⊟Chip 3	-1389	90377	88988	8.67%	-0.015368954
Canada	-10733	35363	24630	2.40%	-0.303509318
France	11529	20784	32313	3.15%	0.554705543
US	-2185	34230	32045	3.12%	-0.063832895
⊟April					
⊟April	-2774	87756	84982	8.28%	-0.031610374
⊟Chip 1	-2774	87756	84982	8.28%	-0.031610374
Canada	1054	19289	20343	1.98%	0.054642542
France	-54	37654	37600	3.66%	-0.001434111

FIGURE 43-50 Use the *GETPIVOTDATA* function to locate April Chip 1 Sales in France.

If you want simply to return total revenue ($1,026,278), you can enter the GETPIVOTDATA(A4,"Sum_of_Revenue") formula (see cell F2).

To see the true power of the *GETPIVOTDATA* function, suppose you want to summarize sales of each product by country for each month of the year in a nice table as shown in Figure 43-51.

J9		fx	April	
	I	J	K	L
8				
9	Month	April		
10				
11				
12		Chip 1	Chip 2	Chip 3
13	Canada	20343	0	0
14	France	37600	0	0
15	US	27039	0	0

FIGURE 43-51 Use *GETPIVOTDATA* to extract April sales of each product in each country.

To begin, create a drop-down box enabling you to enter the month of the year in cell J9. Enter the countries in I13:I15 and the products in J12:L12. In cell J13, copy your previous GETPIVOTDATA formula from E2 and edit it to become =IFERROR(GETPIVOTDATA("Sum_of_Revenue",$A$4,"Month",$J$9,"Product",J$12,"Country",$I13),0). Copying this formula from J13 to J13:L15 pulls the sales of each product during April from the PivotTable. As you copy across, the product pulls changes, and as you copy down, the country pulls changes. In each cell, the chosen month is pulled from cell J9. The use of the *IFERROR* function ensures that if no sales of a product occurred in a country during the selected month, you return a 0 instead of an error message. Imagine how useful this trick would be if you sold 1000 products in 200 countries and regions!

Often, the *GETPIVOTDATA* function is a nuisance. In these cases, you can turn off the option to use it. Suppose you want to refer to data in cells B5:B11 from a PivotTable elsewhere in your workbook. You would probably use the =B5 formula and copy it to the B6:B11 range. Hopefully, this would extract B6, B7, . . . , B11 to the cells you want. Unfortunately, if the *GETPIVOTDATA* option is active, you get a bunch of *GETPIVOTDATA* functions that refer to the same cell. If you want to turn off *GETPIVOTDATA*, click the **File** tab and then click **Options**. Select **Formulas** and, under **Working With Formulas**, clear the **GetPivotData Function For PivotTable References** check box. This ensures that clicking inside a PivotTable yields a formula like =B5 rather than a *GETPIVOTDATA* function. You can also turn off GetPivotData in a particular PivotTable by selecting **PivotTable** from the **Analyze** tab. Select **Options** and, from the drop-down list, clear **Generate GetPivotData**.

Finally, note that you can also combine the *MATCH* and *OFFSET* functions (explained in Chapter 4, "MATCH function," and Chapter 21, "The OFFSET function," respectively) to extract various PivotTable entries.

How can I use the new Excel 2013 Timeline feature to summarize data during different time periods?

Excel 2013 introduces a wonderful new feature, Timeline, that enables you to filter your PivotTable easily based on time periods. Assuming that your data has a column containing actual dates, you can select any subset of consecutive calendar years, quarters, months, or days in your data, and the Timeline feature ensures that all PivotTable calculations include only spreadsheet rows from the selected period.

To illustrate the use of the Timeline feature, look at the Makeuptimeline.xlsx workbook. In the worksheet data, the following information is listed for 1900 makeup transactions: Salesperson, Product, Date, Units, and Revenue. In the worksheet Pivot Table, you see a PivotTable that summarizes sales of each product by each salesperson. After clicking anywhere in the PivotTable, click the **Insert** tab on the ribbon and select **Timeline** from the **Filters** group. You see the timeline shown in Figure 43-52.

	A	B	C	D	E	F	G
1							
2							
3	**Sum of Dollars**	**Column Labels** ▾					
4	**Row Labels** ▾	eye liner	foundation	lip gloss	lipstick	mascara	**Grand Total**
5	Ashley	$5,844.95	$4,186.06	$6,053.68	$3,245.44	$6,617.10	$25,947.24
6	Betsy	$6,046.53	$8,276.84	$5,683.91	$3,968.61	$4,827.25	$28,803.15
7	Cici	$5,982.82	$6,198.25	$5,199.95	$3,148.84	$7,060.71	$27,590.57
8	Colleen	$3,389.63	$6,834.77	$5,573.32	$2,346.41	$6,746.53	$24,890.66
9	Cristina	$5,397.27	$5,290.99	$5,297.98	$2,401.67	$5,461.65	$23,849.56
10	Emilee	$7,587.39	$5,492.80	$5,270.25	$2,189.14	$4,719.30	$25,258.87
11	Hallagan	$6,964.62	$7,256.20	$5,603.12	$3,177.87	$5,703.35	$28,705.16
12	Jen	$7,010.44	$5,747.95	$5,461.61	$3,953.30	$6,877.23	$29,050.53
13	Zaret	$8,270.19	$6,451.65	$5,690.81	$2,448.71	$3,879.95	$26,741.31
14	**Grand Total**	56493.84331	55735.50749	49834.6434	26879.98743	51893.06545	240837.0471
15			**Date**				▾
16							
17			All Periods			QUARTERS ▾	
18			2004		2005	2006	
19			Q1 Q2 Q3	Q4 Q1	Q2 Q3	Q4 Q1 Q2	
20							
21							
22		oic	◀			▶	
23							

FIGURE 43-52 This is the timeline for Makeup data.

By using the Shift key, you can select adjacent quarters that can be used to summarize sales. For example, the Timeline worksheet (see Figure 43-53) summarizes sales during 2004 and the first two quarters of 2005. Clicking the funnel restores a PivotTable based on all data.

	A	B	C	D	E	F	G
1							
2							
3	**Sum of Dollars**	**Column Labels** ▾					
4	**Row Labels** ▾	eye liner	foundation	lip gloss	lipstick	mascara	**Grand Total**
5	Ashley	$2,259.97	$2,064.62	$3,387.84	$1,191.92	$4,773.72	$13,678.07
6	Betsy	$2,714.91	$4,195.09	$2,862.84	$2,223.66	$2,591.12	$14,587.61
7	Cici	$3,310.71	$3,313.91	$2,076.46	$1,676.03	$3,026.36	$13,403.47
8	Colleen	$2,122.76	$4,064.70	$3,190.32	$1,454.87	$3,163.44	$13,996.09
9	Cristina	$3,890.14	$2,047.07	$2,844.16	$1,531.34	$2,708.86	$13,021.57
10	Emilee	$4,086.75	$2,754.36	$2,808.22	$1,180.96	$2,462.89	$13,293.17
11	Hallagan	$4,195.40	$3,622.60	$2,857.48	$2,133.18	$2,309.15	$15,117.81
12	Jen	$3,364.89	$2,830.40	$1,875.47	$1,762.88	$3,866.27	$13,699.91
13	Zaret	$3,188.38	$2,695.03	$3,040.78	$1,659.86	$1,828.48	$12,412.53
14	**Grand Total**	29133.89079	27587.77037	24943.58511	14814.69089	26730.28606	123210.2232
15			**Date**				▾
16							
17			Q1 2004 - Q2 2005			QUARTERS ▾	
18			2004		2005	2006	
19			Q1 Q2 Q3	Q4 Q1	Q2 Q3	Q4 Q1 Q2	
20							
21							
22			◀			▶	
23							

FIGURE 43-53 This timeline summarizes sales for 2004 and first two quarters of 2005.

How I can use a PivotTable to summarize total sales to date during a year?

Using **Value Field Settings** makes it easy to summarize total sales to date during a year. To illustrate this, look at the MonthtoMonth.xlsx file. The Data worksheet contains the Month, Year, and Amount for a number of sales transactions. To begin, in the Year to Date worksheet, summarize monthly sales for each year by dragging **Month** to the **Rows** area, **Year** to the **Columns** area, and **Revenues** to the **Values** area. This yields the PivotTable shown in Figure 43-54.

	A	B	C	D	E
1					
2					
3	**Sum of Revenue**	**Column Labels** ▾			
4	**Row Labels** ▾	**2009**	**2010**	**2011**	**Grand Total**
5	January	10453	84058	45615	140126
6	February	47996	74896	32943	155835
7	March	113126	41689	19821	174636
8	April	69613	59910	39770	169293
9	May	65155	49345	29600	144100
10	June	54814	42355	61331	158500
11	July	34930	87516	38863	161309
12	August	51588	33060	47287	131935
13	September	60835	48963	45559	155357
14	October	85607	36243	30805	152655
15	November	72602	17010	48207	137819
16	December	30043	73381	79733	183157
17	**Grand Total**	**696762**	**648426**	**519534**	**1864722**

FIGURE 43-54 This is a summary of sales by month and year.

This figure shows a sales summary broken down by month and year. From anywhere in the PivotTable, right-click and select **Value Field Settings** and **Show Values As** and choose **Running Total In**. Select **Month**. The resulting PivotTable, shown in Figure 43-55 (see worksheet Year to Date), shows the sales for each month for the given year through that month. For example, sales through February 2010 were $58,449. You may also create the running totals by right-clicking any values cell and choosing **Show Values As**.

	A	B	C	D	E
1					
2					
3	**Sum of Revenue**	**Column Labels**			
4	**Row Labels**	**2009**	**2010**	**2011**	**Grand Total**
5	January	10453	84058	45615	140126
6	February	58449	158954	78558	295961
7	March	171575	200643	98379	470597
8	April	241188	260553	138149	639890
9	May	306343	309898	167749	783990
10	June	361157	352253	229080	942490
11	July	396087	439769	267943	1103799
12	August	447675	472829	315230	1235734
13	September	508510	521792	360789	1391091
14	October	594117	558035	391594	1543746
15	November	666719	575045	439801	1681565
16	December	696762	648426	519534	1864722
17	**Grand Total**				

FIGURE 43-55 Here are year-to-date sales totals.

How can I use a PivotTable to summarize sales this month compared to the same month a year earlier?

Again, you will use the data in the Month to Month workbook. In the Previous Year worksheet, create a PivotTable by dragging **Month** to the **Row** area, **Year** to the **Column** area, and **Sales** to the **Values** area. After right-clicking anywhere in the PivotTable and selecting **Value Field Settings**, filling in the dialog box as shown in Figure 43-56 creates the PivotTable shown in Figure 43-57. Here you see how sales during each month compare to the same month in the previous year. For example, January 2010 sales increased 704.15 percent over January 2009 sales. Again, you can also change the display of sales from actual sales to comparing a month to the same month during the previous year by right-clicking a values cell and selecting **Show Values As**.

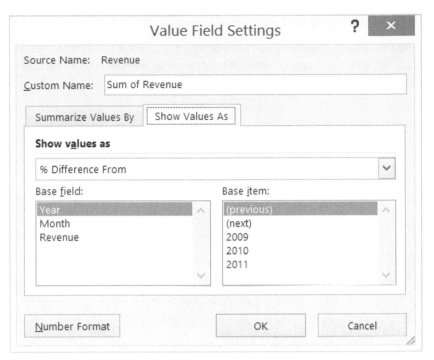

FIGURE 43-56 These are the settings needed to compare a month to the same month in the previous year.

Sum of Revenue	Column Labels			
Row Labels	**2009**	**2010**	**2011**	**Grand Total**
January		704.15%	-45.73%	
February		56.05%	-56.02%	
March		-63.15%	-52.46%	
April		-13.94%	-33.62%	
May		-24.27%	-40.01%	
June		-22.73%	44.80%	
July		150.55%	-55.59%	
August		-35.92%	43.03%	
September		-19.52%	-6.95%	
October		-57.66%	-15.00%	
November		-76.57%	183.40%	
December		144.25%	8.66%	
Grand Total		**-6.94%**	**-19.88%**	

FIGURE 43-57 Comparison of sales to the same month during the previous year.

How can I create a PivotTable based on data in several locations?

Often, the data needed to create a PivotTable can lie in different worksheets or different workbooks. The key to creating a PivotTable from data in different locations is to press ALT+D+P and open the classic **PivotTable And PivotChart Wizard**, shown in Figure 43-58.

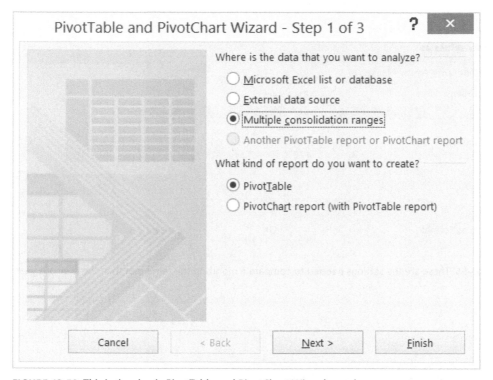

FIGURE 43-58 This is the classic PivotTable and PivotChart Wizard opening page.

To illustrate how to create a PivotTable based on data in different ranges, open the East and West files and, through **View Arrange Tiled**, display them side by side as shown in Figure 43-59. This data represents January, February, and March sales in the East and West. You want to produce a PivotTable that summarizes total sales of each product during each month.

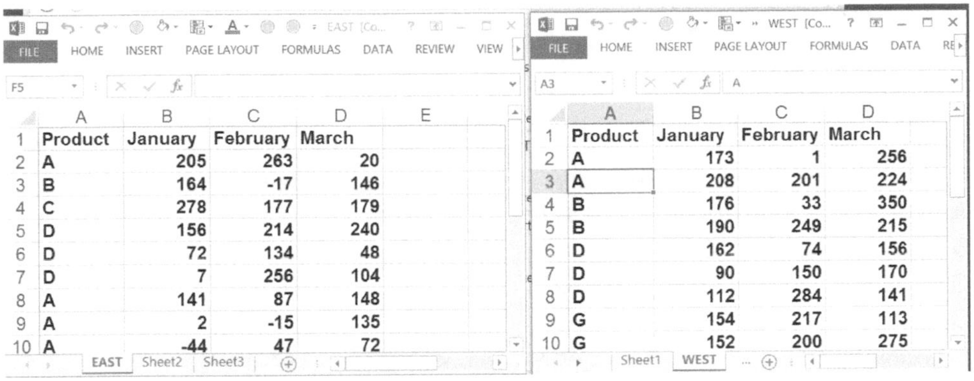

	A	B	C	D
1	Product	January	February	March
2	A	205	263	20
3	B	164	-17	146
4	C	278	177	179
5	D	156	214	240
6	D	72	134	48
7	D	7	256	104
8	A	141	87	148
9	A	2	-15	135
10	A	-44	47	72

	A	B	C	D
1	Product	January	February	March
2	A	173	1	256
3	A	208	201	224
4	B	176	33	350
5	B	190	249	215
6	D	162	74	156
7	D	90	150	170
8	D	112	284	141
9	G	154	217	113
10	G	152	200	275

FIGURE 43-59 Two files will be summarized with a PivotTable.

To begin, press ALT+D+P and select **Multiple Consolidation Ranges**, as shown in Figure 43-58. After selecting **Next**, select **Create A Single Page Field For Me** and, from **Step 2b** of the **PivotTable and PivotChart Wizard**, select, as shown in Figure 43-60, the **East** sales data and click **Add** to add it to the range of data that will be used to create your PivotTable.

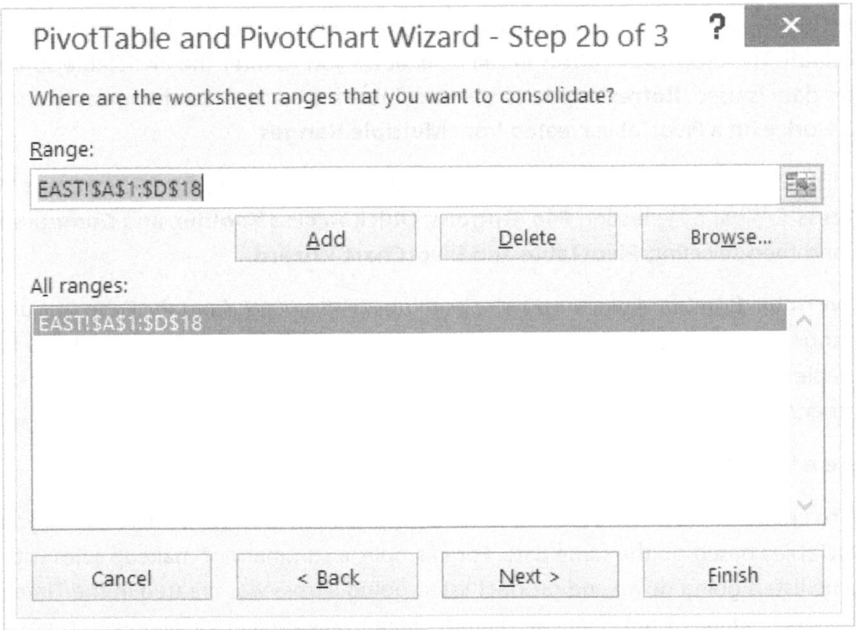

FIGURE 43-60 Add the East data.

Clear the **East** data from the **Range** portion of the page; select the **West** data and add this data to the **All Ranges** section. After clicking **Next**, you can decide whether to place the final PivotTable in a new worksheet or the current worksheet. A new worksheet has been chosen here. After selecting **Finish**, you obtain the PivotTable (see Figure 43-61) in the PT worksheet of West.xlsx workbook.

⬜	A	B	C	D	E
1	Page1	(All) ▾			
2					
3	Sum of Value	Column ▾			
4	Row ▾	January	February	March	Grand Total
5	A	1323	1317	1445	4085
6	B	890	335	812	2037
7	C	1231	922	843	2996
8	D	767	1424	1199	3390
9	E	579	483	371	1433
10	F	597	577	327	1501
11	G	570	850	811	2231
12	H	131	71	266	468
13	Grand Total	6088	5979	6074	18141

FIGURE 43-61 This PivotTable is summarizing East and West sales.

You find, for example, that total sales of Product A in February were 1317. You can filter on the products by selecting the drop-down arrow in cell A4 and filter on the months by using the drop-down arrow in cell B3. The drop-down arrow in cell B1 enables you to filter the PivotTable so only East or West sales data is used. **Refresh** updates the PivotTable based on data changes. Slicers and timelines do not work with a PivotTable created from **Multiple Ranges**.

If you do not like the ALT+D+P combination, you can add the **PivotTable And PivotChart Wizard** to the **Quick Access** toolbar by selecting **File**, **Options**, **Quick Access Toolbar**, and **Commands Not on the Ribbon** and then selecting **PivotTable and PivotChart Wizard**.

To create a PivotTable from multiple ranges, the headings (in this case, January, February, and March) in each range must be identical. Chapter 44 discusses a new feature in Excel 2013, the Data Model, which enables you to create PivotTables even when a heading from one source range occurs in none of the other source ranges.

How can I create a PivotTable based on an already created PivotTable?

Often, you want to create a PivotTable based on an already created PivotTable. This enables you to view several PivotTables based on the same data. For example, a summary of makeup sales with each salesperson's name listed going down and product listed going across was created in the Timeline.xlsx workbook (as shown in Figure 43-52). Suppose you also want to create a PivotTable with product listed going down and salesperson going across. With the cursor in the PivotTable worksheet of workbook Makeuptimeline.xls, press ALT+D+P to open the **PivotTable And PivotChart Wizard**. Choose **Another PivotTable or PivotChart Report**. Choose the PivotTable from which you wish to build your new table. The original PivotTable has been chosen: PivotTable10. Now the Field list appears, and you can create a new PivotTable without disturbing your old table. Product has been put in the Row area, Name in the Column area, and Dollars in the Values area. This creates the PivotTable shown in Figure 43-62.

Sum of Dollars	Column Labels									
Row Labels	Ashley	Betsy	Cici	Colleen	Cristina	Emilee	Hallagan	Jen	Zaret	Grand Total
eye liner	$5,844.95	$6,046.53	$5,982.82	$3,389.63	$5,397.27	$7,587.39	$6,964.62	$7,010.44	$8,270.19	$56,493.84
foundation	$4,186.06	$8,276.84	$6,198.25	$6,834.77	$5,290.99	$5,492.80	$7,256.20	$5,747.95	$6,451.65	$55,735.51
lip gloss	$6,053.68	$5,683.91	$5,199.95	$5,573.32	$5,297.98	$5,270.25	$5,603.12	$5,461.61	$5,690.81	$49,834.64
lipstick	$3,245.44	$3,968.61	$3,148.84	$2,346.41	$2,401.67	$2,189.14	$3,177.87	$3,953.30	$2,448.71	$26,879.99
mascara	$6,617.10	$4,827.25	$7,060.71	$6,746.53	$5,461.65	$4,719.30	$5,703.35	$6,877.23	$3,879.95	$51,893.07
Grand Total	25947.23526	28803.147	27590.573	24890.656	23849.559	25258.87	28705.1622	29050.535	26741.31	240837.0471

FIGURE 43-62 Here is a PivotTable based on another PivotTable.

Problems

1. Contoso, Ltd. produces microchips. Five types of defects (labeled 1–5) have been known to occur. Chips are manufactured by two operators (A and B), using four machines (1–4). You are given data about a sample of defective chips, including the type of defect, the operator, machine number, and day of the week the defect occurred. Use this data to chart a course of action that would lead, as quickly as possible, to improved product quality. You should use a PivotTable to stratify the defects with respect to type of defect, day of the week, machine used, and operator working. You might even want to break down the data by machine, operator, and so on. Assume that each operator and machine made an equal number of products. You'll find this data in the Contoso.xlsx file.

2. You own a fast-food restaurant and have done some market research in an attempt to understand your customers better. For a random sample of customers, you are given the income, gender, and number of days per week that residents go out for fast food. Use this information to determine how gender and income influence the frequency with which a person goes out to eat fast food. The data is in the McDonalds.xlsx file

3. Students at the School of Fine Art apply to study either English or Science. You have been assigned to determine whether the School of Fine Art discriminates against women in admitting students to the school of their choice. You are given the following data on the School of Fine Art's students:

   - Female or male

   - Major applied for: English (Eng) or Science (Sci)

   - Admit? Yes or No

   Assuming that women are as qualified for each major as men are, does this data indicate that the college discriminates against women? Be sure you use all available information. The data is in the Finearts.xlsx file.

4. You have been assigned to evaluate the quality of care given to heart attack patients at Emergency Room (ER) and Chicago Hope (CH). For the past month, you are given the following patient data:

- Hospital (ER or CH).

- Risk category (high or low). High-risk people are less likely to survive than low-risk people.

- Patient outcome (live or die).

Use this data to determine which hospital is doing a better job of caring for heart attack patients. Hint: Use all the data. The data is in the Hospital.xlsx file.

5. You are given the monthly level of the Dow Jones Index for years 1947 to 1992. Does this data indicate any unusual seasonal patterns in stock returns? Hint: You can extract the month (January, February, and so on) by using the TEXT(A4,"mmm") formula copied to any column. The data is in the Dow.xlsx file.

6. The Makeupdb.xlsx file contains information about the sales of makeup products. For each transaction, you are given the following information:

- Name of salesperson

- Date of sale

- Product sold

- Units sold

- Transaction revenue

Create a PivotTable to compile the following information:

- The number of sales transactions for each salesperson.

- For each salesperson, the total revenue by product.

- Using your answer to the previous question, create a function that always yields Jen's lipstick sales.

- Total revenue generated by each salesperson broken down by location.

- Total revenue by salesperson and year. (Hint: You need to group the data by year.)

7. For years 1985 to 1992, you are given monthly interest rates on bonds that pay money one year after the day they're bought. It's often suggested that interest rates are more volatile—tend to change more—when interest rates are high. Does the data in the Intratevol-volatility.xlsx file support this statement? (Hint: PivotTables can display standard deviations.)

8. For the grocery example, prepare a chart that summarizes the trend over time of the sales at each store.

9. For the grocery example, create a calculate field that computes an average per unit price received for each product.

10. For the grocery example, create a PivotChart that summarizes the sales of each product at each store for years 2005 and 2006.

11. For the data in the Calcitemdata.xlsx file, create calculated items that summarize sales of dessert (cakes + puddings) and fruits (apples + grapes).

12. In the chip PivotTable example, create a PivotTable that summarizes monthly sales of Chips 1 and 3 in France and the United States.

13. In the customer PivotTable example, show the top 15 customers in one table and the bottom 5 customers in another table.

14. The Ptablepartsdata.xlsx file contains sales of various parts. Each part code begins with either Part (for computer part) or Comp (for computer). Create a PivotTable that shows only sales of Parts. (Hint: Use a labels filter.)

15. For the data in problem 14, summarize the total sales of parts and computers.

16. The Cigarettedata.xlsx file contains the age of a sample of Americans, whether they smoke cigarettes or cigars, and whether they died during the current year. What can you conclude from this data?

17. The Collegedata.xlsx file tells you the following information about students who applied to graduate school at Kelley University: gender, desired major, whether accepted or rejected. If you construct the appropriate PivotTable, you will find fewer women are accepted than men are. Do you think Kelley discriminates against women?

18. The AnalyzeSurveydata.xlsx file contains answers on a 1–7 scale to various questions on a teaching evaluation survey. Create a PivotChart that charts the fraction of the time each value 1–7 occurs for each question. Filter the chart to show the breakdown for any set of three questions you choose.

19. Using the data in the MonthtoMonth.xlsx file, create a PivotTable that shows how each month's sales differs from the previous month for the year 2010.

CHAPTER 44

The Data Model

Questions answered in this chapter:

- What is the Data Model feature and why do I need to learn about it?

- How can I add data to the Data Model?

- How can I create relationships within the Data Model?

- How can I use the Data Model to create PivotTables?

- How does the Quick Explore option work?

- How can I add new data to a Data Model?

- How can I remove data from the Data Model?

- How can I use the Data Model to create a new PivotTable?

- How can I edit or delete relationships?

- How does the *DISTINCT COUNT* function work?

Answers to this chapter's questions

This section provides the answers to the questions that are listed at the beginning of the chapter.

What is the Data Model feature and why do I need to learn about it?

The Data Model feature is new in Excel 2013. (It was an add-in in Excel 2010.) The Data Model provides an easy way to load data beyond the ordinary capabilities of Excel 2013 (1,048,576 rows of data) and use this data to create PivotTables. The Data Model also enables you to combine data that comes from sources outside of Excel (including Access and SQL Server) with data from Excel. Finally, an understanding of the Data Model will make it easier for you to grasp the amazing capabilities of PowerPivot (see Chapter 45, "PowerPivot"), which is available if you have access to Excel 2013 Pro Plus or Office 365.

In Chapter 43, "Using PivotTables and slicers to describe data," you learned how to use the Excel PivotTable feature to summarize data. You saw how to create PivotTables based on data in disparate locations, but this approach required the data in each location to have the same column headings.

This is often not the case. For example, the Datamodeltemp.xlsx workbook contains two worksheets. The Reps worksheet (shown on the left in Figure 44-1) contains a list of salespeople ID numbers and the state where they sell your products. The Sales worksheet (shown on the right in Figure 44-1) shows unit sales generated by each employee. Naturally, you would like to use a PivotTable to summarize sales by state. The problem is that the data in the Sales worksheet does not know each salesperson's state. You could add a column by using VLOOKUP formulas to insert the states in the Sales worksheet. If you had several hundred thousand rows of data, however, these VLOOKUPs would greatly slow down your spreadsheet performance. The Excel Data Model enables you to work around the VLOOKUPs by easily creating a relationship that tells Excel the state for each salesperson without the need of slow VLOOKUPs.

Data must be included in the Data Model to create amazing graphics with Power View. (See Chapter 46, "Power View," for a discussion of Power View.) Finally, if you want to mash up data from different sources such as databases, the web, text files, and Excel spreadsheets, you want to use PowerPivot (discussed in Chapter 45). When you understand the Data Model, PowerPivot becomes much easier to understand. Power View and PowerPivot are only available if you have the Pro Plus or Office 365 edition of Excel 2013, but the Data Model is included in all editions of Excel 2013.

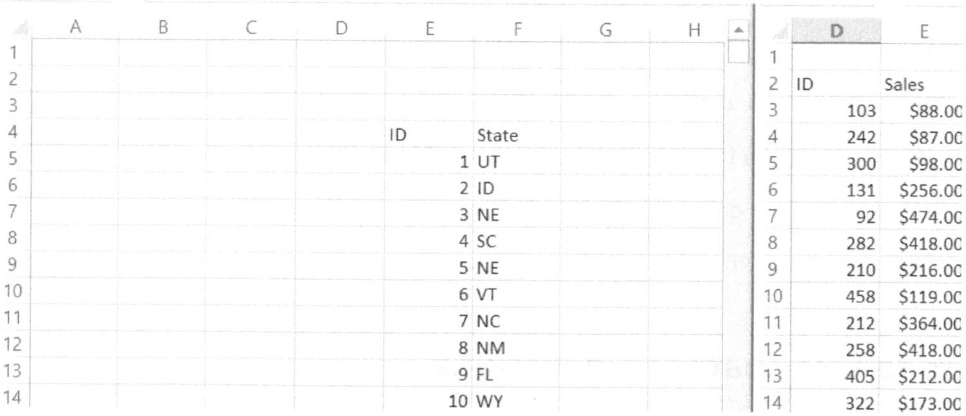

	E	F
4	ID	State
5	1	UT
6	2	ID
7	3	NE
8	4	SC
9	5	NE
10	6	VT
11	7	NC
12	8	NM
13	9	FL
14	10	WY

	D	E
2	ID	Sales
3	103	$88.0C
4	242	$87.0C
5	300	$98.0C
6	131	$256.0C
7	92	$474.0C
8	282	$418.0C
9	210	$216.0C
10	458	$119.0C
11	212	$364.0C
12	258	$418.0C
13	405	$212.0C
14	322	$173.0C

FIGURE 44-1 This is the data used in the Data Model example.

How can I add data to the Data Model?

Before adding any data to the Data Model, you should make the data a table (see Chapter 25, "Tables"). First, select the data, including column headers, in the Reps worksheet and use Ctrl+T to make the data a table. From Table Tools, name the table **Reps**. Then, as shown in Figure 44-2, select **PivotTable** from the **Insert** tab and select the **Add This Data To The Data Model** check box. This ensures that the data in the Reps worksheet is included in the Data Model. In a similar fashion, select the data in the Sales worksheet and name the table **Sales**. Add the Sales table to the Data Model.

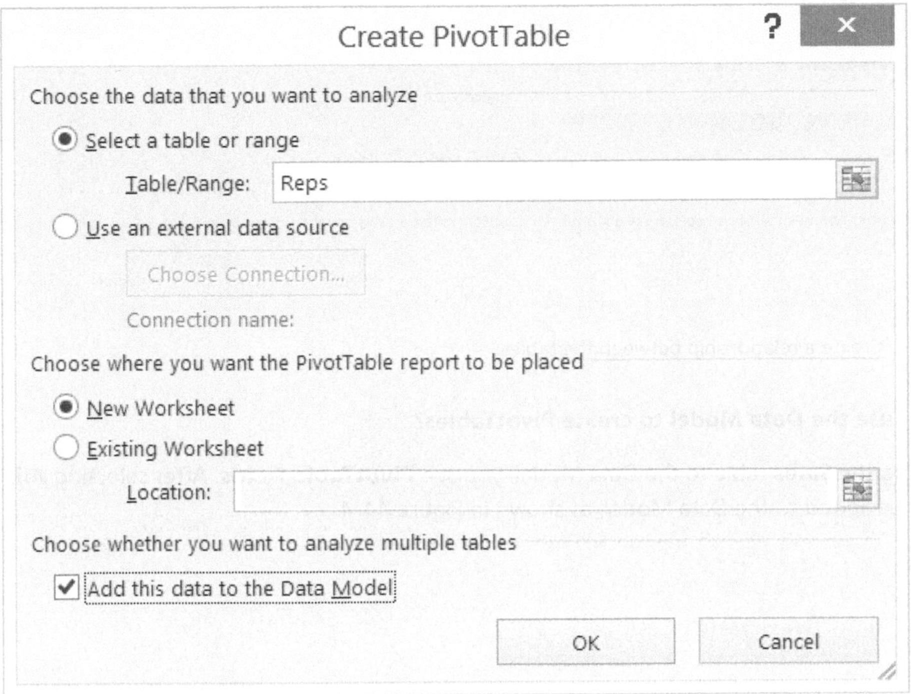

FIGURE 44-2 Add data to the Data Model.

How can I create relationships within the Data Model?

If you want to summarize sales by state, you have a problem. At present, there is no way for Excel to know each salesperson's state. Somehow, you need to create a relationship that enables Excel to determine the state for each row of data in the Sales table. After adding the Sales table to the Data Model, you can create the needed relationship by selecting **Relationships** from the **Data** tab. After clicking **Relationships**, selecting **New** opens the **Create Relationship** dialog box shown in Figure 44-3. The Primary Column must be the column of data that involves a one-to-one relationship that can be mapped into the Foreign Column. Because the Reps table has a state for each sales rep in your example, the Primary Column must be the ID column in the Reps table. Make the Foreign Column the ID column from the Sales table. These settings are shown in Figure 44-3. Now if you try to create a PivotTable that summarizes sales by state, you will be fine because, for each ID number in the Sales table, Excel will know to pull the correct state from the Reps table.

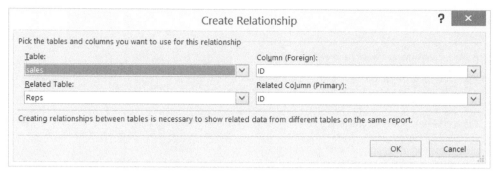

FIGURE 44-3 Create a relationship between the tables.

How can I use the Data Model to create PivotTables?

After adding the **Sales** table to the Data Model, you see **PivotTable Fields**. After selecting **All**, you see all tables added to the Data Model, as shown in Figure 44-4.

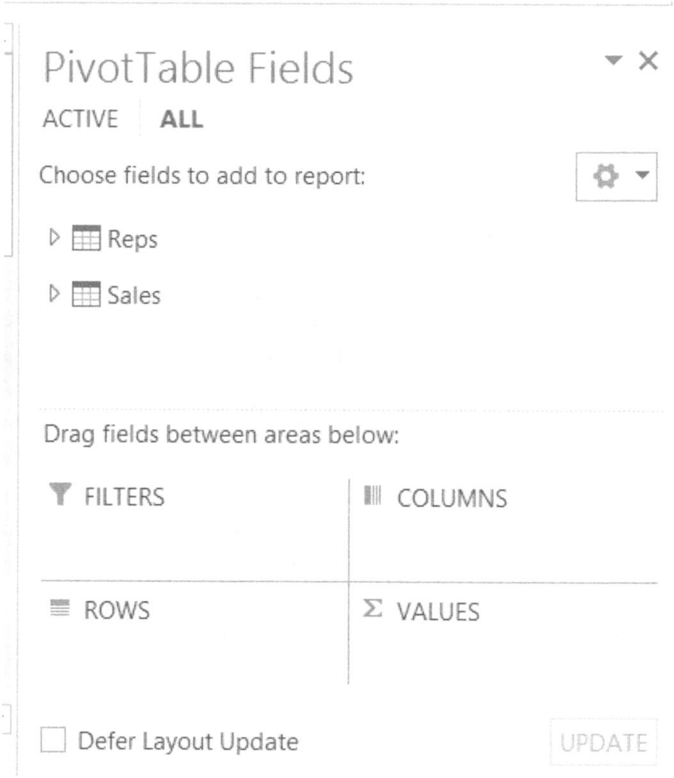

PivotTable Fields   ▼ ×

ACTIVE   **ALL**

Choose fields to add to report: ⚙ ▼

▷ ⊞ Reps

▷ ⊞ Sales

Drag fields between areas below:

▼ FILTERS   ‖‖ COLUMNS

≡ ROWS   Σ VALUES

☐ Defer Layout Update   UPDATE

FIGURE 44-4 This is the field list for the Data Model example.

After clicking the triangles to the left of the Reps and Sales tables, you see all columns from the Reps and Sales tables. To create a PivotTable that computes total sales in each state, drag **States** to the **Rows** zone and **Sales** to the **Values** zone, as shown in Figure 44-5. You obtain the PivotTable shown in Figure 44-6.

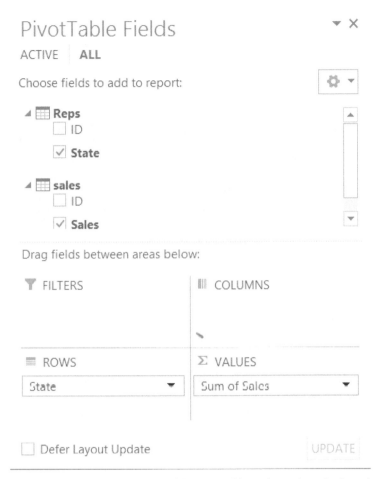

FIGURE 44-5 This is the creation of the PivotTable to determine sales in each state.

For example, 10,846 units were sold in Alaska; 24,147 units were sold in Georgia, and so on.

If you had tried to create the PivotTable before creating the relationship shown in Figure 44-3, Excel would have had no way to figure out the state for each row of the Sales table. Excel would have therefore prompted you to create the needed relationship.

Row Labels	Sum of Sales
AK	10846
AL	23517
AR	24948
AZ	10532
CA	16646
CO	17447
CT	15350
DE	27179
FL	15424
GA	24147
HI	15966
IA	9172
ID	16656
IL	21525
IN	4706
KS	13875
KY	16254
LA	13465
MA	11816
MD	10899

FIGURE 44-6 This figure shows the unit sales in each state.

How does the Quick Explore option work?

If you click the total sales for any state (Alaska here) you see the Quick Explore Icon shown in Figure 44-7. Clicking the drop-down arrow to the right of the icon opens the box shown in Figure 44-8. Quick Explore suggests drilling down by ID. Clicking **Drill To ID** shows the sales for all salespeople associated with Alaska sales (see Figure 44-9).

Row Labels	Sum of Sales	
AK	10846	
AL	23517	🔎
AR	24948	

FIGURE 44-7 This is what the Quick Explore icon looks like.

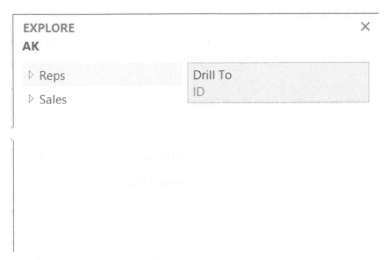

FIGURE 44-8 Quick Explore suggests drilling down to Salesperson ID.

	A	B
3	Row Labels ▼	Sum of Sales
4	11	1387
5	35	588
6	39	1631
7	151	1801
8	383	1388
9	395	2520
10	459	1531
11	**Grand Total**	**10846**

FIGURE 44-9 This figure shows Alaska salespeople and sales.

How can I add new data to a Data Model?

If you want to add a new set of data to the Data Model, make the data a table and select **Insert PivotTable**. You can select **Add This Data To Data Model** and, if you select **All** (instead of Active), you can now use the new data in your PivotTable.

You may also add a newly created Excel Table to a Data Model by clicking the **Data** tab on the ribbon and selecting **Connections**. The **Workbook Connections** dialog box opens. After selecting **Add**, the **Existing Connections** dialog box opens. After choosing **Tables**, you can add your new table to the Data Model.

If adding new data means adding new rows to tables already included in the Data Model, select **Refresh** from the **Workbook Connections** dialog box after selecting **Connections** from the **Data** tab to ensure that your PivotTables will update to include the new data.

How can I remove data from a Data Model?

To remove data from a Data Model, click the **Data** tab on the ribbon and then select **Connections**. As shown in Figure 44-10, you can select a Table (Reps is selected) and choose **Remove** to remove the table from the Data Model.

How can I use the Data Model to create a new PivotTable?

To use existing data to create a new PivotTable, proceed as follows:

1. Open the **Create PivotTable** dialog box by selecting **PivotTable** from the **Insert** tab.

2. Select **Use An External Data Source** and then select **Choose Connection**.

3. From the **Existing Connections** tab, select **Tables** and then choose **Tables In Workbook Data Model**. You see the dialog box shown in Figure 44-11.

4. If you now select **Open**, you are returned to the **Create PivotTable** dialog box, and you can now create a PivotTable.

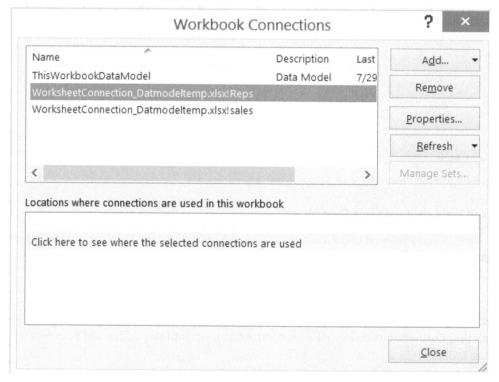

FIGURE 44-10 The Workbook Connections dialog box is set to remove the Reps table from the Data Model.

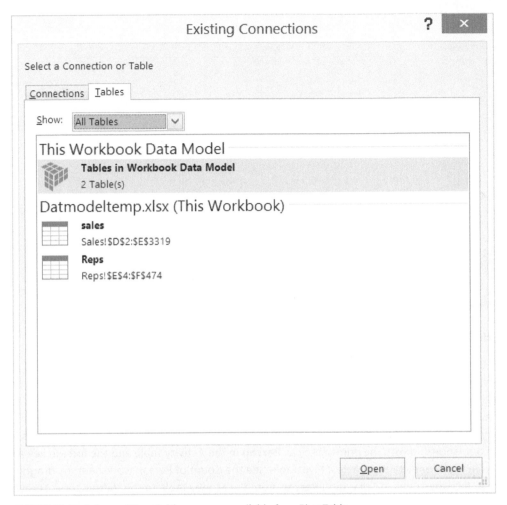

FIGURE 44-11 Sales and Reps tables are now available for a PivotTable.

How can I edit or delete relationships?

To edit or delete relationships, select **Relationships** from the **Data** tools group on the **Data** tab. This opens the **Manage Relationships** dialog box shown in Figure 44-12. From this dialog box, you can edit or delete relationships or create new relationships.

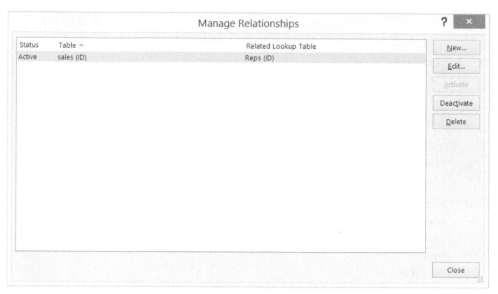

FIGURE 44-12 This is the Manage Relationships dialog box.

How does the *DISTINCT COUNT* function work?

In the DISTINCTCOUNTemp.xlsx file, you are given (as shown in Figure 44-13) a list of athletes (1–100) and salary payments received. Because many athletes received more than one payment, they occur more than once on the list. You are also given the sport each athlete plays. Suppose you want to determine how many athletes played each sport. First, make the data in E3:F466 a table named **Money** and the data in the K6:L106 range a table named **Activity**; add each table to the Data Model. Create a relationship with the primary key as **Person** in the Activity table and the foreign key as **Person** in the Money table. Create a PivotTable (see the Count of Person worksheet) by dragging **Sport** to the **Row** zone and dragging **Person** from the Money table to the **Values** zone. This yields the PivotTable shown in Figure 44-14. Because there are only 100 athletes, you see that each person is counted multiple times. To fix this problem, right-click any value cell in the PivotTable and choose **Value Field Settings**. If you scroll to the bottom, you find, as shown in Figure 44-15, that the last (but not least!) choice is Distinct Count. This choice ensures that each athlete is counted only once and yields the PivotTable shown in Figure 44-16 and worksheet Distinct Count. This PivotTable shows exactly how many athletes play each sport!

	E	F	G	H	I	J	K	L
1								
2	**Person** ▾	**Salary** ▾						
3	32	6						
4	66	4						
5	15	4						
6	53	7					**Person** ▾	**Sport** ▾
7	26	9					1	Basketball
8	56	9					2	Hockey
9	80	7					3	Lacrosse
10	29	7					4	Football
11	63	4					5	Football
12	84	5					6	Lacrosse
13	79	4					7	Lacrosse
14	82	6					8	Baseball
15	69	6					9	Hockey
16	60	8					10	Lacrosse
17	59	8					11	Lacrosse
18	66	4					12	Football
19	6	10					13	Lacrosse
20	91	6					14	Baseball

FIGURE 44-13 This is the data for the DISTINCT COUNT example.

	A	B
1		
2		
3	**Row Labels** ▾	**Count of Person**
4	Baseball	85
5	Basketball	96
6	Football	84
7	Hockey	72
8	Lacrosse	127
9	**Grand Total**	**464**

FIGURE 44-14 This PivotTable counts each athlete multiple times.

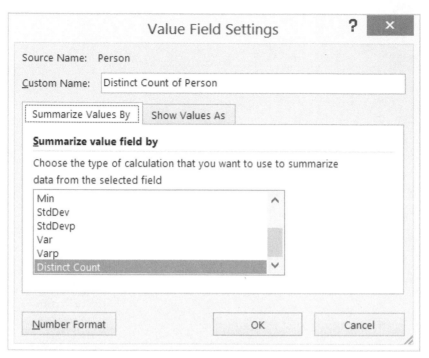

FIGURE 44-15 Choose Distinct Count to obtain a unique list of the number of athletes playing each sport.

Row Labels	Distinct Count of Person
Baseball	21
Basketball	19
Football	20
Hockey	14
Lacrosse	26
Grand Total	**100**

FIGURE 44-16 This is the distinct count of how many athletes play each sport.

Problems

TheFaberu.xlsx file contains salaries, travel expenses, Faculty ID, Department code, and Faculty code for all business school faculty. Use this data to answer the following questions. (No VLOOKUPS allowed!)

1. Use the Data Model to create a PivotTable that gives average salary broken down by department.

2. Use the Data Model to create a PivotTable that gives average salary broken down by type of faculty member and department.

3. Use the Data Model to create a PivotTable that gives average travel expenses by departments.

CHAPTER 45

PowerPivot

Questions answered in this chapter:

- How can I load data into PowerPivot?

- How can I use PowerPivot to create a PivotTable?

- How can I use slicers with PowerPivot?

- What are *DAX* functions?

Microsoft PowerPivot was first introduced as a downloadable add-in for Excel 2010. If you have Excel 2013 Pro Plus or Office 365, PowerPivot for Excel is available to you. PowerPivot for Microsoft Excel 2013 is an add-in that enables you to:

- Store and query large volumes of data (think hundreds of millions of rows) efficiently that you can combine from multiple data sources and multiple data formats. For example, some of your data might come from a Microsoft Access database, some from a text file, some from several Excel files, and some from live data imported from a website.

- Create calculated columns (beyond field definitions). For example, if each row of your source data contained revenue and costs, you could create a calculated column to compute Profit = Revenue – Costs. PowerPivot contains many *DAX* (Data Expression Language) functions that facilitate the creation of calculated columns.

- Create calculated fields that aggregate data from different rows. For example, a calculated field could compute total profit as the sum of profit from each transaction.

- Create KPIs (Key Performance Indicators) that make it easy for an organization to track performance against targets. For example, a PowerPivot KPI could be used to determine for each year and salesperson how his actual sales compared to his sales quota.

- PowerPivot can be used as a data source for workbook reports (PivotTables, Charts, *CUBE* functions, Power View, and so on). Power View is covered in Chapter 46, "Power View."

- PowerPivot reports can be published to Microsoft SharePoint to allow automatic data refresh, facilitate sharing, and enable IT monitoring. When published, it can be used as a data source for other analytic and reporting experiences (such as publishing to SharePoint, a deployment process).

This chapter introduces PowerPivot. For a more complete explanation of how PowerPivot works, read *Microsoft PowerPivot for Excel 2013: Give Your Data Meaning* (Microsoft Press 2013) by Marco Russo and Alberto Ferrari.

To enable the PowerPivot add-in, select **File** from the ribbon. Select **Options** followed by **Add-ins**. At the bottom of the **Add-ins** dialog box, select **COM Add-ins** and then click **GO**. From **COM Add-ins**, select **Microsoft Office PowerPivot For Excel 2013** and click **OK**. You now see a PowerPivot tab on the ribbon.

Answers to this chapter's questions

This section provides the answers to the questions that are listed at the beginning of the chapter.

How can I load data into PowerPivot?

After you enable PowerPivot, you see a PowerPivot tab on the ribbon. Click the **PowerPivot** tab and click the **Manage** button to display the options shown in Figure 45-1. After choosing **Home**, you see the Home tab shown in Figure 45-2.

FIGURE 45-1 This figure shows the PowerPivot options.

FIGURE 45-2 This figure shows the PowerPivot window Home ribbon tab.

On the **Home** tab, you can import data from multiple data sources and formats, for example:

- If you select **From Database**, PowerPivot loads data from an Access or SQL Server database.
- If you select **From Report**, PowerPivot loads data from a SQL Server Reporting Services report.
- If you select **From Data Feeds**, you can read data from a website that has an OData feed.
- For more information on ODATA feeds, see *http://mdn.microsoft.com/en-us/magazine/ff714561.aspx*.
- Choose **Other Sources** to load data from all supported data sources, including Excel files, text files, and many other types of databases such as Oracle and Teradata.
- After making Excel data into a table, you can select **Paste** to link the data to PowerPivot.

To illustrate how to download data from multiple sources into PowerPivot, use the Storesales.txt text file, in which is listed sales transactions from 20 stores. A subset of the data is shown in Figure 45-3.

You can see that for each transaction, you are given the store number, the product sold, sale date, units sold, and revenue. You want to summarize this data by state, but the state for each store is listed in a different file, States.xlsx. The location of each store is shown in Figure 45-4.

storesales - Notepad

File Edit Format View Help

```
Store   Product Date        Units   Revenue
20      food    3/15/2011       37      $16.28
10      cds     11/29/2014      70      $19.60
6       dvds    8/11/2010       68      $39.44
4       dvds    5/11/2012       120     $92.40
6       food    7/8/2011        129     $101.91
6       books   9/7/2011        16      $2.24
5       magazines       1/4/2014        101     $72.72
18      cds     9/27/2011       67      $8.04
15      magazines       9/29/2014       132     $105.60
13      food    1/27/2011       38      $23.18
7       books   4/13/2014       103     $17.51
3       books   2/17/2010       127     $21.59
16      food    6/6/2014        129     $29.67
18      dvds    11/30/2011      149     $80.46
```

FIGURE 45-3 This figure shows the sales data to be loaded into PowerPivot.

	F	G
7	Store	State
8	1	IND
9	2	IND
10	3	ILL
11	4	ILL
12	5	ILL
13	6	ILL
14	7	ILL
15	8	ILL
16	9	MICH
17	10	MICH
18	11	MICH
19	12	MICH
20	13	MICH
21	14	MICH
22	15	KY
23	16	KY
24	17	KY
25	18	KY
26	19	IOWA
27	20	IOWA

FIGURE 45-4 This figure shows the location of each store by state.

You want to create a PivotTable that enables you to slice and dice your data so that you can view how you performed selling each product in each state. To begin, click the **PowerPivot** tab and then click **Manage** to open the **PowerPivot** window. See the Home tab shown in Figure 45-2. Because you want to import a text file, select **From Text** (it is the last choice) from **From Other Sources**. As shown in Figure 45-5, you can then browse to the Storesales.txt file. You do not need to enter anything in the Friendly connection name section of the dialog box, but the **PowerPivot Text File** name is chosen here. Because the first row of data contains column headers, select **Use First Row As Column Headers**. In the **Column Separator** list, select **Tab** because the data fields in the text file is tab delimited. Click **Finish** and then **Close** to complete the process of importing the text file's data into PowerPivot.

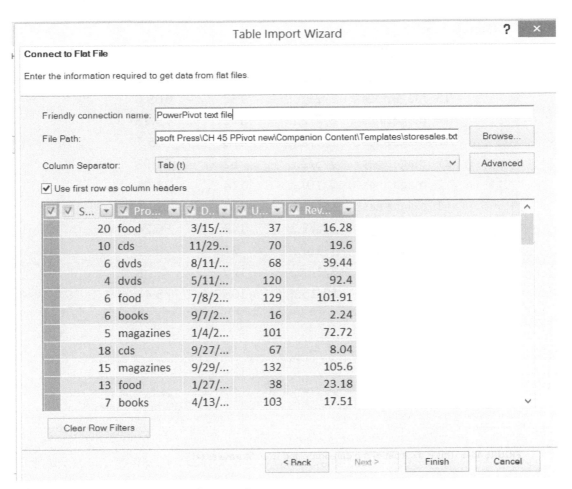

FIGURE 45-5 Set up a text file import for PowerPivot.

Figure 45-6 shows the result after the text data is imported into PowerPivot. A subset of the data is shown. At the bottom, you can see a tab indicating that the source of the data is Storesales.txt. The tab is the table name, and you could have created a name during the import process.

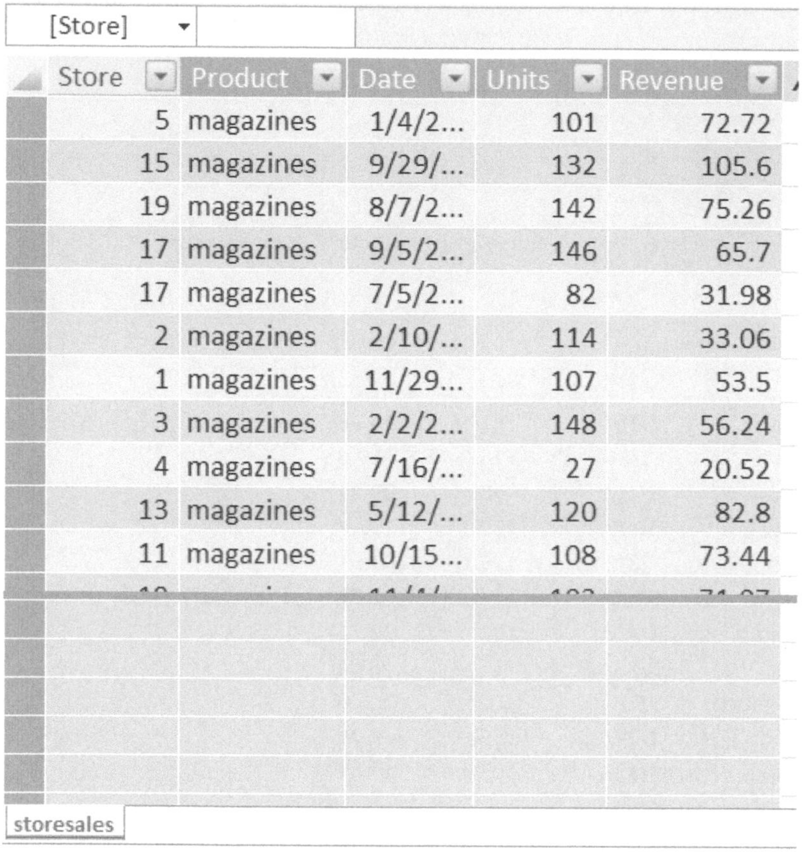

Store	Product	Date	Units	Revenue
5	magazines	1/4/2...	101	72.72
15	magazines	9/29/...	132	105.6
19	magazines	8/7/2...	142	75.26
17	magazines	9/5/2...	146	65.7
17	magazines	7/5/2...	82	31.98
2	magazines	2/10/...	114	33.06
1	magazines	11/29...	107	53.5
3	magazines	2/2/2...	148	56.24
4	magazines	7/16/...	27	20.52
13	magazines	5/12/...	120	82.8
11	magazines	10/15...	108	73.44

[Store] ▾

storesales

FIGURE 45-6 This is a subset of the data imported from Storesales.txt.

Next, you want to import the States.xlsx file so that you can relate to the sales data. To import States.xlsx, return to Excel by clicking the **Switch To Workbook Excel** icon in the upper-left corner (second icon with an X) of the PowerPivot ribbon. Open the States.xlsx file and make the data a table. Copy the data you need. Select **Paste** on the **Home** tab in PowerPivot (see Figure 45-2). The **Paste Preview** dialog box shown in Figure 45-7 opens.

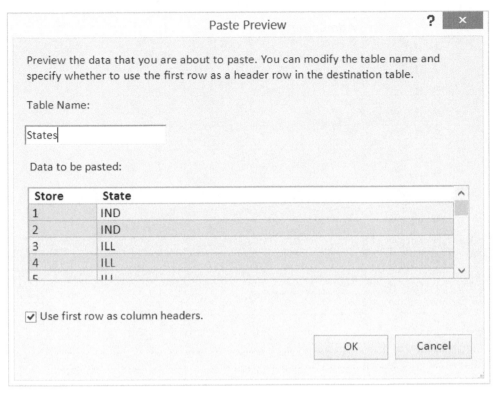

FIGURE 45-7 This is the Paste Preview dialog box.

Select **Use First Row As Column Headers** and change the table name to **States**. After clicking **OK**, the data from States.xlsx is imported into PowerPivot, as shown in Figure 45-8. Note that at the bottom of the window, a tab appears for each table that can be used to create reports.

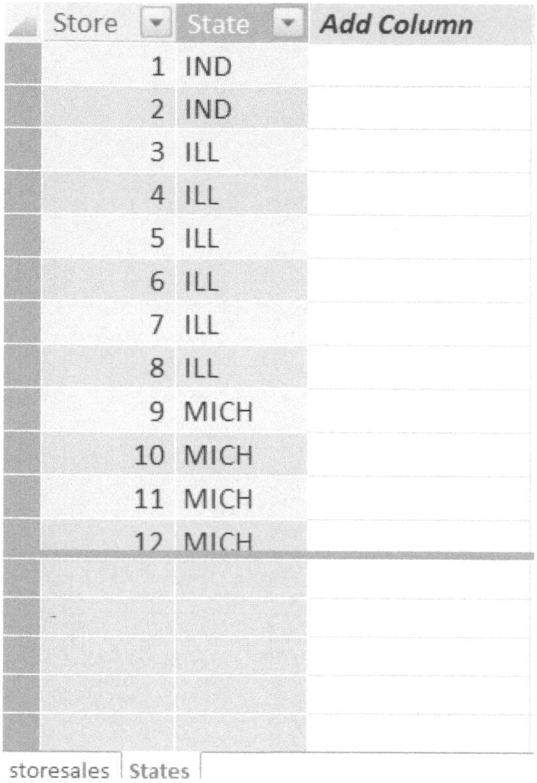

Store ▾	State ▾	Add Column
1	IND	
2	IND	
3	ILL	
4	ILL	
5	ILL	
6	ILL	
7	ILL	
8	ILL	
9	MICH	
10	MICH	
11	MICH	
12	MICH	
	-	

storesales | States

FIGURE 45-8 Data from two sources are now imported into PowerPivot.

Alternatively, the data in the States.xlsx file could have been imported into Excel by selecting **Excel File** from **From Other Sources** and then browsing to the States.xlsx file and selecting the worksheet(s) you want to import.

Recall that you want to analyze sales in different states. The problem is that, at present, PowerPivot does not know that the listing of store locations from States.xlsx corresponds to the stores listed in the text file. To remedy this problem, you must create a relationship between the two data sources. To create this relationship, you can click the **Design** ribbon tab in the PowerPivot window (see Figure 45-2), choose **Create Relationship**, and proceed as shown in Chapter 44, "The Data Model." It is much easier, however, to click **Diagram View** from the **Home** tab and define the needed relationship by dragging (as shown in Figure 45-9) one column on top of another from the many-side to the one-side.

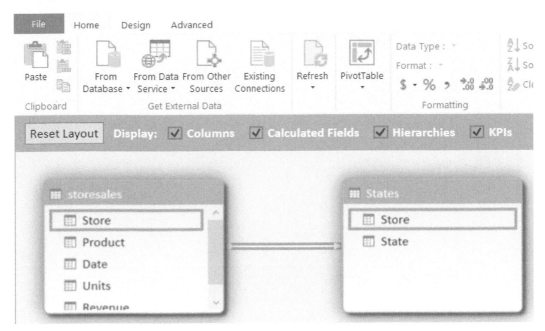

FIGURE 45-9 The relationship diagram enables you to link stores between data sources.

To return to the data view, click the **Data View** icon shown in Figure 45-2.

How can I use PowerPivot to create a PivotTable?

Now you're ready to use PowerPivot to summarize your company's sales data through a PivotTable. For a discussion of other report types that PowerPivot supports, refer again to Ferrari and Russo (2013). Select the **Home** tab in the **PowerPivot** window and then select **PivotTable**. The **Create PivotTable** dialog box opens and prompts you to choose a new worksheet or a location in the current worksheet. Choose a new worksheet. The **PowerPivot Fields** dialog box opens, shown in Figure 45-10.

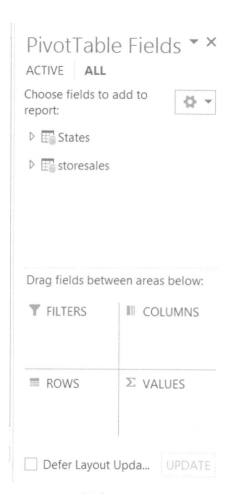

PivotTable Fields ▾ ×

ACTIVE | **ALL**

Choose fields to add to report: ⚙ ▾

▷ ⊞ States

▷ ⊞ storesales

Drag fields between areas below:

▼ FILTERS | ▥ COLUMNS

☰ ROWS | Σ VALUES

☐ Defer Layout Upda... UPDATE

FIGURE 45-10 This figure shows the PowerPivot Fields dialog box.

By clicking the triangles to the left of the States and Storesales tables, you have access to all columns (now referred to as fields) of imported data. The goal is to get a breakdown by state and product of total revenue and units sold. To summarize revenue and units sold, drag the **Revenue** and **Units** fields to the **Values** zone. Drag **State** to the **Rows** zone and **Product** to the **Columns** zone to arrange **PivotTable Fields** as shown in Figure 45-11. Note that the fields used in the PivotTable are selected.

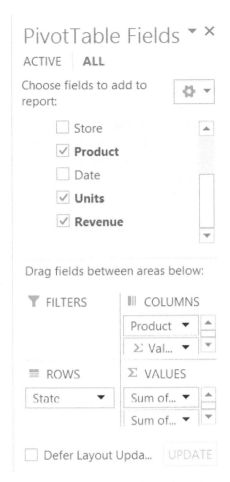

PivotTable Fields ▾ ✕

ACTIVE **ALL**

Choose fields to add to report: ⚙ ▾

- ☐ Store
- ☑ **Product**
- ☐ Date
- ☑ **Units**
- ☑ **Revenue**

Drag fields between areas below:

▼ FILTERS	▥ COLUMNS
	Product ▼ ▲
	Σ Val... ▼ ▼
▤ ROWS	Σ VALUES
State ▼	Sum of... ▼ ▲
	Sum of... ▼ ▼

☐ Defer Layout Upda...   UPDATE

FIGURE 45-11 This figure shows the assignment of fields to create a PivotTable report.

The portion of the PivotTable involving CDs, DVDs, and food is shown in Figure 45-12. As you can see, 3,881 DVDs were sold in Illinois (ILL) for a total revenue of $2,295.76.

	B	C	D	E	F	G	H	I	J
1									
2									
3		Column Labe ▼							
4		books		cds		dvds		food	
5	Row Labe ▼	Sum of Revenu	Sum of Unit	Sum of Revent	Sum of Unit	Sum of Revent	Sum of Unit	Sum of Revent	Sum of Uni
6	ILL	1542.74	4063	1880.44	3881	2295.76	4920	2178.69	4658
7	IND	697.08	1906	799.09	1812	874.89	2009	644.58	1335
8	IOWA	518.61	1341	651.49	1448	480.66	787	364.39	871
9	KY	1654.53	3329	1051.28	2386	1952.7	3696	1224.88	2461
10	MICH	2071.94	4384	1680.84	4236	1320.06	3104	2108.54	4620
11	Grand Total	6484.9	15023	6063.14	13763	6924.07	14516	6521.08	13945

FIGURE 45-12 This figure shows PivotTable breaking down product sales by state.

How can I use slicers with PowerPivot?

In Chapter 43, "Using PivotTables and slicers to describe data," you learned how to use slicers to reveal details and different perspectives in your PivotTable analyses. Here, you create slicers that summarize the data for any subset of products and stores. To do this, you can right-click anywhere in your PivotTable and select **Slicers**. After choosing **Stores** and **Products**, you see the resulting slicers shown in Figure 45-13. (See the Pivotwithslicers.xlsx file.) From **Slicer Tools**, you can modify the appearance of the slicers. For example, you can modify the Stores slicer to have four columns. As described in Chapter 43, you can hold down the Ctrl key as you click to multiselect products, stores, or both. Also, the Shift key can be used to select any contiguous range from a slicer. The PivotTable shown in Figure 45-13 gives the total revenue and units sold of books and food in Stores 7 through 11. Because Stores 7 through 11 are all in Illinois or Michigan, these are the only states shown in the resulting PivotTable.

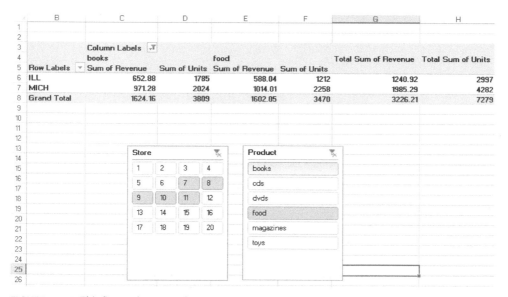

Row Labels	books Sum of Revenue	Sum of Units	food Sum of Revenue	Sum of Units	Total Sum of Revenue	Total Sum of Units
ILL	652.88	1785	588.04	1212	1240.92	2997
MICH	971.28	2024	1014.01	2258	1985.29	4282
Grand Total	1624.16	3809	1602.05	3470	3226.21	7279

FIGURE 45-13 This figure shows Product and Store slicers.

What are *DAX* functions?

Recall from Chapter 43 that you can generate new formulas in a PivotTable by using calculated items or calculated fields. After your data is imported into PowerPivot, you can use DAX formula language to create new calculated columns that make the data model much more meaningful.

> **Note** A full discussion of DAX is beyond the scope of this chapter. *Microsoft PowerPivot for Excel 2013: Give Your Data Meaning* includes an excellent and complete discussion of the DAX language.

To illustrate some DAX formulas, see how to create calculated columns to allow analysis of year, month, and day of the month. To begin, click the **Storessales** tab in the PowerPivot window and select the first blank column. Clicking the **fx** button below the **PowerPivot** ribbon displays a list of *DAX* functions. Many of these (such as *YEAR*, *MONTH*, and *DAY*) are based on Excel functions. Selecting the **Date & Time** category displays the list of *DAX* functions shown in Figure 45-14. The DAX language includes many other powerful functions. For example, the *DISTINCT* function can return a table of distinct values found in a column.

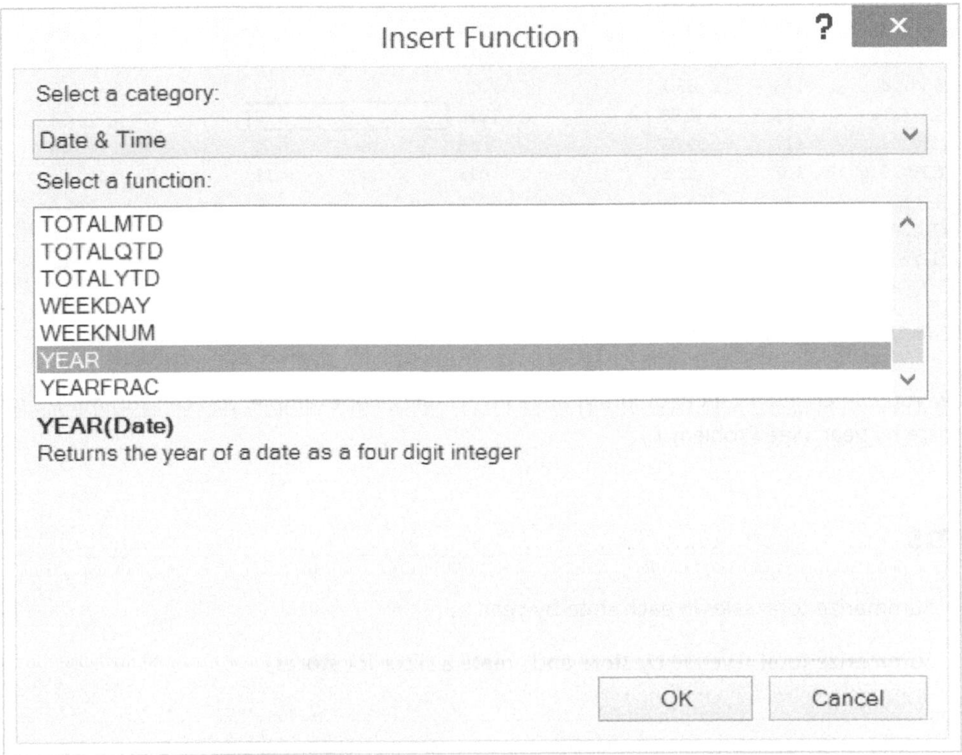

FIGURE 45-14 This is a listing of *DAX* functions.

To place the year, month, and day of the month for each transaction in a separate column, move to the first cell of the first blank column and type **=YEAR(st**. Then you are prompted with the columns from the Data Model tables that you can pass into the *YEAR* function. Select the **Date** column and complete the =YEAR(storesales[Date]) formula. The column is now populated with the year of each sales transaction. By right-clicking the column heading, you can rename the column as **Year**. In the next column, compute the month of the year by entering the =MONTH(storesales[Date]) formula. In the next column, compute the day of the month with the =DAY(storesales[Date]) formula. By right-clicking each column heading, you can rename these columns as **Month** and **Day Of Month**. The table with the calculated columns is shown in Figure 45-15.

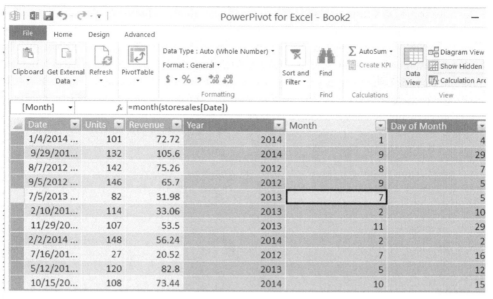

FIGURE 45-15 Year, Month, and Day Of Month calculated columns are created with DAX formulas.

Now you can create a variety of informative PivotTables. For example, you can summarize sales in each state by year. (See Problem 1.)

Problems

1.   Summarize total sales in each state by year.

2.   Summarize total revenue by store and create a slicer for stores.

CHAPTER 46

Power View

Questions answered in this chapter:

- How can I prepare data for Power View?

- What kind of charts can I create with Power View?

- How can I filter Power View charts?

- How can I display sales data by state or country?

- How can I turn a time series scatter chart into an animated experience?

- How can I use Multiples to create many charts easily?

If you have Microsoft Excel 2013 Pro Plus or Office 365, Power View for Excel is available to you. In this chapter, you learn the basics of how Power View can be used to create amazing charts and graphics. Basically, Power View creates a new sheet in your workbook that acts like a blank canvas on which you can create several charts. You can map sales onto a US or world map and even turn a scatter chart of US crimes into an experience that animates the evolution of US crimes over time.

To enable the Power View add-in, select **File** from the ribbon. At the bottom of the **Add-ins** dialog box, select **COM Add-ins** and then click **GO**. From **COM Add-ins**, select **Microsoft Office Power View For Excel 2013** and click **OK**. If you click **Insert** on the ribbon, you see the Power View icon shown in Figure 46-1. On the **Insert** tab, click **Power View** in the **Reports** group (see Figure 46-1) when you want to add a new Power View sheet. If you have not already installed and enabled the Silverlight add-in on your PC, you are prompted to do so. It is a free download.

FIGURE 46-1 This is a view of the ribbon after selecting Insert, including the Power View icon.

Answers to this chapter's questions

This section provides the answers to the questions that are listed at the beginning of the chapter.

How can I prepare data for Power View?

To ready Excel data as the source data for a Power View report, select the data and insert a new Power View sheet. Excel automatically adds the selected range to the workbook data model (see Chapter 44, "The Data Model"). Figure 46-2 shows sales data for an iced tea company (see file Teasales.xlsx) that will be used throughout this chapter. Each row gives the year, state, product sold, and units sold. It is recommended to make all Excel data used as the source for Power View reports into Excel Tables (see Chapter 25, "Tables"). This ensures that new data is automatically included in Power View reports.

If you select **Get External Data** from the **Data** tab on the ribbon, you can also use external databases, text files, and websites as the source data for Power View reports.

To get ready to create charts from this data, select **Power View** from the **Insert** tab.

	C	D	E	F
4	Year	State	Units	Product
5	2010	MO	415	black tea
6	2013	NC	462	black tea
7	2008	IL	662	peach tea
8	2010	AL	279	white tea
9	2012	VA	309	black tea
10	2013	ID	495	black tea
11	2010	MS	645	black tea
12	2008	ND	202	black tea
13	2009	MT	605	black tea
14	2014	NJ	668	white tea
15	2012	WV	667	white tea
16	2009	VT	543	white tea
17	2013	ID	634	peach tea
18	2011	OR	609	white tea
19	2014	SC	603	lemon tea
20	2012	SC	550	black tea
21	2009	ME	537	green tea
22	2014	MA	293	white tea
23	2008	NC	265	lemon tea

FIGURE 46-2 Tea sales data are used to illustrate Power View.

You will see that a blank Power View sheet is added to the workbook (see Figure 46-3), and Power View Fields (based on the Teasales table) appears at the right of the report canvas. Clicking the triangle to the left of Teasales expands the table to display all fields in the Teasales table.

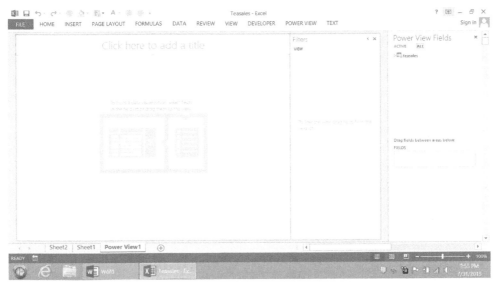

FIGURE 46-3 This is a blank Power View sheet.

Suppose you want to create charts based on the year, units sold, and product sold. After selecting **Year** and **Units** (as shown in Figure 46-4), these fields appear in the **Field** zone. Clicking the drop down arrow to the right of **Year** changes the method of calculation for Year to Do Not Summarize. Otherwise, all rows having the same year will be summed to obtain the entry in the Year column. After typing in a title (**Tea Sales**), you now have a report (see Figure 46-5) consisting of a single table that lists total units sold for each year. Now the table can be transformed into other data visualizations, including charts.

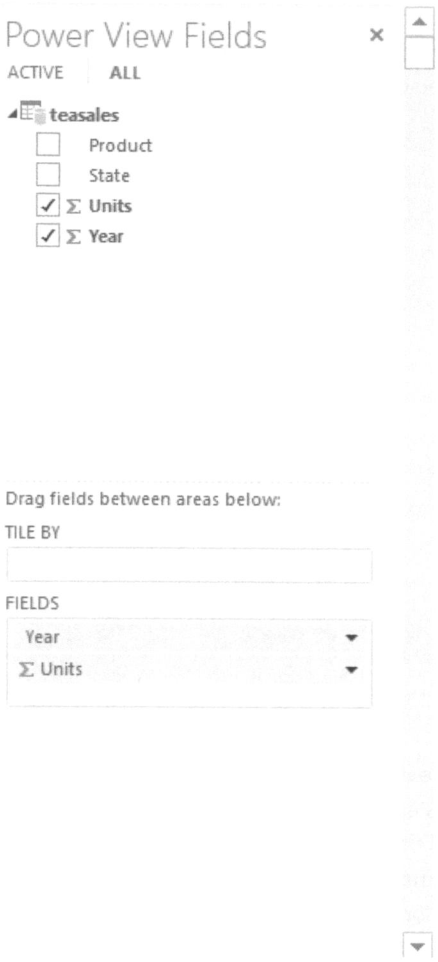

Power View Fields   ×

ACTIVE   ALL

⊿ teasales
  ☐ Product
  ☐ State
  ☑ Σ Units
  ☑ Σ Year

Drag fields between areas below:

TILE BY

FIELDS

Year   ▾
Σ Units   ▾

FIGURE 46-4 Here are Year and Units added to the Fields zone.

Tea Sales

Year	Units
2008	88714
2009	89254
2010	85339
2011	77059
2012	96854
2013	90668
2014	82893
2015	85233
Total	**696014**

FIGURE 46-5 This is the Year and Units table.

What kind of charts can I create with Power View?

If you click the **Design** tab, you see on the left side of the ribbon the Power View arsenal of data visualizations shown in Figure 46-6. Under Other Charts, you see Line, Scatter, and Pie charts. The Map option is explained later in this chapter.

Table   Bar   Column   Other   Map
    ▾   Chart ▾   Chart ▾   Chart ▾
           Switch Visualization

FIGURE 46-6 These are the available Power View charts.

Begin by exploring a Stacked Column chart to display total units sold for each year. Ensure that the table is in focus (select it) and then, on the **Design** tab, select **Stacked Column**. You may resize the chart by dragging the sides or corners of the chart, yielding the chart in Figure 46-7 and sheet Power View 1 of Teasalescharts.xlsx.

Add another chart to your canvas! Suppose you want to create a line chart that shows units sold each year of each product. Click a blank portion of the canvas and then, in **Power View Fields**, select **Year, Units,** and **Products** to create a table consisting of these three fields. Use the **Design** tab to transform the table into the line chart. This results in the charts shown in Figure 46-8.

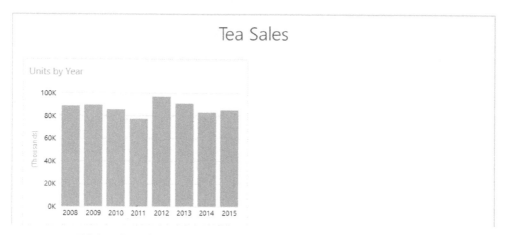

FIGURE 46-7 This is a chart showing tea sales by year.

FIGURE 46-8 This figure shows two charts of Tea Sales data.

How can I filter Power View charts?

In Chapter 43 through Chapter 45, you learned how to use slicers to filter PivotTables, the Data Model, and PowerPivot models. You now learn four ways to filter in Power View:

- Filters

- Slicers

- Filtering by Chart

- Tiles

If you hover inside a chart or table, in the top-right corner, you see the Filter (a funnel) and Pop-Out (or Pop-In) icons (the icon with the arrow to the right of the Filter icon). Clicking the Pop-Out icon makes the chart or table expand to fill the canvas. Clicking the icon again makes the chart or table pop in to revert it to its original size.

Hover inside the chart in the Power View 2 worksheet of the Teasales1.xlsx file and click the Filter icon. On the right of the screen (see Figure 46-10), filter the chart to show only sales through 2012.

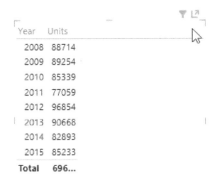

Year	Units
2008	88714
2009	89254
2010	85339
2011	77059
2012	96854
2013	90668
2014	82893
2015	85233
Total	**696...**

FIGURE 46-9 The Filter and Pop-Out icons appear in the upper-right portion of the table or chart.

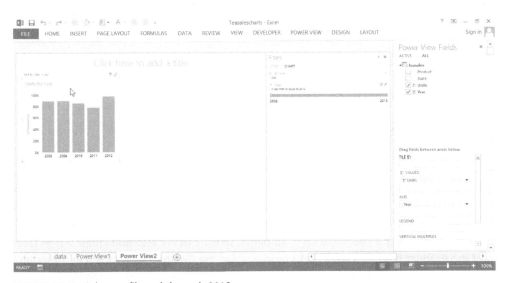

FIGURE 46-10 Sales are filtered through 2012.

A wonderful feature of Power View is the fact that one chart can be used to filter all charts on a Power View worksheet. In the Power View 1 worksheet of the Teasalesfilterbycharts.xlsx workbook, select 2008, 2010, and 2012 on the **Units** chart. As shown in Figure 46-11, the Product chart is also filtered to show only sales in 2008, 2010, and 2012. Selecting 2015 in the **Units By Year** chart restores the unfiltered charts.

FIGURE 46-11 Selecting 2008, 2010, and 2012 on Units By Year filters other charts.

You can also filter a Power View Chart with a slicer. A slicer is created by first defining a single column table and then transforming it into a slicer. It then enables interactive filtering inside the report canvas, and that visually describes the filter selection the report uses. In the PowerView 1 worksheet of the Teasalesslicer.xlsx workbook (see Figure 46-12), use a slicer to filter annual unit sales by product to show only Black Tea and Peach Tea sales. To begin, select a blank area and create a new table consisting of the Product field. You see a list of products. On the **Design** tab, click **Slicer**. To multiselect, press the Ctrl key to select Black Tea and Peach Tea. As shown in Figure 46-12, the slicer causes the chart to show sales results for only black and peach teas. To clear the filter, hover within the slicer and click the Eraser icon located in the top-right corner.

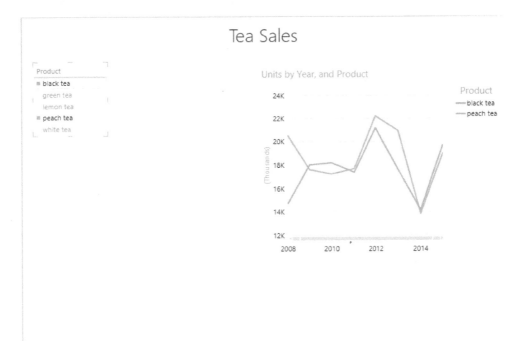

FIGURE 46-12 The slicer shows only Black Tea and Peach Tea sales.

Finally, you can use Tiles to filter on one item of a field at a time. In the Power View 1 worksheet of the Teasalestiles.xlsx workbook, create a tile that enables you to zero in on each state. To begin, create a table showing years, states, and units. Create a line chart that shows sales in each state during each year. This chart is too busy, so add a tile on states by clicking the arrow to the right of **States** in **Power View Fields** and selecting **Add As Tile By**. The chart filtered on the California tile is shown in Figure 46-13.

FIGURE 46-13 The tile is used to show annual California sales.

Any chart that is within the blue lines is filtered by the tile. You can add additional visualizations within this region to have them filter by the tile selection also.

How can I display sales data by state or country?

In the Teasalesmap.xlsx workbook, you want to visualize total sales by state on a US map. To begin, create a table consisting of States and Units, as shown in Figure 46-14.

State	Units
AK	14022
AL	16061
AR	15118
AZ	16484
CA	15696
CO	13128
CT	16664
DE	11874
FL	11279
GA	15833
HI	13244
IA	11461
ID	17028
IL	18825
IN	13024
KS	19196
KY	10522
LA	12486
MA	8523
MD	10304
ME	11477
MI	15651
MN	10829
MO	13682
MS	13362

FIGURE 46-14 This figure shows sales by state that will feed into a map summary.

On the **Design** tab, transform the table to **Map**. Power View uses Bing Maps to draw maps and geocode text locations, and this requires Internet connectivity. You are prompted to allow this connectivity the first time access is required for the workbook session. After you allow access, you see the amazing sales summary shown in Figure 46-15. For each state, there is a bubble whose size represents the state's sales. You can hover your cursor over a bubble to reveal statistics for the state.

FIGURE 46-15 This figure shows unit sales summarized by state.

How can I turn a time series scatter chart into an animated experience?

In 2006, German statistician Hans Rosling gave a TED Talk (*http://www.bing.com/videos/search?q= Ted+talk+animated+movie+data&mid=B8B186BF6A38B76D6F39B8B186BF6A38B76D6F39&view= detail&FORM=VIRE2*) in which he used amazing graphics to summarize the evolution of world economic development. Now Power View empowers you to create similarly amazing animated visualizations to display the evolution of three quantitative variables.

To illustrate the process with US crimes between 1960 and 2009, use the Crimedata.xlsx file, which contains statistics on violent crimes, property crimes, and murders during each of these years. You want to create an animated visualization showing how these quantities change over time. To begin, make the data a table and select **Scatter** from the other chart options. Fill in the field areas as shown in Figure 46-16:

- Placing Violent in the **X Value** zone ensures that violent crimes are represented by the *X* axis value.

- Placing Property in the **Y Value** zone ensures that property crimes are represented by the *Y* axis value.

- Placing murder in the **Size** zone ensures that murders are represented by the size of a bubble.

- Placing Year in the **Details** zone ensures that one point is displayed for each year.

- The optional **Color** zone has been left blank. If it is filled in, the color field is used to categorize each point by color.

- The key is to define Year as the Play Axis field. This results in the addition of a Play button and Time axis at the bottom of the chart. Clicking the **Play** button animates the chart through the years. You can use the Time axis to begin your animation during any year.

FIGURE 46-16 These are the settings you use to create the Crime data movie.

Figure 46-17 shows the final chart. Warning: These charts are addictive!

If you play out the animation shown in Figure 46-17, you see crimes increase for a while and then (thankfully) decline. There is great debate about whether the primary cause of this crime decline is improvement in policy strategies or simply demographics. (Young males commit most crimes, and the number of young males eventually drops.)

FIGURE 46-17 This is an animated summary of crime data.

How can I use Multiples to create many charts easily?

Suppose you want to summarize annual sales of each product in a separate chart. The Power View Multiples feature makes this a snap. To see how, look at the Power View 1 sheet in the Teasalesmultiples.xlsx file. Begin with the summary of Unit Sales shown in Figure 46-7 and then simply drag Product to either the Vertical or Horizontal Multiples zones. Vertical Multiples was chosen here and obtained the following set of charts for each product. The Layout tab enables you to change the appearance of these charts.

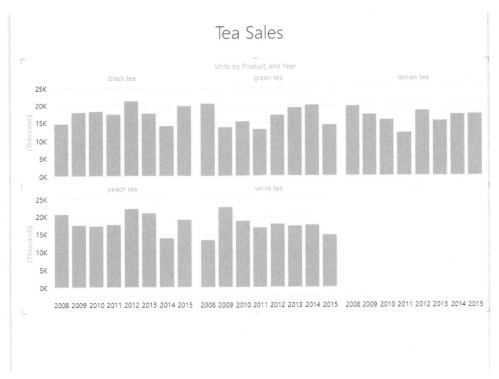

FIGURE 46-18 Here are product charts created with Multiples.

Problems

The Cellphonedata.xlsx file contains the population and number of cell phones for the 20 countries having the most cell phones. Use this data in Problems 1 through 5:

1. Create a column chart that summarizes cell phones by country.

2. Create a scatter chart that plots cell phones versus population.

3. Set up a slicer to filter a clustered column graph of cell phones by country.

4. Set up a tile to filter a column chart that summarizes cell phones by country.

5. Summarize the population data on a map.

6. The Returns.xlsx file contains annual returns on US stocks, T-bills, and bonds for the 1928–2012 period. Create an animation to show the evolution of investment returns over time.

CHAPTER 47

Sparklines

Questions answered in this chapter:

- How can you graphically summarize daily customer counts for each of a bank's branches in a single cell?

- How can you modify sparklines?

- How can you summarize an NFL team's sequence of wins or losses in a single cell?

- Do sparklines automatically update when new data is included?

Sparklines are exciting graphics that can summarize a row or column of data in a single cell. The term *sparkline* was first used by Edward Tufte, a famous expert on the visual presentation of data and its analysis. He described sparklines as "data-intense, design-simple, word-sized graphics." Microsoft Excel 2013 makes it easy to create amazing graphics that reside in a single cell.

Answers to this chapter's questions

This section provides the answers to the questions that are listed at the beginning of the chapter.

How can you graphically summarize daily customer counts for each of a bank's branches in a single cell?

The Sparklines.xlsx file contains daily customer counts at several branches of a New York state bank. See Figure 47-1.

Say that you want to summarize the weekly customer counts by graphing the daily counts for each branch in a single cell. Select the range where you want your sparklines to go (I8:I14 is chosen) and then, from the **Insert** ribbon tab, select **Line** from the **Sparklines** group, which is shown in Figure 47-2.

	C	D	E	F	G	H
6						
7		Monday	Tuesday	Wednesday	Thursday	Friday
8	New York	1176	768	808	864	1235
9	Rochester	475	323	333	356	515
10	Utica	360	250	228	275	378
11	Syracuse	594	412	408	459	618
12	Buffalo	698	475	504	551	803
13	Ossining	306	208	204	234	322
14	Ithaca	437	288	294	299	450

FIGURE 47-1 This figure shows data for sparklines.

Line   Column   Win/
                Loss

Sparklines

FIGURE 47-2 These are the Sparklines choices.

Fill in the following dialog box with the data on which the sparklines are based (D8:H14). See Figure 47-3.

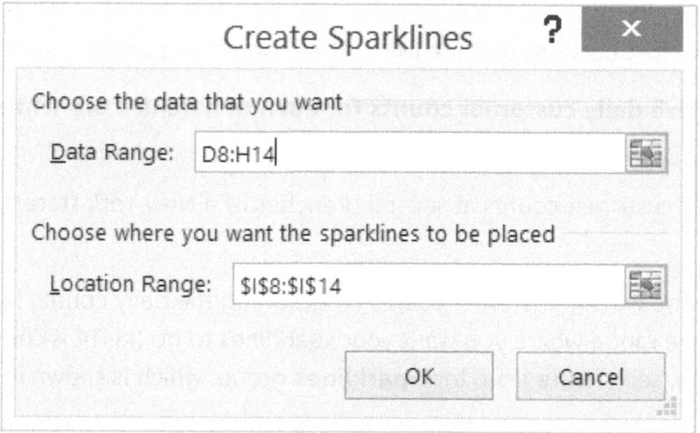

Create Sparklines   ?   ✕

Choose the data that you want

Data Range: D8:H14

Choose where you want the sparklines to be placed

Location Range: $I$8:$I$14

OK   Cancel

FIGURE 47-3 Create line sparklines.

You now see a line graph (Figure 47-4) that summarizes the customer traffic for each branch. You can see this in the Line Sparkline worksheet in the Sparklines.xlsx file.

	C	D	E	F	G	H	I
7		Monday	Tuesday	Wednesday	Thursday	Friday	Summary
8	New York	1176	768	808	864	1235	
9	Rochester	475	323	333	356	515	
10	Utica	360	250	228	275	378	
11	Syracuse	594	412	408	459	618	
12	Buffalo	698	475	504	551	803	
13	Ossining	306	208	204	234	322	
14	Ithaca	437	288	294	299	450	

FIGURE 47-4 Line sparklines are summarizing branch traffic.

You can see that for each branch, Monday and Friday are clearly the busiest days.

How can you modify sparklines?

If you click in any cell containing a sparkline, the **Sparkline Tools Design** tab opens. After selecting the **Design** tab, you can make many changes to your sparklines. For example, as shown in Figure 47-5, you can select the high and low points to be marked.

The resulting sparklines are shown in Figure 47-6. See the High Low worksheet in the Sparklines .xlsx file.

FIGURE 47-5 Select high and low points to mark on sparklines.

	C	D	E	F	G	H	I
7		Monday	Tuesday	Wednesday	Thursday	Friday	Summary
8	New York	1176	768	808	864	1235	
9	Rochester	475	323	333	356	515	
10	Utica	360	250	228	275	378	
11	Syracuse	594	412	408	459	618	
12	Buffalo	698	475	504	551	803	
13	Ossining	306	208	204	234	322	
14	Ithaca	437	288	294	299	450	

FIGURE 47-6 High and low points are marked on sparklines.

These sparklines make it clear that Friday is the busiest day for each branch, and Tuesday or Wednesday is the least busy day.

From the **Design** tab, you can make the following changes to your sparklines:

- Change the type of sparkline (line, column, or win/loss). Column and win/loss sparklines are discussed later in the chapter.

- Use the **Edit Data** command to change the data used to create the sparklines. You can also change the default setting so that hidden data is included in your sparklines.

- Select any combination of the high point, low point, negative points, first point, or last point to be marked.

- Change the style or color associated with the sparklines and sparkline markers.

- By selecting **Axis**, you can change the way the axes are set for each sparkline. For example, you can make the x-axis or y-axis scale the same for each sparkline. The default is to base the scale for each axis on the data for the individual sparkline. This is the scaling used in Figure 47-4. **Custom** enables you to pick an upper and lower limit for each axis.

- When data points occur at irregularly spaced dates, you can select **Data Axis** from **Axis** so that the graphed points are separated by an amount of space proportional to the differences in dates. Figure 47-7 shows company sales at irregularly spaced dates. (See the Date Axis worksheet in the Sparklines.xlsx file.) In cell F12, the sparkline is graphed as though the dates are spaced at regular intervals. After clicking **Axis** and choosing the C10:C13 range to use as the data axis, the sparkline in cell F10 reflects the irregular date spacing.

	C	D	E	F	G
9	Date	Sales			
10	1/1/2010	1000			Date axis
11	6/1/2010	1200			
12	9/1/2012	1400			No date axis
13	1/1/2015	1900			

FIGURE 47-7 Here are sparklines with a date axis.

You can also change line sparklines to column sparklines by clicking any sparkline and then selecting **Column** from the **Sparklines Tools Design** tab. See Figure 47-8 and the Column Sparkline worksheet in the Sparklines.xlsx file.

	C	D	E	F	G	H	I
7		Monday	Tuesday	Wednesday	Thursday	Friday	Summary
8	New York	1176	768	808	864	1235	
9	Rochester	475	323	333	356	515	
10	Utica	360	250	228	275	378	
11	Syracuse	594	412	408	459	618	
12	Buffalo	698	475	504	551	803	
13	Ossining	306	208	204	234	322	
14	Ithaca	437	288	294	299	450	

FIGURE 47-8 This is a column sparkline graph.

How can you summarize an NFL team's sequence of wins or losses in a single cell?

The Nflwinslosses.xlsx file contains the game-by-game performance for each NFL team during the 2009 regular season. A subset of this data is shown in Figure 47-9. (See the Win Loss worksheet.)

	C	D	E	F	G	H	I	J	K	L	M	N	O	P	Q	R	S	T
6			Game															
7		Team	1	2	3	4	5	6	7	8	9	10	11	12	13	14	15	16
8		Arizona Cardinals	-1	1	-1	1	1	1	-1	1	1	1	-1	1	-1	1	1	-1
18		Detroit Lions	-1	-1	1	-1	-1	-1	-1	-1	-1	1	-1	-1	-1	-1	-1	-1
19		Green Bay Packers	1	-1	1	-1	1	1	-1	-1	1	1	1	1	1	-1	1	1
20		Houston Texans	-1	1	-1	1	-1	1	1	1	-1	-1	-1	-1	1	1	1	1
21		Indianapolis Colts	1	1	1	1	1	1	1	1	1	1	1	1	1	1	-1	-1
22		Jacksonville Jaguars	-1	-1	1	1	-1	1	-1	1	1	1	-1	1	-1	-1	-1	-1
23		Kansas City Chiefs	-1	-1	-1	-1	-1	1	-1	-1	1	1	-1	-1	-1	-1	-1	1
24		Miami Dolphins	-1	-1	-1	1	1	-1	1	-1	1	1	-1	1	-1	1	-1	1
25		Minnesota Vikings	1	1	1	1	1	1	-1	1	1	1	-1	1	-1	-1	-1	1
26		New England Patriots	1	-1	1	1	-1	1	1	1	-1	1	-1	-1	1	1	1	-1
27		New Orleans Saints	1	1	1	1	1	1	1	1	1	1	1	1	1	-1	-1	-1
28		New York Giants	1	1	1	1	1	-1	-1	-1	-1	1	-1	1	-1	1	-1	-1
29		New York Jets	1	1	1	-1	-1	-1	1	-1	-1	-1	1	1	1	-1	1	1
30		Oakland Raiders	-1	1	-1	-1	-1	1	-1	-1	-1	1	-1	1	-1	1	-1	-1
31		Philadelphia Eagles	1	-1	1	1	-1	1	-1	1	-1	1	1	1	1	1	1	-1
32		Pittsburgh Steelers	1	-1	1	1	1	1	1	1	-1	-1	-1	-1	1	1	1	1
33		San Diego Chargers	1	-1	1	-1	-1	1	1	1	1	1	1	1	1	1	1	1
34		San Francisco 49ers	1	1	-1	1	-1	-1	-1	-1	1	-1	1	-1	1	-1	1	1
35		Seattle Seahawks	1	-1	-1	-1	1	-1	-1	1	-1	-1	1	1	-1	-1	-1	-1
36		St. Louis Rams	-1	-1	-1	-1	-1	-1	-1	1	-1	-1	-1	-1	-1	-1	-1	-1
37		Tampa Bay Buccaneers	-1	-1	-1	-1	-1	-1	-1	1	-1	-1	-1	-1	1	1	1	-1
38		Tennessee Titans	-1	-1	-1	-1	-1	-1	1	1	1	1	1	-1	1	1	-1	1
39		Washington Redskins	-1	1	-1	1	-1	-1	-1	-1	1	-1	-1	1	-1	-1	-1	-1

FIGURE 47-9 Sparklines summarize wins and losses for NFL teams.

A 1 (one) denotes a win and a –1 a loss. Each win/loss sparkline treats any positive number as an up block and any negative number as a down block. Any 0s are graphed as a gap. To create the win/loss sparklines, select the range where the sparklines should be placed (cell range C8:C39) and then select **Win/Loss** from the **Sparklines** group on the **Insert** menu. Choose the E8:T39 data range. The sparklines make the 2009 NFL season come alive. You can see the amazing starts of the Indianapolis Colts and the New Orleans Saints. You can see that the Tennessee Titans started poorly and then played much better. The New York Giants started well and then hit a rough patch. Win/loss sparklines are great for tracking an organization's progress toward meeting quotas or goals. See Problem 4 at the end of this chapter.

Do Sparklines automatically update when new data is included?

If you want your sparklines to update automatically to include new data, make the data a table (see Chapter 25, "Tables") or convert the data to a dynamic range (see Chapter 21, "The OFFSET function.")

Problems

1. For the bank branch data, make your line sparklines use the same scale for each branch.

2. The Dow.xlsx data contains the values of the Dow Jones Index for January 2 through August 10, 2010. Create a line sparkline to show the ups and downs of the market.

3. Use win/loss sparklines to capture the market's ups and downs. Again, use the Dow.xlsx file.

4. The Goals.xlsx file shows the percentage by which bank branches met or failed to meet their goals each month. Summarize this data with win/loss sparklines.

CHAPTER 48

Summarizing data with database statistical functions

Questions answered in this chapter:

- Joolas is a small makeup company that tracks each sales transaction in a Microsoft Excel 2013 worksheet. Often, it wants to answer questions such as:

  - How many dollars' worth of lip gloss did Jen sell?

  - What was the average number of lipstick units sold each time Jen made a sale in the East region?

  - What was the total dollar amount of all makeup sold by Emilee or in the East region?

  - How many dollars' worth of lipstick were sold by Colleen or Zaret in the East region?

  - How many lipstick transactions were not in the East region?

  - How many dollars' worth of lipstick did Jen sell during 2004?

  - How many units of makeup were sold for a price of at least $3.20?

  - What is the total dollar amount each salesperson sold of each makeup product?

- What helpful tricks can I use to set up criteria ranges?

- I have a database that lists, for each sales transaction, the revenue, the date sold, and the product ID code. Given the date sold and the ID code for a transaction, is there an easy way to extract the transaction's revenue?

As you saw in Chapter 43, "Using PivotTables and slicers to describe data," Excel PivotTables are a great tool for summarizing data. Often, however, a PivotTable gives you much more information than you need. *Database statistical functions* make it easy to answer any reporting question without creating a PivotTable.

You are already familiar with functions such as *SUM, AVERAGE, COUNT, MAX*, and *MIN*. By prefixing a D (which stands for *database*) on these and other functions, you create database statistical functions. However, what does the *DSUM* function do, for example, that the *SUM* function can't? Whereas the *SUM* function adds up every cell in a cell range, the *DSUM* function enables you to specify (by using criteria) a subset of rows to add together in a cell range. For example, suppose you have a sales database for a small makeup company that contains the following information about each sales transaction:

- Name of salesperson

- Transaction date

- Product sold

- Units sold

- Dollars of revenue generated per transaction

- Region of the country where the transaction took place

You can find this data in the Makeupdb.xlsx file, which is shown in Figure 48-1.

Trans Number	Name	Date	Product	Units	Dollars	Location
1	Betsy	4/1/2004	lip gloss	45	$137.20	south
2	Hallagan	3/10/2004	foundatic	50	$152.01	midwest
3	Ashley	2/25/2005	lipstick	9	$ 28.72	midwest
4	Hallagan	5/22/2006	lip gloss	55	$167.08	west
5	Zaret	6/17/2004	lip gloss	43	$130.60	midwest
6	Colleen	11/27/2005	eye liner	58	$175.99	midwest
7	Cristina	3/21/2004	eye liner	8	$ 25.80	midwest
8	Colleen	12/17/2006	lip gloss	72	$217.84	midwest
9	Ashley	7/5/2006	eye liner	75	$226.64	south
10	Betsy	8/7/2006	lip gloss	24	$ 73.50	east
11	Ashley	11/29/2004	mascara	43	$130.84	east
12	Ashley	11/18/2004	lip gloss	23	$ 71.03	west
13	Emilee	8/31/2005	lip gloss	49	$149.59	west
14	Hallagan	1/1/2005	eye liner	18	$ 56.47	south
15	Zaret	9/20/2006	foundatic	-8	$ (21.99)	east
16	Emilee	4/12/2004	mascara	45	$137.39	east
17	Colleen	4/30/2006	mascara	66	$199.65	south
18	Jen	8/31/2005	lip gloss	88	$265.19	midwest
19	Jen	10/27/2004	eye liner	78	$236.15	south
20	Zaret	11/27/2005	lip gloss	57	$173.12	midwest
21	Zaret	6/2/2006	mascara	12	$ 38.08	west
22	Betsy	9/24/2004	eye liner	28	$ 86.51	midwest
23	Colleen	2/1/2006	mascara	25	$ 77.31	midwest

FIGURE 48-1 Use this data to describe how to work with database statistical functions.

By using the *DSUM* function with appropriate criteria, you could, for example, add up the revenue generated only by transactions involving lip gloss sales in the East during 2004. Essentially, the criteria you set up flags those rows you want to include in the total sum. Within these rows, the *DSUM* function acts like the ordinary *SUM* function.

The syntax of the *DSUM* function is DSUM(database,field,criteria):

- *Database* is the cell range that makes up the database. The first row of the list contains labels for each column.

- *Field* is the column containing the values you want the function to add. You can define the field by enclosing the column label in quotation marks. (For example, you would designate the **Dollars** column by entering **"Dollars"**.) The field can also be specified by using the position of the column in the database, measured from left to right. For example, the makeup transaction database would use columns H through M. (The Transactions column was not included as part of the database.) You could specify column H as **field 1** and column M as **field 6**.

- A *criterion* refers to a cell range that specifies the rows on which the function should operate. The first row of a criteria range must include one or more column labels. (The only exception to this rule is *computed criteria*, which is discussed in the last two examples in this chapter.) As the examples illustrate, the key to creating a criteria range is to understand that multiple criteria in the same row are joined by *AND*, whereas criteria in different rows are joined by *OR*.

Now look at some examples (see Figure 48-2) that illustrate the power and versatility of database statistical functions.

Answers to this chapter's questions

This section provides the answers to the questions that are listed at the beginning of the chapter.

How many dollars' worth of lip gloss did Jen sell?

In this example, you want to apply *DSUM* to column 5 of the database. Column 5 contains the dollar volume for each transaction. (The database is named Data, which consists of the H4:M1895 range.) The criteria range in O4:P5 flags all rows in the database in which Name equals Jen *and* Product equals lip gloss. Thus, entering the DSUM(data,5,O4:P5) formula in cell N5 (see Figure 48-2) calculates the total dollar amount of lip gloss sold by Jen. You could have also entered the formula as DSUM(data,"Dollars",O4:P5). Jen sold $5,461.61 worth of lip gloss. In cell N6, you can find the same answer by using the *SUMIFS* function (see Chapter 20, "The *SUMIF, AVERAGEIF, SUMIFS*, and *AVERAGEIFS* functions") with the =SUMIFS(Dollars,Name,"Jen",Product,"lip gloss") formula.

	N	O	P	Q	R
1					
2					
3					
4	Jen lip gloss $	Name	Product		
5	$ 5,461.61	Jen	lip gloss		
6	5461.61479				
7	Jen avg.units lipstick in east	Name	Product	Location	
8	42.25	Jen	lipstick	east	
9	42.25				
10	$s Emilee or east	Name	Location		
11	$ 76,156.48	Emilee			
12			east		
13	$s lipstick by Colleen or Zaret in east	Name	Location	Product	
14	$ 1,073.20	Colleen	east	lipstick	
15	1073.203709	Zaret	east	lipstick	
16	Number of lipstick transactions not in	Product	Location		
17	164	lipstick	<>east	164	
18	total $s jen lipstick in 2004	Name	Product	Date	Date
19	$ 1,690.79	Jen	lipstick	>=1/1/2004	<1/1/2005
20	1690.793115				
21	Units sold for >=$3.20	Big price			
22	1127	FALSE			

FIGURE 48-2 Here are database statistical functions at work.

What was the average number of lipstick units sold each time Jen had a sale in the East region?

You can compute this number by entering the DAVERAGE(data,4,O7:Q8) formula in cell N8. Using 4 as the value for *field* specifies the Units column, and the O7:Q8 criteria range flags all rows in the database in which Name equals Jen, Product equals lipstick, and Location equals East. Using *DAVERAGE* ensures that you average the units sold for the flagged rows. You can see that on average, Jen sold 42.25 units of lipstick in transactions in the East region. In cell N9, you can calculate the same answer by using the =AVERAGEIFS(Units,Name,"Jen",Product,"lipstick",Location,"east") formula.

What was the total dollar amount of all makeup sold by Emilee or in the East region?

In cell N11, you can compute the total dollars ($76,156.48) of sales by Emilee or in the East by using the DSUM(data,5,O10:P12) formula. The criteria in O10:P12 flags sales in the East *or* by Emilee, because criteria in different rows are treated as an *OR* operation. The great programmers at Microsoft have ensured that this formula does not double-count Emilee's sales in the East. Here, you cannot use *SUMIFS* to find the answer easily.

How many dollars' worth of lipstick were sold by Colleen or Zaret in the East region?

The DSUM(data,5,O13:Q15) formula in cell N14 computes the total lipstick revenue generated through Colleen's and Zaret's sales ($1,073.20) in the East. Notice that O14:Q14 specifies criteria that select Colleen's lipstick sales in the East, and O15:Q15 specifies criteria that select Zaret's lipstick sales in the East. Remember that criteria in different rows are joined by *OR*. In cell N15, the answer to this question is calculated with the following formula:

```
=SUMIFS(Dollars,Name,"Colleen",Product,"lipstick",Location,"east")
   +SUMIFS(Dollars,Name,"Zaret",Product,"lipstick",Location,"east")
```

How many lipstick transactions were not in the East region?

In cell N17, you can compute the total number of lipstick transactions (164) outside the East region with the DCOUNT(data,4,O16:P17) formula. You use *DCOUNT* in this problem because you want to specify criteria by which the function will count the number of rows involving lipstick sales and regions other than in the East. Excel treats the *<>East* expression in the criteria range as "not East." For this problem, using *SUMIFS* would require you to have a *SUMIFS* function for each region.

Because the *COUNT* function counts numbers, you need to refer to a column containing numerical values. Column 4, the Units column, contains numbers, so that column is designated in the formula. The DCOUNT(data,3,O16:P17) formula would return 0 because there are no numbers in the database's third column (which is column J in the worksheet). Of course, the DCOUNTA(data,3,O16:P17) formula would return the correct answer because *COUNTA* counts text as well as numbers.

How many dollars' worth of lipstick did Jen sell during 2004?

The trick here is knowing how to flag only sales that occurred in 2004. By including in one row of your criteria range a reference to the **Date** field, using the >=1/1/2004 and <1/1/2005 expressions captures only the 2004 sales. Thus, entering the DSUM(data,5,O18:R19) formula in cell N19 computes the total lipstick sales by Jen ($1,690.79) after January 1, 2004, and before January 1, 2005. In cell N20, the answer to this problem is calculated with the =SUMIFS(Dollars,Date,">=1/1/2004",Date,"<=12/31/2004",Product,"lipstick",Name,"Jen") formula.

How many units of makeup were sold for a price of at least $3.20?

This example involves *computed criteria*. Basically, computed criteria flags rows of the database on the basis of whether a computed condition is true or false for that row. For this question, you want to flag each row that contains Dollars/Units>=$3.20. When setting up a computed criterion (see Figure 48-3), the label in the first row above the computed criteria *must not* be a column label. For example, you can't use Name, Product, or another label from row 4 of this worksheet. The computed criterion is set up to be a formula that returns True based on the first row of information in the database. Thus, to specify rows in which the average price is greater than or equal to $3.20, you need to enter =(L5/K5)>=3.2 in your criterion range below a heading that is not a column label. If the first row of data does not satisfy this condition, you will see FALSE in the worksheet, but Excel will still flag all rows having a unit price that's greater than or equal to $3.20. Entering the DSUM(data,4,O21:O22) formula in N22 computes the total number of units of makeup sold (1,127) in orders for which the unit price was greater than or equal to $3.20. Note that cell O22 contains the =(L5/K5)>=3.2 formula.

	N	O
21	Units sold for >=$3.20	Big price
22		1127 FALSE

FIGURE 48-3 This figure shows a computed criterion.

What is the total dollar amount each salesperson sold of each makeup product?

For this problem, you could use a *DSUM* function whose criteria range is based on both the Name and Product columns. Using a data table, you can easily loop through all possible combinations of Name and Product in the criteria range and compute the total revenue for each Name and Product combination.

Begin by entering any name in cell X26 and any product in cell Y26. Enter the DSUM(data,5,X25:Y26) formula in cell Q25, which computes total sales revenue for (in this case) Betsy and eyeliner. Enter each salesperson's name in the Q26:Q33 cell range and each product in the R25:V25 cell range. Now select the data table range (Q25:V33). On the **Data** tab, in the **Data Tools** group, click **What-If Analysis** and then click **Data Table**. Choose cell X26 as the column input cell and Y26 as the row input cell. You then obtain the results shown in Figure 48-4. Each entry in the data table computes the revenue generated for a different name and product combination because the data table causes the names to be placed in cell X26 and the products to be placed in cell Y26. For example, Ashley sold $3,245.45 worth of lipstick.

	Q	R	S	T	U	V	W	X	Y
21									
22									
23									
24									
25	6046.5343	lip gloss	foundatic	lipstick	mascara	eye liner		Name	Product
26	Betsy	5675.65	8043.49	3968.61	4827.25	6046.53		Betsy	eye liner
27	Hallagan	5603.1194	6985.73	3177.87	5703.35	6964.62			
28	Zaret	5670.3293	6451.65	2448.71	3879.95	8166.75			
29	Colleen	5573.3237	6834.77	2346.41	6746.53	3389.63			
30	Cristina	5297.9798	5290.99	2401.67	5461.65	5397.27			
31	Jen	5461.6148	5628.65	3953.3	6887.17	7010.44			
32	Ashley	6053.6846	4186.06	3245.44	6617.1	5844.95			
33	Emilee	5270.2503	5313.79	2189.14	4719.3	7587.39			
34									
35									
36		lip gloss	foundatic	lipstick	mascara	eye liner			
37	Betsy	5675.65	8043.49	3968.61	4827.25	6046.53			
38	Hallagan	5603.1194	6985.73	3177.87	5703.35	6964.62			
39	Zaret	5670.3293	6451.65	2448.71	3879.95	8166.75			
40	Colleen	5573.3237	6834.77	2346.41	6746.53	3389.63			
41	Cristina	5297.9798	5290.99	2401.67	5461.65	5397.27			
42	Jen	5461.6148	5628.65	3953.3	6887.17	7010.44			
43	Ashley	6053.6846	4186.06	3245.44	6617.1	5844.95			
44	Emilee	5270.2503	5313.79	2189.14	4719.3	7587.39			

FIGURE 48-4 Combine data tables with a *DSUM* function.

This example shows how combining data tables with database statistical functions can quickly generate many statistics of interest. Note that you could also have solved this problem by copying the =SUMIFS(Dollars,Name,$Q37,Product,R$36) formula from cell R37 to R37:V45.

What helpful tricks can I use to set up criteria ranges?

Here are some examples of little tricks that might help you set up an appropriate criteria range. Suppose the column label in the first row of the criteria range refers to a column containing text (for example, column H).

- *Allie* will flag records containing the text string Allie in column H.

- A?X will flag a record if the record's column H entry begins with A and contains X as its third character. (The second character can be anything!)

- <>*B* will flag a record if column H's entry does not contain any Bs.

If a column (for example, column I) contains numerical values,

- >100 will flag a record if column I contains a value greater than 100.

- <>100 will flag a record if column I contains a value not equal to 100.

- >=1000 will flag a record if column I contains a value greater than or equal to 1,000.

I have a database that lists, for each sales transaction, the revenue, the date sold, and the product ID code. Given the date sold and the ID code for a transaction, is there an easy way to capture the transaction's revenue?

The Dget.xlsx file (see Figure 48-5) contains a database that lists revenues, dates, and product ID codes for a series of sales transactions. If you know the date and the product ID code for a transaction, how can you find the transaction's revenue? With the *DGET* function, it's simple. The syntax of the *DGET* function is DGET(database,field#,criteria). Given a cell range for *database* and a value for *field#* in the database (counting columns from left to right across the range), the *DGET* function returns the entry in column *field#* from the database record satisfying the criteria. If no record satisfies the criteria, the *DGET* function returns the #VALUE error message. If more than one record satisfies the criteria, the *DGET* function returns the #NUM! error message.

Suppose that you want to know the revenue for a transaction involving product ID code 62426 that occurred on 1/9/2006. Assuming that there is only one transaction involving this product on the given date, the DGET(B7:D28,1,G5:H6) formula (entered in cell G9) yields the transaction's revenue of $169. Note that 1 was used for the *field#* argument because Revenue is listed in the first column of the database (which is contained in the B7:D28 cell range). The G5:H6 criteria range ensures that you find a transaction involving product 62426 on 1/9/2006.

	B	C	D	E	F	G	H	I
2	Example of DGET Function							
3								
4								
5						date	id code	
6						1/9/2006	62426	
7	revenue	date	id code					
8	$ 856.00	2/2/2000	89550			revenue		
9	$ 461.00	4/12/2003	34506			169		
10	$ 662.00	2/6/1999	57664					
11	$ 522.00	9/25/2005	25449					
12	$ 228.00	7/12/2006	26461					
13	$ 997.00	6/9/2008	73945					
14	$ 857.00	7/30/2006	78607					
15	$ 454.00	12/5/1999	8605					
16	$ 571.00	2/6/2001	33684					
17	$ 690.00	5/17/2006	81984					
18	$ 467.00	10/17/2008	4530					
19	$ 281.00	8/6/2000	72489					
20	$ 965.00	11/17/2003	66050					
21	$ 169.00	1/9/2006	62426					
22	$ 378.00	10/21/2001	34422					
23	$ 273.00	2/28/2001	41064					
24	$ 628.00	6/15/2006	29231					
25	$ 382.00	12/11/2005	9625					
26	$ 896.00	10/16/1999	66644					
27	$ 260.00	3/8/2002	3346					
28	$ 344.00	11/4/2002	38858					

FIGURE 48-5 This figure shows the usage of the *DGET* function.

Problems

1. How many units of lip gloss did Zaret sell during 2004 and 2005?

2. Create a data table that contains each person's total revenue and units sold.

3. How many units of lip gloss did Colleen sell outside the West region?

4. Using the data in the Makeupdb.xlsx file, create a data table that shows the average per-unit revenue generated by each person for sales in which the average per-unit price exceeded $3.30.

5. Use the data in the Sales.xlsx file to determine the following:

   • Total dollar sales in the Midwest

   • Total dollars that Heather sold in the East

   • Total dollars that Heather sold or that were sold in the East

- Total dollars sold in the East by Heather or John

- Number of transactions in the East region

- Number of transactions with greater than average sales

- Total sales not in the Midwest

6. The Housepricedata.xlsx file contains the following information for selected homes:

- Square footage

- Price

- Number of bathrooms

- Number of bedrooms

Use this information to answer the following questions:

- What is the average price of all homes having a total number of bathrooms and bedrooms greater than or equal to six?

- How many homes sell for more than $300,000 and have a total number of bedrooms and bathrooms less than or equal to five?

- How many homes have at least three bathrooms, but the total number of bedrooms and bathrooms is less than or equal to six?

- What Is the highest price of a home having at most 3,000 square feet and a total number of bedrooms and bathrooms less than or equal to six? (Hint: Use the *DMAX* function to solve this problem.)

7. The Deciles.xlsx file contains the unpaid balance for 20 accounts. Use *DBASE* functions to compute the total unpaid balances in each decile.

CHAPTER 49

Filtering data and removing duplicates

Questions answered in this chapter:

Joolas is a small company that manufactures makeup. Its managers track each sales transaction in a Microsoft Excel 2013 worksheet. Sometimes they want to extract, or filter out, a subset of their sales data. For example, they might want to identify sales transactions that answer the following questions:

- How can I identify all transactions in which Jen sold lipstick in the East region?

- How can I identify all transactions in which Cici or Colleen sold lipstick or mascara in the East or South region?

- How can I copy all transactions in which Cici or Colleen sold lipstick or mascara in the East or South region to a different worksheet?

- How can I clear filters from a column or database?

- How can I identify all transactions that involved sales greater than $280 and greater than 90 units?

- How can I identify all sales occurring in 2005 or 2006?

- How can I identify all transactions in the last three months of 2005 or the first three months of 2006?

- How can I identify all transactions for which the salesperson's first name starts with C?

- How can I identify all transactions for which the cell containing the product name is colored in red?

- How can I identify all transactions in the top 30 revenue values in which Hallagan or Jen was the salesperson?

- How can I easily obtain a complete list of salespeople?

- How can I view every combination of salesperson, product, and location that occurs in the database?

- If my data changes, how can I reapply the same filter?

- How can I extract all foundation transactions in the first six months of 2005 for which Emilee or Jen was the salesperson and the average per-unit price was more than $3.20?

Excel 2013 has filtering capabilities that make identifying any subset of data a snap. Excel also makes it easy to remove duplicate records from a list. You'll find the work for this chapter in the Makeupfilter.xlsx file. For the 1,891 sales transactions listed in this file (Figure 49-1 shows a subset of the data), you have the following information:

- Transaction number

- Name of the salesperson

- Date of the transaction

- Product sold

- Units sold

- Dollar amount of the transaction

- Transaction location

	C	D	E	F	G	H	I
3	Transaction number	Name	Date	Product	Units	Dollars	Location
4	1	Betsy	4/1/2004	lip gloss	45	$ 137.20	south
5	2	Hallagan	3/10/2004	foundatior	50	$ 152.01	midwest
6	3	Ashley	2/25/2005	lipstick	9	$ 28.72	midwest
7	4	Hallagan	5/22/2006	lip gloss	55	$ 167.08	west
8	5	Zaret	6/17/2004	lip gloss	43	$ 130.60	midwest
9	6	Colleen	11/27/2005	eye liner	58	$ 175.99	midwest
10	7	Cristina	3/21/2004	eye liner	8	$ 25.80	midwest
11	8	Colleen	12/17/2006	lip gloss	72	$ 217.84	midwest
12	9	Ashley	7/5/2006	eye liner	75	$ 226.64	south
13	10	Betsy	8/7/2006	lip gloss	24	$ 73.50	east
14	11	Ashley	11/29/2004	mascara	43	$ 130.84	east
15	12	Ashley	11/18/2004	lip gloss	23	$ 71.03	west
16	13	Emilee	8/31/2005	lip gloss	49	$ 149.59	west
17	14	Hallagan	1/1/2005	eye liner	18	$ 56.47	south
18	15	Zaret	9/20/2006	foundatior	-8	$ (21.99)	east
19	16	Emilee	4/12/2004	mascara	45	$ 137.39	east
20	17	Colleen	4/30/2006	mascara	66	$ 199.65	south
21	18	Jen	8/31/2005	lip gloss	88	$ 265.19	midwest
22	19	Jen	10/27/2004	eye liner	78	$ 236.15	south

FIGURE 49-1 Here is the makeup sales data.

In what follows, any rectangular range of cells with headings in the first row of each column is referred to as a *database*. Each column (C through I) of your database (cell range C4:I1894) is called a *field*. Each row of the database that contains data is called a *record*. (Thus, the records in your database are contained in the C4:I1894 cell range.) The first row of each field must contain a field name. For example, the name of the field in column F is Product. By using the Excel AutoFilter, you can query the database using *AND* criteria to identify a subset of records. This means that you can use queries of the "Find all records where Field 1 satisfies certain conditions, *and* Field 2 satisfies certain conditions, *and* Field 3 satisfies certain conditions" form. This chapter's examples illustrate the capabilities of the Excel AutoFilter.

Answers to this chapter's questions

This section provides the answers to the questions that are listed at the beginning of the chapter.

How can I identify all transactions in which Jen sold lipstick in the East region?

To begin, place your cursor anywhere in the database and select **Filter** in the **Sort & Filter** group on the **Data** tab on the ribbon. As shown in Figure 49-2, each column of the database now has an arrow in the heading row (see the Data worksheet).

	C	D	E	F	G	H	I
3	Transaction number	Name	Date	Product	Units	Dollars	Locatio
4	1	Betsy	4/1/2004	lip gloss	45	$ 137.20	south
5	2	Hallagan	3/10/2004	foundatior	50	$ 152.01	midwest
6	3	Ashley	2/25/2005	lipstick	9	$ 28.72	midwest
7	4	Hallagan	5/22/2006	lip gloss	55	$ 167.08	west
8	5	Zaret	6/17/2004	lip gloss	43	$ 130.60	midwest
9	6	Colleen	11/27/2005	eye liner	58	$ 175.99	midwest
10	7	Cristina	3/21/2004	eye liner	8	$ 25.80	midwest
11	8	Colleen	12/17/2006	lip gloss	72	$ 217.84	midwest
12	9	Ashley	7/5/2006	eye liner	75	$ 226.64	south
13	10	Betsy	8/7/2006	lip gloss	24	$ 73.50	east
14	11	Ashley	11/29/2004	mascara	43	$ 130.84	east
15	12	Ashley	11/18/2004	lip gloss	23	$ 71.03	west
16	13	Emilee	8/31/2005	lip gloss	49	$ 149.59	west
17	14	Hallagan	1/1/2005	eye liner	18	$ 56.47	south
18	15	Zaret	9/20/2006	foundatior	-8	$ (21.99)	east
19	16	Emilee	4/12/2004	mascara	45	$ 137.39	east
20	17	Colleen	4/30/2006	mascara	66	$ 199.65	south
21	18	Jen	8/31/2005	lip gloss	88	$ 265.19	midwest
22	19	Jen	10/27/2004	eye liner	78	$ 236.15	south
23	20	Zaret	11/27/2005	lip gloss	57	$ 173.12	midwest

FIGURE 49-2 This figure shows the AutoFilter heading arrows.

After clicking the arrow for the **Name** column, you see the choices shown in Figure 49-3. You could choose **Text Filters**, which enables you to filter based on characteristics of the person's name (more on this later). For now, you just want to work with data for Jen, so first clear the **Select All** check box, select the check box for **Jen**, and then click **OK**. You now see only those records for which Jen was the salesperson. Next, at the **Product** column, select the **lipstick** check box. At the **Location** column, select the **East** check box. You now see only those transactions for which Jen sold lipstick in the East region. (See Figure 49-4 and the Lipstick Jen East worksheet.) Notice that the arrow has changed to a funnel in the columns in which you set up filtering criteria.

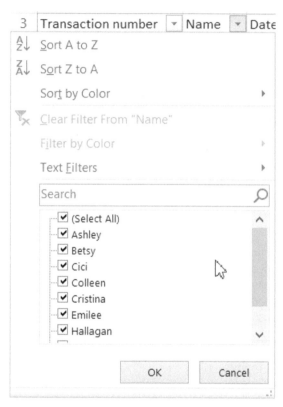

FIGURE 49-3 These are the choices for filtering the Name column.

	C	D	E	F	G	H	I
3	Transaction number ⏷	Name ⏷	Date ⏷	Product ⏷	Units ⏷	Dollars ⏷	Location ⏷
503	500	Jen	3/19/2005	lipstick	6	$ 20.04	east
509	506	Jen	2/17/2004	lipstick	67	$ 202.62	east
691	688	Jen	3/6/2006	lipstick	36	$ 110.26	east
763	760	Jen	1/23/2005	lipstick	12	$ 37.85	east
846	843	Jen	7/27/2006	lipstick	34	$ 103.40	east
1232	1229	Jen	9/24/2004	lipstick	92	$ 277.63	east
1781	1778	Jen	8/31/2005	lipstick	24	$ 74.61	east
1815	1812	Jen	5/22/2006	lipstick	67	$ 203.18	east

FIGURE 49-4 Jen sells lipstick in the East region.

How can I identify all transactions in which Cici or Colleen sold lipstick or mascara in the East or South region?

You select Cici and Colleen from the **Name** column list, **lipstick** and **mascara** from the **Product** column list, and **East** and **South** from the **Location** column list. The records meeting these filtering criteria are shown in Figure 49-5. (See the Cici Colleen Lipstick And Masc worksheet.)

	C	D	E	F	G	H	I
3	Transaction number ⏷	Name ⏷	Date ⏷	Product ⏷	Units ⏷	Dollars ⏷	Locatio ⏷
20	17	Colleen	4/30/2006	mascara	66	$ 199.65	south
84	81	Cici	6/13/2006	lipstick	-3	$ (7.62)	south
106	103	Cici	11/18/2004	mascara	38	$ 115.86	south
139	136	Cici	9/24/2004	mascara	89	$ 269.40	east
143	140	Cici	3/8/2005	lipstick	37	$ 113.65	east
174	171	Colleen	5/26/2004	lipstick	60	$ 182.02	east
191	188	Colleen	2/6/2004	mascara	-5	$ (12.90)	east
201	198	Colleen	2/6/2004	mascara	60	$ 181.94	east
237	234	Colleen	7/9/2004	lipstick	-3	$ (7.40)	south
239	236	Cici	7/9/2004	mascara	5	$ 17.20	east
244	241	Colleen	11/3/2006	mascara	64	$ 194.25	east
253	250	Colleen	2/14/2005	lipstick	65	$ 196.49	south
255	252	Cici	7/16/2006	mascara	-1	$ (1.93)	south
317	314	Colleen	3/17/2006	lipstick	43	$ 130.95	south
337	334	Colleen	2/14/2005	lipstick	15	$ 46.64	east
339	336	Cici	7/18/2005	mascara	85	$ 257.29	south
400	397	Colleen	2/17/2004	mascara	91	$ 274.81	south
435	432	Cici	3/19/2005	mascara	27	$ 83.00	south
442	439	Cici	1/15/2004	mascara	4	$ 14.17	east

FIGURE 49-5 Here are the transactions in which Cici or Colleen sold lipstick or mascara in the East or South region.

How can I copy all transactions in which Cici or Colleen sold lipstick or mascara in the East or South region to a different worksheet?

The trick here is first to press F5, click **Special**, and then select **Visible Cells Only**. Now when you copy your data, Excel includes only the visible rows (in this case, the rows selected by the filtering criteria). Select all the filtered cells in the worksheet (Cici, Colleen, lipstick, and mascara) and paste them into a blank worksheet. You can create a blank worksheet in your workbook by right-clicking any worksheet tab, clicking **Insert**, selecting **Worksheet**, and then clicking **OK**. The Visible Cells Copied worksheet contains the records where Cici or Colleen sold lipstick or mascara in the East.

How can I clear filters from a column or database?

Clicking **Filter** on the **Data** tab removes all filters. Clicking the funnel for any column for which you created a filter displays an option to clear the filter from that column.

How can I identify all transactions that involved sales greater than $280 and greater than 90 units?

After clicking **Filter** on the **Data** tab, first click the **Units** column arrow to display the options shown in Figure 49-6.

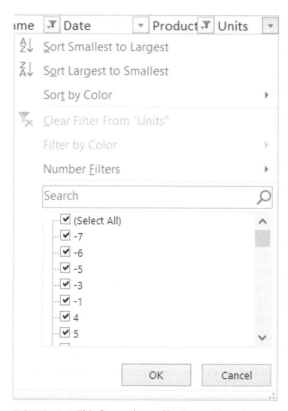

FIGURE 49-6 This figure shows filtering options for a numerical column.

You can select any subset of numerical unit values (for example, all transactions for which sales were −10 or −8 units). Number Filters is chosen here to display the choices in Figure 49-7.

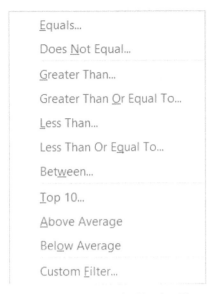

Equals...

Does Not Equal...

Greater Than...

Greater Than Or Equal To...

Less Than...

Less Than Or Equal To...

Between...

Top 10...

Above Average

Below Average

Custom Filter...

FIGURE 49-7 Here are the Number Filters options.

Most of the options you see in the figure are self-explanatory. Here, you choose **Is Greater Than** and then fill in the dialog box as shown in Figure 49-8.

FIGURE 49-8 Select all records where units sold is greater than 90.

Next, at the **Dollars** column, click to include only records where the dollar amount is greater than $280. You obtain the records shown in Figure 49-9. (See the Sales > 90 units dollars > $280 worksheet.) Note that all selected records have both units greater than 90 and dollars greater than $280.

	C	D	E	F	G	H	I
3	Transaction number	Name	Date	Product	Units	Dollars	Location
40	37	Ashley	8/9/2005	mascara	93	$ 280.69	east
57	54	Cici	6/17/2004	eye liner	95	$ 287.76	midwest
64	61	Emilee	12/21/2004	eye liner	95	$ 287.05	midwest
65	62	Ashley	11/16/2005	lipstick	93	$ 280.77	west
165	162	Betsy	10/14/2005	foundation	93	$ 280.17	west
217	214	Betsy	9/13/2004	foundation	94	$ 283.74	west
284	281	Emilee	11/16/2005	foundation	94	$ 283.85	midwest
289	286	Betsy	7/27/2006	mascara	94	$ 284.14	west
314	311	Jen	5/15/2004	eye liner	94	$ 283.88	east
338	335	Ashley	5/26/2004	mascara	94	$ 283.62	midwest
340	337	Colleen	11/18/2004	lip gloss	95	$ 286.86	west
406	403	Jen	6/4/2005	mascara	93	$ 281.17	south
450	447	Cici	10/1/2006	mascara	94	$ 283.45	west
545	542	Ashley	4/19/2006	foundation	93	$ 281.17	midwest
579	576	Emilee	4/10/2005	lipstick	93	$ 280.80	midwest
587	584	Emilee	1/15/2004	foundation	94	$ 284.61	east
599	596	Colleen	10/3/2005	mascara	94	$ 284.25	east
632	629	Hallagan	7/31/2004	mascara	94	$ 283.88	east

FIGURE 49-9 This shows the transactions where more than 90 units were sold for a total of more than $280.

How can I identify all sales occurring in 2005 or 2006?

After clicking **Filter** on the ribbon, click the arrow for the **Date** column to display the choices in Figure 49-10.

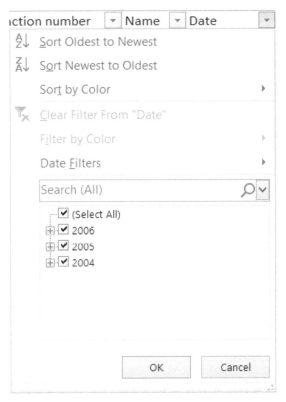

FIGURE 49-10 These are filtering options for the Date column.

After selecting 2005 and 2006, you see only those records involving sales in 2005 or 2006, as shown in Figure 49-11. (See the Sales In 2005 And 2006 worksheet.)

	C	D	E	F	G	H	I
Transaction number ▾		Name ▾	Date ▾	Product ▾	Units ▾	Dollars ▾	Location ▾
	3	Ashley	2/25/2005	lipstick	9	$ 28.72	midwest
	4	Hallagan	5/22/2006	lip gloss	55	$ 167.08	west
	6	Colleen	11/27/2005	eye liner	58	$ 175.99	midwest
	8	Colleen	12/17/2006	lip gloss	72	$ 217.84	midwest
	9	Ashley	7/5/2006	eye liner	75	$ 226.64	south
	10	Betsy	8/7/2006	lip gloss	24	$ 73.50	east
	13	Emilee	8/31/2005	lip gloss	49	$ 149.59	west
	14	Hallagan	1/1/2005	eye liner	18	$ 56.47	south
	15	Zaret	9/20/2006	foundatior	-8	$ (21.99)	east
	17	Colleen	4/30/2006	mascara	66	$ 199.65	south
	18	Jen	8/31/2005	lip gloss	88	$ 265.19	midwest
	20	Zaret	11/27/2005	lip gloss	57	$ 173.12	midwest
	21	Zaret	6/2/2006	mascara	12	$ 38.08	west
	23	Colleen	2/1/2006	mascara	25	$ 77.31	midwest
	24	Emilee	12/6/2006	lip gloss	24	$ 74.62	west
	26	Cristina	9/22/2005	foundatior	77	$ 233.05	midwest
	27	Cristina	3/28/2006	lip gloss	53	$ 161.46	midwest
	29	Zaret	9/9/2006	mascara	19	$ 59.15	west

FIGURE 49-11 This figure shows sales during 2005 and 2006.

Note that you could also have selected **Date Filters** to display the options shown in Figure 49-12.

Most of these options are self-explanatory as well. **Custom Filter** enables you to select any range of dates as your filtering criteria.

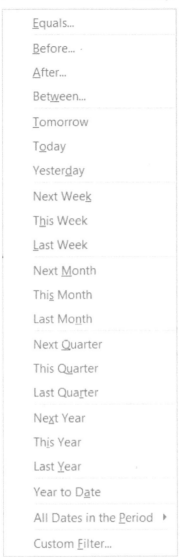

Makeupf

- Equals...
- Before...
- After...
- Between...
- Tomorrow
- Today
- Yesterday
- Next Week
- This Week
- Last Week
- Next Month
- This Month
- Last Month
- Next Quarter
- This Quarter
- Last Quarter
- Next Year
- This Year
- Last Year
- Year to Date
- All Dates in the Period ▸
- Custom Filter...

FIGURE 49-12 These are the Date filtering options.

How can I identify all transactions in the last three months of 2005 or the first three months of 2006?

After clicking the arrow for the **Date** column, you see the list of years shown in Figure 49-10. Clicking the + sign to the left of the year displays a list of months. You can select October through December of 2005 and then January through March of 2006 to show all sales during those months. (See Figure 49-13 and the Filter By Months worksheet.)

	C	D	E	F	G	H	I
1			last 3 months 05 and first 3 months 06				
2							
3	Transaction number ▾	Name ▾	Date ▾	Product ▾	Units ▾	Dollars ▾	Location ▾
9	6	Colleen	11/27/2005	eye liner	58	$ 175.99	midwest
23	20	Zaret	11/27/2005	lip gloss	57	$ 173.12	midwest
26	23	Colleen	2/1/2006	mascara	25	$ 77.31	midwest
30	27	Cristina	3/28/2006	lip gloss	53	$ 161.46	midwest
33	30	Cici	2/23/2006	foundation	-9	$ (24.63)	west
53	50	Cristina	12/8/2005	lip gloss	8	$ 26.24	midwest
55	52	Colleen	11/16/2005	foundation	62	$ 189.25	midwest
61	58	Hallagan	11/5/2005	foundation	63	$ 191.37	south
65	62	Ashley	11/16/2005	lipstick	93	$ 280.77	west
70	67	Colleen	3/6/2006	foundation	-2	$ (3.94)	west
75	72	Jen	1/10/2006	lip gloss	69	$ 208.69	east
82	79	Zaret	12/19/2005	eye liner	26	$ 80.30	south
93	90	Colleen	1/21/2006	lip gloss	75	$ 226.74	south
94	91	Betsy	10/3/2005	eye liner	74	$ 224.23	west
98	95	Jen	3/17/2006	lipstick	-8	$ (22.11)	west

FIGURE 49-13 This figure shows all sales from October 2005 through March 2006.

How can I identify all transactions for which the salesperson's first name starts with C?

Click the **Name** column arrow and choose **Text Filters**. Select **Begins With** and, in the dialog box shown in Figure 49-14, choose **Begins With C**.

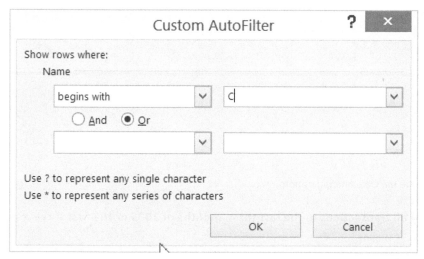

FIGURE 49-14 This is the Custom AutoFilter dialog box set up to select all records for which the salesperson's name begins with C.

How can I identify all transactions for which the cell containing the product name is colored in red?

Click the **Product** column arrow and then choose **Filter By Color**. You can now select the color to use as a filter. As shown in Figure 49-15, only the rows for which the product is colored in red are included here. Figure 49-16 shows the resulting records (see the Filter By Color worksheet).

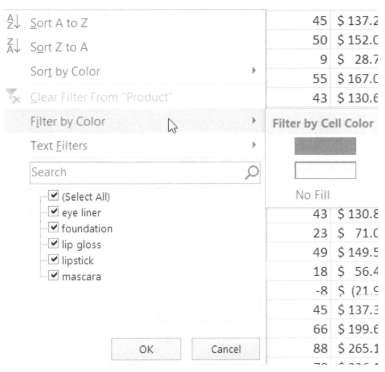

FIGURE 49-15 This is the dialog box for filtering by cell color.

	C	D	E	F	G	H	I
2							
3	Transaction number ▾	Name ▾	Date ▾	Product ▾	Units ▾	Dollars ▾	Locatio ▾
11	8	Colleen	12/17/2006	lip gloss	72	$ 217.84	midwest
247	244	Ashley	9/24/2004	foundatior	84	$ 253.29	east
292	289	Zaret	5/26/2004	lipstick	56	$ 169.19	south

FIGURE 49-16 Here are all the records where the product cell color is red.

How can I identify all transactions in the top 30 of all revenue values for which Hallagan or Jen was the salesperson?

After clicking **Filter** on the ribbon, you click the **Name** column arrow and then select the check boxes for **Hallagan** and **Jen**. Click the arrow for the **Dollar** column and choose **Number Filters**. From the **Number Filters** list, select **Top 10** and then fill in the dialog box as shown in Figure 49-17. You have now filtered all records in the top 30 revenue values in which Jen or Hallagan is the salesperson. See the results in Figure 49-18 (and the Top 30 $s With Hallagan Or Jen worksheet). Note that only five of the top 30 sales had Hallagan or Jen as the salesperson. You can also select **Top 5** percent, **Bottom 20** percent, and so on for any numerical column.

FIGURE 49-17 This is the dialog box in which to select the top 30 records by dollar value.

	D	E	F	G	H	I
1						
2						
3	Name	Date	Product	Units	Dollars	Locatio
314	Jen	5/15/2004	eye liner	94	$ 283.88	east
722	Hallagan	6/13/2006	lip gloss	95	$ 286.68	midwest
797	Hallagan	8/18/2006	foundatior	95	$ 287.80	midwest
1259	Hallagan	4/8/2006	lip gloss	95	$ 286.76	midwest
1619	Hallagan	7/29/2005	eye liner	95	$ 287.15	west

FIGURE 49-18 These are the top 30 records by dollar value for which Jen or Hallagan was the salesperson.

How can I easily obtain a complete list of salespeople?

Here, you want a list of all the salespeople without anybody's name repeated. Begin by selecting **Remove Duplicates** on the **Data** tab on the ribbon to display the **Remove Duplicates** dialog box shown in Figure 49-19. After choosing **Unselect All**, select only the **Name** check box and then click **OK**. This setting filters the data for only the first record involving each salesperson's name. See the results in Figure 49-20 and in the Name Duplicates Removed worksheet.

> **Important** Because selecting Remove Duplicates removes some of your data, I recommend making a copy of your data before selecting Remove Duplicates.

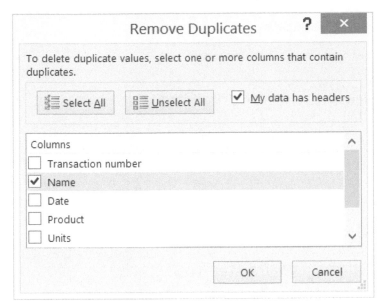

FIGURE 49-19 This is the Remove Duplicates dialog box with the Name column selected.

	C	D	E	F	G	H	I
3	Transaction number	Name	Date	Product	Units	Dollars	Location
4	1	Betsy	4/1/2004	lip gloss	45	$ 137.20	south
5	2	Hallagan	3/10/2004	foundation	50	$ 152.01	midwest
6	3	Ashley	2/25/2005	lipstick	9	$ 28.72	midwest
7	5	Zaret	6/17/2004	lip gloss	43	$ 130.60	midwest
8	6	Colleen	11/27/2005	eye liner	58	$ 175.99	midwest
9	7	Cristina	3/21/2004	eye liner	8	$ 25.80	midwest
10	13	Emilee	8/31/2005	lip gloss	49	$ 149.59	west
11	18	Jen	8/31/2005	lip gloss	88	$ 265.19	midwest
12	28	Cici	6/17/2004	mascara	41	$ 125.27	west

FIGURE 49-20 This figure shows the list of salespersons' names.

How can I view every combination of salesperson, product, and location that occurs in the database?

Here again, you need to click **Remove Duplicates** on the **Data** tab to begin. Fill in the **Remove Duplicates** dialog box as shown in Figure 49-21.

Figure 49-22 lists the first record for each combination of person, product, and location occurring in the database. (See the Unique Name Product Location worksheet.) One hundred eighty unique combinations occurred. Note that the twentieth record was omitted because it included Zaret selling lip gloss in the Midwest, and the fifth record had already picked up this combination.

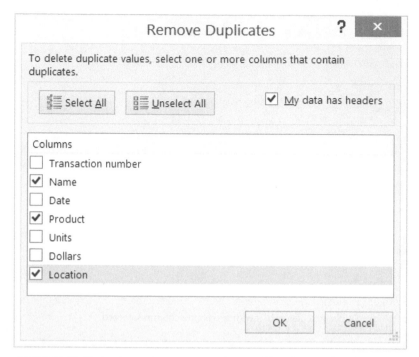

FIGURE 49-21 Find unique salesperson, product, and location combinations.

	C	D	E	F	G	H	I
3	Transaction number	Name	Date	Product	Units	Dollars	Location
4	1	Betsy	4/1/2004	lip gloss	45	$ 137.20	south
5	2	Hallagan	3/10/2004	foundatior	50	$ 152.01	midwest
6	3	Ashley	2/25/2005	lipstick	9	$ 28.72	midwest
7	4	Hallagan	5/22/2006	lip gloss	55	$ 167.08	west
8	5	Zaret	6/17/2004	lip gloss	43	$ 130.60	midwest
9	6	Colleen	11/27/2005	eye liner	58	$ 175.99	midwest
10	7	Cristina	3/21/2004	eye liner	8	$ 25.80	midwest
11	8	Colleen	12/17/2006	lip gloss	72	$ 217.84	midwest
12	9	Ashley	7/5/2006	eye liner	75	$ 226.64	south
13	10	Betsy	8/7/2006	lip gloss	24	$ 73.50	east
14	11	Ashley	11/29/2004	mascara	43	$ 130.84	east
15	12	Ashley	11/18/2004	lip gloss	23	$ 71.03	west
16	13	Emilee	8/31/2005	lip gloss	49	$ 149.59	west
17	14	Hallagan	1/1/2005	eye liner	18	$ 56.47	south
18	15	Zaret	9/20/2006	foundatior	-8	$ (21.99)	east
19	16	Emilee	4/12/2004	mascara	45	$ 137.39	east
20	17	Colleen	4/30/2006	mascara	66	$ 199.65	south
21	18	Jen	8/31/2005	lip gloss	88	$ 265.19	midwest
22	19	Jen	10/27/2004	eye liner	78	$ 236.15	south
23	21	Zaret	6/2/2006	mascara	12	$ 38.08	west

FIGURE 49-22 This is a list of unique salesperson, product, and location combinations.

If my data changes, how can I reapply the same filter?

Right-click any cell in your filtered results, point to **Filter**, and then click **Reapply**. Any changes to your data are reflected in the filtered data.

How can I extract all foundation transactions in the first six months of 2005 for which Emilee or Jen was the salesperson and the average per-unit price was more than $3.20?

The AutoFilter feature (even with Custom) is limited to *AND* queries across columns. This means, for example, that you cannot find all transactions for lipstick sales by Jen during 2005 *or* foundation sales by Zaret during 2004. To perform more-complex queries such as this one, you need to use the Advanced Filter feature. To use Advanced Filter, you set up a criteria range that specifies the records you want to extract. (This process is described in detail in Chapter 48, "Summarizing data with database statistical functions.") After specifying the criteria range, you tell Excel whether you want the records extracted to the current location or to a different location. To identify all foundation transactions in the first six months of 2005 for which Emilee or Jen was the salesperson and for which the average per-unit price was more than $3.20, you can use the criteria range shown in the O4:S6 range in Figure 49-23. (See the Jen + Emilee worksheet in the Advancedfilter.xlsx file.)

	O	P	Q	R	S
1					
2					
3					
4	Name	Date	Date	Price	Product
5	Jen	>=1/1/2005	<=6/30/2005	FALSE	Foundation
6	Emilee	>=1/1/2005	<=6/30/2005	FALSE	Foundation

FIGURE 49-23 Set up a criteria range to use with an advanced filter.

In cells R5 and R6, enter the =(L5/K5)>3.2 formula. Recall from Chapter 48 that this formula creates computed criteria that flag each row in which the per-unit price is more than $3.20. Also, remember that your heading for a computed criterion must not be a field name. Price was used here as the field heading. The criteria in O5:S5 flag all records in which Jen is the salesperson, the date is between 1/1/2005 and 6/30/2005, the product sold is foundation, and the per-unit price is more than $3.20. The criteria in O6:S6 flag all records in which Emilee is the salesperson, the date is between 1/1/2005 and 6/30/2005, the product sold is foundation, and the per-unit price is more than $3.20. The O4:S6 criteria range flags exactly the records you want. Remember that criteria in different rows are joined by *OR*.

You can now select any cell within the database range and select **Advanced** in the **Sort & Filter** group on the **Data** tab. Fill in the dialog box as shown in Figure 49-24.

FIGURE 49-24 These are the Advanced Filter dialog box settings.

With these settings, you are telling Excel to extract all records in the database (the G4:M1895 cell range) that satisfy the criteria specified in O4:S6. These records should be copied to a range whose upper-left corner is cell O14. The records extracted are shown in the O14:U18 cell range. Only the four records shown in Figure 49-25 meet the defined criteria. (See the Jen + Emilee worksheet again.)

	O	P	Q	R	S	T	U
14	Trans Number	Name	Date	Product	Units	Dollars	Location
15	392	Jen	2/25/2005	foundation	8	$ 26.31	south
16	479	Emilee	5/24/2005	foundation	2	$ 7.68	east
17	1035	Emilee	4/10/2005	foundation	8	$ 26.40	east
18	1067	Jen	3/19/2005	foundation	1	$ 4.86	east

FIGURE 49-25 Here are the Advanced Filter results.

If you select **Unique Records Only** in the **Advanced Filter** dialog box, no duplicate records are returned. For example, if Jen had another foundation transaction in the East region on 3/19/2005 for one unit for $4.88, only one of those transactions would be extracted.

Problems

1. Find all transactions in which Hallagan sold eyeliner in the West region.

2. Find all transactions that rank in the top 5 percent with regard to units sold.

3. Find the top 20 revenue-generating transactions that involve foundation sales.

4. Find all transactions involving sales of at least 60 units during 2004 for which the per-unit price was a maximum of $3.10.

5. Find all foundation transactions during the first three months of 2004 for which the per-unit price was larger than the average price received for foundation during the entire period.

6. Find all transactions in which Zaret or Betsy sold either lipstick or foundation.

7. Find all unique combinations of product and salesperson's name.

8. Find all the top 30 sales (by units) occurring in 2005 that involved lip gloss or mascara.

9. Find all sales by Jen between August 10 and September 15, 2005.

10. Find all sales of lipstick sold by Colleen for which the number of units sold is higher than the average number of units in a lipstick transaction.

11. Find all unique combinations of name, product, and location occurring during the first three months of 2006.

12. Find all records in which the product cell is colored yellow.

CHAPTER 50

Consolidating data

Question answered in this chapter:

- My company sells products in several regions of the United States. Each region keeps records of the number of units of each product sold during the months of January, February, and March. Is there an easy way to create a master workbook that always combines each region's sales and gives a tally of the total amount of each product sold in the United States during each month?

A business analyst often receives worksheets that tally the same information (such as monthly product sales) from different affiliates or regions. To determine the company's overall profitability, the analyst usually needs to combine or consolidate this information in a single Microsoft Excel workbook. PivotTables built from multiple consolidation ranges can be used to accomplish this goal, but the little-known Consolidate command (on the Data tab on the ribbon) is another way to accomplish this goal. With Consolidate, you can ensure that changes in the individual worksheets are automatically reflected in the consolidated worksheet.

Answer to this chapter's question

This section provides the answer to the question that is listed at the beginning of the chapter.

My company sells products in several regions of the United States. Each region keeps records of the number of units of each product sold during the months of January, February, and March. Is there an easy way to create a master workbook that always combines each region's sales and gives a tally of the total amount of each product sold in the United States during each month?

The East.xlsx file (shown in Figure 50-1) displays monthly unit sales of Products A–H in the eastern United States during January, February, and March. Similarly, the West.xlsx file (shown in Figure 50-2) displays monthly unit sales of Products A–H in the western United States from January through March. Your need is to create a consolidated worksheet that tabulates each product's total sales by month.

	A	B	C	D	E	F
1	Product	January	February	March		East Sales
2	A	205	263	20		
3	B	164	-17	146		
4	C	278	177	179		
5	D	156	214	240		
6	D	72	134	48		
7	D	7	256	104		
8	A	141	87	148		
9	A	2	-15	135		
10	A	-44	47	72		
11	B	7	-81	2		
12	E	25	120	171		
13	E	197	90	124		
14	E	221	121	48		
15	A	84	103	134		
16	G	-13	250	51		
17	D	-5	159	70		
18	E	136	152	28		

FIGURE 50-1 Here are East region sales from January through March.

	A	B	C	D	E	F	G
1	Product	January	February	March			
2	A	173	1	256			
3	A	208	201	224		West sales	
4	B	176	33	350			
5	B	190	249	215			
6	D	162	74	156			
7	D	90	150	170			
8	D	112	284	141			
9	G	154	217	113			
10	G	152	200	275			
11	G	277	183	372			
12	H	131	71	266			
13	F	294	211	249			
14	F	146	125	5			
15	A	115	214	141			

FIGURE 50-2 Here are the West region sales from January through March.

Before you use the Consolidate command, it's helpful to see both worksheets together on the screen. To do this, open both workbooks, click **Arrange All** in the **Window** group on the **View** tab and select **Tiled**. Your screen should look like Figure 50-3.

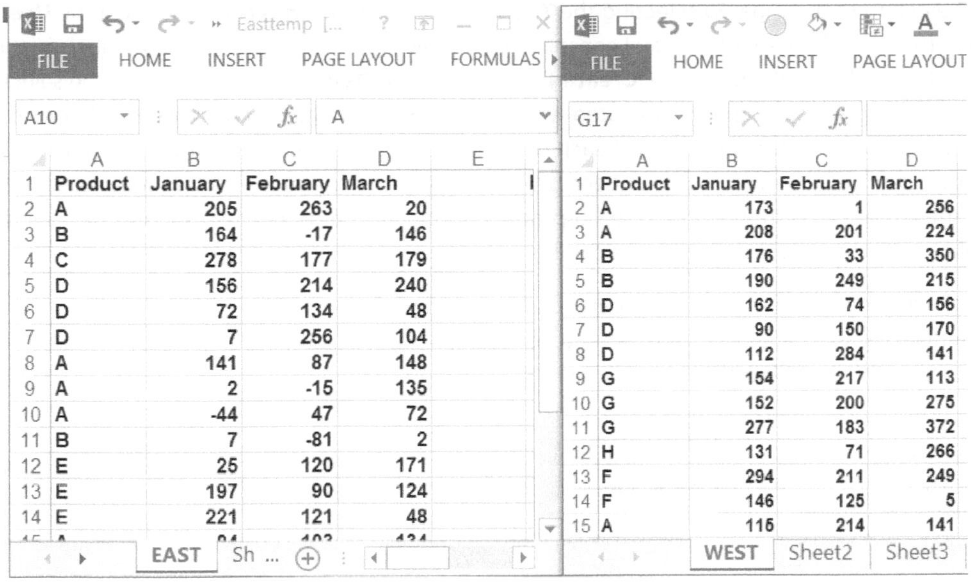

FIGURE 50-3 East and West sales are arranged on the same screen.

Now open a blank worksheet in a new workbook and then click **Arrange All** and **Tiled** again. In the blank worksheet, click **Consolidate** in the **Data Tools** group on the **Data** tab, and you see the **Consolidate** dialog box, shown in Figure 50-4.

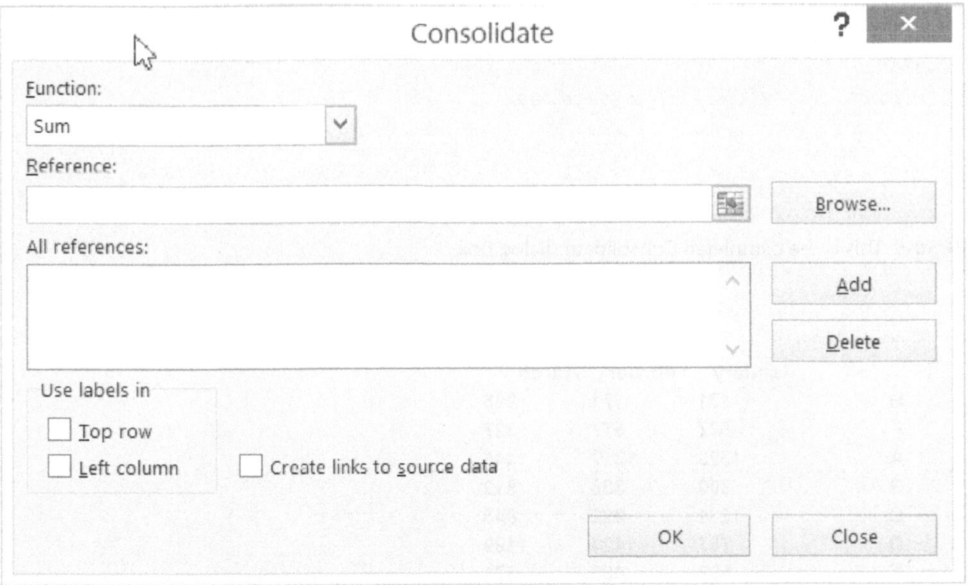

FIGURE 50-4 This is the Consolidate dialog box.

To consolidate the data from the East and West regions in your new, blank worksheet, enter the ranges you want to consolidate in the **Reference** box of the **Consolidate** dialog box, clicking **Add** after selecting each range. By selecting the **Top Row** and **Left Column** check boxes in the **Use Labels In** area, you ensure that Excel consolidates the selected ranges by looking at labels in the top row and left column of each range. **Create Links To Source Data** enables changes in the selected ranges to be reflected in the consolidated worksheet. Select **Sum** in the **Function** box because you want Excel to add up the total sales of each product by month. Selecting **Count**, for instance, would count the number of transactions for each product during each month; selecting **Max** would compute the largest sales transaction for each product during each month. The **Consolidate** dialog box should be filled out as shown in Figure 50-5.

After clicking **OK**, the new worksheet looks like the one shown in Figure 50-6. (See file Eastandwestconsolidated.xlsx.) You can see, for example, that 1,317 units of Product A were sold in February, 597 units of Product F were sold in January, and so on.

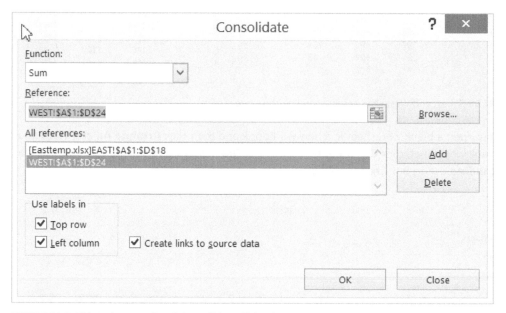

FIGURE 50-5 This is the completed Consolidate dialog box.

		A	B	C	D	E	F
	1			January	February	March	
+	3	H		131	71	266	
+	7	F		597	577	327	
+	18	A		1323	1317	1445	
+	24	B		890	335	812	
+	30	C		1231	922	843	
+	39	D		767	1424	1199	
+	44	E		579	483	371	
+	49	G		570	850	811	

FIGURE 50-6 Here is the total sales data after consolidation.

Now, in cell C2 of East.xlsx, change the **February Product A** sales from 263 to 363. Notice that in the consolidated worksheet, the entry for February Product A sales has also increased by 100 (from 1,317 to 1,417). This change occurs because **Create Links To Source Data** was selected in the **Consolidate** dialog box. (By the way, if you click the **2** right below the workbook name in the consolidated worksheet, you see how Excel grouped the data to perform the consolidation.) The result is contained in the Eastandwestconsolidated.xlsx file. Of course, you could also summarize data from different worksheets by using PivotTables with Multiple Consolidation Ranges (see Chapter 43, "Using PivotTables and slicers to describe data").

If you frequently download new data to your source workbooks (in this case, East.xlsx and West.xlsx), it's a good idea to name the ranges, including your data as a table. Then new data is automatically included in the consolidation. You might also choose to select some blank rows below the current data set. When you populate the blank rows with new data, Excel picks up the new data when it performs the consolidation. A third choice is to make each data range a dynamic range. (See Chapter 21, "The OFFSET function," for more information.)

Problems

The following problems refer to the data in the Jancon.xlsx and Febcon.xlsx files. Each file contains the unit sales, dollar revenues, and product sold for each transaction during the month:

1. Create a consolidated worksheet that gives the total unit sales and dollar revenue for each product by region.

2. Create a consolidated worksheet that gives the largest first-quarter transaction for each product by region from the standpoint of revenue and units sold.

CHAPTER 51

Creating subtotals

Questions answered in this chapter:

- Is there an easy way to set up a worksheet to calculate total revenue and units sold by region?

- Can I also obtain a breakdown by salesperson of sales in each region?

Joolas is a small company that manufactures makeup. For each transaction, it tracks the name of the salesperson, the location of the transaction, the product sold, the units sold, and the revenue. The managers want answers to questions such as those that are the focus of this chapter.

PivotTables can be used to slice and dice data in Microsoft Excel. Often, however, you'd like an easier way to summarize a list or a database within a list. In a sales database, for example, you might want to create a summary of sales revenue by region, a summary of sales revenue by product, and a summary of sales revenue by salesperson. If you sort a list by the column in which specific data is listed, the Subtotal command enables you to create a subtotal in a list on the basis of the values in the column. For example, if you sort the makeup database by location, you can calculate total revenue and units sold for each region and place the totals just below the last row for that region. As another example, after sorting the database by product, you can use the Subtotal command to calculate total revenue and units sold for each product and display the totals below the row in which the product changes. Unfortunately, if you have made a range of cells an Excel table (see Chapter 25, "Tables"), you cannot use that table to create subtotals.

In the next section, you see how easy it is to use Subtotals to summarize Excel data.

Answers to this chapter's questions

This section provides the answers to the questions that are listed at the beginning of the chapter.

Is there an easy way to set up a worksheet to calculate total revenue and units sold by region?

The data for this question is in the Makeupsubtotals.xlsx file. In Figure 51-1, you can see a subset of the data as it appears after sorting the list by the Location column.

To calculate revenue and units sold by region, place the cursor anywhere in the database and then click **Subtotal** in the **Outline** group on the **Data** tab. In the **Subtotal** dialog box, fill in the values as shown in Figure 51-2.

By selecting **Location** from the **At Each Change In** list, you ensure that subtotals are created at each point in which the value in the **Location** column changes. This corresponds to the different regions. Selecting **Sum** from the **Use Function** dialog box tells Excel to create totals for each region based on any set of columns. By selecting **Units** and **Dollars** in the **Add Subtotal To** area, you indicate that subtotals should be created for these columns. **Replace Current Subtotals** causes Excel to remove any previously computed subtotals. Because you haven't created any subtotals, it doesn't matter whether this option is selected for this example. If **Page Break Between Groups** is selected, Excel inserts a page break after each subtotal. Selecting the **Summary Below Data** check box causes Excel to place subtotals below the data. If this option is not selected, the subtotals are created above the data used for the computation. Clicking **Remove All** removes subtotals from the list.

	A	B	C	D	E	F	G
	Trans Number	Name	Date	Product	Units	Dollars	Location
	10	Betsy	8/7/2006	lip gloss	24	$ 73.50	east
	11	Ashley	11/29/2004	mascara	43	$ 130.84	east
	15	Zaret	9/20/2006	foundation	-8	$ (21.99)	east
	16	Emilee	4/12/2004	mascara	45	$ 137.39	east
	45	Emilee	9/20/2006	lip gloss	2	$ 7.85	east
	46	Ashley	8/9/2005	mascara	93	$ 280.69	east
	58	Cristina	4/12/2004	foundation	34	$ 104.09	east
	60	Jen	10/27/2004	mascara	89	$ 269.09	east
	69	Cristina	1/23/2005	eye liner	73	$ 221.41	east
	77	Cristina	1/15/2004	mascara	27	$ 83.29	east
	81	Jen	1/10/2006	lip gloss	69	$ 208.69	east
	86	Jen	8/9/2005	eye liner	-2	$ (4.24)	east
	87	Emilee	8/31/2005	eye liner	5	$ 17.03	east
	98	Jen	4/12/2004	lip gloss	92	$ 277.54	east
	108	Cici	8/31/2005	lip gloss	-10	$ (28.41)	east
	114	Betsy	9/22/2005	lipstick	77	$ 233.33	east
	116	Zaret	6/24/2006	eye liner	22	$ 68.07	east
	119	Colleen	5/22/2006	eye liner	20	$ 62.37	east
	131	Jen	11/29/2004	mascara	56	$ 168.87	east
	133	Betsy	7/9/2004	mascara	11	$ 34.42	east
	140	Jen	6/28/2004	eye liner	80	$ 242.50	east
	145	Cici	9/24/2004	mascara	89	$ 269.40	east

FIGURE 51-1 After sorting a list by the values in a specific column, you can easily create subtotals for that data.

A sample of the Subtotals results is shown in Figure 51-3. You can see that 18,818 units were sold in the East region, earning revenue of $57,372.09.

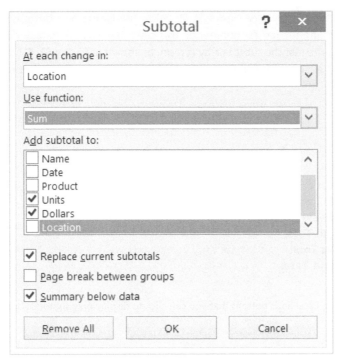

FIGURE 51-2 This is the Subtotal dialog box.

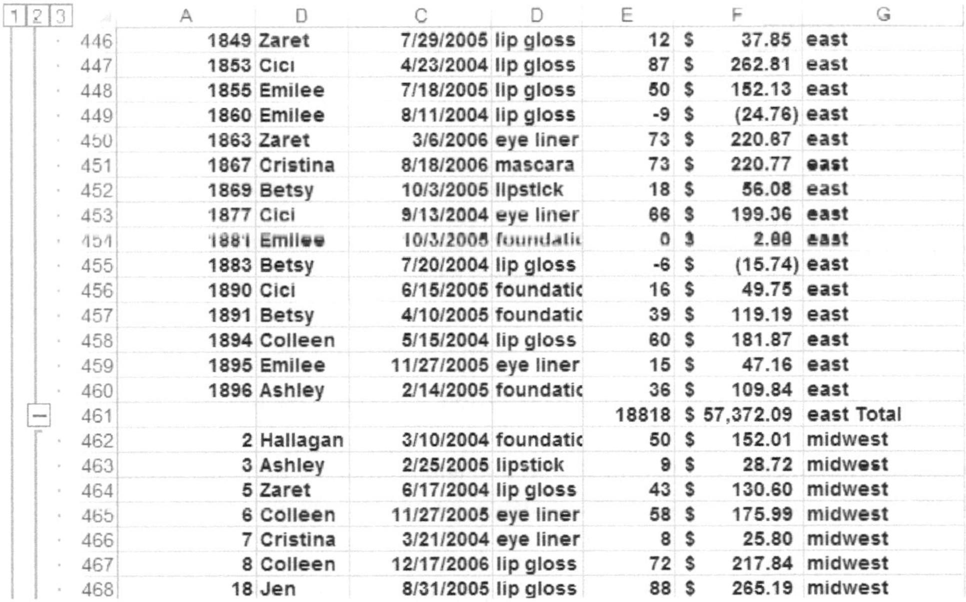

	A	B	C	D	E	F	G
446	1849	Zaret	7/29/2005	lip gloss	12	$ 37.85	east
447	1853	Cici	4/23/2004	lip gloss	87	$ 262.81	east
448	1855	Emilee	7/18/2005	lip gloss	50	$ 152.13	east
449	1860	Emilee	8/11/2004	lip gloss	-9	$ (24.76)	east
450	1863	Zaret	3/6/2006	eye liner	73	$ 220.87	east
451	1867	Cristina	8/18/2006	mascara	73	$ 220.77	east
452	1869	Betsy	10/3/2005	lipstick	18	$ 56.08	east
453	1877	Cici	9/13/2004	eye liner	66	$ 199.36	east
454	1881	Emilee	10/3/2005	foundatic	0	3 2.88	east
455	1883	Betsy	7/20/2004	lip gloss	-6	$ (15.74)	east
456	1890	Cici	6/15/2005	foundatic	16	$ 49.75	east
457	1891	Betsy	4/10/2005	foundatic	39	$ 119.19	east
458	1894	Colleen	5/15/2004	lip gloss	60	$ 181.87	east
459	1895	Emilee	11/27/2005	eye liner	15	$ 47.16	east
460	1896	Ashley	2/14/2005	foundatic	36	$ 109.84	east
461					18818	$ 57,372.09	east Total
462	2	Hallagan	3/10/2004	foundatic	50	$ 152.01	midwest
463	3	Ashley	2/25/2005	lipstick	9	$ 28.72	midwest
464	5	Zaret	6/17/2004	lip gloss	43	$ 130.60	midwest
465	6	Colleen	11/27/2005	lip gloss	58	$ 175.99	midwest
466	7	Cristina	3/21/2004	eye liner	8	$ 25.80	midwest
467	8	Colleen	12/17/2006	lip gloss	72	$ 217.84	midwest
468	18	Jen	8/31/2005	lip gloss	88	$ 265.19	midwest

FIGURE 51-3 These are the subtotals for the East region.

Notice that in the left corner of the window (see Figure 51-3), below the **Name** box, buttons with the numbers 1, 2, and 3 appear. Clicking the largest number (in this case, 3) yields the data and subtotals. If you click the **2** button, you see just the subtotals by region, as shown in Figure 51-4. Clicking the **1** button yields the Grand Total, as shown in Figure 51-5. In short, clicking a lower number reduces the level of detail shown.

	E	F	G
1			
2			
3			
4	Units	Dollars	Location
461	18818	$ 57,372.09	east Total
886	17985	$ 54,805.41	midwest Total
1408	21083	$ 64,296.35	south Total
1899	20821	$ 63,438.82	west Total
1900	78707	$ 239,912.67	Grand Total
1901			

FIGURE 51-4 When you create subtotals, Excel adds buttons that you can click to display only subtotals or both subtotals and details.

	E	F	G
1			
2			
3			
4	Units	Dollars	Location
1900	78707	$ 239,912.67	Grand Total

FIGURE 51-5 Display the overall total without any detail.

Can I also obtain a breakdown by salesperson of sales in each region?

If you want to, you can nest subtotals. In other words, you can obtain a breakdown of sales by each salesperson in each region, or you can even get a breakdown of how much each salesperson sold of each product in each region. (See the Nestedsubtotals.xlsx file.) To demonstrate the creation of nested subtotals, create a breakdown of sales by each salesperson in each region.

To begin, you must sort your data first by **Location** and then by **Name**. This gives a breakdown for each salesperson of units sold and revenue within each region. If you sort first by **Name** and then by **Location**, you would get a breakdown of units sold and revenue for each salesperson by region. After sorting the data, you proceed as before and create the subtotals by region. Click **Subtotal** again and fill in the dialog box as shown in Figure 51-6.

You now want a breakdown by **Name**. Clearing the **Replace Current Subtotals** check box ensures that you will not replace your regional breakdown. You can now see the breakdown of sales by each salesperson in each region as shown in Figure 51-7.

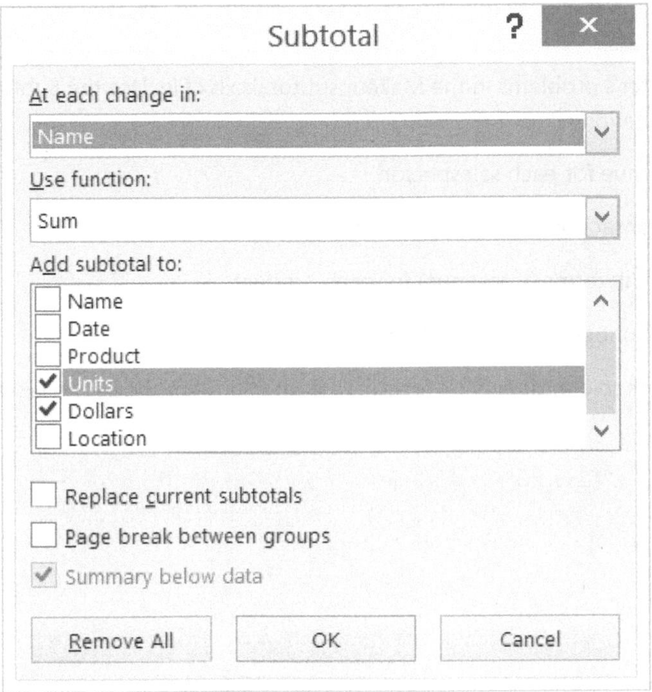

FIGURE 51-6 Create nested subtotals.

	A	B	C	D	E	F	G
1							
2							
3							
4	Trans Number	Name	Date	Product	Units	Dollars	Location
56		**Ashley Total**			2558	$ 7,772.70	
122		**Betsy Total**			2879	$ 8,767.43	
173		**Cici Total**			1951	$ 5,956.32	
220		**Colleen Total**			1874	$ 5,713.07	
261		**Cristina Total**			1348	$ 4,126.27	
312		**Emilee Total**			2064	$ 6,295.47	
355		**Hallagan Total**			1626	$ 4,965.62	
409		**Jen Total**			2282	$ 6,949.21	
469		**Zaret Total**			2236	$ 6,826.00	
470					18818	$ 57,372.09	**east Total**
511		**Ashley Total**			1635	$ 4,985.90	
555		**Betsy Total**			1598	$ 4,878.09	
616		**Cici Total**			2671	$ 8,129.62	
670		**Colleen Total**			2159	$ 6,586.14	
721		**Cristina Total**			1923	$ 5,870.03	
766		**Emilee Total**			1852	$ 5,642.20	
809		**Hallagan Total**			2431	$ 7,378.32	
862		**Jen Total**			2092	$ 6,381.32	
903		**Zaret Total**			1624	$ 4,953.80	
904					17985	$ 54,805.41	**midwest Total**

FIGURE 51-7 Here is an example of nested subtotals.

Problems

You can find the data for this chapter's problems in the Makeupsubtotals.xlsx file. Use the Subtotal command for the following computations:

1. Find the units sold and revenue for each salesperson.

2. Find the number of sales transactions for each product.

3. Find the largest transaction (in terms of revenue) for each product.

4. Find the average dollar amount per transaction by region.

5. Display a breakdown of units sold and revenue for each salesperson that shows the results for each product by region.

CHAPTER 52

Charting tricks

Questions answered in this chapter:

- How can I create combination charts?

- How can I create a secondary axis?

- How can I handle missing data?

- How can I handle the appearance of hidden data?

- How can I use pictures to add bling to my column graphs?

- I charted annual sales data in a column graph, and the years do not show up as column labels. What did I do wrong?

- How can I include data labels and data tables in my charts?

- How can I use Excel 2013 to place data labels on a chart based on the contents of cells?

- How can I track sales force performance over time?

- How can I create a band chart to check whether inventory is within acceptable levels?

- How can I store a chart as a template?

- How can I use a thermometer chart to portray progress against a target?

- How can I create dynamic chart labels?

- How can I use check boxes to control which series are charted?

- How can I use a list box to choose the series to be charted?

- How can I create a Gantt chart?

- How can I create a chart based on sorted data?

- How can I create a histogram that automatically updates when I include new data?

- How can I add conditional colors to a chart?

- How can I use waterfall charts to track progress toward a sales target or break down components of sales price?

- How can I use the *GETPIVOTDATA* function and the Excel Table feature to create dynamic dashboards?

- How can I create a Pareto chart?

- How can I insert a vertical line in a chart to separate pre-merger and post-merger performance?

- How can I use a radar chart to portray how basketball team members differ in strength, speed, and jumping ability?

- I know I can use a scatter plot to display how two variables change. How can I use a bubble chart to summarize the variation of three variables?

An old Chinese proverb says a picture is worth a thousand words. Excel can create many amazing charts, and this chapter shows you many examples of charting tips and tricks. Be aware that charting in Excel 2013 has changed a lot from previous versions.

Answers to this chapter's questions

This section provides the answers to the questions that are listed at the beginning of the chapter.

How can I create combination charts?

The Combinationstemp.xlsx file contains Actual and Target sales for January through July. You would like to create a chart that shows each month's actual and target sales. First, select the F5:H12 range and, from the **Insert** tab, select **Column Charts** and choose the first 2D (clustered) column chart, shown in Figure 52-1. Using two columns makes it difficult to see the contrast between the actual and target sales, so use a combination chart in which one series is charted as a line and the other as a column. To create this chart, right-click on either series and select **Change Chart Type**. After choosing **Combo** (a new choice in Excel 2013) choose the first choice as shown in Figure 52-2. This yields the combination chart shown in Figure 52-3.

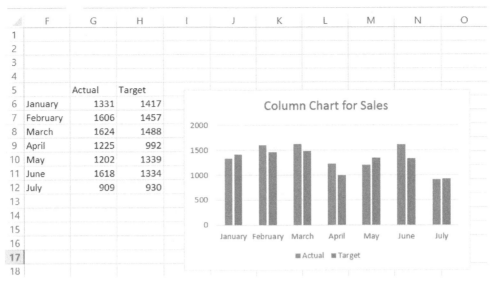

FIGURE 52-1 This is a column chart for actual and sales target.

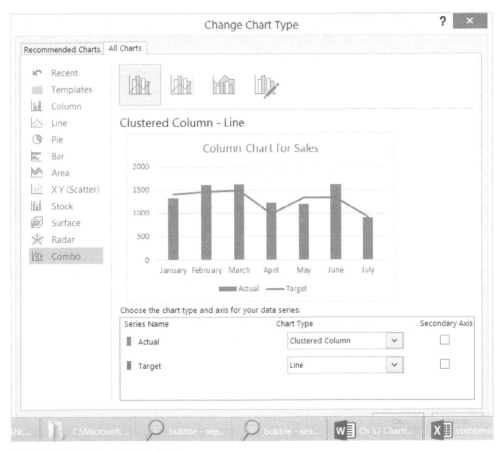

FIGURE 52-2 Select a Combo chart.

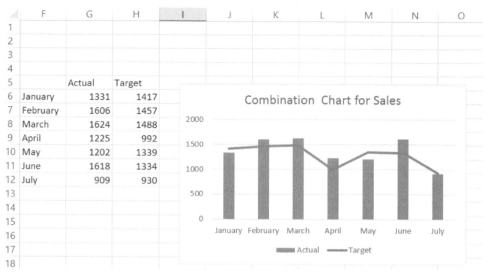

FIGURE 52-3 This is a combination chart.

How can I create a secondary axis?

When charting two quantities of differing magnitude, a secondary axis is often needed to make sense of the chart. To illustrate the idea, Figure 52-6 (see the Secondaryaxis.xlsx file) shows monthly revenues and units sold. If you show this data on a single *Y*-axis, monthly revenues would be hardly visible. To remedy this problem, begin by selecting the (D7:F16) range that you want charted. From the **Insert** tab, select the **Combo Chart** icon shown in Figure 52-4.

FIGURE 52-4 This is the Combo Chart icon.

From the drop-down arrow, select **Create Custom Combo Chart** and fill in the dialog box as shown in Figure 52-5.

The resulting chart summarizes Revenue on a secondary axis (the right-side vertical axis) with a line chart. The resulting chart in 52-6 shows clearly that monthly revenues and units sold change in a virtually lockstep fashion.

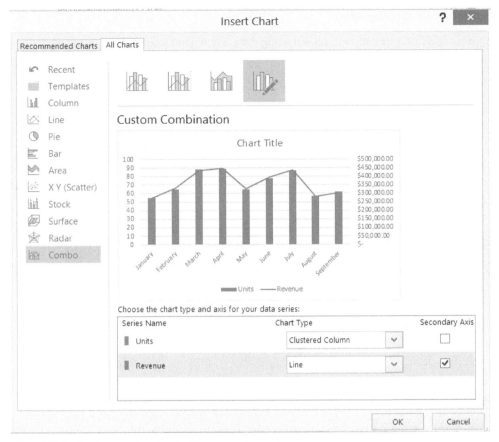

FIGURE 52-5 Create a combo chart with a secondary axis.

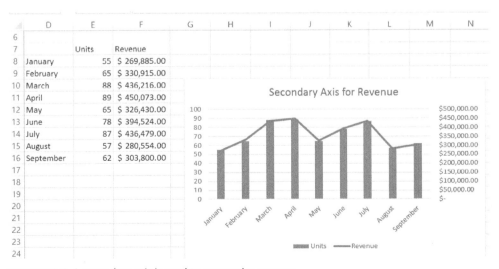

	Units	Revenue
January	55	$ 269,885.00
February	65	$ 330,915.00
March	88	$ 436,216.00
April	89	$ 450,073.00
May	65	$ 326,430.00
June	78	$ 394,524.00
July	87	$ 436,479.00
August	57	$ 280,554.00
September	62	$ 303,800.00

FIGURE 52-6 A secondary axis is used to summarize revenue.

How can I handle missing data?

Often, some rows of a spreadsheet have missing data. Excel gives you three ways to chart missing data:

- Show the data as zeroes.

- Show the data as blanks (gaps).

- Replace a missing data point by a line joining adjacent data points.

To illustrate how things work, the Missingdata.xlsx file contains hourly temperatures, but several values are missing. After plotting the data as a line chart, right-click the data and choose **Select Data**. This opens the dialog box shown in Figure 52-7.

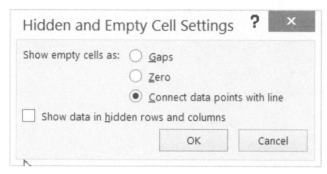

FIGURE 52-7 This figure shows the Hidden And Empty Cell Settings dialog box.

After selecting **Connect Data Points With Line**, you obtain the graph shown in Figure 52-8. Choose the **Line Graph** with dots and lines so you can pick out the missing data because missing data points have no markers.

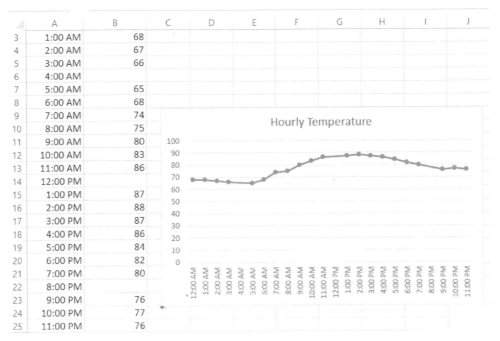

	A	B	C	D	E	F	G	H	I	J
3	1:00 AM	68								
4	2:00 AM	67								
5	3:00 AM	66								
6	4:00 AM									
7	5:00 AM	65								
8	6:00 AM	68								
9	7:00 AM	74								
10	8:00 AM	75								
11	9:00 AM	80								
12	10:00 AM	83								
13	11:00 AM	86								
14	12:00 PM									
15	1:00 PM	87								
16	2:00 PM	88								
17	3:00 PM	87								
18	4:00 PM	86								
19	5:00 PM	84								
20	6:00 PM	82								
21	7:00 PM	80								
22	8:00 PM									
23	9:00 PM	76								
24	10:00 PM	77								
25	11:00 PM	76								

FIGURE 52-8 Missing data are replaced by lines.

How can I handle the appearance of hidden data?

Often, we plot data such as daily sales and filter the data in the spreadsheet. In this situation, Excel gives you a choice either to continue showing all the data in the chart or just show the filtered data. The Hidden.xlsx file contains daily sales of a product for a year. If you graph the data as a line chart, you see the chart shown in Figure 52-9. If you right-click the data and select **Show Data In Hidden Rows And Columns**, shown in Figure 52-7, even if you filter the data, all data points will still be displayed in the chart. For example, as shown in Figure 52-10, the data is filtered to show only December sales, but the chart still shows all daily sales for the entire year. If you did not select **Show Data In Hidden Rows And Columns**, only December sales would be visible in the chart.

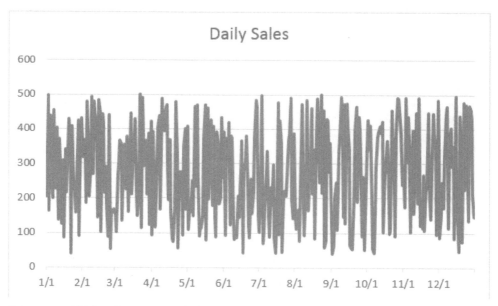

FIGURE 52-9 This is a chart showing daily product sales.

	A	B	C	D	E	F	G	H	I	J
1										
2	**Date**	**Sales**								
337	12/1	361								
338	12/2	86								
339	12/3	152								
340	12/4	246								
341	12/5	173								
342	12/6	320								
343	12/7	442								
344	12/8	466								
345	12/9	115								
346	12/10	361								
347	12/11	403								
348	12/12	292								
349	12/13	351								
350	12/14	83								
351	12/15	496								

FIGURE 52-10 Data is filtered, but the chart is not.

How can I use pictures to add bling to my column graphs?

Usually, the magnitude of product sales are summarized with boring columns or bars in which the height of the column or width of the bar is proportional to the product sales. Wouldn't it be more fun to summarize product sales with a picture of your product, scaled proportionally to actual sales? To illustrate the idea, check out the Picturegraph.xlsx file and the chart shown in Figure 52-11.

In this example, you assume that your company sells soda, so you wish to summarize monthly sales with a soda bottle whose size reflects the magnitude of monthly sales. To begin, select the C5:D8 range and, from the **Insert** tab, select the first 2D column chart option (Clustered Column). Then right-click any column and hover over **Format Data Series**. Select **Fill** and then **Picture**, and you see the window shown in Figure 52-12. After selecting soda and pressing Enter, you are presented with many pictures of soda. After selecting the desired soda bottle and clicking **Insert**, the picture is inserted in the graph as shown in Figure 52-11, with the height of the soda bottle proportional to actual sales.

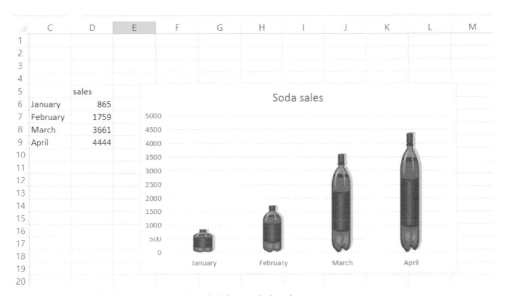

FIGURE 52-11 Soda sales are summarized with a soda bottle.

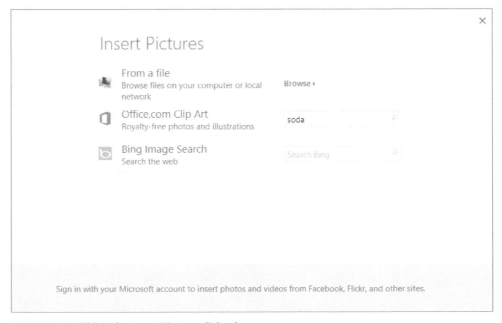

FIGURE 52-12 This is the Insert Pictures dialog box.

I charted annual sales data in a column graph, and the years do not show up as column labels. What did I do wrong?

The Categorylabel.xlsx file contains annual product sales for years 2007 through 2010. When you create a column graph with D5:E9 as the chart data source, the chart fails to show the year on the *x*-axis because Excel thinks you want the year charted as a series. If you omit the Year category label in the upper-left corner of the source range and use the D20:E24 range as the range for the chart, your chart shows the year on the *x*-axis, as desired.

FIGURE 52-13 Omitting a category label helps the column graph the chart correctly.

How can I include data labels and data tables in my charts?

Often, you want to insert data labels next to your columns or bars or perhaps show a table below your chart. To illustrate this process, look at the Labelsandtables.xlsx file. (Also see Figure 52-1.) In this file, you are given sales during the current month of four product categories. To begin, summarize this data in a column graph and place a label containing the product name and actual sales above the column. After creating a column graph in the usual fashion, select the column series and click the + sign to the right of the chart. Select **Data Labels** and **More Options** and choose **Label Options.** Now fill in the Label options as shown in Figure 52-14.

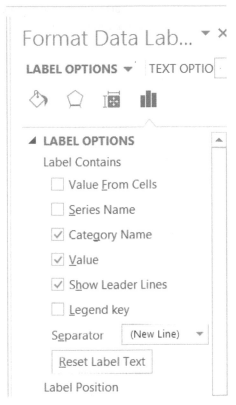

FIGURE 52-14 These settings are needed to show sales and series name on a separate line.

You now see the chart shown in Figure 52-15, which shows the category names and values for each column on separate lines.

FIGURE 52-15 Category names and sales are included in the chart.

You now see how to place a data table summarizing sales below the chart. Simply select the category axis and click the + sign to the right of the chart. After clicking **Data Tables**, you see the data table shown in Figure 52-16.

FIGURE 52-16 Sales are summarized with a data table.

If you want to see more Data Table options, select the triangle to the right of Data Table.

How can I use Excel 2013 to place data labels on a chart based on the contents of cells?

Excel 2013 now makes it possible to place data labels from cells directly on charts. To illustrate the idea, examine the Labelsfromcells.xlsx file shown in Figure 52-17.

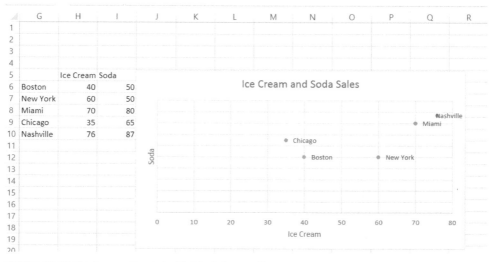

FIGURE 52-17 This is a scatterplot with labels from cells.

To begin creating this graph, select the H5:I10 cell range and choose the first **Scatter Plot** choice from the **Insert** tab. (Scatter Plot is the icon with dots next to the pie chart.) This creates the scatter plot in Figure 52-17 without the city labels. To create the city labels, select the chart. From the **Design** tab, select **Add Chart Element**, choose **Data Labels** and then **More Data Label Options**. Select the first-choice **Value** from **Cells** and clear **Y Value**. Now you can select the G6:G10 cell range to insert the city labels in the chart as shown in Figure 52-17.

How can I track sales force performance over time?

The Salestracker.xlsx file lists monthly sales by your outstanding sales force from January through May (see Figure 52-18).

	D	E	F	G	H	I
1	p	h	up			
2	q	i	down			
3	u	g	flat			
4						
5		January	February	March	April	May
6	Lebron	85	66	81	61	56
7	Wade	82	63	74	78	75
8	Dirk	45	100	115	127	150
9	Manning	75	88	89	76	83
10	Brady	96	90	98	76	93
11	Halliday	75	73	79	91	95
12	Britney	98	91	109	99	84
13	Lindsay	83	84	97	81	98
14	Paris	106	98	84	93	82
15	JLO	104	88	109	101	115
16	Emma	115	94	105	101	107
17	Melo	118	98	128	126	108
18	KD	100	114	104	116	131
19	Vick	112	122	102	124	107
20	Rodgers	127	114	116	139	108

FIGURE 52-18 Here is the monthly sales data.

You want to use icons (up, down, or flat arrow) to track during each month whether a salesperson's ranking has improved, declined, or stayed the same. You could use Excel icon sets (described in Chapter 23, "Conditional formatting"), but then you would have to insert a set of icons for each month, which is a tedious task. A more efficient (although not as aesthetically pleasing) way to create these icons is to enter an *h* when you want an up arrow, enter an *i* when you want a down arrow, and enter a *g* when you want a flat arrow. Then if you change the font to Wingdings 3, you have the desired arrows because the letters of the alphabet correspond in Wingdings 3 to the symbols shown in Figure 52-19.

	J	K
22	Letter	Wingding
23	a	⇨
24	b	⇦
25	c	⇨
26	d	⇦
27	e	⇨
28	f	←
29	g	→
30	h	↑
31	i	↓
32	j	↖
33	k	↗
34	l	↙
35	m	↘
36	n	↔
37	o	↕
38	p	▲
39	q	▼
40	r	△
41	s	▽
42	t	◀
43	u	▶
44	v	◁
45	w	▷
46	x	◣
47	y	◢
48	z	◤

FIGURE 52-19 This is the correspondence between letters and Wingdings 3 symbols.

To create the icons shown in Figure 52-20, proceed as follows:

- Copying the RANK(E6,E$6:E0,0) formula from J6 to J6:N20 computes each person's sales rank during each month.

- Copying the IF(K6<J6,"h",IF(K6>J6,"i","g")) formula from O6 to O7:R20 creates an *h* if the person's rank has improved, an *i* if the person's rank has declined, and a *g* if the salesperson's rank has stayed the same.

- After changing the font in the O6:R20 range to Wingdings 3, you see the icons shown in Figure 52-20.

The advantage of this approach is that you can use IF statements to customize the conditions easily that define the icons.

	January	February	March	April	May	rank January	rank February	rank March	rank April	rank May	trend Feb	trend March	trend April	trend May
p	h	up												
q	i	down												
u	g	flat												
Lebron	85	66	81	61	56	10	14	13	15	15	↓	↑	↓	→
Wade	82	63	74	78	75	12	15	15	12	14	↓	→	↑	↓
Dirk	45	100	115	127	150	15	4	3	2	1	↑	↑	↑	↑
Manning	75	88	89	76	83	13	10	11	13	12	↑	↓	↓	↑
Brady	96	90	98	76	93	9	9	9	13	10	→	→	↓	↑
Halliday	75	73	79	91	95	13	13	14	10	9	→	↓	↑	↑
Britney	98	91	109	99	84	8	8	4	8	11	→	↑	↓	↓
Lindsay	83	84	97	81	98	11	12	10	11	8	↓	↑	↓	↑
Paris	106	98	84	93	82	5	5	12	9	13	→	↓	↑	↓
JLO	104	88	109	101	115	6	10	4	6	3	↓	↑	↓	↑
Emma	115	94	105	101	107	3	7	6	6	6	↓	↑	→	→
Melo	118	98	128	126	108	2	5	1	3	4	↓	↑	↓	↓
KD	100	114	104	116	131	7	2	7	5	2	↑	↓	↑	↑
Vick	112	122	102	124	107	4	1	8	4	6	↑	↓	↑	↓
Rodgers	127	114	116	139	108	1	2	2	1	4	↓	→	↑	↓

FIGURE 52-20 These are the icons that track change in salesperson performance.

How can I create a band chart to check whether inventory is within acceptable levels?

Often, you need to track a quantity (inventory, cash on hand, number of accidents) and want to track whether the quantity is remaining between historical upper and lower limits. A band chart provides a useful tool to monitor how a process changes over time. Figure 52-21 shows an example of a band chart. (See the Bandchart.xlsx file.)

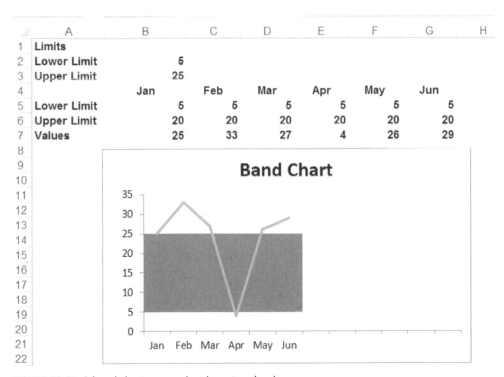

FIGURE 52-21 A band chart summarizes inventory levels.

To create the band chart, proceed as follows:

1. You entered your lower limit on inventory (5) in B2 and your upper limit (25) on inventory in B3.

2. In row 5, you enter the lower limit for each month by copying the =$B$2 formula from B5 to C5:G5.

3. Copying the =$B$3-$B$2 formula from B6 to C6:G6 computes the upper limit–lower limit. Label this row Upper Limit because this row will be used to generate the line representing your upper inventory limit of 25 units.

4. Select the B5:G7 range and select a **Stacked** area chart (the second 2D area option).

5. Select the **Value** series, right-click **Chart Change Type**, and choose the first line-chart option.

6. Add a secondary axis to the **Values** series and then delete it.

7. Right-click the **Lower Limit** series and select **Fill**. From the **Fill** menu, select **No Fill**.

Your band chart shows that you are having great difficulty maintaining inventory levels between the desired lower and upper limits.

How can I store a chart as a template?

You just created a beautiful band chart. You might think that each time you want to create a band chart, you need to repeat the previously described steps. This is not the case. You can save the band (or any other chart) as a template and pull up the chart settings whenever you desire. To illustrate the idea, open the Bandchart.xlsx file, right-click the chart, select **Save As Template**, and give the chart any name you want. (Band was chosen here.) Now suppose you want a band chart just for the months of January to March. Select the data A4:D7 range and, from the **Insert** tab, select the arrow in the lower-right corner of the **Chart** group. Select **All Charts** and **Templates**. Browse to the desired chart template, click **OK**, and you are done!

How can I use a thermometer chart to portray progress against a target?

A thermometer chart shows actual values of a quantity such as revenues stacked within a column that shows a target value. The resulting chart (shown in Figure 52-22) resembles a thermometer, hence the name.

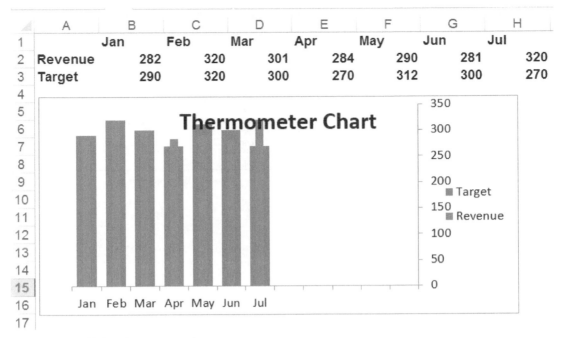

FIGURE 52-22 This is a thermometer chart.

To create a thermometer chart, proceed as follows:

1. Select the A1:H3 range and a **Clustered Column** 2D chart.

2. Select the **Revenue** series and then right-click and select **Format Data Series**. Add a secondary axis and then delete it.

3. Select the **Revenue** series and again right-click and select **Format Data Series**. Set **Overlap** to **0%** and **Gap** width to **48%**.

4. Select the **Target** series and again right-click and select **Format Data Series**. Set **Overlap** to **0%** and **Gap** width to **261%**.

5. You now see the chart shown in Figure 52-22. You might have to adjust the gap widths to obtain a chart you like. Making the Target gap width smaller, for example, makes the red bars wider; making the Revenue gap width larger makes the blue bars narrower.

How can I create dynamic chart labels?

You have probably encountered workbooks with charts in which you change a worksheet input, and the chart labels do not change. This often causes confusion. Now learn how to link series labels and chart titles to worksheet cells. To illustrate the idea (see workbook DynamicLabels.xlsx and Figure 52-23), suppose you want to chart future GDP in the United States and China. You want the chart title to contain the year in which China's GDP passes US GDP and the series label to contain the annual growth rate for each nation. In C5 and C8, you can change the estimated growth rates from their current values of 3% for US GDP and 10% for China GDP.

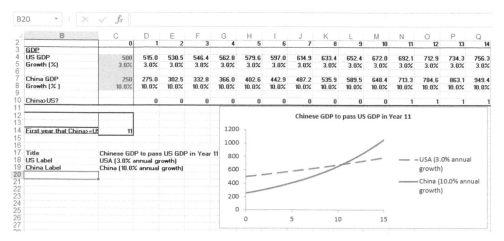

FIGURE 52-23 Create dynamic labels.

The key idea is to link your chart title and labels to cells that change when the growth rates change. Proceed as follows:

1. Copying the IF(D7>=D4,1,0) formula from D10 to E10:R10 enters a 1 if China GDP is at least as big as US GDP.

2. In cell C14, determine the year in which China passes the United States with the IFERROR(MATCH(1,D10:R10,0),"none") formula. Note that if China never passes the United States, this formula returns "none".

3. In cell C17, the =IF(C14="none","US stays on top","Chinese_GDP_to_pass_US_GDP_in _Year"&TEXT(C14,"0")) formula creates your desired chart title. Note that if China never passes the United States, your chart title will be US Stays on Top. Otherwise, your chart title is linked to C14, so the chart title will contain the year in which China passes the United States. The "0" in the *TEXT* function ensures that the year is formatted as an integer.

4. In cell C18, the "USA("&TEXT(C5,"0.0%")&"annual_growth)" formula creates the chart title for the USA series. The "0.0%" portion of the text function ensures that the growth rate is format-ted as a percentage.

5. In cell C19, the ="China("&TEXT(C8,"0.0%")&"annual_growth)" formula creates the chart title for the China series.

6. Now you are ready to create the chart with dynamic labels.

7. Press Ctrl, select the noncontinuous C2:R2, C4:R4, C7:R7 range, and create a **scatter** chart (third option).

8. Select **Add Chart Element** from the **Design** tab and select **Centered Overlay Title**. In the formula bar, type an equals (=) sign, point to cell C17, and press Enter. You now have a dynamic chart label.

9. Select **Series 1** (the USA GDP series) and right-click and choose **Select Data**. Click **Edit** and fill in the **Edit Series** dialog box as follows:

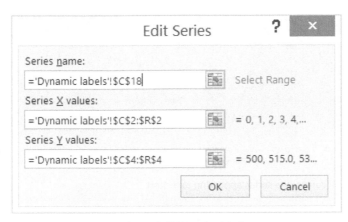

FIGURE 52-24 Create a dynamic USA series label.

This links the USA series label to cell C18, which contains the annual growth rate. In a similar fashion, you link the China series label to cell C19. You now have completed a chart with dynamic labels.

How can I use check boxes to control which series are charted?

You might recall from Chapter 26, "Spin buttons, scroll bars, option buttons, check boxes, combo boxes, and group list boxes," that a check box can be used to toggle the contents of a cell between TRUE and FALSE. It turns out that if Excel sees an #N/A error in a cell, the cell will not generate a point appearing in the chart. Therefore, if you do not want to chart a series, simply use an IF formula to make the charted series #N/A when the check box puts a False in a cell.

To begin, use the methods described in Chapter 26 to create two check boxes, one to control the 2010 series and another to control the 2011 series. The 2010 check box controls cell B1, and the 2011 check box controls cell C1. The original data is in E6:L7. Copying the IF($B$1,F6,NA()) formula from F10 to F11:L11 simply returns the original data for the year if the year's check box is selected or returns #N/A if the year's check box is cleared. You now select the E9:L11 cell range as the source data for a **Line With Markers** chart. Now clearing a year's check box hides a year's data in the chart, and selecting the check box shows the year's data in the chart.

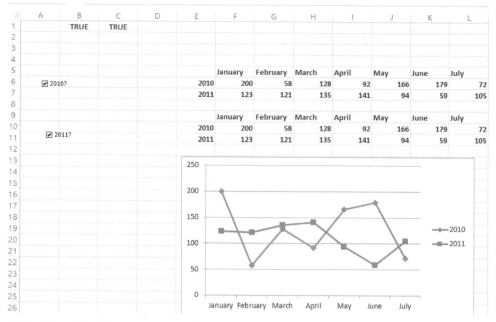

FIGURE 52-25 Check boxes can control the series appearing in a chart.

How can I use a list box to choose the series to be charted?

Suppose your spreadsheet (see Listbox.xlsx) contains 2007–2011 sales in the East, West, Midwest, and South. You want an easy way to control which series is charted. A list box (see Chapter 26) provides an easy way to choose the series to be charted. To begin, on the **Developer** tab, from the **Insert** group, select **List Box** (fifth icon in the top row) from **Form Controls**. When you see the pointer, right-click and select **Format Control**. Select **$A$14:$A$17** as **Input Range** and **Cell Link $H$2**. Now, with an intelligent use of the *INDEX* function, you can use cell H2 to control the charted series.

Copying the INDEX($H$16:$K$21,G7,$H$2) formula from I7 to I8:I10 retrieves the correct series. For example, in the list box shown in Figure 52-26, the East region was selected. This places a 1 in cell H2. Your *INDEX* function retrieves the first column (column H) of data as desired. Now select the H7:Y11 range and create a scatter chart, and you see that when you click a region in the list box, the selected series is charted.

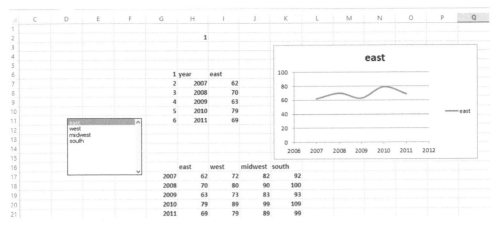

FIGURE 52-26 Use a list box to control the charted series.

How can I create a Gantt chart?

Often, a project requires a number of projects to be completed. A Gantt chart portrays the time each project begins. Shown in Figure 52-27 (see file Gantt.xlsx) is a Gantt chart for a project consisting of five activities. To create this chart, proceed as follows:

1. Select the F3:H8 cell range and create a **Stacked** 2D bar chart (second option).

2. Right-click the **Start** series and, after selecting **Fill**, choose **No Fill** to hide the Start series.

3. Right-click the vertical axis and, after selecting **Format Axis**, select **Categories In Reverse Order** to ensure that Task 1 is listed first instead of last.

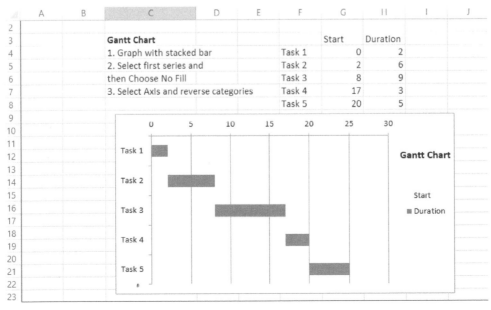

FIGURE 52-27 This is a Gantt chart.

How can I create a chart based on sorted data?

Suppose you have sales in a number of states (see Figure 52-28 and file Sortedgraphx.xlsx), and you want the graph to list the states in descending order of sales as shown in Figure 52-29. To create this chart, you need to reorganize the data in columns J to L so the sales data is sorted in descending order. To accomplish this goal, proceed as follows:

1. Copying the RANK(F9,$F$9:$F$23,0) formula from G9 to G10:G22 computes the rank of each state's sales. For example, NY ranks sixth. Note, however, that KY, Ala, and Ari have the same level of sales. To sort the states in descending order of sales, you need to associate a unique rank with each state.

2. Copying the G9+COUNTIF($G$8:G8,G9) formula from H9 to H10:H22 creates a unique rank for each state by increasing the rank of a state with a tied rank each time a tied rank occurs.

3. Copying the INDEX(E$9:E$23,MATCH($J9,$H$9:$H$23,0),1) formula from K9 to K9:L23 sorts the States and Sales based on descending sales.

4. Now creating a column graph based on K9:L23 yields the graph shown in Figure 52-29.

	E	F	G	H	I	J	K	L
5								
6								
7								
8	State	Sales	Original rank	Revised		Rank	State	Sales
9	NJ	40	1	1		1	NJ	40
10	NY	18	6	6		2	Wva	20
11	Ind	14	10	10		3	Min	19
12	Cal	15	9	9		4	Mic	19
13	KY	10	13	13		5	Fla	19
14	Ari	10	13	14		6	NY	18
15	Ala	10	13	15		7	Va	17
16	Min	19	3	3		8	Mo	16
17	Ill	13	11	11		9	Cal	15
18	Mic	19	3	4		10	Ind	14
19	Mo	16	8	8		11	Ill	13
20	Fla	19	3	5		12	Pa	13
21	Pa	13	11	12		13	KY	10
22	Wva	20	2	2		14	Ari	10
23	Va	17	7	7		15	Ala	10

FIGURE 52-28 This is sales data for a sorted graph.

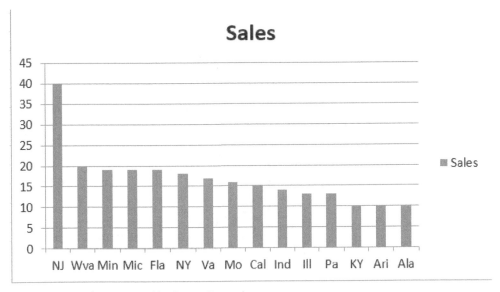

FIGURE 52-29 Sales are sorted in descending order.

How can I create a histogram that automatically updates when I include new data?

In Chapter 42, "Summarizing data by using descriptive statistics," you learned how to use the Analysis Toolpak to create a histogram. Unfortunately, histograms created with the Analysis Toolpak will not update if existing data is changed or if new data is added. By using the Excel Table feature, you can easily create histograms that automatically adjust to changes in the source data. The Dynamichistograms.xlsx file illustrates the idea (see Figure 52-30). Column E contains NBA player salaries in millions of dollars for the 2003–2004 season. To begin, select the E5:E446 range and make that range a table. Enter the bin ranges for your histogram in the H7:H28 range. Note that row 28 will calculate the number of salaries that are larger than $20 million. Use the *FREQUENCY* function to count how many salaries fall into each bin range. The *FREQUENCY* function (see Chapter 87, "Array formulas and functions") is an array function. To use this function, you need to select the range the function populates (in this case, I7:I28) first, enter the function syntax, and then press Ctrl+Shift+Enter. After selecting I7:I28, type in the =**FREQUENCY(E6:E446,H7:H27)** formula and press Ctrl+Shift+Enter. Excel now enters the number of players (0) with a salary less than or equal to 0 in I7, in I8 the number of salaries >0 and <=1 million (124), . . . , in I27 the number of players with salaries >19 and <=20 million (2), and in I28 the number of players with a salary >20 million. To create the dynamic histogram, select the H7:I28 cell range and create a column graph. You now have a dynamic histogram that automatically updates to account for changes in the source data. To prove that the histogram updates, add a few salaries of $30 million. You now see a new spike occur on the right side of the graph.

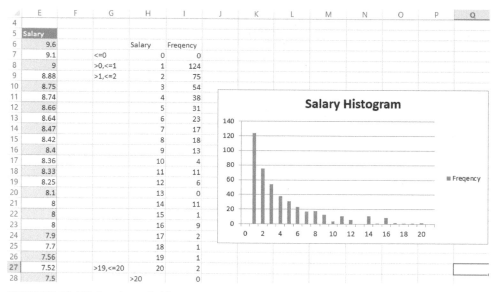

FIGURE 52-30 This is a dynamic histogram.

How can I add conditional colors to a chart?

Suppose you are charting actual and targeted sales for each month, and you want months that perform at 90 percent of target or better in blue, 75 percent of target or worse in green, and other months in red. The Cond colors.xlsx file (Figure 52-31) shows how this is done. The trick to create this chart is to put the data for each color in a different row. To begin, place sales you want colored blue in row 19 by copying the =IF(F13/F14>F15,F13/F14," ") formula from F19 to G19:M19. Then, to place the sales you want colored red in row 20, copy the =IF(AND(G13/G14>G16,G13/G14<=G15),G13/G14," ") formula from F20 to G20:M20. Finally, place the sales for months that should appear in green in row 20 by copying the =IF(AND(G13/G14>G16,G13/G14<=G15),G13/G14," ") formula from F21 to G21:M21. Now select the E18:M21 range and create a column chart. If you want to change the color for any series, select the series and click the paintbrush to the right of the chart; select **Color** and choose the color of your choice.

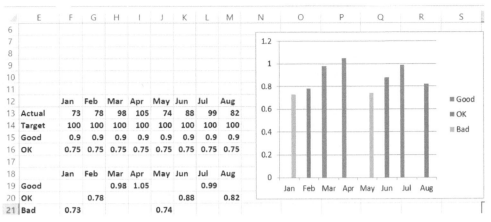

	Jan	Feb	Mar	Apr	May	Jun	Jul	Aug
Actual	73	78	98	105	74	88	99	82
Target	100	100	100	100	100	100	100	100
Good	0.9	0.9	0.9	0.9	0.9	0.9	0.9	0.9
OK	0.75	0.75	0.75	0.75	0.75	0.75	0.75	0.75

	Jan	Feb	Mar	Apr	May	Jun	Jul	Aug
Good			0.98	1.05			0.99	
OK		0.78				0.88		0.82
Bad	0.73				0.74			

FIGURE 52-31 Blue indicates a good month, green a bad month, and red a so-so month.

How can I use waterfall charts to track progress toward a sales target or break down components of sales price?

Waterfall charts, originally developed by the McKinsey consulting firm, are often used to show progress toward a final cash position or a breakdown of a company's total revenue into cost components and profit. The Waterfallcharts.xlsx file contains several examples of waterfall charts. In the All Positive worksheet (see Figure 52-32), you create a waterfall chart for a situation in which all cash flows are positive. You want the chart to show the monthly progress toward your cash flow goal of $3,270. After entering your cash flows in column C, you need to track your cumulative cash flow in column B. Copying the B2+C2 formula from B3 to B4:B7 computes the cumulative cash flow through the end of each month. Next, select the A1:C7 cell range and create a stacked column chart. Selecting the **Base** series and choosing **No Fill** yields the waterfall chart shown in Figure 52-32.

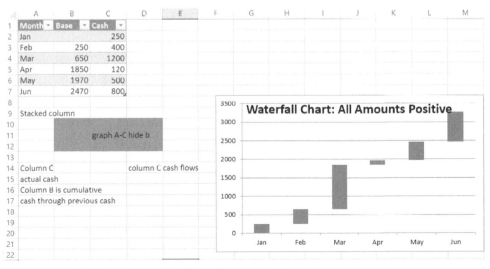

FIGURE 52-32 In this waterfall chart, all cash flows are positive.

Figure 52-33 (see worksheet Positive and Negative) shows a waterfall chart when some cash flows are negative.

After entering the positive cash flows in column C and negative cash flows in column D, compute the total cash flow through the end of each month by copying the E1+C2-D2 formula from E2 to E3:E7. Next, in column B, by copying the E1-D2 formula from B2 to B3:B7, compute the cumulative cash flow through last month, adjusted by the current month's negative cash flow. After selecting the A1:D7 range and creating a column chart, all you have to do is hide column B, and you have the waterfall chart shown in Figure 52-33.

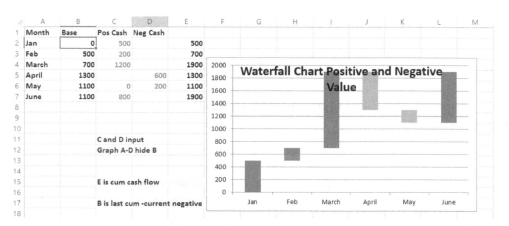

FIGURE 52-33 This is a waterfall chart when some cash flows are positive and some are negative.

By following the method used in the Positive and Negative worksheet, you can easily break down a company's revenue into its cost components (including profit). See worksheet Profitability Waterfall and Figure 52-34.

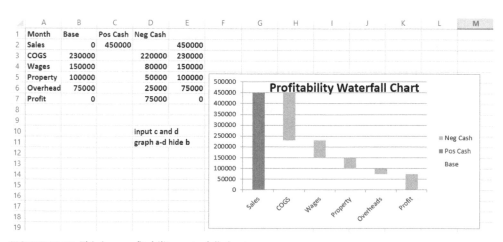

FIGURE 52-34 This is a profitability waterfall chart.

How can I use the *GETPIVOTDATA* function and the Excel Table feature to create dynamic dashboards?

Often, you might download monthly, quarterly, or weekly sales data and want to summarize the sales data in charts that automatically update to include new data. Knowledge of the Excel *GETPIVOTDATA* function (see Chapter 43, "Using PivotTables and slicers to describe data") and Excel Table feature (see Chapter 25, "Tables") make this relatively straightforward (see file Randy.xlsx). Suppose you download weekly sales data for four product categories, Filtrate, Tape, Command, and Abrasives, at four stores: Menards, Target, Lowe's, and Home Depot. Your goal is to set up a dashboard that enables you to chart weekly sales to data at a given store quickly and give you control of which product categories appear in the chart. As shown in Figure 52-35, your data is downloaded in columns D–G. Make the D4:G243 range a table. This ensures that a PivotTable based on this data automatically updates to include new data when you refresh the table.

WEEK	Category	Store	Revenue
3	Abrasives	Lowes	2043
12	Safety	Menards	2343
3	Tape	Home Depo	1414
12	Command	Target	1820
0	Tape	Home Depo	943
7	Tape	Target	1219
7	Command	Menards	1156
11	Abrasives	Lowes	2127
12	Safety	Menards	1315
3	Tape	Target	1580
10	Abrasives	Home Depo	1598
4	Command	Lowes	1000
7	Tape	Menards	1087
7	Abrasives	Menards	1728
1	Abrasives	Target	1911
7	Abrasives	Menards	1563
2	Tape	Target	2482
7	Safety	Lowes	1534
12	Safety	Menards	1471
2	Abrasives	Lowes	990

FIGURE 52-35 Here are sales data for dynamic dashboards.

You now create a PivotTable by dragging **Week** to the **Rows** zone, **Store** and **Category** to the **Columns** zone, and **Revenues** to the **Values** zone. This PivotTable (shown in Figure 52-36) summarizes weekly sales for each category in each store.

Sum of Revenue	Column Labels										
	⊟Lowes				Lowes Total	⊟Menards				Menards Total	⊟Home Depot
Row Labels	Abrasives	Safety	Tape	Command		Abrasives	Safety	Tape	Command		Abrasives
1		1065		1247	2312	3772	526	3466		7764	3272
2	2349	4510			6859	6220	3296	2159		11675	1921
3	2797	1233	2046	6335	12411	3472		959	2369	6800	
4	1501	3822	1180	1000	7503	6018	2212			8230	
5	1940		833	2945	5718	708		501	597	1806	1758
6			1918	6494	8412	4145	6205	4653		15003	
7	3049	3228			6277	3291	2303	6472	1156	13222	3580
8	4208	2890	1873		8971	910		1494	3776	6180	2445
9			2052	2825	4877	6265		1888		8153	
10	6117		1875		7992			2138		2138	4807
11	2127	1971	4461	2394	10953	3596	1169			4765	
12		1542	4786	850	7178	1124	7565	7264	2431	18384	2471
13				1196	1196				3400	3400	
14	1455				1455						
Grand Total	25543	20261	21024	25286	92114	39521	23276	30994	13729	107520	20254

FIGURE 52-36 PivotTable is summarizing category sales by store.

Now you are ready to use the *GETPIVOTDATA* function to extract the data needed to create the desired charts. To begin, create a drop-down box (see Chapter 40, "Validating data") in cell AG8 that can be used to select a store. Create check boxes (see Chapter 26) for each category that can be used to control the AH9:AK9 range. These cells control which categories appear in your chart. Copy the IF(AH$9=FALSE,NA(),IFERROR(GETPIVOTDATA("Revenue",$I$11,"WEEK",$AG11,"Category",AH$10, "Store",$AG$8)," ")) formula from AG11 to the AG11:AK23 range. If you select the check box for a category, this formula extracts the weekly sales for the category; if the category is cleared, #N/A is entered in the cell. Also, if 0 sales occurred, the IFERROR portion of the formulas ensures that sales of 0 are entered. Make the AG10:AK24 range a table so any charts based on this range update automatically to include new data. Figure 52-37 shows how the source data for your chart appears if you want to summarize Abrasive, Safety, and Tape sales at Lowe's.

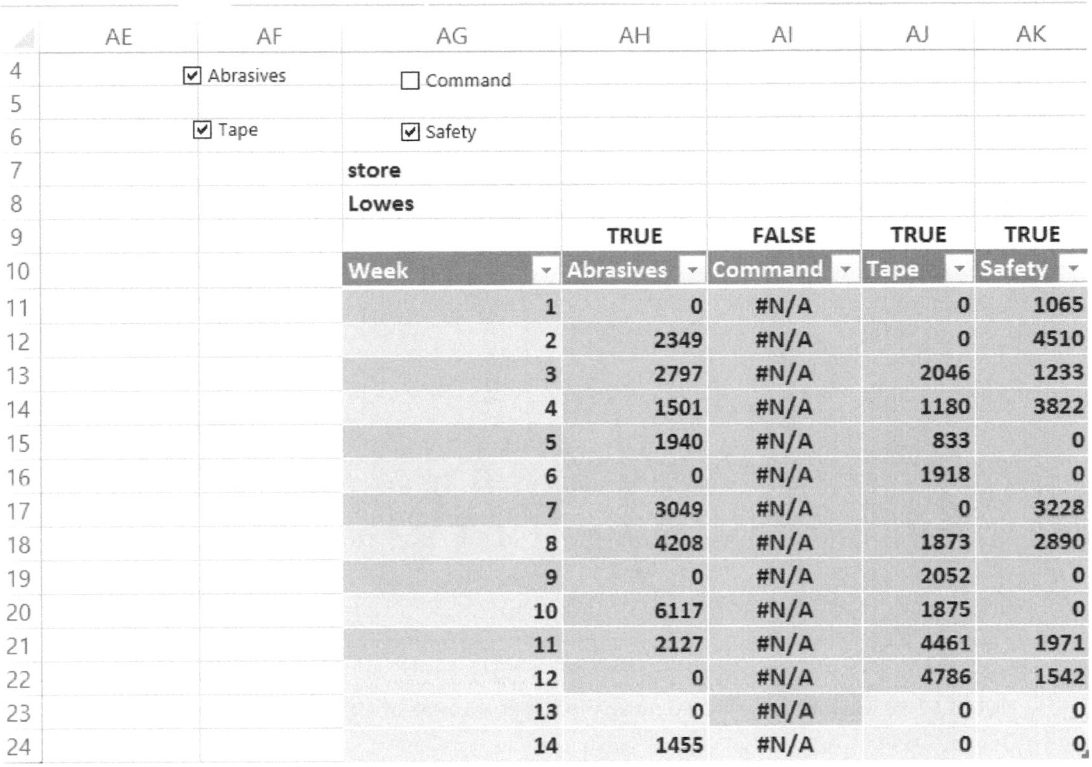

	AE	AF	AG	AH	AI	AJ	AK
4		☑ Abrasives	☐ Command				
5							
6		☑ Tape	☑ Safety				
7			**store**				
8			**Lowes**				
9				TRUE	FALSE	TRUE	TRUE
10			Week ▾	Abrasives ▾	Command ▾	Tape ▾	Safety ▾
11			1	0	#N/A	0	1065
12			2	2349	#N/A	0	4510
13			3	2797	#N/A	2046	1233
14			4	1501	#N/A	1180	3822
15			5	1940	#N/A	833	0
16			6	0	#N/A	1918	0
17			7	3049	#N/A	0	3228
18			8	4208	#N/A	1873	2890
19			9	0	#N/A	2052	0
20			10	6117	#N/A	1875	0
21			11	2127	#N/A	4461	1971
22			12	0	#N/A	4786	1542
23			13	0	#N/A	0	0
24			14	1455	#N/A	0	0

FIGURE 52-37 This is the source data for your chart.

Now for the payoff! Select the AG10:AK24 range and create a scatter plot with smooth lines. The finished chart is shown in Figure 52-38. This chart can show sales at any store of any category combination and update when new data is downloaded.

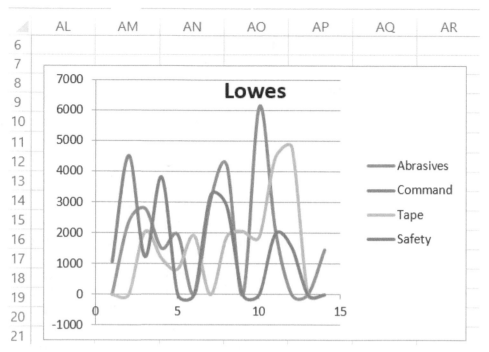

FIGURE 52-38 A dynamic dashboard summarizes sales at Lowe's of Abrasives, Tape, and Safety.

How can I create a Pareto chart?

Companies often summarize problems reported by customers with a Pareto chart. A Pareto chart shows a list of problems on the *x*-axis and, on the *y*-axis, the fraction of problems associated with each problem and the cumulative percentage of problems caused by the listed problems. The Pareto.xlsx file (see Figure 52-39) illustrates the idea. To begin, sort the problems so they are listed in descending order based on the number of times the problem was reported. Copying the E5/ SUM($E$5:$E$10) formula from F5 to F6:F10 computes the percentage of all problems for each type of problem. For example, Set Up caused 31 percent of all problems. Copying the SUM($F$5:F5) formula from G5 to G6:G10 computes the cumulative percentage of problems. For example, the first three listed problems caused 80 percent of all reported problems. After selecting the D4:D10 range, hold down the Ctrl key and select the F4:G10 range. After selecting the combo chart settings shown in Figure 52-40, you have the desired Pareto chart.

Often, Pareto charts can be used to display the 80/20 rule. Some manifestations of the 80/20 rule are as follows:

- 20 percent of different customer complaints cause 80 percent of reported problems.

- 20 percent of people have 80 percent of total income.

- 20 percent of your products generate 80 percent of your profit.

- 20 percent of your salespeople generate 80 percent of your sales.

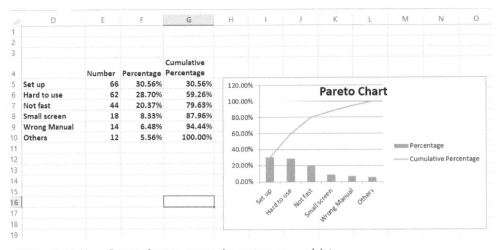

FIGURE 52-39 Use a Pareto chart to summarize customer complaints.

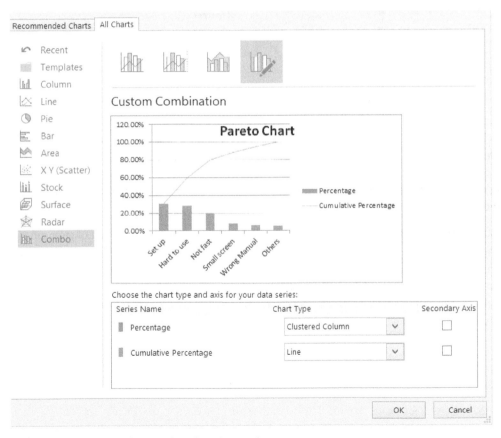

FIGURE 52-40 Here are chart settings for a Pareto chart.

How can I insert a vertical line in a chart to separate pre-merger and post-merger performance?

Suppose (see file Verticalline.xlsx and Figure 52-41) your company was merged with another company on January 10, 2011, and you are charting daily sales. You might want to insert a vertical line in your graph to indicate the date of the merger. If you draw the vertical line with the Excel Shapes feature, and the chart is moved, the line will be in the wrong place. To remedy this problem, begin by selecting the E10:F32 range; create a scatter chart with lines (third option). In the B15:C16 range, enter the date of the merger and the lower and upper limits on the *y* coordinates for your vertical line. (In this case, the lower limit = 0, and the upper limit = 120.) Copy the B15:C16 range and right-click your chart. Clicking the **Paste** icon inserts the vertical line on the January 10 date.

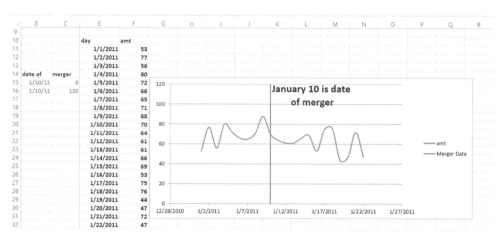

FIGURE 52-41 The vertical line indicates that January 10, 2011 was the merger date.

How can I use a radar chart to portray how basketball team members differ in strength, speed, and jumping ability?

The Radar.xlsx file (see Figure 52-42) summarizes four athletes in the dimensions of strength, speed, and agility. Select the C2:F6 range and, from the **Insert** tab, select the **Radar** chart icon shown in Figure 52-43. From the drop-down menu, select **Radar Chart with Markers**, and you will have the radar chart shown in Figure 52-42. The center of the radar chart indicates a score of 0, and the farther a marker is from the center, the better the score. The chart makes it easy to see, for example, that Max scores poorly on all measures, and Christian scores well on all three measures.

A	B	C	D	E	F	G	H	I	J
1			**Radar Chart**						
2				Speed	Strength	Agility			
3			Greg	10	3	9			
4			Dan	4	10	5			
5			Max	3	2	1			
6			Christian	9	8	10			
7									
8									
9					Radar chart with Markers				
10									
11									
12				—Speed —Strength —Agility					
13					Greg				
14					10				
15					5				
16				Christian	0 Dan				
17									
18					Max				
19									

FIGURE 52-42 This is a radar chart with markers.

FIGURE 52-43 This is a radar chart icon.

I know I can use a scatter plot to display how two variables change. How can I use a bubble chart to summarize the variation of three variables?

Whereas a scatter plot shows you how two variables vary, a bubble chart enables you to summarize three variables visually. The Bubble.xlsx file (see Figure 52-44) contains, for several countries, the percentage variance in sales relative to budget, the annual growth in sales, and each country's market size. To summarize this data in a bubble chart, select the D9:F14 range, click the drop-down arrow by **Scatter Plot** from the **Insert** tab, and choose the first **Bubble Chart** option. After adding (as described earlier in the chapter) a data label for each bubble based on the country (cell range C10:C14) and placing the labels above each bubble, you obtain the bubble chart shown in Figure 52-44. The areas of the bubbles are proportional to the market size of each country. For example, the US bubble contains 50 percent more area than the China bubble.

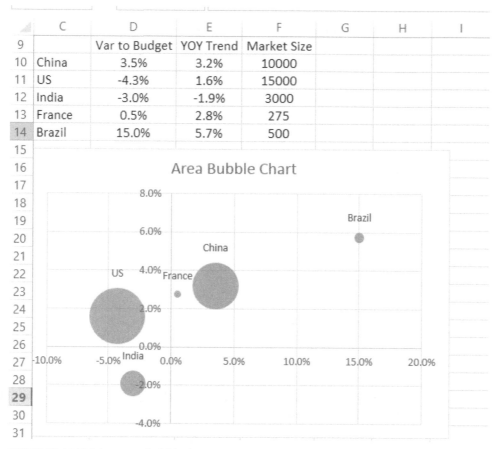

⊿	C	D	E	F	G	H	I
9		Var to Budget	YOY Trend	Market Size			
10	China	3.5%	3.2%	10000			
11	US	-4.3%	1.6%	15000			
12	India	-3.0%	-1.9%	3000			
13	France	0.5%	2.8%	275			
14	Brazil	15.0%	5.7%	500			

FIGURE 52-44 This is an area bubble chart.

Problems

The Cakes.xlsx file contains the number of salespeople and revenue for a bakery for each month. Use this data for problems 1 to 4:

1. Create a combination chart with a secondary axis to summarize monthly salespeople and revenues.

2. Graph monthly revenue and insert data labels on the chart.

3. Graph the number of salespeople and insert a data table below the chart.

4. Plot monthly sales by using a cake chart rather than a column chart.

The Hiddenpivot.xlsx file contains sales of candy between 2009 and 2017. Use this data for problems 5 and 6:

5. Filter the data so that only 2013 sales appear in the spreadsheet, but all data appears in the chart.

6. Summarize each year's sales in a PivotTable and show the percentage improvement in sales from year to year.

7. By using the data in the Salestracker.xlsx file, highlight the top two salespeople each month with an up arrow, the bottom two with a down arrow, and the others with a flat arrow.

8. The Indiana University basketball team considers at least 50 deflections per game a good performance and 30 or fewer deflections a poor performance. In the past six games, Indiana had 25, 55, 45, 43, 59, and 39 deflections. Plot this data on a band chart.

9. Plot the data of problem 8 on a column chart in which good defensive games are highlighted in green, bad games in red, and other games in orange.

10. During its first year of operation, a firm's revenue was $5 million and expenses were $6 million. For different assumed growth rates in expenses and revenues, plot 10 years of revenues and expenses and ensure that the graph title shows the year that revenues first exceed expenses.

The Crimedata.xlsx file contains annual violent crimes, property crimes, and murders in the United States. Use this data for problems 11 and 12:

11. Create a graph showing the number of crimes each year. Use check boxes to control which series are plotted.

12. To summarize murders, create a histogram that updates automatically when new data is included.

13. The following table contains the performance reviews of five employees. Use a radar chart to summarize the performance reviews:

Person	Hardworking	Collegial	Completes tasks on time	Punctual
Wayne	1	2	3	4
Vivian	5	6	7	8
Greg	10	9.5	9	8.5
Jen	9	2	9	4
Wanda	1	1.5	2	2.5

14. A project consists of five activities. The start time and duration of each activity are given. Summarize this data in a Gantt chart:

Activity	Start time	Duration
A	0	4
B	3	6
C	5	7
D	6	8
E	3	6

15. The profit, revenue, and cost breakdown for a year are given in the following table. Summarize this data in a waterfall chart:

Item	Amount
Revenue	$300,000
Profit	$65,000
Labor Costs	$100.000
Material Costs	$80,000
Overhead Costs	$55,000

16. The Paretodata.xlsx file contains product sales at a hardware store. Create a Pareto chart for revenue by product. Does the 80/20 rule appear to hold for this data?

CHAPTER 53

Estimating straight-line relationships

Questions answered in this chapter:

- How can I determine the relationship between monthly production and monthly operating costs?

- How accurately does this relationship explain the monthly variation in plant operating costs?

- How accurate are my predictions likely to be?

- When estimating a straight-line relationship, which functions can I use to get the slope and intercept of the line that best fits the data?

Suppose you manage a plant that manufactures small refrigerators. National headquarters tells you how many refrigerators to produce each month. For budgeting purposes, you want to forecast your monthly operating costs and need answers to the questions that are the focus of this chapter.

Every business analyst should have the ability to estimate the relationship between important business variables. In Microsoft Excel, the trend curve, which is discussed in this chapter as well as in Chapter 54, "Modeling exponential growth," and Chapter 55, "The power curve," is often helpful in determining the relationship between two variables. The variable that analysts try to predict is called the *dependent variable*. The variable you use for prediction is called the *independent variable*. Here are some examples of business relationships you might want to estimate:

Independent variable	Dependent variable
Units produced by plant in a month	Monthly cost of operating plant
Dollars spent on advertising in a month	Monthly sales
Number of employees	Annual travel expenses
Company revenue	Number of employees (headcount)
Monthly return on the stock market	Monthly return on a stock (for example, Dell)
Square feet in home	Value of home

The first step in determining how two variables are related is to graph the data points (by using **Scatter Chart**) so that the independent variable is on the *x*-axis, and the dependent variable is on the *y*-axis. With the chart selected, click a data point (all data points are then displayed in blue), click

Trendline in the **Analysis** group on the **Chart Tools Layout** tab, and then click **More Trendline Options** (or right-click and select **Add Trendline**). You see the **Format Trendline** dialog box, which is shown in Figure 53-1.

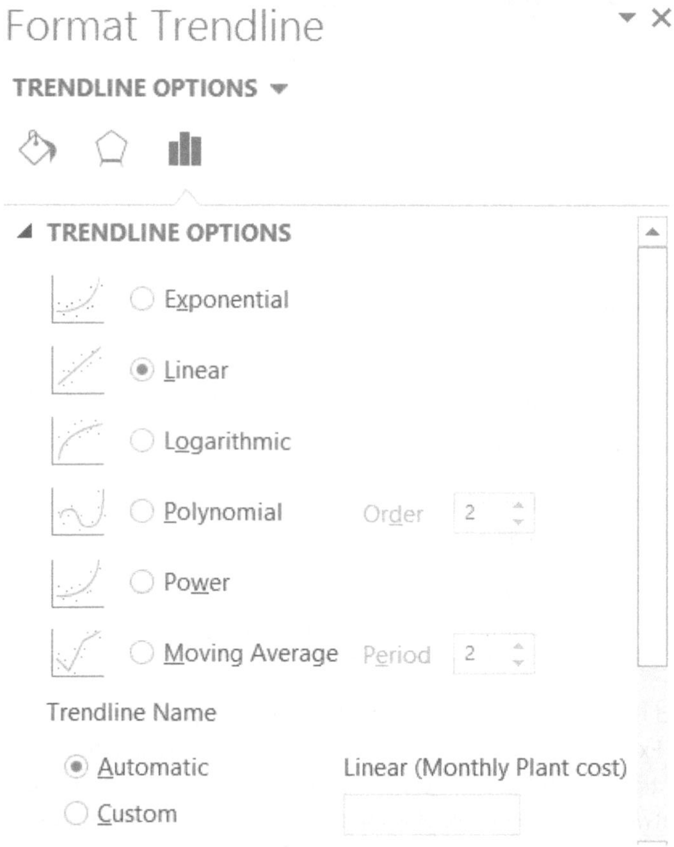

FIGURE 53-1 These are the Format Trendline dialog box options.

If your graph indicates that a straight line is a reasonable fit to the points, choose **Linear**. If the graph indicates that the dependent variable increases at an accelerating rate, **Exponential** (or perhaps **Power**) probably fits the relationship. If the graph shows that the dependent variable increases at a decreasing rate, or that the dependent variable decreases at a decreasing rate, **Power** is probably the most relevant.

This chapter focuses on the Linear option. Chapter 54 discusses the Exponential option, and Chapter 55 covers the Power option. Chapter 62, "Using moving averages to understand time series," discusses the moving average curve, and Chapter 85 "Pricing products by using subjective demand," discusses the polynomial curve. (The logarithmic curve is of little value in this discussion, so it is not addressed.)

Answers to this chapter's questions

This section provides the answers to the questions that are listed at the beginning of the chapter.

How can I determine the relationship between monthly production and monthly operating costs?

The Costestimate.xlsx file, shown in Figure 53-2, contains data about the units produced and the monthly plant operating cost for a 14-month period. You are interested in predicting monthly operating costs from units produced, which helps the plant manager determine the operating budget and understand better the cost to produce refrigerators.

	B	C	D	E	F
1				sum errors	-0.0304
2	Month	Units Produced	Monthly Plant cost	Predicted cost	Error
3	1	1260	123118	118872.66	4245.34
4	2	1007	99601	102612.68	-3011.68
5	3	1296	132000	121186.33	10813.7
6	4	873	80000	94000.671	-14000.7
7	5	532	52000	72085.044	-20085
8	6	476	58625	68485.997	-9861
9	7	482	74624	68871.609	5752.39
10	8	1273	110000	119708.15	-9708.15
11	9	692	81000	82368.036	-1368.04
12	10	690	73507	82239.499	-8732.5
13	11	564	95024	74141.642	20882.4
14	12	470	88004	68100.385	19903.6
15	13	676	70000	81275.468	-11275.5
16	14	870	110253	93807.865	16445.1
17	15	1100		108589.67	
18					

FIGURE 53-2 This is the plant operating data.

Begin by creating an XY chart (or a scatter plot) that displays the independent variable (units produced) on the *x*-axis and the dependent variable (monthly plant cost) on the *y*-axis. The column of data that you want to display on the *x*-axis must be located to the left of the column of data you want to display on the *y*-axis. To create the graph, select the data in the C2:D16 range (including the labels in cells C2 and D2). Click **Scatter** in the **Charts** group on the **Insert** tab and select the first option (**Scatter With Only Markers**) as the chart type. You see the graph shown in Figure 53-3.

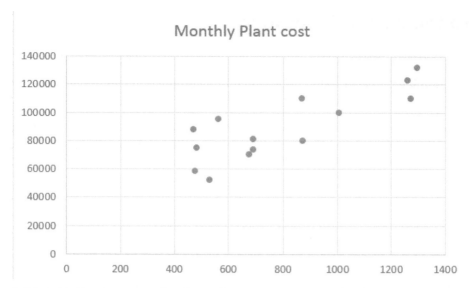

FIGURE 53-3 Here is a scatter plot of operating cost versus units produced.

When you look at the scatter plot, it seems reasonable that a straight line (or linear relationship) exists between units produced and monthly operating costs. You can see the straight line that fits the points best by adding a trendline to the chart. Click within the chart to select it and then click a data point. All the data points are displayed in blue, with an X covering each point. Right-click and then click **Add Trendline**. In the **Format Trendline** dialog box, select **Linear** and then select the **Display Equation On Chart** and the **Display R-Squared Value On Chart** check boxes, as shown in Figure 53-4.

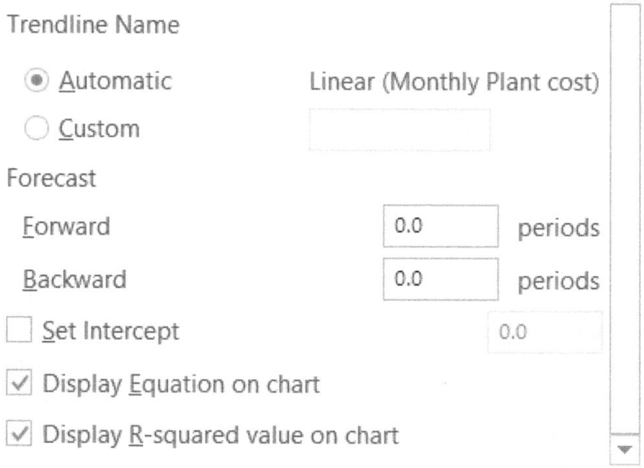

Trendline Name

    ◉ <u>A</u>utomatic   Linear (Monthly Plant cost)

    ○ <u>C</u>ustom

Forecast

    <u>F</u>orward   0.0   periods

    <u>B</u>ackward   0.0   periods

    ☐ Set <u>I</u>ntercept   0.0

    ☑ Display <u>E</u>quation on chart

    ☑ Display <u>R</u>-squared value on chart

FIGURE 53-4 Select trendline options.

After clicking **Close** and adding axis labels and a chart title, you see the results shown in Figure 53-5. A title was added to the chart and labels for the x-axis and y-axis by selecting **Chart Tools** and, from the **Design** tab, selecting **Add Chart Element**.

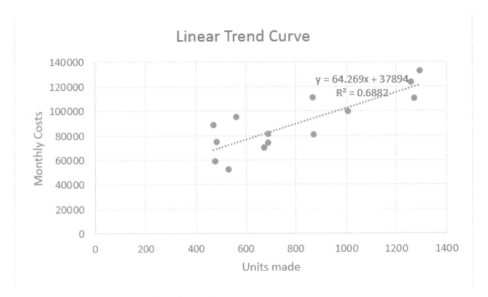

FIGURE 53-5 This is the completed trendline.

If you want to add more decimal points to the values in the equation, you can select the trendline equation and, after selecting **Format from Chart Tools**, choose **Format Selection**. After selecting **Number**, you can choose the number of decimal places to be displayed.

How does Excel determine the best-fitting line? It chooses the line that minimizes (over all lines that could be drawn) the sum of the squared vertical distance from each point to the line. The vertical distance from each point to the line is called an *error*, or *residual*. The line Excel creates is called the *least-squares line*. You minimize the sum of squared errors rather than the sum of the errors because in simply summing the errors, positive and negative errors can cancel each other out. For example, if you add errors, a point 100 units above the line and a point 100 units below the line cancel each other. If you square errors, however, Excel uses the fact that your predictions for each point are wrong to find the best-fitting line.

Thus, Excel calculates the best-fitting straight line for predicting monthly operating costs from monthly units produced as follows:

`(Monthly operating cost)=37,894.0956+64.2687(Units produced)`

By copying the 64.2687*C3+37894.0956 formula from cell E3 to the E4:E16 cell range, you compute the predicted cost for each observed data point. For example, when 1,260 units are produced, the predicted cost is $123,118. (See Figure 53-2.)

You should not use a least-squares line to predict values of an independent variable that lie outside the range for which you have data. The line in this example should only be used to predict monthly plant operating costs during months in which production is between approximately 450 and 1,300 units.

The intercept of this line is $37,894.10, which can be interpreted as the *monthly fixed cost.* Therefore, even if the plant does not produce any refrigerators during a month, this graph estimates that the plant will still incur costs of $37,894.10. The slope of this line (64.2687) indicates that each extra refrigerator produced increases monthly costs by $64.27. Thus, the *variable cost* of producing a refrigerator is estimated to be $64.27.

The errors (or residuals) for each data point were computed in cells F3:F16. The error for each data point was defined as the amount by which the point varies from the least-squares line. For each month, error equals the observed cost minus the predicted cost. Copying the D3-E3 formula from F3 to F4:F16 computes the error for each data point. A positive error indicates a point is above the least-squares line, and a negative error indicates that the point is below the least-squares line, The sum of the errors was computed in cell F1 and yielded −0.03. In reality, for any least-squares line, the sum of the errors should equal 0. (−0.03 was obtained because the equation was rounded to four decimal points.) The fact that errors sum to 0 implies that the least-squares line has the intuitively satisfying property of splitting the points in half.

How accurately does this relationship explain the monthly variation in plant operating cost?

Clearly, each month, both the operating cost and the units produced vary. A natural question is, "What percentage of the monthly variation in operating costs is explained by the monthly variation in units produced?" The answer to this question is the R^2 value (0.69 shown in Figure 53-5). You can state that the linear relationship explains 69 percent of the variation in monthly operating costs. This implies that 31 percent of the variation in monthly operating costs is explained by other factors. Using *multiple regression* (see Chapters 57 through 59), you can try to determine other factors that influence operating costs.

People always ask what a good R^2 value is. There is really no definitive answer to this question. With one independent variable, of course, a larger R^2 value indicates a better fit of the data than a smaller R^2 value. A better measure of the accuracy of your predictions is the *standard error of the regression*, which is described in the next section.

How accurate are my predictions likely to be?

When you fit a line to points, you obtain a standard error of the regression that measures the spread of the points around the least-squares line. The standard error associated with a least-squares line can be computed with the *STEYX* function. The syntax of this function is STEYX(yrange,xrange), where *yrange* contains the values of the dependent variable, and *xrange* contains the values of the independent variable. In cell K1, the standard error of the cost estimate line in the Costestimate.xlsx file was computed by using the STEYX(D3:D16,C3:C16) formula. The result is shown in Figure 53-6.

Approximately 68 percent of the points should be within one standard error of regression (SER) of the least-squares line, and about 95 percent of the points should be within two SER of the least-squares line. These measures are reminiscent of the descriptive statistics rule of thumb that was described in Chapter 42, "Summarizing data by using descriptive statistics." In this example, the absolute value of around 68 percent of the errors should be $13,772 or smaller, and the absolute value of around 95 percent of the errors should be $27,544 (or 2*13,772) or smaller. By looking at the errors in column F, you can see that 10 out of 14, or 71 percent, of the points are within one SER of the least-squares line, and all (100 percent) of the points are within two standard SER of the least-squares line. Any point that is more than two SER from the least-squares line is called an *outlier*. Looking for causes of outliers can often help you improve the operation of your business. For example, a month in which actual operating costs are $30,000 higher than anticipated would be a cost outlier on the high side. If you could ascertain the cause of this high cost outlier and prevent it from recurring, you would clearly improve plant efficiency. Similarly, consider a month in which actual costs are $30,000 less than expected. If you could ascertain the cause of this low cost outlier and ensure that it occurred more often, you would improve plant efficiency.

	H	I	J	K
1	slope	64.2687	std err	13771.9
2	intercept	37894.1		
3	RSq	0.6882		

FIGURE 53-6 This is the computation of slope, intercept, R squared (RSQ) values, and standard error of regression.

When estimating a straight-line relationship, which functions can I use to get the slope and intercept of the line that best fits the data?

The Excel *SLOPE(yrange,xrange)* and *INTERCEPT(yrange,xrange)* functions return the slope and intercept, respectively, of the least-squares line. Thus, entering the SLOPE(D3:D16,C3:C16) formula in cell I1 (see Figure 53-6) returns the slope (64.27) of the least-squares line. Entering the INTERCEPT(D3:D16,C3:C16) formula in cell I2 returns the intercept (37,894.1) of the least-squares line. By the way, the *RSQ(yrange,xrange)* function returns the R^2 value associated with a least-squares line. So, entering the RSQ(D3:D16,C3:C16) formula in cell I3 returns the R^2 value of 0.6882 for the least-squares line.

Problems

The Delldata.xlsx file contains monthly returns for the Standard & Poor's stock index and for Dell stock. The *beta* of a stock is defined as the slope of the least-squares line used to predict the monthly return for a stock from the monthly return for the market:

1. Estimate the beta of Dell.

2. Interpret the meaning of Dell's beta.

3. If you believe a recession is coming, would you rather invest in a high-beta or a low-beta stock?

4. During a month in which the market goes up 5 percent, you are 95 percent sure that Dell's stock price will increase between which range of values?

The Housedata.xlsx file gives the square footage and sales prices for several houses in Bellevue, Washington:

5. You will build a 500-square-foot addition to your house. How much do you think your home value will increase as a result?

6. What percentage of the variation in home value is explained by variation in house size?

7. A 3,000-square-foot house is selling for $500,000. Is this price out of line with typical real estate values in Bellevue? What might cause this discrepancy?

8. We know that 32 degrees Fahrenheit is equivalent to 0 degrees Celsius and that 212 degrees Fahrenheit is equivalent to 100 degrees Celsius. Use the trend curve to determine the relationship between Fahrenheit and Celsius temperatures. When you create your initial chart, before clicking Finish, you must indicate that data is in columns and not rows because with only two data points, Excel assumes different variables are in different rows.

9. The Betadata.xlsx file contains the monthly returns on the Standard & Poor's index as well as the monthly returns on Cinergy, Dell, Intel, Microsoft, Nortel, and Pfizer. Estimate the beta of each stock.

10. The Electiondata.xlsx file contains, for several elections, the percentage of votes Republicans gained from voting machines (counted on election day) and the percentage Republicans gained from absentee ballots (counted after election day). Suppose that during an election, Republicans obtained 49 percent of the votes on election day and 62 percent of the absentee ballot votes. The Democratic candidate cried "fraud." What do you think?

11. The Oldfaithful.xlsx file gives the duration between eruptions of the Old Faithful geyser and the length of the next eruption. Suppose it has been 4 minutes since the last eruption. You are 95 percent sure that the length of the next eruption is between _____ and _____.

12. The Dailydow.xlsx file gives daily values for the Dow Jones index from 1996 to 2010. What is the R squared value when you predict tomorrow's Dow Jones index from today's? Does this high R squared value mean that the market is easy to predict?

CHAPTER 54

Modeling exponential growth

Question answered in this chapter:

- How can I model the growth of a company's revenue over time?

If you want to value a company, it's important to have some idea about its future revenues. Although the future might not be like the past, you often begin a valuation analysis of a corporation by studying the company's revenue growth during the recent past. Many analysts like to fit a trend curve to recent revenue growth. To fit a trend curve, you plot the year on the *x*-axis (for example, the first year of data is Year 1, the second year of data is Year 2, and so on), and on the *y*-axis, you plot the company's revenue.

Usually, the relationship between time and revenue is not a straight line. Recall that a straight line always has the same slope, which implies that when the independent variable (in this case, the year) is increased by 1, the prediction for the dependent variable (revenue) increases by the same amount. For most companies, revenue grows by a fairly constant percentage each year. If this is the case, as revenue increases, the annual increase in revenue also increases. After all, revenue growth of 10 percent of $1 million means revenue grows by $100,000. Revenue growth of 10 percent of $100 million means revenue grows by $10 million. This analysis implies that a trend curve for forecasting revenue should grow more steeply and have an increasing slope. The *exponential function* has the property that as the independent variable increases by 1, the dependent variable increases by the same percentage. This relationship is exactly what you need to model revenue growth.

The equation for the exponential function is $y = ae^{bx}$. Here, *x* is the value of the independent variable (in this example, the year), whereas *y* is the value of the dependent variable (in this case, annual revenue). The value *e* (approximately 2.7182) is the base of natural logarithms. If you select **Exponential** from the Excel trendline options, Excel calculates the values of *a* and *b* that best fit the data. Look at an example.

Answer to this chapter's question

This section provides the answer to the question that is listed at the beginning of the chapter.

How can I model the growth of a company's revenue over time?

The Ciscoexpo.xlsx file, shown in Figure 54-1, contains the revenues for Cisco for years 1990 through 1999. All revenues are in millions of dollars. In 1990, for example, Cisco's revenues were $103.47 million.

◢	A	B	C	D
1		Year 1=1990		
2				
3	Year	Sales	Prediction	Ratio
4	1	70	103.471229	
5	2	183	182.848984	1.767148
6	3	340	323.121233	1.767148
7	4	649	571.003071	1.767148
8	5	1243	1009.04699	1.767148
9	6	1979	1783.13546	1.767148
10	7	4096	3151.06443	1.767148
11	8	6440	5568.39749	1.767148
12	9	8459	9840.18301	1.767148
13	10	12154	17389.0606	1.767148
14				
15	16		529558.325	

FIGURE 54-1 This figure shows Cisco's annual revenues for the years 1990 through 1999.

To fit an exponential curve to this data, begin by selecting the A3:B13 cell range. Next, on the **Insert** tab, in the **Charts** group, click **Scatter**. Selecting the first chart option (**Scatter With Only Markers**) creates the chart shown in Figure 54-2.

Because the slope of a straight line is constant, fitting a straight line to this data would be ridiculous. When a graph's slope is rapidly increasing, as in this example, an exponential growth will usually provide a good fit to the data.

To obtain the exponential curve that best fits this data, right-click a data point (all the points turn blue) and then click **Add Trendline**. In the **Format Trendline** dialog box, select **Exponential** in the **Trendline Options** area and select the **Display Equation On Chart** and **Display R-Squared Value On Chart** check boxes. After you click **Close**, you see the trend curve shown in Figure 54-3.

The estimate of Cisco's revenue in year x (remember that $x = 1$ is year 1990) is computed from the following formula:

`Estimated Revenue=58.552664e.`^{569367x}

Compute estimated revenue in the C4:C13 cell range by copying the =58.552664*EXP(0.569367*A4) formula from C4 to C5:C13. For example, the estimate of Cisco's revenue in 1999 (year 10) is $17.389 billion.

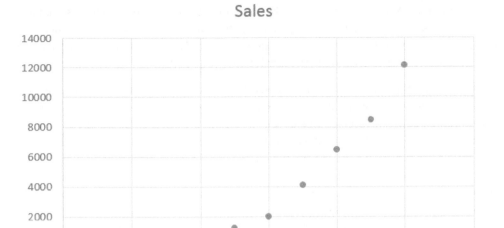

FIGURE 54-2 This is a scatter plot for the Cisco trend curve.

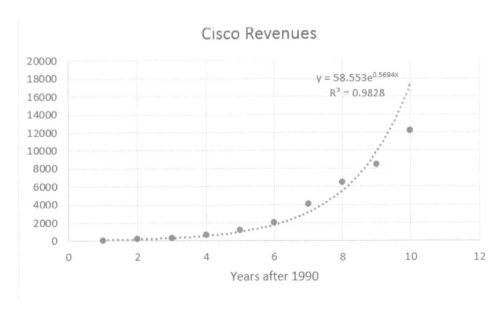

FIGURE 54-3 This is the exponential trend curve for Cisco revenues.

Notice that most of the data points are very close to the fitted exponential curve. This pattern indicates that exponential growth does a good job of explaining Cisco's revenue growth during the 1990s. The fact that the R^2 value (0.98) is very close to 1 is also consistent with the visual evidence of a good fit.

Remember that whenever x increases by 1, the estimate from an exponential curve increases by the same percentage. You can verify this fact by computing the ratio of each year's estimated revenue to the previous year's estimated revenue. To compute this ratio, copy the =C5/C4 formula from D5 to D6:D13. You find that the estimate of Cisco's growth rate is 76.7 percent per year, which is the best estimate of Cisco's annual growth rate for years 1990 through 1999.

Of course, to use this estimated annual revenue growth rate in a valuation analysis, you need to ask yourself whether it's likely that this growth rate can be maintained. Be forewarned that exponential growth cannot continue forever. For example, if you use the exponential trend curve to forecast revenues for 2005 (year 16), Cisco's 2005 predicted revenues would be $530 billion. If this estimate were realized, Cisco's revenues would have tripled the 2005 revenues of the world's largest company (Walmart). This seems highly unrealistic. The moral is that during its early years, the revenue growth for a technology company follows exponential growth. After a while, the growth rate slows down. If Wall Street analysts had understood this fact during the late 1990s, the Internet stock bubble might have been avoided. Note that during 1999, Cisco's actual revenue fell well short of the trend curve's estimated revenue. This fact might well have indicated the start of the technology slowdown, which began during late 2000.

By the way, why must you use $x = 1$ instead of $x = 1990$? If you used $x = 1990$, Excel would have to juggle numbers around the size of e^{1990}. A number this large causes Excel a great deal of difficulty.

Problems

The Exponentialdata.xlsx file contains annual sales revenue for Staples, Walmart, and Intel. Use this data to work through the first five problems for this chapter:

1. For each company, fit an exponential trend curve to its sales data.

2. For which company does exponential growth have the best fit with its revenue growth?

3. For which company does exponential growth have the worst fit with its revenue growth?

4. For each company, estimate the annual percentage growth rate for revenues.

5. For each company, use your trend curve to predict 2003 revenues.

6. The Impalas.xlsx file contains the prices of 2009, 2008, 2007, and 2006 Impalas during 2010. From this data, what can you conclude about how a new car loses its value as it grows older?

CHAPTER 55

The power curve

Question answered in this chapter:

■ As my company produces more of a product, it learns how to make the product more efficiently. Can I model the relationship between units produced and the time needed to produce a unit?

A power curve is calculated with the equation $y = ax^b$. In the equation, a and b are constants. Using a trend curve, you can determine the values of a and b that make the power curve fit a scatter plot diagram best. In most situations, a is greater than 0. When this is the case, the slope of the power curve depends on the value of b, as follows:

■ For $b>1$, y increases as x increases, and the slope of the power curve increases as x increases.

■ For $0<b<1$, y increases as x increases, and the slope of the power curve decreases as x increases.

■ For $b = 1$, the power curve is a straight line.

■ For $b<0$, y decreases as x increases, and the power curve flattens out as x increases.

Here are examples of different relationships that can be modeled by a power curve. These examples are contained in the Powerexamples.xlsx file.

If you are trying to predict total production cost as a function of units produced, you might find a relationship similar to that shown in Figure 55-1. Notice that b equals 2. As mentioned previously, with this value of b, the cost of production increases with the number of units produced. The slope becomes steeper, which indicates that each additional unit costs more to produce. This relationship might occur because increased production requires more overtime labor, which costs more than regular labor.

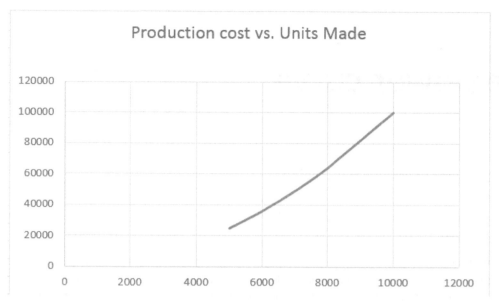

FIGURE 55-1 Predict cost as a function of the number of units produced.

If you are trying to predict sales as a function of advertising expenditures, you might find a curve similar to that shown in Figure 55-2.

FIGURE 55-2 The plot shows sales as a function of advertising.

Here, b equals 0.5, which is between 0 and 1. When b has a value in this range, sales increase with increased advertising but at a decreasing rate. Thus, the power curve enables you to model the idea of diminishing return—that each additional dollar spent on advertising will provide less benefit.

If you are trying to predict the time needed to produce the last unit of a product based on the number of units produced to date, you often find a scatter plot similar to that shown in Figure 55-3.

Here you find that b equals −0.1. Because b is less than 0, the time needed to produce each unit decreases, but the rate of decrease—that is, the rate of learning—slows down. This relationship means that during the early stages of a product's life cycle, huge savings in labor time occur. As you make more of a product, however, savings in labor time occur at a slower rate. The relationship between cumulative units produced and time needed to produce the last unit is called the *learning* or *experience* curve.

FIGURE 55-3 Plot the time needed to produce a unit based on cumulative production.

A power curve has the following properties:

- **Property 1** If x increases by 1 percent, y increases by approximately b percent.

- **Property 2** Whenever x doubles, y increases by the same percentage.

Suppose that demand for a product as a function of price can be modeled as $1000(\text{Price})^{-2}$. Property 1 then implies that a 1 percent increase in price will lower demand (regardless of price) by 2 percent. In this case, the exponent b (without the negative sign) is called the *elasticity*. Elasticity is discussed further in Chapter 83, "Estimating a demand curve." With this background, take a look at how to fit a power curve to data.

Answer to this chapter's question

This section provides the answer to the question that is listed at the beginning of the chapter.

As my company produces more of a product, it learns how to make the product more efficiently. Can I model the relationship between units produced and the time needed to produce a unit?

The Fax.xlsx file contains data about the number of fax machines produced and the unit cost (in 1982 dollars) of producing the last fax machine made during each year. In 1983, for example, 70,000 fax machines were produced, and the cost of producing the last fax machine was $3,416. The data is shown in Figure 55-4.

	A	B	C	D	E	F	G
1	Learning curve FAX data						
2							
3	Year	Production	Cumulative Production	Unit Cost	Forecast		
4	1982	64000	64000	$ 3,700.00	3955.81		
5	1983	70000	134000	$ 3,416.00	3280.54		
6	1984	100000	234000	$ 3,125.00	2848.51		
7	1985	150000	384000	$ 2,583.00	2512.63		
8	1986	175000	559000	$ 2,166.00	2284.66		
9	1987	400000	959000	$ 1,833.00	1992.72		
10	1988	785000	1744000	$ 1,788.00	1712.60		
11	1989	1000000	2744000		1526.85		learning
12		double	3488000		1436.83		percentage
13		cumulative production					0.83897516
14							

FIGURE 55-4 This is the data used to plot the learning curve for producing fax machines.

Because a learning curve tries to predict either cost or the time needed to produce a unit from data about cumulative production, the cumulative number of fax machines produced by the end of each year is calculated in column C. In cell C4, refer to cell B4 to show the number of fax machines produced in 1982. By copying the SUM($B$4:B4) formula from C5 to C6:C10, you can compute cumulative fax machine production for the end of each year.

You can now create a scatter plot that shows cumulative units produced on the *x*-axis and unit cost on the *y*-axis. After creating the chart, you click one of the data points (the data points will be displayed in blue) and then right-click and click **Add Trendline**. In the **Format Trendline** dialog box, select **Power** and then select the **Display Equation On Chart** and **Display R-Squared Value On Chart** check boxes. With these settings, you obtain the chart shown in Figure 55-5. The curve drawn represents the power curve that fits the data best.

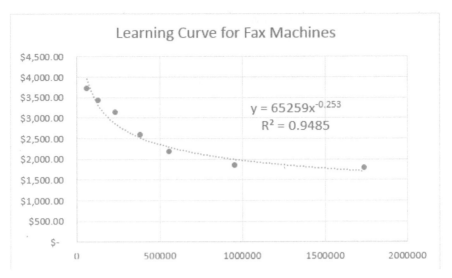

FIGURE 55-5 This is the learning curve for producing fax machines.

The power curve predicts the cost of producing a fax machine as follows:

```
Cost of producing fax machine=65,259(cumulative units produced)⁻·²⁵³³
```

Notice that most data points are near the fitted power curve and that the R^2 value is nearly 1, indicating that the power curve fits the data well.

By copying the 65259*C4^−0.2533 formula from cell E4 to E5:E10, you compute the predicted cost for the last fax machine produced during each year. (The carat symbol [^], which is located over the 6 key, is used to raise a number to a power.)

If you estimated that 1,000,000 fax machines were produced in 1989, after computing the total 1989 production (2,744,000) in cell C11, you can copy the forecast equation to cell E11 to predict that the last fax machine produced in 1989 cost $1,526.85.

Remember that Property 2 of the power curve states that whenever x doubles, y increases by the same percentage. By entering twice cumulative 1988 production in cell C12 and copying your forecast formula in E10 to cell E12, you'll find that doubling cumulative units produced reduces the predicted cost to 83.8 percent of its previous value (1,516.83/1,712.60). For this reason, the current learning curve is known as an 84-percent learning curve. Each time you double units produced, the labor required to make a fax machine drops by 16.2 percent.

If a curve becomes steeper, the exponential curve might fit the data as well as the power curve does. A natural question is which curve fits the data better? In most cases, this question can be answered simply by eyeballing the curves and choosing the one that looks like it's a better fit. More precisely, you could compute the sum of squared errors (SSE) for each curve (obtained by adding up the square of the curve value minus the actual value for each data point) and choose the curve with the smaller SSE.

The learning curve was discovered in 1936 at Wright-Patterson Air Force Base in Dayton, Ohio, when it was found that whenever the cumulative number of airplanes produced doubled, the time required to make each airplane dropped by around 15 percent.

Wikipedia gives the following learning curve estimates for various industries:

- Aerospace: 85 percent

- Shipbuilding: 80–85 percent

- Complex machine tools for new models: 75–85 percent

- Repetitive electronics manufacturing: 90–95 percent

- Repetitive machining or punch-press operations: 90–95 percent

- Repetitive electrical operations: 75–85 percent

- Repetitive welding operations: 90 percent

- Raw materials: 93–96 percent

- Purchased parts: 85–88 percent

Problems

1. Use the fax machine data to model the relationship between cumulative fax machines produced and total production cost.

2. Use the fax machine data to model the relationship between cumulative fax machines produced and average production cost per machine.

3. A marketing director estimates that total sales of a product as a function of price will be as shown in the following table. Estimate the relationship between price and demand and predict demand for a $46 price. A 1 percent increase in price will reduce demand by what percentage?

Price	Demand
$30.00	300
$40.00	200
$50.00	110
$60.00	60

4. The brand manager for a new drug believes that the annual sales of the drug as a function of the number of sales calls on doctors will be as shown in the following table. Estimate sales of the drug if 80,000 sales calls are made on doctors:

Sales calls	Units sold
50,000	25,000
100,000	52,000
150,000	68,000
200,000	77,000

5. The time needed to produce each of the first ten airplanes is as follows:

Unit	Hours
1	1,000
2	800
3	730
4	630
5	600
6	560
7	560
8	500
9	510
10	510

Estimate the total number of hours needed to produce the next ten airplanes.

CHAPTER 56

Using correlations to summarize relationships

Question answered in this chapter:

■ How are monthly stock returns for Microsoft, GE, Intel, GM, and Cisco related?

Trend curves are a great help in understanding how two variables are related. Often, however, you need to understand how more than two variables are related. Looking at the correlation between any pair of variables can provide insights into how multiple variables move up and down in value together.

The correlation (usually denoted by r) between two variables (call them x and y) is a unit-free measure of the strength of the linear relationship between x and y. The correlation between any two variables is always between –1 and +1. Although the exact formula used to compute the correlation between two variables isn't very important, being able to interpret the correlation between the variables is.

A correlation near +1 means that x and y have a strong positive linear relationship. That is, when x is larger than average, y tends to be larger than average, and when x is smaller than average, y also tends to be smaller than average. When a straight line is applied to the data, there will be a straight line with a positive slope that does a good job of fitting the points. As an example, for the data shown in Figure 56-1 (x = *units produced* and y = *monthly production cost*), x and y have a correlation of +0.9. (See the Correlationexamples.xlsx file for Figures 56-1 through 56-3.)

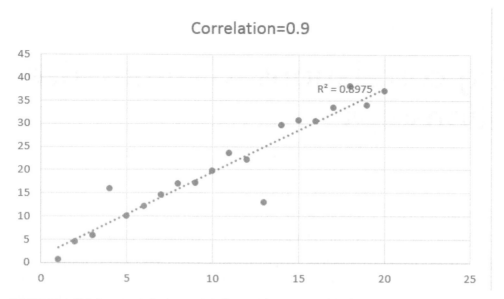

FIGURE 56-1 This is a correlation near +1, indicating that two variables have a strong positive linear relationship.

However, a correlation near –1 means that there is a strong negative linear relationship between x and y. That is, when x is larger than average, y tends to be smaller than average, and when x is smaller than average, y tends to be larger than average. When a straight line is applied to the data, the line has a negative slope that does a good job of fitting the points. As an example, for the data shown in Figure 56-2, x and y have a correlation of –0.9.

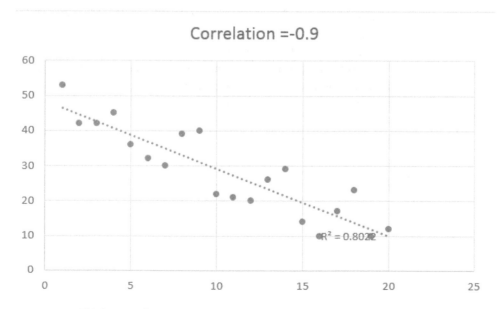

FIGURE 56-2 This is a correlation near –1, indicating that two variables have a strong negative linear relationship.

A correlation near 0 means that x and y have a weak linear relationship. That is, knowing whether x is larger or smaller than its mean tells you little about whether y will be larger or smaller than its mean. Figure 56-3 shows a graph of the dependence of unit sales (y) on years of sales experience (x). Years of experience and unit sales have a correlation of 0.003. In this data set, the average experience is 10 years. You can see that when a person has more than 10 years of sales experience, his sales can be either low or high. You can also see that when a person has fewer than 10 years of sales experience, sales can be low or high. Although experience and sales have little or no linear relationship, there is a strong nonlinear relationship (see the fitted curve) between years of experience and sales. Correlation does not measure the strength of nonlinear relationships.

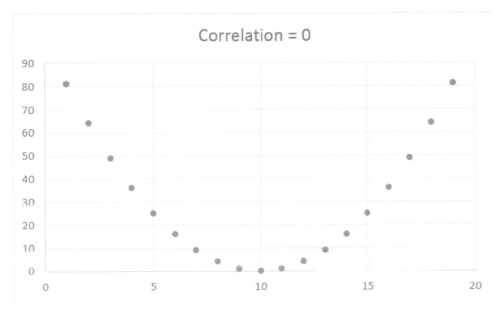

FIGURE 56-3 This is a correlation of 0, indicating a weak linear relationship between two variables.

Answer to this chapter's question

This section provides the answer to the question that is listed at the beginning of the chapter.

How are monthly stock returns for Microsoft, GE, Intel, GM, and Cisco related?

The Stockcorrel.xlsx file (see Figure 56-4) shows monthly stock returns for Microsoft, GE, Intel, GM, and Cisco during the 1990s. You can use correlations to understand how movements in these stocks are related.

To find the correlations between each pair of stocks, click **Data Analysis** in the **Analysis** group on the **Data** tab and then select **Correlation**. You must install the Analysis ToolPak (as described in Chapter 41, "Summarizing data by using histograms," and Chapter 42, "Summarizing data by using descriptive statistics") before you can use this feature. Click **OK** and then fill in the **Correlation** dialog box as shown in Figure 56-5.

▲	A	B	C	D	E	F
51	Date	MSFT	GE	INTC	GM	CSCO
52	3/30/1990	0.122	0.040	0.037	0.022	0.011
53	4/30/1990	0.047	-0.004	-0.054	-0.035	0.011
54	5/31/1990	0.259	0.084	0.222	0.116	0.042
55	6/29/1990	0.041	0.005	-0.026	-0.021	0.071
56	7/31/1990	-0.125	0.034	-0.053	-0.021	-0.038
57	8/31/1990	-0.075	-0.134	-0.250	-0.131	-0.029
58	9/28/1990	0.024	-0.113	-0.004	-0.088	-0.091
59	10/31/1990	0.012	-0.046	0.008	0.014	0.311
60	11/30/1990	0.133	0.053	0.119	0.014	0.339
61	12/31/1990	0.042	0.057	0.027	-0.058	0.136
62	1/31/1991	0.304	0.115	0.188	0.055	0.304
63	2/28/1991	0.057	0.070	0.044	0.101	-0.043
64	3/28/1991	0.023	0.024	-0.021	-0.044	-0.129
65	4/30/1991	-0.067	0.016	0.053	-0.053	0.221
66	5/31/1991	0.109	0.099	0.132	0.217	0.084
67	6/28/1991	-0.069	-0.042	-0.166	-0.055	-0.054
68	7/31/1991	0.079	-0.010	0.011	-0.025	0.287
69	8/30/1991	0.160	0.022	0.053	-0.034	0.156

FIGURE 56-4 These are monthly stock returns during the 1990s.

Correlation ? ✕

Input

Input Range: $B$51:$F$181

Grouped By: ● Columns
○ Rows

☑ Labels in first row

Output options
● Output Range: $H$52
○ New Worksheet Ply:
○ New Workbook

OK
Cancel
Help

FIGURE 56-5 This is the Correlation dialog box.

The easiest way to enter the input range is to select the upper-left cell of the range (B51) and then press Ctrl+Shift+right arrow followed by Ctrl+Shift+down arrow. Select **Labels In First Row** if the first row of the input range contains labels. Enter cell H52 as the upper-left cell of the output range. After clicking **OK**, you get the results shown in Figure 56-6.

	H	I	J	K	L	M
51						
52		*MSFT*	*GE*	*INTC*	*GM*	*CSCO*
53	MSFT	1.000				
54	GE	0.445	1.000			
55	INTC	0.517	0.324	1.000		
56	GM	0.069	0.380	0.317	1.000	
57	CSCO	0.513	0.376	0.488	0.159	1.000
58						

FIGURE 56-6 Here are the stock return correlations.

The correlation between Cisco and Microsoft is 0.513, for example, whereas the correlation between GM and Microsoft is 0.069. The analysis shows that returns on Cisco, Intel, and Microsoft are most closely tied together. Because the correlation between each pair of these stocks is around 0.5, these stocks exhibit a moderate positive relationship. In other words, if one stock does better than average, it is likely (but not certain) that the other stocks will do better than average. Because Cisco, Intel, and Microsoft stock returns are closely tied to technology spending, their fairly strong correlation is not surprising. You can also see that the monthly returns on Microsoft and GM are virtually uncorrelated. This relationship indicates that when Microsoft stock does better than average, you really can't tell whether GM stock will do better or worse than average. Again, this trend is not surprising because GM is not really a high tech company and is more susceptible to the vagaries of the business cycle.

Filling in the correlation matrix

As you can see in this example, Excel left some entries in the correlation matrix blank. For example, the correlation between Microsoft and GE (which is equal to the correlation between GE and Microsoft) is omitted. If you want to fill in the entire correlation matrix, right-click the matrix and then click **Copy**. Right-click a blank portion of the worksheet and then click **Paste Special**. In the **Paste Special** dialog box, select **Transpose**. This flips the data on its side. Now right-click the flipped data and click **Copy**. Right-click the original correlation matrix and click **Paste Special** again. In the **Paste Special** dialog box, select **Skip Blanks** and then click **OK**. The transposed data is copied to the original matrix, but pasting the data does not copy the blank cells from the transposed data. The full correlation matrix is shown in Figure 56-7.

	H	I	J	K	L	M	N
48		correl function					
49		0.159					
50							
51			Full correlation matrix				
52		*Date*	*MSFT*	*GE*	*INTC*	*GM*	*CSCO*
53	Date	1.000	-0.101	0.073	-0.019	0.011	-0.126
54	MSFT	-0.101	1.000	0.445	0.517	0.069	0.513
55	GE	0.073	0.445	1.000	0.324	0.380	0.376
56	INTC	-0.019	0.517	0.324	1.000	0.317	0.488
57	GM	0.011	0.069	0.380	0.317	1.000	0.159
58	CSCO	-0.126	0.513	0.376	0.488	0.159	1.000
59							
60							
61		1.000	-0.101	0.073	-0.019	0.011	-0.126
62			1.000	0.445	0.517	0.069	0.513
63				1.000	0.324	0.380	0.376
64					1.000	0.317	0.488
65						1.000	0.159
66							1.000
67							
68			Transposed correlations				

FIGURE 56-7 This is the complete correlation matrix.

Using the *CORREL* function

As an alternative to using **Correlation** from the **Analysis ToolPak**, you can use the *CORREL* function. For example, entering the CORREL(E52:E181,F52:F181) formula in cell I49 confirms that the correlation between monthly returns on Cisco (shown in column F) and GM (shown in column E) is 0.159.

Relationship between correlation and R^2

In Chapter 53, "Estimating straight-line relationships," you found an R^2 value for units produced and monthly operating cost of 0.688. How is this value related to the correlation between units produced and monthly operating costs? The correlation between two sets of data is simply:

$$\sqrt{R^2 value}$$

for the trendline, where you choose the sign for the square root to be the same as the sign of the slope of the trendline. Thus, the correlation between units produced and monthly operating cost for the data in Chapter 53 is

$$+ \sqrt{.688} = + .829$$

Correlation and regression toward the mean

You have probably heard the phrase, "regression toward the mean." Essentially, this statement means that the predicted value of a dependent variable will be in some sense closer to its average value than the independent variable. More precisely, suppose you try to predict a dependent variable y from an independent variable x. If x is k standard deviations above average, your prediction for y will be rk standard deviations above average. (Here, r = *correlation* between x and y.) Because r is between -1 and $+1$, this means that y is fewer standard deviations away from the mean than x. This is the real definition of "regression toward the mean." See Problem 5 for an interesting application of the concept of regression toward the mean.

Problems

The data for the following problems is in file Ch56data.xlsx:

1. The Problem 1 worksheet contains the number of cars parked each day both in the outdoor lot and in the parking garage near the Indiana University Kelley School of Business. Find and interpret the correlation between the number of cars parked in the outdoor lot and in the parking garage.

2. The Problem 2 worksheet contains daily sales volume (in dollars) of laser printers, printer cartridges, and school supplies. Find and interpret the correlations between these quantities.

3. The Problem 3 worksheet contains annual returns on stocks, T-bills, and T-bonds. Find and interpret the correlations between the annual returns on these three classes of investments.

Here are two more problems:

4. The Dow.xlsx file contains the monthly returns between the 30 stocks comprising the Dow Jones Index. Find the correlations between all stocks. Then, for each stock, use conditional formatting to highlight the three stocks most correlated with that stock. (Of course, you should not highlight a stock as correlated with itself.)

5. NFL teams play 16 games during the regular season. Suppose the standard deviation of the number of games won by all teams is 2, and the correlation between the number of games a team wins in two consecutive seasons is 0.5. If a team goes 12 and 4 during a season, what is your best prediction for how many games that team will win next season?

CHAPTER 57

Introduction to multiple regression

Questions answered in this chapter:

- Our factory manufactures three products. How can I predict the cost of running the factory based on the number of units produced?

- How accurate are my forecasts for predicting monthly cost based on units produced?

- I know how to use the Data Analysis command to run a multiple regression. Is there a way to run the regression without using this command and place the regression's results in the same worksheet as the data?

Answers to this chapter's questions

This section provides the answers to the questions that are listed at the beginning of the chapter.

Our factory manufactures three products. How can I predict the cost of running the factory based on the number of units produced?

Chapter 53 through Chapter 55 described how to use the trend curve in Microsoft Excel 2013 to predict one variable (called *y*, or the *dependent* variable) from another variable (called *x*, or the *independent* variable). However, you often want to use more than one independent variable (called independent variables $x1, x2, \ldots xn$) to predict the value of a dependent variable. In these cases, you can use either the multiple regression option in the Excel Data Analysis feature or the *LINEST* function to estimate the relationship you want.

Multiple regression assumes that the relationship between *y* and $x1, x2, \ldots xn$ has the following form:

```
Y=Constant+B1x1+B2x2+...Bnxn
```

Excel calculates the values of *Constant*, *B1*, *B2*, . . . *Bn* to make the predictions from this equation as accurate (in the sense of minimizing the sum of squared errors) as possible. The following example illustrates how multiple regression works.

The Data worksheet in the Mrcostest.xlsx file (see Figure 57-1) contains the cost of running a plant over 19 months as well as the number of units of Product A, Product B, and Product C produced during each month.

	A	B	C	D	E
3	Month	Cost	A Made	B Made	C Made
4	1	44439	515	541	928
5	2	43936	929	692	711
6	3	44464	800	710	824
7	4	41533	979	675	758
8	5	46343	1165	1147	635
9	6	44922	651	939	901
10	7	43203	847	755	580
11	8	43000	942	908	589
12	9	40967	630	738	682
13	10	48582	1113	1175	1050
14	11	45003	1086	1075	984
15	12	44303	843	640	828
16	13	42070	500	752	708
17	14	44353	813	989	804
18	15	45968	1190	823	904
19	16	47781	1200	1108	1120
20	17	43202	731	590	1065
21	18	44074	1089	607	1132
22	19	44610	786	513	839

FIGURE 57-1 This is the data for predicting monthly operating costs.

You would like to find the best forecast for monthly operating cost that has the following form (which is referred to as Form 1):

```
Monthly operating cost=Constant+B1*(Units A produced)+B2*(Units B produced)
    +B3*(Units C produced)
```

The Excel Data Analysis feature can find the equation for this form that best fits your data. Click **Data Analysis** in the **Analysis** group on the **Data** tab and then select **Regression**. Fill in the **Regression** dialog box as shown in Figure 57-2.

Note If you haven't previously installed the Analysis ToolPak, click the **File** tab, click **Options**, and then click **Add-Ins**. With **Excel Add-ins** selected in the **Manage** dialog box, click **Go**, select the **Analysis ToolPak** check box, and then click **OK**.

FIGURE 57-2 This is the Regression dialog box.

- Input Y Range (B3:B22 in this example) contains the dependent variable or data (including the Cost label) that you want to predict.

- Input X Range (C3:E22) contains the data or independent variables (including the A Made, B Made, and C Made labels) that you want to use in the prediction. Excel has a limit of 15 independent variables, which must be in adjacent columns.

- Because both the Input X and Input Y ranges include labels, select the **Labels** check box.

- The output was placed in a new worksheet, titled Regression.

- Selecting the **Residuals** check box causes Excel to list, for each observation, the prediction from Form 1 and the residual, which equals the observed cost minus the predicted cost.

After clicking **OK** in the **Regression** dialog box, you obtain the output shown in Figure 57-3 and Figure 57-4. (See the Regression worksheet.)

	A	B	C	D	E	F	G	H	I
1	SUMMARY OUTPUT								
2									
3	*Regression Statistics*								
4	Multiple R	0.803398744							
5	R Square	0.645449542							
6	Adjusted R Square	0.57453945							
7	Standard Error	1252.763898							
8	Observations	19							
9									
10	ANOVA								
11		*df*	*SS*	*MS*	*F*	*Significance F*			
12	Regression	3	42856229.89	14285410	9.102365	0.001126532			
13	Residual	15	23541260.74	1569417.4					
14	Total	18	66397490.63						
15									
16		*Coefficients*	*Standard Error*	*t Stat*	*P-value*	*Lower 95%*	*Upper 95%*	*Lower 95.0%*	*Upper 95.0%*
17	Intercept	35102.90045	1837.226911	19.106459	6.11E-12	31186.94158	39018.8593	31186.94158	39018.85932
18	A Made	2.065953296	1.664981779	1.2408264	0.233727	-1.482873542	5.61478013	-1.48287354	5.614780134
19	B Made	4.176355531	1.681252566	2.4840738	0.025288	0.592848311	7.75986275	0.592848311	7.759862751
20	C Made	4.790641037	1.789316107	2.6773587	0.017223	0.97680169	8.60448038	0.97680169	8.604480385

FIGURE 57-3 Here is the original multiple regression output.

	A	B	C
24	**RESIDUAL OUTPUT**		
25			
26	*Observation*	*Predicted Cost*	*Residuals*
27	1	42871.99	1567.01
28	2	43318.35	617.65
29	3	43668.36	795.64
30	4	43575.81	-2042.81
31	5	45342.07	1000.93
32	6	44685.80	236.20
33	7	42784.48	418.52
34	8	43662.85	-662.85
35	9	42753.82	-1786.82
36	10	47339.70	1242.30
37	11	46550.10	-1547.10
38	12	43484.02	818.98
39	13	42668.27	-598.27
40	14	44764.61	-411.61
41	15	45329.26	638.74
42	16	47574.96	206.04
43	17	44179.19	-977.19
44	18	45310.78	-1236.78
45	19	42888.56	1721.44

FIGURE 57-4 Here is the original multiple regression residual output.

What is the best prediction equation? You'll find in the Coefficients column (column B of the summary output) that the best equation of Form 1 that can be used to predict monthly cost is the following:

```
Predicted monthly cost=35,102.90+2.07(AMade)+4.18(BMade)+4.79(CMade)
```

A natural question is which of your independent variables are useful for predicting monthly cost? After all, if you choose the number of games the Seattle Mariners won during a one-month period as an independent variable, you would expect that this variable would have little effect on predicting monthly operating cost. When you run a regression, each independent variable has a p-value between 0 and 1. Any independent variable with a p-value (see column E) of less than or equal to 0.05 is considered useful for predicting the dependent variable. Thus, the smaller the p-value, the higher the predictive power of the independent variable. Your three independent variables have p-values of 0.23 (for A Made), 0.025 (for B Made), and 0.017 (for C Made). These p-values can be interpreted as follows:

- When you use B Made and C Made to predict monthly operating cost, you have a 77 percent chance $(1 - 0.23)$ that A Made adds predictive power.

- When you use A Made and C Made to predict monthly operating cost, there is a 97.5 percent chance $(1 - 0.025)$ that B Made adds predictive power.

- When you use A Made and B Made to predict monthly operating cost, there is a 98.3 percent chance $(1 - 0.017)$ that C Made adds predictive power.

Your p-values indicate that A Made does not add much predictive power to B Made and C Made, which means that if you know B Made and C Made, you can predict monthly operating cost about as well as you can if you include A Made as an independent variable. Therefore, you can opt to delete A Made as an independent variable and use just B Made and C Made for your prediction. Copy the data to the A Removed worksheet and delete the A Made column (column C). Adjust the Input X range to be C3:D22. In the NoA worksheet, you can see the regression output shown in Figure 57-5 and Figure 57-6.

	A	B	C	D	E	F	G	H	I
1	SUMMARY OUTPUT								
2									
3	*Regression Statistics*								
4	Multiple R	0.780421232							
5	R Square	0.609057299							
6	Adjusted R Square	0.560189461							
7	Standard Error	1273.715391							
8	Observations	19							
9									
10	ANOVA								
11		*df*	*SS*	*MS*	*F*	*Significance F*			
12	Regression	2	40439876.29	2E+07	12.46336	0.000545638			
13	Residual	16	25957614.34	1622351					
14	Total	18	66397490.63						
15									
16		*Coefficients*	*Standard Error*	*t Stat*	*P-value*	*Lower 95%*	*Upper 95%*	*Lower 95.0%*	*Upper 95.0%*
17	Intercept	35475.30255	1842.860853	19.2501	1.72E-12	31568.61295	39381.99216	31568.61295	39381.99216
18	B Made	5.320968077	1.429095476	3.72331	0.001849	2.291421689	8.350514465	2.291421689	8.350514465
19	C Made	5.417137848	1.745311648	3.10382	0.006825	1.717243277	9.117032419	1.717243277	9.117032419

FIGURE 57-5 Multiple regression output with A Made data removed as an independent variable.

	A	B	C
23	**RESIDUAL OUTPUT**		
24			
25	*Observation*	*Predicted Cost*	*Residuals*
26	1	43381.05021	1057.949794
27	2	43008.99747	927.002527
28	3	43716.91148	747.0885248
29	4	43173.14649	-1640.146495
30	5	45018.33547	1324.664528
31	6	45352.53278	-430.5327792
32	7	42634.5734	568.4265963
33	8	43497.43576	-497.4357601
34	9	43096.66501	-2129.665007
35	10	47415.43478	1166.565215
36	11	46525.80688	-1522.806879
37	12	43366.11226	936.8877388
38	13	43312.00414	-1242.004144
39	14	45093.11881	-740.1188117
40	15	44751.5519	1216.448104
41	16	47438.12957	342.8704271
42	17	44383.92553	-1181.925527
43	18	44837.33022	-763.3302206
44	19	42749.93783	1860.062168

FIGURE 57-6 This is residual output calculated when A Made data is removed as an independent variable.

You can see that B Made and C Made have very low p-values (0.002 and 0.007, respectively). These values indicate that both these independent variables have useful predictive power. By using the new coefficients in column B, you can now predict monthly operating cost by using the following equation:

```
Predicted monthly operating cost=35,475.3+5.32(BMade)+5.42(CMade)
```

How accurate are my forecasts for predicting monthly cost based on units produced?

In the regression output in cell B5 of the NoA worksheet (see Figure 57-5), R^2 equals 0.61. An R^2 value such as this one means that together, B Made and C Made explain 61 percent of the variation in monthly operating costs. Notice that in the original regression, which included A Made as an independent variable, R^2 equals 0.65. This indicates that the addition of A Made as an independent variable explains only 4 percent more variation in monthly operating costs. Having such a minor difference is consistent with the decision to delete A Made as an independent variable.

In the regression output in cell B7 in the NoA worksheet, the standard error for the regression with B Made and C Made as independent variables is 1,274. You would expect about 68 percent of your multiple regression forecasts to be accurate within one standard error and 95 percent to be accurate within two standard errors. Any forecast that differs from the actual value by more than two standard errors is considered an outlier. Thus, if your forecasted operating cost is in error by more than $2,548 (2*1274), you consider that observation to be an outlier.

In the Residual portion of the output, shown earlier, in Figure 57-6, you are given for each observation the predicted cost and the residual, which equals the actual cost less the predicted cost. For the first observation, for example, the predicted cost is $43,381.10. The residual of $1,057.95 indicates that the prediction of actual cost was too low by $1,057.95.

I know how to use the Data Analysis command to run a multiple regression. Is there a way to run the regression without using this command and place the regression's results in the same worksheet as the data?

The Excel *LINEST* function can be used to insert the results of a regression analysis directly into a workbook. The *LINEST* function is an example of an array function. (See Chapter 87, "Array formulas and functions," for further discussion of array functions and formulas.) For now, here is an introduction to array functions:

- Before entering an array function, you must always select the cell range in which you want the results of the array function to be located.

- Instead of pressing Enter to perform the calculation, you must press Ctrl+Shift+Enter to complete the entry of an array function.

- After entering an array function, you see a curly bracket in the formula bar when you select a cell in which the array function's results are located. This bracket indicates that the results in the cell were computed with an array function.

- You can't modify data in any part of a range created by an array function.

To use the *LINEST* function when there are *m* independent variables, begin by selecting a blank cell range consisting of five rows and *m* + 1 columns where you want *LINEST* to deposit the results. In the A Removed worksheet, the F5:H9 range was used.

The syntax of the *LINEST* function is LINEST(KnownYs,KnownXs,True,True). If the third argument is changed to False, Excel estimates the equation without a constant term. Changing the fourth argument to False causes the *LINEST* function to omit many regression computations and return only the multiple regression equation.

With the upper-left cell of the target range selected (F5 in this example), select the range of the size you want (in this case, the F5:H9 cell range) and then enter the =LINEST(B4:B22,C4:D22,True, True) formula. Because *LINEST* is an array function at this point, first hold down Ctrl+Shift and *then* press Enter for the function to work correctly. After using this key combination, you obtain the results shown in Figure 57-7. (See the A Removed worksheet.)

◢	F	G	H	I	J
4				\multicolumn{2}{l}{LINEST OUTPUT}	
5	5.417137848	5.320968077	35475.30255		
6	1.745311646	1.429095476	1842.860853		
7	0.609057299	1273.715391	#N/A		
8	12.46335684	16	#N/A		
9	40439876.29	25957614.34	#N/A		
10					
11	Cmadecoef	Bmadecoef	Const		
12	Std err C	Std Err B	Std err const		
13	rsq	std err est			
14	F	df			
15	ssreg	ssresid			

FIGURE 57-7 Use the *LINEST* function to calculate a multiple regression.

In row 5, you find the prediction equation (coefficients read right to left, starting with the intercept) of Predicted monthly cost = 35,475.3 + 5.32(B Made) + 5.43(C Made). Row 6 contains standard errors for each coefficient estimate, but these are not too relevant. Cell F7 contains the R^2 value of 0.61, and cell G7 contains the regression standard error of 1,274. Rows 8 and 9 contain information (F statistic, degrees of freedom, sum of squares regression, and sum of squares residual) that is less important.

Note Problems that you can work with to learn more about multiple regression are available at the end of Chapter 59, "Modeling nonlinearities and interactions."

CHAPTER 58

Incorporating qualitative factors into multiple regression

Questions answered in this chapter:

- How can I predict quarterly US auto sales?

- How can I predict US presidential elections?

- Is there an Excel function I can use to make forecasts easily from a multiple regression equation?

In the first example of multiple regression in Chapter 57, "Introduction to multiple regression," the monthly cost of plant operations was forecasted by using the number of units of each product manufactured at the plant. Because you can quantify exactly the amount of a product produced at a plant, you can refer to the units produced of Product A, Product B, and Product C as *quantitative independent variables*. In many situations, however, independent variables can't be easily quantified. In this chapter, you look at ways to incorporate qualitative factors such as seasonality, gender, or the party of a presidential candidate into a multiple regression analysis.

Answers to this chapter's questions

This section provides the answers to the questions that are listed at the beginning of the chapter.

How can I predict quarterly U.S. auto sales?

Suppose you want to predict quarterly US auto sales to determine whether the quarter of the year affects auto sales. Use the data in the Data worksheet in the Autotemp.xlsx file, shown in Figure 58-1. Sales are listed in thousands of cars, and GNP is in billions of dollars.

	A	B	C	D	E	F
7						
8						
9	Historical data					
10	Year	Quarter	Sales	GNP	Unemp	Int
11	79	1	Sales	2541	5.9	9.4
12	79	2	2910	2640	5.7	9.4
13	79	3	2562	2595	5.9	9.7
14	79	4	2385	2701	6	11.9
15	80	1	2520	2785	6.2	13.4
16	80	2	2142	2509	7.3	9.6
17	80	3	2130	2570	7.7	9.2
18	80	4	2190	2667	7.4	13.6
19	81	1	2370	2878	7.4	14.4
20	81	2	2208	2835	7.4	15.3
21	81	3	2196	2897	7.4	15.1
22	81	4	1758	2744	8.3	11.8
23	82	1	1944	2582	8.8	12.8
24	82	2	2094	2613	9.4	12.4
25	82	3	1911	2529	10	9.3
26	82	4	2031	2544	10.7	7.9
27	83	1	2046	2633	10.4	7.8
28	83	2	2502	2878	10.1	8.4
29	83	3	2238	3051	9.4	9.1
30	83	4	2394	3274	8.5	8.8
31	84	1	2586	3594	7.9	9.2
32	84	2	2898	3774	7.5	9.8

FIGURE 58-1 Here is the auto sales data.

You might be tempted to define an independent variable that equals 1 during the first quarter, 2 during the second quarter, and so on. Unfortunately, this approach would force the fourth quarter to have four times the effect of the first quarter, which might not be true. The quarter of the year is a *qualitative independent variable*. To model a qualitative independent variable, you create an independent variable called a *dummy variable* for all but one of the qualitative variable's possible values. (It is arbitrary which value you leave out. In this example, Quarter 4 was omitted.) The dummy variables tell you which value of the qualitative variable occurs. Thus, you have a dummy variable for Quarter 1, Quarter 2, and Quarter 3 with the following properties:

- Quarter 1 dummy variable equals 1 if the quarter is Quarter 1 or 0 if otherwise.

- Quarter 2 dummy variable equals 1 if the quarter is Quarter 2 or 0 if otherwise.

- Quarter 3 dummy variable equals 1 if the quarter is Quarter 3 or 0 if otherwise.

A Quarter 4 observation will be identified by the fact that the dummy variables for Quarter 1 through Quarter 3 equal 0. You can see why you don't need a dummy variable for Quarter 4. In fact, if you include a dummy variable for Quarter 4 as an independent variable in the regression, Microsoft Excel returns an error message, because if an exact linear relationship exists between any set of independent variables, Excel must perform the mathematical equivalent of dividing by 0 (an impossibility) when running a multiple regression. In this example, if you include a Quarter 4 dummy variable, every data point satisfies the following exact linear relationship:

```
(Quarter 1 Dummy)+(Quarter 2 Dummy)+(Quarter 3 Dummy)+(Quarter 4 Dummy)=1
```

> **Note** An exact linear relationship occurs if there exists constants c0, c1, . . . cN, such that for each data point, c0 + c1x1 + c2x2 + . . . cNxN = 0. Here, x1 through xN are the values of the independent variables.

To create the dummy variable for Quarter 1, copy the IF(B12=1,1,0) formula from G12 to G13:G42. This formula places a 1 in column G whenever a quarter is the first quarter or a 0 in column G whenever the quarter is not the first quarter. In a similar fashion, create dummy variables for Quarter 2 (in H12:H42) and Quarter 3 (in I12:I42). You can see the results of the formulas in Figure 58-2.

	G	H	I	J	K	L
10	Q1	Q2	Q3	LagGNP	LagUnemp	LagInt
11	Q1	Q2	Q3	LagGNP	LagUnemp	LagInt
12	0	1	0	2541	5.9	9.4
13	0	0	1	2640	5.7	9.4
14	0	0	0	2595	5.9	9.7
15	1	0	0	2701	6	11.9
16	0	1	0	2785	6.2	13.4
17	0	0	1	2509	7.3	9.6
18	0	0	0	2570	7.7	9.2
19	1	0	0	2667	7.4	13.6
20	0	1	0	2878	7.4	14.4
21	0	0	1	2835	7.4	15.3
22	0	0	0	2897	7.4	15.1
23	1	0	0	2744	8.3	11.8
24	0	1	0	2582	8.8	12.8
25	0	0	1	2613	9.4	12.4
26	0	0	0	2529	10	9.3
27	1	0	0	2544	10.7	7.9
28	0	1	0	2633	10.4	7.8
29	0	0	1	2878	10.1	8.4
30	0	0	0	3051	9.4	9.1
31	1	0	0	3274	8.5	8.8
32	0	1	0	3594	7.9	9.2

FIGURE 58-2 Use dummy variables to track the quarter in which a sale occurs.

In addition to seasonality, you want to use macroeconomic variables such as gross national product (GNP, in billions of 1986 dollars), interest rates, and unemployment rates to predict car sales. Suppose, for example, that you are trying to estimate sales for the second quarter of 1979. Because values for GNP, interest rate, and unemployment rate aren't known at the beginning of the second quarter in 1979, you can't use second quarter 1979 GNP, interest rate, and unemployment rate to predict Quarter 2 1979 auto sales. Instead, you use the values for GNP, interest rate, and unemployment rate *lagged one quarter* to forecast auto sales. By copying the =D11 formula from J12 to J12:L42, you create the lagged value for GNP, the first of your macroeconomic independent variables. For example, the J12:L12 range contains GNP, unemployment rate, and interest rate for the first quarter of 1979.

You can now run the multiple regression by clicking **Data Analysis** on the **Data** tab and then selecting **Regression** in the **Data Analysis** dialog box. Use C11:C42 as the Input Y Range and G11:L42 as the Input X Range, select the **Labels** option (row 11 contains labels), and select the **Residuals** check box. After clicking **OK**, you obtain the output, which you can see in the Regression worksheet and in Figure 58-3, Figure 58-4, and Figure 58-5.

	A	B	C	D	E	F
1	SUMMARY OUTPUT					
2						
3	*Regression Statistics*					
4	Multiple R	0.884139126				
5	R Square	0.781701994				
6	Adjusted R Square	0.727127492				
7	Standard Error	190.5240756				
8	Observations	31				
9						
10	ANOVA					
11		*df*	*SS*	*MS*	*F*	*Significance F*
12	Regression	6	3119625.193	519938	14.3236	6.79746E-07
13	Residual	24	871186.1616	36299.4		
14	Total	30	3990811.355			
15						

FIGURE 58-3 This is the summary output and ANOVA table for auto sales data.

In Figure 58-4, you can see that the equation (equation 1) used to predict quarterly auto sales is as follows:

```
Predicted quarterly sales=3154.7+156.833Q1+379.784Q2+203.03 6Q3+.174(LAGGNP in billions)
    -93.83(LAGUNEMP)-73.91(LAGINT)
```

Also in Figure 58-4, you see that each independent variable has a p-value less than or equal to 0.15. You can conclude that all independent variables have a significant effect on quarterly auto sales. You interpret all coefficients in a regression equation *ceteris paribus* (which means that each coefficient gives the effect of the independent variable after adjusting for the effects of all other variables in the regression).

	A	B	C	D	E	F	G	H	I
16		*Coefficients*	*Standard Error*	*t Stat*	*P-value*	*Lower 95%*	*Upper 95%*	*Lower 95.0%*	*Upper 95.0%*
17	Intercept	3154.700285	462.6530922	6.81872	4.7E-07	2199.83143	4109.56914	2199.83143	4109.56914
18	Q1	156.833091	98.87110703	1.58624	0.12577	-47.22680256	360.892985	-47.2268026	360.8929846
19	Q2	379.7835116	96.08921514	3.95241	0.00059	181.4651595	578.101864	181.4651595	578.1018637
20	Q3	203.035501	95.40891864	2.12806	0.0438	6.12121161	399.94979	6.12121161	399.9497905
21	LagGNP	0.174156906	0.05842	2.98112	0.00649	0.053583977	0.29472983	0.053583977	0.294729835
22	LagUnemp	-93.83233214	28.32328716	-3.3129	0.00292	-152.2887117	-35.375953	-152.288712	-35.37595254
23	LagInt	-73.9167147	17.78851573	-4.1553	0.00036	-110.6303992	-37.20303	-110.630399	-37.20303022
24									

FIGURE 58-4 This is the coefficient information for the auto sales regression.

Here's an interpretation of each coefficient:

- A $1 billion increase in last quarter's GNP increases quarterly car sales by 174.

- An increase of 1 percent in last quarter's unemployment rate decreases quarterly car sales by 93,832.

- An increase of 1 percent in last quarter's interest rate decreases quarterly car sales by 73,917.

To interpret the coefficients of the dummy variables, you must realize that they tell you the effect of seasonality relative to the value left out of the qualitative variables. Therefore:

- In Quarter 1, car sales exceed Quarter 4 car sales by 156,833.

- In Quarter 2, car sales exceed Quarter 4 car sales by 379,784.

- In Quarter 3, car sales exceed Quarter 4 car sales by 203,036.

You find that car sales are highest during the second quarter (April through June; tax refunds and summer are coming) and lowest during the third quarter (October through December; why buy a new car when winter salting will ruin it?).

From the Summary output shown in Figure 58-3, you can learn the following:

- The variation in the independent variables (macroeconomic factors and seasonality) explains 78 percent of the variation in the dependent variable (quarterly car sales).

- The standard error of regression is 190,524 cars. You can expect around 68 percent of your forecasts to be accurate within 190,524 cars and about 95 percent of your forecasts to be accurate within 381,048 cars (2*190,524).

- Thirty-one observations are used to fit the regression.

The only quantity of interest in the ANOVA table in Figure 58-3 is the significance (0.00000068). This measure implies that there are only 6.8 chances in 10,000,000 that, taken together, all the independent variables are useless in forecasting car sales. Thus, you can be quite sure that the independent variables are useful in predicting quarterly auto sales.

Figure 58-5 shows, for each observation, the predicted sales and residual. For example, for the second quarter of 1979 (observation 1), predicted sales from equation 1 are 2,728.6, and the residual is 181,411 cars (2910 − 2728.6). Note that no residual exceeds 381,000 in absolute value, so you have no outliers.

	A	B	C	D
27	**RESIDUAL OUTPUT**			
28				
29	*Observation*	*Predicted Sales*	*Residuals*	
30	1	2728.588616	181.411384	
31	2	2587.848606	-25.848606	
32	3	2336.034563	48.9654368	
33	4	2339.328281	180.671719	
34	5	2447.266343	-305.26634	
35	6	2400.118977	-270.11898	
36	7	2199.7408	-9.7408001	
37	8	2076.383266	293.616734	
38	9	2276.947422	-68.947422	
39	10	2026.185621	169.814379	
40	11	1848.731191	-90.731191	
41	12	2138.394335	-194.39434	
42	13	2212.298456	-118.29846	
43	14	2014.216596	-103.2166	
44	15	1969.394332	61.6056684	
45	16	2166.640544	-120.64054	
46	17	2440.632301	61.3676994	
47	18	2290.352403	-52.352403	
48	19	2131.386979	262.613021	
49	20	2433.681173	152.318827	
50	21	2739.094517	158.905483	
51	22	2586.877653	-138.87765	
52	23	2362.035446	97.9645544	
53	24	2667.994409	-21.994409	
54	25	2937.601377	50.3986226	
55	26	2838.174893	128.825107	
56	27	2713.079218	-274.07922	
57	28	2887.577992	-289.57799	
58	29	3004.570968	40.4290323	
59	30	2921.225251	291.774749	
60	31	2781.597472	-96.597472	

FIGURE 58-5 These are the residuals for the auto sales data.

How can I predict US presidential elections?

When asked which factors drive presidential elections, presidential advisor James Carville said, "It's the economy, stupid." Yale economist Roy Fair showed that Carville was correct in thinking that the state of the economy has a large influence on the results of presidential elections. Fair's dependent variable (see the Data worksheet in the Preselect12l.xlsx file, shown in Figure 58-6) for each election (1916 through 2012) was the percentage of the two-party vote (ignoring votes received by third-party candidates) that went to the incumbent party. He tried to predict the incumbent party's percentage of the two-party vote by using independent variables such as:

- **Party in power**   In your data, 1 denotes when the Republican party was in power, and 0 denotes when the Democratic party was in power.

- **Percentage growth in GNP during the first nine months of the election year**

- **Absolute value of the inflation rate during the first nine months of the election year**   You use the absolute value because either a positive or a negative inflation rate is bad.

- **Number of quarters during the last four years in which economic growth was strong** Strong economic growth is defined as growth at an annual level of 3.2 percent or more.

- **Length of time an incumbent party has been in office** Fair used 0 to denote one term in office, 1 for two terms, 1.25 for three terms, 1.5 for four terms, and 1.75 for five terms or more. This definition implies that each term after the first term in office has less influence on the election results than the first term in office.

- **Elections during wartime** The elections in 1920 (World War I), 1944 (World War II), and 1948 (World War II was still underway in 1945) were defined as wartime elections. (Elections held during the Vietnam War were not considered to be wartime elections.) During wartime years, the variables related to quarters of good growth and inflation were deemed irrelevant and were set to 0.

- **The current president running for reelection** If this is the case, this variable is set to 1; otherwise, this variable is set to 0. In 1976, Gerald Ford was not considered a president running for reelection because he was not elected either as president or as vice-president.

	A	B	C	D	E	F	G	H	I	J	K	L
					Growth rate in election year	Abs. Value Inflation rate in election year	Quarters Growth>3.2 %	Time Incumbent in Office	Incumbent Party 1 = Republican	War	President Running?	Prediction
6	Candidates	Year	Incumbent Share	Party in Power								
7	Wilson-Hughes	1916	51.7	D	2.2	4.3	3	0	0	0	1	50.3663
8	Harding-Cox	1920	36.1	D	-11.5	0	0	1	0	1	0	38.8315
9	Coolidge-Davis	1924	58.3	R	-3.9	5.2	10	0	1	0	1	57.3373
10	Hoover-Smith	1928	58.8	R	4.6	0.2	7	1	1	0	0	56.9562
11	Hoover-FDR	1932	40.9	R	-14.9	7.1	4	1.25	1	0	1	39.1566
12	FDR-Landon	1936	62.2	D	11.9	2.5	9	0	0	0	1	62.6266
13	FDR-Wilkie	1940	55	D	3.7	0	8	1	0	0	1	55.5384
14	FDR-Dewey	1944	53.8	D	4.1	0	0	1.25	0	1	1	52.886
15	Truman-Dewey	1948	52.3	D	1.8	0	0	1.5	0	1	1	50.4825
16	Ike-Stevenson	1952	44.7	D	0.6	2.3	7	1.75	0	0	0	44.4311
17	Ike-Stevenson	1956	57.1	R	-1.5	1.9	5	0	1	0	1	57.0579
18	Kennedy-Nixon	1960	49.9	R	0.1	1.9	5	1	1	0	0	50.9032
19	Johnson-Goldwater	1964	61.2	D	5.1	1.3	10	0	0	0	1	60.5318
20	Nixon-Humphrey	1968	49.4	D	4.8	3.1	7	1	0	0	0	49.198
21	Nixon-McGovern	1972	61.8	R	6.3	4.8	4	0	1	0	1	59.5453
22	Ford-Carter	1976	49	R	3.7	7.6	5	1	1	0	0	49.3399
23	Carter-Reagan	1980	44.8	D	-3.8	7.9	5	0	0	0	1	45.3556
24	Reagan-Mondale	1984	59.1	R	5.4	5.2	8	0	1	0	1	62.0729
25	Bush-Dukakis	1988	53.8	R	2.1	3	4	1	1	0	0	50.6481
26	Bush-Clinton	1992	46.4	R	2.3	3.3	2	1.25	1	0	1	52.0826
27	Clinton-Dole	1996	54.7	D	2.9	2	4	0	0	0	1	53.3503
28	Gore Bush	2000	50.3	D	2.2	1.6	7	0	0	0	0	51.692
29	Bush Kerry	2004	51.2	R	2	2.2	1	0	1	0	1	55.8358
30	Obama McCain	2008	46.3	R	-2.3	3.1	1	1	1	0	0	44.9453
31	Obama Romney	2012	51.9	D	1.57	1.03	1	0	0	0	1	50.5405

FIGURE 58-6 This is presidential election data.

The data from elections from 1916 through 2000 are now used to develop a multiple regression equation that can be used to forecast future presidential elections. The 2004, 2008, and 2012 elections have been saved as validation points. When fitting a regression to data, it's always a good idea to hold back some of your data for use in validating your regression equation. Holding back data enables you to determine whether your regression equation can do a good job of forecasting data it hasn't seen. Any forecasting tool that poorly forecasts data it hasn't seen should not be used to predict the future.

To run the regression, click **Data Analysis** in the **Analysis** group on the **Data** tab and then select the **Regression** tool in the **Data Analysis** dialog box. C7:C28 was used here as the Input Y Range and E7:L28 as the Input X Range. The **Labels** option (row 6 contains labels) was selected. The output was placed in the Answer worksheet, which you can see in Figure 58-7.

	A	B	C	D	E	F	G	H	I
1	SUMMARY OUTPUT								
2									
3	*Regression Statistics*								
4	Multiple R	0.9568422							
5	R Square	0.91554699							
6	Adjusted R Square	0.87332048							
7	Standard Error	2.45997294							
8	Observations	22							
9									
10	ANOVA								
11		*df*	*SS*	*MS*	*F*	*Significance F*			
12	Regression	7	918.4471912	131.2067	21.68181	1.7115E-06			
13	Residual	14	84.72053612	6.051467					
14	Total	21	1003.167727						
15									
16		*Coefficients*	*Standard Error*	*t Stat*	*P-value*	*Lower 95%*	*Upper 95%*	*Lower 95.0%*	*Upper 95.0%*
17	Intercept	45.2900744	2.68849329	16.84589	1.09E-10	39.5238298	51.056319	39.5238298	51.05631901
18	Growth rate in election year	0.69399917	0.107099273	6.479962	1.45E-05	0.46429408	0.9237043	0.46429408	0.923704269
19	Abs. Value Inflation rate in election year	-0.7125779	0.291266106	-2.44648	0.028234	-1.3372816	-0.087874	-1.3372816	-0.08787422
20	Quarters Growth>3.2%	0.85931756	0.274452907	3.13102	0.007364	0.27067462	1.4479605	0.27067462	1.447960504
21	Time Incumbent in Office	-3.2295242	1.124289507	-2.8725	0.012292	-5.6408854	-0.818163	-5.6408854	-0.81816304
22	Incumbent Party 1 = Republican	5.83057855	1.229673084	4.741568	0.000315	3.19319209	8.467965	3.19319209	8.467965011
23	War	4.75195552	2.738420745	1.735291	0.104638	-1.1213728	10.625284	-1.1213728	10.62528388
24	President Running?	4.0355107	1.256977358	3.210488	0.006288	1.3395624	6.731459	1.3395624	6.731459004

FIGURE 58-7 This is the regression output for predicting presidential elections.

In Figure 58-7, you can see that all independent variables (if you round down the War coefficient to 0.10) have *p*-values less than or equal to 0.10 and should all be used in predictions. From the coefficients section in Figure 58-7, you can determine that the best equation to predict elections is given by the following (equation 1):

```
Predicted presidential election percentage= 45.29 +0.69GROWTH - 0.71ABSINFL +0.86*QTRSGOODGROWTH
- 3.23TIMEINOFFICE + 5.83REPB + 4.75WAR + 4.04PRESRUNNING
```

The coefficients of the independent variables can be interpreted as follows (after adjusting for all other independent variables):

- A 1 percent increase in the annual GNP growth rate during an election year is worth 0.69 percent to the incumbent party.

- A 1 percent deviation from the ideal (0 percent inflation) costs the incumbent party 0.71 percent of the vote.

- Every good quarter of growth during an incumbent's term increases his (maybe her someday soon) vote by 0.86 percent.

- Relative to having one term in office, the second term in office decreases the incumbent's vote by 3.22 percent, and each later term decreases the incumbent's vote by 0.25*(3.22percent) = 0.80 percent.

- A Republican has a 5.83 percent edge over a Democrat.

- The United States at war adds 4.79 percent to the prediction for the incumbent vote share.

- If the president is running, you should add 4.04 percent to your prediction for the incumbent vote share.

	A	B	C	D	E
28	RESIDUAL OUTPUT				
29					
30	Observation	Predicted Incumbent Share	Residuals	Year	
31	1	50.36625104	1.333748965	1916	
32	2	38.83151521	-2.731515209	1920	
33	3	57.33733746	0.962662542	1924	
34	4	56.9562323	1.843767704	1928	
35	5	39.15663792	1.743362078	1932	
36	6	63.5365886	-1.336588599	1936	
37	7	55.53839833	-0.53839833	1940	
38	8	52.88603197	0.913968029	1944	
39	9	50.48245282	1.81754718	1948	
40	10	44.43110033	0.268899674	1952	
41	11	57.0578547	0.042145297	1956	
42	12	50.90321848	-1.003218475	1960	
43	13	60.53180525	0.668194754	1964	
44	14	49.1979777	0.202022301	1968	
45	15	59.54525482	2.254745185	1972	
46	16	49.33992153	-0.339921526	1976	
47	17	45.35561071	-0.55561071	1980	
48	18	62.07289465	-2.972894651	1984	
49	19	50.64806358	3.151936419	1988	
50	20	52.08258457	-5.682584573	1992	
51	21	53.35029717	1.349702833	1996	
52	22	51.69197089	-1.391970888	2000	

FIGURE 58-8 These figures are residuals from the presidential election equation.

From cell B5, you see that your regression explains 91.5 percent of the variation in the incumbent's vote share. From the standard error of 2.46 percent, you learn that approximately 95 percent of your forecasts should be accurate within 2*2.46 = 4.92%. Because the margin of error on presidential polls the day of the election is around 3 percent, it is amazing that your model, which does not account for the quality of the candidates, does so well! Look at Figure 58-8; you see that the only outlier was the 1992 Bush–Clinton election, in which Clinton performed 5.68 percent better than expected. This could be attributed to the fact that Clinton was a great campaigner.

Is there an Excel function I can use to make forecasts easily from a multiple regression equation?

It's tedious to make forecasts by using an equation such as equation 1, but the Excel *TREND* function makes it easy to generate forecasts from a multiple regression. You don't even have to run a regression with the Data Analysis command. The syntax of the TREND function is TREND(Known_y's,Known _x's,New_x's,Const). This function will run a regression that attempts to predict Known y's from Known x's. The results of this regression are then applied to the New x's data to generate predictions based on the fitted regression equation. If Const = TRUE, the regression intercept is calculated normally, whereas if Const= FALSE, the regression equation is fit without an intercept.

The *TREND* function is an example of an *array function*. A brief introduction to array functions was provided in Chapter 57, "Introduction to multiple regression," and a more complete discussion of array functions is offered in Chapter 87, "Array formulas and functions."

To illustrate the use of the *TREND* function, how to generate forecasts for the 1916 through 2012 elections is described by using data from only the 1916 through 2000 elections. Begin, as described in Chapter 57, by selecting the cell range (in this example, L17:L31) where you want your forecasts to go. With the pointer in the first cell of this range (cell L17), enter the =TREND(C7:C28,E7:K28,E7:K31,TRUE) formula. Next, as described in Chapter 57, press Ctrl+Shift+Enter. You now see (see Figure 58-6) the forecast for each election, generated in cells L7:L31. Note that in 2004, the incumbent (Bush) performed 4.6 percent worse than expected, and in 2008 and 2012, the candidates of the party in power (McCain and Obama) performed 1.4 percent better than expected.

Note Problems that you can work through to learn more about multiple regression are available at the end of Chapter 59, "Modeling nonlinearities and interactions."

Modeling nonlinearities and interactions

Questions answered in this chapter:

- What does it mean when we say that an independent variable has a nonlinear effect on a dependent variable?

- What does it mean when we say that the effects of two independent variables on a dependent variable interact?

- How can I test for the presence of nonlinearity and interaction in a regression?

Answers to this chapter's questions

This section provides the answers to the questions that are listed at the beginning of the chapter.

What does it mean when we say that an independent variable has a nonlinear effect on a dependent variable?

An independent variable often influences a dependent variable through a nonlinear relationship. For example, if you try to predict product sales by using an equation such as Sales = 500 − 10*Price, price influences sales linearly. This equation indicates that a unit increase in price will (at any price level) reduce sales by 10 units. If the relationship between sales and price were governed by an equation such as Sales = 500 + 4*Price − .40*Price^2, price and sales would be related nonlinearly. As shown in Figure 59-1, larger increases in price result in larger decreases in demand (see the Nonlinearity worksheet in the Interactions.xlsx file). In short, if the change in the dependent variable caused by a unit change in the independent variable is not constant, there is a nonlinear relationship between the independent and dependent variables.

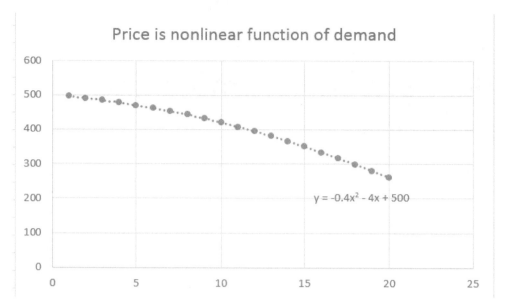

$$y = -0.4x^2 - 4x + 500$$

FIGURE 59-1 This figure shows a nonlinear relationship between demand and price.

What does it mean when we say that the effects of two independent variables on a dependent variable interact?

If the effect of one independent variable on a dependent variable depends on the value of another independent variable, you can say that the two independent variables exhibit *interaction*. For example, suppose you try to predict sales by using price and the amount spent on advertising. If the effect of changing the level of advertising dollars is large when the price is small and small when the price is high, price and advertising exhibit interaction. If the effect of changing the level of advertising dollars is the same for any price level, sales and price do not exhibit any interaction.

How can I test for the presence of nonlinearity and interaction in a regression?

To see whether an independent variable has a nonlinear effect on a dependent variable, you simply add an independent variable to the regression that equals the square of the independent variable. If the squared term has a low *p*-value (less than 0.15), you have evidence of a nonlinear relationship.

To check whether two independent variables exhibit interaction, add a term to the regression that equals the product of the independent variables. If the term has a low *p*-value (less than 0.15), you have evidence of interaction.

To illustrate, try to determine how gender and experience influence salaries at a small manufacturing company. For each employee, you are given the following set of data. You can find the information in the Data worksheet in the Interactions.xlsx file, shown in Figure 59-2:

- Annual salary (in thousands of dollars)

- Years of experience working in the manufacturing business

- Gender (1 = female, 0 = male)

Use this data to predict salary (the dependent variable) based on years of experience and gender. To test whether years of experience has a nonlinear effect on salary, add the term Experience Squared by copying the B2^2 formula from D2 to D3:D98. To test whether experience and gender have a significant interaction, add the term Experience*Gender by copying the B2*C2 formula from E2 to E3:E98. Run a regression with an Input Y Range of A1:A98 and an Input X Range of B1:E98. After selecting **Labels** in the **Regression** dialog box and clicking **OK**, you should obtain the results shown in Figure 59-3.

	A	B	C	D	E
1	Salary	Exp	Gender	Exp^2	Exp*Gender
2	55.92	5	1	25	5
3	62.40	15	0	225	0
4	67.85	12	0	144	0
5	64.81	19	0	361	0
6	58.30	9	0	81	0
7	51.94	3	0	9	0
8	36.34	12	1	144	12
9	28.39	15	1	225	15
10	73.58	8	0	64	0
11	44.17	12	1	144	12
12	57.03	1	1	1	1
13	61.59	5	0	25	0
14	63.22	14	0	196	0
15	58.16	1	1	1	1
16	47.48	3	1	9	3
17	44.43	6	1	36	6
18	59.11	4	0	16	0
19	64.56	9	0	81	0
20	64.66	18	0	324	0
21	49.10	7	1	49	7
22	69.01	14	0	196	0
23	65.00	16	0	256	0
24	37.56	11	1	121	11

FIGURE 59-2 This is the data for predicting salary based on gender and experience.

You can see that gender is insignificant (its p-value is greater than 0.15). All other independent variables are significant (meaning they have a p-value less than or equal to 0.15). You can delete the insignificant gender variable as an independent variable. To do this, copy the data into a new worksheet called **FinalRegression**. (Right-click any worksheet tab, click **Move Or Copy**, and then select the **Create A Copy** check box.) After deleting the Gender column, you obtain the regression results included in the FinalRegression worksheet and shown in Figure 59-4.

	H	I	J	K	L	M	N	O	P
4	*Regression Statistics*								
5	Multiple R	0.930645916							
6	R Square	0.866101822							
7	Adjusted R Square	0.860280162							
8	Standard Error	4.530277908							
9	Observations	97							
10									
11	ANOVA								
12		df	SS	MS	F	Significance F			
13	Regression	4	12213.26555	3053.3164	148.7723146	2.77158E-39			
14	Residual	92	1888.154449	20.523418					
15	Total	96	14101.42						
16									
17		Coefficients	Standard Error	t Stat	P-value	Lower 95%	Upper 95%	Lower 95.0%	Upper 95.0%
18	Intercept	58.30311924	1.960660525	29.736468	5.6775E-49	54.40907819	62.19716028	54.40907819	62.19716028
19	Exp	0.860472831	0.381574828	2.2550566	0.02650141	0.102632286	1.618313377	0.102632286	1.618313377
20	Gender	1.119399728	1.94092596	0.5767349	0.565527049	-2.735446764	4.974246221	-2.735446764	4.974246221
21	Exp^2	-0.035148705	0.017761027	-1.978979	0.050808362	-0.070423637	0.000126228	-0.070423637	0.000126228
22	Exp*Gender	-2.164501713	0.180872223	-11.96702	1.86636E-20	-2.523729559	-1.805273866	-2.523729559	-1.805273866

FIGURE 59-3 These are regression results that test for nonlinearity and interaction.

	H	I	J	K	L	M	N	O	P
2	SUMMARY OUTPUT								
3									
4	*Regression Statistics*								
5	Multiple R	0.930386							
6	R Square	0.865618							
7	Adjusted R Squ	0.861283							
8	Standard Error	4.513994							
9	Observations	97							
10									
11	ANOVA								
12		df	SS	MS	F	gnificance F			
13	Regression	3	12206.44	4068.813	199.6852	2.12E-40			
14	Residual	93	1894.981	20.37614					
15	Total	96	14101.42						
16									
17		Coefficient	andard Err	t Stat	P-value	Lower 95%	Upper 95%	ower 95.0%	Upper 95.0%
18	Intercept	59.05744	1.455412	40.57781	6.06E-61	56.16729	61.9476	56.16729	61.94759951
19	Exp	0.781117	0.354624	2.202664	0.03009	0.076905	1.485329	0.076905	1.485329146
20	Exp^2	-0.033594	0.017492	-1.920523	0.057856	-0.06833	0.001142	-0.06833	0.001141843
21	Exp*Gender	-2.073395	0.087774	-23.62185	4.49E-41	-2.247697	-1.899092	-2.247697	-1.899092079

FIGURE 59-4 These are the regression results after deleting the insignificant gender variable.

All independent variables are now significant (have a p-value less than or equal to 0.15). Therefore, you can predict salary (in thousands of dollars) by using the following equation (equation 1):

```
Predicted salary=59.06+.78(EXP)-.033EXP²-2.07(EXP*GENDER)
```

The negative EXP^2 term indicates that each additional year of experience has less impact on salary, which means that experience has a nonlinear effect on salary. In fact, this model shows that after 13 years of experience, each additional year of experience actually reduces salary.

Remember that gender equals 1 for a woman and 0 for a man. After substituting 1 for gender in equation 1, a woman's salary can be predicted as follows:

```
Predicted salary=59.06+78EXP-.033EXP²-2.07(EXP*1)=59.06-.033EXP²-1.29EXP
```

For a man (substituting *gender* = 0), the following equation can be used:

```
Predicted salary=59.06+.78EXP-.033EXP² -2.07(EXP*0)=59.06+.78EXP-.033EXP²
```

Thus, the interaction between gender and experience shows that each additional year of experience benefits a woman an average of 0.78 − (−1.29) = $2,070 less than a man. This indicates that women are not being treated fairly.

Problems for Chapters 57 and 58

Fizzy Drugs wants to optimize the yield from an important chemical process. The company thinks the number of pounds produced each time the process is run depends on the size of the container used, the pressure, and the temperature. The scientists involved believe the effect of changing one variable might depend on the values of other variables. The size of the process container must be between 1.3 and 1.5 cubic meters, pressure must be between 4 and 4.5 mm, and temperature must be between 22 and 30 degrees Celsius. The scientists patiently set up experiments at the lower and upper levels of the three control variables and obtain the data shown in the Fizzy.xlsx file:

1. Determine the relationship among yield, size, temperature, and pressure.

2. Discuss the interactions among pressure, size, and temperature.

3. What settings for temperature, size, and pressure would you recommend?

Here are additional multiple regression problems:

4. For 12 straight weeks, you have observed the sales (in number of cases) of canned tomatoes at Mr. D's Supermarket. (See the Grocery.xlsx file.) Each week, you keep track of the following:

    • Was a promotional notice for canned tomatoes placed in all shopping carts?

    • Was a coupon for canned tomatoes given to each customer?

    • Was a price reduction (none, 1, or 2 cents off) given?

    Use this data to determine how the preceding factors influence sales. Predict sales of canned tomatoes during a week in which you use a shopping cart notice, offer a coupon, and reduce price by 1 cent.

5. The Countryregion.xlsx file contains the following data for several underdeveloped countries:

    • Infant mortality rate

    • Adult literacy rate

    • Percentage of students finishing primary school

    • Per capita GNP

Use this data to develop an equation that can be used to predict infant mortality. Are there any outliers in this set of data? Interpret the coefficients in your equation. Within what value should 95 percent of your predictions for infant mortality be accurate?

6. The Baseball96.xlsx file gives runs scored, singles, doubles, triples, home runs, and bases stolen for each Major League Baseball team during the 1996 season. Use this data to determine the effects of singles, doubles, and other activities on run production.

7. The Cardata.xlsx file provides the following information for 392 car models:

- Cylinders

- Displacement

- Horsepower

- Weight

- Acceleration

- Miles per gallon (MPG)

Determine an equation that can be used to predict MPG. Why do you think all the independent variables are not significant?

8. The Priceads.xlsx file contains weekly unit sales of a product as well as the product price and advertising expenditures. Explain how advertising and product price influence unit sales.

9. The Teams.xlsx file contains runs scored; hit-by-pitcher; and walks, singles, doubles, triples, and home runs for Major League Baseball teams during the 2000–2006 seasons:

- Use this data to build a model that predicts how many runs a team will score based on the team's hitting statistics.

- How accurate is this model for predicting how many runs a team will score during a season?

- Suppose a team had a positive residual exceeding three times the regression's standard error. What might cause such a result?

10. A hitter's on-base percentage (OBP) is calculated as hit-by-pitcher + walks + hits/(at bats + hit-by-pitcher + walks + sacrifice flies). A hitter's slugging percentage (SLG) is total bases (home runs gets credit for four bases, triples get three, doubles two, and singles 1) divided by at-bats. The Opsslug.xlsx file contains hitting data for major league teams during the 2000–2006 seasons.

Use this data to build a model that can be used to predict runs scored by a team from a team's OBP and SLG:

- Would you recommend that a team use this model or the model from problem 9 to predict runs scored?

- How could this model be used to evaluate individual players' hitting abilities?

- Why might you be skeptical if this model was used to evaluate the hitting ability of a truly great hitter such as Albert Pujols of the St. Louis Cardinals?

11. The NFLinfo.xlsx file contains the following data for NFL teams during the 2003–2006 seasons:

- Margin = Number of points by which a team outscores its opponent

- NYP/A = Yards gained passing per pass attempt

- YR/A = Yards gained per rushing attempt

- DNYP/A = Yards gained passing by opponents per pass attempt

- DYR/A = Yards gained rushing by opponents per attempt

- TO = Turnovers by team

- DTO = Turnovers by a team's opponents

Does this data indicate that passing or rushing effectiveness has more impact on team success?

Around how many points does a turnover cost a team?

Many football fans believe you need a good rushing attack to set up the passing game. Does this data give any support to that view?

12. The Qbinfo.xlsx file lists the famous quarterback ratings for NFL quarterbacks during the 2009 season. The quarterback rating is based on the quarterback's completion percentage, percentage of passes that result in a touchdown, yards per pass attempt, and percentage of passes that are intercepted:

- Develop a formula to predict a quarterback's rating based on his season statistics.

- How accurate are your predictions?

CHAPTER 60

Analysis of variance: one-way ANOVA

Questions answered in this chapter:

- The owner of my company, which publishes computer books, wants to know whether the position of our books in the computer book section of bookstores influences sales. More specifically, does it really matter whether the books are placed in the front, back, or middle of the computer book section?

- If I am determining whether populations have significantly different means, why is the technique called *analysis of variance*?

- How can I use the results of one-way ANOVA for forecasting?

Data analysts often have data about several groups of people or items and want to determine whether the data about the groups differs significantly. Here are some examples:

- Is there a significant difference in the length of time that four doctors keep mothers in the hospital after those patients give birth?

- Does the production yield for a new drug depend on whether the size of the container in which the drug is produced is large, small, or medium?

- Does the drop in blood pressure attained after taking one of four drugs depend on the drug taken?

When you're trying to determine whether the means in several sets of data that depend on one factor are significantly different, one-way analysis of variance, or ANOVA, is the correct tool to use. In the preceding examples, the factors are the doctors, the container size, and the drug, respectively. In analyzing the data, you can choose between two hypotheses:

- *Null hypothesis*, which indicates that the means of all groups are identical.

- *Alternative hypothesis*, which indicates a statistically significant difference between the groups' means.

To test these hypotheses in Microsoft Excel, you can use Anova: Single Factor in the Data Analysis dialog box. If the *p*-value Excel computes is small (usually less than or equal to 0.15), you can conclude that the alternative hypothesis is true (the means are significantly different). If the p-value is greater than 0.15, the null hypothesis is true (the populations have identical means). Let's look at an example.

Answers to this chapter's questions

This section provides the answers to the questions that are listed at the beginning of the chapter.

The owner of my company, which publishes computer books, wants to know whether the position of our books in the computer book section of bookstores influences sales. More specifically, does it really matter whether the books are placed in the front, back, or middle of the computer book section?

The publishing company wants to know whether its books sell better when a display is set up in the front, back, or middle of the computer book section. Weekly sales (in hundreds) were monitored at 12 stores. At five stores, the books were placed in the front; at four stores, in the back; and at three stores, in the middle. Resulting sales are contained in the Signif worksheet in the Onewayanova.xlsx file, which is shown in Figure 60-1. Does the data indicate that the location of the books has a significant effect on sales?

	A	B	C		D	E
1	One-Way ANOVA					
2						
3		Front	Back		Middle	
4		7		12	10	
5		10		13	11	
6		8		15	12	
7		9		16		
8		11				

FIGURE 60-1 Book sales data.

You can assume that the 12 stores have similar sales patterns and are approximately the same size. This assumption enables you to use one-way ANOVA because you believe that at most one factor (the position of the display in the computer book section) is affecting sales. (If the stores were different sizes, you would need to analyze the data with two-way ANOVA, which is discussed in Chapter 61, "Randomized blocks and two-way ANOVA.")

To analyze the data, on the **Data** tab, click **Data Analysis** and then select **Anova: Single Factor**. Fill in the dialog box as shown in Figure 60-2.

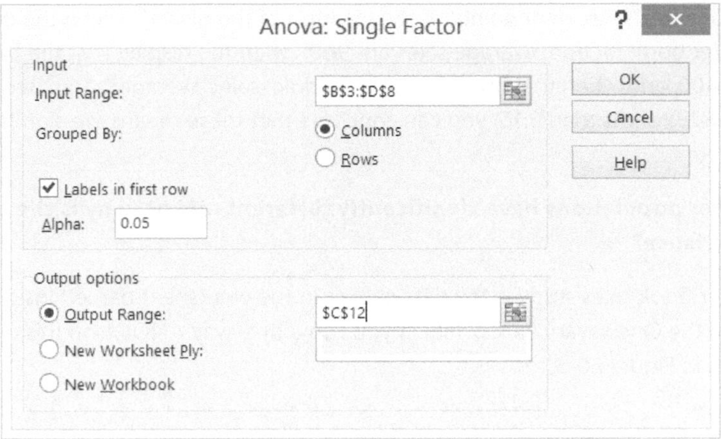

FIGURE 60-2 Anova: Single Factor dialog box.

Use the following configurations:

- The data for your input range, including labels, is in cells B3:D8.

- Select **Labels In First Row** because the first row of the input range contains labels.

- Select **Columns** because the data is organized in columns.

- Select **C12** as the upper-left cell of the output range.

- The selected alpha value is not important. You can use the default value.

After clicking **OK**, you obtain the results shown in Figure 60-3.

	C	D	E	F	G	H	I
12	**Anova: Single Factor**						
13							
14	**SUMMARY**						
15	*Groups*	*Count*	*Sum*	*Average*	*Variance*		
16	**Front**	5	45	9	2.5		
17	**Back**	4	56	14	3.333333		
18	**Middle**	3	33	11	1		
19							
20							
21	**ANOVA**						
22	*Source of Variation*	*SS*	*df*	*MS*	*F*	*P-value*	*F crit*
23	**Between Groups**	55.66667	2	27.83333	11.38636	0.00343	4.25649
24	**Within Groups**	22	9	2.444444			
25							
26	**Total**	77.66667	11				
27							
28	**est std error**	1.563472					

FIGURE 60-3 One-way ANOVA results.

In cells F16:F18, you see average sales, depending on the location of the display. When the display is at the front of the computer book section, average sales are 900; when the display is at the back of the section, sales average 1,400; and when the display is in the middle, sales average 1,100. Because the p-value of 0.003 (in cell H23) is less than 0.15, you can conclude that these means are significantly different.

If I am determining whether populations have significantly different means, why is the technique called analysis of variance?

Suppose that the data in your book sales study is the data shown in the worksheet named Insig, shown in Figure 60-4 (and in the Onewayanova.xlsx file). If you run a one-way ANOVA on this data, you obtain the results shown in Figure 60-5.

	A	B	C	D
1				
2				
3		Front	Back	Middle
4		7	2	3
5		20	16	19
6		8	25	11
7		8	13	
8		2		

FIGURE 60-4 Book store data for which the null hypothesis is accepted.

Note that the mean sales for each part of the store are exactly as before, yet the p-value of .66 indicates that you should accept the null hypothesis and conclude that the position of the display in the computer book section doesn't affect sales. The reason for this strange result is that in the second data set, you have much more variation in sales when the display is at each position in the computer book section. In the first data set, for example, the variation in sales when the display is at the front is between 700 and 1,100, whereas in the second data set, the variation in sales is between 200 and 2,000. The variation of sales within each store position is measured by the sum of the squares of data within a group. This measure is shown in cell D24 in the first data set and in cell F24 in the second. In the first data set, the sum of squares of data within groups is only 22, whereas in the second data set, the sum of squares within groups is 574! This large variation within the data points at each store position masks the variation between the groups (store positions) themselves and makes it impossible to conclude for the second data set that the difference between sales in different store positions is significant.

	E	F	G	H	I	J	K
12	**Anova: Single Factor**		Overall mean				
13			11.1666667				
14	**SUMMARY**						
15	*Groups*	*Count*	*Sum*	*Average*	*Variance*		
16	**Front**	5	45	9	44		
17	**Back**	4	56	14	90		
18	**Middle**	3	33	11	64		
19							
20							
21	**ANOVA**						
22	*Source of Variation*	*SS*	*df*	*MS*	*F*	*P-value*	*F crit*
23	**Between Groups**	55.66667	2	27.83333	0.436411	0.659334	4.25649
24	**Within Groups**	574	9	63.77778			
25							
26	**Total**	629.6667	11				
27							
28	est std err	7.986099					

FIGURE 60-5 ANOVA results accepting the null hypothesis.

How can I use the results of a one-way ANOVA for forecasting?

If there is a significant difference between group means, the best forecast for each group is simply the group's mean. Therefore, in the first data set, you predict the following:

- Sales when the display is at the front of the computer book section will be 900 books per week.

- Sales when the display is at the back will be 1,400 books per week.

- Sales when the display is in the middle will be 1,100 books per week.

If there is no significant difference between the group means, your best forecast for each observation is simply the overall mean. Thus, in the second data set, you predict weekly sales of 1,117, independent of where the books are placed.

You can also estimate the accuracy of your forecasts. The square root of the Within Groups MS (mean square) is the standard deviation of the forecasts from a one-way ANOVA. As shown in Figure 60-3, the standard deviation of forecasts for the first data set is 1.56 (see the Signif worksheet again). By rule of thumb, this means that you would expect, for example:

- During 68 percent of all the weeks in which books are placed at the front of the computer book section, sales will be between 900 − 156 = 744 and 900 + 156 = 1,056 books.

- During 95 percent of all weeks in which books are placed at the front of the computer book section, sales will be between 900 − 2(156) = 588 books and 900 + 2(156) = 1,212 books.

Problems

You can find the data for the following problems in the Chapter60data.xlsx file:

1. For patients of four cardiologists, you are given the number of days the patients stayed in the hospital after open-heart surgery:

   - Is there evidence that the doctors have different discharge policies?

   - You are 95 percent sure that a patient of Doctor 1 will stay in the hospital between what range of days?

2. A drug can be produced by using a 400-degree, 300-degree, or 200-degree oven. You are given the pounds of the drug yielded when various batches are baked at different temperatures:

   - Does temperature appear to influence the process yield?

   - What is the range of pounds of the product that you are 95 percent sure will be produced with a 200-degree oven?

   - If you believe that pressure within the container also influences process yield, does this analysis remain valid?

Randomized blocks and two-way ANOVA

Questions answered in this chapter:

- I am trying to analyze the effectiveness of my sales force. The problem is that in addition to a sales representative's effectiveness, the amount that a representative sells depends on the district to which he is assigned. How can I incorporate the district assignments of my representatives into my analysis?

- Based on my knowledge of sales representatives and districts, how can I forecast sales? How accurate are my sales forecasts?

- How can I determine whether varying the price and the amount of advertising affects the sales of a video game? How can I determine whether price and advertising interact significantly?

- How can I interpret the effects of price and advertising on sales when significant interaction between price and advertising is absent?

In many sets of data, two factors can influence a dependent variable. Here are some examples:

Factors	Dependent variable
Sales representative and district assignment	Sales
Product price and advertising expenditure	Sales
Temperature and pressure	Production yield
Surgeon and brand of stent used	Health of patient after open-heart surgery

When two factors might influence a dependent variable, randomized blocks or two-way analysis of variance (ANOVA) can be used to determine which, if any, of the factors have a significant influence on the dependent variable. With two-way ANOVA, you can also determine whether two factors exhibit a significant interaction. For example, suppose you are trying to predict sales by using product price and advertising budget. Price and advertising interact significantly if the effect of advertising depends on the product price.

In a randomized block model, you observe each possible combination of factors exactly once. You can't test for interactions in a randomized block design. In a two-way ANOVA model, you observe each combination of factors the same number of times (call it k). In this case, k must be greater than 1. In a two-way ANOVA model, you can easily test for interactions.

Answers to this chapter's questions

This section provides the answers to the questions that are listed at the beginning of the chapter.

I am trying to analyze the effectiveness of my sales force. The problem is that in addition to a sales representative's effectiveness, the amount that a representative sells depends on the district to which she is assigned. How can I incorporate the district assignments of my representatives into my analysis?

Suppose you want to determine how a sales representative and the sales district to which the representative is assigned influence product sales. To answer the question in this example, you can have each of four sales reps spend a month selling in each of five sales districts. The resulting sales are given in the *Randomized Blocks* worksheet in the Twowayanova.xlsx file and shown in Figure 61-1. For example, Rep 1 sold 20 units during the month she was assigned to District 4.

	C	D	E	F	G
5		Rep 1	Rep 2	Rep 3	Rep 4
6	Dist 1	1	3	10	12
7	Dist 2	17	12	16	14
8	Dist 3	17	21	22	25
9	Dist 4	20	10	17	23
10	Dist 5	22	21	37	32

FIGURE 61-1 Data for the randomized blocks example.

This model is called a *two-way ANOVA without replication* because two factors (district and sales representative) can influence sales, and you have only a single instance pairing each representative with each district. This model is also called a *randomized block* design because you'd like to randomize (chronologically) the assignment of representatives to districts. In other words, you'd like to ensure that the month during which Rep 1 is assigned to District 1 is equally likely to be the first, second, third, fourth, or fifth month. This randomization hopefully lessens the effect of time (a representative presumably becomes better over time) on your analysis; in a sense, you are blocking the effect of districts when you try to compare sales representatives.

To analyze this data in Microsoft Excel, click **Data Analysis** on the **Data** tab and then select **Anova: Two-Factor Without Replication**. Fill in the dialog box as shown in Figure 61-2.

You can use the following information to set up this analysis:

■ The input range data is in cells C5:G10.

■ Select **Labels** because the first row of the input range contains labels.

■ Enter **B12** as the upper-left cell of the output range.

- The alpha value determines the number shown in the F Crit column. You will not need the information in the F Crit column so, throughout this chapter, you can use the default alpha value of 0.05.

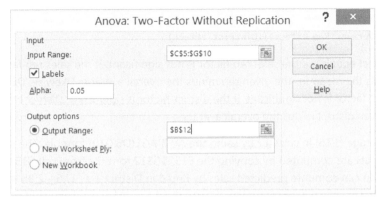

FIGURE 61-2 Anova: Two-Factor Without Replication dialog box for setting up a randomized blocks model.

The output you obtain is shown in Figure 61-3. (The results in cells G12:G24 were not created by the Excel Data Analysis feature. Formulas were entered in those cells, as is explained later in the chapter.)

B	C	D	E	F	G	H
12 Anova: Two-Factor Without Replication					17.6	
13						
14 SUMMARY	Count	Sum	Average	Variance		
15 Dist 1	4	26	6.5	28.33333	-11 1	
16 Dist 2	4	59	14.75	4.916667	-2.85	
17 Dist 3	4	85	21.25	10.91667	3.65	
18 Dist 4	4	70	17.5	31	-0.1	
19 Dist 5	4	112	28	60.66667	10.4	
20					-17.6	
21 Rep 1	5	77	15.4	69.3	-2.2	
22 Rep 2	5	67	13.4	59.3	-4.2	
23 Rep 3	5	102	20.4	104.3	2.8	
24 Rep 4	5	106	21.2	67.7	3.6	
25						
26						
27 ANOVA						
28 Source of Variation	SS	df	MS	F	P-value	F crit
29 Rows	1011.3	4	252.825	15.87598	9.74E-05	3.25917
30 Columns	216.4	3	72.13333	4.529566	0.024095	3.49029
31 Error	191.1	12	15.925			
32		stdev	3.990614			
33 Total	1418.8	19				

FIGURE 61-3 Randomized blocks output.

To determine whether the row factor (districts) or column factor (sales representatives) has a significant effect on sales, just look at the p-value. If the p-value for a factor is low (less than .15), the factor has a significant effect on sales. The row p-value (.0000974) and column p-value (.024) are both less than .15, so both the district and the representative have a significant effect on sales.

Based on my knowledge of sales representatives and districts, how can I forecast sales? How accurate are my sales forecasts?

How should you predict product sales? You can predict sales during a month by using equation 1, shown here:

```
Predicted sales=Overall average+(Rep effect)+(District effect)
```

In this equation, *Rep effect* equals 0 if the sales rep factor is not significant. If the sales rep factor is significant, *Rep effect* equals the mean for the given rep minus the overall average. Likewise, *District effect* equals 0 if the district factor is not significant. If the district factor is significant, *District effect* equals the mean for the given district minus the overall average.

Compute the overall average (17.6) in cell G12 by using the AVERAGE(D6:G10) formula. The representative and district effects are computed by copying the E15–$G$12 formula from cell G15 to G16:G24. As an example, you can compute predicted sales by Rep 4 in District 2 as 17.6 − 2.85 + 3.6 = 18.35. This value is computed in cell D38 (see Figure 61-4) with the G12+G16+G24 formula. If the district effect is significant and the sales representative effect is not, predicted sales for Rep 4 in District 2 would be 17.6 − 2.85 = 14.75.

	C	D	E
36	District 2		
37	Rep 4 Forecast		
38	Mean	18.35	
39	Lower	10.3688	
40	Upper	26.3312	

FIGURE 61-4 Forecast for sales in District 2 by Rep 4.

As in one-way ANOVA, the standard deviation of the forecast errors is the square root of the mean square error shown in cell E31. You can compute this standard deviation in cell E32 with the SQRT(E31) formula. Thus, you can be 95 percent sure that if Rep 4 is assigned to District 2, monthly sales will be between 18.35 − 2(3.99) = 10.37 and 18.35 + 2(3.99) = 26.33. These limits are computed in cell D39 and D40 with the D38−2*E32 and D38+2*E32 formulas, respectively.

How can I determine whether varying the price and the amount of advertising affects the sales of a video game? How can I determine whether price and advertising interact significantly?

When you have more than one observation for each combination of the row and column factors, you have a two-factor ANOVA *with* replication. To perform this sort of analysis, Excel requires you to have the same number of observations for each row-and-column combination.

In addition to testing for the significance of the row and column factors, you can also test for significant interaction between them. For example, if you want to understand how price and advertising affect sales, an interaction between price and advertising would indicate that the effect of an advertising change would depend on the price level (or, equivalently, the effect of a price change would depend on the advertising level). A lack of interaction between price and advertising would mean that the effect of a price change would not depend on the level of advertising.

As an example of two-factor ANOVA with replication, suppose you want to determine how price and advertising level affect the monthly sales of a video game. In the Two Way ANOVA No Interaction worksheet in the Twowayanova.xlsx file, you can find the data shown in Figure 61-5. During the three months in which advertising was low and price was medium, for example, 21, 20, and 16 units were sold.

	B	C	D	E	F	G
1		Average	25.04			
2		Price				
3			Low	Medium	High	Effect
4		Low	41	21	10	-5.593
5	Adv		25	20	11	
6			23	16	8	
7		Medium	28	28	11	-1.815
8			30	22	22	
9			32	18	18	
10		High	35	26	21	7.4074
11			45	40	26	
12			47	32	20	
13		Effect	8.963	-0.2593	-8.7	

FIGURE 61-5 Video game sales data; no interaction.

Notice that for each price/advertising combination, there are exactly three observations. In cell D1, the overall average (25.037) of all observations with the AVERAGE(D4:F12) formula is computed. In cells G4, G7, and G10, the effect for each level of advertising is computed. For example, the effect of having a low level of advertising equals the average for low advertising minus the overall average. In cell G4, the low advertising effect of 5.59 with the AVERAGE(D4:F6)–$D$1 formula is computed. In a similar fashion, the effect of each price level by copying the AVERAGE(D4:D12)–$D$1 formula from D13 to E13:F13 is computed.

To analyze this data, click **Data Analysis** on the **Data** tab, and then select **Anova: Two-Factor With Replication** in the **Data Analysis** dialog box. Fill in the dialog box as shown in Figure 61-6.

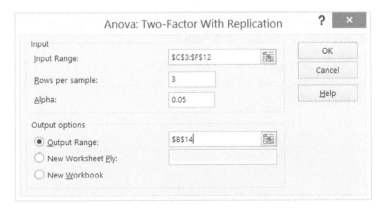

FIGURE 61-6 Anova: Two-Factor With Replication dialog box for running a two-factor ANOVA with replication.

You can use the following information to set up the analysis:

- The input range data, including labels, is in C3:F12. In two-way ANOVA with replication, Excel requires a label for each level of the column effect in the first row of each column in the input range. Thus, you can enter Low, Medium, and High in cells D3:F3 to indicate the possible price levels. Excel also requires a label for each level of the row effect in the first column of the input range. These labels must appear in the row that marks the beginning of the data for each level. Thus, you can place labels corresponding to low, medium, and high levels of advertising in cells C4, C7, and C10.

- In the Rows Per Sample box, enter 3 because you have three replications for each combination of price and advertising level.

- The upper-left cell of your output range is B14.

The only important portion of the output is the ANOVA table, which is shown in Figure 61-7.

	B	C	D	E	F	G	H	I
42	ANOVA							
43	*Source of Variation*	*SS*	*df*	*MS*	*F*	*P-value*	*F crit*	*F crit*
44	Sample	804.963	2	402.481	13.5	0.0003	3.5546	3.55456109
45	Columns	1405.407	2	702.704	23.6	9E-06	3.5546	3.55456109
46	Interaction	50.59259	4	12.6481	0.42	0.7888	2.9277	2.92774871
47	Within	536	18	29.7778				
48								
49	Total	2796.963	26					

FIGURE 61-7 Two-way ANOVA with replication output; no interaction.

As with randomized blocks, an effect (including interactions) is significant if it has a p-value that's less than .15. Here, Sample (this is the row for advertising effect) and Price (shown in the row labeled Columns) are highly significant, and there is no significant interaction. (The interaction p-value is .79!) Therefore, you can conclude that price and advertising influence sales and that the effect of advertising on sales does not depend on the price level. Figure 61-8 graphs average sales for each price advertising combination, and demonstrates the fact that price and advertising do not exhibit a significant interaction. (See the Graph No Interaction worksheet.)

Notice that as advertising increases, average sales increase at roughly the same rate, whether the price level is low, medium, or high. Basically, you can recognize No Interaction by the fact that the series for each price level are nearly parallel.

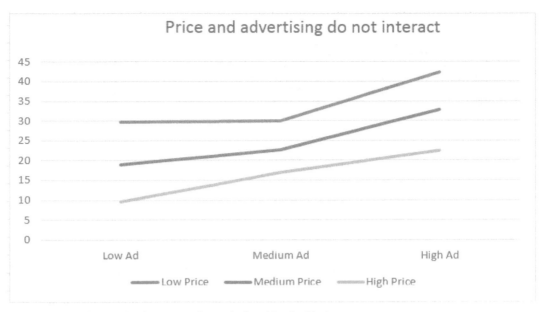

FIGURE 61-8 No interaction between price and advertising in this data set.

How can I interpret the effects of price and advertising on sales when significant interaction between price and advertising is absent?

In the absence of a significant interaction, you can forecast sales in a two-factor ANOVA with replication in the same way that you do in a two-factor ANOVA without replication. Here's the equation to use (equation 2):

```
Predicted sales=Overall average+[Row or advertising effect(if significant)]
   +[Column or price effect(if significant)]
```

This analysis assumes that price and advertising are the only factors that affect sales. If sales are highly seasonal, seasonality would need to be incorporated into the analysis. (Seasonality is discussed in Chapter 63, "Winters's method," and Chapter 65, "Forecasting in the presence of special events.") For example, when price is high and advertising is medium, predicted sales are given by 25.037 + (–1.814) + (–8.704) = 14.52. (See cell E54 in Figure 61-9, which shows the Two Way ANOVA No Interaction worksheet again.) In Figure 61-5, shown earlier, you can see that the overall average is equal to 25.037, the medium advertising effect equals –1.814, and the high price effect equals –8.704.

	B	C	D	E	F	G	H	I
42	ANOVA							
43	*Source of Variation*	*SS*	*df*	*MS*	*F*	*P-value*	*F crit*	*F crit*
44	Sample	804.963	2	402.481	13.5	0.0003	3.5546	3.55456109
45	Columns	1405.407	2	702.704	23.6	9E-06	3.5546	3.55456109
46	Interaction	50.59259	4	12.6481	0.42	0.7888	2.9277	2.92774871
47	Within	536	18	29.7778				
48								
49	Total	2796.963	26					
50								
51				Stdev	5.4569			
52				Medium Ad				
53				High Price				
54				Mean	14.5185			
55				Lower	3.60471			
56				Upper	25.4323			

FIGURE 61-9 Forecasts for sales with high price and medium advertising.

The standard deviation of the forecast errors equals the square root of your mean squared within error:

$$\sqrt{29.78} = 5.46$$

You can be 95 percent sure that the forecast is accurate within 10.92 units. In other words, you are 95 percent sure that sales during a month with high price and medium advertising will be between 3.60 and 25.43 units.

In the Two Way ANOVA with Interaction worksheet, the data from the previous example was changed to the data shown in Figure 61-10. After running the analysis for a two-factor ANOVA with replication, the results shown in Figure 61-11 were obtained.

	C	D	E	F	G
1					
2				Price	
3					
4			Low	Medium	High
5		Low	41	21	15
6	Adv		25	20	14
7			23	16	13
8		Medium	28	28	14
9			30	22	13
10			32	18	12
11		High	50	34	13
12			51	40	13
13			52	32	13

FIGURE 61-10 Sales data with interaction between price and advertising.

	C	D	E	F	G	H	I
43	ANOVA						
44	*Source of Variation*	*SS*	*df*	*MS*	*F*	*P-value*	*F crit*
45	Sample	828.96	2	414.5	24.22	7.86E-06	3.55456
46	Columns	2498.7	2	1249	73.02	2.31E-09	3.55456
47	Interaction	509.93	4	127.5	7.45	0.001006	2.92775
48	Within	308	18	17.11			
49							
50	Total	4145.6	26				
51		Std dev	4.137				

FIGURE 61-11 Output for the two-factor ANOVA with interaction.

In this data set, the *p*-value for interaction is .001. When you see a low *p*-value (less than .15) for interaction, *you do not even check p-values for row and column factors.* You simply forecast sales for any price and advertising combination to equal the mean of the three observations involving that price and advertising combination. For example, the best forecast for sales during a month with high advertising and medium price is:

$$\frac{34 + 40 + 32}{4} = \frac{106}{3} = 35.555 \; units$$

The standard deviation of forecast errors is again the square root of the mean square within:

$$(\sqrt{17.11} = 4.14)$$

Thus, you can be 95 percent sure that the sales forecast is accurate within 8.26 units.

Figure 61-12 Illustrates why this data exhibits a significant interaction between price and advertising. For a low and medium price, increased advertising increases average sales, but if price is high, increased advertising has no effect on average sales. This explains why you cannot use equation 2 to forecast sales when a significant interaction is present. After all, how can you talk about an advertising effect when the effect of advertising depends on the price?

The key thing to notice about this graph is that the different series are not parallel. This tells you that at different price levels, changes in advertising have different effects on sales.

Two-way ANOVA with significant interaction

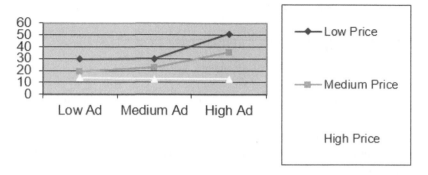

FIGURE 61-12 Price and advertising exhibit a significant interaction in this set of data.

Problems

The data for the following problems is in the Ch61.xlsx file.

1. You believe that pressure (high, medium, or low) and temperature (high, medium, or low) influence the yield of a production process. Given this theory, determine the answers to the following problems:

   - Use the data in the Problem 1 worksheet to determine how temperature and/or pressure influence the yield of the process.

   - With high pressure and low temperature, you're 95 percent sure that process yield will be in what range?

2. You are trying to determine how the particular sales representative and the number of sales calls (one, three, or five) made to a doctor influence the amount (in thousands of dollars) that each doctor prescribes of your drug. Use the data in the Problem 2 worksheet to determine the answers to the following problems:

   - How do the representative and number of sales calls influence sales volume?

   - If Rep 3 makes five sales calls to a doctor, you're 95 percent sure she will generate prescriptions within what range of dollars?

3. Answer the questions in Problem 2 by using the data in the Problem 3 worksheet.

4. The Coupondata.xlsx file contains information on sales of peanut butter for weeks when a coupon was given out (or not) and advertising was done (or not) in the Sunday paper. Describe how the coupon and advertising influence peanut butter sales.

CHAPTER 62

Using moving averages to understand time series

Question answered in this chapter:

- I'm trying to analyze the upward trend in quarterly revenues of Amazon.com since 1996. Fourth quarter sales in the United States are usually larger (because of Christmas) than sales during the first quarter of the following year. This pattern obscures the upward trend in sales. How can I show the upward trend in revenues graphically?

Answer to this chapter's question

This section provides the answer to the question that is listed at the beginning of the chapter.

Time series data simply displays the same quantity measured at different points in time. For example, the data in the Amazon.com.xlsx file, a subset of which is shown in Figure 62-1, displays the time series for quarterly revenues in millions of dollars for Amazon.com. The data covers the time interval from the fourth quarter of 1995 through the third quarter of 2012.

To graph this time series, select the C2:D70 range, which contains the quarter number (the first quarter is Quarter 1, and the last is Quarter 69) and Amazon quarterly revenues (in millions of dollars). Then choose **Chart** on the **Insert** tab and the second option under the **Scatter** chart type (**Scatter With Smooth Lines And Markers**). The time series plot is shown in Figure 62-2.

	A	B	C	D
1				millions
2	Year	Season	Quarter#	Revenue
3	1995	4	1	0.511
4	1996	1	2	0.875
5	1996	2	3	2.23
6	1996	3	4	4.173
7	1996	4	5	8.468
8	1997	1	6	16.005
9	1997	2	7	27.855
10	1997	3	8	37.887
11	1997	4	9	66.04
12	1998	1	10	87.361
13	1998	2	11	115.982
14	1998	3	12	153.649
15	1998	4	13	252.893
16	1999	1	14	293.643
17	1999	2	15	314.376
18	1999	3	16	355.778
19	1999	4	17	676.042
20	2000	1	18	573.889
21	2000	2	19	577.876
22	2000	3	20	637.858

FIGURE 62-1 Quarterly revenues for Amazon.com sales.

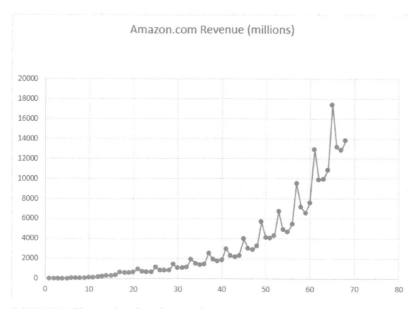

FIGURE 62-2 Time series plot of quarterly Amazon.com revenues.

There is an upward trend in revenues, but the fact that fourth-quarter revenues dwarf revenues during the first three quarters of each year makes it hard to spot the trend. Because there are four quarters per year, it would be nice to graph average revenues during the last four quarters. This is called a *four-period moving average*. Using a four-quarter moving average smooths out the seasonal influence because each average will contain one data point for each quarter. Such a graph is called a *moving average graph* because the plotted average moves over time. Moving average graphs also smooth out random variation, which helps you get a better idea of what is going on with your data.

To create a moving average graph of quarterly revenues, you can modify the chart. Select the graph and then click a data point until all the data points are displayed in blue. Right-click any point, click **Add Trendline**, and then select **Moving Average**. Set the period equal to **4**. Microsoft Excel now creates the four-quarter moving average trend curve that's shown in Figure 62-3. (See the Amazon.com.xlsx file.)

For each quarter, Excel plots the average of the current quarter and the last three quarters. Of course, for a four-quarter moving average, the moving average curve starts with the fourth data point. The moving average curve makes it clear that Amazon.com's revenues had a steady upward trend. In fact, the slope of the four-quarter moving average appears to be increasing. In all likelihood, the slope of this moving average graph will eventually level off, resulting in a graph that looks like an S curve. The Excel Trend Curve feature cannot fit S curves, but the Excel 2013 Solver can be used to fit S curves to data. See *Marketing Analytics* by Wayne Winston (John Wiley, in press) for an explanation of how to fit S curves to data.

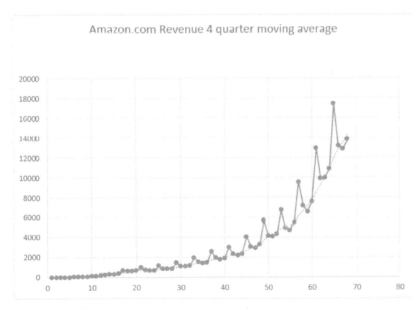

FIGURE 62-3 Four-quarter moving average trend curve.

Problem

1. The Ch62data.xlsx file contains quarterly revenues for GM, Ford, and GE. Construct a four-quarter moving average trend curve for each company's revenues. Describe what you learn from each trend curve.

CHAPTER 63

Winters's method

You often need to predict future values of a time series, such as monthly costs or monthly product revenues. This is usually difficult because the characteristics of any time series are constantly changing. Smoothing or adaptive methods are usually best suited for forecasting future values of a time series. This chapter describes the most powerful smoothing method: *Winters's* method. To help you understand how Winters's method works, I'll use it to forecast monthly housing starts in the United States. Housing starts are simply the number of new homes whose construction begins during a month. I'll begin by describing the three key characteristics of a time series.

Time series characteristics

The behavior of most time series can be explained by understanding three characteristics: base, trend, and seasonality:

- The base of a series describes the series' current level in the absence of any seasonality. For example, suppose the base level for US housing starts is 160,000. In this case, you can believe that if the current month were an average month relative to other months of the year, 160,000 housing starts would occur.

- The trend of a time series is the percentage increase per period in the base. Thus, a trend of 1.02 means that you estimate that housing starts are increasing by 2 percent each month.

- The seasonality (seasonal index) for a period tells you how far above or below a typical month you can expect housing starts to be. For example, if the December seasonal index is .8, then December housing starts are 20 percent below a typical month. If the June seasonal index is 1.3, then June housing starts are 30 percent higher than a typical month.

Parameter definitions

After observing month t, you will have used all data observed through the end of month t to estimate the following quantities of interest:

- L_t = Level of series

- T_t = Trend of series

- S_t = Seasonal index for current month

The key to Winters's method is the following three equations, which are used to update L_t, T_t, and S_t. In the following formulas, *alp*, *bet*, and *gam* are called *smoothing parameters*. You choose the values of these parameters to optimize forecasts. In the following formulas, c equals the number of periods in a seasonal cycle (c = 12 months, for example) and x_t equals the observed value of the time series at time t:

- Formula 1: $L_t = alp(x_t/s_{t-c}) + (1 - alp)(L_{t-1} \cdot T_{t-1})$

- Formula 2: $T_t = bet(L_t/L_{t-1}) + (1 - bet)T_{t-1}$

- Formula 3: $S_t = gam(x_t/L_t) + (1 - gam)s_{t-c}$

Formula 1 indicates that the new base estimate is a weighted average of the current observation (deseasonalized) and the last period's base updated by the last trend estimate. Formula 2 indicates that the new trend estimate is a weighted average of the ratio of the current base to the last period's base (this is a current estimate of trend) and the last period's trend. Formula 3 indicates that you update your seasonal index estimate as a weighted average of the estimate of the seasonal index based on the current period and the previous estimate. Note that larger values of the smoothing parameters correspond to putting more weight on the current observation.

You can define $F_{t,k}$ as your forecast (F) after period t for the period $t+k$. This results in the formula $F_{t,k} = L_t \cdot (T_t)^k s_{t+k-c}$. (I refer to this as formula 4.)

This formula first uses the current trend estimate to update the base k periods forward. Then the resulting base estimate for period $t + k$ is adjusted by the appropriate seasonal index.

Initializing Winters's method

To start Winters's method, you must have initial estimates for the series base, trend, and seasonal indexes. In this example, monthly housing starts for years 1986 and 1987 were used to initialize Winters's method. Smoothing parameters were then chosen to optimize one-month-ahead forecasts for years 1988 through 1996. See Figure 63-1 and the House2.xlsx file. Here are the steps that were followed.

	A	B	C	D	E	F	G	H	I	J
1	DATE	HS							1987 mean	150.45
2	Jan-86	105.4							1986 mean	145.142
3	Feb-86	95.4							Trend	1.003
4	Mar-86	145								
5	Apr-86	175.8								
6	May-86	170.2								
7	Jun-86	163.2								
8	Jul-86	160.7								
9	Aug-86	160.7								
10	Sep-86	147.7					alp	bet	gam	
11	Oct-86	173					0.493579	0.01481	0.2724162	
12	Nov-86	124.1								
13		120.5					seasonal indices			
14	Jan-87	115.6					0.747653			
15	Feb-87	107.2					0.685405			
16	Mar-87	151					1.001381			
17	Apr-87	188.2					1.231428			
18	May-87	186.6					1.207071			
19	Jun-87	183.6					1.17324			
20	Jul-87	172					1.125539			
21	Aug-87	163.8			MAPE	0.0731	1.097798			
22	Sep-87	154					1.020665			
23	Oct-87	154.8					1.108962			
24	Nov-87	115.6	Base	Trend	Forecast	APE	0.810916			
25	Dec-87	113	143	1.003			0.789941			
26	Jan-88	105.1	142	1.003	107.271	0.0207	0.745544			
27	Feb-88	102.8	146.2	1.003	97.6351	0.0502	0.69028			
28	Mar-88	141.2	143.9	1.003	146.844	0.04	0.995969			
29	Apr-88	159.3	136.9	1.002	177.676	0.1154	1.212913			
30	May-88	158	134.1	1.002	165.634	0.0483	1.199217			

FIGURE 63-1 Initialization of Winters's method.

- **Step 1** Estimate, for example, the January seasonal index as the average of January housing starts for 1986 and 1987 divided by the average monthly starts for 1986 and 1987. Therefore, copying the =AVERAGE(B2,B14)/AVERAGE($B$2:$B$25) formula from G14 to G15:G25 generates the estimates of seasonal indexes. For example, the January estimate is 0.75, and the June estimate is 1.17.

- **Step 2** To estimate the average monthly trend, divide the twelfth root of the 1987 mean starts by the 1986 mean starts. Compute this in cell J3 (and copy it to cell D25) with the =(J1/J2)^(1/12) formula.

- **Step 3** Going into January 1987, estimate the base of the series as the deseasonalized December 1987 value. This was computed in C25 with the =(B25/G25) formula.

Estimating the smoothing constants

Now you're ready to estimate smoothing constants. In column C, you can update the series base; in column D, the series trend; and in column G, the seasonal indexes. In column E, compute the forecast for next month and, in column F, compute the absolute percentage error for each month. Finally, use the Solver to choose values for the smoothing constants that minimize the sum of the absolute percentage errors. Here's the process:

- **Step 1** In G11:I11, enter trial values (between 0 and 1) for the smoothing constants.

- **Step 2** In C26:C119, compute the updated series level with formula 1 by copying the =alp*(B26/G14)+(1−alp)*(C25*D25) formula from C26 to C27:C119.

- **Step 3** In D26:D119, use formula 2 to update the series trend, copying the =bet*(C26/C25)+(1–bet)*D25 formula from D26 to D27:D119.

- **Step 4** In G26:G119, use formula 3 to update the seasonal indexes, copying the =gam*(B26/C26)+(1–gam)*G14 formula from G26 to G27:G119.

- **Step 5** In E26:E119, use formula 4 to compute the forecast for the current month by copying the =(C25*D25)*G14 formula from E26 to E27:E119.

- **Step 6** In F26:F119, compute the absolute percentage error for each month by copying the =ABS(B26-E26)/B26 formula from F26 to F27:F119.

- **Step 7** Compute the average absolute percentage error for years 1988 through 1996 in F21 with the =AVERAGE(F26:F119) formula.

- **Step 8** Now use Solver to determine smoothing parameter values that minimize the average absolute percentage error. The Solver Parameters dialog box is shown in Figure 63-2.

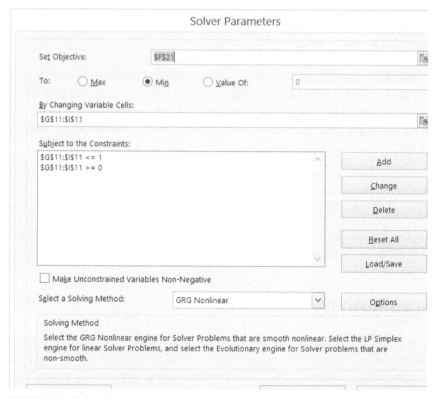

FIGURE 63-2 Solver Parameters dialog box for Winters's model.

Smoothing parameters (G11:I11) were used to minimize the average absolute percentage error (cell F21). The Solver ensures that you find the best combination of smoothing constants. Smoothing constants must be between 0 and 1. Here, *alp* = .50, *bet* = .01, and *gam* = .27 minimize the average absolute percentage error. You might find slightly different values for the smoothing constants, but you should obtain a mean absolute percentage error (MAPE) close to 7.3 percent. In this example, many combinations of the smoothing constants give forecasts having approximately the same MAPE. Your one-month-ahead forecasts are off by an average of 7.3 percent.

Remarks

- Instead of choosing smoothing parameters to optimize one-period forecast errors, you could, for example, choose to optimize the average absolute percentage error incurred in forecasting total housing starts for the next six months.

- If at the end of month t you want to forecast sales for the next four quarters, you would simply add $f^{t,1} + f^{t,2} + f^{t,3} + f^{t,4}$. If you want, you could choose smoothing parameters to minimize the absolute percentage error incurred in estimating sales for the next year.

Problems

All the data for the following problems is in the Quarterly.xlsx file:

1. Use Winters's method to forecast one-quarter-ahead revenues for Apple.

2. Use Winters's method to forecast one-quarter-ahead revenues for Amazon.com.

3. Use Winters's method to forecast one-quarter-ahead revenues for Home Depot.

4. Use Winters's method to forecast total revenues for the next two quarters for Home Depot.

CHAPTER 64

Ratio-to-moving-average forecast method

Questions answered in this chapter:

- What is the trend of a time series?

- How can I define seasonal indexes for a time series?

- Is there an easy way to incorporate trend and seasonality into forecasting future product sales?

Often, you need a simple, accurate method to predict future quarterly revenues of a corporation or future monthly sales of a product. The *ratio-to-moving-average method* provides an accurate, easy-to-use forecasting method for these situations.

In the Ratioma.xlsx file, you are given data for sales of a product during 20 quarters (shown later in Figure 64-1 in rows 5 through 24), and you want to predict sales during the next four quarters (quarters 21–24). This time series has both trend and seasonality.

Answers to this chapter's questions

This section provides the answers to the questions that are listed at the beginning of the chapter.

What is the trend of a time series?

A trend of 10 units per quarter means, for example, that sales are increasing by 10 units per quarter, whereas a trend of –5 units per quarter means that sales tend to decrease 5 units per quarter.

How do I define seasonal indexes for a time series?

We know that Walmart sees a large increase in its sales during the fourth quarter (because of the holiday season). If you do not recognize this, you would have trouble coming up with good forecasts of quarterly Walmart revenues. The concept of seasonal indexes helps you understand a company's sales pattern better. The quarterly seasonal indexes for Walmart revenues are as follows:

- Quarter 1 (January through March): .90

- Quarter 2 (April through June): .98

- Quarter 3 (July through September): .96

- Quarter 4 (October through December): 1.16

These indexes imply, for example, that sales during a fourth quarter are typically 16 percent higher than sales during an average quarter. *Seasonal indexes must average out to 1.*

To see whether you understand seasonal indexes, try to answer the following question: Suppose that during Quarter 4 of 2013, Walmart has sales of $200 billion, and during Quarter 1 of 2014, Walmart has sales of $180 billion. Are things getting better or worse for Walmart? The key idea here is to *deseasonalize* sales and express each quarter's sales in terms of an average quarter. For example, the Quarter 4 2013 sales are equivalent to selling 200/1.16 = $172.4 billion in an average quarter, and the Quarter 1 2014 sales are equivalent to selling 180/.9 = $200 billion in an average quarter. Thus, even though Walmart's actual sales decreased 10 percent, sales appear to be increasing by (200/172.4) − 1 = 16 percent per quarter. This simple example shows how important it is to understand your company's or product's seasonal indexes.

Is there an easy way to incorporate trend and seasonality into forecasting future product sales?

Now let's turn to the simple ratio-to-moving-average forecasting method. This technique enables you to estimate a time series' trend and seasonal indexes easily and makes it easy to generate forecasts of future values of the time series. The work done for this question is shown in Figure 64-1 and the Ratioma.xlsx file.

	B	C	D	E	F	G	H	I	J	K	L
1				slope	6.9387868						
2				intercept	30.166176				quarter	seasonal index	normalized
3									1	0.818547	0.8137368
4	Quarter#	Year	Quarter	Sales	4 period MA	Centered MA	Actual/CMA	Forecast	2	0.93934	0.9338196
5	1	1	1	24					3	1.067364	1.0610914
6	2	1	2	44	52				4	1.198394	1.1913522
7	3	1	3	61	58	55.00	1.11				
8	4	1	4	79	63.5	60.75	1.30				
9	5	2	1	48	71	67.25	0.71				
10	6	2	2	66	77.5	74.25	0.89				
11	7	2	3	91	82.5	80.00	1.14				
12	8	2	4	105	87.25	84.88	1.24				
13	9	3	1	68	89.5	88.38	0.77				
14	10	3	2	85	94.5	92.00	0.92				
15	11	3	3	100	104.25	99.38	1.01				
16	12	3	4	125	114.25	109.25	1.14				
17	13	4	1	107	123.75	119.00	0.90				
18	14	4	2	125	132.25	128.00	0.98				
19	15	4	3	138	139.25	135.75	1.02				
20	16	4	4	159	146.75	143.00	1.11				
21	17	5	1	135	156	151.38	0.89				
22	18	5	2	155	164.25	160.13	0.97				
23	19	5	3	175							
24	20	5	4	192							
25	21	6	1			175.880699		143.121			
26	22	6	2			182.819485		170.72			
27	23	6	3			189.758272		201.351			
28	24	6	4			196.697059		234.335			

FIGURE 64-1 Data for the ratio-to-moving-average example.

You begin by trying to estimate the deseasonalized level of the series during each period (using centered moving averages). Then you can fit a trend line to your deseasonalized estimates (in column G). Next, determine the seasonal index for each quarter. Finally, estimate the future level of the series by extrapolating the trend line and then predict future sales by reseasonalizing the trend line estimate:

- **Calculating moving averages**   To begin, compute a four-quarter moving average (four quarters eliminates seasonality) for each quarter by averaging the prior quarter, the current quarter, and the next two quarters. To do this, copy the AVERAGE(E5:E8) formula from F6 to F7:F22. For example, for Quarter 2, the moving average is .25*(24 + 44 + 61 + 79) = 52.

- **Calculating centered moving averages**   The moving average for Quarter 2 is centered at Quarter 2.5, whereas the moving average for Quarter 3 is centered at Quarter 3.5. Averaging these two moving averages gives a centered moving average, which estimates the level of the process at the end of Quarter 3. Copying the AVERAGE(F6:F7) formula from cell G7 gives you an estimate of the level of the series during each series—without seasonality!

- **Fitting a trend line to the centered moving averages**   You use the centered moving averages to fit a trend line that can be used to estimate the future level of the series.

  In F1, use the SLOPE(G7:G22,B7:B22) formula to find the slope of the trend line and, in cell F2, use the INTERCEPT(G7:G22,B7:B22) formula to find the intercept of the trend line. You can now estimate the level of the series during Quarter t to be $6.94t + 30.17$. Copying the Intercept+Slope*B23 formula from G25 to G26:G28 computes the estimated level of the series from Quarter 21 onward.

- **Computing the seasonal indexes**   Recall that a seasonal index of, say, 2 for a quarter means sales in that quarter are twice sales during an average quarter, and a seasonal index of .5 for a quarter means that sales during that quarter are half of an average quarter. To determine the seasonal indexes, begin by calculating *actual sales/centered moving average* for each quarter for which you have sales. To do this, copy the =E7/G7 formula from cell H7 to H8:H22. You'll see, for example, that during each first quarter, sales were 77, 71, 90, and 89 percent of average, so you can estimate the seasonal index for Quarter 1 as the average of these four numbers (82 percent). To calculate the initial seasonal index estimates, copy the AVERAGEIF($D$7: $D$22,J3,$H$7:$H$22) formula from cell K5 to K6:K8. This formula averages the four estimates you have for Quarter 1 seasonality.

  Unfortunately, the seasonal indexes do not average exactly to 1. To ensure that the final seasonal indexes average to 1, copy the K3/AVERAGE($K$3:$K$6) formula from L3 to L4:L6.

- **Forecasting sales during Quarters 21–24**   To create the sales forecast for each future quarter, you simply multiply the trend line estimate for the quarter's level (from column G) by the appropriate seasonal index. Copying the VLOOKUP(D25,season,3)*G25 formula from cell G25 to G26:G28 computes the final forecast for Quarters 21–24.

If you think the trend of the series has changed recently, you can estimate the series' trend based on more recent data. For example, you could use the centered moving averages for Quarters 13–18 to get a more recent trend estimate with the SLOPE(G17:G22,B17:B22) formula. This yields an estimated trend of 8.09 units per quarter. If you want to forecast Quarter 22 sales, for example, you would add 4(8.09) to the last centered moving average you have (from Quarter 18) of 160.13 to estimate the level of the series in Quarter 22. Then multiplying by the Quarter 2 seasonal index of .933 yields a final forecast for Quarter 22 sales of (160.13 + 4(8.09))*(.933) = 179.6 units.

Problem

1. The Walmartdata.xlsx file contains quarterly revenues of Walmart during years 1994–2009. Use the ratio-to-moving-average method to forecast revenues for Quarters 3 and 4 in 2009 and Quarters 1 and 2 in 2010. Use Quarters 53–60 to create a trend estimate that you use in your forecasts.

CHAPTER 65

Forecasting in the presence of special events

Questions answered in this chapter:

- How can I determine whether specific factors influence customer traffic?

- How can I evaluate forecast accuracy?

- How can I check whether my forecast errors are random?

For a student project in the early 1990s (before direct deposit!), a class and I attempted to forecast the number of customers visiting the Eastland Plaza Branch of the Indiana University (IU) Credit Union each day. Interviews with the branch manager made it clear that the following factors affected the number of customers:

- Month of the year

- Day of the week

- Whether the day was a faculty or staff payday

- Whether the day before or the day after was a holiday

Answers to this chapter's questions

This section provides the answers to the questions that are listed at the beginning of the chapter.

How can I determine whether specific factors influence customer traffic?

The data collected is contained in the Original worksheet in the Creditunion.xlsx file, shown in Figure 65-1. If you try to run a regression on this data by using dummy variables (as described in Chapter 58, "Incorporating qualitative factors into multiple regression"), the dependent variable would be the number of customers arriving each day (the data in column E). You would need 19 independent variables:

- Eleven to account for the month (12 months minus 1)

- Four to account for the day of the week (5 business days minus 1)

- Two to account for the types of paydays that occur each month

- Two to account for whether a particular day follows or precedes a holiday

Microsoft Excel 2013 allows only 15 independent variables, so it appears that you're in trouble.

	B	C	D	E	F	G	H	I	J
1								RSQ	0.7712
2									
3	MONTH	DAYMON	DAYWEEK	CUST	SPECIAL	SP	FAC	BH	AH
4	1	2	2	1825	SP,FAC,AH	1	1	0	1
5	1	3	3	1257		0	0	0	0
6	1	4	4	969		0	0	0	0
7	1	5	5	1672	SP		1	0	0	0
8	1	8	1	1098		0	0	0	0
9	1	9	2	691		0	0	0	0
10	1	10	3	672		0	0	0	0
11	1	11	4	754		0	0	0	0
12	1	12	5	972		0	0	0	0
13	1	15	1	816		0	0	0	0
14	1	16	2	717		0	0	0	0
15	1	17	3	728		0	0	0	0
16	1	18	4	711		0	0	0	0
17	1	19	5	1545	SP		1	0	0	0
18	1	22	1	873		0	0	0	0
19	1	23	2	713		0	0	0	0
20	1	24	3	626		0	0	0	0
21	1	25	4	653		0	0	0	0
22	1	26	5	1080		0	0	0	0
23	1	29	1	650		0	0	0	0
24	1	30	2	644		0	0	0	0
25	1	31	3	803		0	0	0	0
26	2	1	4	1282	FAC		0	1	0	0

FIGURE 65-1 Data used to predict credit union customer traffic.

When a regression forecasting model requires more than 15 independent variables, you can use the Excel Solver to estimate the coefficients of the independent variables. You can also use Excel to compute the R-squared values between forecasts and actual customer traffic and the standard deviation for the forecast errors. To analyze this data (see Figure 65-2), a forecasting equation was created by using a lookup table to locate the day of the week, the month, and other factors. Then Solver was used to choose the coefficients for each level of each factor that yields the minimum sum of squared errors. (Each day's error equals actual customers minus forecasted customers.) Here are the particulars.

Begin by creating indicator variables (in columns G through J) for whether the day is a staff payday (SP), faculty payday (FAC), before a holiday (BH), or after a holiday (AH). (See Figure 65-1.) For example, in cells G4, H4, and J4, enter 1 to indicate that January 2 was a staff payday, faculty payday, and after a holiday. Cell I4 contains 0 to indicate that January 2 was not before a holiday.

The forecast is defined by a constant (which helps center the forecasts so that they will be more accurate) and effects for each day of the week, each month, a staff payday, a faculty payday, a day occurring before a holiday, and a day occurring after a holiday. Insert trial values for all these parameters (the Solver changing cells) in the O4:O26 cell range, shown in Figure 65-2. Solver will then choose values that make the model fit the data best. For each day, the forecast of customer count will be generated by the following equation:

```
Predicted customer count=Constant+(Month effect)+(Day of week effect)
  +(Staff payday effect, if any)+(Faculty payday effect, if any)+
  (Before holiday effect, if any)+(After holiday effect, if any)
```

Using this model, you can compute a forecast for each day's customer count by copying the following formula from K4 to K5:K257:

```
$O$26+VLOOKUP(B4,$N$14:$O$25,2)+VLOOKUP(D4,$N$4:$O$8,2) +G4*$O$9+H4*$O$10+I4*$O$11+J4*$O$12
```

Cell O26 picks up the constant term. VLOOKUP(B4,$N$14:$O$25,2) picks up the month coefficient for the current month, and VLOOKUP(D4,$N$4:$O$8,2) picks up the day of the week coefficient for the current week. G4*$O$9+H4*$O$10+I4*$O$11+J4*$O$12 picks up the effects (if any) when the current day is coded as SP, FAC, BH, or AH.

By copying the (E4-K4)^2 formula from L4 to L5:L257, you can compute the squared error for each day. Then, in cell L2, compute the sum of squared errors with the SUM(L4:L257) formula.

	G	H	I	J	K	L	M	N	O	P	Q	R
1			RSQ	0.7712		stdeverr	163.17722					
2					SSE	6736582.1						
3	SP	FAC	BH	AH	Forecast	Sq Err	Error	Day of Week			average	
4	1	1	0	1	1766.78	3389.5598	58.219926	1	103.3575		dayweek	0
5	0	0	0	0	709.6035	299642.97	547.39654	2	-139.1922		month	-3.86E-09
6	0	0	0	0	745.698	49863.782	223.302	3	-150.342			
7	1	0	0	0	1557.221	13174.184	114.77885	4	-114.2475			
8	0	0	0	0	903.303	18143.294	134.69705	5	300.4243			
9	0	0	0	0	720.7533	885.25683	-29.753206 SP		396.8513			
10	0	0	0	0	709.6035	1414.0205	-37.603463 FAC		394.8944			
11	0	0	0	0	745.698	68.923168	8.3019979 BH		205.2928			
12	0	0	0	0	1160.37	35483.189	-188.36982 AH		254.2811			
13	0	0	0	0	963.303	21698.16	-147.30295 Month					
14	0	0	0	0	720.7533	14.087005	-3.7532659	1	-110.6898			
15	0	0	0	0	709.6035	338.43256	18.396537	2	-75.71538			
16	0	0	0	0	745.698	1203.9514	-34.698002	3	-40.34092			
17	1	0	0	0	1557.221	149.35654	12.221151	4	0.02839			
18	0	0	0	0	963.303	8154.6235	-90.302954	5	87.8157			
19	0	0	0	0	720.7533	60.113132	-7.7532659	6	133.341			
20	0	0	0	0	709.6035	6989.5391	-83.603463	7	115.8034			
21	0	0	0	0	745.698	8592.9196	-92.698002	8	28.77429			
22	0	0	0	0	1160.37	6459.3078	-80.369819	9	-87.56315			

FIGURE 65-2 Changing cells and customer forecasts.

In cell R4, average the day of the week changing cells with the AVERAGE(O4:O8) formula, and in cell R5, average the month changing cells with the AVERAGE(O14:O25) formula. Later, you can constrain the average month and day of the week effects to equal 0, which ensures that a month or day of the week with a positive effect has a higher than average customer count, and a month or day of the week with a negative effect has a lower than average customer count.

You can use the Solver settings shown in Figure 65-3 to choose the forecast parameters to minimize the sum of squared errors.

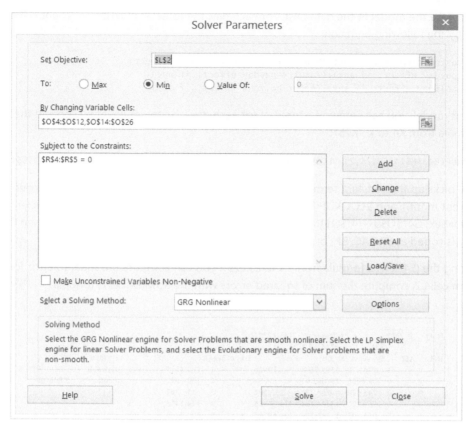

FIGURE 65-3 Solver Parameters dialog box for determining forecast parameters.

The Solver model changes the coefficients for the month, day of the week, BH, AH, SP, FAC, and the constant to minimize the sum of square errors. You can also constrain the average day of the week and month effect to equal 0. Use the Solver to obtain the results shown in Figure 65-2. For example, Friday is the busiest day of the week, and June is the busiest month. A staff payday raises the forecast (all else being equal—in the Latin, ceteris paribus) by 397 customers.

How can I evaluate forecast accuracy?

To evaluate the accuracy of the forecast, you compute the R-squared value between the forecasts and the actual customer count in cell J1. The formula you use is RSQ(E4:E257,K4:K257). This formula computes the percentage of the actual variation in customer count that is explained by the forecasting model. Here, the independent variables explain 77 percent of the daily variation in customer count.

You compute the error for each day in column M by copying the E4–K4 formula from M4 to M5:M257. A close approximation to the standard error of the forecast is given by the standard deviation of the errors. This value is computed in cell M1 by using the STDEVS(M4:M257) formula. Thus, approximately 68 percent of the forecasts should be accurate within 163 customers, 95 percent accurate within 326 customers, and so on.

Try to spot any outliers. Recall that an observation is an outlier if the absolute value of a forecast error exceeds two times the standard error of the regression. Select the M4:M257 range and then click **Conditional Formatting** on the **Home** tab. Next, select **New Rule** and, in the **New Formatting Rule** dialog box, choose **Use A Formula To Determine Which Cells To Format**. Fill in the rule description in the dialog box as shown in Figure 65-4. (For more information about conditional formatting, see Chapter 23, "Conditional formatting.")

FIGURE 65-4 Using conditional formatting to spot forecast outliers.

After you choose a format with a red font, the conditional formatting settings will display in red any error that exceeds 2*(standard deviation of errors) in absolute error. Looking at the outliers, you can see that the model often under-forecasts the customer count for the first three days of the month. Also, during the second week in March (spring break), the model over-forecasts, and the day before spring break, it greatly under-forecasts.

To remedy this problem, in the 1st Three Days worksheet, changing cells were added for each of the first three days of the month and for spring break and the day before spring break. Trial values were added for these new effects in cells O26:O30. By copying the following formula from K4 to K5:K257:

```
$O$25+VLOOKUP(B4,$N$13:$O$24,2)+VLOOKUP(D4,$N$4:$O$8,2)+G4*$O$9+H4*$O$10+I4*$O$11+J4*$O$12
   +IF(C4=1,$O$26,IF(C4=2,$O$27,IF(C4=3,$O$28,0)))
```

the effects of the first three days of the month are included. (The term IF(C4=1,$O$26, IF(C4=2,$O$27,IF(C4=3,$O$28,0))) picks up the effect of the first three days of the month.) The spring break coefficients were entered manually in cells K52:K57. For example, in cell K52, +O29 was added to the formula, and in cells K53:K57, +O30 was added.

After including the new changing cells in the Solver dialog box, you get the results shown in Figure 65-5. Notice that the first three days of the month greatly increase customer count (probably because of government support and Social Security checks) and that spring break reduces customer count. Figure 65-5 also shows the improvement in the forecasting accuracy. The R squared value (RSQ) has improved to 87 percent, and the standard error is reduced to 122 customers.

	I	J	K	L	M	N	O	P	Q	R
1	RSQ	0.8715		stdeverr	122.28505					
2			SSE	3783269.1						
3	BH	AH	Forecast	Sq Err	Error	Day of Week			average	
4	0	1	1879.631	2984.5423	-54.630964		1	107.7063	dayweek	0
5	0	0	995.4	68434.536	261.59995		2	-138.9312	month	2.49E-14
6	0	0	722.9341	60548.436	246.06592		3	-153.3158		
7	0	0	1554.449	13818.155	117.55065		4	-115.0831		
8	0	0	945.7235	23188.13	152.27649		5	299.6238		
9	0	0	699.0859	65.38256	-8.0859483	SP		416.8083		
10	0	0	684.7014	161.32604	-12.701419	FAC		96.64418		
11	0	0	722.9341	965.09124	31.065918	BH		196.4566		
12	0	0	1137.641	27436.946	-165.64102	AH		299.1159		
13	0	0	945.7235	16828.189	-129.72351		1	-105.511		
14	0	0	699.0859	320.91325	17.914052		2	-81.76339		
15	0	0	684.7014	1874.7671	43.298581		3	-27.85624		
16	0	0	722.9341	142.42232	-11.934082		4	-7.28922		
17	0	0	1554.449	89.290215	-9.44935		5	83.84527		
18	0	0	945.7235	5288.7086	-72.723508		6	130.6715		
19	0	0	699.0859	193.60084	13.914052		7	106.6161		
20	0	0	684.7014	3445.8566	-58.701419		8	13.26009		
21	0	0	722.9341	4890.7759	-69.934082		9	-64.68717		
22	0	0	1137.641	3322.4867	-57.641016		10	-68.30456		
23	0	0	945.7235	87452.393	-295.72351		11	-33.75333		

FIGURE 65-5 Forecast parameters and forecasts including spring break and the first three days of the month.

By looking at the forecast errors for the week of 12/24 through 12/31 (see Figure 65-6), you can see that the model has greatly over-forecasted the customer counts for the days in this week. It also under-forecasted customer counts for the week before Christmas. Further examination of the forecast errors (often called *residuals*) also shows the following:

- Thanksgiving is different from a normal holiday in that the credit union is far less busy than expected the day after Thanksgiving.

- The day before Good Friday is really busy because people leave town for Easter.

- Tax day (April 16) is also busier than expected.

- The week before Indiana University starts fall classes (last week in August) was not busy, probably because many staff and faculty take a summer fling vacation before the hectic onrush of the fall semester.

	B	C	D	K	L	M
3	MONTH	DAYMON	DAYWEEK	Forecast	Sq Err	Error
253	12	24	1	1302.463	130655.51	-361.46301
254	12	26	3	1144.1	21054.062	-145.10018
255	12	27	4	883.2169	69810.592	-264.21694
256	12	28	5	1297.924	130266.04	-360.92387
257	12	31	1	1302.463	24480.674	-156.46301

FIGURE 65-6 Errors for Christmas week.

In the Christmas week worksheet, changing cells were added to incorporate the effects of these factors. After adding the new parameters as changing cells, run Solver again. The results you should get are shown in Figure 65-7. The RSQ is up to 92 percent, and the standard error is down to 98.61 customers! Note that the post–Christmas week effect reduced daily customer count by 359, the day before Thanksgiving added 607 customers, the day after Thanksgiving reduced customer count by 161, and so on.

	RSQ	0.9164	stdeverr	98.6147			cutoff	110.5626225		
			SSE	2460389.93			actual	125		
BH	AH	Forecast	Sq Err	Error	Day of Week		sign changes	average		
0	1	1981.1	24363.9878	-156.09		1	108.12	dayweek	-9E-14	
0	0	976.08	78914.9655	280.918		2	-154.6	1 month	1E-06	
0	0	717.68	63163.5973	251.324		3	-164.8	0		
0	0	1539.4	17577.988	132.582		4	-121.1	0		
0	0	946.87	22839.2211	151.127		5	332.32	0		
0	0	684.18	46.5595293	6.82345	SP		368.34	0		
0	0	673.98	3.92565751	-1.9813	FAC		97.12	1		
0	0	717.68	1319.41047	36.3237	BH		272.64	1		
0	0	1171.1	39631.6252	-199.08	AH		477.85	1		
0	0	946.87	17127.8712	-130.07		1	-111.1	0		
0	0	684.18	1077.37916	32.8235		2	-82.13	1		
0	0	673.98	2918.01701	54.0187		3	-26.37	0		
0	0	717.68	44.5731119	-6.6763		4	-34.81	1		
0	0	1539.4	31.1507703	5.502		5	71.042	1		
0	0	946.87	5457.29293	-73.873		6	127.4	1		
0	0	684.18	830.791521	28.8235		7	93.987	1		
0	0	673.98	2302.20776	47.981		8	60.872	1		
0	0	717.68	4183.02504	-64.676		9	-75.35	0		
0	0	1171.1	8295.00769	-91.077		10	-67.92	0		
0	0	946.87	88133.8709	-296.87		11	-35.91	0		
0	0	684.18	1614.15482	-40.177		12	80.332	0		
0	0	673.98	16645.8179	129.019	constant		949.9	1		
0	0	1387.9	11207.1434	-105.86	d1		544.05	1		
0	0	1922	14631.6477	120.961	d2		353.6	1		
0	0	975.89	28935.8732	170.105	d3		302.1	0		
0	0	713.2	718.369947	26.8024	day before sp break		183.24	0		
0	0	703	25.0235784	-5.0024	sp break		-55.21	1		
0	0	746.7	2672.61495	-51.697	christmas week		-359	0		
0	0	1200.1	1689.04256	-41.098	before xmas week		182.94	0		
0	0	975.83	3004.37094	-54.855	before thanks		606.81	0		
0	0	713.2	3003.30571	54.8024	after thanks		-161.2	1		
0	0	703	2401.23102	-49.002	good thurday		319.93	1		
0	0	746.7	12388.2822	111.303	summerfling		-165.1	1		
0	0	1568.4	6171.82676	78.561	tax day		243.75	0		

FIGURE 65-7 Final forecast parameters.

Notice also how the forecasting model is improved by using outliers. If your outliers have something in common (such as being the first three days of the month), include the common factor as an independent variable, and your forecasting error will drop.

How can I check whether my forecast errors are random?

A good forecasting method should create forecast errors or residuals that are random. By random errors, I mean that your errors exhibit no discernible pattern. If forecast errors are random, the sign of your errors should change (from plus to minus or minus to plus) approximately half the time. Therefore, a commonly used test to evaluate the randomness of forecast errors is to look at the number of sign changes in the errors. If you have n observations, nonrandomness of the errors is indicated if you find either fewer than:

$$\frac{n-1}{2} - \sqrt{n}$$

or more than:

$$\frac{n-1}{2} + \sqrt{n}$$

changes in sign. In the Christmas week worksheet, as shown in Figure 65-7, the number of sign changes was determined in the residuals by copying the IF(M5*M4<0,1,0) formula from cell P5 to P6:P257. A sign change in the residuals occurs if and only if the product of two consecutive residuals is negative. Therefore, this formula yields 1 whenever a change in the sign of the residuals occurs. There were 125 changes in sign. In cell P1:

$$\frac{254-1}{2} - \sqrt{254} = 110.6$$

changes were computed in sign as the cutoff for nonrandom residuals. Therefore, you have random residuals.

A similar analysis was performed to predict daily customer counts for dinner at a major restaurant chain. The special factors corresponded to holidays. The study found that Super Sunday (the day of the NFL's Super Bowl) was the least busy day, and Valentine's Day and Mother's Day were the busiest. Also, Saturday was the busiest day of the week for dinner, and Friday was the busiest day of the week for lunch.

Problems

1. How can you use the techniques outlined in this chapter to predict the daily sales of pens at Staples?

2. If you had several years of data, how would you incorporate a trend in the analysis?

CHAPTER 66

An introduction to random variables

Questions answered in this chapter:

- What is a random variable?

- What is a discrete random variable?

- What is the mean, variance, and standard deviation of a random variable?

- What is a continuous random variable?

- What is a probability density function?

- What are independent random variables?

In today's world, the only thing that's certain is that we face a great deal of uncertainty. In the next nine chapters, you find some powerful techniques you can use to incorporate uncertainty in business models. The key building block in modeling uncertainty is understanding how to use random variables.

Answers to this chapter's questions

This section provides the answers to the questions that are listed at the beginning of the chapter.

What is a random variable?

Any situation whose outcome is uncertain is called an *experiment*. The value of a random variable is based on the (uncertain) outcome of an experiment. For example, tossing a pair of dice is an experiment, and a random variable might be defined as the sum of the values shown on each die. In this case, the random variable could assume any of the values of 2, 3, and so on up to 12. As another example, consider the experiment of selling a new video game console, for which a random variable might be defined as the market share for this new product.

What is a discrete random variable?

A random variable is discrete if it can assume a finite number of possible values. Here are some examples of discrete random variables:

- Number of potential competitors for your product

- Number of aces drawn in a five-card poker hand

- Number of car accidents you have (hopefully zero!) in a year

- Number of dots showing on a die

- Number of free throws out of 12 that Phoenix Sun's star Steve Nash makes during a basketball game

What is the mean, variance, and standard deviation of a random variable?

In Chapter 42, "Summarizing data by using descriptive statistics," the mean, variance, and standard deviation for a data set was discussed. In essence, the mean of a random variable (often denoted by μ) is the average value of the random variable you would expect if you performed an experiment many times. The mean of a random variable is often referred to as the random variable's *expected* value. The variance of a random variable (often denoted by σ^2) is the average value of the squared deviation from the mean of a random variable that you would expect if you performed an experiment many times. The standard deviation of a random variable (often denoted by σ) is simply the square root of its variance. As with data sets, the mean of a random variable is a summary measure for a typical value of the random variable, whereas the variance and standard deviation measure the spread of the random variable about its mean.

As an example of how to compute the mean, variance, and standard deviation of a random variable, suppose you believe that the return on the stock market during the next year is governed by the following probabilities:

Probability	Market return
.40	+20 percent
.30	0 percent
.30	-20 percent

Hand calculations show the following:

```
μ = .40*(.20) + .30*(.00) + .30*(-.20) = .02 or 2 percent
```

```
σ² = .4*(.20 - .02)2 + .30*(.0 - .02)2 + .30*(-.20 - .02)2 = .0276
```

Then σ = .166 or 16.6 percent.

In the Meanvariance.xlsx file (shown in Figure 66-1), these computations are verified.

	A	B	C	D	E
1					
2					
3		Value	Probability	Squared deviation	
4		0.2	0.4	0.0324	
5		0	0.3	0.0004	
6		-0.2	0.3	0.0484	
7					
8					
9		Mean	0.02		
10		Variance	0.0276		
11		Standard deviation	0.16613248		

FIGURE 66-1 Computing the mean, standard deviation, and variance of a random variable.

The mean of the market return was computed in cell C9 with the SUMPRODUCT(B4:B6,C4:C6) formula. This formula multiplies each value of the random variable by its probability and sums up the products.

To compute the variance of the market return, the squared deviation of each value of the random variable was determined from its mean by copying the (B4–$C$9)^2 formula from D4 to D5:D6. Then, in cell C10, the variance of the market return was computed as the average squared deviation from the mean with the SUMPRODUCT(C4:C6,D4:D6) formula. Finally, the standard deviation of the market return was computed in cell C11 with the SQRT(C10) formula.

What is a continuous random variable?

A continuous random variable is a random variable that can assume a very large number or, to all intents and purposes, an infinite number of values. Here are some examples of continuous random variables:

- Price of Microsoft stock one year from now

- Market share for a new product

- Market size for a new product

- Cost of developing a new product

- Newborn baby's weight

- Person's IQ

- Dirk Nowitzki's three-point shooting percentage during next season

What is a probability density function?

A discrete random variable can be specified by a list of values and the probability of occurrence for each value of the random variable. Because a continuous random variable can assume an infinite number of values, you can't list the probability of occurrence for each value of a continuous random variable. A continuous random variable is completely described by its *probability density function*. For example, the probability density function for a randomly chosen person's IQ is shown in Figure 66-2.

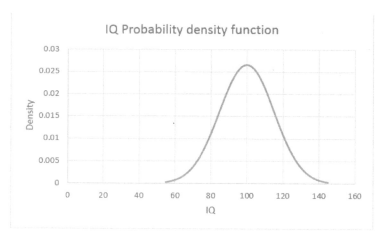

FIGURE 66-2 Probability density function for IQs.

A probability density function (pdf) has the following properties:

- The value of the pdf is always greater than or equal to 0.

- The area under the pdf equals 1.

- The height of the density function for a value x of a random variable is proportional to the likelihood that the random variable assumes a value near x. For example, the height of the density for an IQ of 83 is roughly half the height of the density for an IQ of 100. This tells you that IQs near 83 are approximately half as likely as IQs around 100. Also, because the density peaks at 100, IQs around 100 are most likely.

- The probability that a continuous random variable assumes a range of values equals the corresponding area under the density function. For example, the fraction of people having IQs from 80 through 100 is simply the area under the density from 80 through 100.

- Note that a discrete random variable that assumes many values is often modeled as a continuous random variable. (See Chapter 69, "The normal random variable.") For example, although the number of half gallons of milk sold in a single day by a small grocery store is discrete, it proves more convenient to model this discrete random variable as a continuous random variable.

What are independent random variables?

A set of random variables is independent if knowledge of the value of any of its subsets tells you nothing about the values of the other random variables. For example, the number of games the Indiana University football team won during a year is independent of the percentage return on Microsoft during the same year. Knowing that Indiana did very well would not change your view of how Microsoft stock did during the year.

However, the returns on Microsoft stock and Intel stock are not independent. If you are told that Microsoft stock had a high return in one year, in all likelihood, computer sales were high, which tells you that Intel probably had a good year as well.

Problems

1. Identify the following random variables as discrete or continuous:

   - Number of games the Seattle Seahawks win next season

   - Number that comes up when spinning a roulette wheel

   - Unit sales of Microsoft Surface tablets next year

   - Length of time that a light bulb lasts before it burns out

2. Compute the mean, variance, and standard deviation of the number of dots showing when a die is tossed.

3. Determine whether the following random variables are independent:

   - Daily temperature and sales at an ice cream store

   - Suit and number of a card drawn from a deck of playing cards

   - Inflation and return on the stock market

   - Price charged for and the number of units sold of a car model

4. The current price of a company's stock is $20. The company is a takeover target. If the takeover is successful, the company's stock price will increase to $30. If the takeover is unsuccessful, the stock price will drop to $12. Determine the range of values for the probability of a successful takeover that would make it worthwhile to purchase the stock today. Assume your goal is to maximize your expected profit. Hint: Use the Goal Seek command, which is discussed in detail in Chapter 17, "The Goal Seek command."

5. When a roulette wheel is spun, the possible outcomes are 0, 00, 1, 2, . . . , 36. If you bet on a number coming up, you win $35 if your number comes up, and you lose $1 otherwise. What are the mean and standard deviation of your winnings on a single play of the game?

CHAPTER 67

The binomial, hypergeometric, and negative binomial random variables

Questions answered in this chapter:

- What is a binomial random variable?

- How can I use the BINOM.DIST function to compute binomial probabilities?

- If equal numbers of people prefer Coke to Pepsi and Pepsi to Coke and I ask 100 people whether they prefer Coke to Pepsi, what is the probability that exactly 60 people prefer Coke to Pepsi and the probability that between 40 and 60 people prefer Coke to Pepsi?

- Of all the elevator rails my company produces, 3 percent are considered defective. We are about to ship a batch of 10,000 elevator rails to a customer. To determine whether the batch is acceptable, the customer will randomly choose a sample of 100 rails and check whether each sampled rail is defective. If two or fewer sampled rails are defective, the customer will accept the batch. How can I determine the probability that the batch will be accepted?

- Airlines do not like flights with empty seats. Suppose that, on average, 95 percent of all ticket holders show up for a flight. If the airline sells 105 tickets for a 100-seat flight, what is the probability that the flight will be overbooked?

- The local Village Deli knows that 1,000 customers come for lunch each day. On average, 20 percent order the specialty vegetarian sandwich. These sandwiches are premade. How many should the deli make if it wants to have a 5 percent chance of running out of vegetarian sandwiches?

- What is the hypergeometric random variable?

- What is the negative binomial random variable?

Answers to this chapter's questions

This section provides the answers to the questions that are listed at the beginning of the chapter.

What is a binomial random variable?

A *binomial random variable* is a discrete random variable used to calculate probabilities when all three of the following apply:

- n independent trials occur.

- Each trial results in one of two outcomes: success or failure.

- In each trial, the probability of success (p) remains constant.

In such a situation, the binomial random variable can be used to calculate probabilities related to the number of successes in a given number of trials. We let x be the random variable denoting the number of successes occurring in n independent trials when the probability of success on each trial is p. Here are some examples in which the binomial random variable is relevant:

- **Coke or Pepsi** Assume that equal numbers of people prefer Coke to Pepsi and Pepsi to Coke. You ask 100 people whether they prefer Coke to Pepsi. You're interested in the probability that exactly 60 people prefer Coke to Pepsi and the probability that from 40 through 60 people prefer Coke to Pepsi. In this situation, you have a binomial random variable defined by the following:

  - Trial: survey individuals

  - Success: prefer Coke

  - p equals 0.50

  - n equals 100

  Let x equal the number of people sampled who prefer Coke. You want to determine the probability that $x = 60$ and $40 \leq x \leq 60$.

- **Elevator rails** Of all the elevator rails you produce, 3 percent are considered defective. You are about to ship a batch of 10,000 elevator rails to a customer. To determine whether the batch is acceptable, the customer will randomly choose a sample of 100 rails and check whether each sampled rail is defective. If two or fewer sampled rails are defective, the customer will accept the batch. You want to determine the probability that the batch will be accepted.

  You have a binomial random variable defined by the following:

  - Trial: look at a sampled rail

  - Success: rail is defective

- p equals 0.03

- n equals 100

Let x equal the number of defective rails in the sample. You want to find the probability that $x \leq 2$.

■ **Airline overbooking**   Airlines don't like flights with empty seats. Suppose that, on average, 95 percent of all ticket holders show up for a flight. If the airline sells 105 tickets for a 100-seat flight, what is the probability that the flight will be overbooked?

You have a binomial random variable defined by the following:

- Trial: individual ticket holders

- Success: ticket holder shows up

- p equals 0.95

- n equals 105

Let x equal the number of ticket holders who show up. Then you want to find the probability that $x \geq 101$.

How can I use the *BINOM.DIST* function to compute binomial probabilities?

Microsoft Excel 2013 includes the *BINOM.DIST* function, which you can use to compute binomial probabilities. If you want to compute the probability of x or fewer successes for a binomial random variable having n trials with probability of success p, simply enter **BINOM.DIST(x,n,p,1)**. If you want to compute the probability of exactly x successes for a binomial random variable having n trials with probability of success of p, enter **BINOM.DIST(x,n,p,0)**. Entering 1 as the last argument of *BINOM .DIST* yields a cumulative probability; entering 0 yields the probability mass function for any particular value. (Note that a last argument of True can be used instead of a 1, and a last argument of False can be used instead of a 0.) *Previous versions of Excel will not recognize the BINOM.DIST function.* In previous versions of Excel, you can use the *BINOMDIST* function, which has exactly the same syntax as the *BINOM.DIST* function. Let's use the *BINOM.DIST* function to calculate some probabilities of interest. You'll find the data and analysis in the Binomialexamples.xlsx file, which is shown in Figure 67-1.

	B	C
1		
2		
3	Coke vs. Pepsi	Binom.dist
4	Probability exactly 60 people prefer Coke to Pepsi	0.010843867
5	Probability from 40 through 60 people prefer Coke to Pepsi	0.9647998
6		
7	Elevator Rails	
8	Probability 2 or fewer of 100 rails are defective	0.419775083
9	Airline Overbooking	
10	Probability flight is overbooked if 105 tickets are sold	0.392433721

FIGURE 67-1 Using the binomial random variable.

If equal numbers of people prefer Coke to Pepsi and Pepsi to Coke and I ask 100 people whether they prefer Coke to Pepsi, what is the probability that exactly 60 people prefer Coke to Pepsi and the probability that between 40 and 60 people prefer Coke to Pepsi?

You have n = 100 and p = 0.5. You seek the probability that x = 60 and the probability that $40 \le x \le 60$, where x equals the number of people who prefer Coke to Pepsi. First, you find the probability that x = 60 by entering the BINOM.DIST(60,100,0.5,0) formula. Excel returns the value 0.011.

To use the *BINOM.DIST* function to compute the probability that $40 \le x \le 60$, you can note that the probability that $40 \le x \le 60$ equals the probability that $x \le 60$ minus the probability that $x \le 39$. Thus, you can obtain the probability that from 40 through 60 people prefer Coke by entering the BINOM.DIST(60,100,0.5,1)–BINOM.DIST(39,100,0.5,1) formula. Excel returns the value 0.9648. So, if Coke and Pepsi are equally preferred, it is very unlikely that in a sample of 100 people, Coke or Pepsi would be more than 10 percent ahead. If a sample of 100 people shows Coke or Pepsi to be more than 10 percent ahead, you should probably doubt that Coke and Pepsi are equally preferred.

Of all the elevator rails my company produces, 3 percent are considered defective. We are about to ship a batch of 10,000 elevator rails to a customer. To determine whether the batch is acceptable, the customer will randomly choose a sample of 100 rails and check whether each sampled rail is defective. If two or fewer sampled rails are defective, the customer will accept the batch. How can I determine the probability that the batch will be accepted?

If you let x equal the number of defective rails in a batch, you have a binomial random variable with n = 100 and p = 0.03. You seek the probability that $x \le 2$. Simply enter the BINOM.DIST(2,100,0.03,1) formula in cell C8. Excel returns the value 0.42. Thus, the batch will be accepted 42 percent of the time.

Really, your chance of success is not exactly 3 percent on each trial. For example, if the first 10 rails are defective, the chance the next rail is defective has dropped to 290/9,990; if the first 10 rails are not defective, the chance the next rail is defective is 300/9,990. Therefore, the probability of success on the eleventh trial is not independent of the probability of success on one of the first 10 trials. Despite this fact, the binomial random variable can be used as an approximation when a sample is drawn and the sample size is less than 10 percent of the total population. Here, the population equals 10,000, and the sample size is 100. Exact probabilities involving sampling from a finite population can be calculated with the hypergeometric random variable, which is discussed later in this chapter.

Airlines do not like flights with empty seats. Suppose that, on average, 95 percent of all ticket holders show up for a flight. If the airline sells 105 tickets for a 100-seat flight, what is the probability that the flight will be overbooked?

Let x equal the number of ticket holders who show up for the flight. You have $n = 105$ and $p = 0.95$. You seek the probability that $x \geq 101$. Note that the probability that $x \leq 101$ equals 1 minus the probability that $x \leq 100$. So, to compute the probability that the flight is overbooked, you enter the 1–BINOM.DIST(100,105,0.95,1) formula in cell C10. Excel yields 0.392, which means there is a 39.2 percent chance that the flight will be overbooked.

The local Village Deli knows that 1,000 customers come for lunch each day. On average, 20 percent order the specialty vegetarian sandwich. These sandwiches are premade. How many should the deli make if it wants to have a 5 percent chance of running out of vegetarian sandwiches?

In Excel 2013, the *BINOM.INV* function, with the BINOM.INV(trials, probability of success, alpha) syntax, determines the smallest number x for which the probability of less than or equal to x successes is at least *alpha*. In earlier versions of Excel, the CRITBINOM(trials, probability of success, alpha) function yielded the same results as *BINOM.INV*. In this example, trials equals 1,000, probability of success equals 0.2, and *alpha* equals .95. As shown in Figure 67-2, if the deli orders 221 sandwiches, the probability that demand will be less than or equal to 221 is at least 0.95. Also, the probability that 220 or fewer sandwiches will be demanded is less than 0.95.

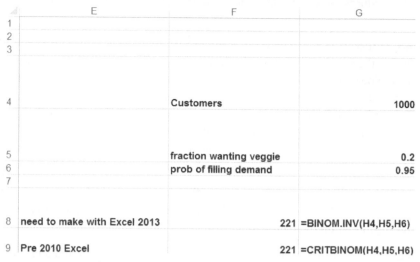

FIGURE 67-2 Example of *BINOM.INV* function.

What is the hypergeometric random variable?

The *hypergeometric random variable* governs a situation such as the following:

- An urn contains *N* balls.

- Each ball is one of two types (called success or failure).

- There are *s* successes in the urn.

- A sample of size *n* is drawn from the urn.

Look at an example in the Hypergeom.dist.xlsx file, which is shown in Figure 67-3. The Excel 2013 HYPERGEOM.DIST(x,n,s,N,0) formula gives the probability of *x* successes if *n* balls are drawn from an urn containing *N* balls, of which *s* are marked as success. The Excel 2013 HYPERGEOM.DIST(x,n,s,N,1) formula gives the probability of less than or equal to *x* successes if *n* balls are drawn from an urn containing *N* balls, of which *s* are marked as success. (As with the *BINOM.DIST* function, True can be used to replace 1 and False to replace 0.)

For example, suppose that 40 of the *Fortune* 500 companies have a woman CEO. The 500 CEOs are analogous to the balls in the urn (N = 500), and the 40 women are representative of the *s* successes in the urn. Then, copying the HYPERGEOM.DIST(C8,Sample_size,Population_women,Population_size,0) formula from D8 to D9:D18 gives the probability that a sample of 10 *Fortune* 500 companies will have 0, 1, 2, . . . , 10 women CEOs. Here, *Sample_size* equals 10, *Population_women* equals 40, and *Population_size* equals 500.

Finding a woman CEO is a success. In the sample of 10, for example, there's a probability of 0.431 that no women CEOs will be in the sample. By the way, you could have approximated this probability with the BINOM.DIST(0,10,0.08,0) formula, yielding 0.434, which is very close to the true probability of 0.431. In cell F10, the probability that at most 2 of the 10 people in the sample would be women was computed with the HYPGEOM.DIST(2,Sample_Size,Population_women,Population_size,TRUE) formula. Thus, there is a 96.2 percent chance that at most two people in the sample will be women. Of course, you could have obtained this answer by adding the shaded cells (D8:D10) together.

	C	D	E	F
1				
2				
3	Population size	500		
4	Sample Size	10		
5	Population women	40		Binomial approximation
6				0.434388454
7	Number of women	Probability		
8		0 0.430956908		
9		1 0.382223421		<=2 women in sample
10		2 0.148407545		ABS(M6)>2*$M$1
11		3 0.033197861		
12		4 0.004734717		
13		5 0.000449538		
14		6 2.87533E-05		
15		7 1.2224E-06		
16		8 3.30288E-08		
17		9 5.11702E-10		
18		10 3.44843E-12		

FIGURE 67-3 Using the hypergeometric random variable.

What is the negative binomial random variable?

The *negative binomial random variable* applies to the same situation as the binomial random variable, but the negative binomial random variable gives the probability of f failures occurring before the sth success. Thus, =NEGBINOM.DIST(f,s,p,0) gives the probability that exactly f failures will occur before the sth success when the probability of success is p for each trial, and =NEGBINOM.DIST(f,s,p,1) gives the probability that at most f failures will occur before the sth success when the probability of success is p for each trial. For example, consider a baseball team that wins 40 percent of its games (see the Negbinom.dist.xlsx file and Figure 67-4). Copying the =NEGBINOM.DIST(D9,2,0.4,False) formula from E9 to E34 gives the probability of 0, 1, 2, . . . , 25 losses occurring before the second win. Note here that success equals a game won. For example, there is a 19.2 percent chance the team will lose exactly one game before winning two games. In cell G10, the =NEGBINOM.DIST(3,2,0.4,TRUE) formula was used to compute the chance that at most three losses will occur before your team wins two games (0.663). Of course, you could have obtained this answer by simply adding up the shaded cells (E9:E12).

	D	E	F	G	H	I
4	40% chance of success					
5						
6						
7						
8	Losses before 2nd win	prob		Probability <=3 failures		
9	0	0.16		before 2nd win		
10	1	0.192		0.66304		
11	2	0.1728				
12	3	0.13824				
13	4	0.10368				
14	5	0.07465				
15	6	0.05225				
16	7	0.03583				
17	8	0.02419				
18	9	0.01612				
19	10	0.01064				
20	11	0.00697				
21	12	0.00453				
22	13	0.00293				
23	14	0.00188				
24	15	0.0012				
25	16	0.00077				
26	17	0.00049				
27	18	0.00031				
28	19	0.00019				
29	20	0.00012				
30	21	7.7E-05				
31	22	4.8E-05				
32	23	3E-05				
33	24	1.9E-05				
34	25	1.2E-05				

FIGURE 67-4 Using the negative binomial random variable.

Problems

1. Suppose that, on average, 4 percent of all CD drives received by a computer company are defective. The company has adopted the following policy: Sample 50 CD drives in each shipment and accept the shipment if none are defective. Using this information, determine the following:

   - What fraction of shipments will be accepted?
   - If the policy changes so that a shipment is accepted if only one CD drive in the sample is defective, what fraction of shipments will be accepted?
   - What is the probability that a sample size of 50 will contain at least 10 defective CD drives?

2. Using the airline overbooking data:

   - Determine how the probability of overbooking varies as the number of tickets sold varies from 100 through 115. Hint: Use a one-way data table.
   - Show how the probability of overbooking varies as the number of tickets sold varies from 100 through 115, and the probability that a ticket holder shows up varies from 80 percent through 95 percent. Hint: Use a two-way data table.

3. Suppose that during each year, a given mutual fund has a 50 percent chance of beating the Standard & Poor's 500 Stock Index (S&P Index). In a group of 100 mutual funds, what is the probability that at least 10 funds will beat the S&P Index during at least 8 out of 10 years?

4. Professional basketball player Steve Nash is a 90-percent foul shooter:

   - If he shoots 100 free throws, what is the probability that he will miss more than 15 shots?

   - How good a foul shooter would Steve Nash be if he had only a 5 percent chance of making fewer than 90 free throws out of 100 attempts? Hint: Use Goal Seek.

5. When tested for extra sensory perception (ESP), participants are asked to identify the shape on a card from a 25-card deck. The deck consists of five cards with each of five shapes. If a person identifies 12 cards correctly, what would you conclude?

6. Suppose that in a group of 100 people, 20 have the flu and 80 do not. If you randomly select 30 people, what is the chance that at least 10 people have the flu?

7. A student is selling magazines for a school fundraiser. There is a 20 percent chance that a given house will buy a magazine. He needs to sell five magazines. Determine the probability that he will need to visit 5, 6, 7, . . . , 100 houses to sell five magazines.

8. Use the *BINOM.DIST* function to verify that the *BINOM.INV* function yields the correct answer to your Village Deli example.

9. In the seventeenth century, French mathematicians Pierre de Fermat and Blaise Pascal were inspired to formulate the theory of modern probability after trying to solve the Problem of the Points. Here is a simple example: Pascal and Fermat take turns tossing coins. Fermat wins a point if a head is tossed, and Pascal wins a point if a tail is tossed. If Pascal is ahead 8–7 and the first player with 10 points wins, what is the chance that Pascal will win?

CHAPTER 68

The Poisson and exponential random variable

Questions answered in this chapter:

- What is the Poisson random variable?

- How can I compute probabilities for the Poisson random variable?

- If the number of customers arriving at a bank is governed by a Poisson random variable, what random variable governs the time between arrivals?

Answers to this chapter's questions

This section provides the answers to the questions that are listed at the beginning of the chapter.

What is the Poisson random variable?

The *Poisson random variable* is a discrete random variable that is useful for describing probabilities for situations in which events (such as customer arrivals at a bank or orders placed for a product) have a small probability of occurring during a short time interval. More specifically, during a short time interval, denoted as t, either zero or one event will occur, and the probability of one event occurring during a short interval of length t is (for some λ) given by λt. Here, λ is the mean number of occurrences per time unit.

Situations in which the Poisson random variable can be applied include the following:

- Number of units of a product demanded during a month.

- Number of deaths per year by horse kick in the Prussian army.

- Number of car accidents you have during a year.

- Number of copies of *The Seat of the Soul* ordered today at Amazon.com.

- Number of worker's compensation claims filed at a company this month.

- Number of defects in 100 yards of string. (Here, 1 yard of string plays the role of time.)

How can I compute probabilities for the Poisson random variable?

You can use the Microsoft Excel 2013 *POISSON.DIST* function to compute probabilities involving the Poisson random variable. In earlier versions of Excel, the *POISSON* function yielded POISSON probabilities. Just remember that in a length of time *t*, the mean of a Poisson random variable is *t*. The syntax of the *POISSON* function is as follows:

POISSON.DIST(x,Lambda,True_or_1) calculates the probability that a Poisson random variable with a mean equal to *Lambda* is less than or equal to *x*.

POISSON.DIST(x,Lambda,False_or_0) calculates the probability that a Poisson random variable with a mean equal to *Lambda* is equal to *x*.

Here are some examples of how to compute probabilities for Poisson random variables. You can find these examples in the Poisson.xlsx file, shown in Figure 68-1.

	B	C
1	Calls per hour	30
2	Mean	60
3		
4	Prob 60 calls in two hours	0.051432
5	Prob<= 60 calls in two hours	0.534262
6	Prob between 50 and 100 calls(inclusive) in two hours	0.915592

FIGURE 68-1 Using the Poisson random variable.

Suppose that my consulting business receives an average of 30 phone calls per hour. During a two-hour period, I want to determine the following:

- The probability that exactly 60 calls will be received in the next two hours

- The probability that the number of calls received in the next two hours will be fewer than or equal to 60

- The probability that from 50 through 100 calls will be received in the next two hours

During a two-hour period, the mean number of calls is 60. In cell C4, I find the probability (0.05) that exactly 60 calls will be received in the next two hours by using the POISSON.DIST(60,C2,False) formula. In cell C5, I find the probability (0.534) that at most 60 calls will be received in two hours with the POISSON.DIST(60,C2,True) formula. In cell C6, I find the probability (0.916) that from 50 through 100 calls will be received in two hours with the POISSON.DIST(100,C2,True)–POISSON.DIST(49,C2,True) formula.

Note You can always use 1 instead of True as an argument in any Excel function.

If the number of customers arriving at a bank is governed by a Poisson random variable, what random variable governs the time between arrivals?

The time between arrivals can be any value, which means that the time between arrivals is a continuous random variable. If an average of arrivals occurs per time unit, the time between arrivals follows an exponential random variable having the probability density function (pdf) of $f(t) = \lambda^{-\lambda t}$. This random variable has a mean, or average, value equal to $1/\lambda$. For $\lambda = 30$, a graph of the exponential pdf is shown in Figure 68-2. You can find this chart and the data for this example in the Density worksheet in the Exponentialdist.xlsx file.

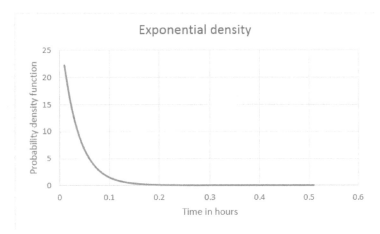

FIGURE 68-2 Exponential probability density function.

Recall from Chapter 66, "An introduction to random variables," that for a continuous random variable, the height of the pdf for a number x reflects the likelihood that the random variable assumes a value near x. You can see in Figure 68-2 that extremely short times between bank arrivals (for example, less than 0.05 hours) are very likely, but that for longer times, the pdf drops off sharply.

Even though the average time between arrivals is $1/30 = 0.033$ hours, there's a reasonable chance that the time between arrivals will be as much as 0.20 hours. The Excel 2013 EXPON.DIST(x,1/mean,True_or_1) formula will give the probability that an exponential random variable with a given *mean* will assume a value less than or equal to x. Thus, the second argument to the *EXPON.DIST* function is the rate per time unit at which events occur. For example, to compute the probability that the time between arrivals is at least 5, 10, or 15 minutes, you can copy the 1–EXPON.DIST(C5,$D$2,True_or_1) formula from cell D5 to D7. In earlier versions of Excel, the *EXPONDIST* function yields the same results as *EXPON.DIST*.

Note that minutes were first converted to hours (5 minutes equals 1/12 hour and so on). Also, the mean time between arrivals is 0.033 hours, so 1/Mean = 1/.033 = 30 was entered in the formula. In short, the arrival rate per time unit was entered, as you can see in Figure 68-3.

	B	C	D	E
1		mean	0.033333333	
2		1/mean	30	
3				
4		x = Time between arrivals	Prob time >=x	
5	5 minutes	0.0833333	0.082084999	
6	10 minutes	0.1666667	0.006737947	
7	15 minutes	0.25	0.000553084	

FIGURE 68-3 Computations of exponential probabilities.

Problems

1. Beer drinkers order an average of 40 pitchers of beer per hour at Nick's Pub in Bloomington, Indiana:

   - What is the probability that at least 100 pitchers are ordered in a two-hour period?

   - What is the chance that the time between ordered pitchers will be 30 seconds or less?

2. Suppose that teenage drivers have an average of 0.3 accidents per year:

   - What is the probability that a teenager will have no more than one accident during a year?

   - What is the probability that the time between accidents will be six months or less?

3. I am next in line at a fast-food restaurant in which customers wait in a single line, and the time to serve a customer follows an exponential distribution with a mean of 3 minutes. What is the chance that I will have to wait at least 5 minutes to be served?

4. Since 1900, a fraction (.00124) of all Major League Baseball games have resulted in no-hitters. A team plays 162 games in a season. What is the chance that a team pitches two or more no-hitters during a season?

CHAPTER 69

The normal random variable

Questions answered in this chapter:

- What are the properties of the normal random variable?

- How can I use Excel to find probabilities for the normal random variable?

- Can I use Excel to find percentiles for normal random variables?

- Why is the normal random variable appropriate in many real-world situations?

Answers to this chapter's questions

This section provides the answers to the questions that are listed at the beginning of the chapter.

What are the properties of the normal random variable?

In Chapter 66, "An introduction to random variables," you learned that continuous random variables can be used to model quantities such as the following:

- Price of Microsoft stock one year from now

- Market share for a new product

- Market size for a new product

- Cost of developing a new product

- Newborn baby's weight

- A person's IQ

Remember that if a discrete random variable (such as sales of Big Macs during 2014) can assume many possible values, you can approximate the value by using a continuous random variable as well. As described in Chapter 66, any continuous random variable X has a probability density function (pdf). The pdf for a continuous random variable is a nonnegative function with the following properties (a and b are arbitrary numbers):

- The area under the pdf is 1.

- The probability that $X < a$ equals the probability that $X \leq a$. This probability is represented by the area under the pdf to the left of a.

- The probability that $X > b$ equals the probability that $X \geq b$. This probability is shown in the area under the pdf to the right of b.

- The probability that $a < X < b$ equals the probability that $a \leq X \leq b$. This probability is the area under the pdf between a and b.

Thus, the area under a continuous random variable's pdf represents probability. Also, the larger the value of the density function at X, the more likely the random variable will take on a value near X. For example, if the density function of a random variable at 20 is twice the density function of the random variable at 5, then the random variable is twice as likely to take on a value near 20 than a value near 5.

For a continuous random variable, the probability that X equals *any value* will always equal 0. For example, some people are from 5.99999 feet through 6.00001 feet tall, but no person can be exactly 6 feet tall. This explains why you can replace the less-than sign (<) with the less-than or equal-to sign ($\leq$) in the probability statements.

Figure 69-1 displays the pdf for $X = IQ$ of a randomly chosen person. The area under this pdf is 1. If you want to find the probability that a person's IQ is less than or equal to 90, you simply find the area to the left of 90. If you want to find the probability that a person's IQ is from 95 through 120, you find the area under the pdf from 95 through 120. If you want to find the probability that a person's IQ is more than 130, you find the area under the density function to the right of 130. (See the IQ Density worksheet in the Normalexamples.xlsx file.)

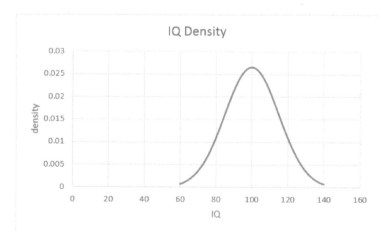

FIGURE 69-1 IQ pdf.

Actually, the density plotted in Figure 69-1 is an example of the *normal random variable*. The normal random variable is specified by its mean and standard deviation. IQs follow a normal random variable with $\mu = 100$ and $\sigma = 15$. This is the pdf displayed in Figure 69-1. The normal random variable has the following properties:

- The most likely value of a normal random variable is μ (as indicated by the pdf peaking at 100 in Figure 69-1).

- As the value x of the random variable moves away from μ, the probability that the random variable is near x sharply decreases.

- The normal random variable is symmetric about its mean. For example, IQs near 80 are as likely as IQs near 120.

- A normal random variable has 68 percent of its probability within σ of its mean, 95 percent within 2σ of its mean, and 99.7 percent within 3σ of its mean. These measures should remind you of the rule of thumb described in Chapter 42, "Summarizing data by using descriptive statistics." In fact, the rule of thumb is based on the assumption that data is sampled from a *normal distribution*, which explains why the rule of thumb does not work as well when the data fails to exhibit a symmetric histogram.

For a larger σ, a normal random variable is more spread out about its mean. This pattern is illustrated in Figures 69-2 and 69-3. (See the Sigma of 5 and 15 worksheet in the Normalexamples.xlsx file.)

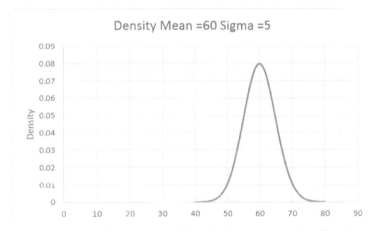

FIGURE 69-2 Normal random variable pdf with a mean equal to 60 and a standard deviation equal to 5.

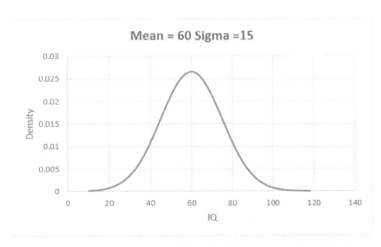

FIGURE 69-3 Normal random variable pdf with a mean equal to 60 and a standard deviation equal to 15.

How can I use Excel to find probabilities for the normal random variable?

Consider a normal random variable X with a mean μ and standard deviation σ. Suppose for any number x, you want to find the probability that $X \leq x$, which is called the *normal cumulative function*. To use Microsoft Excel 2013 to find the probability that $X \leq x$, enter the NORM.DIST(x,μ,σ,1) formula. Of course, the fourth argument of 1 could be replaced by True.

The argument 1 tells Excel to compute the normal cumulative. If the last argument of the function is 0, Excel returns the actual value of the normal random variable pdf. Excel 2013 statistical functions (such as *NORM.DIST*) have been modified or redesigned completely to provide better accuracy than their counterparts (such as *NORMDIST*) in previous versions of Excel.

You can use the *NORM.DIST* function to answer many questions concerning normal probabilities. You can find examples in the Normal worksheet in the Normalexamples.xlsx file, which is shown in Figure 69-4 and in the following three scenarios.

	B	C	D
1			
2		Prob	
3	IQ<90	0.25249254	
4	95<IQ<120	0.53934744	
5	IQ>130	0.02275013	
6			
7	99 %ile Prozac	71.6317394	
8	10% Bloomington income	19747.5875	

FIGURE 69-4 Calculating normal probability.

- **What fraction of people have an IQ of less than 90?** Let X equal the IQ of a randomly chosen person. Then you seek the probability that $X < 90$, which is equal to the probability that $X \leq 90$. Therefore, you can enter the NORM.DIST(90,100,15,1) formula in cell C3 of the Normal worksheet, and Excel returns 0.252. Thus, 25.2 percent of all people have an IQ less than 90.

- **What fraction of all people have IQs from 95 through 120?** When finding the probability that $a \leq X \leq b$, you use the (area under the normal density function to the left of b) – (area under normal density function to the left of a) formula. Thus, you can find the probability that $a \leq X \leq b$ by entering the NORM.DIST(b,μ,s,1)–NORM.DIST(a,μ,s,1) formula. You can answer the question about IQs from 95 through 120 by entering the NORMDIST(120,100,15,1)–NORMDIST(95,100,15,1) formula in cell C4 of the Normal worksheet. Excel returns the probability 0.539, so 53.9 percent of all people have an IQ from 95 through 120.

- **What fraction of all people have IQs of at least 130?** To find the probability that $X \geq b$, note that the probability that $X \geq b$ equals 1 – probability $X < b$. You can compute the probability that $X \geq b$ by entering the 1–NORM.DIST(b,μ,σ,1) formula. You seek the probability that $X \geq 130$. This equals 1 – probability X < 130. You enter the 1–NORM.DIST(130,100,15,1) formula in cell C5 of the Normal worksheet. Excel returns 0.023, so you know that 2.3 percent of people have an IQ of at least 130.

Can I use Excel to find percentiles for normal random variables?

Consider a given normal random variable X with mean and standard deviation. In many situations, you want to answer questions such as the following:

- A drug manufacturer believes that next year's demand for its popular antidepressant will be normally distributed, with mean equal to 60 million days of therapy (DOT) and sigma equal to 5 million DOT. How many units of the drug should be produced this year if the company wants to have only a 1 percent chance of running out of the drug?

- Family income in Bloomington, Indiana, is normally distributed, with mean equal to $30,000 and sigma equal to $8,000. The poorest 10 percent of all families in Bloomington are eligible for federal aid. What should the aid cutoff be?

In the first example, you want to determine the ninety-ninth percentile of demand for the antidepressant. That is, you seek the number x such that there is only a 1 percent chance that demand will exceed x and a 99 percent chance that demand will be less than x. In the second example, you want the tenth percentile of family income in Bloomington. That is, you seek the number x such that there is only a 10 percent chance that family income will be less than x and a 90 percent chance that family income will exceed x.

Suppose you want to find the pth percentile (expressed as a decimal) of a normal random variable X with a mean and a standard deviation. In Excel 2013, simply enter the NORM.INV(p,μ,σ) formula. This formula returns a number x such that the probability that $X \leq x$ equals the specified percentile. You now can solve your examples. You'll find these exercises on the Normal worksheet in the Normalexamples.xlsx file.

For the drug manufacturing example, let X equal annual demand for the drug. You want a value x such that the probability that $X \geq x$ equals 0.01 or the probability that $X < x$ equals 0.99. Again, you seek the ninety-ninth percentile of demand, which you find (in millions) by entering the NORM.INV(0.99,60,5) formula in cell C7. Excel returns 71.63, so the company must produce 71,630,000 DOT. This assumes, of course, that the company begins the year with no supply of the drug on hand. If, for example, it had a beginning inventory of 10 million DOT, it would need to produce 61,630,000 DOT during the current year.

To determine the cutoff for federal aid, if X equals the income of a Bloomington family, you seek a value of x such that the probability that $X \leq x$ equals 0.10, or the tenth percentile of Bloomington family income. You find this value with the NORM.INV(0.10,30000,8000) formula. Excel returns $19,747.59, so aid should be given to all families with incomes smaller than $19,749.59.

Why is the normal random variable appropriate in many real-world situations?

A well-known mathematical result called the *central limit theorem* indicates that if you add together many (usually at least 30 is sufficient) independent random variables, their sum is normally distributed. This result holds true even if the individual random variables are not normally distributed. Many quantities (such as measurement errors) are created by adding together many independent random variables, which explains why the normal random variable occurs often in the real world. Here are some other situations in which you can use the central limit theorem:

- The total demand for pizzas during a month at a supermarket is normally distributed even if the daily demand for pizzas is not.

- The amount of money you win if you play craps 1,000 times is normally distributed, even though the amount of money you win on each individual play is not.

Another important mathematical result shows how to find the mean, variance, and standard deviations of sums of independent random variables. If you are adding together independent random variables $X_1, X_2, \ldots, X_n$ where mean $X_i = \mu_i$, and standard deviation $X_i = \sigma_i$ then the following are true:

1. Mean $(X_1 + X_2 + \ldots X_n) = \mu_1 + \mu_2 + \ldots \mu_n$

2. Variance $(X_1 + X_2 + \ldots X_n) = s_1^2 + s_2^2 + \ldots s_n^2$

3. Standard deviation $(X_1 + X_2 + \ldots X_n) = \sqrt{\sigma_1^2 + \sigma_2^2 + \ldots \sigma_n^2}$

Note that 1 is true even when the random variables are not independent. By combining 1 through 3 with the central limit theorem, you can solve many complex probability problems, such as the following: Suppose daily demand for pizza is not normally distributed but has a mean of 45 and sigma of 10. What is the probability that at least 1,400 pizzas will be sold during a month? Your pizza solution is in the Central Limit worksheet in the Normalexamples.xlsx file, which is shown in Figure 69-5.

	C	D
1		
2	Daily frozen pizza demand	
3	mean	45
4	sigma	12
5		
6	30 day	
7	mean	1350
8	variance	4320
9	sigma	65.72671
10		
11	Probability more than 1400 sold	0.225689
12	1% chance of running out	1502.903

FIGURE 69-5 Using the central limit theorem.

Even though the daily demand for frozen pizzas is not normally distributed, you know from the central limit theorem that the 30-day demand for frozen pizzas is normally distributed. Given this, the preceding 1 through 3 imply the following:

- From 1, the mean of a 30-day demand equals 30(45) = 1,350.

- From 2, the variance of a 30-day demand equals 30(12)2 = 4,320.

- From 3, the standard deviation of a 30-day demand equals = 65.73.

Thus, the 30-day demand for pizzas can be modeled following a normal random variable with a mean of 1,350 and a standard deviation of 65.73. In cell D11, the probability that at least 1,400 pizzas are sold is computed as the probability that the normal approximation is at least 1,399.5 (note that a demand of 1,399.6, for example, would round up to 1,400) with the 1–NORM .DIST(1399.5,D7,D9,TRUE) formula. You find the probability that demand in a 30-day period for at least 1,400 pizzas is 22.6 percent.

The number of pizzas that you must stock to have only a 1 percent chance of running out of pizzas is just the ninety-ninth percentile of the demand distribution. You determine the ninety-ninth percentile of the demand distribution (1,503) in cell D12 with the NORM.INV(0.99,D7,D9) formula. Therefore, at the beginning of a month, you should bring your stock of pizzas up to 1,503 if you want to have only a 1 percent chance of running out of pizzas.

Problems

1. Suppose you can set the mean number of ounces of soda that is put into a can. The actual number of ounces has a standard deviation of 0.05 ounces:

   - If you set the mean at 12.03 ounces, and a soda can is acceptable if it contains at least 12 ounces, what fraction of cans is acceptable?

   - What fraction of cans have less than 12.1 ounces?

   - What should you set the mean to if you want at most 1 percent of your cans to contain at most 12 ounces? Hint: Use the Goal Seek command.

2. Annual demand for a drug is normally distributed with a mean of 40,000 units and a standard deviation of 10,000 units:

   - What is the probability that annual demand is from 35,000 through 49,000 units?

   - If you want to have only a 5 percent chance of running out of the drug, at what level should you set annual production?

3. The probability of winning a game of craps is 0.493. If I play 10,000 games of craps and bet the same amount on each game, what is the probability that I'm ahead? Begin by determining the mean and standard deviation of the profit on one game of craps. Then use the central limit theorem.

4. Weekly sales of Volvo's Cross Country station wagons are normally distributed with a mean of 1,000 and standard deviation of 250:

   - What is the probability that, during a week, from 400 through 1,100 station wagons are sold?

   - There is a 1 percent chance that fewer than what number of station wagons is sold during a week?

CHAPTER 70

Weibull and beta distributions: modeling machine life and duration of a project

Questions answered in this chapter:

- How can I estimate the probability that a machine will work without failing for at least 20 hours?

- How can I estimate the probability that hanging drywall in a building will take more than 200 hours?

The *Weibull random variable* is a continuous random variable that is often used to model the lifetime of a machine. If you have data about how long similar machines have lasted in the past, you can estimate the two parameters (*alpha* and *beta*) that define a Weibull random variable. You can then use the *WEIBULL.DIST* function in Microsoft Excel 2013 to determine probabilities of interest such as an estimate of how long a machine will run without failing.

The *beta random variable* is a continuous random variable that's often used to model the duration of an activity. Given estimates of the minimum duration, maximum duration, mean duration, and the standard deviation of the duration, you can use the *BETA.DIST* function in Excel 2013 to determine probabilities of interest.

Answers to this chapter's questions

This section provides the answers to the questions that are listed at the beginning of the chapter.

How can I estimate the probability that a machine will work without failing for at least 20 hours?

Suppose you have observed the lifetime of seven similar machines. The data collected about the machines is contained in the Weibullest.xlsx file, shown in Figure 70-1.

	A	B	C
16		Machine 1	8.5
17		Machine 2	12.54
18		Machine 3	13.75
19		Machine 4	19.75
20		Machine 5	21.46
21		Machine 6	26.34
22		Machine 7	28.45

FIGURE 70-1 Machine lifetime data.

Reliability engineers have found that the Weibull random variable is usually appropriate for modeling machine lifetimes. The Weibull random variable is specified by two parameters: *alpha* and *beta*. Based on the data, you can determine (using the *AVERAGE* and *STDEV.S* functions in cells B13 and B14) that, on average, a machine lasts 18.68 hours, with a standard deviation of 7.40 hours. By copying these values to cells G6 and G11 and running the Solver with the settings shown in Figure 70-2, you can find estimates of alpha and beta that ensure that the Weibull random variable will have a mean and standard deviation matching the data. In this case, alpha equals 2.725 and beta equals 21.003, as you can see in Figure 70-3. Any value you enter for alpha and beta in cells E2 and E3 for a Weibull random variable yields a mean (computed in cell E6) and standard deviation (computed in cell E11). The Solver model varies alpha and beta until the mean and standard deviation of the Weibull distribution equal the mean and standard deviation of machine lifetime computed from your data. The Multistart option for the GRG Nonlinear engine is recommended for this. The Multistart engine works best with upper and lower bounds on the changing cells. A lower bound of 0.010 on alpha and beta will always work. An upper bound of 1,000 for alpha and beta was tried. If the Solver makes alpha or beta bump up against your upper bound, you should relax the bound.

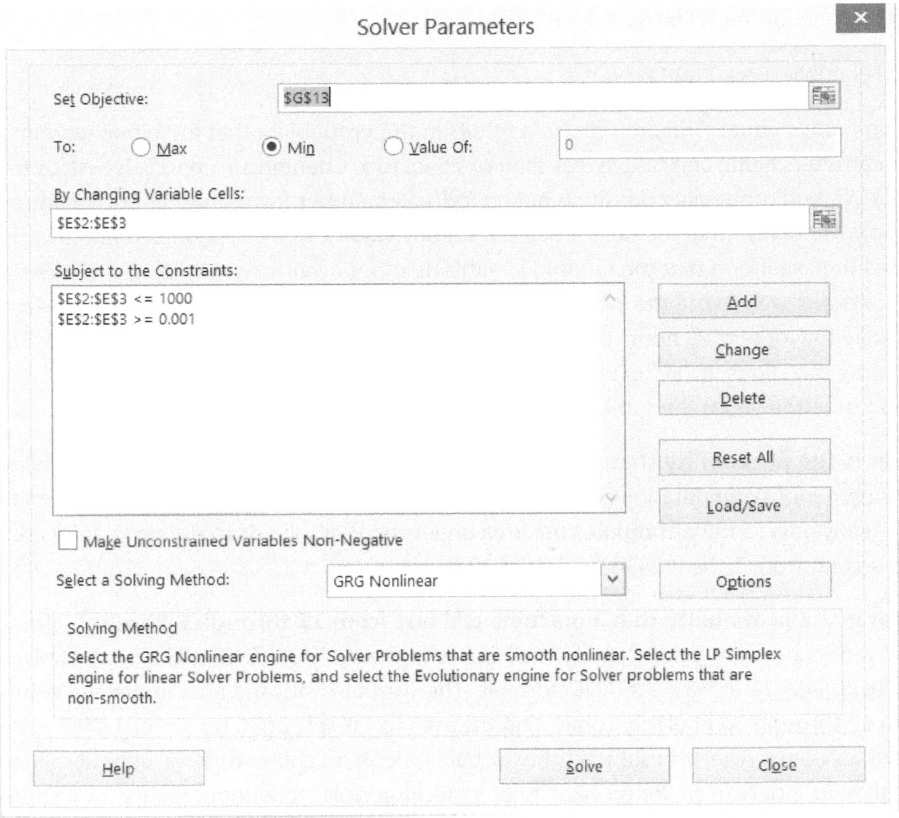

FIGURE 70-2 Solver settings for determining parameters for a Weibull random variable.

	A	B	C	D	E	F	G	H
1								
2				alpha	2.725265			
3				beta	21.00372			
4								
5							assumed	Sq Err
6				mean	18.68428 =		18.68429	1.48E-11
7				variance parts	441.1562			
8					0.915493			
9					0.88957			
10				variance	54.77313			
11				sigma	7.400887 =		7.400885	6.07E-12
12								
13	mean	18.68428571				SSE	2.09E-11	
14	sigma	7.40088476						
15								
16		Machine 1	8.5			Prob>-20 hours	0.416832	
17		Machine 2	12.54					
18		Machine 3	13.75			Prob between 15 and 30 hours	0.599417	
19		Machine 4	19.75					
20		Machine 5	21.46					
21		Machine 6	26.34					
22		Machine 7	28.45					

FIGURE 70-3 Estimates of alpha and beta for a Weibull random variable.

Here's the syntax of the *WEIBULL.DIST* function:

```
WEIBULL.DIST(x,alpha,beta,Cumulative)
```

When *Cumulative* equals True, this formula results in the probability that a Weibull random variable with parameters alpha and beta is less than or equal to *x*. Changing True to False yields the height of the Weibull probability density function (pdf). Remember from Chapter 66, "An introduction to random variables," that the height of a pdf for any value *x* of a continuous random variable indicates the likelihood that the random variable assumes a value near *x*. Thus, if the Weibull density for 20 hours were twice the Weibull density for 10 hours, you would know that a machine is twice as likely to work for 20 hours before failing than to work for 10 hours before failing. Before answering some questions involving probabilities of interest, note that in prior versions of Excel, the *WEIBULLDIST* function yields the same results as *WEIBULL.DIST*:

- **What is the probability that a machine will last at least 20 hours?** This probability (41.7 percent) is computed in cell G16 with the 1–WEIBULL.DIST(20,alpha,beta,1) formula. Essentially, this formula computes the area under the Weibull pdf to the right of 20 hours by subtracting from 1 the area to the left of 20 hours.

- **What is the probability that a machine will last from 15 through 30 hours?** This probability (66.9 percent) is computed in cell G18 with the WEIBULL.DISTL(30,alpha,beta,TRUE)–WEIBULL.DIST(15,alpha,beta,TRUE) formula. This formula finds the area under the Weibull pdf from 15 through 30 hours by computing the area to the left of 30 hours minus the area to the left of 15 hours. After you subtract the probability of a machine working without failure for less than 15 hours from the probability of a machine working without failure for less than or equal to 30 hours, you are left with the probability that a machine will work without failure from 15 through 30 hours.

How can I estimate the probability that hanging drywall in a building will take more than 200 hours?

Since the development of the Polaris missile in the 1950s, project managers have modeled activity durations with the beta random variable. To specify a beta random variable, you need to specify a minimum value, a maximum value, and two parameters (alpha and beta). The data in the Beta.xlsx file (see Figure 70-4) can be used to estimate the parameters of a beta distribution.

Suppose that you believe that the time needed to hang drywall in a building is sure to be between 0 and 600 hours. These are your minimum and maximum values, entered in cells C7 and C8. The F8:F22 cell range contains the lengths of time needed to hang drywall in 15 buildings of a similar size. In cell F5, the AVERAGE function was used to compute the mean time (78.49 hours) needed to hang drywall in these 15 buildings. In cell F6, the STDEV function was used to determine the standard deviation (47.97 hours) of the time needed to hang drywall in these buildings. Any choice of values of alpha and beta determine the shape of the beta distribution's pdf and the mean and standard deviation for the corresponding beta random variable. If you can choose alpha and beta values to match the mean and standard deviation of the drywall installation times computed from this data, it seems reasonable that these alpha and beta values will yield probabilities consistent with the observed data. After you enter the mean and standard deviation for the drywall installation data in cells C9 and C10, the worksheet computes values for alpha (2.20) in cell C5 and beta (14.66) in cell C6 that ensure that the mean and standard deviation of the beta random variable match the mean and standard deviation of the data.

Fit a beta			
alpha	2.196262	mean	78.486
beta	14.59335	sigma	47.967
lower	0		Data
upper	600		26.257
mean	78.48647		91.840
sigma	47.96749		66.543
transformed mean	0.130811		53.893
transformed var	0.006391		222.437
			72.054
			75.357
Probability>=200 hours	0.020502		78.274
Probability <=80 hours	0.583238		99.044
Probability between 30 and 150 hours	0.771058		90.476
			47.000
			16.215
			117.277
			69.935
			50.694

FIGURE 70-4 Determining probabilities with the beta random variable.

The BETA.DIST(x,alpha,beta,True_or_1,lower,upper) function determines the probability that a beta random variable ranging from lower through upper, with parameters alpha and beta, assumes a value less than or equal to x. The last two parameters are optional, and if they are omitted, Excel assumes lower equals 0 and upper equals 1. The BETA.DIST(x,alpha,beta,False_or_0,lower,upper) function returns the pdf for a random variable following a beta distribution. You can now use the *BETA.DIST* function to determine probabilities of interest.

To compute the probability that hanging drywall will take at least 200 hours, you can use the formula in cell C15, 1–BETA.DIST(200,alpha,beta,True_or_1,lower,upper). The result is 2.1 percent. This formula simply computes the probability that hanging drywall will take at least 200 hours as *1 – probability dry walling takes less than or equal to 200 hours.*

The probability that hanging drywall will take at most 80 hours (58.3 percent) can be computed with the formula in cell C16, BETA.DIST(80,alpha,beta,True,lower,upper). And to compute the probability that the task will take from 30 through 150 hours (77.1 percent), in cell C17, use the BETA.DIST(150,alpha,beta,True,lower,upper)–BETA.DIST(30,alpha,beta,True,lower,upper) formula. This formula computes the probability that dry walling takes from 30 through 150 hours as the probability that dry walling takes less than or equal to 150 hours minus the probability that dry walling takes less than or equal to 30 hours. The difference between these probabilities counts only instances when dry walling takes from 30 through 150 hours.

Problems

The data for this chapter's problems are contained in the Ch70data.xlsx file:

1. In the Problem 1 worksheet, you are given data about the duration of a machine's lifetime:

   - What is the probability that the machine will last at least 10 hours?

   - What is the probability that the machine will last from 1 through 5 hours?

   - What is the probability that the machine will fail within 6 hours?

2. You need to clean your house today. In the Problem 2 worksheet, you are given data about how long it has taken to clean your house in the past. If you start cleaning at noon, what are the chances that you'll be finished in time to leave at 7:00 P.M. for a movie?

CHAPTER 71

Making probability statements from forecasts

Questions answered in this chapter:

- On what basis do we evaluate forecasts?

- If a drug company forecasts that it will sell 60 million units of a drug next year, what is the chance it will sell more than 65 million units of that drug next year?

Each day, we are constantly inundated by forecasts. Here are some examples:

- The government predicts the GNP will grow by 4 percent during the next year.

- The Eli Lilly marketing department predicts that during the next year, demand for a given drug will be 400,000,000 DOT (days of therapy).

- A Wall Street guru predicts the Dow will go up 20 percent during the next 12 months.

- The bookmakers forecast that the Indiana Pacers will beat the Houston Rockets by 6 in the opening game of the 2015 NBA season.

Although the forecasts we receive might be the best available, they are almost sure to be incorrect. For example, the bookmaker's prediction that the Pacers will win by 6 points is incorrect unless the Pacers win by exactly 6 points. In short, any single value (or point forecast) implies a distribution for the quantity being forecasted. How can you find a random variable that correctly models the uncertainty inherent in the point forecast? The key to putting a distribution around a point forecast is to have some historical data about the accuracy of past forecasts of the quantity of interest. For example, with regard to the forecast for the Dow industrial average, you might have, for the past 10 years, the forecast made in January of each year for the percentage change in the Dow and the actual change in the Dow for each of the 10 years.

Answers to this chapter's questions

This section provides the answers to the questions that are listed at the beginning of the chapter.

On what basis do we evaluate forecasts?

You can begin by seeing whether past forecasts exhibit any *bias*. For each past forecast, you determine the actual value and forecasted value. Then you average these ratios. If your forecasts are *unbiased*, this average should be around 1. Any significant deviation from 1 indicates a significant bias. For example, if the average of actual and forecasted is 2, actual results tend to be around twice the forecast. To correct for a bias, you should automatically double your forecast. If the average of actual and forecasted is .5, actual results tend to be around half the actual forecast, so to eliminate bias, you should automatically halve your forecast. After you eliminate forecast bias, you look at the standard deviation of the percentage errors of the unbiased forecast and use the following normal random variable to model the quantity being forecasted:

- Mean = the unbiased forecast

- Standard deviation = (unbiased forecast)*(standard deviation of the percentage errors associated with the unbiased forecasts)

The standard deviation of the percentage errors measures the accuracy of the past forecasts. Clearly, a smaller standard deviation of percentage forecast errors is preferred to a larger standard deviation.

The Drugfore.xlsx file (see Figure 71-1) illustrates the ideas of forecast bias and forecast accuracy. The file contains actual and forecasted sales (in millions of DOT) for years 2005 through 2012. First, these forecasts will be shown to be biased, and then they'll be corrected for the bias.

	B	C	D	E	F	G	H	I
1							mean	std dev
2				mean	0.91803		5E-17	0.11375
3								
4		Year	Actual Sales	Forecast	A/F	Unbiased forecast	%age error	
5		2005	17	22	0.77273	20.19668	-16%	
6		2006	59	61	0.96721	55.9999	5%	
7		2007	46	51	0.90196	46.81959	-2%	
8		2008	85	86	0.98837	78.95067	8%	
9		2009	98	103	0.95146	94.5572	4%	
10		2010	94	118	0.79661	108.3277	-13%	
11		2011	24	22	1.09091	20.19668	19%	
12		2012	14	16	0.875	14.6885	-5%	
13								
14								
15				Mean 2013	55.0819			
16				Sigma 2013	6.2657			

FIGURE 71-1 Correcting for forecast bias and measuring forecast accuracy.

To begin, in cells F5:F12, check for bias by computing actual sales and forecasted sales for each year. To do this, copy the D5/E5 formula from F5 to F6:F12.

Next, in cell F2, compute the bias of the original forecasts by averaging each year's actual and forecasted value with the AVERAGE(F5:F12) formula. Actual sales tend to come in 8 percent under forecast. To correct past biased forecasts, multiply them by .92 by copying the $F$2*E5 formula from G5 to G6:G12. In H5:H12, compute each year's percentage error for the unbiased forecast by copying the (D5-G5)/G5 formula from H5 to H6:H12. As you can see, for example, 2005 actual sales were 16 percent less than the unbiased forecast, whereas in 2011, actual sales were 19 percent larger than the unbiased forecast.

Now evaluate the accuracy of the forecast errors in cell I2 by computing the standard deviation of the percentage errors with the STDEV.S(H5:H12) formula. The standard deviation of past unbiased forecasts has been around 11.4 percent of the unbiased forecast.

If a drug company forecasts that it will sell 60 million units of a drug in 2013, what is the chance it will sell more than 65 million units of the drug in 2013?

Forecast errors often follow a normal random variable. Therefore, after correcting for bias, you can assume that forecast errors follow a normal random variable with:

- Mean = the unbiased forecast.

- Standard deviation = (unbiased forecast)*(standard deviation of the percentage errors associated with the unbiased forecasts).

In your example, this means that you should model drug sales in 2013 as a normal random variable with mean = 60(.918) = 55.08 million and standard deviation = (.11375)*55.08 = 6.27 million. You can now use the Excel *NORM.DIST* function to compute, in cell E18 (see Figure 71-2), the chance of selling at least 65 million units in 2013 with the 1-NORM.DIST(65,F15,F16,TRUE) formula. There is a 5.7 percent chance of selling more than 65 million units of the drug.

	D	E	F	G	H
15		Mean 2013	55.0819		
16		Sigma 2013	6.2657		
17					
18	Probability	0.05671928			
19	we sell >65 million	1-NORM.DIST(65,F15,F16,TRUE)			
20	units				

FIGURE 71-2 Chance of selling more than 65 million units of the drug.

Problems

1. In Game 7 of the Boston Celtics–Los Angeles Lakers 2010 NBA finals, the Lakers were favored by seven points. By looking at past NBA games, you will find that bookmakers' forecasts are unbiased. In addition, the standard deviation of bookmaker forecasts in past NBA games is

12 points. Before the game, what would you have estimated as the probability that the Lakers would win the game?

2. A leading cell phone company forecasts that it will sell 3 million units next year of its bestselling phone. In the past, actual sales have been unbiased, with forecast errors having a standard deviation equal to 10 percent of forecasted sales. What are the chances that fewer than 2.5 million phones will be sold next year?

3. The USC.xlsx file contains the USC football team's margins of victory for years 2005 through 2009 and the bookmaker's forecast (before the game) for the USC margin of victory. Do these data indicate that the bookmaker's forecasts are unbiased? If USC is favored by 10 points, estimate the chance that USC wins the game.

CHAPTER 72

Using the lognormal random variable to model stock prices

Questions answered in this chapter:

- What is the lognormal random variable?

- Is there a reason stock prices might follow a lognormal random variable?

- How can I model the future price of any stock as a lognormal random variable?

- How can I compute the probability that the Microsoft stock price will exceed $38 six months from now?

- How can I compute the median price of Microsoft in six months?

Many people are interested in modeling the future price of a stock, a commodity such as oil or wheat, or a future exchange rate. For the past 40 years, the *lognormal random variable* has been the random variable most often used to model stock prices. In this chapter, you learn why the lognormal random variable is a reasonable model for stock prices and how to determine the appropriate lognormal parameters for any stock. The chapter closes by showing how the Excel *LOGNORM.DIST* and *LOGNORM.INV* functions can be used to calculate probabilities that involve the future price of a stock.

Answers to this chapter's questions

This section provides the answers to the questions that are listed at the beginning of the chapter.

What is a lognormal random variable?

A random variable Y follows a lognormal random variable if $\ln Y$ follows a normal random variable. When using the Excel *LOGNORM.DIST* and *LOGNORM.INV* functions, a lognormal random variable Y is characterized by two parameters: a mean Mu equal to the expected value of $\ln Y$ and a standard deviation Sigma equal to the standard deviation of $\ln Y$.

Is there a reason stock prices might follow a lognormal random variable?

Let Y equal the price of a stock n days from now, P equal the stock's price today, and X_t equal the percentage change in the stock's price during day t. Then $Y = P * X_1 * X_2 * \ldots X_n$. Because the logarithm of a product is the sum of the logarithms, it's true that $\ln Y = \ln P + \ln X_1 + \ln X_2 + \ldots \ln X_n$. Suppose the changes in prices on different days are independent random variables. Recall from Chapter 69, "The normal random variable," that the central limit theorem implies that the sum of many independent random variables will be a normal random variable, even if the individual random variables are not normally distributed. This explains why $\ln Y$ is likely to be a normal random variable, and this implies that Y is a lognormal random variable.

How can I model the future price of any stock as a lognormal random variable?

At the close of trading on August 9, 2013, the price of Microsoft stock was $32.70. Suppose you are interested in modeling the price of Microsoft stock in six months as a lognormal random variable. How can you estimate Mu and Sigma? Luckily, information is easily available on the Internet to help you model the future price of a stock. The Ivolatility.com website provides an estimate of a stock's annual volatility (call it Sigma_). The annual volatility is a surrogate for a stock's riskiness or variability. At the close of trading on August 9, 2013, you can find from Ivolatility.com that the Microsoft implied volatility was 22.27 percent. To represent Sigma_ as a decimal, you write Sigma_ = .2227. (The method used to compute implied volatility is discussed in Chapter 78, "Pricing stock options.")

From the Investment section of finance.yahoo.com, you can find the consensus opinion of analysts for the price of Microsoft in a year, shown in Figure 72-1.

Price Target Summary	
Mean Target:	34.92
Median Target:	35.00
High Target:	41.00
Low Target:	28.00
No. of Brokers:	31

FIGURE 72-1 Analysts' forecasts for Microsoft stock price in one year.

Let S equal today's stock price and S_1 equal the estimated mean price in one year. Then Mu_, a surrogate for the annual mean return on the stock, can be estimated by Mu_ = $\ln(S_1/S_0)$.

You know that S equals $32.70, and S_1 equals $34.92. Therefore (as computed in cell F7 of the Lognormal.xlsx file; see Figure 72-2), Mu_ = $\ln(34.92/32.70) = 0.06568$.

	E	F	G
1			
2	**Microsoft August 9, 2013**		
3			
4	Price today	$ 32.70	
5	Forecast in a year	$ 34.92	
6	sigma_	0.2227	
7	Mu_	0.065685	
8	time(years)	0.5	
9	Mu for t	3.507819	
10	Sigma for t	0.157473	
11			
12	**In 6 months**		
13	Chance price >=$38	0.204952	
14	Chance price <=$20	0.000573	
15	Median Price	33.37538	

FIGURE 72-2 Using lognormal to model the price of Microsoft stock in six months.

If you want to model the price of Microsoft stock t years in the future, you need to know Mu_t = Mean of ln of Microsoft stock price in t years and $Sigma_t$ = Standard deviation of ln of Microsoft stock price in t years. It turns out that:

Mu_t = ln S + t($Mu\_$ − .5Sigma_^2) and Sigma = Sigma_*$\sqrt{t}$.

For six months, t =.5 years. In cell E9, $Mu_{.5}$ was computed as ln(32.7) +.5*(.06568) − .5*(.2227)^2 = 3.507819.

In cell E10, you compute $Sigma_{.5}$ = (.227)*$\sqrt{.5}$ = 0.157473.

Therefore, you can model the price of Microsoft in six months as a lognormal random variable with Mu = 3.507819 and Sigma = 0.157473.

How can I compute the probability that the Microsoft stock price will exceed $38 six months from now?

The Excel 2013 *LOGNORM.DIST(x,Mean,Sigma,True_or_1)* function computes the probability that a lognormal random variable with parameters Mean and Sigma is less than or equal to x. Changing True (or 1) to False (or 0) returns the height of the lognormal pdf at x.

In previous versions of Excel, the *LOGNORMDIST* function returns the same results as *LOGNORM .DIST*. In cell F13, you can determine the chance that the price of a share of Microsoft will exceed $38. This is calculated by 1 − Probability that share is >=$38, so use the 1-LOGNORM.DIST(38,F9,F10,True) formula. There is a 20.5 percent chance that a share of Microsoft will sell for more than $38 in six months.

In cell F14, you can determine the chance that a share of Microsoft will sell for less than or equal to $20 in six months with the LOGNORM.DIST(20,F9,F10,True) formula. There is less than a one percent chance that a share of Microsoft will sell for $20 or less in six months.

How can I compute the median price of Microsoft in six months?

The LOGNORM.INV(p,Mu,Sigma) function returns the value x of a lognormal random variable with parameters Mu and Sigma such that there is a probability p that the lognormal random variable is less than or equal to x.

Suppose you want to determine the median price of Microsoft stock in six months. This is a price $\$x$ such that there is a 50 percent chance that the Microsoft stock price in six months will be less than or equal to $\$x$. In cell F15, you find the median price in six months with the LOGNORM.INV(0.5,F9,F10) formula. The median price in six months is $33.38.

Remarks

The famous Black-Scholes option-pricing formula is discussed in Chapter 78. It assumes that the price of a stock does follow a lognormal random variable.

In recent years, it has become apparent that for many stocks, future stock prices take on extremely high or low values more often than the lognormal random variable predicts. This has caused analysts to search for other random variables with fat tails that can be used to model future stock prices. For more details on this topic, see Nicholas Taleb's best-selling book, *The Black Swan* (New York: Random House, 2010). Also, an alternative method for modeling stock prices that does not assume that future stock prices follow a lognormal random variable is discussed in Chapter 75, "Simulating stock prices and asset allocation modeling."

Problems

Suppose a stock sells for $30 today. The annual volatility of the stock is 35 percent, and analysts predict the expected price of the stock in a year will be $35. Use this information to answer the following questions:

1. What is the probability that in two years the stock will sell for more than $45?

2. What is the probability that in two years the stock will sell for less than $25?

3. You are 95 percent sure that the price of the stock in two years will be between what two values? Hint: Use .025 and .975 as the first arguments in the *LOGNORM.INV* function.

CHAPTER 73

Introduction to Monte Carlo simulation

Questions answered in this chapter:

- Who uses Monte Carlo simulation?

- What happens when I type =RAND() in a cell?

- How can I simulate values of a discrete random variable?

- How can I simulate values of a normal random variable?

- How can a greeting card company determine how many cards to produce?

Data analysts would like to estimate the probabilities of uncertain events accurately. For example, what is the probability that a new product's cash flows will have a positive net present value (NPV)? What is the risk factor of an investment portfolio? Monte Carlo simulation enables you to model situations that present uncertainty and then play them out on a computer thousands of times.

Note The term *Monte Carlo simulation* comes from the computer simulations performed during the 1930s and 1940s to estimate the probability that the chain reaction needed for an atom bomb to detonate would work successfully. The physicists involved in this work were big fans of gambling, so they gave the simulations the code name Monte Carlo.

In the next five chapters, examples are provided of how you can use Microsoft Excel 2013 to perform Monte Carlo simulations.

Answers to this chapter's questions

This section provides the answers to the questions that are listed at the beginning of the chapter.

Who uses Monte Carlo simulation?

Many companies use Monte Carlo simulation as an important part of their decision-making process. Here are some examples:

- General Motors, Proctor and Gamble, Pfizer, Bristol-Myers Squibb, and Eli Lilly use simulation to estimate both the average return and the risk factor of new products. At GM, former CEO Rick Waggoner used this information to determine which products came to market.

- GM uses simulation for activities such as forecasting net income for the corporation, predicting structural and purchasing costs, and determining its susceptibility to different kinds of risk (such as interest rate changes and exchange rate fluctuations).

- Lilly uses simulation to determine the optimal plant capacity for each drug.

- Proctor and Gamble uses simulation to model and optimally hedge foreign exchange risk.

- Sears uses simulation to determine how many units of each product line should be ordered from suppliers—for example, the number of pairs of Dockers trousers that should be ordered this year.

- Oil and drug companies use simulation to value real options such as the value of an option to expand, contract, or postpone a project.

- Financial planners use Monte Carlo simulation to determine optimal investment strategies for their clients' retirement.

What happens when I type =RAND() in a cell?

When you type the =RAND() formula in a cell, you get a number that is equally likely to assume any value between 0 and 1. Thus, around 25 percent of the time, you should get a number less than or equal to 0.25; around 10 percent of the time, you should get a number that is at least 0.90, and so on. To demonstrate how the *RAND* function works, take a look at the Randdemo.xlsx file, shown in Figure 73-1.

	B	C	D	E	F
1					
2	Trial			mean	0.495952
3	1	0.813262			
4	2	0.288988		Fraction	
5	3	0.939361		0-.25	0.2575
6	4	0.786287		.25-.50	0.2425
7	5	0.91443		.50-.75	0.2475
8	6	0.26157		.75-1	0.2525
9	7	0.336107			
10	8	0.503733			
11	9	0.105186			
12	10	0.956549			
13	11	0.857657			
14	12	0.126325			
15	13	0.558723			
16	14	0.351238			
17	15	0.856488			
18	16	0.77694			
19	17	0.626955			
20	18	0.552412			
21	19	0.718024			
22	20	0.548031			

FIGURE 73-1 Demonstrating the *RAND* function.

Note When you open the Sheet1 worksheet in the Randdemo.xlsx file, you will not see the same random numbers shown in Figure 73-1. The *RAND* function always recalculates the numbers it generates when a worksheet is opened or when new information is entered in the worksheet. The values in the Frozen worksheet are fixed to correspond to Figure 73-1.

The =RAND() formula was copied from cell C3 to C4:C402; the C3:C402 range was named Data. Then, in column F, you can track the average of the 400 random numbers (cell F2) and use the *COUNTIF* function to determine the fractions that are between 0 and 0.25, 0.25 and 0.50, 0.50 and 0.75, and 0.75 and 1. When you press the F9 key, the random numbers are recalculated. Notice that the average of the 400 numbers is always approximately 0.5 and that around 25 percent of the results are in intervals of 0.25. These results are consistent with the definition of a random number. Also note that the values RAND generates in different cells are independent. For example, if the random number generated in cell C3 is a large number (for example, 0.99), that tells you nothing about the values of the other random numbers generated.

How can I simulate values of a discrete random variable?

Suppose the demand for a calendar is governed by the following discrete random variable:

Demand	Probability
10,000	0.10
20,000	0.35
40,000	0.3
69,000	0.25

How can you have Excel play out, or simulate, this demand for calendars many times? The trick is to associate each possible value of the *RAND* function with a possible demand for calendars. The following assignment ensures that a demand of 10,000 will occur 10 percent of the time, and so on:

Demand	Random number assigned
10,000	Less than 0.10
20,000	Greater than or equal to 0.10, and less than 0.45
40,000	Greater than or equal to 0.45, and less than 0.75
69,000	Greater than or equal to 0.75

To demonstrate the simulation of demand, look at the Sim worksheet in the Discretesim.xlsx file (or its Frozen version shown in Figure 73-2).

	A	B	C	D	E	F	G
1						Cutoffs	Demand
2	Trial		rand			0	10000
3		1	40000	0.632005		0.1	20000
4		2	20000	0.341745		0.45	40000
5		3	60000	0.755492		0.75	60000
6		4	20000	0.222393			
7		5	20000	0.135		Fraction of time	
8		6	20000	0.381374		10000	0.12
9		7	40000	0.723522		20000	0.3325
10		8	20000	0.106238		40000	0.2925
11		9	40000	0.499416		60000	0.255
12		10	10000	0.06099			
13		11	10000	0.063153			
14		12	20000	0.237575			
15		13	60000	0.851849			
16		14	40000	0.592454			
17		15	40000	0.549156			
18		16	60000	0.938556			

FIGURE 73-2 Simulating a discrete random variable.

The key to this simulation is to use a random number to initiate a lookup from the F2:G5 table range (named Lookup). Random numbers greater than or equal to 0 and less than 0.10 will yield a demand of 10,000; random numbers greater than or equal to 0.10 and less than 0.45 will yield a demand of 20,000; random numbers greater than or equal to 0.45 and less than 0.75 will yield a demand of 40,000; and random numbers greater than or equal to 0.75 will yield a demand of 69,000. Four hundred random numbers were generated by copying the RAND() formula from C3 to C4:C402. Then 400 trials, or iterations, of calendar demand were generated by copying the VLOOKUP(C3,lookup,2) formula from B3 to B4:B402. This formula ensures that any random number less than 0.10 generates a demand of 10,000; any random number between 0.10 and 0.45 generates a demand of 20,000; and so on. In the F8:F11 cell range, the *COUNTIF* function was used to determine the fraction of the 400 iterations yielding each demand. When you press F9 to recalculate the random numbers, the simulated probabilities are close to the assumed demand probabilities.

How can I simulate values of a normal random variable?

If you type the NORM.INV(rand(),mu,sigma) formula in any cell, you generate a simulated value of a normal random variable having a mean Mu and standard deviation sigma. This procedure is illustrated in the Sim worksheet in the Normalsim.xlsx file. (See Figure 73-3 for the Frozen version.)

	A	B	C	D	E	F	G
1				mean	40000		
2				sigma	10000		
3	Trial	Normal Rv	Rand				
4	1	51474.28518	0.8744			sim mean	39917.206
5	2	47174.57061	0.76345			sim sigma	10090.233
6	3	28679.63394	0.12881				
7	4	38347.61662	0.43438				
8	5	35589.45315	0.32959				
9	6	21426.72175	0.03163				
10	7	45611.61787	0.71266				
11	8	49758.08713	0.83542				
12	9	74377.58134	0.99971				
13	10	43021.64238	0.61874				
14	11	52902.32552	0.90152				
15	12	23891.34524	0.0536				
16	13	51007.7462	0.8645				
17	14	44679.22699	0.68008				
18	15	51143.83646	0.86744				

FIGURE 73-3 Simulating a normal random variable.

Suppose you want to simulate 400 trials for a normal random variable with a mean of 40,000 and a standard deviation of 10,000. (These values are typed in cells E1 and E2, and these cells are named mean and sigma, respectively.) Copying the =RAND() formula from C4 to C5:C403 generates 400 random numbers. Copying the NORM.INV(C4,mean,sigma) formula from B4 to B5:B403 generates 400 trial values from a normal random variable with a mean of 40,000 and a standard deviation of 10,000. When you press the F9 key to recalculate the random numbers, the mean remains close to 40,000 and the standard deviation close to 10,000.

Essentially, for a random number p, the NORM.INV(p,mean,sigma) formula generates the pth percentile of a normal random variable with a mean Mu and a standard deviation Sigma. For example, the random number 0.87 in cell C4 (see Figure 73-3) generates approximately the eighty-seventh percentile of a normal random variable with a mean of 40,000 and a standard deviation of 10,000 in cell B4.

How can a greeting card company determine how many cards to produce?

This section demonstrates how Monte Carlo simulation can be used as a decision-making tool. Suppose that the demand for a Valentine's Day card is governed by the following discrete random variable:

Demand	Probability
10,000	0.10
20,000	0.35
40,000	0.3
69,000	0.25

The greeting card sells for $4.00, and the variable cost of producing each card is $1.50. Leftover cards must be disposed of at a cost of $0.20 per card. How many cards should be printed?

Basically, you simulate each possible production quantity (10,000; 20,000; 40,000; or 69,000) many times (for example, one thousand iterations). Then you determine which order quantity yields the maximum average profit over the one thousand iterations. You can find the data for this section in the Sim worksheet in the Valentine.xlsx file. (The Frozen version is shown in Figure 73-4.) The range names in cells B1:B11 were assigned to cells C1:C11. The name Lookup was assigned to the G3:H6 cell range. The sales price and cost parameters are entered in cells C4:C6.

	B	C	G	H
1	produced	40000		
2	rand#	0.91064647		
3	demand	60000	0	10000
4	unit prod cost	$ 1.50	0.1	20000
5	unit price	$ 4.00	0.45	40000
6	unit disp cost	$ 0.20	0.75	60000
7				
8	revenue	$ 160,000.00		
9	total var cost	$ 60,000.00		
10	total disposing cost	$ -		
11	profit	$ 100,000.00		

FIGURE 73-4 Valentine's Day card simulation.

Enter a trial production quantity (40,000 in this example) in cell C1. Create a random number in cell C2 with the =RAND() formula. As previously described, demand for the card in cell C3 is simulated with the VLOOKUP(rand,lookup,2) formula. (In the VLOOKUP formula, rand is the cell name assigned to cell C3, not the *RAND* function.)

The number of units sold is the smaller of the production quantity and demand. In cell C8, compute revenue with the MIN(produced,demand)*unit_price formula. In cell C9, compute total production cost with the produced*unit_prod_cost formula.

If more cards are produced than are in demand, the number of units left over equals production minus demand; otherwise, no units are left over. Compute the disposal cost in cell C10 with the unit_disp_cost*IF(produced>demand,produced−demand,0) formula. Finally, in cell C11, compute profit as revenue − total_var_cost-total_disposing_cost.

It would be nice to have an efficient way to press F9 many times (for example, one thousand) for each production quantity and tally the expected profit for each quantity. This situation is one in which a two-way data table comes to the rescue. (See Chapter 16, "Sensitivity analysis with data tables," for details about data tables.) The data table used in this example is shown in Figure 73-5.

	A	B	C	D	E	F
13	mean	25000	45506	58042	43614	
14	st dev	0	12989.25266	47856	72526.3	
15	16000	10000	20000	40000	60000	production quantity
16	1	25000	50000	-26000	-18000	
17	2	25000	50000	-26000	150000	
18	3	25000	8000	16000	-18000	
19	4	25000	8000	100000	-18000	
20	5	25000	50000	100000	66000	
21	6	25000	50000	100000	66000	
22	7	25000	50000	100000	150000	
23	8	25000	50000	16000	-18000	
24	9	25000	50000	16000	66000	
25	10	25000	50000	100000	-60000	
26	11	25000	50000	16000	-18000	
27	12	25000	50000	100000	-18000	
28	13	25000	50000	16000	66000	
29	14	25000	50000	-26000	-18000	
30	15	25000	50000	-26000	66000	
31	16	25000	50000	16000	-18000	
32	17	25000	50000	16000	66000	
33	18	25000	8000	100000	-60000	
34	19	25000	50000	100000	-18000	
35	20	25000	50000	16000	66000	
36	21	25000	8000	16000	-18000	

FIGURE 73-5 Two-way data table for greeting card simulation.

In the A16:A1015 cell range, enter the numbers 1 to 1,000 (corresponding to the 1,000 trials). One easy way to create these values is to start by entering 1 in cell A16. Select the cell and then, on the **Home** tab in the **Editing** group, click **Fill** (the icon with the down arrow), and select **Series** to open the **Series** dialog box. In the **Series** dialog box, shown in Figure 73-6, enter a step value of 1 and a stop value of 1,000. In the **Series In** area, select **Columns** and then click **OK**. The numbers 1 through 1,000 will be entered in column A, starting in cell A16.

FIGURE 73-6 Using the Series dialog box to fill in the trial numbers 1 through 1,000.

Enter the possible production quantities (10,000; 20,000; 40,000; 69,000) in cells B15:E15. You want to calculate profit for each trial number (1 through 1,000) and each production quantity. Refer to the formula for profit (calculated in cell C11) in the upper-left cell of the data table (A15) by entering **=C11**.

You can now trick Excel into simulating one thousand iterations of demand for each production quantity. Select the table range (A15:E1015) and then, in the **Data Tools** group on the **Data** tab, click **What If Analysis** and then select **Data Table**. To set up a two-way data table, choose the production quantity (cell C1) as the row input cell and select any blank cell (cell I14 was chosen here) as the column input cell. After you click **OK**, Excel simulates one thousand demand values for each order quantity.

To understand why this works, consider the values placed by the data table in the C16:C1015 cell range. For each of these cells, Excel uses a value of 20,000 in cell C1. In C16, the column input cell value of 1 is placed in a blank cell, and the random number in cell C2 recalculates. The corresponding profit is then recorded in cell C16. Then the column input cell value of 2 is placed in a blank cell, and the random number in C2 again recalculates. The corresponding profit is entered in cell C17.

By copying the AVERAGE(B16:B1015) formula from cell B13 to C13:E13, you can compute average simulated profit for each production quantity. By copying the STDEV(B16:B1015) formula from cell B14 to C14:E14, you can compute the standard deviation of the simulated profits for each order quantity. Each time you press F9, one thousand iterations of demand are simulated for each order quantity. Producing 40,000 cards always yields the largest expected profit, so producing 40,000 cards appears to be the proper decision.

The impact of risk on your decision

If you produce 20,000 instead of 40,000 cards, the expected profit drops approximately 22 percent, but risk (as measured by the standard deviation of profit) drops almost 73 percent. Therefore, if you are extremely averse to risk, producing 20,000 cards might be the right decision. Incidentally, producing 10,000 cards always has a standard deviation of 0 cards because if you produce 10,000 cards, you will always sell all of them without any leftovers.

Note In this workbook, I set the Calculation option to Automatic Except For Tables. (Use the Calculation command in the Calculation group on the Formulas tab.) This setting ensures that the data table does not recalculate unless you press F9, which is a good idea because a large data table will slow down your work if it recalculates every time you type something in your worksheet. Note that in this example, whenever you press F9, the mean profit changes. This happens because each time you press F9, a different sequence of one thousand random numbers is used to generate demands for each order quantity.

Confidence interval for mean profit

A natural question to ask in this situation is, "Into what interval will I be 95 percent sure that the true mean profit will fall?" This interval is called the *95 percent confidence interval for mean profit*. A 95 percent confidence interval for the mean of any simulation output is computed by the following formula:

$$\text{Mean Profit } \pm \frac{1.96 * \text{profitst.dev.}}{\sqrt{\text{number iterations}}}$$

In cell J11, you can compute the lower limit for the 95 percent confidence interval on mean profit when 40,000 calendars are produced with the D13–1.96*D14/SQRT(1000) formula. In cell J12, the upper limit for the 95 percent confidence interval was computed with the D13+1.96*D14/SQRT(1000) formula. These calculations are shown in Figure 73-7.

	I	J	K
9	95% CI for mean profit		
10	ordering 40,000 calendars		
11	Lower	55075.9	
12	Upper	61008.1	

FIGURE 73-7 Ninety-five percent confidence interval for mean profit when 40,000 calendars are ordered.

You can be 95 percent sure that your mean profit when 40,000 calendars are ordered is between $55,076 and $61,008.

Problems

1. An auto dealer believes that demand for 2015 model cars will be normally distributed with a mean of 200 and a standard deviation of 30. His cost of receiving an Envoy is $25,000, and he sells an Envoy for $40,000. Half of all the Envoys not sold at full price can be sold for $30,000. He is considering ordering 200, 220, 240, 269, 280, or 300 Envoys. How many should he order?

2. A small supermarket is trying to determine how many copies of *People* magazine it should order each week. The owner believes the demand for *People* is governed by the following discrete random variable:

Demand	Probability
15	0.10
20	0.20
25	0.30
30	0.25
35	0.15

The supermarket pays $1.00 for each copy of *People* and sells it for $1.95. Each unsold copy can be returned for $0.50. How many copies of *People* should the store order?

Calculating an optimal bid

Questions answered in this chapter:

- How can I simulate a binomial random variable?

- How can I determine whether a continuous random variable should be modeled as a normal random variable?

- How can I use simulation to determine the optimal bid for a construction project?

When bidding against competitors on a project, the two major sources of uncertainty are the number of competitors and the bids submitted by each competitor. If your bids are high, you'll make a lot of money on each project, but you'll get very few projects. If your bids are low, you'll work on lots of projects but make very little money on each one. The optimal bid is somewhere in the middle. Monte Carlo simulation is a useful tool for determining the bid that maximizes expected profit.

Answers to this chapter's questions

This section provides the answers to the questions that are listed at the beginning of the chapter.

How can I simulate a binomial random variable?

The BINOM.INV(n,p,rand()) formula simulates the number of successes in n independent trials, each of which has a probability of success equal to p. As explained in Chapter 73, "Introduction to Monte Carlo simulation," the *RAND* function generates a number equally likely to assume any value between 0 and 1. As shown in the Binomialsim.xlsx file (see Figure 74-1), when you press F9, the BINOM.INV(100,0.9,D3) formula entered in cell C3 simulates the number of free throws that Steve Nash (a 90-percent foul shooter in the NBA) makes in 100 attempts. The BINOM.INV(100,0.5,D4) formula in cell C4 simulates the number of heads tossed in 100 tosses of a fair coin. In cell C5, the BINOM.INV(3,0.4,D5) formula simulates the number of competitors entering the market during a year in which there are three possible entrants and each competitor is assumed to have a 40 percent chance of entering the market. Of course, the RAND() formula was entered in D3:D5.

	B	C	D
1			
2			Rand#
3	Number of free throws Steve Nash makes out of 100	96	0.984165
4	Number of heads in 100 tosses	50	0.484458
5	Number of competitors entering market; p =4 n= 3	1	0.355209

FIGURE 74-1 Simulating a binomial random variable.

How can I determine whether a continuous random variable should be modeled as a normal random variable?

Suppose that you think the most likely bid by a competitor is $50,000. Recall that the normal probability density function (pdf) is symmetric about its mean. Therefore, to determine whether a normal random variable can be used to model a competitor's bid, you need to test for symmetry about the bid's mean. If the competitor's bid exhibits symmetry about the mean of $50,000, bids of $40,000 and $60,000, $45,000 and $55,000, and so on should be approximately equally likely. If the symmetry assumption seems reasonable, you can then model each competitor's bid as a normal random variable with a mean of $50,000.

How can you estimate the standard deviation of each competitor's bid? Recall from the rule of thumb discussed in Chapter 42, "Summarizing data by using descriptive statistics," that data sets with symmetric histograms have roughly 95 percent of their data within two standard deviations of the mean. Similarly, a normal random variable has a 95 percent probability of being within two standard deviations of its mean. Suppose that you are 95 percent sure that a competitor's bid will be between $30,000 and $70,000. This implies that 2*(standard deviation of competitor's bid) equals $20,000, or the standard deviation of a competitor's bid equals $10,000.

If the symmetry assumption is reasonable, you can now simulate a competitor's bid with the NORM.INV(rand(),50000,10000) formula. (See Chapter 73 for details about how to model normal random variables, using the *NORM.INV* function.)

How can I use simulation to determine the optimal bid for a construction project?

Assume that you're bidding on a construction project that will cost you $25,000 to complete. It costs $1,000 to prepare your bid. You have six potential competitors, and you estimate that there is a 50 percent chance that each competitor will bid on the project. If a competitor places a bid, its bid is assumed to follow a normal random variable with a mean equal to $50,000 and a standard deviation equal to $10,000. Also suppose you are only preparing bids that are exact multiples of $5,000. What should you bid to maximize expected profit? Remember, the low bid wins! You'll find the work for this question in the Bidsim.xlsx file, shown in Figure 74-2 and Figure 74-3.

	D	E	F	G
1	costproject	25000		
2	cost bid	1000	rand#	
3	Number bidders	3	0.633253	
4	mybid	40000		
5				
6				
7				
8	Bidder #	In	Bid	rand#
9	1	yes	47976.61	0.419826
10	2	yes	55099.54	0.694958
11	3	yes	44049.77	0.275914
12	4	no	100000	0.262327
13	5	no	100000	0.038515
14	6	no	100000	0.585372
15				
16	Do I win?			
17	yes			
18	Profit			
19	14000			

FIGURE 74-2 Bidding simulation model.

	D	E	F	G	H	I	J	K
21	mean	3630	7290	8240	5680	3175	2120	225
22	14000	30000	35000	40000	45000	50000	55000	60000
23	1	4000	9000	-1000	19000	-1000	-1000	-1000
24	2	4000	9000	-1000	19000	-1000	-1000	-1000
25	3	-1000	9000	-1000	-1000	-1000	-1000	-1000
26	4	4000	9000	14000	-1000	24000	-1000	-1000
27	5	4000	9000	14000	19000	-1000	-1000	-1000
28	6	4000	-1000	-1000	-1000	24000	-1000	-1000
29	7	4000	9000	14000	-1000	-1000	-1000	-1000
30	8	4000	9000	-1000	-1000	-1000	-1000	-1000
31	9	4000	9000	14000	-1000	-1000	-1000	-1000
32	10	4000	9000	-1000	19000	24000	-1000	-1000
33	11	4000	9000	14000	-1000	-1000	-1000	-1000
34	12	4000	-1000	-1000	-1000	-1000	29000	-1000
35	13	4000	9000	-1000	-1000	24000	-1000	-1000
36	14	4000	9000	14000	-1000	-1000	-1000	-1000
37	15	4000	9000	14000	-1000	24000	-1000	-1000
38	16	4000	-1000	14000	-1000	-1000	-1000	-1000
39	17	4000	9000	14000	-1000	-1000	-1000	34000
40	18	4000	9000	14000	-1000	-1000	-1000	-1000
41	19	4000	9000	14000	-1000	24000	-1000	-1000
42	20	4000	9000	14000	-1000	-1000	-1000	-1000

FIGURE 74-3 Bidding simulation data table.

Your strategy should be as follows:

- Generate the number of bidders.

- For each potential bidder who actually bids, use the normal random variable to model the bid. If a potential bidder does not bid, you assign a large bid (for example, $100,000) to ensure that he does not win the bidding.

- Determine whether you are the low bidder.

- If you are the low bidder, you earn a profit equal to your bid, less project cost, less $1,000 (the cost of making the bid). If you are not the low bidder, you lose the $1,000 cost of the bid.

- Use a two-way data table to simulate each possible bid (for example, $30,000, $35,000, . . . , $60,000) one thousand times and then choose the bid with the largest expected profit.

To begin, assign the names in the D1:D4 cell range to the E1:E4 range. Determine in cell E3 the number of bidders with the BINOM.INV(6,0.5,F3) formula. Cell F3 contains the RAND() formula. Determine which of the potential bidders actually bid by copying the IF(D9<=Number_bidders,"yes","no") formula from E9 to E10:E14.

Generate a bid for each bidder (nonbidders are assigned a bid of $100,000) by copying the IF(E9="yes",NORM.INV(G9,50000,10000),100000) formula from cell F9 to F10:F14. Each cell in the G9:G14 cell range contains the *RAND* function. In cell D17, determine whether you are the low bidder and win the project with the IF(mybid<=MIN(F9:F14),"yes","no") formula. In cell D19, compute profit with the IF(D17="yes",mybid−costproject−cost_bid,−cost_bid) formula, recognizing that you receive only the amount of the bid and pay project costs if you win the bid.

Now you can use a two-way data table (shown in Figure 74-3) to simulate one thousand bids between $30,000 and $60,000. Copy the profit to cell D22 by entering the =D19 formula. Select the D22:K1022 table range. On the **Data** tab, in the **Data Tools** group, click **What-If Analysis** and then click **Data Table** to specify the input values for the data table. The column input cell is any blank cell in the worksheet, and the row input cell is E4 (the location of the bid). Clicking **OK** in the Data Table dialog box simulates the profit from each bid one thousand times.

Copying the AVERAGE(E23:E1022) formula from E21 to F21:K21 calculates the mean profit for each bid. Each time you press F9, you see that the mean profit for one thousand trials is maximized by bidding $40,000.

Problems

1. How would the optimal bid change if you had 12 competitors?

2. Suppose you are bidding for an oil well that you believe will yield $40 million (including the cost of developing and mining the oil) in profits. Three competitors are bidding against you, and each competitor's bid is assumed to follow a normal random variable with a mean of $30 million and a standard deviation of $4 million. What should you bid (within $1 million)?

3. A commonly used continuous random variable is the uniform random variable. A uniform random variable—written as $U(a,b)$—is equally likely to assume any value between two given numbers a and b. Explain why the $a + (b - a)*RAND()$ formula can be used to simulate $U(a,b)$.

4. Investor Peter Fischer is bidding to take over a biotech company. The company is equally likely to be worth any amount between $0 and $200 per share. Only the company itself knows its true value. Peter is such a good investor that the market will immediately estimate the firm's value at 50 percent more than its true value. What should Peter bid per share for this company?

5. Seattle Mariner baseball player Ichiro Suzuki is asking for salary arbitration on his contract. Salary arbitration in Major League Baseball works as follows: The player submits a salary that he thinks he should be paid, as does the team. The arbitrator (without seeing the salaries submitted by the player or the team) estimates a fair salary. The player is then paid the submitted salary that is closer to the arbitrator's estimate. For example, suppose Ichiro submits a $12 million offer, and the Seattle Mariners submit a $7 million offer. If the arbitrator says a fair salary is $10 million, Ichiro will be paid $12 million, whereas if the arbitrator says a fair salary is $9 million, Ichiro will be paid $7 million. Assume that the arbitrator's estimate is equally likely to be anywhere between $8 and $11 million, and the team's offer is equally likely to be anywhere between $6 million and $9 million. Within $1 million, what salary should Ichiro submit?

CHAPTER 75

Simulating stock prices and asset allocation modeling

Questions answered in this chapter:

- I recently bought 100 shares of GE stock. What is the probability that during the next year this investment will return more than 10 percent?

- I'm trying to determine how to allocate my investment portfolio among stocks, T-bills, and bonds. What asset allocation over a five-year planning horizon will yield an expected return of at least 10 percent and minimize risk?

The past few years have shown that future returns on investments are highly uncertain. Chapter 72, "Using the lognormal random variable to model stock prices," showed how to use the lognormal random variable to model stock prices. Many financial experts have been critical of using the lognormal random variable to model stock prices because the lognormal underestimates the probability of extreme events (often called black swans). This chapter explains a relatively simple approach to assessing uncertainty in future investment returns. This approach is based on the idea of *bootstrapping*. Essentially, bootstrapping simulates future investment returns by assuming that the future will be similar to the past. For example, if you want to simulate the stock price of GE in one year, you can assume that each month's percentage change in price is equally likely to be one of, for example, the percentage changes for the previous 60 months. This method allows you to generate thousands of scenarios for the future value of your investments easily. In addition to scenarios that assume that future variability and average returns will be similar to the recent past, you can easily adjust bootstrapping to reflect a view that future returns on investments will be less or more favorable than in the recent past.

After you've generated future scenarios for investment returns, it's a simple matter to use the Microsoft Excel Solver to work out the asset allocation problem—that is, how should you allocate your investments to attain the level of expected return you want but with minimum risk?

The following two examples demonstrate the simplicity and power of the bootstrapping approach.

Answers to this chapter's questions

This section provides the answers to the questions that are listed at the beginning of the chapter.

I recently bought 100 shares of GE stock. What is the probability that during the next year this investment will return more than 10 percent?

Suppose that GE stock is currently selling for $28.50 per share. Data for the monthly returns on GE (as well as for Microsoft and Intel) for the months between August 1997 and July 2002 is included in the Gesim.xlsx file, shown in Figure 75-1. For example, in the month ending on August 2, 2002 (basically, this is July 2002), GE lost 12.1 percent. These returns include dividends (if any) paid by each company.

	C	D	E	F
3	mean	0.014746	0.006237	0.008828
4		MSFT	INTC	GE
5	8/2/2002	-0.08316	-0.15397	-0.12112
6	7/2/2002	-0.12285	0.028493	0.108434
7	6/2/2002	0.074445	-0.33853	-0.06139
8	5/2/2002	-0.02583	-0.03464	-0.01276
9	4/2/2002	-0.13348	-0.05894	-0.15658
10	3/2/2002	0.033768	0.064867	-0.02849
11	2/2/2002	-0.08429	-0.18514	0.041088
12	1/2/2002	-0.03834	0.114295	-0.07314
13	12/1/2001	0.031771	-0.03709	0.045898
14	11/1/2001	0.104213	0.337433	0.057167
15	10/1/2001	0.136408	0.194417	-0.02102
16	9/1/2001	-0.10307	-0.26889	-0.08653
17	8/1/2001	-0.13809	-0.06181	-0.05957
18	7/1/2001	-0.09329	0.019172	-0.10944
19	6/1/2001	0.055218	0.082654	0
20	5/1/2001	0.021107	-0.12601	0.009701
21	4/1/2001	0.238801	0.174658	0.159413
22	3/1/2001	-0.07305	-0.07886	-0.09653
23	2/1/2001	-0.03374	-0.22808	0.011168

FIGURE 75-1 GE, Microsoft, and Intel stock data.

The price of GE stock in one year is uncertain, so how can you get an idea about the range of variation in the price of GE stock one year from now? The bootstrapping approach simply estimates a return on GE during each of the next 12 months by assuming that the return during each month is equally likely to be any of the returns for the 60 months listed. In other words, the return on GE next month is equally likely to be any of the numbers in the F5:F64 cell range. To implement this idea, you use the RANDBETWEEN(1,60) formula to choose a scenario for each of the next 12 months. For example, if this function returns 7 for next month, you use the return for GE in cell F11 (4.1 percent), which is the seventh cell in the range, as next month's return. The results are shown in Figure 75-2. (You'll see different values because the *RANDBETWEEN* function automatically recalculates random values when you open the worksheet.)

To begin, you enter GE's current price per share ($28.50) in cell J6. Then you generate a scenario for each of the next 12 months by copying the RANDBETWEEN(1,60) formula from K6 to K7:K17. Use a lookup table to obtain the GE return based on your scenario. To do this, you simply copy the VLOOKUP(K6,lookup,5) formula from L6 to L7:L17. As the formula indicates, the B5:F64 range is named lookup, with the returns for GE in the fifth column of the lookup range. In the scenarios shown in Figure 75-2, you can see, for example, that the return for GE six months into the future is equal to the 12/1/2001 data point, that is, a 4.6 percent return. (Compare cell L11 in Figure 75-2 with cell F13 in Figure 75-1.)

	I	J	K	L	M
3					
4	GE				
5	Month	Start price	Scenario	Return	End price
6	1	28.5	23	-0.052040634	27.01684
7	2	27.0168419	60	0.088162457	29.39871
8	3	29.3987131	43	-0.043722304	28.11333
9	4	28.1133336	26	-0.024746687	27.41762
10	5	27.4176218	32	-0.133960753	23.74474
11	6	23.7447365	9	0.04589818	24.83458
12	7	24.8345767	5	-0.156577885	20.94603
13	8	20.9460312	38	-0.035371538	20.20514
14	9	20.2051379	8	-0.073139975	18.72733
15	10	18.7273346	13	-0.05956848	17.61178
16	11	17.6117757	43	-0.043722304	16.84175
17	12	16.8417483	25	0.134065934	19.09965

FIGURE 75-2 Simulating GE stock price in one year.

Copying the (1+L6)*J6 formula from M6 to M7:M17 determines each month's ending GE price. The formula takes the form of (1 + month's return)*(GE's beginning price). Finally, copying the =M6 formula from J7 to J8:J17 computes the beginning price for each month as equal to the previous month's ending price.

You can now use a data table to generate one thousand scenarios for GE's price in one year and the one-year percentage return on your investment. The data table is shown in Figure 75-3. In cell J19, you copy the ending price with the =M17 formula. In cell K19, you enter the (M17-$J$6)/$J$6 formula to compute the one-year return as (Ending GE price – Beginning GE price)/Beginning GE price.

Next, select the (J19:K1019) table range, click **What-If Analysis** in the **Data Tools** group on the **Data** tab, and then select **Data Table**. You set up a one-way data table by selecting a blank cell as the column input cell. After you click **OK** in the Data Table dialog box, Excel generates one thousand scenarios for GE's stock price in one year. (The calculation option for this workbook has been set to Automatic Except For Tables on the Formulas tab in the Excel Options dialog box. You need to press F9 if you want to see the simulated prices change.)

	J	K	L	M
18	**End Price**	**End Return**		
19	19.099653	-0.329836736	Mean	0.106679
20	23.7177891	-0.167796874	Prob lose money	0.403
21	25.8389085	-0.093371631	Prob make more than 10%	0.451
22	26.3086531	-0.076889363	Make between 0 and 10%	0.146
23	28.6928527	0.00676676	Lose between 0 and 10%	0.121
24	26.582571	-0.06727821	Lose More than 10%	0.282
25	51.0550021	0.791403584		
26	18.7384374	-0.342510967		
27	24.4760342	-0.141191781		
28	48.0968093	0.687607345		
29	37.2935418	0.308545327		
30	20.4767428	-0.281517797		
31	32.3495125	0.135070615		
32	24.4546509	-0.141942075		
33	36.8287092	0.292235411		
34	25.4360206	-0.107508048		
35	35.9101469	0.260005153		
36	20.4142444	-0.283710722		
37	49.6962638	0.743728555		

FIGURE 75-3 Data table for GE simulation.

In cells M20:M24, use the *COUNTIF* function (see Chapter 19, "The *COUNTIF, COUNTIFS, COUNT, COUNTA*, and *COUNTBLANK* functions") to summarize the range of returns that can occur in one year. For example, in cell M20, you can compute the probability of losing money in one year with the COUNTIF(returns,"<0")/1000 formula. (The range containing the one thousand simulated returns is named Returns.) The simulation indicates that, based on the data for 1997–2002, there is roughly a 40 percent chance that your GE investment will lose money during the next year. You can also see the following results:

- There is a 45 percent probability that returns will be more than 10 percent.

- There is a 15 percent probability that returns will be between 0 and 10 percent.

- There is a 12 percent chance that the investment will lose between 0 and 10 percent.

- There is a 28 percent chance that the investment will lose more than 10 percent.

- The average return for the next year will be approximately 10.7 percent.

Many pundits believe that future stock returns will not be as good as in the recent past. Suppose you feel that in the next year, GE will perform on average 5 percent worse per year than it performed during the 1997–2002 period for which you have data. You can easily incorporate this assumption into a simulation by changing the final price formula for GE in cell M17 to (1 + L17)*J17 − 0.05*J6. This simply reduces the ending GE price by 5 percent of its initial price, which reduces your returns for the next year by 5 percent. You can see these results in the Gesimless5.xlsx file, shown in Figure 75-4.

Note that the estimate is now a 49 percent chance that the price of GE stock will decrease during the next year. The average is not exactly 5 percent lower than the previous simulation because each time you run one thousand iterations, the simulated values change.

	L	M
19	Mean	0.056828
20	Prob lose money	0.487
21	Prob make more than 10%	0.39
22	Make between 0 and 10%	0.123
23	Lose between 0 and 10%	0.14
24	Lose More than 10%	0.347

FIGURE 75-4 Pessimistic view of the future.

I'm trying to determine how to allocate my investment portfolio among stocks, T-bills, and bonds. What asset allocation over a five-year planning horizon will yield an annual expected return of at least 8 percent and minimize risk?

A key decision made by individuals, mutual fund managers, and other investors is how to allocate assets among different asset classes, given the future uncertainty about returns for these asset classes. A reasonable approach to asset allocation is to use bootstrapping to generate one thousand simulated values for the future values of each asset class and then use the Excel Solver to determine an asset allocation that yields an expected return yet minimizes risk. As an example, suppose you are given annual returns on stocks, T-bills, and bonds during the period from 1973 to 2012. You are investing for a five-year planning horizon, and based on the historical data, you want to know which asset allocation yields a minimum risk (as measured by standard deviation) of annual returns and yields an annual expected return of at least 10 percent. You can see this data in the Assetallsim.xlsx file, shown in Figure 75-5. (Not all the data is shown.)

	A	B	C	D
5				
6		Annual Returns on Investments in		
7	Year	Stocks	T.Bills	T.Bonds
8	1973	-14.31%	5.07%	3.66%
9	1974	-25.90%	7.45%	1.99%
10	1975	37.00%	7.15%	3.61%
11	1976	23.83%	5.44%	15.98%
12	1977	-6.98%	4.35%	1.29%
13	1978	6.51%	6.07%	-0.78%
14	1979	18.52%	9.08%	0.67%
15	1980	31.74%	12.04%	-2.99%
16	1981	-4.70%	15.49%	8.20%
17	1982	20.42%	10.85%	32.81%
18	1983	22.34%	7.94%	3.20%
19	1984	6.15%	9.00%	13.73%
39	2004	10.88%	8.51%	1.02%
40	2005	4.91%	7.81%	1.20%
41	2006	15.79%	1.19%	2.98%
42	2007	5.49%	9.88%	4.66%
43	2008	-37.00%	25.87%	1.60%
44	2009	26.46%	-14.90%	0.10%
45	2010	14.82%	0.13%	8.46%
46	2011	2.07%	0.03%	16.04%
47	2012	15.83%	0.05%	2.97%

FIGURE 75-5 Historical returns on stocks, T-bills, and bonds.

To begin, you use bootstrapping to generate one thousand simulated values for stocks, T-bills, and bonds in five years. Assume that each asset class has a current price of $1. (See Figure 75-6.)

For each asset class, you enter an initial unit price of $1 in the H10:J10 cell range. Next, by copying the RANDBETWEEN(1973,2012) formula from K10 to K11:K14, you generate a scenario for each of the next five years. For example, for the data shown, next year will be similar to 1973, the following year will be similar to 1996, and so on. Copying the H10*(1+VLOOKUP($K10,lookup,L$8)) formula from L10 to L10:N14 generates each year's ending value for each asset class. For stocks, for example, this formula computes the following:

```
(Ending year t stock value)=(Beginning year t stock value)*(1+Year t stock return)
```

	G	H	I	J	K	L	M	N
8						2	3	4
9	Year	Stock value	Bill value	Bond value	Scenario	End stock	End bill	End bond
10	1	1	1	1	1973	0.8569	1.0507	1.0366
11	2	0.8569	1.0507	1.0366	1996	1.061014	1.104706	1.051423
12	3	1.061014	1.10470598	1.051423	1975	1.453589	1.183692	1.08938
13	4	1.453589	1.183692458	1.08938	1980	1.914958	1.326209	1.056807
14	5	1.914958	1.326209029	1.056807	1989	2.517786	1.433234	1.243757
15			5 yr stock	5 year bill	5 yr bond			
16			2.517786289	1.433234	1.243757			
17		1	1.508853822	1.406814	1.789437			
18		2	1.054555961	1.354346	1.615356			
19		3	1.654135076	1.53994	1.271061			
39		23	2.386475348	1.291398	1.147029			
40		24	1.796697533	1.343019	1.119824			
41		25	2.767582382	1.327434	1.635493			
42		26	1.172540276	1.317047	1.032606			
43		27	0.577441389	1.853421	1.570944			
44		28	1.805844675	1.416967	1.559975			
45		29	0.46286768	1.30509	1.005424			
46		30	0.929987568	1.704876	1.324592			

FIGURE 75-6 Simulating five-year returns on stocks, T-bills, and bonds.

Copying the =L10 formula from H11 to H11:J14 computes the value for each asset class at the beginning of each successive year.

You can now use a one-way data table to generate one thousand scenarios of the value of stocks, T-bills, and bonds in five years. Begin by copying the Year 5 ending value for each asset class to cells I16:K16. Select the (H16:K1015) table range, click **What If Analysis** on the **Data** tab, and then click **Data Table**. Use any blank cell as the column input cell to set up a one-way data table. After clicking **OK** in the Data Table dialog box, you obtain one thousand simulated values for the value of stocks, T-bills, and bonds over five years. It is important to note that this approach models the fact that stocks, T-bills, and bonds do not move independently. In each of the five years, the stock, T-bill, and bond returns are always chosen from the same row of data. This enables the bootstrapping approach to reflect the interdependence of returns on these asset classes that has been exhibited during the recent past. (See Problem 7 at the end of this chapter for concrete evidence that bootstrapping appropriately models the interdependence between the returns on your three asset classes.)

With this setup, you're ready to find the optimal asset allocation, which is calculated in the Assetallocationopt.xlsx file, shown in Figure 75-7. To start, copy the one thousand simulated five-year asset values and paste them into a blank worksheet. (Here, the C4:E1003 cell range was chosen.) In cells C2:E2, enter trial fractions of your assets allocated to stocks, T-bills, and bonds, respectively. In cell F2, add these asset allocation fractions with the SUM(C2:E2) formula. Later, you can add the F2=1 constraint to the Solver model, which ensures that you invest 100 percent of your money in one of the three asset classes.

	B	C	D	E	F	G	H	I
1		stock	bill	bond	total			
2		0.253439	0.72496	0.0216	1			
3	Iteration#	5 yr stock	5 yr bill	5 yr bond	final value	annual return	mean	0.08
4	1	1.918188	1.59811	1.62557	1.6798239	0.109309548	stdev	0.023464
5	2	1.45762	1.51918	1.49623	1.5030832	0.084917222		
6	3	1.813346	1.36737	1.55269	1.4844033	0.082207102		
7	4	0.708188	1.47771	1.23432	1.2774272	0.050188442		
8	5	1.798887	1.38551	1.49665	1.4926739	0.08341037		
9	6	1.471543	1.27084	1.07473	1.3174699	0.056691324		
10	7	2.312032	1.26426	1.32571	1.531136	0.088936998		
11	8	1.233231	1.29627	1.40951	1.2827384	0.05106027		
12	9	1.714351	1.15937	1.31493	1.3033822	0.05442175		
13	10	1.347237	1.31543	0.91343	1.3148118	0.056264583		
14	11	1.738629	1.40943	1.57053	1.4963423	0.08394237		
15	12	2.142478	1.33612	1.67409	1.5477795	0.091294125		
16	13	2.137394	1.33905	1.99864	1.5556246	0.092398166		
17	14	2.606492	1.4452	1.20512	1.734334	0.11641727		
18	15	1.387836	1.4837	1.11544	1.4514483	0.077358678		
19	16	1.987707	1.46462	1.99573	1.6086637	0.099747678		
20	17	2.022934	1.23382	1.36683	1.4366833	0.07515779		
21	18	1.774454	1.40583	1.52824	1.5018999	0.084746354		
22	19	1.46821	1.38864	1.52959	1.411849	0.071414829		

FIGURE 75-7 Optimal asset allocation model.

Next, you want to determine the final portfolio value for each scenario. To make this calculation, you can use a formula such as (Final portfolio value) = (Final value of stocks) + (Final value of T-bills) + (Final value of bonds). Copying the SUMPRODUCT(C4:E4,$C$2:$E$2) formula from cell F4 to F5:F1003 determines the final asset position for each scenario.

The next step is to determine the annual return over the five-year simulated period for each scenario that Excel generated. Note that $(1 + \text{Annual return})^5$ equals (Final portfolio value)/(Initial portfolio value). Because the initial portfolio value is just $1, this tells you that Annual return equals (Final portfolio value)$^{1/5} - 1$.

By copying the (F4/1)^(1/5)–1 formula from cell G4 to G5:G1003, you can compute the annual return for each scenario during the five-year simulated period. After naming the G4:G1003 range (which contains the simulated annual returns) Returns, you can compute the average annual return in cell I3 with the AVERAGE(returns) formula and the standard deviation of the annual returns in cell I4 with the STDEV.S(returns) formula.

Now you're ready to use Solver to determine the set of allocation weights that yields an expected annual return of at least 8 percent, yet minimizes the standard deviation of the annual returns. The Solver Parameters dialog box set up to perform this calculation is shown in Figure 75-8.

FIGURE 75-8 Solver Parameters dialog box set up for your asset allocation model.

- You try to minimize the standard deviation of the annual portfolio return (cell I4).

- The changing cells are the asset allocation weights (cells C2:E2).

- You must allocate 100 percent of the money you have to the three asset classes (F2=1).

- The expected annual return must be at least 8 percent (I3>=0.08).

- You assume that no short sales are allowed, which is modeled by forcing the fraction of the money in each asset class to be nonnegative. To implement this, select the **Make Unconstrained Variables Non-Negative** check box.

- The minimum risk asset allocation is 25.3 percent stocks, 72.5 percent T-bills, and 2.2 percent bonds. This portfolio yields an expected annual return of 8 percent and an annual standard deviation of 2.3 percent.

Suppose you believe that the next 5 years will, on average, produce returns for stocks that are 5 percent worse than they've been for the past 30 years. It is easy to incorporate these expectations into the simulation. (See Problem 4 at the end of the chapter.)

Problems

Problems 1–3 use data in the Gesim.xlsx file:

1. Assume that the current price of Microsoft stock is $28 per share. What is the probability that in two years the price of Microsoft stock will be at least $35?

2. Solve Problem 1 again, this time with the assumption that during the next two years, Microsoft will on average perform 6 percent better per year than it performed during the 1997–2002 period for which you have data.

3. Assume that the current price of Intel is $20 per share. What is the probability that during the next three years, you will earn at least a 30 percent return (for the three-year period) on a purchase of Intel stock?

Problems 4 through 7 use data in the Assetallsim.xlsx file:

4. Suppose you believe that over the next five years, stocks will produce returns that are 5 percent worse per year, on average, than the 1973–2009 data. Find an asset allocation among stocks, T-bills, and bonds that yields an expected annual return of at least 6 percent yet minimizes risk.

5. Suppose you believe that it is two times more likely that investment returns for each of the next five years will be more like the period from 1992 to 2001 than the period from 1972 to 1991. For example, the chance that next year will be like 1993 has twice the probability that next year will be like 1980. This belief causes your bootstrapping analysis to give more weight to the recent past. How would you factor this belief into your portfolio optimization model?

6. Many mutual funds and investors hedge the risk that stocks will go down by purchasing put options. (See Chapter 78, "Pricing stock options," for more discussion of put options.) How could an asset allocation model be used to determine an optimal hedging strategy that uses puts?

7. Determine the correlations (based on the 1973–2009 data) among annual returns on stocks, T-bills, and bonds. Then determine the correlation (based on the one thousand scenarios created by bootstrapping) among the final values for stocks, T-bills, and assets. Does it appear that the bootstrapping approach picks up the interdependence among the returns on stocks, T-bills, and bonds?

CHAPTER 76

Fun and games: simulating gambling and sporting event probabilities

Questions answered in this chapter:

- What is the probability of winning at craps?

- In five-card draw poker, what is the probability of getting three of a kind?

- Going into the NCAA basketball Final Four, what is the probability of each team winning the tournament?

Gambling and following sporting events are popular pastimes. I think gambling and sports are exciting because you never know what's going to happen. Monte Carlo simulation is a powerful tool that you can use to approximate gambling and sporting event probabilities. Essentially, you estimate probability by playing out a gambling or sporting event situation multiple times. If, for example, you have Microsoft Excel play out the game of craps 10,000 times and you win 4,900 times, you would estimate the probability of winning at craps to equal 4,900/10,000, or 49 percent. If you play out the 2003 NCAA men's Final Four 1,000 times and Syracuse wins 300 of the iterations, you would estimate Syracuse's probability of winning the championship as 300/1,000, or 30 percent.

Answers to this chapter's questions

This section provides the answers to the questions that are listed at the beginning of the chapter.

What is the probability of winning at craps?

In the game of craps, a player rolls two dice. If the combination is 2, 3, or 12, the player loses. If the combination is 7 or 11, the player wins. If the combination is a different number, the player continues rolling the dice until he either matches the number thrown on the first roll (called the *point*) or rolls 7. If the player rolls the point before rolling 7, the player wins. If the player rolls 7 before rolling the point, the player loses. By complex calculations, you can show that the probability of a player winning at craps is 0.493. You can use Excel to simulate the game of craps many times (two thousand was chosen for this example) to approximate this probability.

In this example, it is crucial to keep in mind that you don't know how many rolls the game will take. This example shows that the chance of a game requiring more than 50 rolls of the dice is highly unlikely, so you'll play out 50 rolls of the dice. After each roll, the game status is tracked as follows:

- 0 equals the game is lost.

- 1 equals the game is won.

- 2 equals the game continues.

The output cell keeps track of the status of the game after the fiftieth roll by recording 1 to indicate a win and 0 to indicate a loss. You can review the work done in the Craps.xlsx file, shown in Figure 76-1.

	A	B	C	D	E	F	G	H	AX	AY
1	TOSS#		1	2	3	4	5	6	7	49	50
2	Die Toss 1		5	4	2	3	5	5	1	4	6
3	Die Toss 2		5	6	5	4	4	5	3	4	3
4	Total		10	10	7	7	9	10	4	8	9
5	GAME STATUS		2	1	1	1	1	1	1	1	1

FIGURE 76-1 Simulating a game of craps.

In cell B2, use the *RANDBETWEEN* function to generate the number on the first die on the first roll by using the RANDBETWEEN(1,6) formula. The *RANDBETWEEN* function ensures that each of its arguments is equally likely, so each die has an equal (1/6) chance of yielding 1, 2, 3, 4, 5, or 6. Copying this formula to the B2:AY3 range generates 50 rolls of the dice. (In Figure 76-1, rolls 8 through 48 were hidden.)

In the B4:AY4 cell range, compute the total dice combination for each of the 50 rolls by copying the SUM(B2:B3) formula from B4 to C4:AY4. In cell B5, determine the game status after the first roll with the IF(OR(B4=2,B4=3,B4=12),0,IF(OR(B4=7,B4=11),1,2)) formula. Remember that a roll of 2, 3, or 12 results in a loss (entering 0 in the cell); a roll of 7 or 11 results in a win (1); and any other roll results in the game continuing (2).

In cell C5, compute the status of the game after the second roll with the IF(OR(B5=0,B5=1),B5, IF(C4=$B4,1,IF(C4=7,0,2))) formula. If the game ends on the first roll, maintain the status of the game. If a roll makes your point, record a win with 1. If a roll is a 7, record a loss. Otherwise, the game continues. A dollar sign was added in the reference to column B ($B4) in this formula to ensure that each roll tries to match the point thrown on the first roll. Copying this formula from C5 to D5:AY5 records the game status after rolls 2 through 50.

The game result is in cell AY5, which is copied to C6 so that you can easily see it. Use a one-way data table to play out the game of craps two thousand times. In cell E9, enter the =C6 formula, which tracks the outcome of the game (0 if a loss or 1 if a win). Next, select the (D9:E2009) table range, click **What-If Analysis** in the **Data Tools** group on the **Data** tab, and then click **Data Table**. Here, a one-way table was chosen with any blank cell as the column input cell. After you press F9, Excel simulates the game of craps two thousand times.

In cell E8, you can compute the fraction of the simulations that result in wins with the AVERAGE(E10:E2009) formula. For the two thousand iterations, you win 49.25 percent of the time. If you had run more trials (for example, 10,000 iterations), you would have come closer to the true probability of winning at craps (49.3%). For information about using a one-way data table, see Chapter 16, "Sensitivity analysis with data tables."

In five-card draw poker, what is the probability of getting three of a kind?

An ordinary deck of cards contains four cards of each type—four aces, four deuces, and so on up to four kings. To estimate the probability of getting a particular poker hand, you can assign the value of 1 to an ace, 2 to a deuce, and on up through the deck so that a jack is assigned the value of 11, a queen is assigned 12, and a king is assigned 13.

In five-card draw poker, you are dealt five cards. Many probabilities are of interest but use simulation to estimate the probability of getting three of a kind, which requires you to have three of one type of card and no pairs. (If you have a pair and three of a kind, the hand is a full house.) To simulate the five cards drawn, you proceed as follows. (See the Poker.xlsx file, shown in Figure 76-2.)

- Associate a random number with each card in the deck.

- The five cards chosen will be the five cards associated with the five smallest random numbers, which gives each card an equal chance of being chosen.

- Count how many of each card (ace through king) are drawn.

	A	B	C	D	E	F	G	H	I	J
1										
2		Drawn hand	Rank		Rand#				How many	
3	1	10	6	1	0.1218				1	0
4	2	5	19	1	0.3298				2	1
5	3	9	49	1	0.9124				3	0
6	4	8	11	1	0.1885				4	0
7	5	2	16	2	0.2217				5	1
8			26	2	0.392				6	0
9			5	2	0.0852				7	0
10			18	2	0.3266				8	1
11			29	3	0.4122				9	1
12			40	3	0.7127				10	1
13			20	3	0.3365				11	0
14			23	3	0.3691				12	0
15			24	4	0.3751				13	0
16			27	4	0.396					
17			28	4	0.4063		three of kind?			0
18			33	4	0.603					
19			2	5	0.0211					0
20			15	5	0.2134		prob 3 of kind		1	0
21			48	5	0.8786		0.019		2	0
22			25	5	0.3778				3	0
23			34	6	0.6514				4	0
24			46	6	0.8659				5	0
25			12	6	0.1987				6	0
26			14	6	0.2054				7	0

FIGURE 76-2 Estimating the probability that you'll draw three of a kind in a poker game.

To begin, list all the cards in the deck in cells D3:D54: four 1s, four 2s, and so on up to four 13s. Copy the *RAND* function from cell E3 to E4:E54 to associate a random number with each card in the deck. Copying the RANK.EQ(E3,$E$3:$E$54,1) formula from C3 to C4:C54 gives the rank (ordered from smallest to largest) of each random number. For example, in Figure 76-2, you can see that the fourth 3 in the deck (row 14) is associated with the 23rd smallest random number. (You will see different results in the worksheet because the random numbers are automatically recalculated when you open the worksheet.)

The syntax of the *RANK.EQ* function is RANK.EQ(*number,array,1_or_0*). If the last argument of the *RANK.EQ* function is 1, the function returns the rank of the number in the array, with the smallest number receiving a rank of 1, the second smallest number a rank of 2, and so on. If the last argument of the *RANK.EQ* function is 0, the function returns the rank of the number in the array, with the largest number receiving a rank of 1, the second largest number receiving a rank of 2, and so on.

In ranking random numbers, no ties can occur (because the random numbers would have to match 16 digits).

Suppose, for example, that you are ranking the numbers 1, 3, 3, and 4 and that the last argument of the *RANK.EQ* function was 1. Excel would return the following ranks:

Number	Rank (smallest number has rank of 1)
1	1
3	2
3	2
4	4

Because 3 is the second smallest number, 3 would be assigned a rank of 2. The other 3 would also be assigned a rank of 2. Because 4 is the fourth smallest number, it would be assigned a rank of 4. Understanding the treatment of ties by the *RANK.EQ* function will help you complete Problem 1 at the end of the chapter.

By copying the VLOOKUP(A3,lookup,2,FALSE) formula from cell B3 to B4:B7, you can draw five cards from the deck. This formula draws the five cards corresponding to the five smallest random numbers. (The lookup table range C3:D54 has been named lookup.) FALSE was used in the *VLOOKUP* function because the ranks need not be in ascending order.

Having assigned the range name Drawn to the drawn cards (the B3:B7 range), copying the COUNTIF(drawn,I3) formula from J3 to J4:J15 counts how many of each card are in the hand drawn. In cell J17, determine whether the hand includes three of a kind with the IF(AND(MAX(J3:J15)=3,COUNT IF(J3:J15,2)=0),1,0) formula. This formula returns a 1 if and only if the hand has three of one kind and no pairs.

Now, use a one-way data table to simulate four thousand poker hands. In cell J19, recopy the results of cell J17 with the J17 formula. Select the table range (I19:J4019). After clicking **What-If Analysis** in the **Data Tools** group on the **Data** tab and then clicking **Data Table**, you set up a one-way data table by selecting any blank cell as the column input cell. After you click OK, Excel simulates four thousand poker hands. In cell G21, record the estimated probability of three of a kind with the

AVERAGE(J20:J4019) formula. Estimate the chance of three of a kind at 1.9 percent. (Using basic probability theory, you can show that the true probability of drawing three of a kind is 2.1 percent.)

Going into the 2003 NCAA men's basketball Final Four, what was the probability of each team winning the tournament?

You can rate college basketball teams by using the methodology described in Chapter 34, "Using Solver to rate sports teams," but it is difficult to get the scores of all past games. The highly respected Sagarin ratings (available at sagarin.com) always gives up-to-date ratings for all college basketball teams. On the eve of the 2003 men's Final Four, the Sagarin ratings of the four teams were Syracuse (led by Carmelo Anthony), 91.03; Kansas, 92.76; Marquette (led by Dwayne Wade), 89.01; and Texas, 90.66. Given this information, you can play out the Final Four several thousand times to estimate the chance that each team will win.

The mean prediction for the number of points by which the home team wins is *favorite rating–underdog rating*. In the Final Four, there is no home team, but if there was one, you would add five points to the home team's rating. (In professional basketball, the home edge is four points, and in college and professional football, the home edge is three points.) Then you can use the *NORM.INV* function to simulate the outcome of each game. (See Chapter 69, "The Normal random variable," for a discussion about using the *NORM.INV* function to simulate a normal random variable.)

The likely outcome of the 2003 Final Four was calculated in the Final4sim.xlsx file, shown in Figure 76-3. The semifinals pitted Kansas against Marquette and Syracuse against Texas.

	C	D	E	F	G	H	I	J	K	L	M
1											
2			Semifinals								
3		Rating	Outcome	rand#							
4	KU	92.76	12.059202	0.796991	Final	rand#	Forecast	Outcome	Winner		
5	MARQ	89.01			KU	0.0809	92.76	-12.26	SYR		
6					SYR		91.03				
7											
8	SYR	91.03	5.2529429	0.687329							
9	TEX	90.66									
10											
11							odds		PROB WIN		SYR
12							1.702703	KU	0.37	1	TEX
13							3.514673	TEX	0.2215	2	KU
14							2.773585	SYR	0.265	3	KU
15							5.968641	MARQ	0.1435	4	TEX
16										5	TEX
17										6	KU
18										7	MARQ
19										8	KU
20										9	KU
21										10	MARQ
22										11	KU
23										12	MARQ
24							1.631579			13	SYR
25										14	SYR

FIGURE 76-3 Simulating the outcome of the NCAA 2003 Final Four.

To begin, enter each team's name and rating in the C4:D5 and C8:D9 cell ranges. In cell F4, use the *RAND* function to enter a random number for the Marquette–Kansas game and, in cell F8, enter a random number for the Syracuse–Texas game. The simulated outcome is always relative to the top team listed.

In cell E4, determine the outcome of the Kansas–Marquette game (from the standpoint of Kansas) with the NORM.INV(F4,D4–D5,10) formula. Note that Kansas is favored by D4–D5 points. In cell E8, determine the outcome of the Texas–Syracuse game (from the standpoint of Syracuse) with the NORM.INV(F8,D8–D9,10) formula. (The standard deviation for the difference between the actual winning margin and point spread of a college basketball game is 10 points.)

In cells G5 and G6, ensure that the winner of each semifinal game moves on to the finals. A semifinal outcome of greater than 0 causes the top listed team to win; otherwise, the bottom listed team wins. Thus, in cell G5, you enter the winner of the first game by using the IF(E4>0,"KU","MARQ") formula. In cell G6, enter the winner of the second game by using the IF(E8>0,"SYR","TEX") formula.

In cell H5, enter a random number to simulate the outcome of the championship game. Copying the VLOOKUP(G5,$C$4:$D$9,2,FALSE) formula from I5 to I6 obtains the rating for each team in the championship game. Next, in cell J5, compute the outcome of the championship game (from the reference point of the top listed team in cell G5) with the NORM.INV(H5,I5–I6,10) formula. Finally, in cell K5, determine the actual champion with the IF(J5>0,G5,G6) formula.

Now you can use a one-way data table in the usual fashion to play out the Final Four two thousand times. The simulated winners are in the M12:M2011 cell range. Copying the COUNTIF($M$12:$M$2011,J12)/2000 formula from K12 to K13:K15 computes the predicted probability of each team winning: 37 percent for Kansas, 27 percent for Syracuse, 22 percent for Texas, and 14 percent for Marquette. These probabilities can be translated to odds by using the following formula:

$$\text{Odds against team winning} = \frac{\text{prob team loses}}{\text{prob team wins}}$$

For example, the odds against Kansas are 1.63 to 1:

$$(1 - 0.37)/0.37 = 1.63$$

This means that if you placed $1 on Kansas to win and a bookmaker paid you $1.63 for a Kansas championship, the bet is fair. Of course, the bookie will lower these odds slightly to ensure that he makes money. (See Problem 6 at the end of this chapter for a related exercise.)

This methodology can easily be extended to simulate the entire NCAA tournament. Just use IF statements to ensure that each winner advances and use *VLOOKUP* functions to find each team's rating. See the Ncaa2003.xlsx file for a simulation of the 2003 tournament. The analysis gave Syracuse (the eventual winner) a 4 percent chance to win at the start of the tournament.

In this worksheet comments were used to explain the work, which you can see in Figure 76-4. Here is some background about using comments:

- To insert a comment in a cell, first select the cell. On the **Review** tab, in the **Comments** group, click **New Comment** and then type your comment text. You see a small red mark in the upper-right corner of any cell containing a comment.

- To edit a comment, right-click the cell containing the comment and click **Edit Comment**.

- To make a comment always visible, right-click the cell and click **Show/Hide Comments**. Clicking **Hide Comment** when the comment is displayed hides the comment unless the pointer is in the cell containing the comment.

- If you want to print your comments, click the **Page Setup** dialog box launcher (the small arrow in the bottom-right corner of the group) on the **Page Layout** tab to open the **Page Setup** dialog box. In the **Comments** box on the **Sheet** tab, you can indicate whether you want comments printed as displayed on the sheet or at the end of the sheet.

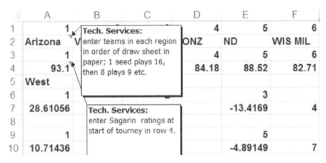

FIGURE 76-4 Comments in a worksheet.

Problems

1. Suppose 30 people are in a room. What is the probability that at least two of them have the same birthday?

2. What is the probability of being dealt one pair in five-card draw poker?

3. What is the probability of being dealt two pairs in five-card draw poker?

4. In the game of Keno, 80 balls (numbered 1 through 80) are mixed up, and then 20 balls are randomly drawn. Before the 20 balls are drawn, a player chooses 10 different numbers. If at least 5 of the numbers are drawn, the player wins. What is the probability of winning?

5. Going into the 2003 NBA finals, the rating system described in Chapter 34 rated the San Antonio Spurs three points higher than the New Jersey Nets. Teams play until one team wins four games. The first two games were at San Antonio, the next three at New Jersey, and the final two games were scheduled for San Antonio. What is the probability that San Antonio will win the series?

6. What odds should the bookmaker give on Kansas winning the Final Four if the bookmaker wants to earn an average of 10 cents per dollar bet?

7. What is the probability of being dealt a flush in five-card draw poker?

8. If you break a 1-inch stick in two places that are randomly chosen, you have three smaller sticks. What are the chances that the three sticks form a triangle?

9. Suppose each hitter on a baseball team has a 50 percent chance of hitting a home run and a 50 percent chance of striking out. On average, how many runs will this team score in an inning?

CHAPTER 77

Using resampling to analyze data

Question answered in this chapter:

- I produced nine batches of a product by using a high temperature and seven batches by using a low temperature. What is the probability that the product yield is better at the high temperature?

Data analysts often need to address questions such as these:

- What is the probability that a new teaching technique improves student learning?

- What is the probability that aspirin reduces the incidence of heart attacks?

- What is the probability that Machine 1 is the most productive of our three machines?

You can use a simple yet powerful technique known as *resampling* to make inferences from data. To make statistical inferences by using resampling, you regenerate data many times by sampling with replacement from your data. Sampling with replacement from data means that the same data point can be chosen more than once. You then make inferences based on the results of this repeated sampling. A key tool in implementing resampling is the *RANDBETWEEN* function. Entering the RANDBETWEEN(*a*,*b*) function yields with equal probability any integer between *a* and *b* (inclusive). For example, RANDBETWEEN(1,9) is equally likely to yield one of the numbers 1 through 9, inclusive.

Answer to this chapter's question

This section provides the answer to the question that is listed at the beginning of the chapter.

I produced nine batches of a product by using a high temperature and seven batches by using a low temperature. What is the probability that the product yield is better at the high temperature?

The Resampleyield.xlsx file, shown in Figure 77-1, contains the product yield from nine batches of a product manufactured at a high temperature and seven batches manufactured at a low temperature.

The mean yield at a high temperature is 39.74, and the mean yield at a low temperature is 32.27. This difference does not prove, however, that mean yield at a high temperature is better than mean yield at a low temperature. You want to know, based on your sample data, the probability that yield at a high temperature is better than at a low temperature. To answer this question, you can randomly generate nine integers between 1 and 9, which creates a resampling of the high-temperature yields.

For example, if you generate the random number 4, the resampled data for high-temperature yields will include a yield of 41.40; if you generate the random number 2, the resampled data will generate a yield of 39.93, and so on. Next, you randomly generate seven integers between 1 and 7, which creates a resampling of the low-temperature yields. You can then check the resampled data to see whether the high-temperature mean is larger than the low-temperature mean and then use a data table to repeat this process several hundred times. (The process was repeated 400 times in this example.) In the resampled data, the fraction of the time that the high-temperature mean is larger than the low-temperature mean estimates the probability that the high-temperature process is superior to the low-temperature process.

	C	D	E
1			
2			
3	mean	39.74	32.27
4	Number	High Temp	Low Temp
5	1	17.55	37.37
6	2	39.93	43.20
7	3	48.98	34.85
8	4	41.40	31.22
9	5	35.70	26.59
10	6	42.24	42.67
11	7	54.75	10.00
12	8	46.96	
13	9	30.19	

FIGURE 77-1 Product yields at high and low temperature.

To begin, you generate a resampling of the high-temperature data by copying the RANDBETWEEN(1,9) formula from cell C16 to C17:C24, as shown in Figure 77-2. A given observation can be chosen more than once or not chosen at all. Copying the VLOOKUP(C16,lookup,2) formula from cell D16 to D17:D24—the range C4:E13 has been named lookup—generates the yields corresponding to the random resampling of the data. Next, generate a resampling from the low-temperature yields. Copying the RANDBETWEEN(1,7) formula from E16 to E17:E22 generates a resampling of seven observations from the original low-temperature data. Copying the VLOOKUP(E16,lookup,3) formula from F16 to F17:F22 generates the seven actual, resampled, low-temperature yields.

In cell D26, compute the mean of the resampled high-temperature yields with the AVERAGE(D16:D24) formula. Similarly, in cell F26, compute the mean of the resampled low-temperature yields with the AVERAGE(F16:F22) formula. In cell D29, determine whether the resampled mean for high temperature is larger than the resampled mean for low temperature with the IF(D26>F26,1,0) formula.

	C	D	E	F
15	Resampled	High Temp	Resampled	Low Temp
16	3	48.98	1	37.37
17	9	30.19	2	43.20
18	6	42.24	4	31.22
19	5	35.70	1	37.37
20	2	39.93	5	26.59
21	2	39.93	7	10.00
22	4	41.40	7	10.00
23	2	39.93		
24	4	41.40		
25				
26	Average	39.97		27.96
27				
28				
29	High better	1		
30				Prob high better
31		1		0.905
32	1	0		
33	2	1		
34	3	1		
35	4	1		
36	5	1		
37	6	1		

FIGURE 77-2 Implementation of resampling.

To replay the resampling 400 times, you can use a one-way data table. Iteration numbers 1 through 400 were put in the C32:431 cell range. (See Chapter 73, "Introduction to Monte Carlo simulation," for an explanation of how to use the Fill Series command to create a list of iteration values easily.) By typing **=D29** in cell D31, create the formula that records whether high-temperature mean is larger than low-temperature mean in the output cell for the data table. After selecting the table range (C31:D431) and then selecting **Data Table** from the **What-If Analysis** menu in the **Data Tools** group on the **Data** tab, choose any blank cell in the worksheet as the column input cell. You have now tricked Microsoft Excel into playing out the resampling 400 times. Each iteration with a value of 1 indicates a resampling in which high temperature has the larger mean. Each iteration with a value of 0 indicates a resampling for which low temperature has a larger mean. In cell F31, determine the fraction of time that high-temperature yield has a larger mean by using the AVERAGE(D32:D431) formula. In Figure 77-2, the resampling indicates a 91 percent chance that high temperature has a larger mean than low temperature. Of course, pressing F9 will generate a different set of 400 resamplings and give you a slightly different estimate of the probability that high-temperature yield is superior to low-temperature yield.

Problems

1. You are testing a new flu drug. Out of 24 flu victims who were given the drug, 20 felt better and 4 felt worse. Out of 9 flu victims who were given a placebo, 6 felt better and 3 felt worse. What is the probability that the drug is more effective than the placebo?

2. A talk on the dangers of high cholesterol was given to eight workers. Each worker's cholesterol was tested both before and after the talk, with the following results. What is the probability that the talk caused the workers to undertake lifestyle changes that reduced their cholesterol?

Cholesterol before	Cholesterol after
220	210
195	198
250	210
200	199
220	224
260	212
175	179
198	184

3. The beta of a stock is simply the slope of the best-fitting line used to predict the monthly return on the stock from the monthly return given in the Standard & Poor's (S&P) 500 index. A beta that is larger than 1 indicates that a stock is more cyclical than the market, whereas a beta of less than 1 indicates that a stock is less cyclical than the market. The Betaresampling .xlsx file contains more than 12 years of monthly returns on Microsoft (MSFT), Pfizer (PFE), other stocks, and the S&P index. Use this data to determine the probability that Microsoft has a lower beta than Pfizer. You will need to use the Excel *SLOPE* function to estimate the beta for each iteration of resampling.

4. The Lawdata.xlsx file gives the LSAT scores and law school GPA for 15 law school students. Based on this data, you are 95 percent sure the correlation between LSAT score and GPA is between which two values?

CHAPTER 78

Pricing stock options

Questions answered in this chapter:

- What are call and put options?

- What is the difference between an American and a European option?

- As a function of the stock price on the exercise date, what do the payoffs look like for European calls and puts?

- What parameters determine the value of an option?

- How can I estimate the volatility of a stock based on historical data?

- How can I use Excel to implement the Black–Scholes formula?

- How do changes in key parameters change the value of a call or put option?

- How can I use the Black–Scholes formula to estimate a stock's volatility?

- I don't want somebody changing my neat option-pricing formulas. How can I protect the formulas in my worksheet so that nobody can change them?

- How can I use option pricing to help my company make better investment decisions?

During the early 1970s, economists Fischer Black, Myron Scholes, and Robert Merton derived the Black–Scholes option-pricing formula, which enables you to derive a value for a European call or put option. Scholes and Merton were awarded the 1997 Nobel Prize in Economics for their efforts. (Black died before 1997, and Nobel prizes are not awarded posthumously.) The work of these economists revolutionized corporate finance. This chapter introduces you to their important work.

Note For an excellent technical discussion of options, see David G. Luenberger's book, *Investment Science*, 2nd ed. (Oxford University Press, 2013).

Answers to this chapter's questions

This section provides the answers to the questions that are listed at the beginning of the chapter.

What are call and put options?

A *call option* gives the owner of the option the right to buy a share of stock for the *exercise price*. A *put option* gives the owner of the option the right to sell a share of stock for the exercise price.

What is the difference between an American and a European option?

An *American option* can be exercised on or before a date known as the *exercise date* (often referred to as the *expiration date*). A *European option* can be exercised only on the exercise date.

As a function of the stock price on the exercise date, what do the payoffs look like for European calls and puts?

Let's look at cash flows from a six-month European call option on shares of IBM with an exercise price of $110. Let P equal the price of IBM stock in six months. The payoff from a call option on these shares is $0 if $P \le 110$ and $P - 110$ if $P > 110$. With a value of P below $110, you would not exercise the option. If P is greater than $110, you would exercise the option to buy stock for $110 and immediately sell the stock for P, thereby earning a profit of $P - 110$. Figure 78-1 shows the payoff from this call option. In short, a call option pays $1 for every dollar by which the stock price exceeds the exercise price. The payoff for this call option can be written as $\text{Max}(0, P - 110)$. Notice that the call option graph in Figure 78-1 (see the Call worksheet in the Optionfigures.xlsx file) has a slope 0 for a value of P smaller than the exercise price. Its slope is 1 for a value of P greater than the exercise price.

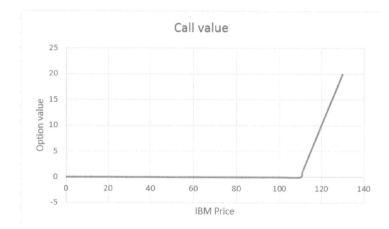

FIGURE 78-1 Cash flows from a call option.

You can show that if a stock pays no dividends, it is never optimal to exercise an American call option early. Therefore, for stock that does not pay a dividend, an American and a European call option both have the same value.

Now look at cash flows from a six-month European put option on shares of IBM with an exercise price of $110. Let P equal the price of IBM in six months. The payoff from the put option is $0 if P ≥ 110 and P – 110 if P < 110. For a value of P below $110, you would buy a share of stock for P and immediately sell the stock for $110. This yields a profit of 110 – P. If P is larger than $110, it would not be profitable to buy the stock for P and sell it for $110, so you would not exercise the option to sell the stock for $110.

Figure 78-2 displays the payoff from this put option (see the Put worksheet in the Optionfigures .xlsx file). In short, a put option pays $1 for each dollar by which the stock price is below the exercise price. A put payoff can be written as Max(0,110 – P). Note that the slope of the put payoff is –1 for a value of P less than the exercise price, and the slope of the put payoff is 0 for a value of P greater than the exercise price.

FIGURE 78-2 Cash flows from a put option.

An American put option can be exercised early, so the cash flows from an American put option cannot be determined without knowledge of the stock price at times before the expiration date.

What parameters determine the value of an option?

In their derivation of the Black–Scholes option-pricing model, Black, Scholes, and Merton showed that the value of a call or put option depends on the following parameters:

- Current stock price.

- The option's exercise price.

- Time (in years) until the option expires (referred to as the option's *duration*).

- Interest rate (per year on a compounded basis) on a risk-free investment (usually T-bills) throughout the duration of the investment. This rate is called the *risk-free rate*. For example, if three-month T-bills are paying 5 percent, the risk-free rate is computed as ln(1 + 0.05). (Calculating the logarithm transforms a simple interest rate into a compounded rate.)

Compound interest simply means that at every instant, you are earning interest on your interest.

■ Annual rate (as a percentage of the stock price) at which dividends are paid. If a stock pays 2 percent of its value each year in dividends, the dividend rate is 0.02.

■ Stock *volatility* (measured on an annual basis). An annual volatility of, for example, 30 percent means that (approximately) the standard deviation of the annual percentage changes in the stock's price is expected to be around 30 percent. During the Internet bubble of the late 1990s, the volatility of many Internet stocks exceeded 100 percent. You can estimate this important parameter in two ways.

The Black–Scholes pricing formula requires the price of the stock to follow a lognormal random variable. See Chapter 72, "Using the lognormal random variable to model stock prices," for further discussion of the lognormal random variable.

How can I estimate the volatility of a stock based on historical data?

To estimate the volatility of a stock based on data about the stock's monthly returns, you can proceed as follows:

■ Determine the monthly return on the stock for a period of several years.

■ Determine for each month ln(1 + monthly return).

■ Determine the standard deviation of ln(1 + monthly return). This calculation gives you the monthly volatility.

■ Multiply the monthly volatility by $\sqrt{12}$ to convert monthly volatility to an annual volatility.

This procedure is illustrated in the Dellvol.xlsx file, which estimates the annual volatility of Dell stock, using monthly prices in the period from August 1988 through May 2001. (See Figure 78-3, in which several rows of data are hidden.)

	A	B	C	D	E	F	G	H
1	Date	Dell Price	Return	1+Return	ln(1+Return)			
2	5/1/01	24.36	-0.07165	0.9283537	-0.074342521			
3	4/1/01	26.24	0.021509	1.0215085	0.021280472		monthly vol	0.16688
4	3/1/01	25.6875	0.174286	1.1742857	0.16066006		annual vol	0.57808
5	2/1/01	21.875	-0.16268	0.8373206	-0.177548278			
148	3/1/89	0.0742	-0.09512	0.904878	-0.099955097			
149	2/1/89	0.082	-0.17172	0.8282828	-0.188400603			
150	1/1/89	0.099	-0.0499	0.950096	-0.051192279			
151	12/1/88	0.1042	-0.08032	0.9196823	-0.083727039			
152	11/1/88	0.1133	-0.08407	0.9159256	-0.087820111			
153	10/1/88	0.1237	0.15824	1.1582397	0.146901353			
154	9/1/88	0.1068	0.282113	1.2821128	0.248509377			
155	8/1/88	0.0833						

FIGURE 78-3 Computing the historical volatility for Dell.

Copying the (B2–B3)/B3 formula from cell C2 to C3:C154 computes each month's return on Dell stock. Then copying the 1+C2 formula from D2 to D3:D154 computes for each month 1 + month's return. Next, compute ln(1 + month's return) for each month by copying the LN(D2) formula from E2 to E3:E154 and compute the monthly volatility in cell H3 with the STDEV.S(E2:E154) formula. Finally, compute an estimate of Dell's annual volatility with the SQRT(12)*H3 formula. Dell's annual volatility is estimated to be 57.8 percent.

How can I use Excel to implement the Black–Scholes formula?

To apply the Black–Scholes formula in Microsoft Excel, you need input values for the following parameters:

- S = Today's stock price

- t = Duration of the option (in years)

- X = Exercise price

- r = Annual risk-free rate (This rate is assumed to be continuously compounded.)

- σ = Annual volatility of stock

- y = Percentage of stock value paid annually in dividends

Given these input values, the Black–Scholes price for a European call option can be computed as follows.

Define:

$$d_1 = \frac{Ln(\frac{S}{X})+(r-y+\frac{\sigma^2}{2})t}{\sigma\sqrt{t}}$$

and:

$$d_2 = d_1 - \sigma\sqrt{t}$$

Then the call price C is given by:

$$C = Se^{-yt}N(d_1) - Xe^{-rt}N(d_2)$$

Here, $N(x)$ is the probability that a normal random variable with a mean of 0 and a σ equal to 1 is less than or equal to x. For example, $N(-1)$ = .16, $N(0)$ = .5, $N(1)$ = .84, and $N(1.96)$ = .975. A normal random variable with a mean of 0 and a standard deviation of 1 is called a *standard normal*. The cumulative normal probability can be computed in Excel 2013 with the *NORM.S.DIST* function. Entering NORM.S.DIST(x,True_or_1) returns the probability that a standard normal random variable is less than or equal to x. For example, entering the NORM.S.DIST(-1,True) formula in a cell will yield 0.16, which indicates that a normal random variable with a mean of 0 and a standard deviation of 1 has a 16 percent chance of assuming a value less than –1.

The price of a European put P can be written as:

$$P = Se^{-yt}(N(d_1) - 1) - Xe^{-rt}(N(d_2) - 1)$$

In the Bstemp.xlsx file (see Figure 78-4) is a template that computes the value for a European call or put option. Enter the parameter values in B5:B10 and read the value of a European call in D13 and a European put in D14.

	A	B	C	D	E
4	Input data				
5	Stock price	20			
6	Exercise price	24			
7	Duration	7			
8	Interest rate	0.04879			
9	dividend rate	0			
10	volatility	0.5			
11					
12				Predicted	
13	Call price			$10.64	
14	put			$7.69	
15					
16					
17	Other quantities for option price				
18	d1	0.781789		N(d1)	0.7828
19	d2	-0.54109		N(d2)	0.2942
20					

FIGURE 78-4 Valuing European calls and puts.

> **Note** Valuing American options is beyond the scope of this book. Interested readers should refer to Luenberger's excellent textbook.

As an example, suppose that Cisco stock sells for $20 today and that you've been issued a seven-year European call option. Assume that the annual volatility of Cisco stock is 50 percent, and the risk-free rate during the seven-year period is estimated at 5 percent per year. Compounded, this translates to $\ln(1 + .05) = .04879$. Cisco does not pay dividends, so the annual dividend rate is 0. The value of the call option is calculated to be $10.64. A seven-year put option with an exercise price of $24 would be worth $7.69.

How do changes in key parameters change the value of a call or put option?

- In general, the effect of changing an input parameter on the value of a call or put is given in the following table:

Parameter	European call	European put	American call	American put
Stock price	+	-	+	-
Exercise price	-	+	-	+
Time to expiration	?	?	+	+

Volatility	+	+	+	+
Risk-free rate	+	-	+	-
Dividends	-	+	-	+

An increase in today's stock price always increases the value of a call and decreases the value of a put.

■ An increase in the exercise price always increases the value of a put and decreases the value of a call.

■ An increase in the duration of an option always increases the value of an American option. In the presence of dividends, an increase in the duration of an option can either increase or decrease the value of a European option.

■ An increase in volatility always increases option value.

■ An increase in the risk-free rate increases the value of a call because higher rates tend to increase the growth rate of the stock price (which is good for the call). This situation more than cancels out the fact that the option payoff is worth less as a result of the higher interest rate. An increase in the risk-free rate always decreases the value of a put because the higher growth rate of the stock tends to hurt the put, as does the fact that future payoffs from the put are worth less. Again, this assumes that interest rates do not affect current stock prices, but they do.

■ Dividends tend to reduce the growth rate of a stock price, so increased dividends reduce the value of a call and increase the value of a put.

By using one-way and two-way data tables (see Chapter 16, "Sensitivity analysis with data tables," for details about how to work with data tables), you can, if you want, explore the specific effects of parameter changes on the value of calls and puts.

How can I use the Black–Scholes formula to estimate a stock's volatility?

Earlier in this chapter, you saw how to use historical data to estimate a stock's annual volatility. The problem with a historical volatility estimate is that the analysis looks backward. What you really want is an estimate of a stock's volatility looking forward. The *implied volatility* approach *implied volatility* approach simply estimates a stock's volatility as the volatility value that will make the Black–Scholes price match the option's market price. In short, implied volatility extracts the volatility value implied by the option's market price.

You can easily use the Goal Seek command and the input parameters you've been using to compute an implied volatility. On July 22, 2003, Cisco was selling for $18.43. An October 2003 call option with a $17.50 exercise price was selling for $1.85. This option expires on October 18 (89 days in the future). Thus, the option has a duration of 89/365 = 0.2438 years. Cisco does not expect to pay dividends; assume a T-bill rate of 5 percent and a corresponding risk-free rate of ln(1 + .05) = 0.04879. To determine the volatility for Cisco implied by this option price, you enter the relevant parameters in cells B5:B10 of the Ciscoimpvol.xlsx file, which is shown in Figure 78-5.

	A	B	C	D	E	F
4	Input data					
5	Stock price	18.43				
6	Exercise price	17.5				
7	Duration	0.24384				
8	Interest rate	0.04879				
9	dividend rate	0				
10	volatility	0.34036				
11						
12				Predicted		
13	Call price			$1.85		
14	put			$0.71		
15						
16						
17	Other quantities for option price					
18	d1	0.4629		N(d1)	0.678281	
19	d2	0.29483		N(d2)	0.615937	

FIGURE 78-5 Using implied volatility to estimate Cisco's volatility.

Next, use the **Goal Seek** dialog box (see Figure 78-6) to determine the volatility (the value in cell B10) that makes the call price (the formula in D13) hit a value of $1.85.

FIGURE 78-6 Goal Seek settings to find implied volatility.

This option implies an annual volatility for Cisco of 34 percent, as you can see in Figure 78-5.

> **Note** The *www.Ivolatility.com* website provides an estimate of the volatility of any stock, either historical or implied.

I don't want somebody changing my neat option-pricing formulas. How can I protect the formulas in my worksheet so that nobody can change them?

Surely, you have sent a worksheet to someone who then changed your carefully constructed formulas. Sometimes you want to protect a worksheet so that another user can only enter input data but not modify the worksheet's formulas. You can see how to protect all the formulas in the Black–Scholes template in the following example. (See the Bstemp.xlsx and Bstempprotected.xlsx files.)

Begin by unlocking all the cells in the worksheet and then lock the cells you want to protect. First, click the gray box in the upper-left corner of the worksheet, where the row and column headings intersect (next to the A and the 1). After you click this box, any format changes you make affect the entire worksheet. For example, if you select a bold format after clicking this box, all the cells in the worksheet will use the bold format.

After selecting the entire worksheet, click the **Font** dialog box launcher (the small arrow) on the **Home** tab. This opens the **Format Cells** dialog box, shown in Figure 78-7. On the **Protection** tab, clear the **Locked** check box, as shown in Figure 78-7, and then click **OK**. Now all cells in the worksheet are unlocked, which means that even if the worksheet is protected, you can still access these cells.

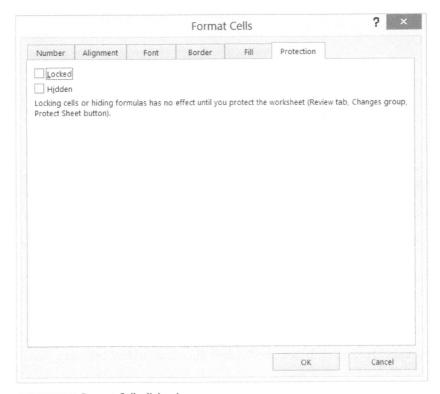

FIGURE 78-7 Format Cells dialog box.

Next, select all the formulas in the worksheet. To do this, press F5, which opens the **Go To** dialog box. Click **Special**, select **Formulas**, and click **OK**. Click the **Format Cells** dialog box launcher again and, on the **Protection** tab, select the **Locked** check box. Selecting this box locks all the formulas.

Now you can protect the worksheet, which will prevent a user from changing your formulas. Click **Protect Sheet** in the **Changes** group on the **Review** tab. In the **Protect Sheet** dialog box, select the **Select Unlocked Cells** check box, as shown in Figure 78-8. This option allows users of a template to select unlocked cells, but the formulas will be off-limits.

Now, when you click any formula, you cannot see or change its contents. Go ahead and try to mess up a formula! The result of protecting this workbook is saved in the Bstempprotected.xlsx file.

FIGURE 78-8 Allowing users to access unlocked cells.

How can I use option pricing to help my company make better investment decisions?

Option pricing can be used to improve a company's capital budgeting or financial decision-making process. The use of option pricing to evaluate actual investment projects is called *real options*. The idea of real options is credited to Judy Lewent, the former chief financial officer of Merck. Essentially, real options let you put an explicit value on managerial flexibility, which is often missed by traditional capital budgeting. The following two examples illustrate the concepts of real options.

> **Note** Refer to Luenberger's book for a more detailed discussion of real options.

You own an oil well. Today, your best guess is that the oil in the well is worth $50 million. In five years (if you own the well), you will make a decision to develop the oil well, at a cost of $70 million. A wildcatter is willing to buy the well today for $10 million. Should you sell the well?

Of course, the value of the oil in five years might increase. Even if you assume that the value of the oil would increase by 5 percent a year, the oil would be worth only $63.81 million in five years. Traditional capital budgeting says that the well is worthless because the cost to develop it is more than the value of the oil in the well. But wait; in five years' time, the value of the oil in the well will be different because many things (such as the global oil price) might change. There's a chance that the oil will be worth at least $70 million in five years. If the oil is worth $80 million in five years, developing the well in five years would return $10 million.

Essentially, you own a five-year European call option on this well because the payoff from the well in five years is the same as the payoff on a European call option with a stock price of $50 million, an exercise price of $70 million, and a duration of five years. You can assume an annual volatility similar to the volatility of a typical oil company stock (for example, 30 percent). If you use a T-bill rate of 5 percent, corresponding to a risk-free rate of 4.879 percent, in the Oilwell.xlsx file (see Figure 78-9), you can determine that the value of this call option is $11.47 million, which means that you should not sell the well for $10 million.

Of course, you do not know the actual volatility for this oil well. Therefore, you can use a one-way data table to determine how the value of the option depends on a volatility estimate. (See Figure 78-9.) From the data table, you can see that as long as the oil well's volatility is at least 27 percent, your oil well option is worth more than $10 million.

	A	B	C	D	E	F	G	H	I
1	Call with dividends								
2									
3									
4	Input data								
5	Stock price	50							
6	Exercise price	70							
7	Duration	5							
8	Interest rate	0.05							
9	dividend rate	0					Volatility	$11.47	
10	volatility	0.3					0.1	2.635248	
11							0.11	3.064456	
12				Predicted			0.12	3.498668	
13	Call price			$11.47			0.13	3.936575	
14	put			$16.32			0.14	4.377212	
15							0.15	4.819845	
16							0.16	5.263906	
17	Other quantities for option price						0.17	5.708942	
18	d1	0.2		N(d1)	0.5783		0.18	6.15459	
19	d2	-0.47		N(d2)	0.318		0.19	6.600548	
20							0.2	7.046562	
21							0.21	7.492419	
22							0.22	7.937931	
23							0.23	8.382936	
24							0.24	8.82729	
25							0.25	9.270862	
26							0.26	9.713537	
27							0.27	10.15521	
28							0.28	10.59577	

FIGURE 78-9 Oil well real options.

As a second example, consider a biotech drug company that is developing a drug for a pharmaceutical firm. The biotech company currently believes the value of the drug is $50 million. Of course, the value of the drug might drop over time. To protect against a price drop, the biotech company wants the drug to have a guaranteed value of $50 million in five years. If an insurance company wants to underwrite this liability, what is a fair price to charge?

Essentially, the biotech company is asking for a payment of $1 million in five years for each $1 million by which the value of the drug in five years is below $50 million. This is equivalent to a five-year put option on the value of the drug. Assuming a T-bill rate is 5 percent and the annual volatility on comparable drug stocks is 40 percent (see the Drugabandon.xlsx file, shown in Figure 78-10), the value of this option is $10.51 million. This type of option is often referred to as an *abandonment option*, but it is equivalent to a put option. (Figure 78-10 displays a one-way data table to show how the value of the abandonment option depends on the assumed volatility, ranging from 30 to 45 percent of the drug's value.)

	A	B	C	D	E	F	G	H	I
1	Call with dividends								
2									
3									
4	Input data								
5	Stock price	50							
6	Exercise price	50							
7	Duration	5							
8	Interest rate	0.0488							
9	dividend rate	0					Volatility	$10.51	
10	volatility	0.4					0.3	7.03399	
11							0.31	7.383411	
12				Predicted			0.32	7.732875	
13	Call price			$21.34			0.33	8.082211	
14	put			$10.51			0.34	8.431265	
15							0.35	8.779894	
16							0.36	9.127966	
17	Other quantities for option price						0.37	9.475362	
18	d1	0.72		N(d1)	0.764		0.38	9.821968	
19	d2	-0.174		N(d2)	0.431		0.39	10.16768	
20							0.4	10.51241	
21							0.41	10.85605	
22							0.42	11.19853	
23							0.43	11.53976	
24							0.44	11.87967	
25							0.45	12.21819	

FIGURE 78-10 Calculating an abandonment option.

Problems

1. Use the monthly stock returns in the Volatility.xlsx file to determine estimates of annual volatility for Intel, Microsoft, and GE.

2. A stock is selling today for $42. The stock has an annual volatility of 40 percent, and the annual risk-free rate is 10 percent:

    - What is a fair price for a six-month European call option with an exercise price of $40?

    - How much does the current stock price have to increase for the purchaser of the call option to break even in six months?

    - What is a fair price for a six-month European put option with an exercise price of $40?

    - How much does the current stock price have to decrease for the purchaser of the put option to break even in six months?

    - What level of volatility would make the $40 call option sell for $6? (Hint: Use the Goal Seek command.)

3. On September 25, 2000, JDS Uniphase stock sold for $106.81 per share. On the same day, a $100 European put expiring on January 20, 2001, sold for $11.875. Compute an implied volatility for JDS Uniphase stock based on this information. Use a T-bill rate of 5 percent.

4. On August 9, 2002, Microsoft stock was selling for $48.58 per share. A $35 European call option expiring on January 17, 2003, was selling for $13.85. Use this information to estimate the implied volatility for Microsoft stock. Use a T-bill rate of 4 percent.

5. You have an option to buy a new plane in three years for $25 million. Your current estimate of the value of the plane is $21 million. The annual volatility for the change in the plane's value is 25 percent, and the risk-free rate is 5 percent. What is the option to buy the plane worth?

6. The current price of copper is 95 cents per pound. The annual volatility for copper prices is 20 percent, and the risk-free rate is 5 percent. In one year, you have the option (if you want it) to spend $1.25 million to mine 8 million pounds of copper. The copper can be sold at whatever the copper price is in one year. It costs 85 cents to extract a pound of copper from the ground. What is the value of this situation to you?

7. You own the rights to a biotech drug. Your best estimate is that the current value of these rights is $50 million. Assuming that the annual volatility of biotech companies is 90 percent and the risk-free rate is 5 percent, what is the value of an option to sell the rights to the drug five years from now for $40 million?

8. Merck is debating whether to invest in a pioneer biotech project. The company estimates that the worth of the project is –$56 million. Investing in the pioneer project gives Merck the option to own, if it wants to, a much bigger technology that will be available in four years. If Merck does not participate in the pioneer project, it cannot own the bigger project. The bigger project will require $1.5 billion in cash four years from now. Currently, Merck estimates the net present value (NPV) of the cash flows from the bigger project to be $597 million. Assuming a risk free rate of 10 percent and that the annual volatility for the bigger project is 35 percent, what should Merck do? (This is the problem that started the whole field of real options!)

9. Develop a worksheet that uses the following inputs to compute annual profit:

   - Annual fixed cost

   - Unit cost

   - Unit price

   - Annual demand = 10,000 – 100*(price)

   Protect the cells used to compute annual demand and annual profit.

CHAPTER 79

Determining customer value

Questions answered in this chapter:

- A credit card company currently has an 80 percent retention rate. How will the company's profitability improve if the retention rate increases to 90 percent or higher?

- A long-distance phone company gives the competition's customers an incentive to switch. How large an incentive should it give?

Many companies undervalue their customers. When valuing a customer, a company should look at the net present value (NPV) of the long-term profits that the company earns from the customer. (For detailed information about net present value, see Chapter 7, "Evaluating investments by using net present value criteria.") Failure to look at the long-term value of a customer often causes a company to make poor decisions. For example, a company might cut its customer service staff by 10 percent to save $1 million, but the resulting decrease in service quality might cause it to lose much more than $1 million in customer value, which would, of course, result in the company being less profitable. The following two examples show how to compute customer value.

Answers to this chapter's questions

This section provides the answers to the questions that are listed at the beginning of the chapter.

A credit card company currently has an 80 percent retention rate. How will the company's profitability improve if the retention rate increases to 90 percent or higher?

This example is based on a discussion in Frederick Reichheld's excellent book, *The Loyalty Effect* (Harvard Business School Press, 2001). You can find the sample data for this example in the Loyalty .xlsx file, shown in Figure 79-1. Reichheld estimates the profitability of a credit card customer based on the number of years the customer has held a card. For example, during the first year a customer has the credit card, the cardholder generates –$40 profit, which is the result of customer acquisition costs and the cost of setting up the customer's account. During each successive year, the profit generated by the customer increases until a customer who has owned a card for 20 or more years generates $161 per year in profits.

The credit-card company wants to determine how the value of a customer depends on the company's retention rate. Currently, the company has an 80 percent retention rate, which means that at the end of each year, 20 percent (1 – 0.80) of all customers do not renew their card. (The 20 percent of customers who don't renew can be referred to as the annual *churn rate*.) The credit card company wants to determine the long-term value of a customer for retention rates of 80 percent, 85 percent, 90 percent, 95 percent, and 99 percent.

	A	B	C	D	E	F	G
4				npv per customer	141.7181		
5							
6		retention rate	0.8				
7		Interest rate	0.15				
8	Year	Mean Profit(if still here)	Number	Profit		retention rate	141.7181
9	1	($40.00)	100	($4,000.00)		0.8	141.7181
10	2	$66.00	80	$5,280.00		0.85	193.1495
11	3	$72.00	64	$4,608.00		0.9	269.3474
12	4	$79.00	51.2	$4,044.80		0.95	390.7125
13	5	$87.00	40.96	$3,563.52		0.99	548.5771
14	6	$92.00	32.768	$3,014.66			
15	7	$96.00	26.2144	$2,516.58			
16	8	$99.00	20.97152	$2,076.18			
17	9	$103.00	16.77722	$1,728.05			
18	10	$106.00	13.42177	$1,422.71			
19	11	$111.00	10.73742	$1,191.85			
20	12	$116.00	8.589935	$996.43			
21	13	$120.00	6.871948	$824.63			
22	14	$124.00	5.497558	$681.70			
23	15	$130.00	4.398047	$571.75			
24	16	$137.00	3.518437	$482.03			
25	17	$142.00	2.81475	$399.69			
26	18	$148.00	2.2518	$333.27			

FIGURE 79-1 Value of a credit card customer.

To determine the long-term value of a customer, you start with a cohort of, for example, 100 customers. (A *cohort* is a group of individuals having a statistical factor in common. The size 100 is arbitrary here, but round numbers make it easier to follow the analysis.) Then you determine how many of these customers are still around each year with the (Customers around for year $t + 1$) = (Retention rate)*(Customers around for year t) formula. You can assume that customers quit only at the end of each year. Then you use the NPV function to determine the total NPV (assuming a 15 percent discount rate) generated by the original cohort of 100 customers. The 15 percent discount rate implies that $1 earned one year from now is worth the same as $1.00/$1.15 of profit earned now. Dividing this number by the number of customers in the original cohort (100) gives you the value of an individual customer.

First, assign the names in the B6:B7 cell range to the C6:C7 cell range. Enter the number of original customers (100) in cell C9. Copying the retention_rate*C9 formula from cell C10 to the C11:C38 range generates the number of customers present for each year. For example, 80 customers will be present in Year 2.

Compute the profit earned each year by multiplying the number of remaining customers by each customer's profit. To make this calculation, copy the C9*B9 formula from cell D9 to D10:D38. In cell E4, compute the average NPV generated by an individual customer with the (1+Interest_rate)*NPV(Interest_rate,D9:D38)/100 formula. Assume cash flows at the beginning of the year and a 15 percent annual discount rate. The portion of the formula that reads NPV(Interest _rate,D9:D38) computes the average NPV generated by an individual customer, assuming end-of-year cash flows. Multiplying by (1 + Interest_rate) converts the end-of-year cash flow NPV to a beginning-of-year NPV.

With an 80 percent retention rate, the average customer is worth $141.72. To determine how the value of an individual customer varies with a change in annual retention rate, use a one-way data table. Enter the relevant annual retention rates in the F9:F13 cell range. In cell G8, enter the formula you want the data table to calculate (NPV per customer) with the =E4 formula. Select the table range (F8:G13) and then choose **Data Table** from the **What-If Analysis** command on the **Data** tab. After entering a column input cell of C6, you obtain the profit calculations shown in Figure 79-1. Notice that increasing the retention rate from 80 percent to 90 percent nearly doubles the value of each customer, which strongly argues for being nice to these customers and against pinching pennies on activities related to customer service. Understanding the value of a customer gives most companies a crucial lever that can be used to increase their profitability.

A long-distance phone company gives the competition's customers an incentive to switch. How large an incentive should it give?

You work for a phone company in which the average long-distance customer spends $400 per year, and the company generates a 10 percent profit margin on each dollar spent. At the end of each year, 50 percent of the company's customers switch to the competition, and without any incentives, 30 percent of the competition's customers switch to your company. You're considering giving the competition's customers a one-time incentive to switch companies. How large an incentive can you give and still break even?

The key to analyzing this problem (which you can find in the Phoneloyalty.xlsx file, shown in Figure 79-2) is to look at the NPV for two situations:

- **Situation 1**   100 customers begin with the competition.

- **Situation 2**   You pay the 100 customers who are with the competition a certain amount to switch to your company.

By following through each situation for a period of time (for example, 20 years), you can use the Goal Seek command to determine the dollar amount x paid to a person switching to your company that makes you indifferent about the following two situations:

- **Situation 1**   You have just paid 100 unloyal customers $x each to switch to your company.

- **Situation 2**   The market consists of 100 unloyal customers.

Assume that the analysis begins on June 30, 2014, and that customers switch companies at most once per year. Assign the range names in cells A2:A6 to cells B2:B6. The key step in the analysis is to realize that (year $t + 1$ customers with us) = .3*(year t competitor customers) + .5*(year t our customers). Similarly (year $t + 1$ customers with competition) = .7*(year t competition customers) + .5*(year t our customers).

	A	B	C	D	E	F	G	H	I	J
2	switch fee	34.22193			pay-no pay	0				
3	probleave	0.5								
4	probcome	0.3								
5	annrevenue	400	NPV	13674.36			13674.36			
6	profitmargin	0.1		Pay them			Do not pay them			
7		Date	Year	Number with us	Number with them	Profit	Number with us	Number with them	Profit	
8		initial								
9		6/30/2014	1	100	0	577.81	30	70	1200	
10		6/30/2015	2	50	50	2000	36	64	1440	
11		6/30/2016	3	40	60	1600	37.2	62.8	1488	
12		6/30/2017	4	38	62	1520	37.44	62.56	1498	
13		6/30/2018	5	37.6	62.4	1504	37.488	62.512	1500	
14		6/30/2019	6	37.52	62.48	1500.8	37.4976	62.5024	1500	
15		6/30/2020	7	37.504	62.496	1500.2	37.49952	62.5005	1500	
16		6/30/2021	8	37.5008	62.4992	1500	37.4999	62.5001	1500	
25		6/30/2030	17	37.5	62.5	1500	37.5	62.5	1500	
26		6/30/2031	18	37.5	62.5	1500	37.5	62.5	1500	
27		6/30/2032	19	37.5	62.5	1500	37.5	62.5	1500	
28		6/30/2033	20	37.5	62.5	1500	37.5	62.5	1500	

FIGURE 79-2 Phone incentive analysis.

Enter 100 in cell D9 (customers with us) and 0 in cell E9 (customers with the competition). This customer alignment corresponds to the situation right after the incentive is offered to 100 customers. Assume that customers who receive the incentive must stay with the company for at least one year. Copying the (1–probleave)*D9+probcome*E9 formula from D10 to D11:D28 generates the number of customers during each year. (Years 2022 through 2029 are hidden in Figure 79-2.) Copying the probleave*D9+(1–probcome)*E9 formula from E10 to E11:E28 calculates the number of customers with the competition during each year.

In cell F9, generate the profit earned during the first year with the D9*annrevenue*profitmargin–switch_fee*100 formula. Note that the cost of paying the 100 customers with the competition to switch has been subtracted. Copying the D10*annrevenue*profitmargin formula from F10 to F11:F28 generates profit during later years. In cell D5, compute the NPV of the profits associated with the incentive by using the XNPV(0.1,F9:F28,B9:B28) formula. (See Chapter 7 for a discussion of the XNPV function.)

In a similar fashion, in the G8:I28 cell range, generate the profits earned each year from 100 customers who were originally with the competition. On June 30, 2014, 30 of these 100 customers will have switched (even without incentives). In cell F2, compute the difference between the NPV with the incentive and the NPV without the incentive.

Finally, use the Goal Seek command to vary the size of the incentive (cell B2) to set F2 equal to 0. The Goal Seek dialog box is shown in Figure 79-3. An incentive of $34.22 makes the NPV of the two situations identical. Therefore, you could give incentives of up to $34.22 for a customer to switch and still have increased profitability.

FIGURE 79-3 Goal Seek settings to determine the maximum incentive that increases profitability.

Problems

1. Whirlswim Appliance is considering giving each of its customers free maintenance on each DVD player purchased. The company estimates that this proposal will require it to pay an average of $2.50 for each DVD player sold today (the cost in today's dollars). Currently, the market consists of 72,000 consumers whose last purchase was from Whirlswim and 86,000 consumers whose last purchase was from a competitor. In a given year, 40 percent of all consumers purchase a DVD player. If their last purchase was a Whirlswim, there is a 60 percent chance that their next purchase will be a Whirlswim. If their last purchase was not a Whirlswim, there is a 30 percent chance that their next purchase will be a Whirlswim. A purchase during the current year will lead to a $20 profit. The contribution to profit (and maintenance cost per purchaser) from a purchaser grows at 5 percent per year. Profits (over a 30-year horizon) are discounted at 10 percent per year.

    Suppose that you provide free maintenance. If the customer's last purchase was a Whirlswim, the probability that the customer's next purchase will be a Whirlswim will increase by an unknown amount between 0 percent and 10 percent. Similarly, if you give free maintenance and the customer's last purchase was not a Whirlswim, the probability that her next purchase is a Whirlswim will increase by an unknown amount between 0 percent and 10 percent. Do you recommend that Whirlswim adopt the free maintenance policy?

2. Mr. D's Supermarket is determined to please its customers with a customer advantage card. Currently, 30 percent of all shoppers are loyal to Mr. D's. A loyal Mr. D's customer shops at Mr. D's 80 percent of the time. An unloyal Mr. D's customer shops at Mr. D's 10 percent of the time. A typical customer spends $150 per week, and Mr. D's is running on a 4 percent profit margin.

    The customer advantage card will cost Mr. D's an average of $0.01 per dollar spent. You believe Mr. D's share of loyal customers will increase by an unknown amount between 2 percent and 10 percent. You also believe that the fraction of the time a loyal customer shops at Mr. D's will increase by an unknown amount between 2 percent and 12 percent. Should Mr. D's adopt a customer advantage card? Should Mr. D's adopt the card if its profit margin is 8 percent instead of 4 percent?

CHAPTER 80

The economic order quantity inventory model

Questions answered in this chapter:

- An electronics store sells 10,000 cell phones per year. Each time an order is placed for a supply of cell phones, the store incurs an order cost of $10. The store pays $100 for each cell phone, and the cost of holding a cell phone in inventory for a year is assumed to be $20. When the store orders cell phones, how large an order should it make?

- A computer manufacturing plant produces 10,000 servers per year. The cost to produce each server is $2,000. The cost to set up a production run of servers is $200, and the cost to hold a server in inventory for a year is $500. The plant can produce 25,000 servers per year if it wants to. When the plant produces servers, how large a batch should it produce?

When a store orders an item repeatedly, a natural question is what quantity the store should order each time. If the store orders too many items, it incurs excessive inventory or holding costs. If the store orders too few items, it incurs excessive reordering costs. Somewhere, there must be a happy medium that minimizes the sum of annual inventory and order costs.

Similarly, consider a manufacturing plant that produces batches of a product. What batch size minimizes the sum of annual inventory and setup costs? The two examples in this chapter show how to use the economic order quantity formula (developed in 1913 by F. Harris of Westinghouse Corporation) to answer these questions.

Answers to this chapter's questions

This section provides the answers to the questions that are listed at the beginning of the chapter.

An electronics store sells 10,000 cell phones per year. Each time an order is placed for a supply of cell phones, an order cost of $10 is incurred. The store pays $100 for each cell phone, and the cost of holding a cell phone in inventory for a year is assumed to be $20. When the store orders cell phones, how large an order should it make?

The size of an order that minimizes the sum of annual inventory and ordering costs can be determined after the following parameters are known:

- K = Cost per order

- h = Cost of holding one unit in inventory for a year

- D = Annual demand for product

You can follow an example of how to work with these parameters by using the EOQ worksheet in the Eoq.xlsx file, which is shown in Figure 80-1.

	A	B	C
1			
2	cost/order	K	10
3	annual holding cost per unit	h	20
4	annual demand	D	10000
5	order quantity	EOQ	100
6	holding cost per year	annhc	$1,000.00
7	order cost per year	annoc	$1,000.00
8	total annual cost (excluding purchasing	anncost	$2,000.00
9	orders per year	annorders	100

FIGURE 80-1 EOQ template.

If q equals order size, annual inventory cost equals $0.5qh$. (Throughout this example, this equation is referred to as Equation 1.) You derive Equation 1 because the average inventory level ($0.5q$) will be half the maximum inventory level. To see why the average inventory level is $0.5q$, note that you can compute the average inventory level for a cycle (the time between the arrival of orders). At the beginning of a cycle, an order arrives, and the inventory level is q. At the end of the cycle, you are out of stock, and the inventory level is 0. Because demand occurs at a constant rate, the average inventory level during a cycle is simply the average of 0 and q or $0.5q$. Maximum inventory level will equal q because orders are assumed to arrive at the instant that the inventory level is reduced to 0.

Because D/q orders are placed per year, annual ordering cost equals $(D/q)*K$. (Refer to this equation as Equation 2.) Using calculus or the Excel Solver, you can show that the annual sum of inventory and ordering costs is minimized for a value of q equal to the economic order quantity (EOQ), which is calculated using the following formula (Equation 3):

$$EOQ = \sqrt{\frac{2KD}{h}}$$

From this formula, you can see the following:

- An increase in demand or ordering cost will increase the EOQ.

- An increase in holding cost will decrease the EOQ.

In the Eoq.xlsx file, use Equation 3 to determine EOQ in cell C5. Determine annual holding cost in cell C6 by using Equation 1. Determine annual ordering cost in cell C7 with Equation 2. Notice that for EOQ, the annual ordering cost equals the annual holding cost, which will always be the case. In cell C8, determine the total annual cost (ignoring the purchasing cost, which does not depend on your ordering strategy) with the C6+C7 formula.

Of course, you can use one-way and two-way data tables to determine the sensitivity of the EOQ and various costs to variations in K, h, and D. In this example, $K = \$10$, $D = 10,000$ cell phones per year, and $h = \$20$ per cell phone. By inserting these values in cells C2:C4, you find the following:

- Each order should be for 100 cell phones.

- Annual holding and ordering costs each equal $1,000. The EOQ always sets annual holding costs equal to annual ordering costs.

- Total annual costs (exclusive of purchasing costs) equal $2,000.

When you are working with EOQ, keep the following in mind:

- The presence of quantity discounts invalidates the EOQ because the annual purchase cost then depends on the order size.

- The EOQ assumes that demand occurs at a relatively constant rate throughout the year. The EOQ should not be used for products for which there is seasonal demand.

- Annual holding cost is usually assumed to be between 10 percent and 40 percent of a product's unit purchasing cost.

- Included (in the EOQ Protected worksheet in the Eoq.xlsx file) is a version of the EOQ worksheet in which all formulas are protected. When the sheet is protected, nobody can change the formulas. See Chapter 78, "Pricing stock options," for instructions about how to protect a worksheet.

 More Info For more information about inventory modeling, interested readers can refer to my book, *Operations Research: Applications and Algorithms* (Duxbury Press, 2007).

A computer manufacturing plant produces 10,000 servers per year. The cost to produce each server is $2,000. The cost to set up a production run of servers is $200, and the cost to hold a server in inventory for a year is $500. The plant can produce 25,000 servers per year if it wants to. When the plant produces servers, how large a batch should it produce?

With the EOQ model, you assume an order arrives the instant the order is placed. When a company manufactures a product instead of ordering it, an order must be produced and cannot arrive instantaneously. In such situations, instead of computing the cost-minimizing order quantity, you need to determine the cost-minimizing batch size. When a company produces a product internally instead of purchasing the product externally, the batch size that minimizes costs depends on the following parameters:

- K = Cost of setting up a batch for production.

- h = Cost of holding each unit in inventory for a year.

- D = Annual demand for the product.

- R = Annual rate at which the product can be produced. For example, IBM might have the capacity to produce 25,000 servers per year.

If q equals the size of each production batch, the annual holding cost equals $0.5*(q/R)*(R - D)*h$. (Refer to this equation as Equation 4.) Equation 4 follows because each batch takes q/R years to produce, and during a production cycle, inventory increases at a rate of $R - D$. The maximum inventory level, which occurs at the completion of a batch, can be calculated as $(q/R)*(R - D)$. The average inventory level will thus equal $0.5*(q/R)*(R - D)$.

Because D/q batches are produced per year, annual setup cost equals KD/q (referred to as Equation 5). Using calculus or the Excel Solver, you can show that the batch size that minimizes the sum of annual setup and production-run costs is given by the following (referred to as Equation 6). This model is called the economic order batch (EOB) size:

$$EOB = \sqrt{\frac{2KDR}{h(R-D)}}$$

From this formula, you can determine the following:

- An increase in K or D will increase the EOB.

- An increase in h or R will decrease the EOB.

In the Cont Rate EOQ worksheet in the Contrateeoq.xlsx file, a template is constructed to determine the EOB, annual setup, and holding costs. The worksheet is shown in Figure 80-2.

	A	B	C
1			
2	cost per batch	K	$ 200.00
3	annual holding cost per unit	h	$ 500.00
4	annual demand	D	10000
5	annual production rate	rate	25000
6	batch size	EOB	115.470054
7	holding cost per year	annhc	$17,320.51
8	order cost per year	annoc	$17,320.51
9	total annual cost (excluding purchasing	anncost	$34,641.02
10	batches per year	annbatches	86.6025404

FIGURE 80-2 Template for computing EOB.

For this example, $K = \$200$, $h = \$500$, $D = 10{,}000$ units per year, and $R = 25{,}000$ units per year. After entering these parameter values in the C2:C5 cell range, you find the following:

- The batch size that minimizes costs is 115.47 servers. Thus, the company should produce 115 or 116 servers in each batch.

- The annual holding cost and setup costs equal $\$17{,}320.51$. Again, the EOB will always set annual holding cost equal to annual setup cost.

- Total annual cost (exclusive of variable production costs) is $\$34{,}641.02$.

- 86.6 batches per year will be produced.

When you are working with the EOB model, keep the following in mind:

- If the unit variable cost of producing a product depends on the batch size, the EOB model is invalid.

- The EOB assumes that demand occurs at a relatively constant rate throughout the year. The EOB should not be used for products for which there is seasonal demand.

- The annual holding cost is usually assumed to be between 10 percent and 40 percent of a product's unit purchasing cost.

- Included (in the Protected worksheet in the Contrateeoq.xlsx file) is a version of the EOB worksheet in which all formulas are protected. See Chapter 78 for instructions about how to protect a worksheet.

Problems

1. An appliance store sells HDTVs. Annual demand is estimated at 1,000 units. The cost to carry an HDTV in inventory for one year is $\$500$, and the cost to place an order for HDTVs is $\$400$:

   - How many HDTVs should be ordered each time an order is placed?

   - How many orders per year should be placed?

   - What are the annual inventory and ordering costs?

2. Suppose that the Waterford Crystal company can produce up to 100 iced-tea pitchers per day. Further, suppose that the plant is open 250 days per year and that annual demand is for 20,000 pitchers. The cost to hold a pitcher in inventory for a year might be $\$10$, and the cost to set up the facility to produce iced tea pitchers might be $\$40$:

   - What batch size would you recommend for iced-tea pitchers?

   - How many batches per year should be produced?

   - What are the annual setup and inventory costs for iced-tea pitchers?

CHAPTER 81

Inventory modeling with uncertain demand

Questions answered in this chapter:

- At what inventory level should I place an order if my goal is to minimize annual holding, ordering, and shortage costs?

- What does the term *95-percent service level* mean?

Chapter 80, "The economic order quantity inventory model," showed you how to use the economic order quantity (EOQ) to determine an optimal order quantity and production batch size. The examples assumed that demand occurred at a constant rate. Thus, if annual demand occurred at a rate of, for example, 1,200 units per year, monthly demand would equal 100 units. As long as demand occurs at a relatively constant rate, the EOQ is a good approximation of the cost-minimizing order quantity.

In reality, demand during any time period is uncertain. When demand is uncertain, a natural question is how low to let the inventory level go before placing an order. The inventory level at which an order should be placed is called the *reorder point*. Clearly, a high reorder point will decrease shortage costs and increase holding costs. Similarly, a low reorder point will increase shortage costs and decrease holding costs. At some intermediate reorder point, the sum of shortage and holding costs is minimized. The first example in this chapter shows how to determine a reorder point that minimizes expected ordering, shortage, and holding costs based on the following two assumptions:

- Each unit you are short is back ordered by a customer, and you incur the shortage cost c_B. This cost is primarily a measure of the customer's dissatisfaction caused by late receipt of an ordered item.

- Each unit you are short results in a lost sale, and you incur the shortage cost $c_{LS} > c_B$. The lost sales cost includes the profit lost from the lost sale as well as the shortage cost included in c_B.

The second example shows how to determine the optimal reorder point based on a *service level* approach. For example, a 95-percent service level means that you set the reorder point at a level ensuring that, on average, 95 percent of all demand is met on time. It is usually difficult to determine the cost of a shortage in either the back-ordered case or the lost-sales case. For that reason, most companies set reorder points by using the service level approach.

Note On this book's companion website, for the back-ordered and lost-sales models, I've included a worksheet named Protected in which all formulas are protected for both the back-ordered and lost-sales cases. You can use these worksheets as templates.

Answers to this chapter's questions

This section provides the answers to the questions that are listed at the beginning of the chapter.

At what inventory level should I place an order if my goal is to minimize annual holding, ordering, and shortage costs?

As indicated in Chapter 80, the EOQ depends on the following parameters:

- K = Cost per order.

- h = Cost of holding one unit in inventory for a year.

- D = Annual demand for the product. Because demand is now uncertain, you let D stand for the expected annual demand for the product.

The back-order case

See the Reorderpoint_backorder.xlsx file, shown in Figure 81-1, for the data to use in this example. First suppose that each shortage results in the back-ordered units. In other words, a shortage does not result in any lost demand. Also assume that each unit you are short incurs a cost c_B. In this case, the reorder point depends on the following quantities:

- EOQ is the economic order quantity (the quantity ordered each time an order is placed).

- K is the cost per order.

- h is the annual holding cost per unit.

- D is the mean annual demand.

- SOC is the cost per unit short.

- $annsig$ is the standard deviation of annual demand.

- $meanLT$ is the average *lead time*; that is, the average time between placing an order and receiving the order.

- $sigmaLT$ is the standard deviation of lead time.

Say that a department store wants to determine an optimal inventory policy for ordering electric mixers. It has the following information:

- It costs $50 to place an order for mixers.

- It costs $10 to hold a mixer in inventory for a year.

	A	B	C
1			
2	cost/order	K	$ 50.00
3	annual holding cost per unit	h	$ 10.00
4	mean annual demand	D	1000
5	order quantity	EOQ	100
6	orders per year	annorders	10
7	lost sales cost	LSC	$ 40.00
8	annual sigma	annsig	40.8
9	mean lead time	meanLT	0.038461538
10	sigma lead time	sigmaLT	0
11	mean lead time demand	meanLTD	38.46153846
12	sigma lead time demand	sigmaLTD	8.001538314
13	probability of stockout	probout	0.024390244
14	reorder point	RP	54.22861214
15	safety stock	SS	15.76707368

FIGURE 81-1 Determining the reorder point when shortages are backordered.

- On average, the store sells 1,000 mixers per year.

- All customers who try to purchase a mixer when the store is sold out of them return at a later date and buy a mixer when the mixer is in stock. The store incurs a penalty of $20 for each unit it is short.

- The annual demand for mixers (based on historical data) has a standard deviation of 40.8.

- Lead time is always two weeks (0.038 years), with a standard deviation of 0.

After you enter *K*, *h*, and *D* in cells C2:C4, the spreadsheet computes the EOQ (100 mixers) in C5. After you enter *SOC*, *annsig*, *meanLT*, and *sigmaLT* in cells C7:C10, the spreadsheet computes in cell C14 the reorder point that minimizes the sum of expected annual holding and shortage costs (51.63 mixers). Thus, the department store should order 100 mixers whenever its stock decreases to 51.62 (or 52) mixers.

The *safety stock level* associated with a given reorder point is *reorder point–mean lead time demand*. The department store maintains a safety stock level of 51.62 − 38.46 = 13.16 mixers, computed in cell C15. Essentially, the safety stock is always in inventory, resulting in extra holding costs. A higher level of safety stock will, of course, reduce shortages.

The lost-sales case

Now suppose that each shortage results in a lost sale. The cost associated with a lost sale is usually estimated as the back-order penalty plus the profit associated with a unit sold. Suppose that the department store earns a $20 profit on each mixer it sells. The unit shortage cost for the lost-sales case is then $40 ($20 lost profit + $20 back-order penalty).

In the Reorderpoint_lostsales.xlsx file, shown in Figure 81-2, you can see the work done to esti-mate the reorder point for the lost-sales case. After entering the lost-sales cost of $40 in cell C7 of the spreadsheet, you find that the optimal inventory policy is to order 100 mixers and place an order when inventory is down to 54.23 mixers. Your safety stock level is 15.77 mixers, and 2.4 percent of the store's demand for mixers will be unmet. Notice that the assumption of a lost sale has increased the reorder point and reduced the probability of a shortage. This happens because the increased cost of a shortage (from $20 to $40) makes the store more eager to avoid shortages.

	A	B	C
1			
2	cost/order	K	$ 50.00
3	annual holding cost per unit	h	$ 10.00
4	mean annual demand	D	1000
5	order quantity	EOQ	100
6	orders per year	annorders	10
7	unit stockout cost	SOC	$ 20.00
8	annual sigma	annsig	40.8
9	mean lead time	meanLT	0.0384615
10	sigma lead time	sigmaLT	0
11	mean lead time demand	meanLTD	38.461538
12	sigma lead time demand	sigmaLTD	8.0015383
13	probability of stockout	probout	0.05
14	reorder point	RP	51.622898
15	safety stock	SS	13.161359

FIGURE 81-2 Determining the reorder point when sales will be lost.

Increased uncertainty greatly increases the reorder point. For example, in the lost-sales case, if the standard deviation for lead time is one week (0.019 years) rather than 0, the reorder point increases to 79.50 mixers, and the safety stock more than doubles from when your lead time was known with certainty.

What does the term *95 percent service level* mean?

As stated earlier in the chapter, a *95-percent service level* simply means that you want 95 percent of your demand to be met on time. Because estimating the back-order penalty and/or the penalty that results from a lost sale is often difficult, many companies set safety stock levels for products by set-ting a service level. Using the Servicelevelreorder.xlsx file (shown in Figure 81-3), you can determine the reorder point corresponding to any service level you want.

	A	B	C	D	E	F
1	Service level	SL	0.95			
2	cost/order	K	$ 50.00			
3	annual holding cost per unit	h	$ 10.00			
4	mean annual demand	D	1000			
5	order quantity	EOQ	100			
6	orders per year	annorders	10			
7	annual sigma	annsig	69.28			
8	mean lead time	meanLT	0.08333			
9	sigma lead time	sigmaLT	0			
10	mean lead time demand	meanLTD	83.3333			
11	sigma lead time demand	sigmaLTD	19.9994			
12	reorder point	ROP	90.2301			
13	standardized reorder point	SROP	0.34485			DIFF
14	normal loss for stand. ROP	NLSTANDROP	0.25001 =		0.25	6E-08
15	safety stock	SS	6.89674			

FIGURE 81-3 Determination of the reorder point by using the service level approach.

As an example, consider a pharmacy that is trying to determine an optimal inventory policy for a drug it stocks. The pharmacy would like to meet 95 percent of demand for the drug on time. The following parameters are relevant:

- Each order for the drug costs $50.

- The cost to hold a unit of the drug in inventory for a year is $10.

- Average demand per year for the drug is 1,000 units.

- The standard deviation of annual demand is 69.28 units.

- The time required to receive a shipment of the drug always takes exactly one month (0.083 years).

You enter the service level you want (0.95) in cell C1 and all other parameters in cells C2:C4 and C7:C9. To determine the reorder point yielding the service level you want, click **Solver** in the **Data Analysis** group on the **Data** tab. The Solver model (see Figure 81-4) adjusts the reorder point until the percentage of demand met on time matches the service level you want. Under **Options**, choose **Multistart**. (See Chapter 35, "Warehouse location and the GRG Multistart and Evolutionary Solver engines.") Then you put a lower bound of .001 on the reorder point (to keep the Solver from trying a negative reorder point) and an upper bound of 10,000 (fairly arbitrary) on the reorder point. If the Solver bumps up against your upper bound, you should relax the bound. As you can see in Figure 81-3, the pharmacy should order 100 units of the drug whenever its inventory level drops to 90.23 units. This reorder point corresponds to a safety stock level of 6.90 units.

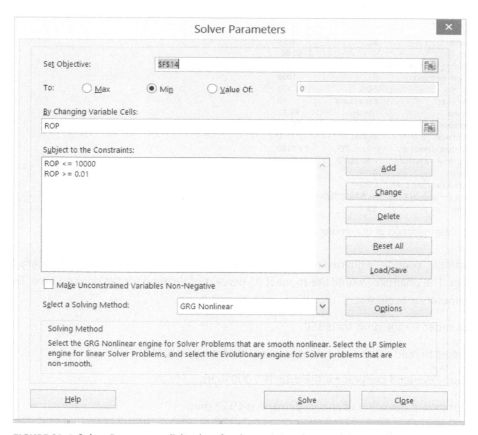

FIGURE 81-4 Solver Parameters dialog box for determining the reorder point for a 95-percent service level.

In the following table, the reorder point and safety stock levels corresponding to service levels between 80 percent and 99 percent are listed:

Service-level percentage	Reorder point/units	Safety stock/units
80	65.34	-17.99
85	71.85	-11.48
90	79.57	-3.76
95	90.23	6.90
99	108.44	25.11

Notice that moving from an 80 percent service level to a 99 percent service level increases the reorder point by almost 67 percent! Also note that you can attain a 90-percent service level with a reorder point less than the mean lead time demand (refer to cell C10 in Figure 81-3). A 90 percent service level results in a negative safety stock level, which is possible because shortages occur only during the lead time, and lead times usually cover a small portion of a year.

Problems

When working with Problems 1 and 2, assume that a restaurant serves an average of 5,000 bottles of wine per year. The standard deviation of the annual demand for wine is 1,000 bottles. The annual holding cost for a bottle of wine is $1. It costs $10 to place an order for wine, and it takes an average of three weeks (with a standard deviation of one week) for the wine to arrive:

1. Assume that when the restaurant is out of wine, it incurs a penalty of $5 as the result of lost goodwill. In addition, the restaurant earns a profit of $2 per bottle of wine. Determine an optimal ordering policy for the wine.

2. Determine an inventory policy for wine that yields a 99-percent service level.

3. A reorder point policy is often referred to as a two-bin policy. How can a reorder point policy be implemented when two bins are used to store inventory?

CHAPTER 82

Queuing theory: the mathematics of waiting in line

Questions answered in this chapter:

- What factors affect the number of people and the time we spend waiting in line?

- What conditions should be met before analyzing the average number of people present or the average time spent in a queuing system?

- Why does variability degrade the performance of a queuing system?

- Can I easily determine the average time a person spends at airport security or waiting in line at a bank?

We have all spent a lot of time waiting in lines, and you'll soon see that a slight increase in service capacity can often greatly reduce the size of the lines we encounter. If you run a business, ensuring that your customers do not spend too much time waiting is important. Therefore, business people need to understand the mathematics of wait time, usually referred to as *queuing theory*. This chapter shows you how to determine the service capacity needed to provide adequate service.

Answers to this chapter's questions

This section provides the answers to the questions that are listed at the beginning of the chapter.

What factors affect the number of people and the time we spend waiting in line?

This chapter addresses queuing problems in which all arriving customers wait in one line for the first available service person. (To keep things simple, service people are referred to as *servers*.) This model is a fairly accurate representation of the situations you face when you wait at a bank, in an airport security line, or at the post office. By the way, the idea of having customers wait in one line started in about 1970, when banks and post-office branches realized that although waiting in one line does not reduce the average time customers spend waiting, it does reduce the variability of the time they spend in line, thereby creating a fairer system.

Three main factors influence the time you spend in a queuing system:

- **The number of servers**   Clearly, the more servers, the less time on average customers spend in line, and fewer people on average will be present in the line.

- **The mean and the standard deviation of the time between arrivals**   The time between arrivals is called interarrival time. If the average interarrival time increases, the number of arrivals decreases, which results in shorter lines and less time spent in a queuing system. As you soon see, an increase in standard deviation of interarrival times increases the average time a customer spends in a queuing system and the average number of customers present.

- **The mean and the standard deviation of the time needed to complete service**   If the average service time increases, you see an increase in the average time a customer spends in the system and in the number of customers present. An increase in the standard deviation of service times increases the average time a customer spends in a queuing system and the average number of customers present.

What conditions should be met before analyzing the average number of people present or the average time spent in a queuing system?

When analyzing the time people spend waiting in lines, mathematicians talk about *steady state* characteristics of a system. Essentially, steady state means that a system has operated for a long time. More specifically, analysts would like to know the value of the following quantities in the steady state:

- W = Average time a customer spends in the system

- W_q = Average time a customer spends waiting in line before the customer is served

- L = Average number of customers present in the system

- L_q = Average number of customers waiting in line

By the way, it is always true that L = (1/mean interarrival time)*W and L_q = (1/mean interarrival time)*W_q.

To discuss the steady state of a queuing system meaningfully, the following must be the case:

- The mean and standard deviation of both the interarrival times and the service times changes little over time. The technical phrase is that the distribution of interarrival and service times is stationary over time.

- (1/mean service time)*(number of servers) > (1/(mean interarrival time)). This will be Equation 1.

Essentially, if Equation 1 is true, you can serve more people per hour than are arriving. For example, if mean service time equals 2 minutes (or 1/30 of an hour), and mean interarrival time equals 1 minute (or 1/60 of an hour), Equation 1 tells you that 30*(number of servers) > 60, or that the number of servers must be greater than or equal to 3 for a steady state to exist. If you cannot serve customers faster than they arrive, eventually you fall behind and never catch up, resulting in an infinite line.

Why does variability degrade the performance of a queuing system?

To see why variability degrades the performance of a queuing system, consider a one-server system in which customers arrive every 2 minutes, and service times always equal 2 minutes. There will never be more than one customer in the system. Now suppose that customers arrive every 2 minutes, but half of all service times are 0.5 minutes and half are 3.5 minutes. Even though arrivals are totally predictable, the uncertainty in service time means that eventually the server falls behind and a line forms. For example, if the first four customers have 3.5-minute service times, after 12 minutes, four customers are waiting, which is illustrated in the following table:

Time	Event	Present after event
0 minutes	Arrival	1 person
2 minutes	Arrival	2 people
3.5 minutes	Service completed	1 person
4 minutes	Arrival	2 people
6 minutes	Arrival	3 people
7 minutes	Service completed	2 people
8 minutes	Arrival	3 people
10 minutes	Arrival	4 people
10.5 minutes	Service completed	3 people
12 minutes	Arrival	4 people

Can I easily determine the average time a person spends at airport security or waiting in line at a bank?

The Model worksheet in the Queuingtemplate.xlsx file contains a template that you can use to determine approximate values for L, W, L_q, and W_q (usually within 10 percent of their true value). The worksheet is shown in Figure 82-1.

	A	B	C
1			
2			
3	Arrival rate	0.077734	per minute
4	Service rate	0.01297	per minute
5	s(servers)	6	
6	Mean interarrival time	12.864	
7	Mean service time	77.102	
8	Standard deviation of interarrival times	4.43908	
9	Standard deviation of service times	48.05051	
10	CV arrive	0.119079	
11	CV service	0.388387	
12	u	5.993412	
13	ro	0.998902	
14	R(s,mu)	0.73554	
15	E_C(s,mu)	0.996956	
16	W_q	2960.658	
17	L_q	230.1434	
18	W	3037.76	
19	L	236.1368	

FIGURE 82-1 Queuing template.

After you enter the following data, the template computes W_q, L_q, W, and L. The parameters in cells B6:B9 can easily be estimated by using past data:

- Number of servers (cell B5)

- Mean interarrival time (cell B6)

- Mean service time (cell B7)

- Standard deviation of interarrival times (cell B8)

- Standard deviation of service times (cell B9)

Here's an example of the template in action. You want to determine how the operating characteristics of an airline security line during the 9:00 A.M. to 5:00 P.M. shift depends on the number of agents working. In the Queuing Data worksheet in the Queuingtemplate.xlsx file, shown in Figure 82-2, interarrival times and service times are tabulated. (Some rows have been hidden.)

By copying the AVERAGE(B4:B62) formula from cell B1 to C1, you find the mean interarrival time is 12.864 seconds, and the mean service time is 77.102 seconds. Because mean service time is almost six times as large as mean interarrival time, you need at least six agents to guarantee a steady state. Copying the STDEV.S(B4:B62) formula from cell B2 to C2 tells you that the standard deviation of the interarrival times is 4.439 seconds, and the standard deviation of the service times is 48.051 seconds.

Return to the queuing template in the Model worksheet. If you enter these values in cells B6:B9 and enter six servers in cell B5, you find that disaster ensues. In the steady state, nearly 236 people will be in line (cell B19). You've probably been at the airport in this situation.

	A	B	C	D
1	mean	12.86440678	77.10169492	seconds
2	sigma	4.43908047	48.05051039	seconds
3		Interarrival time	Service Time	
4		5	95	
5		17	240	
6		12	71	
7		18	68	
8		9	90	
9		16	117	
10		15	291	
11		15	116	
12		10	107	
13		11	100	
14		9	28	
15		15	119	
16		19	98	
17		9	72	
18		16	127	
57		13	74	
58		11	27	
59		13	84	
60		19	90	
61		11	42	
62		18	74	

FIGURE 82-2 Airline interarrival and service times.

Use a one-way data table (shown in Figure 82-3) to determine how changing the number of agents affects the system's performance. In cells F10:F14, enter the number of agents to consider (6 through 10). In cell G9, enter the formula to compute $L(=B19)$ and, in H9, enter the formula to compute $W(=B18)$. Select the table range (F8:H14) and then click **Data Table** from the **What-If Analysis** menu on the **Data** tab. After choosing cell B5 (the number of servers) as the row input cell, you obtain the data table shown in Figure 82-3. Notice that adding just one ticket agent to the original six agents reduces the expected number of customers present in line from 236 to fewer than 7. Adding the seventh agent reduces a customer's average time in the system from 3,038 seconds (50.6 minutes) to 89 seconds (1.5 minutes). This example shows that a small increase in service capacity can greatly improve the performance of a queuing system.

In cells F16:K22, you can use a two-way data table to examine the sensitivity of the average time in the system (W) to changes in the number of servers and standard deviation of service times. The row input cell is B5, and the column input cell is B9. When seven agents are working, an increase in the standard deviation of service times from 40 seconds to 90 seconds results in a 29 percent increase in the mean time in the system (from 86.2 seconds to 111.8 seconds).

	E	F	G	H	I	J	K
6							
7			L	W			
8		Servers	236.1368	3037.76			
9		6	236.1368	3037.76			
10		7	6.917396	88.9882			
11		8	6.262791	80.56709			
12		9	6.092038	78.37046			
13		10	6.031636	77.59342			
14							
15					servers		
16		3037.76	6	7	8	9	10
17		40	2342.086	86.1952	79.75282	78.07234	77.47788
18	service time	50	3225.354	89.74136	80.78666	78.45085	77.62457
19	sigma	60	4304.905	94.07556	82.05026	78.91348	77.80387
20		70	5580.737	99.1978	83.54359	79.46023	78.01577
21		80	7052.851	105.1081	85.26668	80.09109	78.26027
22		90	8721.247	111.8064	87.2195	80.80607	78.53736

FIGURE 82-3 Sensitivity analysis for an airport security line.

Note Readers who are interested in a more extensive discussion of the queuing theory should refer to my book, *Operations Research: Applications and Algorithms* (Duxbury Press, 2007).

Problems

A bank has six tellers. Use the following information to answer Problems 1 to 4:

- Mean service time equals 1 minute.

- Mean interarrival time equals 25 seconds.

- Standard deviation of service times equals 1 minute.

- Standard deviation of interarrival times equals 10 seconds.

1. Determine the average time a customer waits in line.

2. On average, how many customers are present in the bank line?

3. Would you recommend adding more tellers?

4. Suppose it costs $20 per hour to have a teller working, and you value a customer's time at $15 per hour. How many tellers should you have working?

5. Thirty women work on the fifth floor of a business school. Assume each woman uses the restroom three times a day (the office is open from 8 A.M. to 5 P.M.), and each visit takes 180 seconds on average, with a standard deviation of 90 seconds. Assume the standard deviation of time between arrivals to the restroom is 5 minutes. How many toilets would you recommend for the women's restroom?

CHAPTER 83

Estimating a demand curve

Questions answered in this chapter:

- What do I need to know to price a product?

- What is the meaning of *elasticity of demand*?

- Is there any easy way to estimate a demand curve?

- What does a demand curve tell us about a customer's willingness to pay for our product?

Every business must determine a price for each of its products. Pricing a product properly is difficult. Chapter 84, "Pricing products by using tie-ins," and Chapter 85, "Pricing products by using subjectively determined demand," describe some simple models that might aid you in pricing a product to maximize profitability. For further insights into pricing, refer to the excellent book, *Power Pricing*, by Robert J. Dolan and Hermann Simon (Free Press, 1997).

Answers to this chapter's questions

This section provides the answers to the questions that are listed at the beginning of the chapter.

What do I need to know to price a product?

Consider a product such as a candy bar. To determine a profit-maximizing price, you need to know two things:

- The variable cost of producing each unit of the product (call this *UC*).

- The product's demand curve. Simply put, a demand curve tells you the number of units of a product a customer will demand at each price. In short, if you charge a price of $\$p$ per unit, the demand curve gives you a number $D(p)$, which equals the number of units of the product that will be demanded at price $\$p$. Of course, a firm's demand curve is constantly changing and often depends on factors beyond the firm's control (such as the state of the economy and a competitor's price).

After you know *UC* and the demand curve, the profit corresponding to a price of $\$p$ is simply $(p - UC)*D(p)$. After you have an equation for $D(p)$, which gives the quantity of the product demanded at each price, you can use the Microsoft Excel Solver feature to find the profit-maximizing price, which you'll see in Chapter 84 and Chapter 85.

What is the meaning of *elasticity of demand*?

Given a demand curve, the *price elasticity* for demand is the percentage decrease in demand resulting from a 1 percent increase in price. When elasticity is larger than 1 percent, demand is price elastic. When demand is price elastic, a price cut increases revenue. When elasticity is less than 1 percent, demand is price inelastic. When demand is price inelastic, a price cut decreases revenue. Here are some observed estimates of elasticities:

- Salt, 0.1 (very inelastic)

- Coffee, 0.25 (inelastic)

- Legal fees, 0.4 (inelastic)

- TV sets, 1.2 (slightly elastic)

- Restaurant meals, 2.3 (elastic)

- Foreign travel, 4.0 (very elastic)

A 1 percent decrease in the cost of foreign travel, for example, will result in a 4 percent increase in demand for foreign travel.

Is there any easy way to estimate a demand curve?

Using q to represent the quantity demanded of a product, the two most commonly used forms for estimating demand curves are as follows:

- **Linear demand curve**   In this case, demand follows a straight-line relationship of the form $q = a - bp$. For example, $q = 10 - p$ is a linear demand curve. (Here, a and b can be determined by using a method described later in the chapter.) When the demand curve is linear, the elasticity is constantly changing.

- **Power demand curve**   In this situation, the demand curve is described by a power curve of the form $q = ap^b$, $b<0$. (See Chapter 55, "The power curve," for more information.) Again, a and b can be determined by the method described later in the chapter. The equation $q = 100p^{-2}$ is an example of a power demand curve. If demand follows a power curve, for any price the elasticity equals $-b$. Thus, for the demand curve $q = 100p^{-2}$, the price elasticity of demand always equals 2.

Suppose that a product's demand curve follows a linear or power demand curve. If you know the current price and demand for a product and the product's price elasticity of demand, determining the product's demand curve is a simple matter. Here are two examples.

A product is currently selling for $100, and demand equals 500 units. The product's price elasticity for demand is 2. Assuming the demand curve is linear, you want to determine the equation of the demand curve. The solution is in the Linearfit.xlsx file, which is shown in Figure 83-1.

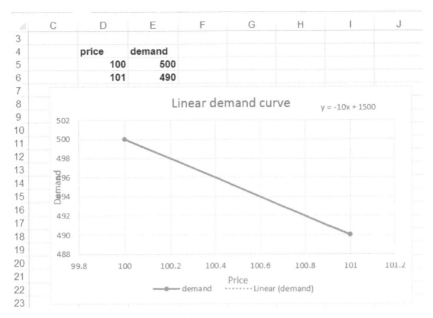

FIGURE 83-1 Fitting a linear demand curve.

Given two points, you know that a unique straight line passes through those two points, and you actually know two points on the demand curve. One point is p = 100, and q = 500. Because elasticity of demand equals 2, a 1 percent increase in price results in a 2 percent decrease in demand. Thus, if p = 101 (a 1 percent increase), demand drops by 2 percent of 500 (10 units) to 490. Thus, p=101, and q – 490 is a second point on the demand curve. You can now use the Excel trendline to find the straight line that passes through the (100,500) and (101,490) points.

You begin by entering these points in the worksheet in the D5:E6 cell range, as shown in Figure 83-1. Select the D4:E6 range and, on the ribbon, in the **Charts** group on the **Insert** tab, choose **Scatter, Scatter With Straight Lines**. After selecting this option for a Scatter chart, you see the graph has a positive slope. This implies that higher prices lead to higher demand, which cannot be correct. The problem is that with only two data points, Excel assumes that the data points you want to graph are in separate columns, not separate rows. To be sure that Excel understands that the individual points are in separate rows, click inside the graph and, on the ribbon, click the **Design** tab in the **Chart Tools** section. Click **Switch Row/Column** in the **Data** section of the **Design** tab. (Note that by clicking the Select Data button, you can change the source data that generates your chart.) Now right-click one of the points, click **Add Trendline**, and then select **Linear** and **Display Equation On Chart**. You see the straight-line plot, complete with the equation shown in Figure 83-1. Because x is price and y is demand, the equation for the demand curve is q = 1500 – 10p. This equation means that each $1 increase in price costs you 10 units of demand. Of course, demand cannot be linear for all values of p because for large values of p, a linear demand curve will yield negative demand. For prices near the current price, however, the linear demand curve is usually a good approximation of the product's true demand curve.

As a second example, again assume that a product is currently selling for $100, and demand equals 500 units. The product's price elasticity for demand is 2. Now fit a power demand curve to this information. See the Powerfit.xlsx file, shown in Figure 83-2.

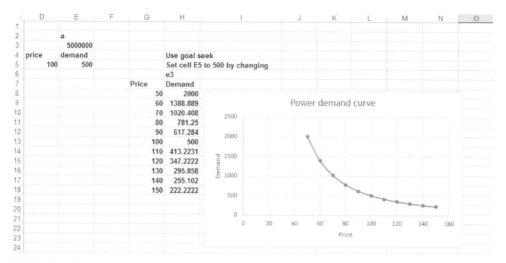

FIGURE 83-2 Power demand curve.

In cell E3, enter a trial value for a. Then, in cell D5, enter the current price of $100. Because elasticity of demand equals 2, you know that the demand curve has the form of $q = ap^{-2}$, where a is unknown. In cell E5, enter the demand for a price of $100, corresponding to the value of a in cell E3, with the a*D5^-2 formula. Now you can use the Goal Seek command (for details, see Chapter 17, "The Goal Seek command") to determine the value of a that makes the demand for price $100 equal to 500 units. Set cell E5 to the value of 500 by changing cell E3. You find that a value for a of 5 million yields a demand of 500 at a price of $100. Thus, the demand curve (graphed in Figure 83-2) is given by $q = 5{,}000{,}000p^{-2}$. For any price, the price elasticity of demand on this demand curve equals 2.

What does a demand curve tell us about a customer's willingness to pay for our product?

Suppose you are trying to sell a software program to a *Fortune* 500 company. Let q equal the number of copies of the program the company demands and let p equal the price charged for the software. Suppose you have estimated that the demand curve for software is given by $q = 400 - p$. Clearly, your customer is willing to pay less for each additional unit of the software program. Locked inside this demand curve is information about how much the company is willing to pay for each unit of the program. This information is crucial for maximizing profitability of sales.

Rewrite the demand curve as $p = 400 - q$. Thus, when $q = 1$, $p = $399 and so on. Now try to figure out the value the customer attaches to each of the first two units of the program. Assuming that the customer is rational, the customer will buy a unit if and only if the value of the unit exceeds your price. At a price of $400, demand equals 0, so the first unit cannot be worth $400. At a price of $399, however, demand equals 1 unit. Therefore, the first unit must be worth something between $399 and $400. Similarly, at a price of $399, the customer does not purchase the second unit. At a price of

$398, however, the customer is purchasing two units, so the customer does purchase the second unit. Therefore, the customer values the second unit somewhere between $399 and $398.

It can be shown that the best approximation of the value of the ith unit purchased by the customer is the price that makes demand equal to $i - 0.5$. For example, by setting q equal to 0.5, the value of the first unit is $400 - 0.5 = 399.50. Similarly, by setting $q = 1.5$, the value of the second unit is $400 - 1.5 = 398.50.

Problems

1. Suppose you are charging $60 for a board game you invented and have sold three thousand units during the past year. Elasticity for board games is known to equal 3. Use this information to determine a linear and power demand curve.

2. For each of your answers in Problem 1, determine the value consumers place on the two thousandth unit purchased of your game.

CHAPTER 84

Pricing products by using tie-ins

Question answered in this chapter:

- How does the fact that customers buy razor blades as well as razors affect the profit-maximizing price of razors?

Certain consumer product purchases frequently result in the purchase of related products, or *tie-ins*. Here are some examples:

Original purchase	Tie-in product
Razor	Razor blades
Men's suit	Shirt and/or tie
Personal computer	Software training manual
Video game console	Video game

Using the techniques described in Chapter 83, "Estimating a demand curve," it's easy to determine a demand curve for the product that's originally purchased. You can then use the Microsoft Excel Solver to determine the original product price that maximizes the sum of the profit earned from the original and the tie-in products. The following example shows how this analysis is done.

Answer to this chapter's question

This section provides the answer to the question that is listed at the beginning of the chapter.

How does the fact that customers buy razor blades as well as razors affect the profit-maximizing price of razors?

Suppose that you're currently charging $5.00 for a razor, and you're selling 6 million razors. Assume that the variable cost of producing a razor is $2.00. Finally, suppose that the price elasticity of demand for razors is 2. What price should you charge for razors?

Assume (incorrectly) that no purchasers of razors buy blades. You determine the demand curve (assuming a linear demand curve) as shown in Figure 84-1. (You can find this data and the chart on the No Blades worksheet in the Razorsandblades.xlsx file.) Two points on the demand curve are price = $5.00, demand = 6 million razors and price = $5.05 (an increase of 1 percent), demand = 5.88 million (2 percent less than 6 million). After drawing a chart and inserting a linear trendline as shown in

Chapter 83, you find the demand curve equation is $y = 18 - 2.4x$. Because x equals price and y equals demand, you can write the demand curve for razors as follows: *demand* (in millions) = $18 - 2.4(price)$.

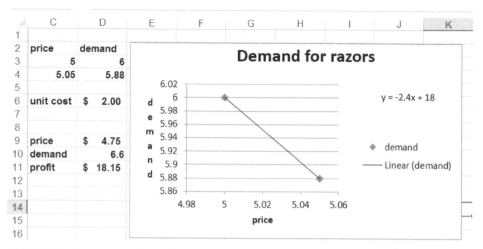

FIGURE 84-1 Determining the profit-maximizing price for razors.

Associate the names in cell C6 and the C9:C11 range with cells D6 and D9:D11. Enter a trial price in D9 and determine demand for that price in cell D10 with the 18-2.4*price formula. Determine in cell D11 the profit for razors by using the demand*(price–unit_cost) formula.

Now, use Solver to determine the profit-maximizing price. The Solver Parameters dialog box is shown in Figure 84-2.

Maximize the profit cell (cell D11) by changing the price (cell D9). The model is not linear because the target cell multiplies two quantities—demand and (price – cost)—each depending on the changing cell. Solver finds that charging $4.75 for a razor maximizes profit. (Maximum profit is $18.15 million.)

Now suppose that the average purchaser of a razor buys 50 blades and that you earn $0.15 of profit per blade purchased. How does this change the price you should charge for a razor? Assume that the price of a blade is fixed. (In Problem 3 at the end of the chapter, the blade price changes.) The analysis is in the Blades worksheet, which is shown in Figure 84-3.

FIGURE 84-2 Solver Parameters dialog box set up for maximizing razor profit.

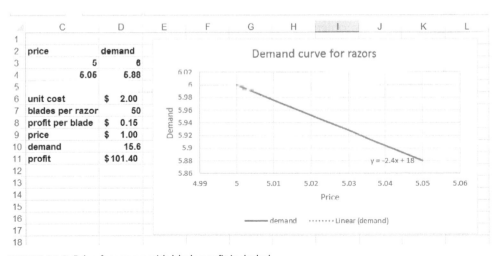

FIGURE 84-3 Price for razors with blade profit included.

Use the **Create From Selection** command in the **Defined Names** group on the **Formulas** tab to associate the names in cells C6:C11 with cells D6:D11. (For example, cell D10 is named Demand.)

> **Note** Astute readers will recall that cell D10 of the No Blades worksheet was also named Demand. What does Excel do when you use the range name Demand in a formula? Excel simply refers to the cell named Demand in the current worksheet. In other words, when you use the range name Demand in the Blades worksheet, Excel refers to cell D10 of that worksheet and not to cell D10 in the No Blades worksheet.

In cells D7 and D8, enter the relevant information about blades. In D9, enter a trial price for razors and, in D10, compute demand with the 18-2.4*price formula. Next, in cell D11, compute total profit from razors and blades with the demand*(price−unit_cost)+demand*blades_per_razor*profit _per_blade formula. Notice that demand*blades_per_razor*profit_per_blade is the profit from blades.

The Solver setup is exactly as was shown earlier, in Figure 84-2: Change the price to maximize the profit. Of course, now the profit formula includes the profit earned from blades. Excel shows that profit is maximized by charging only $1.00 (half the variable cost!) for a razor. This price results from making so much money from blades. You are much better off ensuring that many people have razors even though you lose $1.00 on each razor sold. Many companies do not understand the importance of the profit from tie-in products. This leads them to overprice their primary product and not maximize their total profit.

Problems

> **Note** In all the following problems, assume a linear demand curve.

1. You are trying to determine the profit-maximizing price for a video game console. Currently, you are charging $180 and selling 2 million consoles per year. It costs $150 to produce a console, and price elasticity of demand for consoles is 3. What price should you charge for a console?

2. Now assume that, on average, a purchaser of your video game console buys 10 video games, and you earn $10 profit on each video game. What is the correct price for consoles?

3. In the razor and blade example, suppose the cost to produce a blade is $0.20. If you charge $0.35 for a blade, a customer buys an average of 50 blades. Assume the price elasticity of demand for blades is 3. What price should you charge for a razor and for a blade?

4. You are managing a movie theater that can handle up to eight thousand patrons per week. The current demand, price, and elasticity for ticket sales, popcorn, soda, and candy are given in Figure 84-4. The theater keeps 45 percent of ticket revenues. Unit cost per ticket, popcorn sales, candy sales, and soda sales are also given. Assuming linear demand curves, how can the

theater maximize profits? Demand for food is the fraction of patrons who purchase the given food.

	B	C	D	E	F	G	H	I
2								
3			elasticity	current price	demand	cost	ticket percentage	
4	keep 45%	ticket	3	8	3000	0	0.45	
5		popcorn	1.3	3.5	0.5	0.4		
6		soda	1.5	3	0.6	0.6		
7		candy	2.5	2.5	0.2	1		

FIGURE 84-4 Movie problem data.

5. A prescription drug is produced in the United States and sold internationally. Each unit of the drug costs $60 to produce. In the German market, you are selling the drug for 150 euros per unit. The current exchange rate is 0.667 US dollars per euro. Current demand for the drug is 100 units, and the estimated elasticity is 2.5. Assuming a linear demand curve, determine the appropriate sales price (in euros) for the drug.

CHAPTER 85

Pricing products by using subjectively determined demand

Questions answered in this chapter:

- Sometimes I don't know the price elasticity for a product. In other situations, I don't believe a linear or power demand curve is relevant. Can I still estimate a demand curve and use Solver to determine a profit-maximizing price?

- How can a small drugstore determine the profit-maximizing price for lipstick?

Answers to this chapter's questions

This section provides the answers to the questions that are listed at the beginning of the chapter.

Sometimes I don't know the price elasticity for a product. In other situations, I don't believe a linear or power demand curve is relevant. Can I still estimate a demand curve and use Solver to determine a profit-maximizing price?

When you don't know the price elasticity for a product or don't think you can rely on a linear or power demand curve, a good way to determine a product's demand curve is to identify the lowest price and highest price that seem reasonable. You can then try to estimate the product's demand with the high price, the low price, and a price midway between the high and low prices. Given these three points on the product's demand curve, you can use the Microsoft Excel Trendline feature to fit a quadratic demand curve with the following formula (Equation 1):

```
Demand=a(price)²+b(pri=ce)+c
```

For any three specified points on the demand curve, values of *a*, *b*, and *c* exist that will make Equation 1 exactly fit the three specified points. Because Equation 1 fits three points on the demand curve, it seems reasonable to believe that the equation will give an accurate representation of demand for other prices. You can then use Equation 1 and Solver to determine maximum profit, which is given by the (price−unit cost)*demand formula. The following example shows how this process works.

How can a small drugstore determine the profit-maximizing price for lipstick?

Suppose that a drugstore pays $0.90 for each unit of lipstick it orders. The store is considering charging from $1.50 through $2.50 for a unit of lipstick. The store thinks that at a price of $1.50, it will sell 60 units per week. (See Figure 85-1 and the Lipstickprice.xlsx file.) At a price of $2.00, the store thinks it will sell 51 units per week, and at a price of $2.50, 20 units per week. What price should the store charge for lipstick?

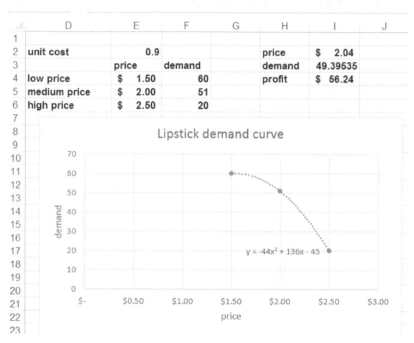

FIGURE 85-1 Lipstick pricing model.

You begin by entering the three points with which you chart the demand curve in the E3:F6 cell range. After selecting E3:F6, click the **Charts** group on the ribbon's **Insert** tab and then select the first option for a **Scatter** chart. You can then right-click a data point and select **Add Trendline**. In the **Format Trendline** dialog box (see Figure 85-2), choose **Polynomial** and select **2** in the **Order** box (to obtain a quadratic curve of the form of Equation 1). Select **Display Equation On Chart**.

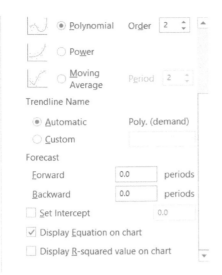

FIGURE 85-2 Configuring the Format Trendline dialog box for selecting a polynomial demand curve.

Excel creates the chart shown in Figure 85-1. The estimated demand curve (Equation 2) is *Demand* = −44*Price² + 136*Price − 45.

Next, you insert a trial price in cell I2. You compute product demand by using Equation 2 in cell I3 with the −44*price^2+136*price−45 formula. (Cell I2 is named Price.) Then you compute weekly profit from lipstick sales in cell I4 with the demand*(price−unit_cost) formula. (Cell E2 is named Unit_Cost, and cell I3 is named Demand.) Then you use Solver to determine the price that maximizes profit. The Solver Parameters dialog box is shown in Figure 85-3. Note that you must constrain the price to be between the lowest and the highest specified prices ($1.50 through $2.50). If you allow Solver to consider prices outside this range, the quadratic demand curve might slope upward, which implies that a higher price would result in larger demand. This result is unreasonable, which is why you should constrain the price.

The result is that the drugstore should charge $2.04 for a unit of lipstick. This yields sales of 49.4 units per week and a weekly profit of $56.24.

The approach to pricing outlined in this chapter requires no knowledge of the concept of price elasticity. Inherently, the Solver considers the elasticity for each price when it determines the profit-maximizing price. This approach can easily be applied by organizations that sell thousands of different products. The only data that needs to be specified for each product is its variable cost and the three given points on the demand curve.

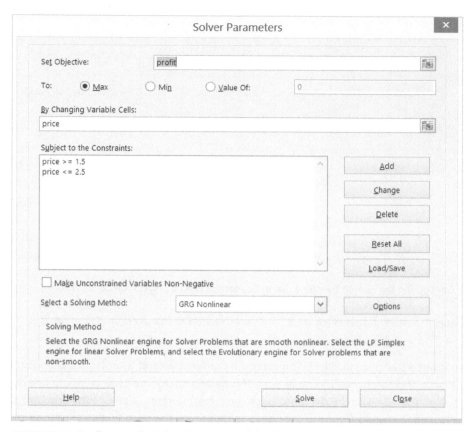

FIGURE 85-3 Configuring the Solver Parameters dialog box to calculate lipstick pricing.

Problems

1. Suppose it costs $250 to produce a video game console. A price from $200 through $400 is under consideration. Estimated demand for the game console is shown in the following table:

Price	Demand (in millions)
$200	2
$300	0.9
$400	0.2

What price should you charge for a game console?

2. This problem uses the demand information given in Problem 1. Each game owner buys an average of 10 video games. You earn $10 profit per video game. What price should you charge for the game console?

3. You are trying to determine the correct price for a new weekly magazine. The variable cost of printing and distributing a copy of the magazine is $0.50. You are thinking of charging from $0.50 through $1.30 per copy. The estimated weekly sales of the magazine are shown in the following table:

Price	Demand (in millions)
$0.50	2
$0.90	1.2
$1.30	0.3

In addition to sales revenue from the magazine, you can charge $30 per one thousand copies sold for each of the 20 pages of advertising in each week's magazine. What price should you charge for the magazine?

CHAPTER 86

Nonlinear pricing

Questions answered in this chapter:

- What is linear pricing?

- What is nonlinear pricing?

- What is bundling, and how can it increase profitability?

- How can I find a profit-maximizing, nonlinear pricing plan?

Answers to this chapter's questions

This section provides the answers to the questions that are listed at the beginning of the chapter.

What is linear pricing?

Chapter 84, "Pricing products by using tie-ins," and Chapter 85, "Pricing products by using sub-jectively determined demand," show how to determine a profit-maximizing price for a product. In those chapters' examples, however, the implicit assumption is made that no matter how many units a customer purchases, she is charged the same amount per unit. This model is known as *linear pricing* because the cost of buying *x* units is a straight-line function of *x*; namely, *cost of x units* = (*unit price*)*x*. You see in this chapter that *nonlinear pricing* can often greatly increase a company's profit.

What is nonlinear pricing?

A *nonlinear pricing* scheme simply means that the cost of buying *x* units is not a straight-line function of *x*. We have all encountered nonlinear pricing strategies. Here are some examples:

- **Quantity discounts** The first five units might cost $20 each and the remaining units $12 each. Quantity discounts are commonly used by companies selling software and computers. An example of the cost of purchasing *x* units is shown in the Nonlinear Pricing Examples work-sheet in the Nlp.xlsx file, which is shown in Figure 86-1. Notice that the graph has a slope of 20 for five or fewer units purchased and a slope of 12 for more than five units purchased.

FIGURE 86-1 Cost of quantity discount plan.

- **Two-part tariff**   When you join a country club, you usually pay a fixed fee for joining the club and then a fee for each round of golf you play. Suppose that your country club charges a membership fee of $500 per year and charges $20 per round of golf. This type of pricing strategy is called a *two-part tariff*. For this pricing policy, the cost of purchasing a given number of rounds of golf is shown in Figure 86-2. Again, look at the Nonlinear Pricing Examples worksheet in Nlp.xlsx. Note that the graph has a slope of 520 from zero through one unit purchased and a slope of 20 for more than one unit purchased. Because a straight line must always have the same slope, you can see that a two-part tariff is highly nonlinear.

FIGURE 86-2 Cost of two-part tariff.

What is bundling, and how can it increase profitability?

Price bundling involves offering a customer a set of products for a price less than the sum of the products' individual prices. To analyze why bundling works, you need to understand how a rational consumer makes decisions. For each product combination available, a rational consumer looks at the value of what you are selling and subtracts the cost to purchase it. This yields the *consumer surplus* of the purchase. A rational consumer buys nothing if the consumer surplus of each available option is negative. Otherwise, the consumer purchases the product combination having the largest consumer surplus.

So how can bundling increase your profitability? Suppose that you sell computers and printers and have two customers. The values each customer attaches to a computer and a printer are shown here:

Customer	Computer value	Printer value
1	$1,000	$500
2	$500	$1,000

You only offer the computer and printer for sale separately. By charging $1,000 for a printer and for a computer, you will sell one printer and one computer and receive $2,000 in revenue. Now suppose that you offer the printer and computer in combination for $1,500. Each customer buys both the computer and the printer, and you receive $3,000 in revenue. By bundling the computer and printer, you can extract more of the consumer's total valuation. Bundling works best if customer valuations for the bundled products are negatively correlated. In this example, the negative correlation between the values for the bundled products results because the customer who places a high value on a printer places a low value on a computer, and the customer who places a low value on a printer places a high value on a computer.

When you go to a theme park such as Disneyland, you don't buy a ticket for each ride. You buy a ticket to enter the theme park or you don't go. This is an example of *pure bundling* because the consumer does not have the option to pay for a subset of the offered products. This approach reduces lines (imagine a line at *every* ride) and results in more profit.

To see why this bundling approach increases profitability, suppose there is only one customer and that the number of rides the customer wants to go on is governed by a demand curve that is calculated as (Number of rides) – 20 – 2*(Price of ride). From the discussion of demand curves in Chapter 83, "Estimating a demand curve," you know that the value the consumer gives to the ith ride is the price that makes demand equal to $i - 0.5$. Thus, you know that $i - 0.5 = 20 - 2*$(value of ride i) or, solving for the value of ride i, that (value of ride i) $= 10.25 - (i/2)$. The first ride is worth $9.75, the second ride is worth $9.25, and so on to the twentieth ride, which is worth $0.25.

Assume you charge a constant price per ride and that it costs $2 in variable costs per ride. You seek the profit-maximizing linear pricing scheme. On the OnePrice worksheet in the Nlp.xlsx file, shown in Figure 86-3, you see how to determine the profit-maximizing price per ride.

Associate the range names in C8:C10 with cells D8:D10. Enter a trial price in cell D8 and compute the number of ride tickets purchased in cell D9 with the 20–(2*D8) formula. Compute the profit in cell D12 with the Demand*(price–unit_cost) formula. You can now use the Solver to maximize the value in D12 (profit) by changing cell D8 (price). A price of $6 results in eight ride tickets being purchased, and you earn a maximum profit of $32.

	B	C	D	E
5				
6	Linear			
7	Pricing			
8		price	$ 6.00	
9		Demand	$ 8.00	
10		unit cost	$ 2.00	
11				
12		profit	$ 32.00	

FIGURE 86-3 Profit-maximizing linear pricing scheme.

Now pretend that you're like Disneyland and offer only a bundle of 20 rides to the customer. You set a price equal to the sum of the customer's valuations for each ride ($9.75 + $9.25 + . . . $0.75 + $0.25 = $100.00). The customer values all 20 rides at $100.00, so the customer will buy a park entry ticket for $100.00. You earn a profit of $100.00 – $2.00(20) = $60.00, which almost doubles your profit from linear pricing.

How can I find a profit-maximizing, nonlinear pricing plan?

In this section, you see how you can determine a profit-maximizing, two-part-tariff pricing plan for the amusement park example. Proceed as follows:

1. Hypothesize trial values for the fixed fee and the price per ride.
2. Determine the value the customer associates with each ride: Value of ride i = 10 – .5(i – .5) = 10.25 – 0.5i.
3. Determine the cumulative value associated with buying i rides.
4. Determine the price charged for i rides: Fixed fee + i*(price per ride).
5. Determine the consumer surplus for buying i rides: Value of i rides – price of i rides.
6. Determine the maximum consumer surplus.
7. Determine the number of units purchased. If the maximum consumer surplus is negative, no units are purchased. Otherwise, use the *MATCH* function to find the number of units yielding the maximum surplus.
8. Use a *VLOOKUP* function to look up revenue corresponding to the number of units purchased.
9. Compute profit as revenue – costs.
10. Use a two-way data table to determine a profit-maximizing fixed fee and price per ride.

The work for this approach is in the Two-Part Tariff worksheet in the Nlp.xlsx file, which is shown in Figure 86-4.

To begin, name cell F2 Fixed and cell F3 LP. Enter trial values for the fixed fee and the price per ride in cells F2 and F3. Next, determine the value the consumer places on each ride by copying the

10.25–(D6/2) formula from cell E6 to E7:E25. You find that the customer places a value of $9.75 on the first ride, $9.25 on the second ride, and so on.

	B	C	D	E	F	G	H	I	J
1							Units bought	15	
2		cost		fixed fee	$ 56.00		Revenue	$ 93.50	
3		$ 2.00		price per ride	$ 2.50		Prod Cost	$ 30.00	
4						Max surplus	0.25		
5			Unit	Value	Cum Value	Price paid	Surplus		Profit
6			1	9.75	9.75	58.5	-48.75		$ 63.50
7			2	9.25	19	61	-42		
8			3	8.75	27.75	63.5	-35.75		
9			4	8.25	36	66	-30		
10			5	7.75	43.75	68.5	-24.75		
11			6	7.25	51	71	-20		
12			7	6.75	57.75	73.5	-15.75		
13			8	6.25	64	76	-12		
14			9	5.75	69.75	78.5	-8.75		
15			10	5.25	75	81	-6		
16			11	4.75	79.75	83.5	-3.75		
17			12	4.25	84	86	-2		
18			13	3.75	87.75	88.5	0.75		
19			14	3.25	91	91	0		
20			15	2.75	93.75	93.5	0.25		
21			16	2.25	96	96	0		
22			17	1.75	97.75	98.5	-0.75		
23			18	1.25	99	101	-2		
24			19	0.75	99.75	103.5	-3.75		

FIGURE 86-4 Determination of optimal two-part tariff.

To compute the cumulative value of the first *i* rides, copy the SUM($E$6:E6) formula from F6 to F7:F25. This formula adds up all values in column E that are in or above the current row. By copying the fixed_fee+price_per_ride*D6 formula from G6 to G7:G25, you can compute the cost of *i* rides. For example, the cost of five rides is $68.50.

Recall that the consumer surplus for *i* rides equals (*Value of i rides*) – (*Cost of i rides*). By copying the F6–G6 formula from cell H6 to the H7:H25 range, you compute the consumer's surplus for purchasing any number of rides. For example, the consumer surplus for purchasing five rides is –$24.75, which is the result of the large fixed fee.

In cell H4, compute the maximum consumer surplus with the MAX(H6:H25) formula. Remember that if the maximum consumer surplus is negative, no units are purchased. Otherwise, the consumer will purchase the number of units yielding the maximum consumer surplus. Therefore, by entering the IF(H4>=0,MATCH(H4,H6:H25,0),0) formula in cell I1, you determine the number of units purchased (in this case, 15). Notice that the *MATCH* function finds the number of rows you need to move down in the H6:H24 range to find the first match to the maximum surplus.

Now name the D5:G25 range lookup. You can then look up total revenue in the fourth column of this range based on the number of units purchased (which is already computed in cell I1). The total revenue is computed in cell I2 with the IF(I1=0,0,VLOOKUP(I1,lookup,4)) formula. Notice that if no rides are purchased, you earn no revenue. Compute total production cost for rides purchased in cell I3 with the I1*C3 formula. In cell J6, compute profit as revenues less costs with the I2–I3 formula.

Now you can use a two-way data table to determine the profit-maximizing combination of fixed fee and price per ride. The data table is shown in Figure 86-5. (Many rows and columns are hidden.) In setting up the data table, the fixed fee was varied between $10.00 and $60.00 (the values in the K10:K60 range), and the price per ride was varied between $0.50 and $5.00 (the values in L9:BE9). Profit was recomputed in cell K9 with the =J6 formula.

Select the table range (cells K9:BE60) and then, on the **Data** tab, in the **Data Tools** group, click **What-If Analysis**. Select **Data Table**. The column input cell is F2 (the fixed fee), and the row input cell is F3 (the price per ride). Clicking **OK** in the **Table** dialog box computes the profit for each fixed fee and price per ride combination represented in the data table.

	J	K	L	M	N	AE	AF	BB	BC	BD	BE
5	Profit				Max Profit						
6	$ 63.50				$ 63.50						
7											
8			Unit	cost							
9		$ 63.50	0.5	0.6	0.7	2.4	2.5	4.7	4.8	4.9	5
10		10	-18.5	-17	-14.7	16	17.5	39.7	38	39	40
11		11	-17.5	-16	-13.7	17	18.5	40.7	39	40	41
12		12	-16.5	-15	-12.7	18	19.5	41.7	40	41	42
13		13	-15.5	-14	-11.7	19	20.5	42.7	41	42	43
14		14	-14.5	-13	-10.7	20	21.5	43.7	42	43	44
15		15	-13.5	-12	-9.7	21	22.5	44.7	43	44	45
16		16	-12.5	-11	-8.7	22	23.5	45.7	44	45	46
17		17	-11.5	-9.6	-7.7	23	24.5	46.7	45	46	47
18		18	-10.5	-8.6	-6.7	24	25.5	47.7	46	47	48
19		19	-9.5	-7.6	-5.7	25	26.5	48.7	47	48	49
20		20	-8.5	-6.6	-4.7	26	27.5	49.7	48	49	50
21		21	-7.5	-5.6	-3.7	27	28.5	50.7	49	50	51
22		22	-6.5	-4.6	-2.7	28	29.5	51.7	50	51	52
23		23	-5.5	-3.6	-1.7	29	30.5	52.7	51	52	53
24		24	-4.5	-2.6	-0.7	30	31.5	53.7	52	53	54
48		48	19.5	21.4	23.3	54	55.5	0	0	0	0
49	Fixed	49	20.5	22.4	24.3	55	56.5	0	0	0	0
50	cost	50	21.5	23.4	25.3	56	57.5	0	0	0	0
51		51	22.5	24.4	26.3	57	58.5	0	0	0	0
52		52	23.5	25.4	27.3	58	59.5	0	0	0	0
53		53	24.5	26.4	28.3	59	60.5	0	0	0	0
54		54	25.5	27.4	29.3	60	61.5	0	0	0	0
55		55	26.5	28.4	30.3	61	62.5	0	0	0	0
56		56	27.5	29.4	31.3	62	63.5	0	0	0	0
57		57	28.5	30.4	32.3	63	0	0	0	0	0
58		58	29.5	31.4	33.3	0	0	0	0	0	0
59		59	30.5	32.4	34.3	0	0	0	0	0	0
60		60	31.5	33.4	35.3	0	0	0	0	0	0

FIGURE 86-5 Two-way data table computing optimal two-part tariff.

To highlight the profit-maximizing two-part tariff, use conditional formatting; select the L10:BE60 range. Click **Conditional Formatting** on the **Home** tab, click **Top/Bottom Rules**, and then click **Top 10 Items**. Change the 10 in the dialog box to a **1** so that only the largest profit is formatted. Here, a fixed fee of $56.00 and a price per ride of $2.50 earns a profit of $63.50, which almost doubles the profit from linear pricing. A fixed fee of $59.00 and a price per ride of $2.30 also yields a profit of $63.50.

Because a quantity-discount plan involves selecting three variables (cutoff, high price, and low price), you cannot use a data table to determine a profit-maximizing quantity-discount plan. You might think you could use a Solver model (with changing cells set to cutoff, high price, and low price) to determine a profit-maximizing quantity-discount strategy. Before Excel 2010, the Solver often had difficulty determining optimal solutions when the target cell is computed by using formulas containing IF statements. The Excel 2013 Solver handles the quantity-discount problem with ease, even with the use of IF statements. In the Qd.xlsx file (see Figure 86-6), use the Evolutionary Solver engine to find the profit-maximizing quantity-discount plan. Assume that all units bought up to a cutoff (called CUT) are sold at a high price (called HP) and that the remaining items are sold at a low price (called LP). The only change in the spreadsheet setup is in column G. After naming cells F1:F3 with the names in E1:E3, compute the amount a person would pay to buy any number of units by copying the IF(D6<=Cut,D6*HP,HP*Cut+(D6-Cut)*LP) formula from G6 to G7:G25. The Solver Parameters dialog box setup is shown in Figure 86-7. As described in Chapter 35, "Warehouse location and the GRG Multistart and Evolutionary Solver engines," use the Evolutionary Solver here because the model uses IF statements that involve changing cells. The Mutation Rate under Evolutionary Solver options was changed to .5. Note that you must constrain the cutoff point to be an integer; use an upper bound of $20 for all the changing cells. Of course, if Solver had chosen a price near $20, you would have relaxed the upper bound on the price changing cells.

The Solver found a maximum profit of $63.97, obtained by charging $18.48 for the first four units purchased and $1.84 for the remaining units. The customers will buy 16 units. If you had run Solver longer, it would have found the true maximum profit, which is $64.00.

	C	D	E	F	G	H	I	J
1			Cut	4		Units bought	16	
2	cost		HP	$ 18.48		Revenue	$ 95.97	
3	$ 2.00		LP	$ 1.84		Prod Cost	$ 32.00	
4					Max surplus	0.03156491		
5		Unit	Value	Cum Value	Price paid	Surplus		Profit
6		1	9.75	9.75	18.4811003	-8.731100274		$ 63.97
7		2	9.25	19	36.9622005	-17.96220055		
8		3	8.75	27.75	55.4433008	-27.69330082		
9		4	8.25	36	73.9244011	-37.9244011		
10		5	7.75	43.75	75.7614039	-32.01140393		
11		6	7.25	51	77.5984068	-26.59840676		
12		7	6.75	57.75	79.4354096	-21.6854096		
13		8	6.25	64	81.2724124	-17.27241243		
14		9	5.75	69.75	83.1094153	-13.35941526		
15		10	5.25	75	84.9464181	-9.946418094		
16		11	4.75	79.75	86.7834209	-7.033420926		
17		12	4.25	84	88.6204238	-4.620423759		
18		13	3.75	87.75	90.4574266	-2.707426592		
19		14	3.25	91	92.2944294	-1.294429425		
20		15	2.75	93.75	94.1314323	-0.381432257		
21		16	2.25	96	95.9684351	0.03156491		
22		17	1.75	97.75	97.8054379	-0.055437923		
23		18	1.25	99	99.6424408	-0.642440755		
24		19	0.75	99.75	101.479444	-1.729443588		
25		20	0.25	100	103.316446	-3.316446421		

FIGURE 86-6 Use of Solver to find the profit-maximizing quantity-discount plan.

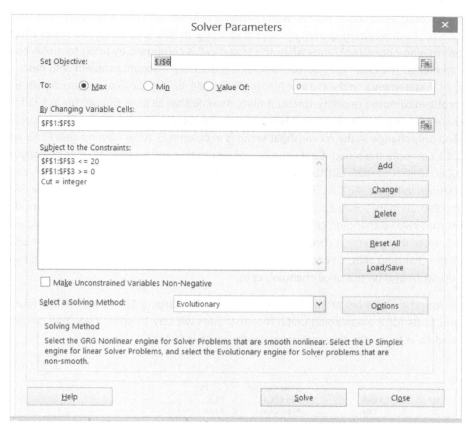

FIGURE 86-7 Solver settings for maximizing a quantity-discount plan.

Problems

You own a small country club and have three types of customers who value each round of golf they play during a month as shown in the following table:

Round no.	Customer type 1	Customer type 2	Customer type 3
1	$60	$50	$40
2	$50	$45	$30
3	$40	$30	$20
4	$30	$15	$10
5	$20	$0	$0
6	$10	$0	$0

1. Find a profit-maximizing two-part tariff.

2. Suppose you will offer a pure bundle. For example, a member can play up to five rounds of golf for $60 per month. The member has no option to choose from other than the pure bundle. What pure bundle maximizes your profit?

CHAPTER 87

Array formulas and functions

Questions answered in this chapter:

- What is an array formula?

- How can I interpret formulas such as (D2:D7)*(E2:E7) and SUM(D2:D7*E2:E7)?

- I have a list of names in one column. These names change often. Is there an easy way to transpose the listed names to one row so that changes in the original column of names are reflected in the new row?

- I have a list of monthly stock returns. Is there a way to determine the number of returns from −30 percent through −20 percent, −10 percent through 0 percent, and so on that will automatically update if I change the original data?

- Can I write one formula that will sum up the second digit of a list of integers?

- Is there a way to look at two lists of names and determine which names occur on both lists?

- Can I write a formula that averages all numbers in a list that exceed the list's median value?

- I have a sales database for a small makeup company that lists the salesperson, product, units sold, and dollar amount for every transaction. I know I can use database statistical functions or *COUNTIFS*, *SUMIFS*, and *AVERAGEIFS* to summarize this data. Can I also use array functions to summarize the data and answer questions such as how many units of makeup a salesperson sold, how many units of lipstick were sold, and how many units were sold by a specific salesperson or were lipstick?

- What are array constants and how can I use them?

- How can I edit array formulas?

- Given quarterly revenues for a toy store, can I estimate the trend and seasonality of the store's revenues?

- Given a list of transactions in different countries, how can I calculate the median size of a transaction in each country?

Answers to this chapter's questions

This section provides the answers to the questions that are listed at the beginning of the chapter.

What is an array formula?

Array formulas often provide a shortcut or more efficient approach to performing complex calculations with Microsoft Excel. An array formula can return a result in either one cell or a range of cells. Array formulas perform operations on two or more sets of values, called *array arguments*. Each array argument used in an array formula must contain exactly the same number of rows and columns.

When you enter an array formula, you must first select the range in which you want Excel to place the array formula's results. Then, after entering the formula in the first cell of the selected range, *you must press Ctrl+Shift+Enter*. If you fail to press Ctrl+Shift+Enter, you'll obtain incorrect or nonsensical results. The process of entering an array formula and then pressing Ctrl+Shift+Enter can be referred to as *array-entering* a formula.

Excel also contains a variety of *array functions*. Chapter 42, "Summarizing data by using descriptive statistics," discusses the *MODE.MULT* array function. You met two array functions (*LINEST* and *TREND*) in Chapter 57, "Introduction to multiple regression," and Chapter 58, "Incorporating qualitative factors into multiple regression." As described in those chapters, to use an array function or formula, you must first select the range in which you want the formula or function's results placed. Then, after entering the function or formula in the first cell of the selected range, you must press Ctrl+Shift+Enter. This chapter introduces you to three other useful array functions: *TRANSPOSE*, *FREQUENCY*, and *LOGEST*. You also learn how to write your own array formulas.

As you'll see, you cannot delete any part of a cell range that contains results computed with an array formula. In addition, you cannot paste an array formula into a range that contains both blank cells and array formulas. For example, if you have an array formula in cell C10 and you want to copy it to the C10:J15 cell range, you cannot simply copy the formula to this range because the range contains both blank cells and the array formula in cell C10. To work around this difficulty, copy the formula from C10 to D10:J10 and then copy the contents of C10:J10 to C11:J15.

The best way to learn how array formulas and functions work is by looking at some examples, so let's get started.

How can I interpret formulas such as (D2:D7)*(E2:E7) and SUM(D2:D7*E2:E7)?

On the Total Wages worksheet in the Arrays.xlsx file is listed the number of hours worked and the hourly wage rates for six employees, as you can see in Figure 87-1.

If you want to compute each person's total wages, you could simply copy the D3*E3 formula from F2 to F3:F7. There is certainly nothing wrong with that approach, but using an array formula provides a more elegant solution. Begin by selecting the F2:F7 range, where you want to compute each person's total earnings. Then enter the =(D2:D7*E2:E7) formula and press Ctrl+Shift+Enter. You see that each person's total wages are correctly computed. Also, if you look at the Formula bar, you see that the formula appears as {=(D2:D7*E2:E7)}. The curly brackets are the way Excel tells you that you've created an array formula. (You don't enter the curly brackets that show up at the beginning and end of an array formula, but the curly brackets indicate that a formula is an array formula in this chapter.)

	C	D	E	F	G
				total owed each	grand total
1		Hours	wage rate	person	owed
2	John	3	$ 6.00	$ 18.00	$ 295.00
3	Jack	4	$ 7.00	$ 28.00	
4	Jill	5	$ 8.00	$ 40.00	
5	Jane	8	$ 9.00	$ 72.00	
6	Jean	6	$ 10.00	$ 60.00	
7	Jocelyn	7	$ 11.00	$ 77.00	

FIGURE 87-1 Using array formulas to compute hourly wages.

To see how this formula works, click in the **Formula** bar, highlight D2:D7 in the formula, and then press F9. You see {3;4;5;8;6;7}, which is the way Excel creates the D2:D7 cell range as an array. Now select E2:E7 in the **Formula** bar and then press F9 again. You see {6;7;8;9;10;11}, which is the way Excel creates an array corresponding to the E2:E7 range. The inclusion of the asterisk (*) tells Excel to multiply the corresponding elements in each array. Because the cell ranges being multiplied include six cells each, Excel creates arrays with six items, and because you selected a range of six cells, each person's total wage is displayed in its own cell. Had you selected a range of only five cells, the sixth item in the array would not be displayed.

Suppose you want to compute the total wages earned by all employees. One approach is to use the =SUMPRODUCT(D2:D7,E2:E7) formula. Again, however, try to create an array formula to compute total wages. Begin by selecting one cell (cell G2 is chosen here) in which to place the result. Then enter the =SUM(D2:D7*E2:E7) formula in cell G2. After pressing Ctrl+Shift+Enter, you obtain (3)(6) + (4)(7) + (5)(8) + (8)(9) + (6)(10) + (7)(11) = 295. To see how this formula works, select the D2:D7*E2:E7 portion in the **Formula** bar and then press F9. You see SUM({18;28;40;83;60;77}), which shows that Excel created a six-element array whose first element is *3*6(18)*, whose second element is *4*7(28)*, and so on, until the last element, which is *7*11(77)*. Excel then adds up the values in the array to obtain the total of $295

I have a list of names in one column. These names change often. Is there an easy way to transpose the listed names to one row so that changes in the original column of names are reflected in the new row?

The Transpose worksheet in the Arrays.xlsx file, shown in Figure 87-2, lists a set of names in cells A4:A8. The goal is to list these names in one row (the C3:G3 cell range). If you knew that the original list of names would never change, you could accomplish this goal by copying the cell range and then using **Transpose** in the **Paste Special** dialog box. (See Chapter 13, "The Paste Special command," for details.) Unfortunately, if the names in column A change, the names in row 3 would not reflect those changes if you use Paste Special, Transpose. What you need in this situation is the *TRANSPOSE* function.

	A	B	C	D	E	F	G
1							
2							
3			Julie	Jason	Jack	Jill	Jane
4	Julie						
5	Jason						
6	Jack						
7	Jill						
8	Jane						

FIGURE 87-2 Using the *TRANSPOSE* function.

The *TRANSPOSE* function is an array function that changes rows of a selected range into columns and vice versa. To begin using *TRANSPOSE* in this example, you select the C3:G3 range, where you want the transposed list of names to be placed. Then, in cell C3, you array-enter the =TRANSPOSE(A4:A8) formula. The list of names is now displayed in one row. More important, if you change any of the names in A4:A8, the corresponding name will change in the transposed range.

I have a list of monthly stock returns. Is there a way to determine the number of returns from –30 percent through –20 percent, –10 percent through 0 percent, and so on that will automatically update if I change the original data?

This problem is a job for the *FREQUENCY* array function. The *FREQUENCY* function counts how many values in an array (called the *data array*) occur within given value ranges (specified by a bin array). The syntax of the *FREQUENCY* function is FREQUENCY (*data_array,bin_array*).

To illustrate the use of the *FREQUENCY* function, look at the Frequency worksheet in the Arrays .xlsx file, shown in Figure 87-3. It lists monthly stock returns for a fictitious stock in the A4:A77 cell range.

	A	B	C	D
1	min	-43.84%		
2	max	52.56%		
3	Returns			
4	43.81%		Total	
5	-8.30%			74
6	-25.12%		Bin values	
7	-43.84%		-0.4	1
8	-8.64%		-0.3	1
9	49.98%		-0.2	2
10	-1.19%		-0.1	5
11	46.74%		0	13
12	31.94%		0.1	11
13	-35.34%		0.2	13
14	29.28%		0.3	12
15	-1.10%		0.4	11
16	-10.67%		0.5	4
17	-12.77%		0.6	1
18	19.17%			0

FIGURE 87-3 Using the *FREQUENCY* function.

You find in cells A1 and A2 (using the *MIN* and *MAX* functions) that all returns are from –44 percent through 53 percent. Based on this information, you can set up bin value boundaries in cells C7:C17, starting at –0.4 and ending at 0.6. Now select the D7:D18 range, where you want the results of the *FREQUENCY* function to be placed. In this range, cell D7 will count the number of data points less than or equal to –0.4, D8 will count the number of data points greater than –0.4 and less than or equal to –0.3, and so on. Cell D17 will count all data points greater than 0.5 and less than or equal to 0.6, and cell D18 will count all the data points that are greater than 0.6.

Enter the =FREQUENCY(A4:A77,C7:C17) formula and then press Ctrl+Shift+Enter. This formula tells Excel to count the number of data points in A4:A77 (the data array) that lie in each of the bin ranges defined in C7:C17. The results show that one return is greater than –0.4 and less than or equal to –0.3. Thirteen returns are greater than 0.1 and less than or equal to 0.2. If you change any of the data points in the data array, the results generated by the *FREQUENCY* function in cells D7:D17 will reflect the changes in your data.

Can I write one formula that will sum up the second digit of a list of integers?

In the A4:A10 cell range in the Sum Up 2nd Digit worksheet in the Arrays.xlsx file, seven integers are listed. (See 87-4.) You would like to write one formula that sums up the second digit of each number. You could obtain this sum by copying the VALUE(MID(A4,2,1)) formula from B4 to B5:B10. This formula returns (as a numerical value) the second character in cell A4. Then you could add up the B4:B10 range and obtain the total of 27.

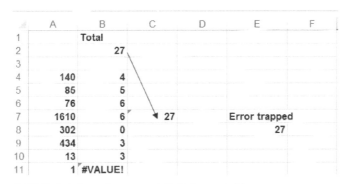

FIGURE 87-4 Summing second digits in a set of integers.

An array function makes this process much easier. Simply select cell C7 and array-enter the =SUM(VALUE(MID(A4:A10,2,1)) formula. Your array formula will return the correct answer, 27.

To see what this formula does, highlight MID(A4:A10,2,1) in the **Formula** bar and then press F9. You see {"4";"5";"6";"6";"0";"3";"3"}. This string of values shows that Excel has created an array consisting of the second digit (viewed as text) in the A4:A10 cell range. The VALUE portion of the formula changes these text strings into numerical values, which are added up by the SUM portion of the formula.

Notice that in cell A11, a number with one digit is entered. Because this number has no second digit, the MID portion of your formula returns #VALUE. How can you modify this array formula to account for the possible inclusion of one-digit integers? Simply array-enter the {SUM(IF(LEN(A4:A11) >=2,VALUE(MID(A4:A11,2,1)),0))} formula in cell E8. This formula replaces any one-digit integer with a 0, so you still obtain the correct sum.

Is there a way to look at two lists of names and determine which names occur on both lists?

In the Matching Names worksheet in the file Arrays.xlsx file, two lists of names appear (in columns D and E), as you can see in Figure 87-5. Here, you want to determine which names on List 1 also appear on List 2. To accomplish this, you select the C5:C28 range and array-enter the ={MATCH(D5:D28,E5:E28,0)} formula in cell C5. This formula loops through the C5:C28 cells. In cell C5, the formula verifies whether the name in D5 has a match in column E. If a match exists, the formula returns the position of the first match in E5:E28. If no match exists, the formula returns #NA (for not available). Similarly, in cell C6, the formula verifies whether the second name on List 1 has a match. You see, for example, that Artest does not appear on the second list but Harrington does (first matched in the second cell in the E5:E28 range).

	B	C	D	E	F
4			List 1	List 2	
5	NO	#N/A	Artest	BMiller	
6	NO	#N/A	Artest	Harrington	
7	YES	2	Harrington	BMiller	
8	NO	#N/A	Artest	Harrington	
9	NO	#N/A	Artest	Harrington	
10	NO	#N/A	Artest	BMiller	
11	YES	2	Harrington	BMiller	
12	NO	#N/A	Artest	Mercer	
13	NO	#N/A	Artest	Harrington	
14	NO	#N/A	Artest	Harrington	
15	YES	8	Mercer	BMiller	
16	NO	#N/A	Artest	Mercer	
17	NO	#N/A	O'Neal	RMiller	
18	NO	#N/A	O'Neal	BMiller	
19	NO	#N/A	O'Neal	RMiller	
20	NO	#N/A	O'Neal	RMiller	
21	YES	13	RMiller	BMiller	
22	NO	#N/A	O'Neal	RMiller	
23	NO	#N/A	O'Neal	RMiller	
24	YES	13	RMiller	BMiller	
25	NO	#N/A	O'Neal	Mercer	
26	NO	#N/A	O'Neal	BMiller	
27	NO	#N/A	O'Neal	RMiller	
28	NO	#N/A	O'Neal	BMiller	

FIGURE 87-5 Finding duplicates in two lists.

To enter Yes for each name in List 1 with a match in List 2, and No for each List 1 name without a match, select the B5:B28 cell range and array-enter the {IF(ISERROR(C5:C28),"No","Yes")} formula in cell B5. This formula displays No for each cell in C5:C28 containing the #NA message and Yes for all cells returning a numerical value. Note that =ISERROR(x) yields True if the formula x evaluates to an error and yields False otherwise.

Can I write a formula that averages all numbers in a list that are greater than or equal to the list's median value?

On the Average Those > Median worksheet in the Arrays.xlsx file, shown in Figure 87-6, the D5:D785 range (named Prices) contains a list of prices. You want to average all prices that are at least as large as the median price. In cell F2, compute the median with the Median(prices) formula. In cell F3, compute the average of numbers greater than or equal to the median by entering the =SUMIF(prices,">=" &F2,prices)/COUNTIF(prices,">="&F2) formula. This formula adds up all prices that are at least as large as the median value (*243*) and then divides by the number of prices that are at least as large as the median. The average of all prices at least as large as the median price is $324.30.

D	E	F	G	H
	median	243		
	answer	324.2977	with formula	
Price				
224				
321		324.2977	with array	
133				
310				
370				
223				
380				
253				
211				
248				
146				
334				

FIGURE 87-6 Averaging prices at least as large as the median price.

An easier approach is to select cell F6 and array-enter the =AVERAGE(IF(prices> =MEDIAN(prices),prices,""))} formula. This formula creates an array that contains the row's price if the row's price is greater than or equal to the median price or a space otherwise. Averaging this array gives you the results you want.

I have a sales database for a small makeup company that lists the salesperson, product, units sold, and dollar amount for every transaction. I know I can use database statistical functions or *COUNTIFS*, *SUMIFS*, and *AVERAGEIFS* to summarize this data. Can I also use array functions to summarize the data and answer questions such as how many units of makeup a salesperson sold, how many units of lipstick were sold, and how many units were sold by a specific salesperson or were lipstick?

The Makeuparray.xlsx file contains a list of 1,900 sales transactions made by a makeup company. For each transaction, the transaction number, salesperson, transaction date, product sold, units sold, and dollar volume are listed. You can see some of the data in Figure 87-7.

	I	J	K	L	M	N
4	Trans Number	Name	Date	Product	Units	Dollars
5	1	Betsy	4/1/2004	lip gloss	45	$ 137.20
6	2	Hallagan	3/10/2004	foundation	50	$ 152.01
7	3	Ashley	2/25/2005	lipstick	9	$ 28.72
8	4	Hallagan	5/22/2006	lip gloss	55	$ 167.08
9	5	Zaret	6/17/2004	lip gloss	43	$ 130.60
10	6	Colleen	11/27/2005	eyeliner	58	$ 175.99
11	7	Cristina	3/21/2004	eyeliner	8	$ 25.80
12	8	Colleen	12/17/2006	lip gloss	72	$ 217.84
13	9	Ashley	7/5/2006	eyeliner	75	$ 226.64
14	10	Betsy	8/7/2006	lip gloss	24	$ 73.50
15	11	Ashley	11/29/2004	mascara	43	$ 130.84
16	12	Ashley	11/18/2004	lip gloss	23	$ 71.03
17	13	Emilee	8/31/2005	lip gloss	49	$ 149.59
18	14	Hallagan	1/1/2005	eyeliner	18	$ 56.47
19	15	Zaret	9/20/2006	foundation	-8	$ (21.99)
20	16	Emilee	4/12/2004	mascara	45	$ 137.39
21	17	Colleen	4/30/2006	mascara	66	$ 199.65
22	18	Jen	8/31/2005	lip gloss	88	$ 265.19
23	19	Jen	10/27/2004	eyeliner	78	$ 236.15
24	20	Zaret	11/27/2005	lip gloss	57	$ 173.12
25	21	Zaret	6/2/2006	mascara	12	$ 38.08

FIGURE 87-7 Makeup database.

This data can easily be summarized by using database statistical functions, as described in Chapter 48, "Summarizing data with database statistical functions," or by using the *COUNTIFS* and *SUMIFS* functions. (See Chapter 19, "The *COUNTIF, COUNTIFS, COUNT, COUNTA*, and *COUNTBLANK* functions," and Chapter 20, "The SUMIF, AVERAGEIF, SUMIFS, and AVERAGEIFS functions"). As you'll see in this section, array functions provide an easy, powerful alternative to these functions:

- **How many units of makeup did Jen sell?** You can easily answer this question by using the *SUMIF* function. In this worksheet, the J5:J1904 cell range is named Name and the M5:M1904 cell range Units. The SUMIF(Name,"Jen",Units) formula was entered in cell E7 to sum up all the units sold by Jen. The total is 9,537 units. You can also answer this question by array-entering the =SUM(IF(J5:J1904="Jen",M5:M1904,0))} formula in cell E6. This formula creates an array that contains the units sold for a transaction made by Jen and a 0 for all other transactions.

Therefore, summing this array also yields the number of units sold by Jen—9,537—as you can see in Figure 87-8.

	A	B	C	D	E	F	G
5					units sold by jen	units lipstick sold by jen	units sold by Jen or lipstick
6				Array function	9537	1299	17061
7				other functions	9537	1299	17061
8							
9					Name	Product	
10					Jen	lipstick	
11							
12					Name	Product	
13					Jen		
14						lipstick	
15							
16		eyeliner	foundation	lip gloss	lipstick	mascara	
17	Ashley	1920	1373	1985	1066	2172	
18	Betsy	1987	2726	1857	1305	1582	
19	Cici	1960	2031	1701	1035	2317	
20	Colleen	1107	2242	1831	765	2215	
21	Cristina	1770	1729	1734	788	1790	
22	Emilee	2490	1803	1725	720	1545	
23	Hallagan	2288	2387	1840	1045	1873	
24	Jen	2302	1883	1792	1299	2261	
25	Zaret	2715	2117	1868	800	1268	

FIGURE 87-8 Summarizing data with array formulas.

■ **How many units of lipstick did Jen sell?** This question requires a criterion that uses two columns (Name and Product). You could answer this question by using the database statistical function formula =DSUM(J4:N1904,4,E9:F10), which is entered in cell F7. This formula shows that Jen sold 1,299 units of lipstick. You can also obtain this answer by using the array formula entered in cell F6, =SUM((J5:J1904="jen")*(L5:L1904="lipstick")*M5:M1904)}.

To understand this formula, you need to know a bit about Boolean arrays. The portion of this formula that reads (J5:J1904="jen") creates a Boolean array. For each entry in J5:J1904 that equals *Jen*, the array includes the value *True*, and for each entry in J5:J1904 that does not equal *Jen*, the array contains *False*. Similarly, the (L5:L1904="lipstick") portion of this formula creates a Boolean array with a True corresponding to each cell in the range that contains the word *lipstick* and a False corresponding to each cell in the range that does not. When Boolean arrays are multiplied, another array is created using the following rules:

- True*True = 1

- True*False = 0

- False*True = 0

- False*False = 0

In short, multiplying Boolean arrays mimics the *AND* operator. Multiplying the product of the Boolean arrays by the values in the M5:M1904 range creates a new array. In any row in which Jen sold lipstick, this array contains the units sold. In all other rows, this array contains a 0. Summing this array yields Jen's total lipstick sales (1,299).

- **How many units were sold by Jen or were lipstick?**   In cell G7, the database statistical function =DSUM(J4:N1904,4,E12:F14) was used to find that all units that were sold by Jen or that were lipstick total 17,061. In cell G6, compute the number of units that were sold by Jen or that were lipstick by array-entering the {SUM(IF((J5:J1904="jen")+(L5:L1904="lipstick"),1,0)*M5:M1904)} formula.

Again, the portion of this formula that reads (J5:J1904="jen")+(L5:L1904="lipstick") creates two Boolean arrays. The first array contains True if and only if Jen (the formula is not case sensitive) is the salesperson. The second array contains True if and only if the product sold is lipstick. When Boolean arrays are added, the following rules are used:

- False + True = 1

- True + True = 1

- True + False = 1

- False + False = 0

In short, adding Boolean arrays mimics the *OR* operator. Therefore, this formula creates an array in which each row where Jen is the salesperson or lipstick is the product sold multiplies the number of units sold by 1. In any other row, the number of units sold is multiplied by 0. The same result is obtained as with the database statistical formula (17,061).

- **Can I summarize the number of units of each product sold by each salesperson?**   Array formulas make answering a question such as this a snap. You begin by listing each salesperson's name in the A17:A25 cell range and each product name in the B16:F16 cell range. Now you array-enter the {SUM(($J$5:$J$1904=$A17)*($L$5:$L$1904=B$16)*$M$5:$M$1904)} formula in cell B17.

This formula counts only units of eyeliner sold by Ashley (1,920 units). By copying this formula to C17:F17, you can compute the units of each product sold by Ashley. Copy the formulas in C17:F17 to C18:C25 and compute the number of units of each product sold by each salesperson. Notice that you must add a dollar sign to A in the reference to cell A17 so that you always pull the person's name, and you add a dollar sign to the 16 in the reference to cell B16 so that you always pull the product.

Note Astute readers might ask why not simply select the formula in B17 and try to copy it in one step to fill in the table. Remember that you cannot paste an array formula into a range that contains both blank cells and array formulas, which is why you must first copy the formula in B17 to C17:F17 and then drag it down to complete the table.

What are array constants and how can I use them?

You can create your own arrays and use them in array formulas. Simply enclose the array values in curly brackets—{ }. You need to enclose text in double quotation marks (" ") as well. You can also include the logical values *True* and *False* as entries in the array. Formulas or symbols such as dollar signs or commas are not allowed in array constants.

As an example of how an array constant might be used, look at the Creating Powers worksheet in the Arrays.xlsx file, shown in Figure 87-9.

	C	D	E	F
3	Sales	Sales^2	Sales^3	Sales^4
4	2	4	8	16
5	4	16	64	256
6	8	64	512	4096
7	10	100	1000	10000
8	14	196	2744	38416
9	20	400	8000	160000

FIGURE 87-9 Creating second and fourth powers of sales.

In this worksheet, you're given sales during six months, and you want to create for each month the second, third, and fourth power of sales. Simply select the D4:F9 range, which is where you want the resulting computation to be placed. Array-enter the =C4:C9^{2,3,4} formula in cell D4. In the D4:D9 cell range, this formula loops through and squares each number in C4:C9. In the E4:E9 cell range, the formula loops through and cubes each number in C4:C9. Finally, in the F4:F9 cell range, the formula loops through and raises each number in C4:C9 to the fourth power. The array constant {2,3,4} is required to let you loop through different power values.

How can I edit array formulas?

Suppose you have an array formula that creates results in multiple cells and you want to edit, move, or delete the results. You cannot edit a single element of the array. To edit an array formula, make a change to any cell within the array and then press Ctrl+Shift+Enter to apply the change. Now, the entire array will be updated.

Given quarterly revenues for a toy store, can I estimate the trend and seasonality of the store's revenues?

The Toysrustrend.xlsx file, shown in Figure 87-10, contains quarterly revenues (in millions of dollars) for a toy store during the years of 1997 through 2002. You would like to estimate the quarterly trend in revenues as well as the seasonality associated with each quarter (first quarter equals January–March; second quarter equals April–June; third quarter equals July–September; fourth quarter equals October–December). A trend of 1 percent per quarter, for example, means that sales are increasing at 1 percent per quarter. A seasonal index for the first quarter of 0.80, for example, means that sales during Quarter 1 are approximately 80 percent of an average quarter.

The trick to solving this problem is to use the *LOGEST* function. Suppose that you are trying to predict a variable y from independent variables $x1, x2, \ldots, xn$, and you believe that for some values of *a, b1, b2, . . . , bn*, the relationship between *y* and *x1, x2, . . . , xn* is given by $y = a(b1)^{x1}(b2)^{x2}(bn)^{xn}$. (Call this Equation 1.)

Year	Quarter	Sales	Quarter#	Q1 dummy	Q2 dummy	Q3 dummy	index Forecast	q3	q2	q1	trend	const
							mean quarter 0.582197 q4			172%		
				1	2	3	index		80% 73%	75%		
1997	1	1646	1	1	0	0	1853.104665	0.467772	0.43	0.435	1.0086	4219.57
1997	2	1738	2	0	1	0	1826.702203					
1997	3	1883	3	0	0	1	2025.018084					
1997	4	4868	4	0	0	0	4366.196216					
1998	1	1924	5	1	0	0	1917.500329					
1998	2	1989	6	0	1	0	1890.180377					
1998	3	2142	7	0	0	1	2095.387765					
1998	4	4383	8	0	0	0	4517.922188					
1999	1	2043	9	1	0	0	1984.133752					
1999	2	2020	10	0	1	0	1955.864428					
1999	3	2171	11	0	0	1	2168.202803					
1999	4	4338	12	0	0	0	4674.920659					
2000	1	2186	13	1	0	0	2053.082697					
2000	2	2204	14	0	1	0	2023.83101					
2000	3	2465	15	0	0	1	2243.548175					
2000	4	5027	16	0	0	0	4837.374851					
2001	1	2319	17	1	0	0	2124.427627					
2001	2	1994	18	0	1	0	2094.15944					
2001	3	2220	19	0	0	1	2321.51181					
2001	4	4799	20	0	0	0	5005.474351					
2002	1	2061	21	1	0	0	2198.251805					
2002	2	2021	22	0	1	0	2166.931793					

FIGURE 87-10 Toy revenue trend and seasonality estimation.

The *LOGEST* function is used to determine values of *a, b1, b2, . . . , bn* that best fit this equation to the observed data. To use the *LOGEST* function to estimate trend and seasonality, note the following:

- *y* equals quarterly revenues.

- *x1* equals the quarter number. (Listed in chronological order, the current quarter is Quarter 1, the next quarter is Quarter 2, and so on.)

- *x2* equals 1 if the quarter is the first quarter of the year and 0 otherwise.

- *x3* equals 1 if the quarter is the second quarter of the year and 0 otherwise.

- *x4* equals 1 if the quarter is the third quarter of the year and 0 otherwise.

You need to choose one quarter to leave out of the model. (The fourth quarter was chosen here.) This approach is similar to the one used with dummy variables in Chapter 58. The model you choose to estimate is then $y = a(b1)^{x1}(b2)^{x2}(b3)^{x3}(b4)^{x4}$. When the *LOGEST* function determines values of *a, b1, b2, b3,* and *b4* that best fit the data, the values are interpreted as follows:

- *a* is a constant used to scale the forecasts.

- *b1* is a constant that represents the average per-quarter percentage increase in toy store sales.

- *b2* is a constant that measures the ratio of first-quarter sales to the omitted quarter's (fourth quarter) sales.

- *b3* is a constant that measures the ratio of second-quarter sales to the omitted quarter's sales.

- *b4* is a constant that measures the ratio of third-quarter sales to the omitted quarter's sales.

To begin, create the dummy variables for Quarters 1–3 in the G6:I27 cell range by copying the IF($D6=G$4,1,0) formula from G6 to G6:I27. Remember that a fourth quarter is known to Excel because all three dummy variables equal 0 during the fourth quarter, which is why you can leave out the dummy variable for this quarter.

Select the K6:O6 cell range, where you want *LOGEST* to place the estimated coefficients. The constant *a* will be placed in the right-most cell, followed by the coefficients corresponding to the ordering of the independent variables. Thus, the trend coefficient will be next to the constant, then the Quarter 1 coefficient, and so on.

The syntax to use for the *LOGEST* function is LOGEST(*y_range,x_range,True,True*). After array-entering the =LOGEST(E6:E27,F6:I27,True,True)} formula in cell K6, you obtain the coefficient estimates shown in Figure 87-10. The equation to predict quarterly revenues (in millions) is as follows:

$$4219.57*(1.0086)^{quarter\ number}*(.435)^{Q1dummy}*(.426)^{Q2dummy}*(.468)^{Q3dummy}$$

During the first quarter, the Q1 dummy equals 1, and the Q2 and Q3 dummies equal 0. (Recall that any number raised to the power 0 equals 1.) Thus, during a first quarter, quarterly revenues are predicted to equal $4219.57*(1.0086)^{quarter\ number}*(.435)$.

During a second quarter, the Q1 dummy and the Q3 dummy equal 0, and the Q2 dummy equals 1. During this quarter, quarterly revenues are predicted to equal $4219.57*(1.0086)^{quarter\ number}*(.426)$. During a third quarter, the Q1 dummy and the Q2 dummy equal 0 and the Q3 dummy equals 1. Quarterly revenues during this quarter are predicted to equal $4219.57*(1.0086)^{quarter\ number}*(.468)$. Finally, during a fourth quarter, the Q1, Q2, and Q3 dummies equal 0. During this quarter, quarterly revenues are predicted to equal $4219.57*(1.0086)^{quarter\ number}$.

In summary, you have estimated a quarterly upward trend in revenues of 0.9 percent (around 3.6 percent annually). After adjusting for the trend, you find the following:

- Quarter 1 revenues average 43.5 percent of Quarter 4 revenues.

- Quarter 2 revenues average 42.6 percent of Quarter 4 revenues.

- Quarter 3 revenues average 46.8 percent of Quarter 4 revenues.

To create a seasonal index for each quarter, you give the omitted quarter (Quarter 4) a value of 1 and find that an average quarter has a weight equal to the following (see cell K2 in Figure 87-10):

$$\frac{.435 + .426 + .468 + 1}{4} = .582$$

Then you can compute the relative seasonal index for Quarters 1–3 by copying the K6/$K$2 formula from K4 to L4:M4. The Quarter 4 seasonality is computed in cell M2 with the 1/K2 formula. After adjusting for the trend, you can conclude the following:

- Quarter 1 sales are 80 percent of a typical quarter.

- Quarter 2 sales are 73 percent of a typical quarter.

- Quarter 3 sales are 75 percent of a typical quarter.

- Quarter 4 sales are 172 percent of a typical quarter.

Suppose you want to generate the forecast for each quarter corresponding to the fitted equation (Equation 1). You can use the Excel *GROWTH* function to create this forecast. The *GROWTH* function is an array function with the GROWTH(*known_ys,known_xs,new_xs,True*) syntax. This formula gives the predictions for the new *xs* when Equation 1 is fitted to the data contained in the ranges specified by *known ys* and *known xs*. Thus, selecting the J6:J27 range and array-entering the ={GROWTH(E6:E27, F6:I27,F6:I27,TRUE)} formula in cell J6 generates forecasts from Equation 1 for each quarter's revenue. For example, the forecast for Quarter 4 of 1997, using Equation 1, is $4.366 billion.

Given a list of transactions in different countries, how can I calculate the median size of a transaction in each country?

The Medians.xlsx (see Figure 87-11) contains the revenue generated by a company's transactions in France, the United States, and Canada. Here, you want to calculate the median size of the transactions in each country. Suppose, for example, you want to compute the median size of a transaction in the United States. An easy way to do this is to create an array that contains only the US revenues and replaces other revenues by a blank space. Then you can have Excel compute the median of this new array. After naming the data in column C Country and naming the data in column D Revenue, you can array-enter the =MEDIAN(IF(Country=F5,Revenue,"")) formula in cell G5 to replace the revenue in each row containing a non-US transaction by a blank space and calculate the median size of US transactions ($6,376.50). Copying this formula from G5 to G6:G7 computes the median transaction size for Canada and France. In effect, this approach develops a *MEDIANIF* function that is analogous to the *AVERAGEIF* function of Chapter 20. Of course, this approach could be used to create a *STDEVIF, PERCENTIF,* or other statistical function that performs calculations on any specified subset of your data.

	C	D	E	F	G
1	Country	Revenue			
2	US	5919			
3	Canada	4005		Median	
4	US	6456		Revenue	
5	France	8328		US	6376.5
6	Canada	9426		Canada	6326
7	US	5929		France	7403
8	France	7746			
9	Canada	9292			
10	US	8839			
11	France	7403			
12	Canada	3911			
13	US	7458			
14	Canada	8094			
15	France	4727			
16	Canada	5675			
17	US	4104			
18	France	7654			

FIGURE 87-11 Finding median transaction size in each country.

Problems

All data for Problems 1 through 5 are in the Chapter87data.xlsx file:

1. The Duplicate worksheet contains two lists of names. Use an array formula to count the number of names appearing on both lists.

2. The Find Errors worksheet contains some calculations. Use an array formula to count the number of cells containing errors. (Hint: Use the *ISERROR* function in your array formula.)

3. The Sales worksheet contains 48 months of sales at a toy store. Create an array formula to add (beginning with Month 3) every fifth month of sales. (Hint: You might want to use the Excel *MOD* function. MOD(number,divisor) yields the remainder after the number is divided by the divisor. For example, MOD(7,5) yields 2.)

4. Use an array function to compute the third, fifth, and seventh power of each month's sales.

5. The Product worksheet contains sales during April through August of Products 1 through 7. Sales for each month are listed in the same column. Rearrange the data so that sales for each month are listed in the same row, and changes to the original data are reflected in the new arrangement you have created.

6. Use the data in the Historicalinvest.xlsx file to create a count of the number of years in which stock, bond, and T-bill returns are from –20 percent through –15 percent, –15 percent through –10 percent, and so on.

7. An M by N matrix is a rectangular array of numbers containing m rows and n columns. For example,

$$\begin{bmatrix} 1 & 2 & 3 \\ 4 & 5 & 6 \\ 7 & 8 & 9 \end{bmatrix}$$

is a 3-by-3 matrix. Consider two matrices, A and B. Suppose that the number of columns in matrix A equals the number of rows in matrix B. Then you can multiply matrix A by matrix B. (The product is written as *AB*.) The entry in row I and column J of *AB* is computed by applying the *SUMPRODUCT* function to row I of A and column J of B. *AB* will have as many rows as A and as many columns as B. The Excel *MMULT* function is an array function with which you can multiply matrices. Use the *MMULT* function to multiply the following matrices:

$$A = \begin{bmatrix} 1 & 2 & 3 \\ 4 & 5 & 6 \\ 7 & 7 & 0 \end{bmatrix} \text{ and } B = \begin{bmatrix} 1 & 2 & 3 \\ 1 & 2 & 0 \\ 3 & 3 & 0 \end{bmatrix}$$

8. A square matrix has the same number of rows and columns. Given a square matrix A, suppose there exists a matrix B whereby *AB* equals a matrix in which each diagonal entry equals 1 and all other entries equal 0. You can then say that B is the inverse of A. The Excel array function *MINVERSE* finds the inverse of a square matrix. Use the *MINVERSE* function to find the inverse for matrices A and B in Problem 7.

9. Suppose you have invested a fraction f_i of your money in investment i ($i = 1,2, \ldots ,n$). In addition, suppose the standard deviation of the annual percentage return on investment i is s_i and the correlation between the annual percentage return on investment i and investment j is $ñ_{ij}$. You would like to know the variance and standard deviation of the annual percentage return on your portfolio. This can easily be computed by using matrix multiplication. Create the following three matrices:

- Matrix 1 equals a 1 by n matrix whose ith entry is $s_i f_i$.

- Matrix 2 equals an n by n matrix whose entry in row i and column j is $ñ_{ij}$.

- Matrix 3 is an n by 1 matrix whose ith entry is $s_i f_i$.

The variance of the annual percentage return on your portfolio is simply (Matrix 1)*(Matrix 2)*(Matrix 3). The data in Historicalinvest.xlsx gives annual returns on stocks, bonds, and T-bills. Use the *MMULT* and *TRANSPOSE* functions to estimate (based on the given historical data) the variance and standard deviation of a portfolio that invests 50 percent in stocks, 25 percent in bonds, and 25 percent in T-bills.

Problems 10 through 13 use the data in the Makeupdb.xlsx file.

10. How many dollars' worth of lip gloss did Jen sell?

11. What was the average number of lipstick units sold by Jen in the East region?

12. How many dollars of sales were made by Emilee or in the East region?

13. How many dollars' worth of lipstick were sold by Colleen or Zaret in the East region?

14. Use the data in the Chapter58data.xlsx file to estimate the trend and seasonal components of the quarterly revenues of Ford and GM.

15. In the toy store example (using the Toysrustrend.xlsx file), use the data for 1999–2001 to forecast quarterly revenues for 2002.

16. The Lillydata.xlsx file contains information from a market research survey that was used to gather insights to aid in designing a new blood pressure drug. Fifteen experts (six from Lilly and nine from other companies—see column N) were asked to compare five sets of four potential Lilly products. The fifth choice in each scenario is that a competitor's drug is chosen over the four listed Lilly drugs.

   For example, in the first scenario, the second option considered would be a Lilly drug that reduced blood pressure 18 points, resulted in 14 percent of side effects, and sold for $16.

   The I5:N21 range contains the choices each expert made for each of the five scenarios. For example, the first expert (who worked for Lilly) chose a competitor's drug when faced with Scenario 1 and chose the first listed drug when faced with Scenario 2. Use this information to answer the following:

   - Enter a formula that can be copied from I2 to I2:M5 that calculates the price for each scenario and option in I2:M5.

   - Enter an array formula in I23 that can be copied to I23:I32 and then to J23:M32 that calculates for each question the frequency of each response (1–5), broken down by Lilly and non-Lilly experts. Thus for Question 1, one Lilly expert responded 1, three responded 2, and two responded 5.

17. The Arrayexam1data.xlsx file contains sales by company and date. Your job is to break sales down on a quarterly basis by using array formulas.

   Summarize (using only array formulas) by company and by quarter as shown in Figure 87-12.

⊿	K	L	M	N	O	P
2						
3						
4		**see pivot table in previous sheet**				
5						
6		1/1/2004	4/1/2004	7/1/2004	10/1/2004	1/1/2005
7	ACS					
8	ActSys Medical, Inc.					
9	Baxter Healthcare Corporation					
10	BioMed Plus, Inc.					
11	Blood Diagnostics, Inc.					
12	Briggs Corporation					
13	Cardinal Health					
14	Gentiva Health Services					
15	Priority Healthcare					
16	Tri State Distribution, Inc.					

FIGURE 87-12 Format for Problem 17 answer.

For example, L7 should contain Quarter 1 (January 1 through March 31) ACS sales, and so on. Verify your answer with a PivotTable.

18. Explain why array-entering the =SUM(1/COUNTIF(Info,Info)) formula will yield the number of unique entries in the Info range. Apply this formula to the data in the Unique.xlsx file and verify that it returns the number of unique entries.

19. The Salaries.xlsx file contains the salaries of NBA players. Write an array formula that adds the four largest player salaries. Hint: Use the array constant {1,2,3,4} in conjunction with the *LARGE* function. Then generalize your formula so that you can enter any positive integer *n*, and your formula will add the *n* largest salaries. Hint: If cell G9 contains an integer *n*, when you array-enter a ROW(Indirect("1:"&G9)) formula, Excel will create an array constant {1,2, . . . ,*n*}.

Index

Symbols

& (and) operator, 38, 164
* (asterisk) wildcard, 164
   for MATCH function, 28
^ (caret symbol), for raising number to a power, 61, 585
: (colon), to indicate time, 112
$ (dollar sign)
   and cell references, 12
   in conditional formatting formula, 211
>= (greater-than or equal-to) character, 164
– (minus) signs, in PivotTable, 395
<> (not equal to) operator, 163
+ (plus) sign, in PivotTable, 395
##############, display of, 112
#DIV/0! value, 104
#N/A (Not Available) response, 16, 18, 129, 191
   and charts, 551
   from MODE function, 372
   from VLOOKUP, 103
#NUM error
   from IRR function, 68, 69
   from XNPV function, 64
#NUM! error, 104, 497
#Per, 76
   in FV function, 77
#REF! error, 104
#VALUE error, 44, 497, 818
#VALUE! error, 104
? (question mark) wildcard, 164
" " (quotation marks)
   for IF statement text, 98
   for MATCH text values, 28
   for text in criteria, 163
_ (underscore), in range names, 13
24-hour military time, 112
{ } (curly brackets), for array formulas, 814

A

abandonment option, 753–754
ABS function, 322
absolute value function, 322
Access database, loading data from, 457
accumulated depreciation, 102
accuracy of forecasts, 574–575
   estimating, 627
   for predicting monthly cost based on units
      produced, 602–603
Add Constraint dialog box, 299
   Bin option, 298
   for product mix solver problem, 277–278
Add-Ins dialog box
   Analysis ToolPak, 361
   COM Add-Ins, 469
addition, with Paste Special, 119
ADDRESS function, 192
Add Scenario dialog box, 156
Advanced Filter dialog box, 518
Advanced Filter feature, 517–518
advertising
   impact on sales, 632, 635
   plot showing sales as function, 582
age
   grouping data by, 412
   influence on travel spending, 412–413
AGGREGATE function, 103
alternative hypothesis, 623
Amazon.com.xlsx file, 641
Amazon.xlsx file, 209
American options, 744, 748
ampersand (&), concatenation with, 38, 164
analysis of variance. See ANOVA (analysis of variance)
Analysis ToolPak
   for histogram, 555
   installing, 598

analytics, 261–266
    difficulties in implementing, 264–265
    importance, 263
    knowledge needed for, 263–264
    predictive, 261–262, 264
    prescriptive, 262–263
    trends in, 265
analytics professionals, certification for, 263
Analyze tab
    Changed Data Source, 409
    Field Items, 421
    PivotChart, 403, 413
and (&) operator, 38, 164
AND operator, 210, 493
    for database criteria, 503
    in IF statement, 97, 98
animated charts, changing time series scatter
        to, 480–482
annual cost of capital, 61
annual holding cost, 766
    assumptions, 765
    minimizing, 770–772
annual revenue, computing, 140
annual setup cost, 766
annual variable cost, 140
annual volatility of stock riskiness, 702
annuity
    number of periods in, 76
    value in future dollars, 77
    value of, 75
ANOVA (analysis of variance)
    one-way, 623–628
    two-way, 629–640
Anova: Single Factor dialog box, 625
ANOVA table
    for auto sales data, 608
    significance, 609
Anova: Two-Factor Without Replication dialog
        box, 631
Applynames.xlsx file, 10
area chart, stacked, 548
argument, error from, 104
array arguments, 814
array constants, 823
array formulas, 814
    editing, 823
    interpreting, 814–815
array functions, 814
    FREQUENCY function, 555, 816–817
    LINEST function, 603–604

MODE.MULT function as, 372
    for summarizing sales database
            transactions, 820–822
    for sum of second digit in integer list, 817–818
    TRANSPOSE function, 815–816
    TREND function, 614
arrays
    of prices greater than median, 819
    Worksheet range name as, 192
Arrays.xlsx file
    Average Those > Median worksheet, 819
    Creating Powers worksheet, 823
    Frequency worksheet, 816
    Matching Names worksheet, 818
    Total Wages worksheet, 814
    Transpose worksheet, 815
ASCII character, function to provide, 38
ASCIIcharacters.xlsx file, 38
Asiansales.xlsx file, 177
Assetallocationopt.xlsx file, 727
Assetallsim.xlsx file, 725
Assign.xlsx file, 330
assumptions
    annual holding cost for inventory, 765
    finding cells affected by, 130–132
    for simulation, 724
    in worksheet models, 139
asterisk (*) wildcard, 164
    for MATCH function, 28
auditing tool, 127–138. See also Inquire add-in
    for multiple worksheets, 134
Audittwosheetstemp.xlsx file, 137
Audittwosheets.xlsx workbook, 134
AutoComplete
    column headings for, 233
    with range names, 9, 355
AutoFill feature, 115
AutoFilter, 503
    limitations, 517
Automatic calculation mode, for data tables, 143
Automatic Except For Data Tables, 143
automatic scaling, for GRG Solver engine, 317
Autotemp.xlsx file, Data worksheet, 605
average
    moving, time series understood with, 641–644
    time waiting inline at airport or at bank, 779–782
AVERAGE function, 632
    for average annual return, 727
    copying, 98, 712
    for bias calculation, 699

for mean interval time, 780
for mean of resampled high-temperature
        yields, 740
for moving averages, 653
#N/A error, 103
sample mean from, 371
TRIMMEAN function vs., 381
AVERAGEIF function, 170, 172
AVERAGEIFS function, 170, 172
average inventory level, 766
average quantity of sales, 172
axes
    secondary, for combo charts, 536–537
    x and y
        of histogram, 361
        label for, 572
        scale for sparkline, 488
        of scatter chart, 569

B

balance sheets, 99–104
balloon loan, 79
balloon payment, 81
band chart, 547–548
Bandchart.xlsx file, 547
Banded Columns tool, 235
Banded Rows tool, 235
bar graph, creating, 44
Baseball.xlsx file, 29
base of time series, 645
basketball team members, abilities, 564–565
Basketball.xlsx file, 214
best-case scenario, 156
BETA.DIST function, 691, 695–696
beta of stock, 742
beta random variable, 691, 694–696
Bezos.xlsx file, 144
bias in past forecasts, 698
bids
    calculating optimal, 715–720
    for construction project, simulation for
        optimal, 716–718
    estimating standard deviation of
        competitors', 716
Bidsim.xlsx file, 716
binary changing cells, in modeling, 298
binary programming problems, solving, 301–302
BINOM.DIST function, 671–672, 672
BINOMDIST function, 671

Binomialexamples.xlsx file, 671
binomial random variable, 670–671
    negative, 675–676
    simulating, 715–716
Binomialsim.xlsx file, 715
BINOM.INV function, 673, 715, 718
bin ranges, 359, 361
    counting units in each, 555
    defining, 360
bin value boundaries, 817
Black, Fischer, 743
Black–Scholes option-pricing formula, 704
    for stock volatility estimates, 749–750
    implementing, 747–748
black swans (extreme events), 721
The Black Swan (Taleb), 704
blank cells, counting, 162, 165
blank rows, adding to PivotTable, 406–407
blank worksheet, creating, 506
bonds, allocating investments, 725–728
Boolean arrays, 821, 822
bootstrapping, 721, 722
    for asset allocation, 725–726
break even
    Goal Seek to determine, 150
    for retailer, 144
    two-way data table for, 145
Bstempprotected.xlsx file, 751
Bstemp.xlsx file, 748
bubble charts, 565
bundling, 804–806
business variables, estimating relationship
        between, 569
butterfly spread, 107
By Changing Cell, for Goal Seek, 149

C

calculated columns, 455
    DAX formulas for, 467
calculated fields, 455
    deleting, 426
    in PivotTable, 421–422
calculated items, 424–427
    deleting, 426
Calculateditem.xlsx file, 424
calculations, moving results of, 117
call option, 744
    impact of key parameter changes, 748–749

call price, 747
capital budgeting
    option pricing to improve, 752
    Solver for, 297–304
caret symbol [^], for raising number to a power, 61,
    585
cascading list selection, 355
case sensitivity, of FIND function, 37
cash flows
    from call option, 744
    comparing, 59
    from European put option, 745
    finding IRR, 68
    finding IRR for irregularly spaced, 71
    net present value of, interest rate and, 67
    number of years for payback of initial investment
        cost, 31–32
Categorylabel.xlsx file, 542
cell ranges. *See also* conditional formatting
    getting statistics describing, 381
    MATCH function to locate position for value
        in, 28
    OFFSET function for reference to, 175–186
    selecting all data in column or row, 120
    value lookup from, 15
cell references
    $ (dollar sign) and, 12
    in INDIRECT function, 187–194
cells
    color of, sorting based on, 226–227
    counting based on characteristics, 165
    counting those containing number, 162
    count of those meeting given criterion, 162
    dependency between, 87. *See also* circular
        references
    extracting data to separate, 41–43, 180
    finding those affected by assumptions, 130–132
    formatting for hours, SUM and, 114
    highlighting dependents for active, 132
    ignoring, 103
    viewing value changes, 130
cell values, shading to display differences, 203–204
centered moving averages, calculating, 653
central limit theorem, 687, 702
central location measures, 371–374
certification for analytics professionals, 263
ceteris paribus, 608
Change Table Name tool, 235
changing cells
    All Different constraints for, 335

bounds on, 329
for forecasting, 657
in modeling, 298
in optimization model, 268
for product mix Solver model, 275
for software project selection problem, 298
for Solver workforce scheduling, 286
for transportation problem, 291
characters. *See also* text strings
    CLEAN function to remove invisible, 39
    count for text string, 37
    FIND function to extract, 41
    maximum number in formulas, 105
CHAR function, 38
Chartdynamicrange.xlsx file, 183
charts, 533–568
    adding trendline, 572
    automatic updates after adding data, 236
    band chart for checking inventory levels,
        547–548
    basing on table, 237
    bubble, 565–566
    changing time series scatter to animated,
        480–482
    check boxes to control series, 551–552
    Clustered Column 2D, 549
    column labels, troubleshooting display, 542
    combination, 534–536
        secondary axis for, 536–537
    conditional colors in, 556–557
    data labels, 542–544
        based on cell contents, 544–547
        dynamic, 549–551
    of data points, 569
    Gantt, 553
    hidden data appearance, 539
    histogram automatic update for new data,
        555–556
    Line With Markers, 551
    list box to select series, 552–553
    missing data and, 538–539
    moving average, 643
    Multiples to create, 482–483
    Pareto, 562–563
    pictures in column graphs, 540–541
    in Power View, 469
        creating, 473–474
        filtering, 474–478
        filtering with slicer, 476–477
        filtering with Tiles, 477

radar, 564–565
resizing, 473
scatter, 569
    of cumulative units produced and unit
        costs, 584–585
    variable changes displayed with, 565
separate for each product, 482–483
sorted data as basis, 554–555
Stacked 2D bar, 553
stacked area, 548
Stacked Column, 473
storing as template, 548
tables in, 542
thermometer for progress display, 548–549
updates automatically, 183
vertical line for separation, 564
waterfall, 557–558
chart titles, linking to cells, 549–551
Chart Tools Layout tab, Analysis, Trendline, 570
check boxes, 246
    for scroll bar, 252
    to control series charting, 551–552
churn rate, 758
circular references, 9, 87–92, 102
    resolving, 88–90
Circular.xlsx file, 88
Ciscoexpo.xlsx file, 577
cities, list of distances between, 23–24
Cleanexample.xlsx file, 44
CLEAN function, 39, 44
clearing
    data validation, 355
    filters from column or database, 506
Clear Rules, for conditional formatting, 197
Clustered Column 2D chart, 549
coefficients
    of dummy variables, 609
    of independent variables, 612
    interpreting in regression equation, 608–609
cohort, 758
collapsing PivotTable fields, 395–396
colon (:), to indicate time, 112
color
    of cell or font, sorting based on, 226–227
    in charts, conditional formatting of, 556–557
    coding monthly stock returns, 207–208
    filtering by, 513
    for sparklines, 488
    for weekend dates, 213
Colorscaleinvestment.xlsx file, 203

color scales, 203–204
    for conditional formatting, 197
COLUMN function, 192
column graphs, pictures in, 540–541
column labels, in charts, troubleshooting
        display, 542
Column Labels zone, in PivotTable Field list, 390
columns
    calculated, 455
    clearing filters from, 506
    copying formula to all cells in, 98
    formula to return last number in, 181
    freezing to keep visible, 97
    hiding, 19
    hiding or unhiding, 144
    INDEX function to reference, 25
    as named range, 9
    realigning data to rows, 118–119
    referencing by name, 90
    selecting all data in, 119
combination charts, 534–536
Combinationstemp.xlsx file, 534
combining text strings, 41
combo box, 246
Combobox.xlsx file, 256
combo charts, secondary axis for, 536–537
comments in worksheets, 736–737
compact form for PivotTable, 393
comparing workbooks, Inquire add-in for, 136–137
compound interest, 745
computed criteria, for database functions, 495
CONCATENATE function, 38, 41
Cond colors.xlsx file, 556
conditional formatting, 195–222
    based on rating for player abilities, 214–215
    chart colors, 556–557
    copying with Format Painter, 218–219
    customizing rules, 199–200
    data bars, 201–202
    dates as basis for, 199
    deleting, 209
    deleting rule, 200
    employee ratings highlighted with, 332–333
    Highlight Cells, 198–199
    icon sets in, 203–204
    options, 196
    order of precedence for rules, 209
    outliers highlighting with, 375–382
    PivotTable with, 407–409
    for profit-maximizing two-part tariff, 808

for revenue quarters, 209–212
selecting cells having, 209
toggling on and off, 252–253
Conditional Formatting Rules Manager dialog
box, 200, 212
formula option, 211
Use A Formula, 210
conditional tests. *See* IF statements
confidence interval, for mean profit, 712
conflict, in conditional formatting rules, 209
Consolidate dialog box, 523
consolidating data, 521–526
constraints
on price, 799
for product mix Solver model, 275
for software project selection problem, 298
Solver handling of, 300
for Solver workforce scheduling, 286
for transportation problem, 291, 292
construction project, simulation for optimal
bid, 716–718
consumer surplus of purchase, 805, 807
continuous random variable, 665
modeling as normal random variable, 716
Contrateeoq.xlsx file, Cont Rate EOQ worksheet, 766
Convert Text To Columns Wizard, 180
extracting data with, 43–47
Convert to Range tool, 235
copying
array formulas, 814
conditional formatting with Format Painter,
218–219
filtered transactions to different worksheet, 506
formatting automatically, 231–235
formulas automatically, 231–235
formula to all cells in column, 98
HLOOKUP function, 331
spinner buttons, 248
worksheets, 236
correlation
and regression toward the mean, 595
relationship to r-squared value, 594
summarizing relationships with, 589–596
Correlation dialog box, 591–592
correlation matrix, 593–594
CORREL function, 594
Costestimate.xlsx file, 571, 574
cost-minimizing batch size, 766–767
cost of capital, 61
IRR vs., 70

cost of goods sold (COGS), 101
costs
of inventory shortage, 769
inventory to minimize annual holding, ordering
and shortage costs, 770–772
of lost sales, 769
minimizing for inventory and orders, 763–765
monthly fixed, 573
operating, explaining monthly variation, 574
predicting for factory production of 3
products, 597–602
variable, 574
COUNTA function, 162, 166, 180
COUNTBLANK function, 162, 165
COUNT function, 162, 165, 495
OFFSET function with, 181
COUNTIF function, 162, 163, 164, 331, 554, 707, 724,
734, 736, 819
serial number for date in, 165
COUNTIFS function, 162, 170
array function alternatives, 820
multiple criteria for, 165
country
calculating median size of revenue, 826–827
displaying sales data by, 478–479
tracking revenues based on, 177–178
craps
determining status after first roll, 99
probability of winning, 731–733
Create From Selection, 4–5
Create Links To Source Data option, for consolidating
data, 524, 525
Create PivotTable dialog box, 388–389, 448, 463
Create Relationship dialog box, 443
Create Sparklines dialog box, 486
credit card company, retention rate, 757–759
Creditunion.xlsx file, Original worksheet, 655
Crimedata.xlsx file, 480
CRITBINOM function, 673
criteria
for database functions, 493
for SUMIF function, rules for, 170
multiple, for COUNTIFS function, 165
multiple for sort, 224
ranges setup, 497
CUMIPMT function, 81–82
CUMPRINC function, 81–82
cumulative cash flow, calculating, 32
curly brackets ({ }), for array formulas, 814
current time, displaying, 113

Custom AutoFilter dialog box, 507, 512
customers
    determining value, 757–762
    factors impacting traffic, 655–658
    graphic summary of daily counts, 485–487
    incentives to switch companies, 759–760
customizing icon sets, 206
Custom Lists dialog box, for custom sort order, 228
cutoffs, computing for outlier, 376

D

dashboards, dynamic, 559–561
data
    changing for sparklines, 488
    consolidating, 521–526
    extracting from PivotTable, 427–429
    extracting to separate cell, 180
    hidden, charts and, 539
    histograms for summarizing, 359–368
    importing
        from Internet, 345–348
        from text file or document, 339–344
    loading into PowerPivot, 456–463
    missing, charts and, 538–539
    preparing for Power View, 470–473
    realigning from row or column, 118–119
    reapplying filter after changes, 517
    sorting for subtotals, 530
    summarizing. *See* descriptive statistics
    validating, 349–358
Data Analysis command, running regression
        without, 603–604
Data Analysis dialog box, 360
    Anova: Single Factor, 623, 624
    Anova: Two-Factor with Replication, 633–634
    Regression, 608, 612
data analysis, resampling for, 739–742
data array, 816. *See also* arrays
data bars, 201–202
    for conditional formatting, 197
    in PivotTable, 407
database, 503
    clearing filters from, 506
    loading data from, 457
    Number Filters for, 507
database statistical functions, 491–500
data entry
    automatic chart updates after adding, 236
    of dates, 53
    on multiple worksheets, 124
    preventing date errors, 351
    preventing nonnumeric value, 352
    state abbreviations list for, 353
    of time and date in one cell, 112
    of times, 112
    tooltips for, 350
    updating calculations after, 409
data labels in charts, 542–544
    based on cell contents, 544–547
Data Model, 441–454
    adding data to, 442–443, 447
    basics, 441–442
    deleting data from, 448
    PivotTable creation with, 444–446, 448–449
    Quick Explore option, 446–447
Datamodeltemp.xlsx file
    Reps worksheet, 442
    Sales worksheet, 442
data points, 359
    graph of, 569
data sets
    defining typical value for, 370–374
    descriptive statistics for comparing, 377
    finding second smallest or largest number in, 379
    measuring spreads, 374–375
    percentile ranking in, 377–379
    range of, 375
    ranking numbers in, 380
    trimmed mean, 380–381
data sources
    creating relationship between, 462–463
Data tab
    Data Analysis, 360, 612
        Anova: Two-Factor Without Replication, 630
        Correlation, 591
        Descriptive Statistics, 369
        Regression, 598
        Solver, 269, 275, 773
    Data Tools
        Consolidate, 523
        Text To Columns, 180
        Text To Columns, Delimited, 43
    Data Validation, 349, 352
        Clear All, 355
    Get External Data, 470
        From Web, 345
    Outline, Subtotal, 527
    Relationships, 443, 449

Remove Duplicates, 514–515
Sort & Filter
    Advanced, 517
    Filter, 503
    Sort, 224
    Sort A To Z, 229
What-If Analysis
    Data Table, 141, 142, 143, 145, 496, 718, 723,
        726, 732, 734, 781
    Goal Seek, 150
    Scenario Manager, 156
Data Table dialog box, 141
data tables
    combining with functions, 143–144
    for EOQ sensitivity, 765
    one-way
        for impact of agent count, 781
        for poker hand simulation, 734
        for resampling, 741
    saving values in, 142
    scenario generation with, 723–724
    two-way, 711
data validation
    clearing, 355
    selecting cells with settings, 355
Data Validation dialog box
    Error Alert tab, 350, 351
    Input Message tab, 350
    list validation in, 353–354
    Settings tab, 350, 351
DATEDIF function, 58–59
Datedv.xlsx file, 351
DATE function, 58
Datelookup.xlsx file, 19
A Date Occurring dialog box, 199
dates
    Autofill for day of week, 115
    calculating in relation to another date, 56
    color for weekend, 213
    conditional formatting based on, 199
    data entry of, 53
    determining number of workdays between
        two, 57
    entry with time in one cell, 112
    extracting month, year, day from, 58
    filtering based on, 508–510
    General format of, 55
    preventing data entry errors, 351
    price lookup based on, 19

sales statistics based on, 495
serial number for, 111
Dates.xlsx file, 54, 57, 58
DATEVALUE function, 55
DAVERAGE function, 494
DAX (Data Expression Language) functions, 455,
    466–468
DAY function, 58
DAY function (DAX), 467
day of week
    Autofill for, 115
    selecting, 256
DCOUNT function, 495
debt. *See also* loans
    computing, 101
debugging, formula segment value display for, 181
decisions, mathematical models for, 262
default settings, number of worksheets in
    workbook, 124
Define Name command, 5–7
degrees of freedom, 604
deleting
    array formulas and, 814
    calculated item or calculated field, 426
    conditional formatting, 197, 200, 209
    data from Data Model, 448
    duplicates from tables, 235
    range names, 6
    relationships, 449–450
    subtotals, 528
delimited option, for importing data, 339, 341
Dellvol.xlsx file, 746
demand
    constraint, 293
    elasticity of, 786
    subjectively determined, for product
        pricing, 797–802
demand curve
    and customer willingness to pay for
        product, 788–789
    estimating, 785–790
demand points, 291
density function of random variable, 684
dependency between cells, 87. *See also* circular
    references
dependents, 130
    highlighting for active cell, 132
dependent variables, 569
    graph for, 571
    influence of two factors, 629

nonlinear effect of independent variable
on, 615–616
depreciation, computing, 102
descriptive statistics, 369–384
data sets comparison with, 377
for range of cells, 381
Descriptive Statistics dialog box, 370
deseasonalization of sales estimates, 652–654
Design tab
Add Chart Element, Data Labels, 545
Layout Group, Report Layout, 393
Map, 479
Table Style Options, Total Row check box, 238
Developer tab
Controls, Insert, 245, 248
Insert, 253, 256
Form Controls, 552
DGET function, 497–498
Dget.xlsx file, 497
disabling Flash Fill, 47
discounted cash flow, 61
discount rate, for cash flows NPV equalizing zero, 72
discrete random variable, 664, 666, 683
simulating values, 708–709
Discretesim.xlsx file, Sim worksheet, 708
Display Equation On Chart option for trendline, 572
Display R-Squared Value On Chart option for
trendline, 572
distances between cities, function to return, 23–24
DISTINCTCOUNTemp.xlsx file, 450
DISTINCT COUNT function, 450–452
DISTINCT function (DAX), 467
distribution problems, Solver for, 291–296
#DIV/0! value, 104
dividends, 101
division
with Paste Special, 119
by zero, 104
document, importing data from, 339–344
dollar sign ($)
and cell references, 12
in conditional formatting formula, 211
"drilling down" in PivotTable, 427–429
Drugfore.xlsx file, 698
DSUM function, 493–494, 821, 822
with criteria range of Name and Product, 496
SUM function vs., 491–492
syntax, 493
dummy variables, 606–607
creating, 825

interpreting coefficients of, 609
duplicates, removing from table, 235
duration of activity, modeling, 691, 694–696
dynamic dashboards, 559–561
Dynamichistograms.xlsx file, 555
dynamic labels, charts with, 549–551
dynamic range, 355, 525
name for, 182
Dynamicrange.xlsx file, 182

E

Eastandwestconsolidated.xlsx file, 525
economic order quantity inventory model, 763–768
economy, influence on presidential elections, 610
Edit Formatting Rule dialog box, 203, 205, 214, 376
editing
array formulas, 823
comments, 737
conditional formatting rule, 209
range names, 6
relationships, 449–450
Edit the Rule Description dialog box, 202
80/20 rule, 562
elasticity, 583
of demand, 786
email addresses, Flash Fill to create, 46
employee ratings, conditional formatting for
highlighting, 332–333
Enable Iterative Calculation, 87, 88, 102
ending balances, for each month, 80
ending time, calculating number of hours between
starting time and, 114
Eoq.xlsx file, EOQ worksheet, 764
error alert, 350
Error Checking, 128
Error Checking dialog box, 129
errors
from dummy variable, 606
in forecasts, 660
randomness of, 661–662
errors (residuals)
for data points, 574
for trendline and data point, 573
Errortrap.xlsx file, 103
Errortypes.xlsx file, 104
error values, 103
#DIV/0! value, 104
#N/A (Not Available), 16, 18, 129, 191, 818

from MODE function, 372
from VLOOKUP, 103
#NUM!, 497
#VALUE, 497, 818
Esc key, stopping Solver with, 321
estimates
accuracy of forecasts, 627
of demand curve, 785–790
deseasonalization for sales, 652
probabilities of uncertain events, 705–714
of revenue trends and seasonality, 823–826
European option, 744
European put options
cash flow from, 745
price of, 748
stock purchase with, 95–96
Evaluate Formula dialog box, 181
Evolutionary Solver engine, 270, 323, 327, 809
penalties and, 329–334
traveling salesperson problem in, 337
worker assignment to workgroups, 330–332
exact linear relationship, 607
Excel 2007, conditional formatting feature
changes, 195
Excel Error Trap capability, 128
Excel Evaluate Formula feature, 181
Excelfinfunctions.xlsx file, 79
Excel Options dialog box
Add-Ins, 135
Solver Add-in, 269
Advanced, 47
Editing Options, 47
Customize Ribbon, Main tabs, 245
Formulas
Automatic Except for Data Tables, 143
Enable Iterative Calculations, 87, 88, 102
Working With Formulas, 429
Use Automatic Scaling, 307
Excel Solver. See Solver
exercise date, 744
exercise price, 744
Existing Connections dialog box, 447
expanding PivotTable fields, 395–396
experience curve, 583
experiment, 663
expiration date, 744
EXPON.DIST function, 681
EXPONDIST function, 681
exponential curve, sum of squared errors for, 585

Exponentialdist.xlsx file, Density worksheet, 681
exponential graph, 570
exponential growth, limitations, 580
exponential growth modeling, 577–580
obtaining best-fitting curve, 578
extracting characters, FIND function for, 41
extracting data
Convert Text To Columns Wizard, 43–47
from PivotTable, 427–429
to separate cell, 41–43, 180
extreme events (black swans), 721
extreme skewness, 380–381

F

Fair, Roy, 610
favorite rating–underdog rating, 735
Fax.xlsx file, 584
feasible solution, 270
fields
assigning to creat PivotTable report, 465
calculated, 455
in database, 503
in PivotTable, collapsing and expanding, 395–396
filtered transactions, copying to different
worksheet, 506
filtering, 501–520
based on date, 508–510
by beginning letter of name, 512
charts
with slicer, 476–477
with Tiles, 477
clearing from column or database, 506
by color, 513
PivotTable fields, 397–403
Power View charts, 474–478
reapplying after data changes, 517
Table slicers for, 240
top 30 revenue values by salesperson, 513–514
transactions, 503–504, 505
transactions by months, 511–512
Final4sim.xlsx file, 735
financial analysts, geometric mean use by, 381
financial functions, 76
CUMIPMT function, 81–82
CUMPRINC function, 81–82
FV function, 77
IPMT function, 79
NPER function, 82

NPV function, 75–76
PMT function, 79
PPMT function, 79
financial planning, Solver for, 305–312
FIND function, 37, 41, 42, 180
Finmathsolver.xlsx file, PMT By Solver
    worksheet, 306
First Column tool, 235
five-card draw poker, probability of three-of-a-kind
    hand, 733–734
fixed costs, monthly, 573
fixed-width option, for importing data, 339, 341
flagging fields, containing text string, 497
Flash Fill, 45
    disabling, 47
    to extract data, 180
Flashfill.xlsx file, 45
Font dialog box, launcher, 751
fonts
    color of, sorting based on, 226–227
    size for histogram, 362
    Wingdings, 546–547
forecasts
    accuracy for predicting monthly cost based on
        units produced, 602–603
    basis for evaluating, 698–700
    errors, 699
        randomness of, 661–662
        standard deviation of, 632
    estimating accuracy, 627
    generating from multiple regression, 613–614
    one-way ANOVA for, 627
    probability statements from, 697–700
    ratio-to-moving-average, 651–654
    sales based on sales representatives and
        districts, 632
    special events impacting, 655–662
Format Cells dialog box, 55, 198, 207
    date display in, 54
    Protection tab, 751
Format Control dialog box, 252
    for check box, 254
    for spinner button, 249
Format Data Series, Fill, Picture, 541
Format Painter, copying conditional formatting
    with, 218–219
formatting. See also conditional formatting
    copying automatically, 231–235
    PivotTable changes, 395

Format Trendline dialog box, 570, 572, 798–799
    Exponential, 578
    Power, 584
forms, displaying controls, 245
Formula Auditing toolbar, 128
Formula AutoComplete, 233
Formula bar, 2
    array formulas in, 814
formulas. See also array formulas
    adding range name to, 8
    auditing tool to trace, 131
    copying automatically, 231–235
    copying results only, 117
    displaying range names in existing, 10
    entry for large column of numbers, 315
    INDIRECT function to read range name portion
        in, 191
    Inquire add-in to display relationships, 137
    maximum number of characters in, 105
    pasting range names into, 165
    protecting from change, 750–751
    range names in, 2
    selecting all in worksheet, 751
    three-dimensional, 123–126
    toggling display with value display, 128
Formulas tab
    Calculation
        Automatic Except For Data Tables, 143
        Calculation, 712
    Create From Selection, 8
    Defined Names, 183, 192
        Create From Selection, 1, 4, 163, 794
        Define Name, Apply Names, 11
        Name Manager, 182
    Formula Auditing, 127
        Evaluate Formula, 181
        Trace Dependents, 130
        Trace Precedents, 134
    Name Manager, 6, 233
        Define Name, 5
FORMULATEXT function, 128
four-period moving average, 642–643
Freeze Panes command, 97, 251–252
FREQUENCY array function, 555, 816–817
F statistic, 604
function keys
    F3 for pasting range names, 165
    F4 for changing dollar signs in cell reference, 211
    F9 for iterations, 712

F9 for recalculation, 143
F9 to display formula segment value, 181
functions
    combining with data table, 143–144
    maximizing in GRG Nonlinear engine, 320
    minimizing in GRG Nonlinear engine, 321
Function Wizard, Help On This Function, 103
future value (Fv), 76
    of PMT function, 79
FV function, 77

G

gambling probabilities simulation, 731–738
Gantt chart, 553
Gauss-Seidel Iteration, 89
gender
    influence on amount spent on travel, 411–412
    nonlinear effect on salary, 617–618
General format of date, 55
genetic algorithms, 323
geometric mean, 381
GEOMMEAN function, 382
Geommean.xlsx file, 381
Gesimless5.xlsx file, 724
GETPIVOTDATA function, 427–429, 559–561
    turning off, 429
Getpivotdata.xlsx file, 427
GET.WORKBOOK macro, 192
Globalwarming2011.xlsx file, 197
Goal Seek command, 149–154, 759, 788
    for algebra story problems, 151–152
    for implied volatility, 749–750
Goal Seek dialog box, 150, 151, 760–761
Go To dialog box, 134, 209, 751
    Special, 355
gradient fill, for data bars, 201
Grand Total, hiding, 426
    in PivotTable, 406
graphic summary, of daily customer counts,
    485–487
graphs. *See* charts
greater-than or equal-to (>=) character, 164
GRG Multistart, 326
GRG nonlinear engine, 269, 317
    minimizing functions in, 321
    optimization models in, 320–323
    trouble in, 322
GRG Nonlinear tab, Multistart option, 321

Groceriespt.xlsx file, 387
    All Row Fields worksheet, 391
    Slicers worksheet, 405
grocery sales at several stores, summaries, 387–388
gross fixed assets, 102
gross national product (GNP), 607
group box, option button in, 255
Grouping dialog box, 413
grouping items, in PivotTable, 423–424
GROWTH function, 826
guess, for IRR function, 68

H

Header Row tool, 235
headings for PivotTable, 388
Help On This Error, 128
Help On This Function, 103
Hidden.xlsx file, 539
hiding
    columns, 19, 144
    Grand Total, 426
    rows, 144
    subtotals in PivotTable, 406–407
Highlight Cells conditional formatting, 196, 198–199
Highlightcells.xlsx file, 198
high points on Sparklines, 487
Histogram dialog box, 361
histograms, 44
    automatic update for new data, 555–556
    common shapes, 363–365
    comparing from different data sets, 366
    for data summaries, 359–368
    gaps between bars, 362
Historicalinvesttemp.xlsx file, 7
Historicalinvest.xlsx file, 206
HLOOKUP function, 16, 19
    copying, 331
holding costs, safety stock and, 771
holidays, WORKDAY function and, 56
Holland, John, 323
Home tab
    Cells, Format, Hide & Unhide, 19, 144
    Conditional Formatting, 197
        Data Bars, 407
        New Rule, 254, 332, 376
        Top/Bottom Rules, 808
    Diagram View, 462
    Editing, Fill, 711

for PowerPivot window, 456
Styles, Conditional Formatting, 196
horizontal lookup, 15
HOUR function, 113
hours
calculating number to complete job, 113
cell formatting, SUM and, 114
HTML table, importing from, 345
HYPERGEOM.DIST function, 674–675
Hypergeom.dist.xlsx file, 674
hypergeometric random variable, 673, 674–675

I

icon sets, 545
for conditional formatting, 197
sorting data based on, 227
IFERROR function, 103, 550, 560
IF statements, 93–110
for break even analysis, 145
nested, 95–96, 105
OR operator, 99
purchase price as function of number of units
purchased, 94–95
Solver and, 809
with ROW and MOD functions, 104
Ifstatement.xlsx file
Craps worksheet, 99
Hedging worksheet, 95
Quantity Discount worksheet, 94
ignored cells, 103
implied volatility approach, 749
importing data
from Internet, 345–348
to PowerPivot, 457
text files for, 459
from text file or document, 339–344
incentives, for customers to switch companies,
759–760
income before taxes, computing, 102
income statements, 99–104
Income.xlsx file, 216
independent random variables, 666
normal distribution of sum, 687
independent variables, 569
coefficients of, 612
graph for, 571
multiple, 597
nonlinear effect on dependent variable, 615–616

predictive power of, 601
p-value of, 601–602, 608
INDEX function, 23–26, 336, 552, 554
MATCH function and, 29
Index.xlsx file, 23
Indirectconsolidate.xlsx file, 191
INDIRECT function, 187–194, 355
product sales summary from, 191–192
to read range name portion in formula, 191
SUM function with, 188
Indirectmultisheet.xlsx file, 189
Indirectsimpleex.xlsx file, 187
industries, learning curve estimates for various, 586
infeasible solution, 281
INFORMS (Institute for Operations Research and
Management Science), 263
input assumptions, in worksheet models, 139
input cells, linking spinner buttons to, 249–250
input range, for histogram, 361
Inquire add-in, 135–138
to display formula relationships, 137
for relationships between worksheets, 137
workbook comparison, 136–137
workbook information from, 136
Inquire tab, 136
Cell Relationship, 137
Worksheet Relationships, 137
Insert Calculated Field dialog box, 421
Insert Calculated Item dialog box, 426
inserting
comments, 736
worksheets in workbook, 124
Insert Pictures dialog box, 541
Insert PivotTable command, 418
Insert tab
Charts
Line, 236
Scatter, 545, 571, 578, 798
Scatter, Bubble Chart, 565
Scatter, Scatter with Straight Lines, 787
Scatter With Smooth Lines And Markers,
641–642
Column Charts, 534
Filters
Slicers, 240
Timeline, 429
PivotTable, 448
Add This Data To The Data Model, 442
Radar chart, 564
Reports, Power View, 469, 470

Slicer, 405
Sparklines
Line, 485
Win/Loss, 490
Tables, 232
PivotTable, 388
Worksheet, 506
installing Analysis ToolPak, 598
integer, for date display, 54
Integer Optimality setting, 301–302
integer programming problems, solving, 301
Interactions.xlsx file
Data worksheet, 616
Nonlinearity worksheet, 615
interaction, testing for presence in regression,
616–619
interarrival time, 778
mean, 780
INTERCEPT function, 575, 653
intercept of line, in straight-line relationship, 575
interest
accumulating for several periods, 81
payment amount in loan, 79
interest expense, computing, 101
interest income, computing, 101
interest rate, 607
calculating for borrowed amount, 81
and cash flows NPV, 67
interest rate per period, 76
internal rate of return (IRR), 67–74
finding for irregularly spaced cash flows, 71
modified, 71
Internet Explorer, Export To Microsoft Excel
from, 348
Internet, importing data from, 345–348
invalid data, Excel default response to, 350
invalid range name, 13
inventory
band chart for checking levels, 547–548
economic order quantity inventory model,
763–768
modeling with uncertain demand, 769–776
investments
allocating portfolio among stocks, T-bills, and
bonds, 725–728
calculating number of years for payback given
annual cash flow, 31–32
net present value criteria for evaluating, 59–66
pricing options for decisions, 752–754
probability of gain, 722–724

uncertainty of future returns, 721
invisible characters, CLEAN function to remove, 39
IPMT function, 79
IRR. *See* internal rate of return (IRR)
IRR function, 68
IRR.xlsx file, 68, 72
ISERROR function, 819
ISFORMULA function, 128
ISFORMULATEXT.xlsx file, 128
ISNUMBER function, 352–353
iterations
enabling for calculations, 87, 88
F9 function keys for, 712
simulating, 712

J

James, Bill, 264
job shop scheduling problems, 335

K

keyboard function keys
F3 for pasting range names, 165
F4 for changing dollar signs in cell reference, 211
F9 for iterations, 712
F9 for recalculation, 143
F9 to display formula segment value, 181
KPIs (Key Performance Indicators), 455
Kurtosis, 373

L

labels
charts with dynamic, 549–551
for histogram, 362
for x- and y-axis, 572
Labelsandtables.xlsx file, 542
Labelsfromcells.xlsx file, 544
LARGE function, 31, 379
Last Column tool, 235
Last year.xlsx file, 11
lead time, uncertainty impact, 772
leap year, Excel and 1900, 54
learning curve, 583
discovery, 586
for fax machine production, 585
least-squares line, 573
LEFT function, 37, 40, 42, 180

Lefthandlookup.xlsx file, 177
left-side lookup, 177
Lemonade.xlsx file, 140
LEN function, 37, 41
Lenora.xlsx file, 40
Lewent, Judy, 752
liabilities. *See also* loans
    computing, 101
lifetime of machine, modeling, 691–693
linear demand curve, 786, 787
    alternative, 797
linear equations, Excel iterative procedure for, 89
Linearfit.xlsx file, 786
linear graph, 570
linear models, 279–280, 301
linear pricing, 803
linear problem solving, 319
    optimization, 269
linear relationships, 572
    exact, 607
line charts, creating, 473
LINEST function, 603–604
Lineupsch38.docx file, 339
Lineupsch38.txt file, 340
Line With Markers chart, 551
lipstick, profit-maximizing price for, 798
list boxes, 246
    to choose charted series, 552–553
lists
    comparing for common entries, 818–819
    selecting item from, 256
loans
    calculating monthly payments, 79
    periods for payback, 82
LOGEST function, 823–824
Logicalexamples.xlsx file, 210
logical functions, 210
lognormal random variable, 701–704, 721
LOGNORM.DIST function, 701, 703
LOGNORM.INV function, 701, 704
lookup functions, 15–22. *See also* MATCH function
    * (asterisk) as wildcard, 28
    based on right-most column in range, 177
    HLOOKUP function, 16, 19
    for product price from product ID, 18
    VLOOKUP function, 15–16
lookup, random number to initiate, 708
lost-sales case, for inventory, 772–774
lost sales cost, 769
LOWER function, 38

low points on Sparklines, 487
Loyalty.xlsx file, 757

M

macroeconomic variables, 607
macros, file suffix, 192
Make Unconstrained Variables Non-Negative
    setting, 309
Makeup2007.xlsx file, 170
Makeuparray.xlsx file, 820
Makeupfilter.xlsx file, 502
Makeupsorttemp.xlsx file
    Dates worksheet, 228
    Makeup worksheet, 223, 226
Makeupsort.xlsx file, 229
Makeupsubtotals.xlsx file, 527
Makeuptimeline.xlsx file, 429
Manage dialog box, Excel Add-ins, 598
Manage Relationships dialog box, 449
Manage Rules dialog box, Stop If True option,
    216–218
Manage Rules, for conditional formatting, 197
manufacturing plant, production size, 765–767
MAPE (mean absolute percentage error), 649
market trends, 97
mass-mailing travel brochure, 410–414
Matchex.xlsx file, 28
MATCH function, 27–34, 429, 550, 807, 818
    to compute payback period, 32
    to find highest value in list, 30
    OFFSET function and, 177
mathematical models for decisions, 262
mathematical operations, 41
Matradingrule.xlsx file, 97
matrices, multiplying, 828
MAX function, 101, 744, 807
    to find highest value in list, 30
maximizing function, in GRG Nonlinear engine, 320
maximizing profitability, monthly product mix
    for, 273–282
maximum inventory level, 766
Maximum Time Without Improvement, 329
mean, 371
    forecasting use of, 627
    geometric, 381
    information from, 375
    mode vs., 373
    of normal random variable, 684–685

of random variable, 664–665
regression toward, correlation and, 595
of resampled high-temperature yields, 740
of sums of independent random variables, 688
of time between arrivals, 778
of time needed to complete service, 778
trimmed, 380–381
as unbiased forecast, 698
mean profit, confidence interval for, 712
measures of central location, 371–374
MEDIAN function, 372, 819
MEDIANIF function, 826
median of sample, 372
Medians.xlsx file, 826
merger, indicator on graph, 564
merging scenarios in workbooks, 158
Merton, Robert, 743
metrics in baseball, 264
microchip manufacturer, PivotTables for summarizing data, 417–420
Microsoft Power Query for Excel, 348
Microsoft Word document, importing data from, 339
middle of year, NPV when cash flow occurs at, 62
MID function, 37, 41, 42, 817
military time, 112
MIN function, 326, 710
minimizing functions, in GRG Nonlinear engine, 321
minus (–) signs, in PivotTable, 395
MINUTE function, 113
MINVERSE function, 828
MIRR function, 71
Missingdata.xlsx file, 538
MMULT function, 828
mode, 372–373
mean vs., 373
MODE function, 372
Modefunctions.xlsx file, 372
modeling nonlinearities, 615–622
MODE.MULT function, 372
MODE.SNGL function, 372
MOD function, 104
modified internal rate of return, 71
Monte Carlo simulation, 158
basics, 705–714
for optimal bid calculation, 715
uses, 706
month-day-year format, 54
MONTH function, 58
MONTH function (DAX), 467

monthly fixed cost, 573
monthly operating cost, forecast for, 598
monthly payments, calculating for loans, 79
months
extracting from date, 58
formula to return product sales for specific, 29
sorting chronologically, 228
MonthtoMonth.xlsx file, 431
mortgage
Goal Seek for determining amount based on payments, 150
monthly payment based on loan amount and interest rate, 143–144
Mortgagedt.xlsx file, 143
mortgage payments, Solver to determine for variable interest rate, 306–307
Moviestemp.xlsx file, 179
moving averages
calculating, 653
time series understood with, 641–644
moving-average trading rules, 96–99
Mrcostest.xlsx file, Data worksheet, 597
multiple peaks on histogram, 365
Multiple Ranges, PivotTable slicers and, 436
multiple regression, 574
basics, 597–604
function for forecasting from equation, 613–614
output, 600
qualitative factors in, 605–614
residual output, 600
multiplication
of matrices, 828
with Paste Special, 119
Mutation Rate, 329

N

#N/A (Not Available) response, 16, 18, 129, 191
and charts, 551
from MATCH function, 818
from MODE function, 372
from VLOOKUP, 103
Name box, range name creation with, 2–3
#NAME? error, 104
Name Manager, 6–7, 182, 233
dialog box, 9
names. *See also* range names
filtering by beginning letter of, 512
referencing columns or rows by, 90

navigating worksheets, 391
NCAA men's basketball Final Four, probability of team win, 735–737
negative binomial random variable, 675–676
Negativedatabars.xlsx file, 202
negative kurtosis, 374
negative linear relationship, 590
negatively skewed histogram, 364
negative skew, 373
NEGBINOM.DIST function, 675
Negbinom.dist.xlsx file, 675
nesting
    IF statements, 95, 105
    list selection, 355
    subtotals, 530
net fixed assets, 102
net income after taxes, 102
net present value (NPV), 59–66
    for cash flows
        interest rate and, 67
        at irregular intervals, 62–64
        received at year's beginning, 62
    definition of term, 60–61
    of long-term profits from customer, 757
    projects contributing greatest, 297
NETWORKDAYS function, 57
NETWORKDAYS.INTL function, 57
New Formatting Rule dialog box, 201–202, 407–408
    Use A Formula To Determine Which Cells To Format, 659
New Name dialog box, 5, 12, 183, 192
New Rule, for conditional formatting, 197
New Web Query dialog box, 346
Nfl2009april2010.xlsx file, 313
NFL teams
    point spreads, 314–317
    summarizing sequence of wins or losses, 489–490
95-percent service level, 772–774
Nlp.xlsx file
    Nonlinear Pricing Examples worksheet, 803, 804
    OnePrice worksheet, 805
    Two-Part Tariff worksheet, 806
nonadjacent selections, grouping, 424
nonblank cells, counting, 162, 166
noncontiguous ranges, naming, 3
nonlinearities
    modeling, 615–622
    testing for presence in regression, 616–619

nonlinear pricing, 803–812
    profit-maximizing, 806–810
nonlinear Solver model, 317
nonnumeric value
    preventing data entry of, 352
nonprinting characters, CLEAN function to remove, 39
nonsmooth functions, 270
nonsmooth optimization problems, 323
normal cumulative function, 686
Normalexamples.xlsx file, Normal worksheet, 686
normal random variables, 683–690
    appropriateness for real-world situations, 687–688
    finding probabilities for, 686
    percentiles for, 687
    properties, 683–685, 684–685
    simulating values, 709
NORM.DIST function, 686
NORM.INV function, 709, 687, 735–736
NORM.S.DIST function, 747
not equal to (<>) operator, 163
NOT operator, 210
NOW function, 113
NPER function, 82
NPV. See net present value (NPV)
NPVauditscenario.xlsx file, 155
NPVaudit.xlsx file, 136, 137
    Original Model worksheet, 130
NPV function, 61–62, 75–77, 758
NPVspinnerstemp.xlsx file, Original Model worksheet, 247
NPV.xlsx file, 59
null hypothesis, 623, 626
Number Filters for database, 507
numbers
    assigning icons to range, 205
    converting text to, 41
    converting to text string, 38
    counting cells containing, 162
    count of cells in range containing, 165
    not in ascending order, for lookup, 18
    raising to a power, 61
    ranking in data sets, 380
#NUM error
    from IRR function, 68
    from XNPV function, 64
#NUM! error, 104

O

observations. *See* data points
OData feed, 457
Offsetcost.xlsx file, 178
Offsetexample.xlsx file, 176
OFFSET function, 175–186, 233, 429
    COUNT function with, 181
    dynamic range names from, 183
    MATCH function and, 177
    SUM function with, 178
Oilwell.xlsx file, 752
one-way ANOVA, 623–628
Onewayanova.xls file, Insig worksheet, 626
Onewayanova.xlsx file, 624
one-way data table, 140–141
operating costs
    explaining monthly variation, 574
    production relationship to, 571–574
operating income, computing, 101
optimal bid, calculating, 715–720
optimal product mix, Solver for determining,
      273–284
optimal solution, 270
optimization model
    changing cells in, 268
    GRG nonlinear engine for, 320–323
    problem constraints, 268
    Solver for, 267–272
    target cells, 267–268
option buttons, 246
    for product price selection, 255–256
options
    parameters determining value, 745–746
    pricing for investment decisions, 752–754
Options dialog box. *See* Excel Options dialog box
order costs, minimizing, 770–772
order of precedence, for conditional formatting
      rules, 200, 209
OR operator, 210, 493
    database functions with, 495
    in IF statement, 99
outliers, 375, 574, 603
    computing cutoffs for, 376
    conditional formatting for highlighting, 375–382
    in forecasts, 659–661
outline form, for PivotTable, 394
output cells, in Scenario Manager, 155

P

Page Break Between Groups, 528
Page Setup dialog box, Sheet tab, 737
Pareto chart, 562–563
Pareto.xlsx file, 562
Paste Link, 119
Paste Name dialog box, 2, 8
Paste Preview dialog box, 460–461
Paste Special command, 142
Paste Special dialog box, 117–122
    Transpose, 118, 593, 815
Pastespecial.xlsx file
    Paste Special Divide Before worksheet, 119
    Paste Special Transpose worksheet, 118
    Paste Special Value worksheet, 117
pasting range names into formula, 165
pattern recognition technology, Flash Fill use
      of, 45–47
payback period, 31, 147
Payback.xlsx file, 31
Paymentgs.xlsx file, 150
payment on the principal, 79
payment (Pmt), 76
    in FV function, 77
    present value of, 76
penalties, Evolutionary Solver and, 329–334
#Per, 76
    in FV function, 77
    for PMT function, 79
percentage return, calculating for stock purchase
      with European put options, 95–96
PERCENTILE.EXC function, 377, 378–379
PERCENTILE function, 377, 378
PERCENTILE.INC function, 377, 378
percentiles
    for normal random variables, 687
    ranking in data set, 377–379
PERCENTRANK.EXC function, 377, 379
PERCENTRANK function, 377, 379
PERCENTRANK.INC function, 377, 379
percent values, spinner button for, 250
performance, tracking sales over time, 545–546
periods for loan payback, 82
perpetuity, 83
Peyton.xlsx file, 345
Phoneloyalty.xlsx file, 759
Picturegraph.xlsx file, 540
pictures in column graphs, 540–541
PivotChart, summarizing PivotTable with, 403–404

PivotChart Tools, 414
PivotTable, 521
    adding blank rows, 406–407
    basics, 386–387
    basing on data in several locations, 434–436
    calculated field in, 421–422
    collapsing and expanding fields, 395–396
    conditional formatting in, 407–409
    creating
        based on existing, 436
        with Data Model, 444–446, 448–449
        with PowerPivot, 463–465
    "drilling down" in, 427–429
    extracting data from, 427–429
    field assignments for creating report, 465
    format changes for, 395
    format for scenario summary, 158
    grouping items in, 423–424
    headings for, 388
    hiding subtotals in, 406–407
    layouts, 393–394
    reason for name, 395
    refreshing, 447
    report filter, 404–405, 422
    sales summary for month compared same month
        previous year, 432–433
    slicers for, 405–406, 422
        Multiple Ranges and, 436
    sorting and filtering fields, 397–403
    summarizing
        data by time periods, 429–430
        grocery sales at several stores, 387–388
        total sales to date, 431–432
        with PivotChart, 403–404
PivotTable And PivotChart Wizard, 434–436
    adding to Quick Access toolbar, 436
PivotTable Field list, 390–392
PivotTable Options dialog box, 406
PivotTable Tools Analyze tab, 396
PivotTable Tools Design tab, Blank Rows, 406
plus (+) sign, in PivotTable, 395
PMT function, 79
    in two-way table, 143
    Solver to verify accuracy, 306–307
Pmt (payment), 76
    in FV function, 77
point forecast, 697
point spreads for games, Solver model for, 313
POISSON.DIST function, 680
Poisson random variable, 679–682

poker, probability of three-of-a-kind hand, 733–734
Pop-Out/Pop-In icons, for charts or tables, 475
population, 323
population standard deviation, 375
population variance, 375
portfolio insurance, 96
position, MATCH function to locate for value in
        range, 28
positive kurtosis, 374
positive linear relationship, 589–590
positively skewed histogram, 364
positive skew, 373
power curve, 569, 581–588
power demand curve, 786, 788
    alternative, 797
Powerexamples.xlsx file, 581
power graph, 570
PowerPivot, 442, 455–468
    basics, 455–456
    enabling add-in, 456
    importing data to, 457
    importing text files for, 459
    loading data into, 456–463
    PivotTable creation with, 463–465
    slicers use with, 466
PowerPivot Fields dialog box, 463–464
PowerPivot tab, Manage, 458
Power Query, 348
Power View, 442, 469–484
    blank sheet, 471
    charts
        creating, 473–474
        filtering, 474–478
        filtering with slicer, 476–477
        filtering with Tiles, 477
    data preparation for, 470–473
    displaying sales data by state or country,
        478–479
    Multiples feature, 482–483
PPMT function, 79
precedents, 130
predictions
    accuracy of, 574–575
    of future values of time series, 645–650
    real-time, 265
    of sports outcomes, 313
    US auto sales, 605–609
    US presidential elections, 610–613
predictive analytics, 261–262, 264
prescriptive analytics, 262–263

present value (Pv). *See also* net present value (NPV)
   in FV function, 77
   for PMT function, 79
presidential elections in US, predicting, 610–613
previous year, creating range name for, 12
price elasticity, 786
   unknown, 797
price per unit, computing, 234
pricing
   average of all greater than median, 819
   bundling and, 804–806
   as function of number purchased, 94
   impact of changes, 140
   impact on sales, 632, 635
   linear, 803
   lookup
      based on date, 19
      product ID for, 18–19
   nonlinear, 803–812
   options for investment decisions, 752–754
   products, 785
   profit-maximizing, 142
   stock options, 743–756
   two-part tariff, 804
   with subjectively determined demand, 797–802
   with tie-ins, 791–796
principal
   accumulating for several periods, 81
   payment amount in loan, 79
printing comments, 737
probabilities
   involving sampling, 673
   NCAA men's basketball Final Four, team
      win, 735–737
   for normal random variable, 686
   for Poisson random variable, 680
   simulating for gambling and sporting
      events, 731–738
   statements from forecasts, 697–700
probability density function (pdf), 665–666
   for continuous random variable, 683–684
probability statements, less-than or equal to sign ($\le$)
      in, 684
problem constraints, in optimization model, 268
Prodmixtemp.xlsx file, 136
Prodmix.xlsx file, 283
   Feasible Solution worksheet, 273
product ID, for product price lookup, 18–19
production
   determining appropriate level, 710–712

predicting costs for 3 products, 597–602
relationship to operating costs, 571–574
risk impact on decision, 712
Solver to determine location, 291–294
product life cycle, and labor time savings, 583
Productlookup.xlsx file, 29
products
   formula to return sales for specific month, 29
   pricing, 785
   total cost by development stages, 178–179
profit, 275
   computing, 140
profitability, 140
   bundling and, 804–806
   monthly product mix to maximizing, 273–282
profit-maximizing price, 142
   determining, 785
   for razor, 791–796
pro forma financial statements, debt as plug, 99–104
Proforma.xlsx file, 99
progress
   thermometer chart for displaying, 548–549
   waterfall chart to track, 557–558
projects, Solver to determine acceptable, 297–300
PROPER function, 38
Protect Sheet dialog box, 751
Ptableexample.xlsx file, 417
Ptcustomers.xlsx file, Data worksheet, 398
purchase price. *See* pricing
pure bundling, 805
put option, 744
   impact of key parameter changes, 748–749
   slope of payoff, 745
p-value
   and effect of factor on sales, 631
   of independent variable, 601–602, 608
   and nonlinear relationships, 616
PV function, 75
Pv (present value). *See also* net present value (NPV)
   in FV function, 77
   for PMT function, 79

Q

quadratic demand curve, Trendline to fit, 797
qualitative factors in multiple regression, 605–614
qualitative independent variable, quarter of year
      as, 606
quantitative independent variables, 605

quantity discounts
EOQ and, 765
and nonlinear pricing, 803–804
queries, 503
question mark (?) wildcard, 164
Queuingtemplate.xlsx file
Model worksheet, 779
Queuing Data worksheet, 780
queuing theory, 777–784
average time waiting in line at airport or at bank, 779–782
conditions for analysis, 778–779
variability degrading performance, 779
Quick Access toolbar, adding PivotTable And PivotChart Wizard to, 436
Quick Explore option, in Data Model, 446–447
quotation marks (" ")
for MATCH text values, 28
for text in arrays, 823
for text in criteria, 163
for text in IF statement, 98

R

R2 value, 574, 602
correlation relationship to, 594
for least-squares line, 575
radar chart, 564–565
Radar.xlsx file, 564
raising number to a power, 61, 585
RANDBETWEEN function, 722–723, 726, 732
Randdemo.xlsx file, 706
RAND function, 706–708, 710, 715, 735
randomized blocks, 629–640
output, 631
random variables, 663–668
beta, 691, 694–696
binomial, 670–671
negative, 675–676
simulating, 715–716
continuous, 665
modeling as normal random variable, 716
definition, 663
discrete, 664, 666, 683
simulating values, 708–709
governing time between arrivals, 681
hypergeometric, 673, 674–675
independent, 666
lognormal, 701–704, 721

mean, variance, and standard deviation of, 664–665
normal, 683–690
simulating values, 709
Poisson, 679–682
uniform, 719
Weibull, 691–693
range lookup argument, 16, 18
range names, 1–14
applying to entire worksheet, 11
AutoComplete of, 9
automatically including new data, 182–183
creating, 1–7
with Create From Selection, 4–5
with Define Name, 5–7
with Name box, 2–3
displaying in existing formulas, 10
duplicate in multiple worksheets, 794
error from undefined, 104
for table range, 17
pasting into formula, 165
pasting list into worksheet, 11
restrictions, 13
scope for, 6
range of cells
getting statistics describing, 381
MATCH function to locate position for value in, 28
OFFSET function for reference to, 175–186
selecting all data in column or row, 120
value lookup from, 15
range of data set, 375
RANK.AVG function, 380
RANK.EQ function, 380, 734
RANK function, 380, 546, 554
ranking numbers, in data sets, 380
Rate, 76
in FV function, 77
for PMT function, 79
RATE function, 81
rating for player abilities, conditional formatting based on, 214–215
Ratioma.xlsx file, 651, 652
ratio-to-moving-average forecast method, 651–654
Razorsandblades.xlsx file, No Blades worksheet, 791
razors, profit-maximizing price of, 791–796
real options, 752
real-time predictions, 265
reciprocal cost allocation method, 91
records, 503

rectangular range of cells, naming, 2
reference cells, for OFFSET function, 175
#REF! error, 104
refreshing PivotTables, 447
refresh settings, for web query, 347
regional worksheets, set up for, 124
region, calculating total revenue and units sold
    by, 527–530
regression. *See also* multiple regression
    estimating independent variable coefficients
        for, 656
    standard error for, 602
    sum of squares, 604
    testing for presence of nonlinearity and
        interaction in, 616–619
    toward the mean, correlation and, 595
Regression dialog box, 598, 599
regression equation, holding back data for
    validating, 611
Reichheld, Frederick, 757
relationships
    between correlation and r-squared value, 594
    creating
        within Data Model, 443–444
        between data sources, 462–463
    editing or deleting, 449–450
    power curve for modeling, 581
    of stock returns, 591–593
    straight-line estimates, 569–576
    summarizing, correlations for, 589–596
remainder from division, MOD function to
    return, 105
Remove Duplicates tool, 235, 514–515
removing. *See* deleting
reorder point
    in back-order case, 770–771
    inventory level for, 769
    in lost-sales case, 772
Reorderpoint_lostsales.xlsx file, 772
Repeatedhisto.xlsx file, 44
Replace Current Subtotals, 528
REPLACE function, 38
replication
    two-factor ANOVA with, 632
    two-way ANOVA without, 630
report filters
    limitations of, 405
    for PivotTable, 422
Report Filter zone, in PivotTable Field list, 391
REPT function, 37, 44

Required Bounds On Variables setting, 323
Resampleyield.xlsx file, 739
resampling for data analysis, 739–742
residuals
    for data points, 574
    in forecasts, 660
        randomness of, 661–662
    from presidential election equation, 613
    sum of squares, 604
    for trendline and data point, 573
Resize Table tool, 235
resizing charts, 473
resolving circular references, 88–90
result cells, in Scenario Manager, 155
retailer, profit potential based on revenue and
    expenses, 144–145
retained earnings, computing, 101, 102
retirement planning, 305
    Solver for, 307–309
returned units, totals of, 171
revenue
    calculating median size in each country, 826–827
    calculating total, 233
    calculating total by region, 527–530
    conditional formatting for quarters, 209–212
    estimating trends and seasonality, 823–826
    filtering top 30 values by salesperson, 513
    fitting trend curve to recent growth, 577–580
    moving average graph of, 643
    sorting customers by, 402–403
    tracking based on country, 177–178
Reverse Icon Order, in conditional formatting, 206
Review tab
    Changes, Protect Sheet, 751
    Comments, New Comment, 736
RIGHT function, 37, 43
risk-free rate, 745
risk, impact on production decision, 712
Rock.xlsx file, 162
Rosling, Hans, 480
ROW function, 104, 192
Row Labels zone, in PivotTable Field list, 390
rows
    adding blank in PivotTable, 406–407
    of database, 503
    freezing to keep visible, 97
    hiding or unhiding, 144
    ignoring those with errors, 103
    increasing height of, 248
    INDEX function to reference, 25

realigning data to column, 118–119
referencing by name, 90
selecting all data in, 120
RSQ function, 575

S

safety stock level, 771
Sagarin ratings, 735
salary
    finding highest in list, 29–31
    nonlinear effect of years of experience, 617
    wages*hours formula for computing, 13
sales
    average number of units sold per
        transaction, 172
    average quantity of, 172
    breakdown by salesperson in region, 530–531
    calculating units of, 171
    computing, 101
    deseasonalization of estimates, 652
    forecast based on sales representatives and
        districts, 632
    impact of price and advertising, 632
    interpreting effects of price and advertising
        on, 635
    plotting as function of advertising, 582
    summarizing transactions, 238–240
    summary worksheet by country, 191–192
    total dollar amount based on year, 171
    total dollar amount by salesperson, 170–171
    trends and seasonality in forecasting future, 652
sales database, array functions to summarize,
    820–822
sales force
    analysis of effectiveness, 630–631
    complete list of, 514
sales statistics, database function for, 493–498
Salesstripping.xlsx file, 42
Salestracker.xlsx file, 545
sample standard deviation, 374–375
sample variance, 374–375
sampling, probabilities involving, 673
Sandp.xlsx file, 207
saving
    charts as templates, 548
    values in data table, 142
Scalesiconsdatabars.xlsx file, 204
scaling, for sparkline axis, 488

scatter chart, 564, 569
    for Cisco trend curve, 579
    of cumulative units produced and unit
        costs, 584–585
    with smooth lines and markers, 641–642
    variable changes displayed with, 565
Scenario Manager, 155–160
Scenario Manager dialog box, 157
scenarios, data table to generate, 723–724
Scenario Values dialog box, 157
Scholes, Myron, 743
scope
    for range name, 6
    worksheets vs. workbooks, 9
scroll bars, 246, 247
    check box for, 252
S curve, 643
SEARCH function, 37
seasonal demand, EOQ and, 765
seasonal indexes, 651–652
    computing, 653
seasonality
    in forecasting future sales, 652
    for time period, 645
Secondaryaxis.xlsx file, 536
SECOND function, 113
seconds (time), displaying, 113
Select A Solving Method list, 269
selecting
    all data in column, 120
    all formulas in worksheet, 751
    cells having conditional formatting, 209
    cells with data validation settings, 355
    day of the week, 256
    list items, 256
    noncontiguous ranges, 3
sensitivity analysis, 139–148, 155–160
    with multiple key inputs, spinner buttons
        for, 247–252
sequencing problems, 335
serial number for dates, 54, 111
    in COUNTIF function, 165
series charting, check boxes to control, 551–552
Series dialog box, 711
SERIES function, 184
series in chart, list box to select, 552–553
series labels, linking to cells, 549–551
service level approach, 769
Servicelevelreorder.xlsx file, 772
service time, mean, 780

Set Cell, for Goal Seek, 149, 151
Set Values Do Not Converge result, from Solver
  model, 283
SHEET function, 192
SHEETS function, 192
shipping
  company location for two warehouses, 325–327
  minimizing costs, 293
  Solver to determine location for, 291–294
shortage cost, 769
  minimizing, 770–772
Show Calculation Steps, 128
Show Data In Hidden Rows And Columns, 539
significance, in ANOVA table, 609
Simplex LP engine, 269, 279, 280
simulation
  assumptions for, 724
  of gambling and sporting event
      probabilities, 731–738
  for optimal bid for construction project, 716–718
  of stock prices, 721–730
size of charts, changing, 473
SKEW function, 373
skewness
  extreme, 380–381
  in histogram, 364
  measure, 373
slicers
  filtering charts with, 476–477
  PivotTables with, 405–406, 422
    Multiple Ranges and, 436
  PowerPivot use of, 466
  for tables, 240
Slicer Tools Options tab, 240
  formatting options, 406
Sloan Conference on Sports Analytics, 263
SLOPE function, 575, 653
slope of function
  in GRG Nonlinear engine, 320
  of put payoff, 745
  of straight-line relationship, 575
SMALL function, 31, 379
smoothing parameters in Winters's method, 646
Solver
  for capital budgeting, 297–304
  Esc key for stopping, 321
  estimating independent variable coefficients
      with, 656
  Evolutionary Solver, 323, 327
    penalties and, 329–334

for financial planning, 305–312
lack of solution from, 282–283
linear problem solving, 319
nonlinear model, 317
optimal product mix from, 273–284
optimization with, 267–272
quantity-discount with IF statements, 809
for retirement planning, 307–309
smoothing constants values from, 647–648
sports teams ratings with, 313–318
transportation or distribution problems in,
    291–296
to verify PMT function accuracy, 306–307
workforce scheduling with, 285–290
Solver Add-In, activating, 269–270
Solver Options dialog box, 301–302
Solver Parameters dialog box, 269, 275–277
  for asset allocation model, 728
  for determining forecast parameters, 658
  Evolutionary Solver problem in, 329
  Make Unconstrained Variables Non-Negative
      setting, 309
  for maximizing quantity-discount plan, 809–810
  for maximizing razor profit, 792–793
  for mortgage payments determination, 307
  for NFL ratings, 316
  for One warehouse problem, 325
  for product mix problem, 279
  for profit-maximizing price, 799
  for project selection model, 299
  for reorder point for 95-percent service level, 774
  for retirement planning, 309
  for transportation problem, 293
  for traveling salesperson problem, 337
  for Winters's model, 648
  for workforce problem, 287
Sort dialog box, 224
  sorting without using, 229–230
sorted data, as chart basis, 554–555
Sortedgraphx.xlsx file, 554
sorting, 223–230
  based on cell or font color, 226–227
  custom list for, 228
  data for subtotals, 530
  icon sets as basis for, 227
  months chronologically, 228
  multiple criteria for, 224
  PivotTable fields, 397–403
  transaction data, 223–226

Sort Largest To Smallest command, for PivotTable, 397

Sort Z To A, 397

spaces, removing from text string, 37, 40

Sparklines, 485–490

    automatic updates, 490

    modifying, 487–488

Sparklines.xlsx file, 485

    Line Sparkline worksheet, 486–487

Sparkline Tools Design tab, 487

special events, forecasts impacted by, 655–662

spinner buttons, 246, 247

    copying and pasting, 248

    creating, 248

    for percent values, 250

    linking to input cells, 249–250

sporting events probabilities simulation, 731–738

sports teams ratings, Solver for, 313–318

SQL Server database, loading data from, 457

SQRT function, 324, 325, 632

squared errors, sum of, 657

square matrix, 828

Stacked 2D bar chart, 553

Stacked area chart, 548

Stacked Column chart, 473

standard deviation

    of bids, estimating, 716

    of forecast errors, 632

    information from, 375

    of normal random variable, 684–685

    of random variable, 664–665

    sample, 374–375

    of sums of independent random variables, 688

    of time between arrivals, 778

    of time needed to complete service, 778

    unbiased forecast and, 698

standard error of the regression, 574, 602

standard normal, 747

starting time, calculating number of hours between ending time and, 114

state abbreviations

    list for data entry, 353

    for named ranges, 4, 7

Statedv.xlsx file, 353

states

    displaying sales data by, 478–479

    listing in descending order of sales, 554

Statestemp.xlsx file, 4

States.xlsx file, 6, 7, 460

station wagons, family factors in purchase decision, 414–417

Station.xlsx file, 415

STDEV function, 375, 712

STDEV.P function, 375

STDEV.S function, 375, 727

STDEVS function, 658

steady state characteristics of system, 778–779

STEYX function, 574

Stockcorrel.xlsx file, 591

stock prices

    lognormal random variable for modeling, 701–704

    median in future, 704

    options, 743–756

    simulating, 721–730

stock returns

    color coding, 207–208

    relationship of, 591–593

stocks

    allocating investments, 725–728

    annual volatility of riskiness, 702

    beta of, 742

    purchase with European put options, 95–96

    transaction costs, 99

    website for volatility estimates, 750

Stop If True option, 216–218

stopping Solver, Esc key for, 321

store orders, determining quantity, 763–765

Storesales.txt file, 458

story problems in algebra, Goal Seek for, 151–152

straight-line relationship

    estimates, 569–576

    slope, 575

structure of worksheet model, 127

styles

    for PivotTable, 395

    for sparklines, 488

SUBSTITUTE function, 39–40, 45

Subtotal dialog box, 527–529

subtotals, 527–532

    deleting, 528

    in PivotTable, hiding, 406–407

    nesting, 530

subtraction, with Paste Special, 119

SUM function, 807, 817

    cell formatting for hours, 114

    DSUM function vs., 491–492

    INDIRECT function with, 188

maintaining original range after row insertion, 189–190
OFFSET function with, 177, 178
for retained earnings calculation, 101
SUMIF function, 169, 170, 819, 820
SUMIFS function, 170, 172, 493, 497
array function alternatives, 820
Sumindirect.xlsx file, 188
summarizing
bubble chart for three variables, 565
with database statistical functions, 491–500
graph of daily customer counts, 485–487
grocery sales at several stores, 387–388
NFL team sequence of wins or losses, 489–490
PivotTables, 417–420
data by time periods, 429–430
with PivotChart, 403–404
relationships, correlations for, 589–596
sales database transactions, array functions for, 820–822
sales for month compared same month previous year, 432–433
Subtotal command for, 527–532
total sales to date with PivotTable, 431–432
Summary Below Data, 528
summary report for scenarios, 157
summary worksheet, for sales by country, 191
sum of squared errors (SSE), 657
for exponential curve, 585
sum of squares regression, 604
sum of squares residual, 604
SUMPRODUCT function, 274–275, 286, 292, 298, 815
supply constraint, 292
supply points, 291
Switch To Workbook Excel icon, 460
symbols, in range names, 13
symmetric histogram, 363
symmetry about the mean, testing for, 716

T

Tableexampletemp.xlsx file, 231
Tablemakeuptemp.xlsx file, 238
table range
range names for, 17
for VLOOKUP, 15
tables, 231–244
AutoComplete options for, 233
basing chart on, 237
in charts, 542–544
data source list as, 355
for histogram, 555
removing duplicates from, 235
Table slicers, 240
Table Styles tool, 236
Table Tools contextual tab, 235
Table Tools Design tab, 232
tabular form, for PivotTable, 394
Taleb, Nicholas, The Black Swan, 704
target cells
in optimization model, 267–268
for product mix Solver model, 275
for software project selection problem, 298
for Solver workforce scheduling, 286
for transportation problem, 291, 292
taxes
computing, 102
computing rates based on income, 16–18
T-bills, allocating investments, 725–728
Teasales1.xlsx file, Power View 2 worksheet, 475
Teasalesfilterbycharts.xlsx file, 476
Teasalesmultiples.xlsx file, 482
Teasalesslicer.xlsx file, 476
Teasalestiles.xlsx file, 477
temperature data, visual indicators for, 197
templates, storing charts as, 548
text files
importing data from, 339–344
importing for PowerPivot, 459
text filters, 503, 512
text functions, 35–50
CHAR function, 38
CLEAN function, 39, 44
CONCATENATE function, 38, 41
FIND function, 37, 41, 42
LEFT function, 37, 40, 42
LEN function, 37, 41
LOWER function, 38
MID function, 37, 41, 42
PROPER function, 38
REPLACE function, 38
REPT function, 37, 44
RIGHT function, 37, 43
SEARCH function, 37
SUBSTITUTE function, 39–40, 45
TRIM function, 37, 40
UPPER function, 38
VALUE function, 38, 41, 45
Textfunctions.xlsx file, 36

Text Import Wizard, 339–344
text strings
    character count for, 37
    combining, 41
    converting to number, 38, 41
    converting to time, 113
    finding first occurrence of match in, 27
    flagging fields containing, 497
    quotation marks for, 823
        in IF statement, 98
        in MATCH function, 28
    removing spaces from, 37
    repeating, 37
    returning characters from, 37
Text That Contains option, for conditional
        formatting, 199
thermometer chart, 548–549
three-dimensional formulas, 123–126
tie-ins, pricing with, 791–796
Tiles, for filtering charts, 477
time
    between arrivals, random variable
        governing, 681
    calculating number of hours between starting
        and ending, 114
    computations with, 112
    creating sequence of regularly spaced
        intervals, 115
    data entry of, 112
        with date in one cell, 112
    displaying current, 113
    format for displaying, 112
    serial number for, 111
    summarizing PivotTable data by periods,
        429–430
    tracking sales performance over, 545–546
TIME function, 113
Timeline feature, 429–430
time series
    characteristics, 645
    moving averages for understanding, 641–644
    predicting future values, 645–650
    seasonal indexes for, 651–652
    trend of, 651
time series scatter chart, changing to
        animated, 480–482
TIMEVALUE function, 113
Time.xlsx file, 112, 113
title of chart, 572
TODAY function, 55, 113

today's date, formula to automatically display, 55
toggling, 109
    formula display with value display, 128
Tolerance setting, for Solver, 301
tooltips, for data entry, 350
Top 10 Filter dialog box, 401
Top 10 Items, for PivotTable layout, 400
Top/Bottom Rules, for conditional formatting, 197
total assets, 102
total cost of product, by development stages,
        178–179
total hours, SUM function for, 114
total production cost, predicting as function of units
        produced, 581
total revenue, computing, 233
total sales to date, summarizing with
        PivotTable, 431–432
To Value, for Goal Seek, 149
Toysrustrend.xlsx file, 823
Trace Dependents, 130, 132
Trace Errors, 129
Trace Precedents, 130, 132–133
transactions
    costs for stock, 99
    filtering, 503–504, 505
    filtering by color, 513
    filtering by months, 511 512
    sorting data, 223–226
transportation problems, Solver for, 291–296
Transport.xlsx file, 291
TRANSPOSE function, 815–816
Transpose option for Paste Special, 118
travel brochure, mass-mailing, 410–414
Traveldata.xlsx file, Data worksheet, 410
traveling salesperson problem (TSP), 336–337
trend curves, 569
    for relationship of variables, 589
TREND function, 613–614
trendlines
    adding to chart, 572
    determining best-fitting, 573
    to fit quadratic demand curve, 797
    fitting to centered moving averages, 653
trends
    in forecasting future sales, 652
    of time series, 645
TRIM function, 37, 40
TRIMMEAN function, 381
Trimmean.xlsx file, 381
trimmed mean of data set, 380–381

Tsp.xlsx file, 336
Tufte, Edward, 485
two-part tariff, 804
  determining optimal, 807
two-way ANOVA, 629–640
  with replication, 632
    sales forecasts with, 635
Twowayanova.xlsx file, Randomized Blocks
    worksheet, 630
two-way data table, 140, 142, 143
  for break even point, 145

U

unbiased forecasts, 698
uncertain demand, inventory modeling with,
    769–776
uncertain events, estimating probabilities, 705–714
uncertainty, modeling inherent, in point
    forecast, 697
underscore (_), in range names, 13
unemployment rates, 607
Unfreeze Panes command, 97, 252
Ungroup command, 424
unhiding columns or rows, 144
uniform random variable, 719
unique internal rate of return, 68–69
  guaranteeing, 70
  use of, 70–71
Unique Records Only option for filter, 518
US auto sales, predicting, 605–609
US cities, approximate distance between, 324
US presidential elections, predicting, 610–613
units produced, predicting total production cost as
    function of, 581
units sold, calculating total by region, 527–530
UPPER function, 38
Use A Formula To Determine Which Cells To Format
    setting, 332
Use Function dialog box, 528
user forms, 245
  menu, 248

V

Valentine.xlsx file, Sim worksheet, 710
validating data, 349–358
validating regression equation, holding back data
    for, 611

#VALUE error, 44
#VALUE! error, 104
Value Field Settings command, 391
Value Field Settings dialog box, 416, 419–420
  Average, 411–412
  Number Format, 395
VALUE function, 38, 41, 45, 817
value of customer, determining, 757–762
Values field, display choices, 421
values, toggling formula display with, 128
Values zone, in PivotTable Field list, 390
VAR function, 375
variable cost, 574
variable interest rate, Solver to determine mortgage
    payments, 306–307
variables
  correlation between, 589
  estimating relationship between, 569
  independent vs. dependent, 569
  macroeconomic, 607
  nonlinear effect of independent variable on
      dependent, 615–616
  random, 663–668
  scatter chart for displaying changes, 565
variance. *See also* ANOVA (analysis of variance)
  of random variable, 664–665
  sample, 374–375
  of sums of independent random variables, 688
VAR.P function, 375
VAR.S function, 375
vertical line for chart separator, 564
Verticalline.xlsx file, 564
vertical lookup, 15
View tab
  Freeze Panes, 251–252
  Unfreeze Panes, 252
  Windows
    Arrange All, 522
    Freeze Panes, 97
Visible Cells Only option for copying, 506
visiblity of comments, 737
VLOOKUP function, 15–16, 315, 709, 710, 657, 723,
    734, 736
  * (asterisk) as wildcard, 28
  Excel Data Model vs., 442
  to find highest value in list, 30
  for tax rate based on income, 16–18
volatility of stocks, 746–747
  Black–Scholes formula for estimating, 749–750
  website for estimates, 750

W

waiting in line
    factors affecting time spent, 777–778
    mathematics of, 777–784
Walmartrev.xlsx file, 104
warehouse location for shipping company, 323
Warehouseloc.xlsx file
    One warehouse worksheet, 323
    Two warehouses worksheet, 325
Watch Window, 130
waterfall charts, 557–558
Waterfallcharts.xlsx file, All Positive worksheet, 557
web query, refresh settings for, 347
WEEKDAY function, 58, 213
weekend
    color for dates, 213
    customizing definition of, 57
WEIBULL.DIST function, 691, 694
Weibull random variable, 691–693
What-If Analysis, 141
    Data Table, 141, 142, 143, 145, 496, 718, 723, 726,
        732, 734, 781
    Goal Seek, 150
    Scenario Manager, 156
wildcards
    * (asterisk) in MATCH function, 28
    in database function criteria, 497
    ? (question mark) as, 164
Wingdings font, 546–547
win/loss sparkline, 490
Winters's method, 645–650
    initializing, 646–647
    parameter definitions, 645–646
    smoothing constants estimates, 647–649
Word document, importing data from, 339
Workbook Analysis Report dialog box, 136
Workbook Connections dialog box, 447, 448
workbooks
    combining region sales in, 521–526
    creating blank worksheet in, 506
    displaying all range names in, 2
    Inquire add-in information on, 136
    Inquire add-in to compare, 136–137
    inserting worksheets, 124
    listing all worksheets in, 192–193
    merging scenarios in, 158
    scope vs. worksheet scope, 9
WORKDAY function, 56
WORKDAY.INTL function, 56

workdays, determining the number between two
    dates, 57
workforce scheduling
    Evolutionary Solver for, 330–332
    Solver for, 285–290
worksheets
    assumptions in models, 139
    comments in, 736–737
    copying, 236
    copying filtered transactions to different, 506
    displaying multiple, 522
    duplicate range names in multiple, 794
    formulas for cells in multiple, 123–126
    Inquire add-in for relationships between, 137
    inserting in workbook, 124
    listing all in workbook, 192–193
    navigating, 391
    pasting range names list into, 11
    scope vs. workbook scope, 9
    structure of model, 127

X

x-axis
    of histogram, 361
    label for, 572
    scale for sparkline, 488
    of scatter chart, 569
XIRR function, 71
.xlsm file suffix, 192
XNPV function, 62, 760
XY chart, 571. *See also* scatter chart

Y

y-axis
    label for, 572
    scale for sparkline, 488
    of scatter chart, 569
YEAR function, 58
YEAR function (DAX), 467
years of experience, nonlinear effect on salary,
    617–618

Z

zero, division by, 104
zones, in PivotTable Field list, 390–392

About the author

WAYNE L. WINSTON is Professor Emeritus at the Indiana University Kelley School of Business and is presently a Visiting Professor at the Bauer College of Business at the University of Houston. He has won over 45 teaching awards, has taught Excel and Excel modeling to thousands of business analysts at Fortune 500 companies, and has consulted with many organizations, including the Dallas Mavericks and New York Knicks NBA teams. He has written 15 books on Excel, management science, and operations research, including *Mathletics*, which describes the math behind the exciting new field of sports analytics.

Now that you've read the book...

Tell us what you think!

Was it useful?
Did it teach you what you wanted to learn?
Was there room for improvement?

Let us know at http://aka.ms/tellpress

Your feedback goes directly to the staff at Microsoft Press,
and we read every one of your responses. Thanks in advance!

CPSIA information can be obtained at www.ICGtesting.com
Printed in the USA
LVOW01s2242080114

368605LV00002BA/2/P